D0008269

SIXTH EDITION

SIMON & SCHUSTER
HANDBOOK
FOR
WRITERS

LYNN QUITMAN TROYKA

Prentice
Hall

UPPER SADDLE RIVER, NEW JERSEY 07458

Library of Congress Cataloging-in-Publication Data
Troyka, Lynn Quitman
  Simon & Schuster handbook for writers / Lynn Quitman Troyka.—6th ed.
    p. cm.
  Includes index.
  ISBN 0-13-184679-5
    1. English language—Rhetoric—Handbooks, manuals, etc. 2. English
language—Grammar—Handbooks, manuals, etc. 3. Report writing—Handbooks, manuals,
etc. I. Title: Handbook for writers. II. Title.

  PE1408 .T696 2001
  808'.042—dc21

                                                                              2001034007
Editor in Chief: Leah Jewell
Development Editors: Harriet Prentiss and Stephanie Carpenter
VP/Director of Production and Manufacturing: Barbara Kittle
Senior Managing Editor: Mary Rottino
Senior Project Manager: Shelly Kupperman
Manufacturing Manager: Nick Sklitsis
Prepress and Manufacturing Buyer: Mary Ann Gloriande
Creative Design Director: Leslie Osher
Interior and Cover Designer: Ximena P. Tamvakopoulos
Line Art Coordinator: Guy Ruggiero
Artist: Maria Piper
Marketing Director: Beth Gillett Mejia
Editorial Assistants: Jennifer Collins and Christine Berger
Senior Marketing Manager: Brandy Dawson
Cover Art: Vincent van Gogh, Dutch (1853–1890), *View of Arles with Irises*. Van Gogh
Museum, Amsterdam, Netherlands/SuperStock.

This book was set in 10/11 New Caledonia by Carlisle Communications, Ltd. and printed
and bound by Quebecor/World Color. The cover was printed by Phoenix Color.

© 2002, 1999, 1996, 1993, 1990, 1987 by Lynn Quitman Troyka
Published by Pearson Education, Inc.
Upper Saddle River, NJ 07458

Printed in the United States of America

10   9   8   7   6   5   4   3   2

ISBN 0-13-184679-5 (Student Version)
ISBN 0-13-041626-6 (Annotated Instructor's Edition)

Pearson Education LTD., London
Pearson Education Australia PTY, Limited, Sydney
Pearson Education Singapore, Pte. Ltd
Pearson Education North Asia Ltd, Hong Kong
Pearson Education Canada, Ltd., Toronto
Pearson Educación de Mexico, S.A. de C.V.
Pearson Education of Japan, Tokyo
Pearson Education Malaysia, Pte. Ltd
Pearson Education, Upper Saddle River, New Jersey

CONTENTS

Contents

Contents

8   Verbs   181

9   Pronouns: Case and Reference   210

Contents

Contents

PART FIVE: WRITING RESEARCH 479

31 Using Sources and Avoiding Plagiarism 480

32 Research Writing as a Process 502

Contents

33 Successful Library Research 527

34 Successful Online Research 544

35 MLA Documentation with Case Study 561

PART SIX: WRITING ACROSS THE CURRICULUM 707

39 Comparing the Disciplines 708

40 Writing About Literature 712

41 Writing in the Social Sciences and Natural Sciences 732

SOCIAL SCIENCES 732

PREFACE

In writing the *Simon & Schuster Handbook for Writers,* Sixth Edition, I remain convinced that students are empowered by knowledge and deserve unwavering respect as emerging writers.

As in previous editions, I've designed this revision of the *Simon & Schuster Handbook for Writers* for three purposes: as a classroom text, a self-instruction manual, and a reference book. My greatest wish for students who use the *Handbook* is that they succeed as writers and joyfully fulfill their potentials in academic, personal, workplace, and public settings.

In writing the book, I've sought to be inclusive of all people. Role stereotyping and sexist language are avoided; *man* is never used generically for human race (rare exceptions are in quotations from published writers); male and female writers are represented equally in examples; and many ethnic groups are represented in the mix of student and professional writing examples.

Additionally, I have relaxed my tone, revised into active voice most passive voice structures, and at times used first person to help me communicate with students more directly. This update of audience awareness derives from the stance of many modern scholars of writing style, such as Joseph M. Williams in *Style: Ten Lessons in Clarity and Grace,* Fifth Edition (Longman, 1997). It also follows the spirit of this awareness found in the *MLA Handbook for Writers of Research Papers,* Sixth Edition (MLA, 2003): "Effective writing depends as much on clarity and readability as on content. . . . The key to successful communication is using the right language for the audience you are addressing" (42).

To unify this new edition of the *Handbook,* my stance throughout is that writing emerges from context, not from isolated components. I've written the exercises in connected discourse, not in random sentences collected together. As students work the exercises, they experience what real writers face when they revise and edit. For exercise content, I've drawn from subjects across the curriculum, choosing those with intrinsic interest for all students. Similarly, I've formed clusters of examples with related content so that students can focus on the instruction instead of on a new topic with each new example.

This new edition adds extensive new material while it retains the core features of the previous editions. To acquaint you with the Sixth Edition, the rest of this introduction is divided into sections:

- **"How to Locate" Guide** lists the navigation tools that help students easily locate what they want to find.

- **New Features** lists the abundant, exciting additions to the Sixth Edition.
- **Core Features** lists the many popular elements that I have retained from my previous editions.

But first, a personal note: When I was an undergraduate years ago, handbooks for student writers weren't widely available or used. Questions about writing nagged at me, but I couldn't find a book to answer them. On top of my being curious about the "why" of English and its conventions, my less-than-precise ear for language annoyed me. I worried that I guessed too often, and I felt frustrated by my ignorance. The semester before I graduated, I happily discovered a thin book on a dusty, little-used library shelf that answered some—though not all—of my questions. Back then, I could never have imagined that someday I myself might write a considerably expanded, modern version of a handbook for writers. Once I completed the *Simon & Schuster Handbook for Writers* (I started writing the First Edition in 1983, and it was published in 1987), I was amazed that I had had the nerve to begin. This proves to me—and I hope to students—that with persistence and patience, anyone can master English and writing.

In that spirit, I hope faculty and students alike will join in the conversation my pages seek to invite. Please e-mail me at <LQTBook@aol.com>. I look forward to your starting our conversation.

Lynn Quitman Troyka

"HOW TO LOCATE" GUIDE FOR THE SIXTH EDITION

HOW TO LOCATE LISTS OF THE BOOK'S CONTENTS

The Overview of Contents inside the front cover is a condensed version of the entire contents. Students can open the book to see instantly what chapter and section they are seeking. A complete Table of Contents precedes this preface. Also, a highly detailed Index starts on page 844.

HOW TO LOCATE THE BOOK'S SEVEN MAJOR TOPICS

Each of the seven Parts of this handbook contains one major topic: Writing an Essay; Understanding Grammar and Writing Correct Sentences; Writing Effective Sentences and Using Effective Words; Using Punctuation and Mechanics; Writing Research; Writing Across the Curriculum; and Writing When English Is a Second Language. The top edge of the pages of each Part are tinted a different color, which gives students speedy visual access to the Part they need. The seven colors show on the upper edge of the closed book and again on the banner at the top of each opened page. A complete guide to these and other color-coded elements in the handbook appears on next to last page.

HOW TO LOCATE A SPECIFIC CHAPTER

The chapters in this handbook are numbered in sequence from 1 to 50. Within each chapter, the comprehensive coverage is divided into short "chunks" of information. Each section, or chunk, is assigned a number-letter code: the chapter number followed by a lowercase letter, beginning with *a* and continuing in alphabetical order to the end of the chapter. (For example, in Chapter 1, the sections are 1a, 1b, 1c, up to 1g; and in Chapter 50, the sections are 50a to 50c.) Each number-letter code is followed by a heading in question form. These number-letter codes are also used to cross-reference to sections of the book where students can find more information. Number-letter codes also sit at the top outside corner of each page as well as in all contents lists.

HOW TO LOCATE MATERIAL ON EACH PAGE

FAQs (Frequently Asked Questions)—a new feature in the Sixth Edition—now form the main headings of the sections in each chapter. Friendly in tone, these FAQs echo the questions students ask themselves when looking for information. Also, the last FAQ on the page is repeated in the running head at the top of every right-hand page. For more detail about navigating a page in the Sixth Edition, see How to Use This Handbook, which is on inside back cover.

HOW TO USE THE BOOK'S SPECIAL ELEMENTS

The 195 boxes in this book are one of its special elements. The boxes, numbered sequentially throughout the book, are thumbnail sketches or summaries of key information. A symbol at the upper-left corner of each box carries a message: ⊙ means the box is a summary; ▇ says the box presents a pattern; and ≣ tells that the box is a checklist. Other special elements on some pages are small icons to signal students about related information. The ⊚ symbol means an Alert that prompts students to recall a related point in the context of the topic being discussed (for example, in a sentence-style discussion, an Alert points out a comma rule that applies); ▣ indicates a Computer Tip; and ⊕ announces an ESL Note for students for whom English is a second (or third, etc.) language. Additionally, SMALL CAPITAL LETTERS in the text signal that a term is defined in the Terms Glossary, located immediately before the Index at the back of the handbook. This identification feature allows students to concentrate on the material at hand, with the assurance that a needed definition is always at hand.

NEW FEATURES OF THE SIXTH EDITION

NEW ⓦ COMPREHENSIVE, INTERACTIVE WEB SITE, FREE, to accompany the *Simon & Schuster Handbook for Writers,* Sixth Edition, and accessible to each student who uses the personal access code bound into the new book or purchased separately. Designed specifically to help anyone using a Lynn Quitman Troyka *Handbook or Quick Access Reference for Writers,* it includes numerous components:

■ A complete e-book, linked to all the exercises and other Web material, which is easily searchable by keyword, index, or section number-letter code for a rule or other information.

■ Hundreds of application exercises for self-grading, including editing, fill-in-the-blank, essay, multiple choice, and matching.

■ "Blue Pencil" exercises, providing grammar and punctuation practice in the context of complete paragraphs.

■ Several comprehensive diagnostic tests for students to assess their strengths and weaknesses in all areas of grammar and punctuation.

■ Helpful Web links (URLs) for every Part or major topic to offer supplemental resources and activities.

■ An online reference library that provides information on how to search, evaluate, and document online sources.

■ A **new,** innovative section dedicated to helping students write different types of papers. It provides students with tips, book references, sample student papers, and more.

To assist students even if they aren't navigating the site via a particular chapter, it's organized two different ways: (1) "What type of paper are you writing?" and (2) "Where are you in the writing process?"

NEW Main headings in each chapter are worded as FAQs (Frequently Asked Questions). Carefully constructed and based on research into how students phrase questions to themselves, the FAQs facilitate naturalistic interactions between student and handbook. Additionally, each chapter now starts by posing the first, basic question students ask: for example "Why write?" "What is 'agreement'?" "What is a sentence fragment?" "What is the role of the comma?"

NEW Coverage of Research Writing has been expanded by 60 percent, with eight chapters instead of five.

- A **new** separate chapter on "Successful Library Research," with information about creating a search strategy; using reference works, books, and periodicals; and evaluating print sources (Chapter 33).

- A **new** separate chapter on "Successful Online Research," with information about searching the Internet and the World Wide Web, narrowing a search, avoiding plagiarism, and evaluating online sources (Chapter 34).

- A **new** separate chapter on MLA-style documentation, with expanded coverage of online and electronic sources coupled with an updated student MLA sample paper (Chapter 35).

- A **new** separate chapter on APA-style documentation, with expanded coverage of online and electronic sources coupled with an updated student APA sample paper (Chapter 36).

- A **new** section on Columbia Online Style (COS) documentation, in the same chapter with the styles of the Chicago Manual (CM) and Council of Biology Editors (CBE) (Chapter 37).

- A **new** separate chapter on "Effective Document Design," with many examples of how to incorporate graphics into papers, format business reports, and design a Web site (Chapter 38).

- **Updated** Chapter 31, "Using Sources and Avoiding Plagiarism," now with a brief summary of the entire research section.

- **Revised** Chapter 32, "Research Writing as a Process," streamlined to emphasize the processes of research writing, now featuring a section on the role of new technologies in research.

NEW Separate chapter on "Oral Presentations" explains how to analyze the audience, pick and research a topic, organize material, use visual aids, and deliver speeches and other talks (Chapter 44).

NEW Public writing, incorporated into the chapter on "Business and Public Writing," now offers guidelines on composing letters, reports, proposals, and e-mail messages in and outside of the formal business environment (Chapter 42).

NEW The Usage Glossary has been moved from the end of the book, and its now placed in its own chapter (Chapter 20). This positions the glossary near related material on language, and it also provides an easier, more logical reference point for students.

NEW Two separate chapters, "Misplaced and Dangling Modifiers" (Chapter 14) and "Shifting and Mixed Sentences" (Chapter 15), now split the former four-topic Chapter 15 to adjust the pace for covering these complex concepts.

NEW Revised chapter on pronouns unites pronoun case and pronoun reference into one chapter (Chapter 9), instead of the former two chapters (Chapters 9 and 10).

NEW A section on tools for writers (Chapter 1) talks about computers, a personal bookshelf of reference volumes, and other resources for writers.

NEW Chapter 4 on "Writing Paragraphs" has been revised to follow students' natural composing progression from introductory paragraphs, to body paragraphs, to concluding paragraphs.

NEW Jargon-free, revised coverage of "Sentence Fragments" (Chapter 12), "Comma Splices and Run-on Sentences" (Chapter 13), and "Parallelism" (Chapter 18) goes along with the naturalistic, plain-language questions students ask themselves about these topics.

NEW Sample science report discusses the efficacy of antibiotics in "Writing in the Social Sciences and Natural Sciences" (Chapter 41).

NEW Over 30 percent of the exercise content is new for this edition, with many exercises featuring options for both individual and collaborative work.

NEW Each Part Opener, seven parts in total, highlights a specific reference to the Troyka Web site, <www.prenhall.com/troyka>, as well as to a general URL that can supplement the Part's discussion.

NEW Images accompany the "Focus on Revising" features (at the end of Chapters 8, 12, 13, and 15) to encourage students in visualizing the essay's context.

NEW Additional Computer Tips, ESL Notes, and Alerts throughout the text help students incorporate technology, assist students for whom English is a second language, and highlight interactions between two or more grammatical and rhetorical issues.

CORE FEATURES OF THE SIXTH EDITION

- Starts with six chapters about writing essays, explaining that the writing process is rarely linear, always varying with the writer, the topic, and the writing situation.

- Illustrates a variety of writing processes with *ten* complete student essays: one with an informative purpose (Chapter 3); two with a persuasive purpose (Chapter 6); one as a critical response to a reading (Chapter 5); two MLA-style research papers, one on a general topic (Chapter 35) and one on a literary topic (Chapter 40); one APA-style research paper (Chapter 36); three literature-based papers, including the literary research paper mentioned above; and one **new** science report (Chapter 41).

- Offers detailed explanations of critical thinking and reading, as they relate to writing. Extensively class-tested, Chapter 5 explains the crucial differences between summary and synthesis, with a discussion paced to assist students in grasping each cognitive process and to help them understand the higher level of thinking demanded by synthesis.

- Devotes a full chapter to argument, with two students each taking a different position on the same topic. The Toulmin model and the classical model receive equal coverage.

- Covers all topics of grammar, style, language, punctuation, and mechanics.

- Demonstrates that research writing combines three processes: conducting research, understanding the results of that research, and writing a paper based on that research.

- Contains *two* complete MLA-style research papers. In Chapter 35, a paper about multiple intelligences is accompanied by a narrative of the student's research writing process as well as with annotations and directed commentary alongside each page of the paper. In Chapter 40, a literary research paper discusses the writings of Jamaican poet Claude McKay.

- Includes a complete APA-style research paper about biological clocks, accompanied by a narrative of the student's writing process (Chapter 36).

- Supplies a huge number of MLA and APA documentation examples, with much more for users of Internet and other electronic sources. Also gives directories for examples of in-text citations, similar to those used for MLA Works Cited and APA References.

- Presents six chapters for students to use when they're writing across the curriculum, now including an added chapter on oral communication and an expanded chapter on business writing and public writing.

■ Addresses the concerns of multilingual students, with many ESL Notes throughout the book and a longer discussion in six chapters.

■ Placed across from inside back cover, Response Symbols include proofreading marks in addition to the traditional correction symbols.

SUPPLEMENTS FOR THE SIXTH EDITION

Prentice Hall now offers an *even wider choice* of student supplements and instructor supplements to help faculty augment and customize their courses.

FOR STUDENTS

■ ⓦ COMPREHENSIVE, INTERACTIVE WEB SITE to accompany the *Simon & Schuster Handbook for Writers*, Sixth Edition, <http://www.prenhall.com/troyka>

■ *Simon & Schuster Workbook for Writers*, Sixth Edition, ISBN 0-13-041627-4

■ The New York Times *Themes of the Times*, distributed exclusively by Prentice Hall, ISBN 0-13-690181-6

■ *Rough Drafts: An Activity Book to Accompany the Simon & Schuster Handbook for Writers*, Sixth Edition, ISBN 0-13-041610-X

■ *A Writer's Guide to Research and Documentation*, ISBN 0-13-032641-0

■ *A Writer's Guide to Writing in the Disciplines and Oral Presentations*, ISBN 0-13-018931-6

■ *A Writer's Guide to Document and Web Design*, ISBN 0-13-018929-4

■ *A Writer's Guide to Writing About Literature*, ISBN 0-13-018932-4

■ *English on the Internet 2001: Evaluating Online Resources*, ISBN 0-13-019484-0. Free to students when packaged with text— but the package's ISBN is different: ISBN 0-13-072309-6

■ *The New American Webster Handy College Dictionary*, ISBN 0-13-032870-7. Free to students when packaged with the text—but the package's ISBN is different: ISBN 0-13-071913-7

FOR INSTRUCTORS

■ *Annotated Instructor's Edition (AIE)* for the *Simon & Schuster Handbook for Writers*, Sixth Edition, ISBN 0-13-041626-6

■ *Strategies and Resources for Teaching Writing* with the *Simon & Schuster Handbook for Writers*, Sixth Edition, ISBN 0-13-041628-2

- *Answer Key* to *Simon & Schuster Workbook for Writers*, Sixth Edition, ISBN 0-13-041624-X
- <www.turnitin.com> This innovative online service is FREE to professors using the *Simon & Schuster Handbook for Writers*, Sixth Edition. It greatly simplifies the process when teachers want to find out if students are copying their assignments from the Internet. In addition to helping instructors easily identify instances of Web-based student plagiarism, Turnitin.com also offers a digital archiving system and an online peer review service. Faculty set up a "drop box" at the Turnitin.com Web site where their students submit papers. Turnitin.com then cross-references each submission with millions of possible online sources. Within 24 hours, teachers receive a customized, color-coded "Originality Report," complete with live links to suspect Internet locations, for each submitted paper. For more information, visit <www.prenhall.com/english>.
- *WebCT* 🖋, *BlackBoard*, and *Course Compass* adapted for the *Simon & Schuster Handbook for Writers*, Sixth Edition. They feature extensive content in each of these course platforms, saving instructors time in preparing online courses.
- *Daedalus Online* 📖 is a Web site that provides an online environment for collaboration, with prompts for a variety of writing assignments and other user-friendly material. For more information, visit <http://www.prenhall.com/daedalus>.
- Prentice Hall Resources for Teaching Writing series (available in print and online):
  - *Teaching Writing Across the Curriculum* by Art Young, Clemson University, ISBN 0-13-081650-7
  - *Computers and Writing* by Dawn Rodrigues, University of Texas at Brownsville, ISBN 0-13-084034-3
  - *Portfolios* by Pat Belanoff, State University of New York, Stony Brook, ISBN 0-13-572322-1
  - *Journals* by Christopher C. Burnham, New Mexico State University, ISBN 0-13-572348-5
  - *Collaborative Learning* by Harvey Kail, University of Maine, and John Trimbur, Worcester Polytechnic Institute, ISBN 0-13-028487-4
  - *English as a Second Language* by Ruth Spack, Tufts University, ISBN 0-13-028559-5
  - *Distance Education* by W. Dees Stallings, University of Maryland, University College, ISBN 0-13-088656-4

ACKNOWLEDGMENTS

For me, the best part of writing acknowledgments is my chance to thank publicly the students who generously gave me permission to show their writing as exemplary models in the *Simon & Schuster Handbook for Writers,* Sixth Edition. Each is now officially a "published writer." My congratulations!

I also thank the hundreds of students who have met with me in groups or who have written me to share their experiences with, and suggestions for, my handbooks. I take their words very seriously, and whatever flaws remain on these pages are my responsibility alone.

Central to my composing process for this new edition of the *Simon & Schuster Handbook for Writers* were three exceptional colleagues. Esther DiMarzio, Kishwaukee College, wrote most of the new exercises and shared her wise, creative insights into the teaching and learning of writing. Harriet Prentiss, Development Editor, was the penultimate structural editor and chief consultant as I updated the Sixth Edition. Cynthia Nordberg contributed hugely to the *Annotated Instructor's Edition* of the *Handbook,* as I explain in that volume's Preface.

Additionally, I was privileged to draw on the expertise of top-notch people to participate in the enterprise. I am very grateful to Beverly Buster, University of South Florida, for updating the *Simon & Schuster Workbook for Writers,* Sixth Edition; Lyneé Lewis Gaillet, Georgia State University, for journal updates; Linda Julian, Furman University, for updating *Strategies and Resources for Teaching Writing* to accompany the *Handbook;* Erin Karper, Purdue University, for any early draft of my new chapter on document design; William J. McCleary, retired, State University of New York at Brockport, for collaborative exercises; Sean Nighbert, St. Philip's College, for the first draft of my chapter about online research and for preparing Web site material for <www.prenhall.com/troyka>; Meredith Weisberg, Purdue University, for journal updates; and Christine Manion, Marquette University, for the first draft of my new chapter on oral presentations.

My special thanks go to the faculty reviewers for this Sixth Edition: Stephanie Chamberlain, Southeast Missouri State University; Patrick T. Dolan, Arapahoe Community College; Sarah H. Harrison, Tyler Junior College; Anna R. Holston, Central Texas Community College; Richard F. Johnson, William Rainey Harper College; Mary Lynch Kennedy, State University of New York at Cortland; Charles Poston, Fairmont State College; Lauren Sewell Coulter, University of Tennessee at Chattanooga; Beverly J. Slaughter, Brevard Community College; Dr. Jan E. VanStavern, Dominican College of San Rafael; Stephen Wilhoit, University of Dayton; Heywood L. Williams-Crisson, Longview Community College. I'm grateful, too, to the following students at Kishwaukee College who wrote very helpful reviews: Cheryl Casey, Naomi Campbell Faivre, Amy Houtz, Angela Johanasson, Carolina

Avendano Landaverde, Lauma Ribinska, Tara Senkowski, Harvest Sutherland, Daniel Underwood, and Kim Coleman-Kimberly Wilkerson. I also renew my gratitude for their contributions to my previous handbook editions: Don Jay Coppersmith, Internet Consultant; Jo Ellen Coppersmith, Utah Valley State College; Esther DiMarzio, Kishwaukee College; Ann B. Dobie, University of Southwestern Louisiana; Michael J. Freeman, Director of the Utah Valley State College Library; Scott Leonard, Youngstown State University; Dorothy V. Lindman, Brookhaven College; Alice Maclin, DeKalb College; Barbara Matthies, Iowa State University; Patricia Morgan, Louisiana State University; Kirk Rasmussen, Utah Valley State College; Mary Ruetten and Barbara Gaffney, University of New Orleans; Matilda Delgado Saenz; Paulette Smith, Reference Librarian, Valencia Community College; Judith Stanford, Rivier College; Cy Strom, Colborne Communications Center; and Lisa Lavery Wallace, Attorney at Law.

Behind the pages of this edition reside many voices of wise colleagues. I am particularly grateful to members of the Regional Advisory Boards for Prentice Hall and Lynn Troyka, who set aside precious days in their busy lives to discuss key issues with me. In the Southeast, they were Peggy Jolly, University of Alabama at Birmingham; Stephen Prewitt, David Lipscomb University; Mary Anne Reiss, Elizabethtown Community College; Michael Thro, Tidewater Community College at Virginia Beach; and the late, treasured Sally Young, University of Tennessee at Chattanooga. In the Southwest, they were Jon Bentley, Albuquerque Technical-Vocational Institute; Kathryn Fitzgerald, University of Utah; Maggy Smith, University of Texas at El Paso; Martha Smith, Brookhaven College; and Donnie Yeilding, Central Texas College. In Florida, they are Kathleen Bell, University of Central Florida; David Fear, Valencia Community College; D. J. Henry, Daytona Beach Community College; Marilyn Middendorf, Embry-Riddle Aeronautical University; Phillip Sipiora, University of South Florida; and Valerie Zimbaro, Valencia Community College.

My thanks also to reviewers of my earlier editions: Nancy Westrich Baker, Southeast Missouri State University; Bradley Bleck, University of Nevada; J. Norman Bosley, Ocean Community College; Phyllis Brown, Santa Clara University; Judith A. Burnham, Tulsa Community College; Robert S. Caim, West Virginia University at Parkersburg; Ann L. Camy, Red Rocks Community College; Joe R. Christopher, Tarleton State University; Marilyn M. Cleland, Purdue University, Calumet; Thomas Copeland, Youngstown State University; Rita Eastburg, College of Lake County; Joanne Ferreira, State University of New York at New Paltz and Fordham University; Carol L. Gabel, William Paterson University; Anne Gervasi, DeVry Institute of Technology; Joe Glaser, Western Kentucky University; Michael Goodman, Fairleigh Dickinson University; Mary Multer Greene, Tidewater Community College at Virginia Beach; Julie

Hagemann, Purdue University, Calumet; John L. Hare, Montgomery College; Lory Hawkes, DeVry Institute of Technology, Irving; Lorraine Higgins, University of Pittsburgh; Janet H. Hobbs, Wake Technical Community College; Frank Hubbard, Marquette University; Rebecca Innocent, Southern Methodist University; Ursula Irwin, Mount Hood Community College; Denise Jackson, Southeast Missouri State University; Margo K. Jang, Northern Kentucky University; Margaret Faye Jones, Nashville State Technical Institute; Myra Jones, Manatee Community College; Judith C. Kohl, Dutchess Community College; James C. McDonald, University of Southwestern Louisiana; Darlene Malaska, Youngstown Christian University; Christine Manion, Marquette University; Martha Marinara, University of Central Florida; Michael J. Martin, Illinois State University; Susan J. Miller, Santa Fe Community College; Rosemary G. Moffett, Elizabethtown Community College; Bethany Paige Nowviskie, University of Virginia; Jon F. Patton, University of Toledo; Pamela T. Pittman, University of Central Oklahoma; Nancy B. Porter, West Virginia Wesleyan College; Kirk Rasmussen, Utah Valley State College; Edward J. Reilly, St. Joseph's College; Peter Burton Ross, University of the District of Columbia; Eileen Schwartz, Purdue University, Calumet; Lisa Sebti, Central Texas College; Eileen B. Seifert, DePaul University; John S. Shea, Loyola University at Chicago; Tony Silva, Purdue University; Bill M. Stiffler, Harford Community College; Jack Summers, Central Piedmont Community College; Vivian A. Thomlinson, Cameron University; Matt Turner, Iowa State University; William P. Weiershauser, Iowa Wesleyan College; Joe Wenig, Purdue University; Carolyn West, Daytona Beach Community College; and Roseanna B. Whitlow, Southeast Missouri State University.

My special gratitude goes to a group of eminent colleagues who contributed to the Sixth Edition of the *Annotated Instructor's Edition (AIE)* of the *Simon & Schuster Handbook for Writers*. For their scholarly, bibliographic essays that set the context for my handbook, I thank Barbara Gleason, City College of the City University of New York; Catherine L. Hobbs, University of Oklahoma; Irwin Weiser, Purdue University; Margot I. Soven, La Salle University; and Joy Reid, University of Wyoming. D. J. Henry, Daytona Beach Community College, wrote the description in the margins of Chapter 35 of her practical application of portfolio assessment theory to the first-year composition classroom.

At Prentice Hall, I worked with a heroic, exceedingly intelligent team. Leah Jewell, English Editor in Chief, a visionary gifted with exceptional common sense, was the leader. Shelly Kupperman, Production Editor and Senior Project Manager, shared her amazing ability to care passionately, stay calm and productive in the midst of maelstroms, and polish all details to a lustrous shine. Vivian Garcia, Assistant Editor, was ideal as editorial coordinator because she is astute, dynamic, informed, and a delight to work with; while Stephanie Carpenter, Assistant Development

Editor, jumped on the moving train of my handbook with grace and gusto, quickly becoming indispensable. Brandy Dawson, Senior Marketing Manager, participated beyond what her title suggests, for she is a keen-minded, enthusiastic bard who brings to the table news of the road along with fresh ideas. Others whose support sustained me are Phil Miller, President of Humanities and Social Sciences; Barbara Kittle, Director of Production and Marketing; Mary Rottino, Managing Editor; Leslie Osher, Creative Design Director; Beth Gillett Mejia, Director of Marketing; Ximena P. Tamvakopoulos, Senior Art Director; Mary Ann Gloriande, Assistant Manufacturing Manager; Nick Sklitsis, Manufacturing Manager; Bud Therien, AVP/Publisher; and Editorial Assistant Jennifer M. Collins and Marketing Assistant Christine Moodie. I would also like to thank both Judy Kiveat and Diane Nesin for their sharp eyes and dedication to excellence in copyediting and proofreading this edition.

Family and friends strengthen all facets of my life by allowing me to share their lives and affections. Ida Morea, my Administrative Assistant and friend, is a joy who graces each day with her wonderful warmth, loyalty, excellence, and readiness to dive into whatever is at hand. My sister and friend, Edith Klausner, graces me with her bountiful spirit and outstanding values as a progressive educator. Others I treasure in my family include my sister and brother-in-law Rita and Hy Cohen; my niece, Randi Klausner Friedman, and Kenny, Casey, Max, and Alexandra; my nephew Michael Klausner and Barbara, Jill, Gregory, and Claire; my nephew Steven Klausner and Ariele, Daniel, and Jessica; my cousins Alan Furman and Lynne, Adam, and Joshua; Elaine and Lee Dushoff; Martha and Chuck Schliefer; Zina Rosenthal; the late, sorely missed Gideon Zwas; Tzila Zwas and Gila and Eyal; and my late parents, Belle and Sidney Quitman. My "adopted" family, most especially extraordinary Kristen – and Dan, Lindsey, and Ryan Black, are a cherished, vital part of my life. My dear friends stand by me in ways large and small. They are Susan Bartlestone; Elliot Goldhush; Myra Kogen; JoAnn and Tom Lavery; Betty Renshaw; Magdalena Rogalskaja; Avery Ryan and Jimmy, Gavin, and Ian; Shirley and Don Stearns; Marilyn and Ernest Sternglass; Elsie Tischler; Lisa and Nathaniel Wallace; and Muriel Wolfe. Most of all, I thank my husband and dearest friend, David Troyka, for his vibrant love, unwavering moral support, and energizing spirit of adventure.

CREDITS

ABOUT LYNN QUITMAN TROYKA

Photo: Ida Morea

Lynn Quitman Troyka, Ph.D., taught for many years at the City University of New York (CUNY), including Queensborough Community College; the Center for Advanced Studies in Education at the Graduate School; the graduate program in Language and Literacy at City College; and as Senior Research Associate in the Instructional Resource Center.

Dr. Troyka has published in journals such as *College Composition and Communication, College English, Journal of Basic Writing,* and *Writing Program Administration,* and in books from Southern Illinois University Press, Random House, the National Council of Teachers of English (NCTE), and Heinemann/Boynton/Cook. She is an author in composition/rhetoric for the *Encyclopedia of English Studies and Language Arts,* Scholastic, 1993; and in basic writing for the *Encyclopedia of Rhetoric,* 1994. She served as editor of the *Journal of Basic Writing* from 1985 to 1988. She has also conducted seminars and workshops at hundreds of colleges and at national and international meetings.

Dr. Troyka is the author of numerous textbooks, including the *Simon & Schuster Quick Access Reference for Writers,* Third Edition, Prentice Hall, 2000; the third *Canadian Edition of the Simon & Schuster Handbook for Writers,* Prentice-Hall Canada, 2001; *Structured Reading,* Fifth Edition, (with Joseph W. Thweatt), Prentice Hall, 1999; *Steps in Composition,* Seventh Edition (with Jerrold Nudelman), Prentice Hall, 1999; and seven others.

Dr. Troyka is a past national chair of the Two-Year College English Association (TYCA) of NCTE; the Conference on College Composition and Communication (CCCC), the College Section of NCTE, and the Writing Division of the Modern Language Association (MLA). She is the recipient of the 2001 Exemplar Award of CCCC, the highest award given for scholarship, teaching, and service. She was named 1993 Rhetorician of the Year, and she received the Nell Ann Pickett Award for Service in 1995 from TYCA.

She chaired the Task Force on the Future of CCCC and the CCCC Project Mentor Committee; and she currently serves on the NCTE Leadership Committee for Preparing Future Faculty (PFF), a project of the Council of Graduate Schools and the American Association of Colleges and Universities.

"All this information," says Dr. Troyka, "tells what I've done, not who I am. I am a teacher. Teaching is my life's work, and I love it."

For David,
who makes it all incredibly special

Visit the Troyka Web site for information on:

- Writing effective paragraphs
- Critical reading and writing
- Writing effective arguments

You'll also find access to *Writing Paragraphs* by Dorothy Turner at <www.uottawa.ca/ academic/arts/writcent/hypergrammar/ paragrph.html> Hosted by The University of Ottawa, this comprehensive site divides paragraph writing into easy-to-follow steps including outlining, organizing, and developing your paragraph. (This site uses Canadian spelling.)

PART ONE

WRITING AN ESSAY

1 THINKING ABOUT PURPOSES AND AUDIENCES

1a Why bother to write?

In this age of cell phones, e-mail, and the Internet, why do you need the ability to write well? Surprisingly, today's fast-paced, electronic world demands more, not less, writing. Whether for an entry-level job, for later advancement, or for a professional career, your success potential in workplaces of the twenty-first century relies heavily on how well you write documents. Recent surveys of people working in a variety of jobs and professional fields say that each day they spend an average of 30 percent of the time writing. They write letters, memos, product evaluations, technical manuals, business-trip reports, feasibility reports, lab reports, proposals, minutes, Web pages, newsletters, and brochures (the first four are most common).

Your success in college is another reason to have solid writing ability. Throughout your education, you will be called on to write essays, research papers, lab reports, and other college-related assignments.

Yet another benefit of writing skill comes from the physical activity of writing. In the act of writing, studies show, people significantly increase their insights, understandings, and abilities to remember the subject they're writing about. Here's how this phenomenon operates.

Writing is a way of discovering and learning. The physical act of writing triggers brain processes that lead you to make new connections among ideas. Pleasant shocks of recognition occur as your mind starts from what you already know and leaps to what you did not "see" before. One of my favorite statements comes from world-famous writer E. M. Forster: "How can I know what I mean until I've seen what I said?" Writing activates unique mental pathways that enable you to pursue knowledge, think through complex concepts, and gain solid ownership of your education.

Writing is a way of thinking and reflecting. Only humans can think about thinking. They can reflect on what they know and have experienced, a process greatly accelerated and enhanced during the act of writing. For you as a student, this means that writing forces you to clarify your thinking as you use words to convey your thoughts. And when you revise a draft, you push yourself further so that your writing is as close as possible to what you're thinking.

Writing is a way of owning and sharing knowledge. Few educated people remember specific classroom sessions or chapters from textbooks, but nearly everyone recalls the topics of their research papers. By writing intensively about a topic that you have thought about deeply, you become an authority on that topic. As this happens, others begin to identify you as a disciplined, educated person. On a larger scale, our democratic society can thrive only when people are educated to assess information, raise important questions, evaluate the answers, and exercise their rights and responsibilities as informed citizens.

1b How is writing defined?

Writing communicates a message for a purpose to readers; each of the four key terms in this sentence is important. **Written communication** involves sending a message to a destination. The **message** of writing is its content. The **purpose** of each writing task strongly influences central decisions writers make as they put their ideas into words (1c). **Readers,** or "audience," are the destination for writing (1d).

1c What are the major purposes for writing?

A writer's **purpose** for writing is the motivating force behind what's being written. Some students think their purpose is to fulfill an assignment, but the concept of *purpose* relates to the actual piece of writing. Every writer, whether student or professional, needs to get under way by choosing which of the four major purposes of writing, listed in Box 1, they want to pursue.

◉ **Purposes for writing*** 1

- to express yourself
- to inform a reader
- to persuade a reader
- to create a literary work

* Adapted from James L. Kinneavy, in *A Theory of Discourse* (1971; New York: Norton, 1980).

In this handbook, I concentrate on the two major purposes you need for most academic writing: to inform a reader (1c.2) and to persuade a reader (1c.3). I've chosen them because these two are the most practical and helpful for students. The two remaining purposes listed in Box 1 are important for contributing to human thought and culture, but they relate less to what most college writing involves.

1c.1 What is expressive writing?

Expressive writing is writing to express your personal thoughts and feelings. Largely, expressive writing is meant for the writer's eyes only. When expressive writing is intended as public reading, it falls into the category of *literary writing*. The excerpt here comes from the personal journal of Daniel Casey, the same student whose sample essay I show in Chapter 6 of this handbook. Daniel generously granted me permission to publish this excerpt here.

> When we lived in Maine, the fall and winter holidays were my touchstones—the calendar moved along in comforting sequence. I wrapped the snow and foods and celebrations around me like a soft blanket. I burrowed in. Now that we live in New Mexico, I don't need that blanket. But I sure do miss it.
>
> —Daniel Casey, student

1c.2 What is informative writing?

Informative writing seeks to give information to readers and usually to explain it. This type of writing is also called *expository writing* because it expounds on—sets forth—observations, ideas, facts, scientific data, and statistics. Informative writing is found in textbooks, encyclopedias, technical and business reports, nonfiction books, newspapers, and many magazines.

The essential goal of informative writing is to educate your reading audience about something. Like all good educators, you need to present your information clearly, accurately, completely, and fairly. In section 4i of this handbook, I show you many strategies that writers use for informative writing. I discuss and illustrate narration, description, process, example, definition, analysis and classification, comparison and contrast, analogy, and cause-and-effect analysis. These strategies can help you deliver your message, but above all, your success depends on whether your information can be verified as accurate. Box 2 gives you a checklist to assess your informative writing. But first, here's a paragraph written to inform.

> In 1914 in what is now Addo Park in South Africa, a hunter by the name of Pretorius was asked to exterminate a herd of 140 elephants. He killed all but 20, and those survivors became so cunning at evading him

that he was forced to abandon the hunt. The area became a preserve in 1930, and the elephants have been protected ever since. Nevertheless, elephants now four generations removed from those Pretorius hunted remain shy and strangely nocturnal. Young elephants evidently learn from the adults' trumpeting alarm calls to avoid humans.

—Carol Grant Gould, "Out of the Mouths of Beasts"

As informative writing, this paragraph works because it focuses clearly on its TOPIC* (elephant behavior), presents facts that can be verified (who, what, when, where), and is written in a reasonable TONE.

 Checklist for informative writing　　　　2

- Is its information clear?
- Does it present facts, ideas, and observations that can be verified?
- Does its information seem complete and accurate?
- Is the writer's tone reasonable and free of distortions (1e)?

1c.3　What is persuasive writing?

Persuasive writing, also called *argument writing,* seeks to convince readers about a matter of opinion. When you write to persuade, you deal with debatable topics, ones that can be seen from more than one point of view. Your goal is to change your readers' minds about the topic—or at least to bring your readers' opinions closer to your point of view. To succeed, you want to evoke a reaction in your audience so that they think beyond their present position (for example, reasoning why free speech needs to be preserved) or take action (for example, registering to vote). Examples of persuasive writing include newspaper editorials, letters to the editor, opinion essays in newspapers and magazines, reviews, sermons, books that argue a point of view, and business proposals that advocate certain approaches over others.

In Chapter 4 of this handbook, I show you strategies of paragraph development that effective writers use in their persuasive writing. Also, Chapter 6 is a whole chapter devoted entirely to approaches to writing arguments.

In general terms, persuasive writing means you move beyond merely stating your opinion. You give the basis for that opinion. You

---

* Find the definition of any word printed in small capital letters (such as TOPIC) in the Terms Glossary at the back of this book directly before the index.

support your opinion so that each GENERALIZATION you make is backed up with specific, illustrative details. A generalization is a broad statement without details. The first sentences of 1c.1, 1c.2, and 1c.3 are generalizations. Box 3 gives you a checklist to assess your persuasive writing. But first, here's a paragraph written to persuade.

> The search for some biological basis for math ability or disability is fraught with logical and experimental difficulties. Since not all math underachievers are women, and not all women are mathematics-avoidant, poor performance in math is unlikely to be due to some genetic or hormonal difference between the sexes. Moreover, no amount of research so far has unearthed a "mathematical competency" in some tangible, measurable substance in the body. Since "masculinity" can't be injected into women to test whether or not it improves their mathematics, the theories that attribute such ability to genes or hormones must depend for their proof on circumstantial evidence. So long as about 7 percent of the PhD's in mathematics are earned by women, we have to conclude either that these women have genes, hormones, and brain organization different from those of the rest of us, or that certain positive experiences in their lives have largely undone the negative fact that they're female, or both.
>
> —Sheila Tobias, *Overcoming Math Anxiety*

As persuasive writing, this passage works because it provides undistorted information on math ability; it expresses a point of view that resides in sound reasoning (math ability isn't based on gender); it offers evidence (a logical line of argument); and it tries to get the reader to agree with the point of view.

 Checklist for persuasive writing   **3**

- Does it present a point of view about which opinions vary?
- Does it support its point of view with specifics?
- Does it base its point of view on sound reasoning and logic?
- Are the parts of its argument clear?
- Does it intend to evoke a reaction from the reader?

EXERCISE 1-1

For each paragraph, decide if the dominant purpose is informative or persuasive. Then apply the questions in Box 2 or Box 3 to the paragraph, and explain your answers.

A.   Diabetes mellitus could be treated—at least to the extent of reducing the elevated blood sugar and correcting the acidosis that otherwise led to diabetic coma and death—by the insulin preparation isolated by Banting and Best. Pellagra, a common cause of death among the impoverished rural populations in the South, had become curable with Goldberger's discovery of the vitamin B complex and the subsequent identification of nicotinic acid. Diphtheria could be prevented by immunization against the toxin of diphtheria bacilli and, when it occurred, treated more or less effectively with diphtheria antitoxin.
                                                                —Lewis Thomas, "1933 Medicine"

B.   Efforts to involve the father in the birth process, to enhance his sense of paternity and empowerment as he adjusts to his new role, should be increased. Having the father involved in labor and delivery can significantly increase his sense of himself as a person who is important to his child and to his mate. Several investigators have shown that increased participation of fathers in the care of their babies, increased sensitivity to their baby's cues at one month, and significantly increased support of their wives can result from the rather simple maneuver of sharing the newborn baby's behavior with the new father at three days, using the Neonatal Behavioral Assessment Scale (NBAS). In light of these apparent gains, we would do well to consider a period of paid paternity leave, which might serve both symbolically and in reality as a means of stamping the father's role as critical to his family. Ensuring the father's active participation is likely to enhance his image of himself as a nurturing person and to assist him toward a more mature adjustment in his life as a whole.
                                                    —T. Berry Brazelton, "Issues for Working Parents"

C.   After proposing marriage to a neighbor girl, my grandfather used this hammer to build a house for his bride on a stretch of river bottom in northern Mississippi. The lumber for the place, like the hickory for the handle, was cut on his own land. By the day of the wedding, he had not quite finished the house, and so right after the ceremony, he took his wife home and put her to work. My grandmother had worn her Sunday dress for the wedding, with a fringe of lace tacked on around the hem in honor of the occasion. She removed this lace and folded it away before going out to help my grandfather nail siding on the house. "There she was in her good dress," he told me some fifty-odd years after that wedding day, "holding up them long pieces of clapboard while I hammered, and together we got the place covered up before dark." As the family grew to four, six, eight, and eventually thirteen, my grandfather used this hammer to enlarge his house room by room, like a chambered nautilus expanding its shell.
                                                    —Scott Russell Sanders, "The Inheritance of Tools"

EXERCISE 1-2

Using each topic listed here, work individually or with your peer-response group to think through two different essays: one informative, the second persuasive. Be ready to discuss in some detail how the two essays on each topic would differ. For help, consult section 1c.

diets   tastes in music   current fads in clothing   road rage

1d What does "audience" mean for writing?

Your **audience** consists of everyone who will read your writing. After college, your audiences will be readers of your business, professional, and public writing (Chapter 42). In college, you address a mix of audience types, each of which expects to read **academic writing**—the writing assigned in your courses. Here's a list of overall categories of audiences for academic writing, each of which is detailed in the section listed in parentheses.

- your peers (1d.1)
- a general audience (1d.2)
- a specialist audience (1d.3)
- your instructor (who represents either general or specialized readers) (1d.4)

The more specifics you can assume about your audience for your academic writing, the better your chances of reaching it successfully. The questions in Box 4 can serve as a guide.

◎ **Characteristics of reading audiences**　　　　**4**

What Setting Are They Reading In?
- academic setting?
- workplace setting?
- public setting?

Who Are They?
- age, gender
- ethnic backgrounds, political philosophies, religious beliefs

→

Characteristics of reading audiences *(continued)*   **4**

- roles (student, parent, voter, wage earner, property owner, veteran, and others)
- interests, hobbies

What Do They Know?

- level of education
- amount of general or specialized knowledge about the topic
- probable preconceptions and prejudices brought to the topic

---

When you know or can reasonably assume who will be in your reading audience for each assignment, your chances of reaching it improve. For example, if you're writing a sales report for your supervisor, you can use terms such as *product life cycle, break-even quantity, nonprice competition,* and *markup.* In contrast, if general readers were the audience for the same information, you would want to avoid specialized, technical vocabulary—or if you had to use some essential specialized terms, you would define them in a nontechnical way.

⊕ ESL NOTE: As someone from a non-U.S. culture, you might be surprised—even offended—by the directness with which people speak and write in the United States. If so, I hope you'll read my open letter to multilingual students about honoring their cultures; it starts Part Seven of this handbook. You may come from a written-language tradition that expects elaborate, formal, or ceremonial language; reserves the central point of an academic essay for the middle; requires tactful, indirect discussions (at least in comparison to the U.S. style); and, in some cultures, accommodates digressions that might, or might not, lead back to the main point. In contrast, U.S. writers and readers expect language and style that is very direct, straightforward, and without embellishment (as compared to the styles of many other cultures). U.S. college instructors expect essays in ACADEMIC WRITING to contain a THESIS STATEMENT (usually at the end of the introductory paragraph), to demonstrate a tightly organized presentation of information from one paragraph to the next, to make GENERALIZATIONS that are always backed up with strong supporting details, and to end with a logical concluding paragraph. Also, for writing in the United States you are expected to use so-called *standard English grammar.* This means following the rules used by educated speakers. Actually, the United States has a rich mixture of grammar systems, but academic writing requires standard English grammar. If you want to hear it spoken, listen to the anchors of television and radio news programs. Accurate choice of words and spelling are also expected. ⊕

1d.1 What is a peer audience?

In some writing classes, instructors divide students into **peer-response groups**. People in your *peer group* are fellow students in your class, and all are equal in the right to speak. Peer-response groups can be formed for students to give each other feedback on their writing. (If your instructor does not use peer-response groups, ask if you are permitted to show other students your writing to get their responses. Some instructors have very strict rules about such matters, so ask before you act.)

Participating in a peer-response group makes you part of a respected tradition of colleagues helping colleagues. Professional writers often seek comments from other writers to improve their rough drafts. As a member of a peer-response group, you're not expected to be a writing expert. Rather, you're expected to offer responses as a practiced reader and as a fellow student writer who understands what writers go through.

The role of members of a peer-response group is to react and discuss, not to do the work for someone. Hearing or reading comments from your peers might be your first experience with seeing how others read your writing. This can be very informative, surprising, and helpful. Also, when peers share their writing with the group, each member gets the added advantage of learning about other students' writing for the same assignment.

Peer-response groups are set up in different ways. One arrangement calls for students to pass around and read each other's drafts silently, writing down reactions or questions in the margins or on a response form created by the instructor. In another arrangement, students read their drafts aloud, and then each peer responds either orally or on a response form. Yet another arrangement asks for focused responses to only one or two features of each draft (perhaps each member's thesis statement, or topic sentences and supporting details, or use of transitional words, etc.). Still another method is for the group to BRAINSTORM a topic together before writing, or to discuss various sides of a debatable topic, or to share reactions to an essay or piece of literature the class has read, and so on.

Whatever the arrangement of your group, you want to be clear about exactly what you are expected to do, both as a peer-responder and as a writer. If your instructor gives you guidelines for working in a peer-response group, follow them carefully. If you've never before participated in a peer-response group, or in the particular kind your instructor forms, here are ways to get started: Consult the guidelines in Box 5 at the end of this section; watch what experienced peers do; and ask questions of your instructor (your interest shows a positive, cooperative attitude). Otherwise, just dive in knowing that you will learn as you go.

Now to the sometimes sticky issue of how to take criticism of your writing: Here's my personal advice as a writer for being able (or at least appearing able) to take constructive criticism gracefully. First, know that most students don't like to criticize their peers. They worry about being impolite, inaccurate, or losing someone's friendship. Try, therefore, to cultivate an attitude that encourages your peers to respond as freely and as helpfully as possible. Show, also, that you can listen without getting angry or feeling intruded upon.

Second, realize that most people tend to be a little (or quite a bit) defensive about even the best-intentioned and tactful criticism. Of course, if a comment is purposely mean or sarcastic, you and all others in your peer-response group have every right to say so and not tolerate it. Third, if you don't understand a comment fully, ask for clarification. Otherwise, you might misunderstand what's suggested and go off in the wrong direction.

Finally, no matter what anyone says about your writing, it remains yours alone. You retain "ownership" of your writing always, and you don't have to make every suggested change. Use only the comments that you think can move you closer to reaching your intended audience. Of course, if a comment from your instructor points out a definite problem, and you choose to ignore it, it could have an impact on your grade—though many instructors are open to an explanation of your rationale for deciding to ignore what they said.

⊚ **ALERT:** Some instructors and students use the terms *peer-response group* and *collaborative writing* to mean the same thing. In this handbook, I assign the terms to two different situations. I use *peer-response group* (1d.1) for students getting together in small groups to help each other do many things, as I explain below. I use COLLABORATIVE WRITING (3f) for students writing an essay, a research paper, or a report together. ●

◉ **Guidelines for participating**   **5**
    in peer-response groups

One basic principle should guide your participation in a peer-response group: Take an upbeat, constructive attitude, whether you're responding to someone else's writing or receiving responses from others.

As a Responder

■ Think of yourself in the role of a coach, not a judge.

■ Consider all writing by your peers as "works in progress."

                                                   →

Guidelines for participating   **5**
in peer-response groups *(continued)*

- After hearing or reading a peer's writing, briefly summarize it to check that you and your peer are clear about what the peer said or meant to say.
- Start with what you think is well done. No one likes to hear only negative comments.
- Be honest in your suggestions for improvements.
- Base your responses on an understanding of the writing process, and remember that you're reading drafts, not finished products. All writing can be revised.
- Give concrete and specific responses. General comments such as "This is good" or "This is weak" aren't much help. Say specifically what is good or weak.
- Follow your instructor's system for putting your comments in writing so that your fellow writer can recall what you said. If one member of your group is supposed to take notes, speak clearly so that the person can be accurate. If you're the notetaker, be accurate, and ask the speaker to repeat what he or she said if it went by too quickly.

As a Writer

- Adopt an attitude that encourages your peers to respond freely. Listen and try to resist any urge to interrupt during a comment or to jump in to react.
- Remain open-minded. Your peers' comments can help you see your writing in a fresh way, which, in turn, can help you produce a better revised draft.
- Ask for clarification if a comment isn't clear. If a comment is too general, ask for specifics.
- As much as you encourage your peers to be honest, remember that the writing is yours. You "own" it, and you decide which comments to use or not use.

1d.2 What is a general audience?

A **general audience** of readers is composed of educated, experienced readers—people who regularly read newspapers, magazines, and books. These readers, with general knowledge of many subjects, likely know something about your topic. But, if you get too technical, you are writing for readers who possess specialized knowledge on a particular subject (1d.3). Consequently, avoid specialized or technical terms—though, if you need to use a few, be sure to give everyday definitions.

Also, general readers approach a piece of writing expecting to become interested in it. They hope to learn about a new topic, to add to their store of knowledge about a subject, and, often, to see a subject from a perspective other than their own. As a writer, you need to fulfill those expectations.

1d.3 What is a specialist audience?

A **specialist audience** is composed of readers who have expert knowledge of specific subjects. Many people are experts in their occupational fields, and some become experts in areas that simply interest them, such as amateur astronomy or raising orchids. People from a particular group background (Democrats, Republicans, Catholics, or military veterans, for example) are specialists in those areas.

Specialist readers, however, share more than knowledge: They share assumptions and beliefs. For example, suppose you're writing for an audience of immigrants to the United States who feel strongly about keeping their cultural traditions alive. You can surely assume your readers know those traditions well, so you wouldn't need to describe and explain the basics. On the other hand, whenever you introduce a concept that's likely new to your readers, don't assume they'll understand it right away, even though they are specialists. Explain the new concept thoroughly.

1d.4 What is my instructor's role as audience?

As your audience, your instructor functions in three ways. First, your instructor assumes the role of your target audience: either general or specialist readers (1d.2 and 1d.3). Second, your instructor is like a coach, someone committed to helping you improve your writing. Third, your instructor is the eventual evaluator of your final drafts.

Instructors know that few students are experienced writers or experts on the subjects they write about. Still, instructors expect your writing to reflect your having taken the time to learn something worthwhile about a topic and then to write about it clearly. Instructors are experienced readers; they recognize a minimal effort almost at once.

Also, instructors are members of a group whose professional lives center on intellectual endeavors. You, therefore, want to write within the constraints of academic writing and to write on topics that have some intrinsic intellectual interest (2d).

If you are a relatively inexperienced college writer, you might wrongly assume that your instructor can mentally fill in what's not said. Or you might think that it's wrong, even insulting to your instructor, if you extend your discussion beyond simple statements. Instructors—indeed, all readers—are not mind readers, and they become annoyed when you don't write fully on a topic. It's never wrong to go beyond stating the obvious or to show you know how to develop your material beyond bare-bones basics. By the way, if you think you might be saying too little, ask your peers to read your writing and tell you if your worry is justified.

1e What is "tone" in writing?

Tone is more than what you say; tone is *how* you say it. As a writer, your tone reveals your attitude toward your AUDIENCE as well as the TOPIC. Tone in writing operates like tone of voice, except in writing you can't rely on facial expressions and voice intonations to communicate a tone.

Your DICTION (choice of words), LEVEL OF FORMALITY, and writing style create your tone. You can use SLANG and other highly INFORMAL LANGUAGE in a note to your roommate, but not in ACADEMIC WRITING or BUSINESS WRITING. When you write for an audience about which you know little, use more formality. "More formality," by the way doesn't mean dull and drab. Lively language in a serious discussion can enhance your message and strike the right tone.

In business and professions, if you were to write a memo to your supervisor about a safety hazard in your workplace, you would avoid writing a chatty message with a joke about an accident that could happen. Such a tone directed at your supervisor would be described as "flippant" or "irresponsible." Then again, if you chose to include in the memo all sorts of background information that your supervisor already knows, your supervisor would become impatient and annoyed.

Academic writing usually calls for a medium-to-formal tone (21b). This is a reasonable, even-handed tone, somewhat formal and serious but not pompous. Also, in academic writing, you want to avoid using language to manipulate your readers, especially with distorted facts or SLANTED LANGUAGE (21h). Slanted terms (for example, *the corrupt, deceitful politician*) rather than neutral words (for example, *the politician under investigation for taking bribes*) seem to jump off the page, causing your readers to decide immediately that your message isn't trustworthy.

In all types of writing, use GENDER-NEUTRAL LANGUAGE that represents both men and women fairly (for example, replace *policeman* with *police officer;* replace *doctors' wives* with *doctors' spouses*). Similarly, avoid SEXIST LANGUAGE or words with sexist overtones (21g) so that you don't alienate your readers because you appear to be insensitive to gender issues or simply crude in using language.

Another type of language that carries a message larger than the words themselves is pretentious language (21h). Its use implies either that you're showing off to impress people (it never works) or that you want to obscure a message with an unnecessary pileup of words. Choose straightforward rather than extravagant words (use *concert,* not *orchestral event*) if you want to be taken seriously. Another way your readers can tell you want to hide something is by the use of EUPHEMISMS (use *cutting jobs,* not *downsizing* or *rightsizing*).

Problems with tone can result from combining words into certain phrases. It's the combination and its location, not the words taken separately, that creates a tone. For example, you want to avoid sarcastic language in an academic or business setting that calls for a reasonable tone. If you were to write "He was a regular Albert Einstein" to describe a person interviewed for a paper, the words would say more about you than about the person interviewed. Such a tone implies an overly critical or nasty streak that can't be controlled. Conversely, you could introduce IRONY if you wrote "The chief assistant to Governor George Ghoti claimed the Governor could give me up-to-date information about my topic, but the assistant turned out to know much more than the Governor." Box 6 lists guidelines for handling tone in your writing.

 How to use tone in writing 6

- Reserve a highly informal tone for conversational writing.
- Use a formal or medium level of formality in your academic writing and when you write for supervisors, professionals, and other people you know from a distance.
- Avoid an overly formal, ceremonial tone.
- Avoid sarcasm and other forms of nastiness.
- Choose language appropriate for your topic and your readers.
- Choose words that work with your message, not against it.
- Whatever tone you choose to use, be consistent in each piece of writing.

EXERCISE 1-3

Using the topics listed here, work individually or with your peer-response group to think through specific ways the tone of an essay would differ for these three audiences: a college instructor, a close friend, and a supervisor at a job. Be ready to discuss in some detail how the three essays on each topic would differ. For help, consult sections 1d and 1e.

suggestions for a fair way to evaluate each person's work

benefits of having water sprinklers in every room

an explanation of why you were absent yesterday

1f What does "sources for writing" mean?

Sources for writing consist of material that contains someone else's ideas, not yours. Sources, often called *outside sources*, include credible information on the Internet, library collections, and the spoken words of experts. Sources can add authority to what you write, especially if the topic is open to debate. But be careful: Different instructors have differing policies on outside sources. Some instructors want students to draw on sources only in connection with a research paper (Chapters 31–37). Other instructors encourage "source-based writing" for most assignments. Still others never want students to use outside sources. Find out your instructor's stand on the use of sources so you can fulfill the requirements of your course successfully.

Some students wonder whether consulting sources for their writing suggests that they can't come up with ideas of their own. Actually, the opposite is true. When students use sources well, they demonstrate their ability to locate relevant sources, assess whether the sources are credible and worth using, integrate the material with skill, and credit the sources accurately. To achieve this, follow the guidelines in Box 7 at the end of this section.

Of course, no matter how many outside sources you refer to, you remain your own first source. Throughout your life, you've been building a fund of knowledge by reading, going to school, attending cultural and sports events, hearing speeches by experts, watching television, and exploring the Internet. The basis for your writing is the information you have, as well as your ideas, reflections, reactions, and opinions. Sources offer support and additional information and points of view, but you are always the starting point for your writing.

If you use sources in your writing, never plagiarize. PLAGIARISM occurs when a writer takes ideas or words from a source without revealing that a source was used or what the source was. Always, give credit by using DOCUMENTATION to tell your readers the exact place where your thinking was influenced by a source. According to the DOCUMENTATION STYLE you are using (Chapters 35–37), state the name of the source and where it can be found by anyone else who would wish to consult it.

If you don't document your sources, you are plagiarizing (Chapter 31). Plagiarism is a major academic offense. A student who plagiarizes can instantly fail a course or be asked to leave college. Until recently, students might have felt they could "get away" with plagiarizing because no instructor could have read all the possible sources on a topic. Today, however, at least one WORLD WIDE WEB site—and likely more in the future—can scan documents and search the INTERNET to identify plagiarized material. Such Web sites look at the sites that sell papers, digitized library collections, and all search engine files. A **search engine** is an Internet-specific software program that can look through files at all Internet sites. The search quickly identifies not only exactly what has been plagiarized but also the source from which the material was taken.

◉ Guidelines for using sources in writing   7

- Evaluate sources critically. Not all are accurate, true, or honest. (5g, especially Box 36 on p. 126)
- Represent your sources accurately. Be sure to quote, PARAPHRASE, and summarize well so that you avoid distorting the material. (Chapter 31)
- Never plagiarize. (Chapter 31a)
- Know the difference between writing a SUMMARY and writing a SYNTHESIS. By using sources in your writing, you are expected to synthesize well. A summary means all you do is report the source material. That is not enough. A synthesis means you make intelligent connections between the source and your ideas, or between a variety of sources, or between a variety of sources and your ideas. Synthesizing is what college writers are expected to do. (5e and 5f)
- Credit your sources with DOCUMENTATION that names them clearly and completely. Ask your instructor which DOCUMENTATION STYLE to use. Five widely used styles are presented in Chapters 35–37.

1g What tools can help me as a writer?

Before you begin tackling your college writing assignments, you can benefit greatly from knowing what tools are widely available to help you.

1g.1 A computer for word processing

A computer's **word processing** software can prove a big help at various stages of the WRITING PROCESS (see Box 8, page 21, for summary). Although you can certainly write by hand or at a typewriter, methods writers have been using for many years, you might find that writing on a computer is easier. If you don't own a computer, try to use one in your college's computer lab. Many colleges require final drafts to be typed on a computer, though some make allowances for students who find it impossible.

1g.2 Your personal bookshelf

Your **personal bookshelf** needs to contain three essential volumes: a dictionary, a thesaurus, and a handbook for writers. A **dictionary** is indispensable. If possible, buy one. Most college bookstores offer a good variety of hardback "college dictionaries." Before choosing one, browse through it and read some definitions you want to learn or to understand more clearly. A lightweight paperback abridged dictionary in your book pack can be very handy for checking words on the spot when they're unknown to you. Unabridged dictionaries list all recognized words in standard use in English. They're comprehensive, but heavy and over-sized. The reference section of every library has one (usually on display) that anyone can consult (21e.1).

Another valuable resource for writers is a **thesaurus,** which is a col-lection of synonyms. The easiest to use are arranged alphabetically. Check for this feature, as it is not an automatic arrangement for a the-saurus. *Roget's 21st Century Thesaurus* is an excellent volume arranged alphabetically. If you prefer to start with a paperback, many alphabeti-cally arranged ones are available. Soon, however, you might find a short thesaurus too limited in scope (21e.2).

A **handbook for writers** is also vital for you to have on your per-sonal bookshelf. A handbook—such as the one you're holding as you read this—gives you detailed information about (sometimes forgotten) rules of grammar, punctuation, and other writing conventions. It also offers extensive advice about how to write successfully, whether for col-lege, business, or the public. It shows you step by step how to write and document research papers. Some handbooks, including this one, include guidance on how to write for a variety of courses other than English. You need all this information to write successfully in other courses and in your career after college.

🖳 **COMPUTER TIP:** As I write this, only one highly respected college dictionary—the *Merriam-Webster Collegiate Dictionary*—can be ac-cessed online. The URL is <http://www.m-w.com/netdict.htm>. The same site gives you access to an online thesaurus. To find out what is available when you need it, use your search engine to go to "dictionar-ies." ▣

1g.3 Your college library

A **college library,** sometimes called a *learning resources center,* is fully stocked with all manner of reference books, circulating books, resources for online access, and more. Before you need to use the library, spend some time getting to know what's available. Then you can dive right in when the time comes.

Concentrate most on your college library's reference section. It con-tains dozens, if not hundreds, of volumes. Essential resources include at least one set of encyclopedias; one or more almanacs; various kinds of up-to-date atlases; books of quotations (don't limit yourself to the classic *Bartlett's Familiar Quotations*); indexes to popular and scholarly period-icals; and the *Library of Congress Subject Headings* (*LCSH*), volumes that list all categories of knowledge with subcategories for each. These resources can be centrally important as you write research papers and search out information for other purposes. Today, many—but not all—reference books are available in print and online.

1g.4 Computer tools for writers

Word processing programs, such as WordPerfect and Microsoft Word, include aids for writers. They're built into your software. They offer some advantages, but they also have severe limitations. Become familiar with both. In no case are such tools substitutes for your own careful editing and proofreading. Software, after all, can't "think" and make distinctions between *form* and *from* in spelling, between the way you use or misuse *deep* and *profound,* or between an unjustified and a justified use of a passive construction (8p).

- **Spell-check programs** show you words that don't match the dictionary in the software. These programs are a big help for spotting a misspelling or mistyping (called *typos*), but they won't call your attention to your having typed *west* when you intended to type *rest*.

- **Thesaurus programs,** like their print versions, give you synonyms for words. But they can't tell you which fit well into your particular sentences. Whenever a synonym is unfamiliar or hazy, look it up in your dictionary. You don't want to use words that strike you as attractive options, but which turn out to distort or render meaningless your communication.

- **Grammar** or **style-check programs** check your writing against the software's strict interpretations of rules of grammar, word use, punctuation, and other conventions. You then see an alert signaling those elements of your writing that differ from the program's standards. Can you always rely on those standards? No. While most alerts are useful for getting you to re-think the way you've said something, the final decision about how to deliver your message is yours. You might want to use a semicolon even when the program suggests a period, to retain a word even when the program says you need to be concise, or to accept a long sentence when it follows or is followed by a few very short sentences. Consult this handbook if you're not sure what a program is suggesting or about the justification for your deviation from the program's rules.

www.prenhall.com/troyka

2 PLANNING AND SHAPING

2a What is the writing process?

Many people think that professional writers can sit down at their computers, think of ideas, and magically produce a finished draft, word by perfect word. Experienced writers know better. They know that **writing is a process,** a series of activities that starts the moment they begin thinking about a subject and ends with proofreading the final draft. Experienced writers also know that good writing is rewriting, again and yet again. Their drafts are filled with additions, deletions, rewordings, and rearrangements.

For example, see below how I revised the paragraph you just read. I didn't make all the changes at the same time, even though it looks that way on the example. I went through the paragraph four times before I was sat-

~~Chapter One discusses what writing is. This chapter explains how writing happens.~~ Many people think that professional writers can sit down at their computers, think of ideas, and ⌃*magically* produce a finished draft, word by perfect word. Experienced writers know better. They know that writing is a process. ~~The writing process is~~ a series of activities that starts the moment *they begin*⌃ thinking about a subject ~~begins~~ and ends with⌃ *proofreading* the final draft. Experienced writers also know that good writing is rewriting, again and yet again. *Their drafts are filled with additions, deletions, rewordings, and rearrangements.*

Draft and revision of Lynn Troyka's first paragraph in Chapter 2

isfied with it. Notice that I deleted one sentence, combined two sentences, added a sentence at the end, and changed wording throughout.

Writing is an ongoing process of considering alternatives and making choices. The better you understand the writing process, the better you'll write; and the more you feel in control of your writing, the more you'll enjoy it.

In this chapter, I discuss each part of the writing process separately. In real life, the steps overlap. They loop back and forth, which is why writing is called a *recursive process*. Box 8 lists the steps.

◉ Steps in the writing process 8

- **P** = **Planning** means discovering and compiling ideas for your writing.
- **S** = **Shaping** means organizing your material.
- **D** = **Drafting** means writing your material into sentences and paragraphs.
- **R** = **Revising** means evaluating your draft and then rewriting it by adding, deleting, rewording, and rearranging.
- **E** = **Editing** means checking for correct grammar, spelling, punctuation, and mechanics.
- **P** = **Proofreading** means reading your final copy to eliminate typing or handwriting errors.

Visualizing the writing process

Do you like, as I do, to visualize a process? If so, see the drawing here. The arrows show movement. You might move back before going ahead (perhaps as you revise, you realize you need to plan some more); or you might skip a step and come back to it later (perhaps in the middle of revising, you jump into editing for a few minutes because a punctuation or grammar rule affects how you express your point); and so on.

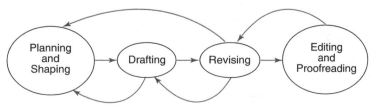

Visualizing the writing process

As you work with the writing process, allow yourself to move freely through each step to see what's involved. Notice what works best for *you*. As you develop a sense of your preferred writing methods, adapt the process to fit each writing situation. No single way exists for applying the writing process.

My most personal advice from one writer to another is this: Most writers struggle some of the time with ideas that are difficult to express, sentences that won't take shape, and words that aren't precise. Be patient with yourself. Don't get discouraged. Writing takes time. The more you write, the easier it will become—though writing never happens magically.

2b What terms describe different kinds of writing?

Terms that describe different types of writing are often used interchangeably. Most instructors attach specific meanings to each one. Listen closely so you can sort out what terms *your* instructor uses. If your instructor's use of terms isn't clear, ask for clarification.

For example, the words *essay, theme,* and *composition* usually—but not always—refer to writing of about 500 to 1,000 words. In this handbook, I use **essay**. Similarly, the word *paper* can mean anything from a few paragraphs to a complex research project. In this handbook, I use **paper** for longer writing projects, such as *research papers*. Also, I sometimes use the general term **piece of writing** to refer to all types of writing.

2c What is a "writing situation"?

The **writing situation** of each assignment is the place to start with thinking about your writing. Its four elements are *topic, purpose, audience,* and *special requirements*. The questions in Box 9 cover each aspect. (*Memory hint:* The first letter of each word (TPAS) will form TOPAS by adding the letter *O* from *topic;* perhaps pronouncing it "to pass" will also help.)

⊙ **Guidelines for analyzing each writing situation: TPAS**   9

- **T** = **Topic:** What topic will you be writing about?
- **P** = **Purpose:** What is your purpose for writing (1c)?
- **A** = **Audience:** Who is your audience (1d)?
- **S** = **Special requirements:** How much time do you have to complete the assignment? What is the length requirement?

A **topic** is the foundation of every writing situation. As you think through a topic, you want to remain within the constraints of academic writing. Whatever your topic, stick to it, and resist any temptation to bend it in another direction.

The **purpose** of most college writing is to inform or persuade (1b and 1c). Some assignments state the writing purpose, while some only imply it. For example, if you were asked, "Describe government restrictions on cigarette advertising," your purpose would be informative. In contrast, if you were asked to respond to the statement "Smoking should (or should not) be banned in all public places," your purpose would be persuasive.

But suppose your assignment doesn't indicate a writing purpose: for example, "Write an essay on smoking." Here, you're expected to choose a purpose and think about what you intend to write on the topic. As you plan how to develop the topic, you'll begin to see whether your purpose is informative or persuasive. It's normal to find yourself deciding to switch purposes midstream to better suit what you are saying.

Your reading **audience** (1d) consists of everyone who will read what you write. According to your assignment and the procedures in your class, your audience includes your peer-response group (1d.1), friends, readers who have specialized knowledge about your topic (1d.3), and your instructor (1d.4). Think through the characteristics and expectations of your audience so that your writing will successfully deliver its intended meaning.

Special requirements are practical matters such as how much time you're given to complete the assignment and how long your writing should be. For example, for an assignment due in one week, your reading audience expects more than one day's work. However, if an assignment is due overnight, your reading audience realizes you had to write in haste, though they never expect sloppy or careless work. Perhaps the highest expectations in a reading audience are applied to an assignment that calls for reading or other research, so be sure to build time for that early in your schedule.

Some instructors put each assignment in writing, either on the board or in a handout. But other instructors give assignments orally during class, expecting you to write them down. Try to record every word. Don't hesitate to ask questions if you don't catch all the words or if something isn't clear—and be sure to write down the answers because they often tend to slip from memory. Listen, too, to questions other students ask, and write down the answers. Such notes can serve as useful springboards when you start writing.

In the rest of this chapter, I present the writing processes of two college students, Carol Moreno and Daniel Casey, as they plan and shape their material. Then, in Chapter 3, you'll see Carol's essay evolving through three separate, complete drafts. Later, in Chapter 6, you'll see how Daniel's essay developed. To start, here are the written assignments each student received.

> **Carol Moreno was given this assignment:** Write an essay of 700 to 800 words discussing a challenge you faced and tried to meet. Your writing purpose can be informative or persuasive. Expect to write three drafts. (1) Your first draft, typed double-spaced, is due two classes from today. (2) Your clean second draft, typed double-spaced, without notes or comments, is due two classes later. Clip to it your first draft showing all notes you made to yourself or from comments your peer-response group made; you can handwrite notes and comments. I'll read your second draft as an "essay in progress" and will make comments to help you toward a third (and final) draft. (3) The third draft, typed double-spaced, is due one week after I return your second draft with my comments.
>
> **Daniel Casey was given this assignment:** Write an essay of 500 to 700 words arguing that holidays in the United States have or have not become too commercialized. Your final draft is due in one week.

Carol's first step was to analyze her writing situation (Box 9). She realized the *topic*—a challenge she faced and tried to meet—would need to be narrowed. She tentatively decided her *purpose* would be informative, though she thought she might have to switch to a persuasive purpose as she went along. She knew that she would share her first draft with her peer-response group to help her toward her second draft. She also understood that her instructor would be her final *audience*. She was aware of the *requirements* for time and length.

Daniel also read his assignment and analyzed his writing situation (Box 9). He saw that the assignment was very structured. The *topic* is given—commercialization of holidays in the United States. The *purpose* is persuasive because students needed to take a position on the topic and argue for it. He knew from experience in this class that his instructor would be his *audience*. The time and length *requirements* were specifically stated.

EXERCISE 2-1

For each assignment below, work individually or with a peer-response group to list the elements in the writing situation. Consult section 2c for help.

1. *English:* Write a 500- to 700-word essay arguing for or against doubling the size of your college's student body. This assignment is due in one week.

2. *Journalism:* Write a 300-word editorial for the student newspaper (to be published next week) praising or criticizing your college's policy of selling parking stickers to students and faculty on a first-come basis. Draw on your personal experience or that of students you know.

3. *Art:* You have twenty minutes in class to compare and contrast Greek and Roman styles of architecture.
4. *Chemistry:* Write a one-paragraph description of the process of hydration.
5. *Economics:* Write a 1,000-word paper on the impact of capitalism since 1989 on the former communist nations of eastern Europe. Draw on your reading. Be sure to cite your sources. This assignment is due in two weeks.

2d How can I think through a writing topic?

Situations vary. Some assignments are very specific. For example, here's an assignment that leaves no room for choice: "Explain how oxygen is absorbed in the lungs." Students need to do precisely what's asked, taking care not to wander off the topic. Only rarely, however, are writing-class assignments as specific as that one. Often, you'll be expected to select your own topic (2d.1), broaden a narrow topic (2d.2), or narrow a broad topic (2d.3). The overriding principle always is **what separates most good writing from bad is the writer's ability to move back and forth between general statements and specific details.**

2d.1 Selecting your own topic

If you have to choose a topic, don't rush. Take time to think through your ideas. Avoid getting so deeply involved in one topic that you cannot change to a more suitable topic in the time allotted.

Not all topics are suitable for ACADEMIC WRITING. Your topic needs to have inherent intellectual interest: ideas and issues meaty enough to demonstrate your thinking and writing abilities. Think through potential topics by breaking each into its logical subsections. Then, make sure you can supply sufficiently specific details to back up each general statement. Conversely, make sure you are not bogged down in so many details you can't figure out what GENERALIZATIONS they support.

Work toward balance by finding a middle ground. Beware of topics so broad they lead to well-meaning but vague generalizations (for example, *Education is necessary for success*). Also, beware of topics so narrow that they lead nowhere after a few sentences (for example, *Jessica Max attends Tower College*).

2d.2 Broadening a narrow topic

You know a topic is too narrow when you realize there's little to say after a few sentences. Or it's too narrow when there's only one point to develop, which makes that one point the topic. When faced with a too-narrow topic, think about underlying concepts. For example, suppose you want to write about Fidel Castro, president of Cuba. If you chose

"Fidel Castro took control of Cuba on January 1, 1959," you'd be working with a single fact rather than a topic. To expand beyond such a narrow thought, you could think about the general area that your fact fits into—say, Cuban political history. Although that is too broad to be a useful topic, you're headed in the right direction. Next, you might think of a topic that relates to Castro's political impact, such as "What impact has Fidel Castro's leadership had on Cuba since he took power on January 1, 1959?" Depending on your writing situation (2c), you might need to narrow your idea further by focusing on Castro's impact in a single area, such as type of government, or education, or the food supply.

2d.3 Narrowing a broad topic

Narrowing a broad topic calls for you to break the topic down into subtopics. Most broad subjects can be broken down in hundreds of ways, but you need not think of all of them. Settle on a topic that interests you, one narrowed enough—but not too much—from a broad topic. For example, if you're assigned "marriage" as the topic for a 1,000-word essay, you'd be too broad if you chose "What makes a successful marriage?" You'd be too narrow if you came up with "Alexandra and Gavin were married by a Justice of the Peace." You'd likely be on target with a subtopic such as "In successful marriages, husbands and wives learn to accept each other's faults." You could use 1,000 words to explain and give concrete examples of typical faults and discuss why accepting them is important. Here are two more examples:

SUBJECT	*music*
WRITING SITUATION	freshman composition class
	informative purpose
	instructor as audience
	500 words; one week
POSSIBLE TOPICS	"How music lifts moods"
	"The main characteristics of country music"
	"The relationships between plots of Puccini's operas"
SUBJECT	*cities*
WRITING SITUATION	sociology course
	persuasive purpose
	peers and then instructor as audience
	950 to 1,000 words; ten days
POSSIBLE TOPICS	"Comforts of city living"
	"Discomforts of city living"
	"Importance of city planning for open spaces"

Carol Moreno knew her assigned topic—"a challenge you faced and tried to meet" (2c)—was too broad. To narrow it, she used these STRUCTURED TECHNIQUES for discovering and compiling ideas: browsing her journal (2f), freewriting (2g), and mapping (2j). They helped her decide to write about the challenge of increasing her strength.

Daniel Casey didn't need to narrow his topic because his assignment (2c) was very specific: to discuss whether "holidays in the United States have or have not become too commercialized." He chose to argue that they have not. He used these structured techniques for discovering and compiling ideas: brainstorming (2h) and "journalist's questions" (2i). He used a subject tree (2p) to check whether he was ready to begin DRAFTING.

2e What can I do if no ideas occur to me?

If you've ever felt you'll never think of anything to write about, don't despair. Instead, use **structured techniques,** sometimes called *prewriting strategies* or *invention techniques,* for discovering and compiling ideas. Professional writers use them to uncover hidden resources in their minds. For a list of the techniques, see Box 10 (the parentheses tell you where to find more explanation and an example). Try out each one. Experiment to find out which techniques suit your style of thinking. Also, even if one technique produces good ideas, try another to see what additional possibilities might turn up.

⊙ Ways to discover and compile ideas for writing　　　　　　　　　**10**

- Keep an idea book and a journal (2f).
- Freewrite (2g).
- Brainstorm (2h).
- Ask the "journalist's questions" (2i).
- Map (2j).
- Talk it over (2k).
- Do an Internet search (2l).
- Incubate (2m).

COMPUTER TIP: Because you never know when an idea you have rejected one moment might become useful later from another point of view, don't delete your work spent discovering and compiling ideas. Save all your "rejected" work in a separate folder. Today's junk can become tomorrow's treasure.◙

🌐 **ESL NOTE:** The STRUCTURED TECHNIQUES discussed here aim to let your ideas flow out of you without judging them right away. If such ways of using language are unfamiliar to you or seem difficult to implement, consider doing them first in your native language and then translating them into English when one idea seems to have potential for your writing.✛

2f How do I use an idea book and a journal?

As you develop the habits of mind and behavior of a writer, your ease with writing will grow. One such habit is keeping an **idea book.** Professional writers are always on the lookout for ideas to write about and details to develop their ideas. They listen, watch, talk with people, and generally keep an open mind. They are always ready to jot down their thoughts and observations in a pocket-size notepad that they carry with them. They know that good ideas can evaporate as quickly as they spring to mind. If you use an idea book throughout your college years, you will see your powers of observation increase dramatically.

Additionally, most professional writers keep a daily writing **journal.** This allows you to have a conversation on paper with yourself. Your audience is you, so the content and tone can be as personal and informal as you wish. Even fifteen minutes a day can be enough. If you don't have that chunk of time, write in your journal before you go to bed, between classes, on a bus.

Unlike a diary, a journal is *not* a record of what you do each day. A journal is for your thoughts from your reading, your observations, even your dreams. You can respond to quotations, react to movies or plays, or reflect on your opinions, beliefs, and tastes. Keeping a journal can help you in three ways. First, writing every day gives you the habit of productivity. The more you write, the more you get used to the feeling of words pouring out of you onto paper, and the easier it will become for you to write in all situations. Second, a journal instills the habit of close observation and discovery, two habits of mind that good writers cultivate. Third, a journal is an excellent source of ideas for assignments.

Here's an excerpt of a journal entry Carol Moreno had made before she got the assignment to write about having faced a challenge (see page 24). Even though she hadn't thought of her entry as a potential subject for a later essay, when she read through her journal for ideas, she realized that improving her physical preparedness for nursing school was indeed a challenge she had faced.

September 30 I got to add 5 more reps today and it's only the sixth weight lifting class. I wasn't really surprised—I can tell I'm stronger. I wonder if I'm strong enough yet to lift Gran into the wheelchair alone. I was so scared last summer when I almost dropped her. Besides being terrified of hurting her, I thought that somehow the admissions committee would find out and tell me I was too weak to be accepted into nursing school. What if I hadn't noticed the weight lifting course for P.E. credit!?! Weight lifting is the best exercise I've ever done and I'm not getting beefy looking either.

Excerpt from Carol Moreno's journal

2g What is freewriting?

Freewriting is writing nonstop. You write down whatever comes into your mind without stopping to wonder whether the ideas are good or the spelling is correct. When you freewrite, don't do anything to interrupt the flow. Don't censor any thoughts or flashes of insight. Don't go back and review. Don't cross out.

Freewriting helps get you used to the "feel" of your pen moving across paper or your fingers rapidly hitting computer keys. Freewriting works best if you set a goal—perhaps writing for fifteen minutes or filling one or two pages. Keep going until you reach that goal, even if you have to write one word repeatedly until a new word comes to mind. Some days when you read over your freewriting, it might seem mindless, but other days your interesting ideas may startle you.

In **focused freewriting,** you write from a specific starting point—a sentence from your general freewriting, an idea, a quotation, or anything else you choose. Except for this initial focal point, focused freewriting is the same as regular freewriting. Write until you meet your time or page limit, and don't censor yourself. If you go off the topic, that's fine: See where your thoughts take you. Just keep moving forward.

29

> *Pumping iron — what the steroid jocks call it and exactly what I DO NOT want to be. — a muscle cube. Great that Prof. Moore told us women's muscles don't bulk up much unless a weight lifting program is really intense — they just get longer. No bulk for me PLEASE. Just want upper body strength — oh, and the aerobic stuff from swimming, which makes me feel great. Lift, sweat, swim, lift, sweat, swim, lift, sweat, swim.*

Excerpt from Carol Moreno's freewriting

Like a journal, freewriting is a good source of ideas and details. When Carol Moreno thought her weight-training course might qualify for her assignment (see page 24), she tried exploring the topic through focused freewriting on "pumping iron" (see above).

2h What is brainstorming?

Brainstorming means listing everything you can think of about a topic. Let your mind range freely, generating quantities of ideas. Write words, phrases, or sentence fragments—whatever comes to you. If you run out of ideas, ask yourself exploratory questions, such as *What is it? What is it the same as? How is it different? Why or how does it happen? How is it done? What causes it or results from it? What does it look, smell, sound, feel, or taste like?* and so on.

After you've compiled a list, go to step two: Look for patterns, ways to group the ideas into categories. You will probably find several categories. Set aside any items that don't fit into a group. If a category interests you but has only a few items, brainstorm that category alone.

You can brainstorm in one concentrated session or over several days, depending on how much time you have for an assignment. Brainstorming in a PEER-RESPONSE GROUP can be especially fruitful: One person's ideas bounce off the next person's, and collectively more ideas come to mind.

🖥 **COMPUTER TIP:** When freewriting (2g) or brainstorming (2h), try "invisible writing" by turning off your computer monitor. A blank screen can help you focus on getting the words out without the temptation to stop and criticize, but the computer will still be recording your words. When you can write no more, turn on the monitor to see what you have. (To do invisible writing by hand, use a worn-out ballpoint pen and a piece of carbon paper between two sheets of paper.)▣

Brainstorming was a technique Daniel Casey used to develop his argument that the commercialization of holidays has advantages (6k). Brainstorming helped him think through his opinion as well as come up with supporting details. The excerpt below shows the random nature of brainstorming. Later, Daniel grouped some items (marked with an asterisk [*]) to support the point he makes in his essay's paragraph four, which is about the good effects of holiday spirit.

EXCERPT FROM DANIEL CASEY'S BRAINSTORMING

people/cheerful*

economy up—good, giving and getting gifts

people give to charities—Salvation Army bell ringers

friendly greetings, even from strangers!*

kids—Santa*

~~the Easter Bunny?~~ nope

festive atmosphere/decorations, music—even elves!*

Xmas cards to old friends*

arousing positive feelings (even in depressed people)

EXERCISE 2-2

Here's a list brainstormed for a business class writing assignment. The topic was "ways to promote a new movie." Working individually or in a peer-response group, look over the list and group the ideas. You'll find that some ideas don't fit into a group. Also, you're welcome to add your own ideas to the list. For help, consult section 2h.

coming attractions	suspense
TV ads	book the movie was based on
provocative	locations
movie reviews	rating
how movie was made	adventure
sneak previews	newspaper ads
word of mouth	stars
director	dialogue
topical subject	excitement
special effects	photography

2i What are the "journalist's questions"?

When journalists report a story, they gather and write about information by asking who did what, where it happened, when it happened, and why and how it happened. The same questions come in handy for writers exploring a topic. The **journalist's questions** are *Who? What? When? Where? Why?* and *How?*

Daniel Casey used the journalist's questions to expand his thinking on the benefits of commercializing holidays. His answers showed him that he had enough material for a good essay.

WHO?	**Who** benefits from commercialized holidays?
WHAT?	**What** are the most commercialized holidays?
WHEN?	**When** did holidays start getting so commercial?
WHERE?	**Where** can evidence be found that commercialized holidays have benefits?
WHY?	**Why** do some people object to commercializing holidays?
HOW?	**How** exactly do we commercialize holidays?

2j What is mapping?

Mapping, also called *clustering* or *webbing,* is a visual form of brainstorming. When some writers actually see ways their ideas connect, they begin to think more creatively. Other writers like mapping to help them check the logical relationships between ideas.

To map, write your topic in the middle of a sheet of paper, and draw a circle around it. Now, moving out from the center, use lines and circles to show ideas that are subtopics of the topic in the center circle. Continue to subdivide and add details, as the example on page 33 shows. At any time, you can move to a blank space on your map and start a new subtopic. Try to keep going without censoring yourself.

Carol Moreno used mapping to prompt herself to discover ideas about women and weight training. When she finished, she was satisfied that she'd have enough to say in her essay.

2k How can "talking it over" help?

Talking it over is based on the notion that two heads are better than one. The expression "bouncing ideas off each other" captures this idea. When you talk it over with someone interested in listening and making suggestions, you often think of new ideas. The "it" can be what you've discovered using this handbook's STRUCTURED TECHNIQUES (2e), or additional specific details to support a general statement, or anything else you want to explore. Ways of approaching a point of discussion include

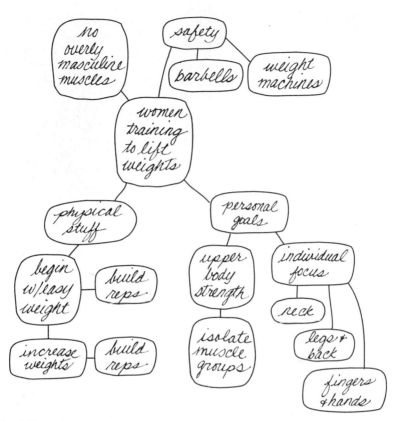

Carol Moreno's mapping

debating, questioning, analyzing (5b), evaluating (5c), synthesizing (5e), and assessing reasoning (5i).

The term "sounding board" in this context means someone you trust to tell you if your ideas are complete and reasonable. If your instructor sets up peer-response groups in your class, you might ask the other members to serve as sounding boards. Otherwise, talk with a good friend or another adult.

21 How can an Internet search help?

An **Internet search** is a good technique for finding ideas to write about; for understanding your subject's categories, from the most general on a given subject to the most specific; and for locating information you can use in your writing. Internet searches scan the WORLD WIDE WEB using **search engines,** software programs that rapidly search and find online information sources. Some instructors want students to think of ideas on their own, without using Internet search engines. If that's the case, don't use them.

Perhaps one of the better search engines for moving from general to specific categories—at least at the time I'm writing this handbook—is <http://www.yahoo.com>. Others include <http://www.hotbot.com> (which is currently part of lycos.com), and <http://altavista.com>. (A fuller list appears in section 34c.2, Box 143).

Click on the "search" function and type in the word you want to explore. If it's more than one word, use BOOLEAN EXPRESSIONS (34c.1) so that the search engine will "understand" what you are looking for.

EXERCISE 2-3

If you have Internet access, go to <http://www.yahoo.com>. Click on the search function, and type in "roses." You'll see a list of categories, one of which is *gardens* or *home and gardens.* Choose it and proceed to make choices as you work your way to ever more specific categories. Be ready to explain the sequence (or "path") you used and what you found with that sequence, keeping in mind idea-gathering techniques summarized in Box 10 (2e). Next, go back to the general category *roses* and make another set of choices (take another path). Be ready to explain this second sequence, what you found, and how the two sequences differ.

2m How can incubation help me?

Incubation refers to giving your ideas time to grow and develop. This technique works especially well when you need to step back and evaluate what you've discovered and compiled for your writing. For example, you might feel you're not seeing how your material can be pulled together. Conversely, if some parts of your essay seem too thin in content, incubation gives you distance from your material so that you can decide what works. Ideally, incubate your ideas overnight or for a couple of days; but even a few hours can help.

One way to start incubation is to turn your attention to something entirely unrelated to your writing. Concentrate hard on that other matter so that your conscious mind is given over to it totally. After a while, relax and guide your mind back to your writing. Often, you'll see what you've discovered and compiled for writing in a different way.

Another strategy for incubation is to allow your mind to wander without thinking about anything in particular. Relax and open your mind to random thoughts, but don't dwell on any one thought very long. After a while, guide your mind back to your writing. Often, you'll see solutions that hadn't occurred to you before.

EXERCISE 2-4

Try each structured technique for discovering and compiling ideas shown in 2e through 2m. Use your own topics or select from the suggestions below.

a dream vacation   meeting deadlines   playing a sport   libraries
what you want in a spouse

2n How can shaping help me?

Shaping writing means organizing your material. Like a story, an essay needs a beginning, a middle, and an end. The essay's introduction sets the stage; the essay's body paragraphs provide the substance of your message in a sequence that makes sense; the conclusion ends the essay logically. The major elements in an informative essay are listed in Box 11. (For the major elements in a persuasive essay using classical argument, see Box 41 in section 6e.)

 Elements in an informative essay 11

1. **Introductory paragraph:** Leads into the topic of the essay and tries to capture the reader's interest.

2. **Thesis statement:** States the central message of the writing. The thesis statement (2q) usually appears at the end of the introductory paragraph.

3. **Background information:** Provides a context for understanding the points a writer wants to make. Background information may be integrated into the introductory paragraph (as in Daniel Casey's introduction, in section 6k.). More complex information may require a separate paragraph of information (as in the second paragraph in Carol Moreno's essay, in section 3g).

4. **Points of discussion:** Support the essay's thesis statement. They are the essential content of the body paragraphs in an essay. Each point of discussion consists of a general statement backed up by specific details.

5. **Concluding paragraph:** Ends the essay smoothly, flowing logically from the rest of the essay (4k).

Each paragraph's length in an essay needs to be in proportion to its function. Introductory and concluding paragraphs are usually shorter than body paragraphs. Body paragraphs need to be somewhat approximate to each other in length. If one body paragraph becomes overly long in relation to the others, consider breaking it into two paragraphs. (I discuss paragraph writing extensively in Chapter 4.)

2o How can looking for "levels of generality" help me?

Generality is a relative term. Concepts exist in the context of—in relationship with—other concepts. More general concepts belong together (can be grouped), while less general concepts belong grouped. When you look for **levels of generality,** you're figuring out which ideas or concepts can be grouped. Levels of generality start with the most general and work down to the most specific. Conversely, **levels of specificity** start with the most specific and work up to the most general. Being aware of levels, particularly when writing body paragraphs, gives you a sensible sequence for presenting your material. Use whichever pattern works for you because each sequence is merely the reverse of the other. Here's an example.

LEVELS OF GENERALITY (BIG TO SMALL) ∇
MOST GENERAL: LEVEL 1   a bank
LESS GENERAL: LEVEL 2   money in the bank
LESS GENERAL: LEVEL 3   bank account
LESS GENERAL: LEVEL 4   checking account
LEAST GENERAL: LEVEL 5   account #123456 at Bank EZCome, EZGo

LEVELS OF SPECIFICITY (SMALL TO BIG) Δ
MOST SPECIFIC: LEVEL 5   account #123456 at Bank EZCome, EZGo
LESS SPECIFIC: LEVEL 4   checking account
LESS SPECIFIC: LEVEL 3   bank account
LESS SPECIFIC: LEVEL 2   money in the bank
LEAST SPECIFIC: LEVEL 1   a bank

2p How can a subject tree help me?

A **subject tree** shows you visually whether you have sufficient content, at varying levels of generality or specificity, to start a first draft of your writing. A subject tree also visually demonstrates whether you have a good balance of general ideas and specific details. If what you have are mostly general ideas—or, the other way around, mostly specific details—go back to techniques for discovering and compiling ideas (2e through 2m) so that you can come up with the sorts of material that are missing.

Daniel Casey used a subject tree to help him shape the third paragraph in his essay (6k).

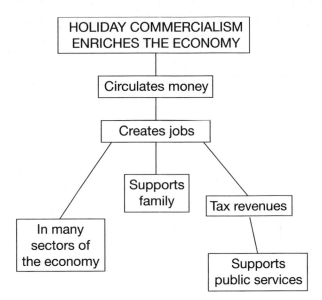

Daniel Casey's subject tree

2q What is a thesis statement?

A **thesis statement** is the central message of an essay. It's the essay's main idea. As a writer, you want to write a thesis statement with great care so that it prepares your readers for what follows in the essay. This means your thesis statement has to reflect with some accuracy the content of your essay. Box 12 lists the basic requirements for a thesis statement.

⊙ Basic requirements for a thesis statement   12

- It states the essay's subject—the topic that you discuss.
- It conveys the essay's purpose—either informative or persuasive.
- It indicates your focus—the assertion that presents your point of view.
- It uses specific language—not vague words.
- It may briefly state the major subdivisions of the essay's topic.

Some instructors add to these basic requirements. You might, for example, be asked to put your thesis statement at the end of your introductory paragraph (as in the final draft of Carol Moreno's essay, in section

37

3g.3). Some instructors require that the thesis statement be contained in one sentence; other instructors permit two sentences if the topic is complex. All requirements, basic and additional, are designed to help you develop a thesis statement that will guide the writing of your essay and help you communicate clearly with your reader. By the way, don't confuse the role of a thesis statement with the role of an essay's title (3c.3).

ESL NOTE: A thesis statement, especially in the introductory paragraph, is commonly found in the ACADEMIC WRITING of North American and some other cultures. If your culture would consider such an early, blunt, and straightforward statement to be rude or crude, respect your tradition but nevertheless write one for classes at North American colleges.

Most writers find that their thesis statement changes somewhat with each successive draft of an essay. Still, when you revise its language, be sure to stick to the essential idea you want to communicate. A thesis statement is a guide; it helps you stay on the topic and develop your ideas in an essay. To start, make an ASSERTION—a sentence stating your topic and the point you want to make about it. This assertion focuses your thinking as you develop a preliminary thesis statement. Next, move toward a final thesis statement that most accurately reflects the content of your essay.

Here is the evolution of Carol Moreno's thesis statement as she moved from a simple assertion to her final version for her essay on weight training. The final version fulfills all the requirements described in Box 12. (For the evolution of Daniel Casey's thesis statement as he moved from an assertion to his final version, see section 6c.)

NO I think women can pump iron like men. [This assertion is a start.]

NO If she is trained well, any woman can "pump iron" well, just like a man. [This can be considered a preliminary thesis because it's more specific (it mentions training), but the word *any* is vague and inaccurate, and the word *well* appears twice.]

NO In spite of most people thinking only men can "pump iron," women can also do it successfully with the right training. [This draft is better because it's more specific, but "most people thinking only men" goes off Carol's intended topic. Also, this draft doesn't mention Carol's central concept of building strength.]

YES With the right training, women can also "pump iron" to build strength. [This is a good thesis statement.]

For essays with an informative purpose (1c.2), here are more examples of thesis statements for 500- to 700-word essays. The NO versions are assertions or preliminary thesis statements. The YES versions are good because they fulfill the requirements in Box 12.

TOPIC *suing for malpractice*

NO There are many kinds of malpractice suits.

YES Many people know about medical malpractice suits, and increasingly people are becoming aware of suits against lawyers, teachers, and even parents.

TOPIC *women artists*

NO Paintings by women are getting more attention.

YES During the past ten years, the works of artists Mary Cassatt and Rosa Bonheur have finally gained widespread critical acclaim.

For essays written with a persuasive purpose (1c.3), here are examples of thesis statements written for 500- to 700-word essays. Again, the NO versions are assertions or preliminary thesis statements. The YES versions fulfill the requirements in Box 12.

TOPIC *discomforts of city living*

NO The discomforts of living in a modern city are many.

YES Rising crime rates, increasingly overcrowded conditions, and rising taxes make living comfortably in a modern city difficult.

TOPIC *deceptive advertising*

NO Deceptive advertising can cause many problems for consumers.

YES Deceptive advertising costs consumers not only money but also their health.

EXERCISE 2-5

Each set of sentences below offers several versions of a thesis statement. Within each set, the thesis statements progress from weak to strong. The fourth thesis statement in each set is the best. Based on the requirements listed in Box 12, work individually or with a peer-response group to explain why the first three choices in each set are weak and the last is best.

A. 1. Advertising is complex.
   2. Magazine advertisements appeal to readers.
   3. Magazine advertisements must be creative.
   4. To appeal to readers, magazine advertisements must skillfully use language, color, and design.
B. 1. Tennis is excellent exercise.
   2. Playing tennis is fun.
   3. Tennis requires various skills.
   4. Playing tennis for fun and exercise requires agility, stamina, and strategy.

C. 1. *Hamlet* is a play about revenge.
   2. Hamlet must avenge his father's murder.
   3. Some characters in the play *Hamlet* want revenge.
   4. In the play *Hamlet,* Hamlet, Fortinbras, and Laertes all seek revenge.
D. 1. Maintaining friendships requires work.
   2. To have good friends, a person must learn how to be a good friend.
   3. To be a good friend, a person must value the meaning of friendship.
   4. Unless a person is sensitive to others and communicates with them honestly, that person will not be able to build strong friendships.
E. 1. Many people aren't interested in politics.
   2. Adults have become increasingly dissatisfied with the political process.
   3. Fewer adults than ever vote in local elections.
   4. Fewer college students participated in state primaries and voted in state elections this year than in either of the last two elections.

EXERCISE 2-6

Here are writing assignments, narrowed topics, and tentative thesis statements. Alone or with your peer-response group, evaluate each thesis statement according to the basic requirements in Box 12.

1. *Marketing assignment:* 700- to 800-word persuasive report on the cafeteria. *Audience:* the instructor and the cafeteria's manager. *Topic:* cafeteria conditions. *Thesis:* The college cafeteria could attract more students if it improved the quality of its food, its appearance, and the friendliness of its staff.
2. *Music assignment:* 300- to 500-word review of a performance. *Audience:* the instructor and other students in the class. *Topic:* the local symphony's final spring concert. *Thesis:* The "Basically Beethoven" program that ended the local symphony's spring season was interesting.
3. *Chemistry assignment:* 800- to 1,000-word informative report about the ozone layer. *Audience:* the instructor and visiting students and instructors attending a seminar at the state college. *Topic:* recent research on the ozone layer. *Thesis:* The United States should increase efforts to slow the destruction of the ozone layer.

4. *Journalism assignment:* 200- to 300-word article about campus crime. *Audience:* the instructor, the student body, and the college administration. *Topic:* recent robberies. *Thesis:* During the fall term, campus robberies at the college equaled the number of robberies that took place in the prior five years combined.
5. *Business writing assignment:* 400- to 500-word persuasive report about the career-counseling services offered by the college. *Audience:* college seniors, career counselors, and the instructor. *Topic:* job placement for seniors. *Thesis:* The college's liberal arts graduates are hired mainly by business and industry.

2r What is outlining?

An **outline** lays out the relationships among ideas in a piece of writing. Outlines can lead writers to see how well their writing is organized. Many instructors require that outlines be handed in either before or with an essay.

Some writers like to outline; others don't. If you don't, but you're required to write one, tackle the job with an open mind. You may be pleasantly surprised at what the rigor of outline writing does to your perception of your essay.

An outline can be *informal* or *formal.* Try outlining at various steps of the WRITING PROCESS: before drafting, to arrange ideas; while you draft, to keep track of your material; while you revise, to check the logical flow of thought or to reveal what information is missing, repeated, or off the topic; or in whatever other ways you find helpful.

Informal outlines

An **informal outline** is a working plan that lays out the major points of an essay. Because it's informal, it doesn't need to use the numbering and lettering conventions of a formal outline. Complete sentences are not required; words and phrases are acceptable.

Carol Moreno used an informal outline for planning her essay (3g). Here's how she roughed out her third paragraph.

CAROL MORENO'S INFORMAL OUTLINE

Thesis statement: With the right training, women can also "pump iron" to build strength.

how to use weights
    safety is vital
    free weights
        don't bend at waist
        align neck and back
        look straight ahead
        weight machines—safety

41

💻 **COMPUTER TIP:** You can create an informal outline on a computer. After your first draft, read what you have written, and put a symbol near what seems most important. Then, copy and paste those sentences to the bottom of your text so that you can see them grouped together. Next, move them around into different sequences to see which point needs to come first, second, and so on. ◙

Formal outlines

A **formal outline** requires you to use the conventions that dictate how to display relationships among ideas. You need to adhere strictly to the numbering and lettering conventions required, as shown below. A formal outline can be either a *topic outline* or a *sentence outline*. In a topic outline, each entry is a word or phrase. In a sentence outline, each entry is a complete sentence. Never mix the two types.

Writers who use formal outlines say that a sentence outline brings them closer to drafting than does a topic outline. This makes sense because topic outlines carry less information. But you have to find out which type works best for you. Box 13 displays the pattern of a formal outline and lists format and wording rules to follow strictly.

◉ **Guidelines for writing an outline**   **13**

Formal Outline Pattern

> *Thesis statement:* (Insert actual statement)
> I. First main idea
>   A. First subdivision of the main idea
>   1. First reason or example
>   2. Second reason or example
>   a. First supporting detail
>   b. Second supporting detail
>   B. Second subdivision of the main idea
> II. Second main idea
> III. Third main idea

Rules for Formatting Outlines

■ **Introductory and concluding paragraphs:** Don't include your introductory and concluding paragraphs in an outline.

■ **Thesis statement:** Place your thesis statement immediately before the outline itself (see examples at end of this chapter).

■ **Indenting numbers, letters, and lines:** Systematically indent all parts of an outline. Use capital roman numerals (I, II, III) to   ➞

What Is Outlining? **2r**

Guidelines for writing an outline *(continued)*   **13**

signal major subdivisions of your topic. Indent capital letters (A, B, C) to signal the next LEVEL OF GENERALITY. Indent even further arabic numbers (1, 2, 3) to show the third level of generality. Finally, indent lowercase letters (a, b, c) to show the fourth level of generality, if there is one. If an outline entry runs longer than one line, indent the second line under the first word of the first line.

■ **Minimum of two entries at each level:** If you can't subdivide a category into at least two parts, eliminate the subdivision or expand it into a minimum of two items. If you use a I, you must have a II; if you use an A, you must have a B; if you use a 1, you must have a 2; and so forth.

NO　　A. Free weights
　　　　　　1. Safe lifting technique
　　　　　B. Weight machines

YES　　A. Free weights
　　　　　B. Weight machines

YES　　A. Free weights
　　　　　　1. Unsafe lifting techniques
　　　　　　2. Safe lifting techniques
　　　　　B. Weight machines

■ **No overlapping headings:** Be sure that what you place in subdivisions I and II is distinct from what you place in subdivisions A and B. Said another way, don't pair a main idea with a supporting detail.

NO　　A. Free weights
　　　　　　1. Weight machines

YES　　A. Free weights
　　　　　　1. Unsafe lifting techniques
　　　　　　2. Safe lifting techniques
　　　　　　　a. Neck and back alignment
　　　　　　　b. Head alignment
　　　　　B. Weight machines

■ **Parallelism:** Keep entries at I and II, A and B, 1 and 2, and a and b grammatically parallel (18f). For example, all might start with an *-ing* form of a VERB.

NO　　A. Free weights
　　　　　B. Using weight machines

→

43

> **Guidelines for writing an outline** (*continued*)   **13**
>
> **YES**   A. Using weight machines
>   B. Using free weights
> **YES**   A. Free weights
>   B. Weight machines
>
> ■ **Capitalization and punctuation:** Capitalize only the first word
> of each entry. Proper nouns are an exception: They are always
> capitalized. In a sentence outline, end each sentence with a
> period. In a topic outline, use no punctuation to end the entries.

Here's a topic outline of the final draft of Carol Moreno's essay on
weight lifting for women (3g.3). A sentence outline follows it so that you
can compare the two types of outlines.

TOPIC OUTLINE

Thesis statement: With the right training, women can "pump iron" to
build strength.

I. Avoidance of massive muscle development
   A. Role of women's biology
      1. Not much muscle-bulking hormone
      2. Muscles get longer, not bulkier
   B. Role of combining exercise types
      1. Anaerobic (weight lifting)
      2. Aerobic (swimming)
II. Safe use of weights
   A. Free weights
      1. Unsafe lifting techniques
      2. Safe lifting techniques
         a. Head alignment
         b. Neck and back alignment
   B. Weight machines
III. Individualized the program based on physical condition
   A. Role of resistance and reps
   B. Characteristics for personalizing the program
      1. Weight
      2. Age
      3. Physical condition
IV. Individualized a weight-training program
   A. Upper body strength
   B. Individual objectives

    1. Mine
    2. Car crash victim's
    3. Physical therapist's

SENTENCE OUTLINE

Thesis statement: With the right training, women can also "pump iron" to build strength.

   I. The right training lets women who lift weights avoid developing massive muscles.
     A. Women's biology plays a role.
       1. Women don't produce much of a specific muscle-bulking hormone.
       2. Women's muscles tend to grow longer rather than bulkier.
     B. Combining different kinds of exercise also plays a role.
       1. Anaerobic exercise, like weight lifting, builds muscle.
       2. Aerobic exercise, like swimming, builds endurance and stamina.
  II. The right training shows women how to use weights safely to prevent injury.
     A. Free weights require special precautions.
       1. Bending at the waist and jerking a barbell up are unsafe.
       2. Squatting and using leg and back muscles to straighten up are safe.
         a. The head is held erect and faces forward.
         b. The neck and back are aligned and held straight.
     B. Weight machines make it easier to lift safely because they force proper body alignment.
 III. The right training includes individualized programs based on a woman's physical condition.
     A. Progress comes from resistance and from repetitions tailored to individual capabilities.
     B. Programs consider a woman's physical characteristics.
       1. Her weight is a factor.
       2. Her age is a factor.
       3. Her physical conditioning is a factor.
 IV. The right training includes individualized programs based on a woman's personal goals.
     A. Certain muscle groups are targeted to increase women's upper body strength.
     B. Other muscle groups are targeted based on individual objectives.
       1. I wanted to strengthen muscles needed for lifting patients.
       2. An accident victim wanted to strengthen her neck muscles.
       3. A physical therapist wanted to strengthen her fingers and hands.

⌨ **COMPUTER TIP:** Be careful with your computer's outlining function. In some word processing programs, the function only places a bullet at the beginning of each paragraph. It pays no attention to levels of generality or whether the material relates to your topic. Other word processing programs do a somewhat better job, but nothing substitutes for the human eye. ▣

EXERCISE 2-7

Here is a sentence outline. Individually or with your peer-response group, revise it into a topic outline. Then, be ready to explain why you prefer using a topic outline or a sentence outline as a guide to writing. For help, consult 2r.

Thesis statement: Common noise pollution, although it causes many problems in our society, can be reduced.

I. Noise pollution comes from many sources.
   A. Noise pollution occurs in many large cities.
      1. Traffic rumbles and screeches.
      2. Construction work blasts.
      3. Airplanes roar overhead.
   B. Noise pollution occurs in the workplace.
      1. Machines in factories boom.
      2. Machines used for outdoor construction thunder.
   C. Noise pollution occurs during leisure-time activities.
      1. Stereo headphones blare directly into eardrums.
      2. Film soundtracks bombard the ears.
      3. Music in discos assaults the ears.
II. Noise pollution causes many problems.
   A. Excessive noise damages hearing.
   B. Excessive noise alters moods.
   C. Constant exposure to noise limits learning ability.
III. Reduction in noise pollution is possible.
   A. Pressure from community groups can support efforts to control excessive noise.
   B. Traffic regulations can help alleviate congestion and noise.
   C. Pressure from workers can force management to reduce noise.
   D. People can wear earplugs to avoid excessive noise.
   E. Reasonable sound levels for headphones, soundtracks, and discos can be required.

3 DRAFTING AND REVISING

In the WRITING PROCESS, drafting and revising come after PLANNING and SHAPING (Chapter 2). **Drafting** means you get ideas onto paper in sentences and paragraphs. In everyday conversation, people use the word *writing* to talk about drafting, but *writing* is too broad a term here. The word *drafting* more accurately describes what you do when you write your first attempt—your first *draft*—to get ideas onto paper. **Revising** means you look over your first draft, analyze and evaluate it for yourself, and then rewrite it by composing a number of subsequent versions, or drafts, to get closer to what you want to say. Revising involves adding, cutting, moving material, and after that, EDITING and PROOFREADING.

3a What can help me write a first draft?

A **first draft** is the initial version of a piece of writing. Before you begin a first draft, seek out places and times of the day that encourage you to write. You might write best in a quiet corner of the library, or at 4:30 a.m. at the kitchen table before anyone else is up, or outside alone with nature or with a steady flow of people walking by. Most experienced writers, myself among them, find they concentrate best when they're alone and writing where they won't be interrupted. But individuals differ, and you may prefer background noise—a crowded cafeteria, hearing the low hum of conversation at the next table or in the next room, for example.

A caution: Don't mislead yourself. You can't produce a useful first draft while talking to friends and stopping only now and then to jot down a sentence. You won't draft smoothly while watching television or being constantly interrupted.

Finally, resist delaying tactics. While you certainly need a computer or a pad of paper and a pen or pencil, you don't need fifteen perfectly sharpened pencils neatly lined up on your desk.

💻 **COMPUTER TIP:** As you write on a computer, experiment to see which writing steps are easier for you to type and which steps you prefer to write by hand. Some writers do all their planning, shaping, drafting, revising, and editing on the computer. Other writers reserve the computer for revising and editing. ◉

Now, dive in. Based on the PLANNING and SHAPING you've done (Chapter 2), start writing. The direction of drafting is forward: Keep pressing ahead. If you wonder about the spelling of a word or a point in grammar, don't stop. Use a symbol or other signal you can revisit later. Use whatever you like: a question mark, an asterisk, an underline, a circle, or all capital letters. If the exact word you need escapes you while you're drafting, substitute an easy synonym and mark it to go back to later. If you question your sentence style or the order in which you present supporting details, type a symbol or the word *Style?* or *Order?* nearby so you can return to it later. If you begin to run dry, reread what you have written—not to start revising prematurely, but only to propel yourself to keep moving ahead with your first draft. Once you finish your draft, you can easily find the symbols or words you've used to alert you to a possible problem by using the "Find" function on your computer.

💻 **COMPUTER TIP:** Use your "Save" function often to protect your work, at least every one or two pages or every ten minutes. This prevents your losing what you have written as you've moved along. Also, print your work regularly so that you have a hard copy in the event that computer problems develop (and they always do, it seems). ◉

A first draft is a preliminary or rough draft. Its purpose is to get your ideas onto disk or into computer memory or on paper. Never are first drafts meant to be perfect. Rather, they're meant to give you something to revise. Box 14 offers a few ways to move into drafting after you have planned and focused (Chapter 2). Experiment to see what works best for you. And be ready to adjust what works according to each writing situation (2c).

◉ **Ways to start drafting** 14

- **Write a discovery draft.** Put aside all your notes from planning and shaping, and write a discovery draft. This means using FOCUSED FREEWRITING (2g) to get ideas on paper and to make connections that spring to mind as you write. Your discovery draft can serve as a first draft or as one more part of your notes when you write a more structured first draft.

→

> ## Ways to start drafting *(continued)* 14
>
> - **Work from your notes.** Sort your notes from planning and shaping (Chapter 2) into groups of subtopics so that when you start writing, you can focus on each subtopic without having to search repeatedly through your pile of notes. Arrange the subtopics in what seems to be a sensible sequence, knowing you can always go back later and re-sequence the subtopics. Now write a first draft by working through your notes on each subtopic. Draft either the entire essay or blocks of a few paragraphs at one time.
> - **Use a combination of approaches.** When you know the shape of your material, write according to that structure. When you feel "stuck" and don't know what to say next, switch to writing as you would for a discovery draft.

3b How can I overcome writer's block?

If you're afraid or otherwise feel unable to start writing, perhaps you're being stopped by writer's block. **Writer's block** is the desire to get started, but not doing so. Often, writer's block occurs because the writer harbors a fear of being wrong. To overcome that fear, or any other cause of your block, think about it honestly so that you can shed light on and gain understanding of whatever is holding you back. Writer's block can strike professional as well as student writers; therefore, a variety of techniques have become popular to overcome it.

The most common cause of writer's block involves a writer's belief in myths about writing. If you are such a writer, look honestly at the truth and overcome the block.

MYTH   Writers are born, not made.

TRUTH   Everyone can write. Writers don't expect to "get it right" the first time. Being a good writer means being a patient rewriter.

MYTH   Writers have to be "in the mood" to write.

TRUTH   If writers always waited for "the mood" to occur, few would write at all. News reporters and other professional writers have deadlines to meet, whether or not they're in the mood to write.

MYTH   Writers have to be really good at grammar and spelling.

TRUTH   Writers don't let spelling and grammar block them. They write, and when they hear that quiet inner voice saying that a word or sentence isn't quite right, they turn to their dictionary or handbook to check.

MYTH Writers don't have to revise.

TRUTH Writers *expect* to revise—several times. Once words are on paper, writers can see what readers will see. This "re-vision" helps writers revise.

MYTH Writing can be done at the last minute.

TRUTH Drafting and revising take time. Ideas don't leap onto paper in final, polished form.

Box 15 lists reliable strategies writers have developed to overcome writer's block. If you feel blocked, experiment to discover what works best for you. Also, try your own ideas about how to get started. As you use the list in Box 15, suspend judgment of your writing. Let things flow. Don't find fault with what you're typing or writing. Your goal is to get yourself under way. You can evaluate and improve your writing when you're revising it. According to research, premature revision stops many writers cold—and they are hit with writer's block. Your reward for waiting to revise until your first draft is finished is the comfort of having in front of you a springboard for your revising.

⊙ **Ways to overcome writer's block**   **15**

- **Check that one of the myths about writing given above isn't stopping you.**

- **Avoid staring at a blank page.** Relax and move your hand across the keyboard or page. Write words, scribble, or draw while you think about your topic. The physical act of getting *anything* on paper can stir up ideas and lead you to begin drafting.

- **Visualize yourself writing.** Many professional writers say that they write more easily if they first picture themselves doing it. Before getting out of bed in the morning or while waiting for a bus or walking to classes, summon up a visual image of yourself in the place where you usually write, with the materials you need, busy at work.

- **Picture an image or a scene, or imagine a sound that relates to your topic.** Start writing by describing what you see or hear.

- **Write about your topic to a friend.** This technique helps you relax and makes drafting nothing more than a chat on paper with someone with whom you feel comfortable.

                                                  →

> ### Ways to overcome writer's block *(continued)*   **15**
>
> - **Try writing your material as if you were someone else.** When they take on a role, many writers feel less inhibited about writing.
> - **Start in the middle.** Begin with a body paragraph, and write from the center of your essay out, instead of from beginning to end.
> - **Use focused freewriting** (2g).
> - **Change your method of writing.** If you usually use a computer, try writing by hand. When you write by hand, treat yourself to good-quality paper so that you can enjoy the pleasure of writing on smooth, strong paper. Often that pleasure propels you to keep going. If you usually use a pen, switch to a pencil or a computer.

3c How do I revise?

Revising is rewriting. When you see the word *revision,* break it down to "re-vision," which means "to see again with fresh eyes." To revise, use the **ECR** (**E**valuate, **C**hange, and **R**eevaluate) system for looking at your draft to figure out ways to improve it. To do this, you need to read your writing honestly, without losing confidence or becoming defensive. After all, what's on the page is ink, not ego. As you work, look at whatever you change and evaluate the revision first on its own and then in the context of the surrounding material. Continue ECR until you're satisfied that your essay is the best you can make it, in light of your specific WRITING SITUATION (2c).

Whenever possible within your time frame, distance yourself from each draft. The best way to distance is to leave a chunk of time between finishing a first draft and starting to revise. Doing so helps you develop an objective sense of your work. Student writers often want to hold on to their every word, especially if they had trouble getting started on a first draft. Resist such a feeling vigorously. Put away your draft, and allow the rosy glow of authorial pride to dim a bit. The classical writer Horace recommended waiting nine years before revising! You might try to wait a few hours or even thirty minutes. Better yet, take a day or two before going back to look at your work with fresh eyes.

Also, as you are revising, don't start EDITING (3d). Editing comes after revising. Research shows that premature editing distracts writers from dealing with the larger issues that revision involves.

⬛ **COMPUTER TIPS:** (1) To move from your first draft to revision, use the Find or Search function to locate each place where you entered an "alert to yourself" (a symbol, a word, an underlining, etc.) as you were DRAFTING (3a). Type into the Find or Search box whatever you used as you drafted to alert yourself of the need to go back and check that spot. Then, click on "Find Next" and you'll come to each place you used your alert. At this point, you can take the time to rethink the matter and decide what to do. (2) As you're revising, if you suspect that you've overused a word or group of words, use the Find or Search (on some computers, the "Replace") function to discover how many times you have indeed used it. If necessary, replace with other words. Beware, however, in using your computer's thesaurus: Lots of words in the thesaurus look attractive, but they do not fit the specific context you have in mind. Always, always check the SYNONYM for its specific meaning in your dictionary.◙

3c.1 Goals and activities during revision

Your goal during revision is to improve your draft at two levels: the *global level*, which involves the whole essay and paragraphs, and the *local level*, which involves sentences and words.

To revise successfully, you need first to expect to revise. The myth that good writers never have to revise is nonsense. Only the opposite is true: Writing *is* revising. Final drafts evolve from first drafts. Here's how to prepare your mind for revising:

- Shift mentally from suspending judgment (during idea gathering and drafting) to making judgments. Read your draft critically to evaluate it.

- Decide whether to write an entirely new draft or to revise the one you have. Be critical as you evaluate your first draft, but don't be overly harsh. Most early drafts provide sufficient raw material for revision to get under way.

- Be systematic. Don't evaluate at random. Most writers work best when they concentrate on each element sequentially. Start with your draft's overall organization; next, move to its paragraphs, then to its sentences, and last to its word choice. If you need practice in being systematic, try using a revision checklist, either one supplied by your instructor or the ones in this handbook in Boxes 18 and 19.

You can engage in the activities of revision, listed in Box 16, using a computer or by revising by hand.

> ## Major activities during revision: ACRM   16
>
> **A = Add.** Insert needed words, sentences, and paragraphs. If your additions require new content, return to the STRUCTURED TECHNIQUES shown in Chapter 2.
>
> **C = Cut.** Get rid of whatever goes off the topic or repeats what has already been said.
>
> **R = Replace.** As needed, substitute new words, sentences, and paragraphs for what you have cut.
>
> **M = Move.** Change the sequence of paragraphs if the material isn't presented in logical order. Move sentences within paragraphs or to other paragraphs when your PARAGRAPH ARRANGEMENT does not allow the material to flow.

COMPUTER TIP: Many writers feel more creative as they revise when they use a computer. Relieved of the tedious work of copying and recopying material, they find their ideas flow more freely. Nevertheless, watch out for the ultimate seduction: A neatly printed page may *look* like a final draft, but it isn't.

3c.2 The role of a thesis statement in revision

The THESIS STATEMENT (2q) of your essay has great organizing power because it controls and limits what your essay can cover. The thesis statement presents the TOPIC of your essay, your particular focus on that topic, and your PURPOSE for writing. Your first draft of a thesis statement is usually only an estimate of what you plan to cover in your essay. Therefore, as you revise, keep checking the accuracy of your thesis statement. Use the thesis statement's controlling power to bring it and your essay in line with each other. When your essay is finished, the thesis statement and what you say in your essay should match. If the two do not, you need to revise either the thesis statement or the essay—or sometimes both.

Every writer's experience with revising a thesis statement varies from essay to essay. Carol Moreno, the student you met in Chapter 2 as she did her planning and shaping, wrote several versions of her thesis statement (shown in 2q, page 38) before she started to draft. After writing her first draft, she checked her thesis statement and decided that it communicated what she wanted to say. But that wasn't the end of it: Carol had to change parts of her essay to conform more closely to her thesis statement. You can read Carol's three complete drafts, along with comments, at the end of this chapter (3g).

3c.3 The role of an essay title during revision

Your essay **title** can also show you what needs revising because it clarifies the overall point of the essay. An effective title sets you on your course and tells your readers what to expect. Some writers like to begin their first drafts with a title at the top of the page to focus their thinking. Then, as they revise drafts, they revise the title. If, however, no title springs to mind, don't be concerned. Often a good title doesn't surface until after drafting, revising, and even editing. It can take that long to come up with a good title. Whatever you do, never tack on a title as an afterthought right before handing in your essay. A title is essential for readers to read first so that they can begin focusing on your essay. You cannot depend on your thesis statement to do the initial job of guiding your reader into your essay.

Titles can be direct or indirect. A **direct title** tells exactly what the essay will be about. A direct title contains key words under which the essay could be cataloged in a library or other database system.

A direct title shouldn't be too broad. For example, Carol's first and second drafts of a title were "Pumping Iron" (3g.1 and 3g.2). By her final draft, Carol realized her early title was too broad, so she revised it to "Women Can Pump Iron, Too." Conversely, a direct title should not be too narrow. Here's a title that Carol might have used that would have been too narrow—and too long: "Women Pump Iron to Meet a Wide Range of Physical and Personal Objectives."

An **indirect title** only hints at the essay's topic. It tries to catch the reader's interest by presenting a puzzle that can be solved by reading the essay. When writing an indirect title, you don't want to be overly obscure or too cute. For example, a satisfactory indirect title for Carol's final draft might be: "On Goals." In contrast, the indirect title "Equal Play" wouldn't work because it's only remotely related to the point of the essay. Also, "Thanks, Granny!" would likely be seen as too cute for ACADEMIC WRITING.

👁 **PUNCTUATION ALERT:** When you write the title at the top of the page or on a title page, never enclose it in quotation marks or underline it. Let your title stand on its own, without decoration, on your title page or at the top center of page 1 of your essay. ●

Whether direct or indirect, your essay title stands alone. It is never the opening sentence of your essay. For example, Carol's essay, "Women Can Pump Iron, Too," would suffer a major blow if the first sentence were "Women certainly can" or "I am the proof." Never does the first sentence of an essay refer to the title. Rather, the first sentence starts the content of the essay flowing. Box 17 offers you guidelines for writing effective essay titles.

Guidelines for writing essay titles **17**

- Don't wait until the last minute and tack a title on your essay. Try writing a title before you begin drafting or while you are revising. Then double-check as you prepare your final draft to see that your essay title clearly relates to your essay's content.

- For a direct title, use key words that relate to your topic, but don't get overly specific and try to reveal your entire essay.

- For an indirect title, be sure that its meaning will become very clear when your readers have finished your essay. Be sure, also, that it isn't too cute.

- Don't use quotation marks with the title or underline it (unless your title includes another title; see section 28d).

- Don't expect your essay title to serve as the first sentence of your essay.

3c.4 The role of unity and coherence in an essay

I need to get ahead of myself for a moment here. Chapter 4 in this handbook shows you many techniques for achieving unity and coherence in an essay, but here I want to preview the concepts because they're central concerns as you revise.

An essay has **unity** (4d) when all parts relate to the THESIS STATEMENT and to each other. You can consider an essay unified when it meets two criteria: First, the thesis statement clearly ties in to all TOPIC SENTENCES. Second, each paragraph contains examples, reasons, facts, and details directly related to its topic sentence and, in turn, to the thesis statement. In a nutshell, as you revise make sure that nothing in the essay is off the topic. An essay achieves **coherence** (4g) through word choice, use of TRANSITIONAL EXPRESSIONS, clear use of PRONOUNS, selective repetition, and effective PARALLELISM.

3c.5 Using revision checklists

A revision checklist focuses your attention as you evaluate and revise your writing. Use such a checklist, either one provided by your instructor or one that you compile on your own based on Boxes 18 and 19. I've designed the boxes to be comprehensive and detailed, so that you can see all the important issues as you adapt them to your personal strengths and weaknesses.

Revision checklist for *global elements:* **18**
Essay and paragraphs

You should be able to answer *yes* to each question below. If you answer *no,* you need to revise. The numbers in parentheses tell you which sections of chapters or whole chapters in this handbook to go to for more information.

Whole Essay

1. Is my essay TOPIC suitable for the WRITING SITUATION (2c)?

2. Does my THESIS STATEMENT (2q) communicate my subject, PURPOSE, and focus (Box 12, page 37)?

3. Does my essay reflect an awareness of who my readers are (1d)?

4. Is my TONE appropriate to my purpose and audience (1e)?

5. Have I covered all that my thesis statement "promises" (2q)?

6. Is my essay well organized (2o), and are my paragraphs logically arranged (4h and 4i)?

7. Is my essay unified (3c.4 and 4d)?

8. Is my reasoning sound (5h and 5i), and do I avoid LOGICAL FALLACIES (5j)?

9. Does my title reflect the content of my essay (3c.3)?

Paragraphs

10. Does my introductory paragraph prepare my readers for what follows (4b)?

11. Does each body paragraph present its main idea in a topic sentence, as needed (4e)?

12. Is each main idea clearly related to my thesis statement (2q)?

13. Is each of my body paragraphs developed with sufficient concrete support for its main idea (4f)?

14. Do I use TRANSITIONS effectively (4g.1 and 4g.5)?

15. Do my paragraphs maintain COHERENCE (3c.4 and 4g)?

16. Does my concluding paragraph provide a sense of completion (4k)?

Revision checklist for *local elements:* **19**
Sentences and words

You should be able to answer *yes* to each question below. If you answer *no*, you need to revise. The numbers in parentheses tell you which chapters or sections of chapters in this handbook to go to for more information.

1. Have I eliminated SENTENCE FRAGMENTS (Chapter 12)?
2. Have I eliminated COMMA SPLICES and RUN-ON SENTENCES (Chapter 13)?
3. Have I eliminated confusing SHIFTS (15a–15e)?
4. Have I eliminated MISPLACED and DANGLING MODIFIERS (Chapter 14)?
5. Have I eliminated mixed and incomplete sentences (15f–15j)?
6. Are my sentences concise (Chapter 16)?
7. Do my sentences show clear relationships among ideas (Chapter 17)?
8. Do I use parallelism to help my sentences deliver their meaning gracefully? And do I avoid faulty PARALLELISM (Chapter 18)?
9. Do I use variety and emphasis in my writing (Chapter 19)?
10. Is my usage correct (Chapter 20)?
11. Have I used exact words (21e)?
12. Is my writing at an appropriate LEVEL OF FORMALITY for my writing situation (21b)?
13. Do I avoid SEXIST LANGUAGE (21g), SLANTED and INFORMAL LANGUAGE (21h), CLICHÉS (21j), and artificial language (21k–21m)?

⊕ ESL NOTE: If English isn't your native language, you may want to consult Part Seven in this handbook to check your use of VERB-PREPOSITION combinations (Chapter 48); ARTICLES (Chapter 46); word order (Chapter 47); VERBALS (Chapter 49); and MODAL AUXILIARIES (Chapter 50).⊕

💻 COMPUTER TIP: "Move," one of the major activities of revision (Box 16), is easy on a computer. First, make a copy of your draft to work with, and leave your original draft as is; you never know when you'll decide that you prefer your original version of a sentence or a section. The copy is for you to experiment with. You can "cut" and "paste" to reorder sentences or rearrange paragraphs. Try, for example, to split up a paragraph, join two paragraphs, or even exchange your first and last paragraphs. Similarly, try to reorder the sequence of some sentences or interchange sentences between paragraphs. Likely, these experiments won't yield anything useful, but they might reveal a few surprises that help you "re-vision" your work. The computer makes such rearranging painless. Beware, however, of being tempted to rearrange endlessly. Set limits, or you'll never finish the assignment.◘

3d How do I edit?

Editing means checking the technical correctness of your writing. You carefully examine your writing for correct grammar, spelling, punctuation, capitalization, and use of numbers, italics, and abbreviations. Some people use the terms *editing* and *revising* interchangeably, but they are very different steps in the writing process. In contrast to revising, editing means looking at each word for its technical correctness. By editing, you fine-tune the surface features of your writing.

Editing is crucial in writing. No matter how much attention you've paid to planning, shaping, drafting, and revising, you need to edit carefully. Slapdash editing distracts and annoys your reader; lowers that reader's opinion of you and what you say in your essay; and, if you're writing for college assignments, usually earns a lower grade.

My best advice to you about editing is this: Don't rush. Editing takes time. Inexperienced writers sometimes rush editing, eager to "get it over with." Resist any impulse to hurry. Be systematic and patient. Checking grammar and punctuation takes your full concentration, along with time to look up and apply the rules in this handbook.

When do you know you've finished revising and are ready to edit? Ask yourself, "Is there anything else I can do to improve the content, organization, development, and sentence structure of this draft?" If the answer is no, you're ready to edit.

▣ **COMPUTER TIPS:** (1) Many word processing programs include tools for writers (a spell-checker, style-checker, thesaurus, readability analyzer, etc.) as they edit. Beware, however. Each tool has shortcomings serious enough to create new errors. Yet, if you use the tools intelligently with their shortcomings in mind, they can be very useful. For a list of these tools for writers, and a description of their advantages and disadvantages, see section 1g.4. (2) Whenever possible, edit on a paper copy of your writing. It's much easier to spot editing errors on a printed page than on a computer screen. After you finish editing, you can transfer your corrections to the computer. (3) Whenever you print your writing, during the editing (or revision) steps, double-space your document before printing it. The extra space gives you room to write in your changes clearly so that you can read them easily later. (4) If you must edit onscreen, highlight every two or three sentences, and read each slowly. By working in small segments, you reduce the tendency to read too quickly and miss errors. ◘

An editing checklist helps you find errors. Using an editing checklist, either one provided by your instructor or one based on Box 20 that you tailor to your particular needs, can help you move through editing systematically.

 Editing checklist 20

You should be able to answer *yes* to each question below. If you answer *no,* you need to edit. The numbers in parentheses tell you which chapters in this handbook to go to for more information.

1. Is your grammar correct (Chapters 7 through 15)?
2. Is your spelling, including hyphenation, correct (Chapter 22)?
3. Have you used commas correctly (Chapter 24)?
4. Have you used all other punctuation correctly (Chapters 23 and 25 through 29)?
5. Have you used capital letters, italics, abbreviations, and numbers correctly (Chapter 30)?

A timesaving method for editing is to create a personal file of editing errors you tend to make repeatedly. If, for example, the difference between *its* and *it's* always escapes you, or if you tend to misuse the colon, your personal file of editing errors can remind you to read your draft over again, looking only for those problems.

3e How do I proofread?

To **proofread,** check your final draft for accuracy and neatness before handing it in. In contrast to editing, which is a check for technical correctness, proofreading is typographical. This is your last chance to catch typing (or handwriting) errors and to make sure what you hand in is a clean transcription of your final draft. No matter how hard you worked on earlier parts of the writing process, your final copy needs to be free of proofreading oversights. Shoddy proofreading distracts and annoys your reader; lowers that reader's opinion of you and what you say in your essay; and, if you're writing for college, usually earns a lower grade.

In proofreading, read your work carefully line by line, looking for typing errors, such as letters or words accidentally omitted, words typed twice in a row, wrong indents to start each paragraph, and similar "slips of the pen" as they were called before computers. Whenever a page has more than one error, consider printing (or rewriting) a new page. Never expect your instructor to make allowances for crude typing (or handwriting); if you can't type well (or write legibly), arrange to have your paper typed properly.

Unless your instructor gives different directions, proofreading calls also for you to type, at the top right of each page, your last name and the page number. At the left margin, and below this information, type your full name, your professor's name (initial for first name only if needed), your course title, your class and section number, and the date (3g.3).

Some techniques for proofreading include (1) using a ruler under each line as you read it to prevent yourself from looking beyond that line; (2) reading backwards, sentence by sentence, to prevent yourself from being distracted by the content of the paper; and (3) proofreading your final draft aloud, to yourself or to a friend, so that you can hear errors that have slipped past your eyes.

When your instructor permits you to handwrite your work, check that every word can be read easily. Make sure that your *e*'s are open and your *i*'s are not; that each sentence starts with a clearly written capital letter (in some handwritings, capitals and small letters look alike); and that you've attended to other matters of legibility.

COMPUTER TIPS: (1) Whenever possible, proofread a paper copy of your writing. It's much easier to spot errors on a printed page than onscreen. After you finish proofreading, transfer your corrections to the computer. (2) Whenever you print your writing from a computer, double-space your document before printing it. The extra space gives you room to write in your changes clearly so that you can read them easily later. (3) If you must proofread onscreen, highlight a section of one or two sentences, and read each slowly. By working in small segments, you reduce the tendency to read too quickly and miss errors.

3f What is collaborative writing?

Some instructors use the term *peer-group writing* interchangeably with the term **collaborative writing.** In this handbook, I use the term *collaborate* to mean "students working together to write a paper." The underlying idea is that two (or more) heads are better than one.

Moreover, writing collaboratively enhances confidence, as writers support one another. Also important, the benefits of acquiring experience in collaborative writing extend beyond your college years. Many professions require participation in writing committees; members of the group must reach general agreement on how to proceed and contribute equally to a written report. Marketing managers, for example, head up teams who conduct consumer research, and then—as a group—write up their findings. Box 21 provides a summary of guidelines for collaborative writing.

 Guidelines for collaborative writing   **21**

Starting

1. Learn each other's names. If the group wishes, exchange e-mail addresses and/or phone numbers so that you can be in touch outside of class.

2. Participate actively in the group process. During discussions, help set a tone that encourages everyone to participate, including people who don't like to interrupt, who want time to think before they talk, or who are shy. Conversely, help the group set limits if someone dominates the discussions or makes all the decisions. If you lack experience contributing in a group setting, plan personal ways you'll take an active role.

3. As a group, assign work to be done between meetings. Distribute the responsibilities as fairly as possible. Also, decide whether to choose one discussion leader or to rotate leadership, unless your instructor assigns a particular procedure.

Planning the Writing

4. After discussing the project, BRAINSTORM (2h) as a group or use STRUCTURED TECHNIQUES for discovering and compiling ideas (Box 10, page 27).

5. Together agree on the ideas that seem best and allow for a period of INCUBATION (2m), if time permits. Then, discuss your group choices again.

6. As a group, divide the project into parts and distribute assignments fairly.

7. As you work on your part of the project, take notes in preparation for giving your group a progress report.

8. As a group, outline (2r) or otherwise sketch an overview of the paper to get a preliminary idea of how best to use material contributed by individuals.

→

Guidelines for collaborative writing *(continued)* 21

Drafting the Writing

9. Draft a THESIS STATEMENT. The thesis statement sets the direction for the rest of the paper. Each member of the group can draft a thesis statement, but you need to agree on one version before getting too far into the rest of the draft. Your group might revise the thesis statement after the whole paper has been drafted, but using a preliminary version gets everyone started in the same direction.

10. Work on the rest of the paper. Decide whether each member of the group should write a complete draft or a different part of the whole. Use photocopies to share work.

Revising the Writing

11. Read over the drafts. Are all the important points included?

12. Use the revision checklists (Boxes 18 and 19 in 3c.5), and work either as a group or by assigning portions to subgroups.

13. Agree on a final version. Assign someone to prepare the final draft and make needed photocopies.

Editing and Proofreading the Writing

14. As a group, review photocopies of the final draft. Don't leave the last stages to a subgroup. Draw on everyone's knowledge of grammar, spelling, and punctuation. Use everyone's eyes for proofreading.

15. Use the editing checklist (Box 20 in 3d) to double-check for errors. If you find more than one or two errors per page, correct and print out the page again. No matter how well the group has worked collaboratively, or how well the group has written the paper, a sloppy final version reflects negatively on the entire group.

3g An essay in three drafts, by Carol Moreno

The following sections look once again at Carol Moreno, a student planning to write on the topic of weight lifting for women. In Chapter 2, you'll find her writing assignment (page 24), how she used an entry in her journal (2f), mapped her ideas (see 2j), wrote her thesis statement (2q), and outlined (2r). During these activities, Carol chose an informative writing purpose (1c.2).

3g.1 Carol Moreno's first draft

Here is Carol's first draft showing her own notes to herself about revisions to make in the second draft. The notes resulted from comments of her peer-response group and from her personal rereading of her draft.

Carol's first draft, with notes to herself based on comments from her peer-response group and her own thinking

What do I mean here?

Pumping Iron

I should say why she needed lifting

[It all] began when my grandmother broke her hip.

I couldn't [lift] her alone when I was helping take care
she does not weigh much, but she was too much for me.
of her. I needed strength, [and] I'm planning to be a

I need to clarify the connection

I have to check when I revise whether this thesis statement fits the rest of my essay

nurse. Then I found out I could satisfy a physical ed

requirement in college with a weight lifting course

Lots of I's — is this only about me?

for women. [I] thought only big, macho men lift weights.

But if she is trained well, any woman can "pump iron"

well, just like a man.

Hoping for strength and endurance

~~The first day of class we did not exercise. We~~

MOVE. This should be my third ¶.

~~talked about who we are and why we wanted to take the~~

can lead to *unless lifters*

~~course. We heard about how to avoid~~ injury by learning

my second ¶ should give background

and weight machines. *Free weights are barbells.*

the safe use of free weights ~~(barbells)~~ To be safe,

no matter how little the weight, lifters must never

grasp
raise a barbell by bending at the waist. Instead, they
should squat, ~~grab~~ the barbell, and then straighten up

To avoid a *that* *serious*
into a standing position. Twists can lead to injury, ~~so~~

I need to go into more detail here

lifters must keep head erect, facing forward, back and

neck aligned. Lifters use weight machines sitting

down, which is a big advantage of the Nautilus and

Universal.

→

happy

(I) was {relieved} that (I) won't develop overly

move up ↑ to be #2 (background)

masculine muscle mass. (We) learned that we can rely on

I have to bring in more than myself to say who we are

women's biology. Our bodies produce only very small

amounts of the hormones that enlarge muscles in men.

I need to tie these together (check 4d)

With normal training, ~muscles

~~Normally,~~ women's ⋀ grow longer rather than bulkier.

Weight lifting is a form of (anareobic) exercise. It

(SP)

does not make people breathe harder or their hearts

(SP)

running, walking, and

beat faster. (Arobic) exercise like ⋀ swimming builds

am I too informal here?

endurance, so I (took up) swimming.

My topic sentence needs work

    After safety comes our needs for physical

strength. A well-planned, progressive weight training

It

a person

program. ~~You~~ ⋀ begins ⋀ with whatever weight ⋀ ~~you~~ can lift

to the base weight as one gets stronger.

comfortably and ~~then~~ gradually add ⋀ What builds

the lifter does,

muscle strength is the number of "reps", ~~we do~~ not

resistance from adding

necessarily an increase in the amount of ~~added~~ ⋀

weight. In my class, we ranged from 18 to 43, scrawny

pudgy   *couch-potato*

to ~~fat~~, and ~~lazy~~ to superstar, and we each developed

I'm not trying here

a program that was (OK) for us. Some women didn't

try

listen to our instructor who urged us not to ~~do~~ ⋀ more

Start sentence here? Not sure

reps or weight than our programs called for, even if

our first workouts

~~it~~ ⋀ seemed too easy. This turned out to be good

advice because those of us who didn't listen woke

the next morning

up ⋀ feeling as though our bodies had been twisted by

evil forces.

→

In addition to
fitting to ~~After meeting~~ her physical capabilities, a

weight lifter needs to design her personal goals.

Most students in my group wanted to improve their

upper body strength. (Each) student learned to use

I need specific examples of students

specific exercises to isolate certain muscle groups,

for example we might work on our arms and (abdomen)

sp?

one day and our shoulders and chest the next day.

~~My goal is nursing, which I want to pursue. I want~~

~~to help others, but I'm also very interested in~~

I'm off the topic

~~the science I'll learn. I hear there is a lot of~~

~~memorization, which I'm pretty good at. I also will~~

~~have "clinical" assignments to give us hands on~~

~~experience in hospitals.~~ Because I had had such

trouble lifting my grandmother, I added exercises to

strengthen my legs and back. Another student added

neck strengthening exercises. Someone else added

finger and hand exercises.

At the end of the course, we had to evaluate

our progress. When I started, I could lift 10 pounds, *over my head for 3 reps.* x

~~but~~ By the end, I could lift 10 pounds, for 20 reps *over my head*

and 18 pounds for 3 reps. I am so proud of my

I forget to talk about my swimming

I need a stronger ending

accomplishments that I work out three or four times *still*

a week. I am proof that any woman can become stronger

and have more stamina.

3g.2 Carol Moreno's second draft

For her second draft, Carol revised by working systematically through the notes she had written on the draft. The notes came from her own thoughts as well as from the comments of a peer-response group with which she had shared her paper.

From the assignment (see page 24), Carol knew that her instructor would consider this second draft an "essay in progress." Her instructor's responses would be designed to help her write a final draft. Carol expected two types of comments: questions to help her clarify and expand on some of her ideas, and references to some of this handbook's section codes (number-letter combinations) to point out errors. Here is her second draft.

Carol's second draft, with her instructor's responses

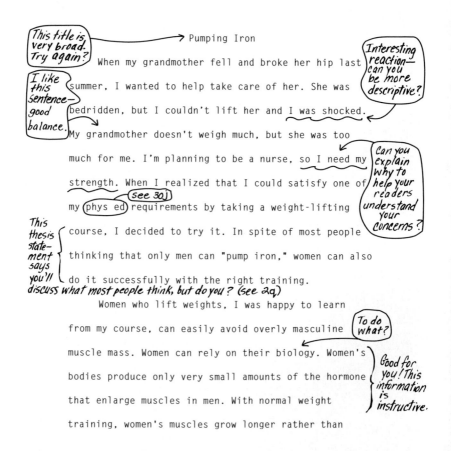

This title is very broad. Try again? → Pumping Iron

Interesting reaction— can you be more descriptive?

When my grandmother fell and broke her hip last summer, I wanted to help take care of her. She was bedridden, but I couldn't lift her and I was shocked. My grandmother doesn't weigh much, but she was too much for me. I'm planning to be a nurse, so I need my strength. When I realized that I could satisfy one of my (phys ed) requirements by taking a weight-lifting course, I decided to try it. In spite of most people thinking that only men can "pump iron," women can also do it successfully with the right training.

I like this sentence— good balance.

Can you explain why to help your readers understand your concerns?

(see 30j)

This thesis statement says you'll discuss what most people think, but do you? (see 2q)

Women who lift weights, I was happy to learn from my course, can easily avoid overly masculine muscle mass. Women can rely on their biology. Women's bodies produce only very small amounts of the hormone that enlarge muscles in men. With normal weight training, women's muscles grow longer rather than

To do what?

Good for you! This information is instructive.

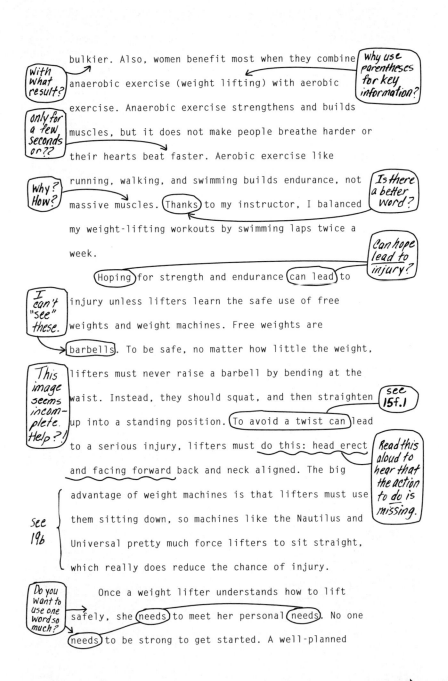

bulkier. Also, women benefit most when they combine

With what result?

anaerobic exercise (weight lifting) with aerobic

Why use parentheses for key information?

exercise. Anaerobic exercise strengthens and builds

only for a few seconds or??

muscles, but it does not make people breathe harder or

their hearts beat faster. Aerobic exercise like

Why? How?

running, walking, and swimming builds endurance, not

Is there a better word?

massive muscles. (Thanks) to my instructor, I balanced

my weight-lifting workouts by swimming laps twice a

week.

Can hope lead to injury?

(Hoping) for strength and endurance (can lead) to

I can't "see" these.

injury unless lifters learn the safe use of free

weights and weight machines. Free weights are

(barbells). To be safe, no matter how little the weight,

This image seems incomplete. Help?!

lifters must never raise a barbell by bending at the

waist. Instead, they should squat, and then straighten

see 15f.1

up into a standing position. (To avoid a twist can) lead

to a serious injury, lifters must do this: head erect

Read this aloud to hear that the action to do is missing.

and facing forward back and neck aligned. The big

advantage of weight machines is that lifters must use

see 19b

them sitting down, so machines like the Nautilus and

Universal pretty much force lifters to sit straight,

which really does reduce the chance of injury.

Do you want to use one word so much?

Once a weight lifter understands how to lift

safely, she (needs) to meet her personal (needs). No one

(needs) to be strong to get started. A well-planned

See 12b

progressive weight training program. It begins with
whatever weight a person can lift comfortably and
gradually adds to the base weight as she gets
stronger. What builds strength is the number of "reps"
the lifter does, not necessarily an increase in the

meaning?

amount of resistance from adding weight. Our
instructor helped the women in our class, who ranged

These adjectives are fun.

from 18 to 43, scrawny to pudgy, couch potato to
superstar, to develop a program that suited us. Our
instructor urged us not to try more reps or weight
than our programs called for, even if our first
workouts seemed too easy. This turned out to be good

Fun again. Your voice (personality) comes through.

advice because those of us who did not listen woke up
the next morning feeling as though our bodies had
been twisted by evil forces.

In addition to fitting a program to her physical

Does one design a goal?

capabilities, a weight lifter needs to design her
personal goals. Most students in my group wanted to
improve their upper body strength, so we focused on

good details

exercises to strengthen our arms, shoulders, abdomens,
and chests. Each student learned to use specific

see 13c

Why important?

exercises to isolate certain muscle groups, for

see 24c

example we might work on our arms and abdomen one
day and our shoulders and chest the next day. Because
I had had such trouble lifting my grandmother, I added

Excellent examples Carol! exercises to strengthen my legs and back. Another

student added neck strengthening exercises. Someone   *Why did she choose this?*

else, planning to be a physical therapist, added

finger and hand-strengthening exercises.

At the end of the course, we had to evaluate our   *How long was it?*

progress. When I started, I could lift 10 pounds over

my head for 3 reps. By the end, I could lift 10 pounds   *Can you communicate your enthusiasm to your reader more effectively?*

over my head for 20 reps and 18 pounds for 3 reps.

see 24c Also I could swim for 20 sustained minutes instead of

the 10 at first. I am so proud of my accomplishments

that I still work out three or four times a week. I am

proof that any woman can benefit from "pumping iron."

Not only will she become stronger and have more

stamina, she will also feel very good.   *Isn't this a bit flat?*

Dear Carol,
You have truly earned the right to feel proud of yourself. You've also inspired me to consider weight training myself!
As you revise for your final draft, I'd urge you to get more voice (your personality) into the essay. To do this, you don't have to become too informal; instead, find how you felt about what you were doing and try to put that into words. Also, think about my questions and the codes that refer you to sections of the Troyka handbook. I will enjoy reading your final draft, I'm sure.
                                                    K.N.

3g.3 Carol Moreno's final draft

For her final draft, Carol worked systematically through her second draft with an eye on her instructor's responses. Also, she revised in places where her instructor hadn't commented. As another check, Carol referred to the revision checklists, Boxes 18 and 19, in section 3c.5.

Next, to edit her final draft, Carol looked up the handbook codes (number-letter combinations) her instructor wrote on her second draft. She also consulted the editing checklist, Box 20 in section 3d. Before she started to proofread, Carol took a break from writing so she could refresh her ability to see typing errors. Distance from her work, she knew, would also help her see it more objectively.

Here is Carol's final draft. I have put notes in the margins to point out to you essay elements that help the essay succeed. My notes are for you only, so of course, don't write any on your final drafts.

Carol's final draft

Moreno 1

Carol Moreno

Professor K. Norris

Freshman Composition 101, Section LR

4 December 2000

TITLE   Women Can Pump Iron, Too

INTRODUCTION: Gets reader's attention with personal anecdote

When my grandmother fell and broke her hip last summer, I wanted to help take care of her. Because she was bedridden, she needed to be lifted at times, but I was shocked to discover that I could not lift her without my mother's or brother's help. My grandmother does not weigh much, but she was too much for me. My pride was hurt, and even more important, I began to worry about my plans to be

Question to add sentence variety

a nurse specializing in the care of elderly people. What if I were too weak to help my patients get around? When I realized that I could satisfy one of my Physical Education requirements by taking a weight-lifting course for women, I decided to try it. Many people picture only big, macho men wanting to lift weights, but times have changed. With

→

THESIS STATEMENT: focus of essay — the right training, women can also "pump iron" to build strength.

BODY PARAGRAPH ONE: Gives background information — Women who lift weights, I was happy to learn from my course, can easily avoid developing overly masculine muscle mass. Women can rely on their biology to protect them. Women's bodies produce only very small amounts of **Refutes possible objection** the hormones that enlarge muscles in men. With normal weight training, women's muscles grow longer rather than bulkier. The result is smoother, firmer muscles, not **Transition to signal additional point** massive bulges. Also, women benefit most when they combine weight lifting, which is a form of anaerobic exercise, with aerobic exercise. Anaerobic exercise strengthens and builds muscles, but it does not make people breathe harder **Specific details of two types of conditioning** or their hearts beat faster for sustained periods. In contrast, aerobic exercises like running, walking, and swimming build endurance, but not massive muscles, because they force a person to take in more oxygen, which increases lung capacity, improves circulatory health, and tones the entire body. Encouraged by my instructor, I balanced my weight-lifting workouts by swimming laps twice a week.

BODY PARAGRAPH TWO: Describes safe use of equipment and lifting techniques — Striving for strength can end in injury unless weight lifters learn the safe use of free weights and weight machines. Free weights are barbells, the metal bars that round metal weights can be attached to at each end. To be safe, no matter how little the weight, lifters must never raise a barbell by bending at the waist, grabbing the bar- **Transition to show contrast** bell, and then straightening up. Instead, they should squat, grasp the barbell, and then use their leg muscles to straighten into a standing position. To avoid a twist that can lead to serious injury, lifters must use this posture: head erect and facing forward, back and neck aligned. The big advantage of weight machines, which use weighted handles and bars hooked to wires and pulleys, is that lifters must use them sitting down. Therefore,

→

machines like the Nautilus and Universal actually force lifters to keep their bodies properly aligned, which drastically reduces the chance of injury.

BODY PARAGRAPH THREE: Describes and explains the design and purpose of weight training programs

Once a weight lifter understands how to lift safely, she needs a weight-lifting regimen personalized to her specific physical needs. Because benefits come from "resistance," which is the stress that lifting any amount of weight puts on a muscle, no one has to be strong to get started. A well-planned, progressive weight-training program begins with whatever weight a person can lift comfortably and gradually adds to the base weight as she gets stronger. What builds muscle strength is the number of repetitions, or "reps," the lifter does, not necessarily an increase for resistance from adding weight.

Specific details for reader to visualize a class

Our instructor helped the women in the class, who ranged from 18 to 43, scrawny to pudgy, and couch potato to superstar, to develop a program that was right for our individual weight, age, and overall level of conditioning. Everyone's program differed in how much weight to start out with and how many reps to do for each exercise. Our instructor urged us not to try more weight or reps than our programs called for, even if our first workouts seemed too easy. This turned out to be good advice because those of us who did not listen woke up the next day feeling as though evil forces had twisted our bodies.

BODY PARAGRAPH FOUR: Explains the need for developing a program to fit individual needs

In addition to fitting a program to her physical capabilities, a weight lifter needs to design an individual routine to fit her personal goals. Most students in my group wanted to improve their upper body strength, so we focused on exercises to strengthen arms, shoulders, abdomens, and chests. Each student learned to use specific exercises to isolate certain muscle groups. Because muscles strengthen and grow when they're rested after a workout, our instructor taught us to work alternate muscle

→

Specific examples to add interest

groups on different days. For example, a woman might work on her arms and abdomen one day and then her shoulders and chest the next day. Because I had had such trouble lifting my grandmother, I added exercises to strengthen my legs and back. Another student, who had hurt her neck in a car crash, added neck-strengthening exercises. Someone else, planning to be a physical therapist, added finger- and hand-strengthening exercises.

CONCLUSION: Reports writer's personal progress

At the end of our 10 weeks of weight training, we had to evaluate our progress. Was I impressed! I felt ready to lift the world. When I started, I could lift only 10 pounds over my head for 3 reps. By the end of the course, I could lift 10 pounds over my head for 20 reps, and I could lift 18 pounds for 3 reps. Also, I could swim laps for 20 sustained minutes instead of the 10 I had barely managed at first. I am so proud of my weight-training accomplishments that I still work out three or four times a week. I am proof that any woman can benefit from "pumping iron." Not only will she become stronger and have more stamina, but she will also feel energetic and confident. After all, there isn't a thing to lose--except maybe some flab.

4 WRITING PARAGRAPHS

4a What is a paragraph?

A **paragraph** is a group of sentences that work together to develop a unit of thought. Paragraphing permits writers to divide material into manageable parts. When a group of paragraphs works together in logical sequence, the result is a complete essay or other whole piece of writing.

To signal the start of a new paragraph, indent the first line about one-half inch. Skip no extra lines between paragraphs. BUSINESS WRITING (Chapter 42) is an exception: It calls for *block format* for paragraphs, which means you do not indent the first line but rather leave a double space between paragraphs. (If you're already double-spacing, then leave two double lines for a total of four lines.)

I explain later in this chapter the rich variety of PARAGRAPH ARRANGE-MENTS (4h) and RHETORICAL STRATEGIES (4i) at your disposal for writing paragraphs. Types of arrangements and rhetorical strategies are culture-bound in that they reflect patterns of thought in Western cultures. But first, let's look at characteristics of paragraphs in general. I start by discussing introductory paragraphs (4b); then, body paragraphs (4c through 4j); and last, concluding paragraphs (4k).

4b How can I write effective introductory paragraphs?

An **introductory paragraph** leads the reader to sense what's ahead. It sets the stage. It also, if possible, attempts to arouse a reader's interest in the topic.

A THESIS STATEMENT can be an important component in an introduction. Many instructors require students to place their thesis statement at the end of the opening paragraph. Doing so disciplines students to state early the central point of the essay. If an introduction points in one direction, and the rest of the essay goes off in another, the essay isn't communicating a clear message. Professional writers don't necessarily include a thesis statement in their introductory paragraphs. Most have the skill to maintain a line of thought without overtly stating a main idea. Introductory paragraphs, as well as concluding paragraphs (4k), are usually shorter than body paragraphs (4c).

Be careful not to tack on a sloppy introduction at the last minute. It plays too important a role to be tossed off with merely a few shallow lines. While many writers prefer to write only a thesis statement as an introduction in an early draft, they always return to write a complete introductory paragraph after the body—main part—of the writing is finished. For a list of specific strategies to use—and pitfalls to avoid for introductory paragraphs,—see Box 22.

 Introductory paragraphs 22

Strategies to Use
- Providing relevant background information
- Relating briefly an interesting story or anecdote
- Giving one or more pertinent—perhaps surprising—statistics
- Asking one or more provocative questions
- Using an appropriate quotation
- Defining a key term (6g)
- Presenting one or more brief examples (4i.4)
- Drawing an analogy (4i.9)

Strategies to Avoid
- Don't write statements about your purpose, such as "I am going to discuss the causes of falling oil prices."
- Don't apologize, as in "I am not sure this is right, but this is my opinion."
- Don't use overworked expressions, such as "Haste makes waste, as I recently discovered" or "Love is grand."

Always integrate an introductory device into the paragraph so that it leads smoothly into the thesis statement. Some examples follow. In this chapter, each example paragraph has a number to its left for your easy reference. Here's an introductory paragraph that uses two brief examples to lead into the thesis statement (shown in italics).

1　On seeing another child fall and hurt himself, Hope, just nine months old, stared, tears welling up in her eyes, and crawled to her mother to be comforted—as though she had been hurt, not her friend. When 15-month-old Michael saw his friend Paul crying, Michael fetched his own teddy bear and offered it to Paul; when that didn't stop Paul's tears, Michael brought Paul's security blanket from another room. *Such small acts of sympathy and caring, observed in scientific studies, are leading researchers to trace the roots of empathy—the ability to share another's emotions—to infancy, contradicting a long-standing assumption that infants and toddlers were incapable of these feelings.*

> —Daniel Goleman, "Researchers Trace Empathy's Roots to Infancy"

In paragraph 2, the opening quotation sets up a dramatic contrast with the thesis statement.

2　"Alone one is never lonely," says May Sarton in her essay "The Rewards of Living a Solitary Life." Most people, however, don't share Sarton's opinion: They're terrified of living alone. They're used to living with others—children with parents, roommates with roommates, friends with friends, spouses with spouses. When the statistics catch up with them, therefore, they're rarely prepared. Chances are high that most adult men and women will need to know how to live alone, briefly or longer, at some time in their lives.

> —Tara Foster, student

In paragraph 3, the writer asks a direct question, and next puts the reader in a dramatic situation to arouse interest in the topic.

3　What should you do? You're out riding your bike, playing golf, or in the middle of a long run when you look up and suddenly see a jagged streak of light shoot across the sky, followed by a deafening clap of thunder. Unfortunately, most outdoor exercisers don't know whether to stay put or make a dash for shelter when a thunderstorm approaches, and sometimes the consequences are tragic.

> —Gerald Secor Couzens, "If Lightning Strikes"

EXERCISE 4-1

Write an introduction for the three essays informally outlined here. Then, for more practice, write one alternative introduction for each. If you have a peer-response group, share the various written introductions and decide which are most effective. For help, see 4b.

1. Reading for fun
   Thesis statement: People read many kinds of books for pleasure.
   Body paragraph 1: murder mysteries and thrillers
   Body paragraph 2: romances and westerns
   Body paragraph 3: science fiction

2. Computer games

   Thesis statement: Interactive video games require players to exercise their skills of dexterity, intelligence, and imagination.

   Body paragraph 1: manual dexterity

   Body paragraph 2: intelligence

   Body paragraph 3: imagination

3. Using credit cards

   Thesis statement: Although credit cards can help people manage their finances wisely, they also offer too much temptation.

   Body paragraph 1: convenience and safety

   Body paragraph 2: tracking of purchases

   Body paragraph 3: overspending dangers

4c What are body paragraphs?

Each **body paragraph,** which belongs between an introductory paragraph (4b) and a concluding paragraph (4k), consists of a main idea and support for that idea. To be effective, a body paragraph needs three characteristics: *unity* (4d and 4e), *development* (4f), and *coherence* (4g). The sections shown in parentheses explain how you can achieve each characteristic. Box 23 gives an overview of all three characteristics.

⊙ **Three characteristics of effective   23
body paragraphs: UDC**

U = Unity Have you made a clear connection between the main idea of the paragraph and the sentences that support the main idea (4d and 4e)?

D = Development Have you included detailed and sufficient support for the main idea of the paragraph (4f)?

C = Coherence Have you progressed from one sentence to the next in the paragraph smoothly and logically (4g)?

Paragraph 4 is an example of an effective body paragraph. It's from an essay called "What's Bugging You?"

The cockroach lore that has been daunting us for years is mostly true. Roaches can live for twenty days without food, fourteen days without

77

water; they can flatten their bodies and crawl through a crack thinner than a dime; they can eat huge doses of carcinogens and still die of old age. They can even survive "as much radiation as an oak tree can," says William Bell, the University of Kansas entomologist whose cockroaches appeared in the movie *The Day After*. They will eat almost anything—regular food, leather, glue, hair, paper, even the starch in bookbindings. (The New York Public Library has quite a cockroach problem.) They sense the slightest breeze, and they can react and start running in .05 second; they can also remain motionless for days. And if all this isn't creepy enough, they can fly too.

4

—Jane Goldman, "What's Bugging You?"

Paragraph 4 has UNITY (4d) in that the main idea (stories we've heard about cockroaches are true), stated in the TOPIC SENTENCE (4e), which is also the first sentence, is supported by detailed examples. It has COHERENCE (4g) in that the content of every sentence ties into the content of the other sentences. Also, the paragraph *coheres*—sticks together—by word choices (repeating *they can* each time to put the emphasis on the interesting facts) and with consistent grammar (a different ACTIVE VERB [see VOICE, 8n through 8p] for each example). It has PARAGRAPH DEVELOPMENT (4c and 4i) in that the details provide support for the main idea.

4d How can I create unity in paragraphs?

A paragraph has **unity** when the connection between the main idea and its supporting sentences is clear. Paragraph 4 in the last section is a good example.

Unity is ruined when any sentence in a paragraph "goes off the topic," which means its content doesn't relate to the main idea or to the other sentences in the paragraph. To show you broken unity, in paragraph 5 I've deliberately inserted two sentences that go off the topic (the fourth and the next to last) which ruin a perfectly good paragraph, shown as paragraph 6. (Neither a personal complaint about stress nor hormones produced by men and women during exercise belong in a paragraph defining different kinds of stress.)

NO

5

Stress has long been the subject of psychological and physiological speculation. In fact, more often than not, the word itself is ill defined and overused, meaning different things to different people. Emotional stress, for example, can come about as the result of a family argument or the death of a loved one. Everyone says, "don't get stressed," but I have no idea how to do that. Environmental stress, such as exposure to excessive heat or cold, is an entirely different phenomenon. Physiologic stress has been described as the outpouring of the steroid hormones from the adrenal glands. During exercise, such as weightlifting, males and females produce different hormones. Whatever its guise, a lack of a firm definition has seriously impeded past research.

YES

6   Stress has long been the subject of psychological and physiological speculation. In fact, more often than not, the word itself is ill defined and overused, meaning different things to different people. Emotional stress, for example, can come about as the result of a family argument or the death of a loved one. Environmental stress, such as exposure to excessive heat or cold, is an entirely different phenomenon. Physiologic stress has been described as the outpouring of the steroid hormones from the adrenal glands. Whatever its guise, a lack of a firm definition has seriously impeded past research.

—Herbert Benson, M.D., *The Relaxation Response*

4e   How do topic sentences help create paragraph unity?

A **topic sentence** contains the main idea of a paragraph. The topic sentence controls the content of the rest of the paragraph. Often, the topic sentence comes at the beginning of a paragraph, though not always. In pieces of writing longer than an essay, two sentences are used to present the main idea.

Professional essay writers, because they have the skill to carry the reader along without explicit signposts, sometimes decide not to use topic sentences. Student writers, however, are usually required by their instructors to use topic sentences. As apprentice writers, students might be more likely to write paragraphs that lack UNITY.

Topic sentence starting a paragraph

In ACADEMIC WRITING, most paragraphs begin with a topic sentence (shown here in italics) so that readers know immediately what to expect. Paragraph 7 is an example.

7   *To travel the streets of Los Angeles is to glimpse America's ethnic future.* At the bustling playground at McDonald's in Koreatown, a dozen shades of kids squirt down the slides and burrow through tunnels and race down the catwalks, not much minding that no two of them speak the same language. Parents of grade-school children say they rarely know the color of their youngsters' best friends until they meet them; it never seems to occur to the children to say, since they have not yet been taught to care.

—Nancy Gibbs, "Shades of Difference"

Sometimes, a topic sentence both starts a paragraph and, in different wording, ends the paragraph. Paragraph 8 is an example.

8   *Burnout is a potential problem for hardworking and persevering students to fight.* A preliminary step for preventing student burnout is for students to work in moderation. Students can concentrate on school every day, if they don't overtax themselves. One method students can use is to avoid concentrating on a single project for an extended period. For example, if students have to read two books for a midterm history test, they should do other assignments at intervals so that the two books will not get boring. Another means to moderate a workload is to regulate how many extracurricular projects to take on. *When a workload is manageable, a student's immunity to burnout is strengthened.*

—Bradley Howard, student

Topic sentence ending a paragraph

Some paragraphs give supporting details first and wait to state the topic sentence at the paragraph's end. This approach is particularly effective for building suspense or for creating a bit of drama. Paragraph 9 is an example.

9   Most people don't lose ten dollars or one hundred dollars when they trade cars. They lose many hundreds or even a thousand. They buy used cars that will not provide them service through the first payment. They overbuy new cars and jeopardize their credit, only to find themselves "hung," unable even to sell their shiny new toys. *The car business is one of the last roundups in America, the great slaughterhouse of wheeling and dealing, where millions of people each year willingly submit to being taken.*

—Remar Sutton, *Don't Get Taken Every Time*

Topic sentence implied, not stated

Some paragraphs are a unified whole even without a single sentence that readers can point to as the topic sentence. Yet, most readers can catch the main idea anyway. Paragraph 10 is an example. What do you think might be a straightforward topic sentence for it?

10   The Romans were entertained by puppets, as were the rulers of the Ottoman Empire with their favorite shadow puppet, Karaghoiz, teller of a thousand tales. In the Middle Ages, puppets were cast as devil and angel in religious mystery and morality plays until cast out entirely by the church. For centuries, a rich puppetry heritage in India has matched that country's multilayered culture. The grace of Bali is reflected in its stylized, ceremonial rod and shadow puppets. The Bunraku puppets of Japan, unequaled for technique anywhere in the world, require a puppet master and two assistants to create one dramatic character on stage.

—Dan Cody, "Puppet Poetry"

EXERCISE 4-2

Working individually or with a peer-response group, identify the topic sentences in the following paragraphs. If the topic sentence is implied, write the point the paragraph conveys. For help, consult section 4e.

A. 11   A good college program should stress the development of high-level reading, writing, and mathematical skills and should provide you with a broad historical, social, and cultural perspective, no matter what subject you choose as your major. The program should teach you not only the most current knowledge in your field but also—just as important—prepare you to keep learning throughout your life. After all, you'll probably change jobs, and possibly even careers, at least six times, and you'll have other responsibilities, too—perhaps as a spouse and as a parent and certainly as a member of a community whose bounds extend beyond the workplace.

—Frank T. Rhodes, "Let the Student Decide"

B. 12   The once majestic oak tree crashes to the ground amid the destructive flames, as its panic-stricken inhabitants attempt to flee the fiery tomb. Undergrowth that formerly flourished smolders in ashes. A family of deer darts furiously from one wall of flame to the other, without an emergency exit. On the outskirts of the inferno, firefighters try desperately to stop the destruction. Somewhere at the source of this chaos lies a former campsite containing the cause of this destruction—an untended campfire. This scene is one of many that illustrate how human apathy and carelessness destroy nature.

—Anne Bryson, student

C. 13   Rudeness isn't a distinctive quality of our own time. People today would be shocked by how rudely our ancestors behaved. In the colonial period, a French traveler marveled that "Virginians don't use napkins, but they wear silk cravats, and instead of carrying white handkerchiefs, they blow their noses either with their fingers or with a silk handkerchief that also serves as a cravat, a napkin, and so on." In the 19th century, up to about the 1830s, even very distinguished people routinely put their knives in their mouths. And when people went to the theater, they would not just applaud politely—they would chant, jeer, and shout. So, the notion that there's been a downhill slide in manners ever since time began is just not so.

—"Horizons," *U.S. News & World Report*

4f   How can I develop my body paragraphs?

You develop a **body paragraph** by supplying detailed support for the main idea of the paragraph communicated by your TOPIC SENTENCE (4e), whether stated or implied. The detailed support is not merely a repetition, using other words, of the main idea. When this happens, you're merely going around in circles. I've deliberately created paragraph 15 to show you a bad example of development. It goes nowhere because all that happens is that one idea is restated three times in different words. Compare it with paragraph 4 that appears earlier in this chapter (4c), which is a well-developed paragraph.

NO The cockroach lore that has been daunting us for years is mostly
14 true. Almost every tale we have heard about cockroaches is correct. The stories about cockroaches have frightened people for
generations.

**What separates most good writing from bad is the writer's
ability to move back and forth between main ideas and specific
details.** To check whether you are providing sufficient detail in a body
paragraph, use the **RENNS Test.** Each letter in the made-up word
RENNS cues you to remember a different kind of supporting detail at
your disposal, as listed in Box 24.

 **The RENNS Test: Checking for supporting
details** **24**

R = **Reasons** provide support.
E = **Examples** provide support.
N = **Names** provide support.
N = **Numbers** provide support.
S = **Senses**—sight, sound, smell, taste, touch—provide support.

Use the RENNS Test to check the quality of your **paragraph development.** Of course, not every paragraph needs all five kinds of RENNS
details, nor do the supporting details need to occur in the order of the
letters in RENNS. Paragraph 15 contains three of the five types of
RENNS details. Identify the topic sentence and as many RENNS as you
can before reading the analysis that follows the paragraph.

15 U.S. shores are also being inundated by waves of plastic debris. On
the sands of the Texas Gulf Coast one day last September, volunteers collected 307 tons of litter, two-thirds of which was plastic, including 31,733
bags, 30,295 bottles, and 15,631 six-pack yokes. Plastic trash is being
found far out to sea. On a four-day trip from Maryland to Florida that
ranged 100 miles offshore, John Hardy, an Oregon State University
marine biologist, spotted "Styrofoam and other plastic on the surface,
most of the whole cruise."

—"The Dirty Seas," *Time*

In paragraph 15, the first sentence serves as the topic sentence.
Supporting details for that main idea include examples, names, and numbers. The writer provides examples of the kinds of litter found washed
up on the beach and floating offshore. The writer names many specific

things: Texas Gulf Coast, September, bags, bottles, six-pack yokes, Maryland, Florida, John Hardy, Oregon State University, marine biologist, and Styrofoam. And the writer uses specific numbers to describe the volume of litter collected (307 tons), to give counts of specific items (such as 31,733 bags), and to tell how far from shore (100 miles) the litter had traveled.

Paragraph 16 contains four of the five types of RENNS. Identify the topic sentence and as many RENNS as you can before you read the analysis that follows the paragraph.

> We live in a changed world from that of 1888, and we are a changed nation. Our founders knew an America with rising expectations, while we see a superpower riddled with self-doubt. Tropical rain forests were a mysterious challenge in 1888. The challenge in 1988 is saving them from disappearance. Automobiles had just been invented, and airplanes were unknown. Would our founders be impressed by rush-hour traffic, a brown cloud over Denver, or aerial gridlock at Chicago's O'Hare Airport? Could they have conceived of a Mexico City with 20 million people in an atmosphere so murky that the sun is obscured, so poisonous that school is sometimes delayed until late morning, when the air clears?
>
> —Gilbert M. Grosvenor, "Will We Mend Our Earth?"

In paragraph 16, the first sentence is the topic sentence. Supporting details for the main idea include examples (disappearing rain forests, cars that cause rush-hour traffic, airplanes that cause gridlock in the air, air pollution); the writer also uses names (America, Denver, Chicago's O'Hare Airport, Mexico City) and numbers (1888, 1988, 20 million people). Sensory details provide more support (seeing the "brown cloud" over Denver and the "murky atmosphere" that obscures the sun in Mexico City).

EXERCISE 4-3

Working individually or with a peer-response group, look again at the paragraphs in Exercise 4-2. Identify the RENNS in each paragraph. For help, consult 4f.

4g How can I write coherent paragraphs?

A paragraph is a **coherent paragraph** when its sentences relate to each other, not only in content but also in choice of words and grammatical structures. A coherent paragraph conveys continuity because the sentences follow naturally from one to the next. Techniques for achieving COHERENCE are listed in Box 25, with the section that offers a complete explanation shown in parentheses.

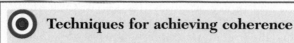

◉ **Techniques for achieving coherence**   **25**

- Using appropriate transitional expressions (4g.1)
- Using pronouns when possible (4g.2)
- Using deliberate repetition of a key word (4g.3)
- Using parallel structures (4g.4)
- Using coherence techniques to create connections between paragraphs (4g.5)

4g.1 Using transitional expressions for coherence

Transitional expressions are words and phrases that signal connections among ideas. **Transitions** are bridges that lead your reader along your line of thought. They offer cues about what follows. Commonly used transitional expressions are listed in Box 26.

◉ **Transitional expressions**   **26**
   and the relationships they signal

ADDITION	also, in addition, too, moreover, and, besides, furthermore, equally important, then, finally,
EXAMPLE	for example, for instance, thus, as an illustration, namely, specifically,
CONTRAST	but, yet, however, nevertheless, nonetheless, conversely, in contrast, still, at the same time, on the one hand, on the other hand,
COMPARISON	similarly, likewise, in the same way,
CONCESSION	of course, to be sure, certainly, granted,
RESULT	therefore, thus, as a result, so, accordingly,
SUMMARY	hence, in short, in brief, in summary, in conclusion, finally,
TIME SEQUENCE	first, second, third, next, then, finally, afterward, before, soon, later, meanwhile, subsequently, immediately, eventually, currently,
PLACE	in the front, in the foreground, in the back, in the background, at the side, adjacent, nearby, in the distance, here, there,

---

👁 **COMMA ALERT:** In academic writing, set off a transitional expression with a comma, unless the expression is one short word (24g). ●

Vary your choices of transitional words. For example, instead of always using *for example,* try *for instance.* Also, when choosing a transitional word, make sure it correctly says what you mean. For example, don't use *however* in the sense of *on the other hand* if you mean *therefore* in the sense of *as a result.* The three brief examples below demonstrate how to use transitional expressions for each context.

COHERENCE BY ADDITION
Woodpeckers use their beaks to find food and to chisel out nests. In addition, they claim their territory and signal their desire to mate by using their beaks to drum on trees.

COHERENCE BY CONTRAST
Most birds communicate by singing. Woodpeckers, however, communicate by the duration and rhythm of the drumming of their beaks.

COHERENCE BY RESULT
The woodpecker's strong beak enables it to communicate by drumming on dry branches and tree trunks. As a result, woodpeckers can communicate across greater distances than songbirds can.

Paragraph 17 demonstrates how transitional expressions (shown in bold) enhance a paragraph's coherence. The topic sentence is the final sentence.

17 Before the days of television, people were entertained by exciting radio shows such as *Superman, Batman,* and "War of the Worlds." **Of course,** the listener was required to pay careful attention to the story if all details were to be comprehended. **Better yet,** while listening to the stories, listeners would form their own images of the actions taking place. When the broadcaster would give brief descriptions of the Martian space ships invading earth, **for example,** every member of the audience would imagine a different space ship. **In contrast,** television's version of "War of the Worlds" will not stir the imagination at all, for everyone can clearly see the actions taking place. All viewers see the same space ship with the same features. Each aspect is clearly defined, and **therefore,** no one will imagine anything different from what is seen. **Thus,** television can't be considered an effective tool for stimulating the imagination.

—Tom Paradis, "A Child's Other World"

4g.2 Using pronouns for coherence

Pronouns—words that refer to NOUNS or other PRONOUNS—allow readers to follow your train of thought from one sentence to the next without boring repetition. Without pronouns, you would have to repeat nouns over and over. For example, this sentence uses no pronouns and therefore has needless repetition: *The woodpecker scratched the woodpecker's head with the woodpecker's foot.* In contrast, with pronouns the sentence can be: *The woodpecker scratched **its** head with **its** foot.* Paragraph 18 illustrates how pronouns (shown in bold) contribute to coherence.

> 18   The funniest people I know are often unaware of just how ticked off **they** are about things until **they** start to kid around about **them.** Nature did not build **these** people to sputter or preach; instead, in response to the world's irritations, **they** create little plays in **their** minds—parodies, cartoons, fantasies. When **they** see how funny **their** creations are, **they** also understand how really sore **they** were at **their** sources. **Their** anger is a revelation, one that works backward in the minds of an audience: the audience starts out laughing and winds up fuming.
>
> —Roger Rosenblatt, "What Brand of Laughter Do You Use?"

4g.3 Using deliberate repetition for coherence

A key word is a strong word that's central to the main idea of the paragraph. **Repetition** of a key word is a useful way to achieve COHERENCE in a paragraph. The word usually appears first in the paragraph's TOPIC SENTENCE (4e) and then again throughout the paragraph. The idea of key-word repetition is to keep a concept in front of the reader.

Use this technique sparingly to avoid being monotonous. Also, limit your selection of a key word to one or at the most two words. The shorter a paragraph, the more likely a repeated key word will seem repetitious, and the less likely it'll be effective. In a longer paragraph, however, the repetition of a key word can be effective. Paragraph 19 contains repeated words (shown in bold) closely tied to emotions, making the paragraph more coherent.

> 19   **Emotions** are, technically speaking, chemical impulses to act. The root of the word ***emotion*** is *motere,* the Latin verb meaning "to move," plus the prefix *e* which means "away," suggesting a tendency to act is implicit in every **emotion.** One of the primary functions of **emotion** is to warn us of danger. Goleman refers to this warning process as an "**emotional** alarm." When you experience an **emotional** alarm, like an unexpectedly loud noise, the **emotional** part of your brain takes over the analytical part of your brain, and you react.
>
> —Carol Carter and Lynn Quitman Troyka, *Majoring in the Rest of Your Life*

4g.4 Using parallel structures for coherence

Parallel structures are created when grammatically equivalent forms are used in series, usually of three or more items, but sometimes only two (see PARALLELISM, Chapter 18). Using parallel structures helps to give a paragraph coherence. The repeated parallel structures reinforce connections among ideas, and add tempo and sound to the sentence.

In paragraph 20, the authors use several parallel structures (shown in bold): a parallel series of words (*the sacred, the secular, the scientific*); parallel PHRASES (*sometimes smiled at, sometimes frowned upon*); and six parallel CLAUSES (the first being *banish danger with a gesture*).

> 20 Superstitions are **sometimes smiled at** and **sometimes frowned upon** as observances characteristic of **the old-fashioned, the unenlightened,** children, peasants, servants, immigrants, foreigners, or backwoods people. Nevertheless, they give all of us ways of moving back and forth among the different worlds in which we live—**the sacred, the secular,** and **the scientific.** They allow us to keep a private world also, where, smiling a little, we can **banish danger with a gesture** and **summon luck with a rhyme, make the sun shine in spite of storm clouds, force the stranger to do our bidding, keep an enemy at bay,** and **straighten the paths of those we love.**
>
> —Margaret Mead and Rhoda Metraux, "New Superstitions for Old"

4g.5 Using coherence techniques to create connections among paragraphs

The same techniques for achieving COHERENCE in a paragraph apply to showing connections among paragraphs in a piece of writing. All four techniques help: transitional expressions (4g.1), pronouns (4g.2), deliberate repetition (4g.3), and parallel structures (4g.4). To see them in action, look over this handbook's student essays (one in 3g, two in 6k, three in 40e), two research papers (35e.2 and 36i.2), and a science report (41h.1).

Example 21 shows two short paragraphs and the start of a third. The writer achieves coherence among the paragraphs by repeating the key word *gratitude* and the related words *grateful, thankful,* and *thank* and by using *then* as a transition into the next paragraph. The writer also uses PARALLELISM within the paragraphs in this example.

> 21 To me, gratitude and inner peace go hand in hand. The more genuinely grateful I feel for the gift of my life, the more peaceful I feel. Gratitude, then, is worthy of a little practice.
>
> If you're anything like me, you probably have many people to be thankful for: friends, family members, people from your past, teachers, gurus, people from work, someone who gave you a break, as well as countless others. You may want to thank a higher power for the gift of life itself, or for the beauty of nature.
>
> As you think of people to be grateful for, remember that it can be anyone—someone who held a door open for you, or a physician who saved your life. . . .

EXERCISE 4-4

Working individually or with a peer-response group, locate the coherence techniques in each paragraph. Look for transitional expressions, pronouns, deliberate repetition, and parallel structures. For help, consult 4g.

A.   Kathy sat with her legs dangling over the edge of the side of the hood. The band of her earphones held back strands of straight copper hair that had come loose from two thick braids that hung down her back. She swayed with the music that only she could hear. Her shoulders raised, making circles in the warm air. Her arms reached out to her side; her open hands reached for the air; her closed hands brought the air back to her. Her arms reached over her head; her opened hands reached for a cloud; her closed hands brought the cloud back to her. Her head moved from side to side; her eyes opened and closed to the tempo of the tunes. Kathy was motion.

22

—Claire Burke, student

B.   Newton's law may have wider application than just the physical world. In the social world, racism, once set into motion, will remain in motion unless acted upon by an outside force. The collective "we" must be the outside force. We must fight racism through education. We must make sure every school has the resources to do its job. We must present to our children a culturally diverse curriculum that reflects our pluralistic society. This can help students understand that prejudice is learned through contact with prejudiced people, rather than with the people toward whom the prejudice is directed.

23

—Randolph H. Manning, "Fighting Racism with Inclusion"

C.   The snow geese are first, rising off the ponds to breakfast in the sorghum fields up the river. Twenty thousand of them, perhaps more, great white birds with black wing tips rising out of the darkness into the rosy reflected light of dawn. They make a sweeping turn, a cloud of wings rising above the cottonwoods. But *cloud* is the wrong word. They don't form a disorderly blackbird rabble but a kaleidoscope of goose formations, always shifting, but always orderly. The light catches them—white against the tan velvet of the hills. Then they're overhead, line after line, layer above layer of formations, and the sky is filled with the clamor of an infinity of geese.

24

—Tony Hillerman, *Hillerman Country*

EXERCISE 4-5

Working individually or with a peer-response group, use RENNS (4f) and techniques for achieving coherence (4g) to develop three of the following topic sentences into paragraphs. When finished, list the RENNS and the coherence techniques you used in each paragraph.

1. Newspaper comic strips reflect current concerns in our culture.
2. The contents of trash in the United States say a great deal about U.S. culture.
3. The car a person owns says much about that person.
4. Doing laundry carelessly can be dangerous to one's clothes.
5. Time management is a lifesaver for college students.

4h In what different ways can I arrange a paragraph?

When you choose a **paragraph arrangement** during DRAFTING, you order its sentences to communicate the paragraph's message most clearly and effectively. Later, during REVISION, experiment with other arrangements to see how else your sentences might be arranged for greatest impact. You may find sometimes that only one possible arrangement can work. For example, if you're explaining how to bake a cake, you want to give the directions in a particular order. But other times, you may find that more than one arrangement is possible. For example, if you're writing about solving a problem and therefore using the problem-to-solution arrangement, you might also use the technique of ordering from least to most important (or its reverse). Box 27 lists the most common ways to arrange a paragraph. More about each arrangement appears in the section in parentheses.

◉ Ways to arrange sentences in a paragraph   27

- by time (4h.1)
- by location (4h.2)
- from general to specific (4h.3)
- from specific to general (4h.4)
- from least to most important (4h.5)
- from problem to solution (4h.6)

4h.1 Arranging by time

In a paragraph arranged according to **time,** or **chronological order,** events are presented in whatever order they took place. For example, when you tell a story, you write what happened first, then second, then

89

third, and so on. Using time sequence is a very natural and easy way to organize a paragraph. Paragraph 25 is an example.

25   Other visitors include schools of dolphin swimming with synchronized precision and the occasional humpback whale. Before 1950, these 14-meter marine mammals were a common sight in the waters of the Great Barrier Reef as they passed on their annual migration between Antarctic waters and the tropics, where their calves were born. Then in the 1950s, whaling stations were set up on the New South Wales and Queensland coasts, and together with the long-established Antarctic hunts by the Soviet Union and America, whales were slaughtered in the thousands. By the time the whaling stations on the eastern Australian coast closed in the early 1960s, it was estimated that only two hundred remained in these waters. Today, their numbers are slowly increasing, but sightings are still rare.

—Allan Moult, "Volcanic Peaks, Tropical Rainforest, and Mangrove Swamps"

4h.2   Arranging by location

A paragraph arranged according to **location,** or **spatial order,** leads the reader's attention from one place to another. The movement can be in any direction—from top to bottom, left to right, inside to outside, and so on. Paragraph 26 traces natural disasters across the United States from west to east.

26   In the United States, most natural disasters are confined to specific geographical areas. For example, the West Coast can be hit by damaging earthquakes at any time. Most Southern and Midwestern states can be swept by devastating tornadoes, especially in the spring, summer, and early fall. The Gulf of Mexico and the Atlantic Ocean can experience violent hurricanes in late summer and fall. These different natural disasters, and others as dangerous, teach people one common lesson—advance preparation can mean survival.

—Dawn Seaford, student

4h.3   Arranging from general to specific

The most common pattern for arranging information is from **general to specific.** Typically, the general statement is the TOPIC SENTENCE, and the supporting details (see RENNS, 4f) explain the specifics. Paragraph 27 is an example.

Unwanted music is privacy's constant enemy. There is hardly an American restaurant, store, railroad station or bus terminal that doesn't gurgle with melody from morning to night, nor is it possible any longer to flee by boarding the train or bus itself, or even by taking a walk in the park. Transistor radios have changed all that. Men, women and children carry them everywhere, hugging them with the desperate attachment that a baby has for its blanket, fearful that they might have to generate an idea of their own or contemplate a blade of grass. Thoughtless themselves, they have no thought for the sufferers within earshot of their portentous news broadcasts and raucous jazz. It's hardly surprising that RCA announced a

27 plan that would pipe canned music and pharmaceutical commercials to 25,000 doctors' offices in eighteen big cities—one place where a decent quietude might be expected. This raises a whole new criterion for choosing a family physician. Better to have a second-rate healer content with the sounds of his stethoscope than an eminent specialist poking to the rhythms of Gershwin.

—William Zinsser, *The Haircurl Papers*

4h.4 Arranging from specific to general

A less common paragraph arrangement moves from **specific to general.** Paragraph 28 is an example. To achieve greatest impact, the paragraph starts with details that support the topic sentence, which ends the paragraph.

Replacing the spark plugs is probably the first thing most home auto mechanics do. But too often, the problem lies elsewhere. In the ignition system, the plug wires, distributor unit, coil, and ignition control unit play just as vital a role as the spark plugs. Moreover, performance prob-

28 lems are by no means limited to the ignition system. The fuel system and emissions control system also contain several components that equal the spark plug in importance. The do-it-yourself mechanic who wants to provide basic care for a car must be able to do more than change the spark plugs.

—Danny Witt, student

4h.5 Arranging from least to most important

A paragraph arranged from **least to most important** uses **climactic order,** which means that the high point—the climax—comes at the end. For a paragraph to be arranged from least to most important, it has to have at least three items: least, better, best. And remember that the last item always packs the greatest impact and is the most memorable. Paragraph 29 is an example.

For a year, Hal and I worked diligently on that boat. At times, it was a real struggle for me to stay on course: as an 11-year-old, my attentions often wandered and the work was not always exciting. But Hal's dedi-

29 cation profoundly influenced me. By his own example, he taught me important lessons about how to be organized, how to set priorities, and how to be responsible. He also, through working with me on the design of the boat's electronics, played a pivotal role in developing my passion for science.

—Patrick Regan Buckley, "Lessons in Boat-Building—and Life"

4h.6 Arranging from problem to solution

In some cases, an effective arrangement for a paragraph is **problem to solution.** Usually, the topic sentence presents the problem. The very next sentence presents the main idea of the solution. Then, the rest of the paragraph covers the specifics of the solution. Paragraph 30 is an example.

> 30   When I first met them, Sara and Michael were a two-career couple with a home of their own, and a large boat bought with a large loan. What interested them in a concept called voluntary simplicity was the birth of their daughter and a powerful desire to raise her themselves. Neither one of them, it turned out, was willing to restrict what they considered their "real life" into the brief time before work and the tired hours afterward. "A lot of people think that as they have children and things get more expensive, the only answer is to work harder in order to earn more money. It's not the only answer," insists Michael. The couple's decision was to trade two full-time careers for two half-time careers, and to curtail consumption. They decided to spend their money only on things that contributed to their major goal, the construction of a world where family and friendship, work and play, were all of a piece, a world, moreover, which did not make wasteful use of the earth's resources.

> —Linda Weltner, "Stripping Down to Bare Happiness"

EXERCISE 4-6

Working individually or with a peer-response group, rearrange the sentences in each paragraph below so that it flows logically. To begin, identify the topic sentence, use it as the paragraph's first sentence, and continue from there. For help, consult 4h.

PARAGRAPH A

1. Remember, many people who worry about offending others wind up living according to other people's priorities.
2. Learn to decline, tactfully but firmly, every request that doesn't contribute to your goals.
3. Of all the timesaving techniques ever developed, perhaps the most effective is the frequent use of the word *no.*
4. If you point out that your motivation isn't to get out of work but to save your time to do a better job on the really important things, you'll have a good chance of avoiding unproductive tasks.

> —Edwin Bliss, "Getting Things Done: The ABC's of Time Management"

PARAGRAPH B

1. After a busy day, lens wearers often don't feel like taking time out to clean and disinfect their lenses, and many wearers skip the chore.
2. When buying a pair of glasses, a person deals with just the expense of the glasses themselves.

3. Although contact lenses make the wearer more attractive, glasses are easier and less expensive to care for.
4. However, in addition to the cost of the lenses themselves, contact lens wearers must shoulder the extra expense of cleaning supplies.
5. This inattention creates a danger of infection.
6. In contrast, contact lenses require daily cleaning and weekly enzyming that inconvenience lens wearers.
7. Glasses can be cleaned quickly with water and tissue at the wearer's convenience.

—Heather Martin, student

PARAGRAPH C

1. The researchers found that the participation of women in sport was a significant indicator of the health and living standards of a country.
2. Today, gradually, women have begun to enter sport with more social acceptance and individual pride.
3. In 1952, researchers from the Finnish Institute of Occupational Health who conducted an intensive study of the athletes participating in the Olympics in Helsinki predicted, "Women are able to shake off civil disabilities which millennia of prejudice and ignorance have imposed upon them."
4. Myths die hard, but they do die.

—Marie Hart, "Sport: Women Sit in the Back of the Bus"

EXERCISE 4-7

Working individually or with a peer-response group, determine the arrangements in these paragraphs. Choose from time, location, general to specific, specific to general, least to most important, or problem to solution. For help, consult 4h.

A.   A combination of cries from exotic animals and laughter and gasps from children fills the air along with the aroma of popcorn and peanuts. A hungry lion bellows for dinner, his roar breaking through the confusing chatter of other animals. Birds of all kinds chirp endlessly at curious children. Monkeys swing from limb to limb, perform-
31 ing gymnastics for gawking onlookers. A comedy routine by orangutans employing old shoes and garments incites squeals of amusement. Reptiles sleep peacefully behind glass windows, yet they send shivers down the spines of those who remember the quick death many of these reptiles can induce. The sights and sounds and smells of the zoo inform and entertain children of all ages.

—Deborah Harris, student

B.   No one even agrees anymore on what "old" is. Not long ago, 30 was middle-aged and 60 was old. Now, more and more people are living into

their 70s, 80s and beyond—and many of them are living well, without
32 any incapacitating mental or physical decline. Today, old age is defined
not simply by chronological years, but by degree of health and well-being.

—Carol Tavris, "Old Age Isn't What It Used to Be"

C. Lately, bee researchers have been distracted by a new challenge
from abroad. It's, of course, the so-called "killer bee" that was imported
into Brazil from Africa in the mid-1950s and has been heading our way
ever since. The Africanized bee looks like the Italian bee but is more
33 defensive and more inclined to attack in force. It consumes much of the
honey that it produces, leaving relatively little for anyone who attempts
to work with it. It travels fast, competes with local bees and, worse,
mates with them. It has ruined the honey industry in Venezuela and now
the big question is: Will the same thing happen here?

—Jim Doherty, "The Hobby That Challenges You to Think Like a Bee"

EXERCISE 4-8

Working individually or with a peer-response group, decide what would be the
best arrangement for a paragraph on each topic listed here. Choose from one
or a combination of time, location, general to specific, specific to general,
least to most important, or problem to solution. For help, consult 4h.

1. ways to make friends
2. automobile accidents
3. how to combine work and college
4. teaching children table manners

4i What rhetorical strategies can I use to write my paragraphs?

Rhetorical strategies, also called *rhetorical patterns,* are techniques
for presenting ideas clearly and effectively. Rhetorical strategies reflect
patterns of thought long in use in our Western culture. You choose a specific rhetorical strategy according to what you want to accomplish. Box 28
lists the common rhetorical strategies at your disposal.

⊙ **Common rhetorical strategies**   28
   (or patterns) for paragraphs

- narrative
- description
- process
- examples
- definition

- analysis
- classification
- comparison and contrast
- analogy
- cause-and-effect analysis

Often, your topic sentence will steer you toward a particular pattern. For example, if a topic sentence is "Grilling a great hot dog is easy," the implied pattern—or rhetorical strategy—is to explain the process of how to grill a hot dog. Or if a topic sentence is "To see many different styles of architecture in one U.S. city, visit Chicago," the implied pattern—or rhetorical strategy—is to give examples.

Sometimes, you need to use a combination of rhetorical strategies. For example, in a paragraph on types of color blindness, you might use a combination of definition (4i.5) and classification (4i.7). A paragraph explaining why one brand of house paint is superior to another might call for comparison and contrast (4i.8) combined with description (4i.2)—and, perhaps, also definition (4i.5) and examples (4i.4).

4i.1 Writing a narrative

Narrative writing is a rhetorical strategy that tells a story. A *narration* deals with what is happening or what has happened. Paragraph 34 is an example.

34 Gordon Parks speculates that he might have spent his life as a waiter on the North Coast Limited train if he hadn't strolled into one particular movie house during a stopover in Chicago. It was shortly before World War II began, and on the screen was a hair-raising newsreel of Japanese planes attacking a gunboat. When it was over the camera operator came out on stage and the audience cheered. From that moment on Parks was determined to become a photographer. During his next stopover, in Seattle, he went into a pawnshop and purchased his first camera for $7.50. With that small sum, Parks later proclaimed, "I had bought what was to become my weapon against poverty and racism." Eleven years later, he became the first black photographer at *Life* magazine.

—Susan Howard, "Depth of Field"

4i.2 Writing a description

Writing a **description** is a rhetorical strategy that appeals to a reader's senses—sight, sound, smell, taste, and touch. *Descriptive writing* paints a picture in words. Paragraph 35 is an example.

35 Walking to the ranch house from the shed, we saw the Northern Lights. They looked like talcum powder fallen from a woman's face. Rouge and blue eye shadow streaked the spires of a white light which exploded, then pulsated, shaking the colors down—like lives—until they faded from sight.

—Gretel Ehrlich, "Other Lives"

4i.3 Writing about a process

Writing about a **process** is a rhetorical strategy that reports a sequence of actions by which something is done or made. A process usually proceeds chronologically—first do this, then do that. A process's complexity dictates the level of detail in the writing. For example, paragraph 36 provides an overview of a complicated process. Paragraph 37, on the other hand, gives explicit step-by-step directions.

36   Making chocolate isn't as simple as grinding a bag of beans. The machinery in a chocolate factory towers over you, rumbling and whirring. A huge cleaner first blows the beans away from their accompanying debris—sticks and stones, coins and even bullets can fall among cocoa beans being bagged. Then they go into another machine for roasting. Next comes separation in a winnower, shells sliding out one side, beans falling from the other. Grinding follows, resulting in chocolate liquor. Fermentation, roasting, and "conching" all influence the flavor of chocolate. Chocolate is "conched"—rolled over and over against itself like pebbles in the sea—in enormous circular machines named conches for the shells they once resembled. Climbing a flight of steps to peer into this huge, slow-moving glacier, I was expecting something like molten mud but found myself forced to conclude it resembled nothing so much as chocolate.

—Ruth Mehrtens Galvin, "Sybaritic to Some, Sinful to Others"

37   Carrying loads of equal weight like paint cans and toolboxes is easier if you carry one in each hand. Keep your shoulders back and down so that the weight is balanced on each side of your body, not suspended in front. With this method, you'll be able to lift heavier loads and also to walk and stand erect. Your back will not be strained by being pulled to one side.

—John Warde, "Safe Lifting Techniques"

4i.4 Writing using examples

A paragraph developed by **examples** presents particular instances of a larger category. For instance, examples of the category "endangered animals" could include the black rhinoceros, South China tiger, Bulmer's fruit bat, and silvery gibbon. Paragraph 38 is an example of this strategy. On the other hand, sometimes one **extended example,** usually called an *illustration,* is called for. Paragraph 39 is an example of this technique.

38   The current revolution in zoo design—the landscape revolution—is driven by three kinds of change that have occurred during this century. First are great leaps in animal ecology, veterinary medicine, landscape design, and exhibit technology, making possible unprecedented realism in zoo exhibits. Second is the progressive disappearance of wilderness—the very subject of zoos—from the earth. Third is knowledge derived from market research and from environmental psychology, making possible a sophisticated focus on the zoo-goer.

—Melissa Greene, "No Rms, Jungle Vu"

39 He was one of the greatest scientists the world has ever known, yet if I had to convey the essence of Albert Einstein in a single word, I would choose *simplicity.* Perhaps an anecdote will help. Once, caught in a downpour, he took off his hat and held it under his coat. Asked why, he explained, with admirable logic, that the rain would damage the hat, but his hair would be none the worse for its wetting. This knack of going instinctively to the heart of the matter was the secret of his major scientific discoveries—this and his extraordinary feeling for beauty.

—Banesh Hoffman, "My Friend, Albert Einstein"

4i.5 Writing using definition

When you define something, you give its meaning. **Definition** is often used together with other rhetorical strategies. If, for example, you were explaining how to organize a seashell collection, you'd probably want to define the two main types of shells: bivalve and univalve. You can also develop an entire paragraph by definition, called an **extended definition.** An extended definition discusses the meaning of a word or concept in more detail than a dictionary definition. If the topic is very abstract, the writer tries to put the definition in concrete terms. Sometimes a definition tells what something is not, as well as what it is, as in paragraph 40.

40 Chemistry is that branch of science that has the task of investigating the materials out of which the universe is made. It is not concerned with the forms into which they may be fashioned. Such objects as chairs, tables, vases, bottles, or wires are of no significance in chemistry; but such substances as glass, wool, iron, sulfur, and clay, as the materials out of which they are made, are what it studies. Chemistry is concerned not only with the composition of such substances, but also with their inner structure.

—John Arrend Timm, *General Chemistry*

4i.6 Writing using analysis

Analysis, sometimes called *division,* divides things up into its parts. It usually starts, often in its topic sentence, by identifying one subject and continues by explaining the subject's distinct parts. Paragraph 41 discusses the parts of the wing of a supersonic aircraft.

41 A wing design is a compromise. For example, if a designer wants a wing for an aircraft that will cruise at supersonic speeds, he must also design the wing to fly at subsonic speeds as well as for takeoffs and landings. Thus, the optimum cruise configuration is compromised to gain other necessary characteristics. Granted, devices such as ailerons, flaps, spoilers, and slats can partially compensate for deficiencies, but these still do not give the optimum performance of a wing designed for a particular flight regime.

—Bill Siuru and John D. Busick, *The Next Generation of Aircraft Technology*

4i.7 Writing using classification

Classification groups items according to an underlying, shared characteristic. Paragraph 42 groups—classifies—interior violations of building-safety codes.

42

A public health student, Marian Glaser, did a detailed analysis of 180 cases of building code violation. Each case represented a single building, almost all of which were multiple-unit dwellings. In these 180 buildings, there were an incredible total of 1,244 different recorded violations—about seven per building. What did the violations consist of? First of all, over one-third of the violations were exterior defects: broken doors and stairways, holes in the walls, sagging roofs, broken chimneys, damaged porches, and so on. Another one-third were interior violations that could scarcely be attributed to the most ingeniously destructive rural southern migrant in America. There were, for example, a total of 160 instances of defective wiring or other electrical hazards, a very common cause of the excessive number of fires and needless tragic deaths in the slums. There were 125 instances of inadequate, defective, or inoperable plumbing or heating. There were 34 instances of serious infestation by rats and roaches.

—William Ryan, "Blaming the Victim"

4i.8 Writing using comparison and contrast

A paragraph developed by *comparison* deals with similarities; a paragraph developed by *contrast* deals with differences. **Comparison and contrast** writing is usually organized one of two ways: You can use *point-by-point organization,* which moves back and forth between the items being compared; or you can use *block organization,* which discusses one item completely before discussing the other. Box 29 lays out the two patterns visually.

   Patterns for comparison and contrast   **29**

Point-by-Point Structure

Student body: college A, college B
Curriculum: college A, college B
Location: college A, college B

Block Structure

College A: student body, curriculum, location
College B: student body, curriculum, location

Paragraph 43 is structured point by point, going back and forth between the two children (whose names are in boldface) being compared.

> My husband and I constantly marvel at the fact that our two sons, born of the same parents and only two years apart in age, are such completely different human beings. The most obvious differences became apparent at their births. Our firstborn, **Mark,** was big and bold—his intense, already wise eyes, broad shoulders, huge and heavy hands, and powerful, chunky legs gave us the impression he could have walked out of the delivery room on his own. Our second son, **Wayne,** was delightfully different. Rather than having the football physique that **Mark** was born with, **Wayne** came into the world with a long, slim, wiry body more suited to running, jumping, and contorting. **Wayne's** eyes, rather than being intense like **Mark's,** were impish and innocent. When **Mark** was delivered, he cried only momentarily, and then seemed to settle into a state of intense concentration, as if trying to absorb everything he could about the strange, new environment he found himself in. Conversely, **Wayne** screamed from the moment he first appeared. There was nothing helpless or pathetic about his cry either—he was darn angry!
>
> —Rosanne Labonte, student

43

Paragraph 44 uses the block pattern for comparison and contrast. The writer first discusses games and then business (each key word is in boldface).

> **Games** are of limited duration, take place on or in fixed and finite sites, and are governed by openly promulgated rules that are enforced on the spot by neutral professionals. Moreover, they're performed by relatively evenly matched teams that are counseled and led through every move by seasoned hands. Scores are kept, and at the end of the game, a winner is declared. **Business** is usually a little different. In fact, if there is anyone out there who can say that the business is of limited duration, takes place on a fixed site, is governed by openly promulgated rules that are enforced on the spot by neutral professionals, competes only on relatively even terms, and performs in a way that can be measured in runs or points, then that person is either extraordinarily lucky or seriously deluded.
>
> —Warren Bennis, "Time to Hang Up the Old Sports Clichés"

44

4i.9 Writing using analogy

An **analogy** is an extended comparison between objects or ideas from different classes—things not normally associated. Analogy is particularly effective in explaining unfamiliar or abstract concepts because a comparison can be drawn between what is familiar and what is not. An analogy often begins with a SIMILE or METAPHOR (21d), as in paragraph 45.

Casual dress, like casual speech, tends to be loose, relaxed, and colorful. It often contains what might be called "slang words": blue jeans, sneakers, baseball caps, aprons, flowered cotton housedresses, and the like. These garments could not be worn on a formal occasion without causing disapproval, but in ordinary circumstances, they pass without remark. "Vulgar words" in dress, on the other hand, give emphasis and

45 get immediate attention in almost any circumstances, just as they do in speech. Only the skillful can employ them without some loss of face, and even then, they must be used in the right way. A torn, unbuttoned shirt or wildly uncombed hair can signify strong emotions: passion, grief, rage, despair. They're most effective if people already think of you as being neatly dressed, just as the curses of well-spoken persons count for more than those of the customarily foul-mouthed do.

—Alison Lurie, *The Language of Clothes*

4i.10 Writing using cause-and-effect analysis

Cause-and-effect analysis examines outcomes and the reasons for those outcomes. Causes lead to an event or an effect, and effects result from causes. (For a discussion of correct logic for assessing CAUSE AND EFFECT, see 5h.) Paragraph 46 discusses how television (the cause) becomes indispensable (the effect) to parents of young children.

Because television is so wonderfully available as child amuser and child defuser, capable of rendering a volatile three-year-old harmless at the flick of a switch, parents grow to depend upon it in the course of their daily lives. And as they continue to utilize television day after day, its importance in their children's lives increases. From a simple source of

46 entertainment provided by parents when they need a break from child-care, television gradually changes into a powerful and disruptive presence in family life. But despite their increasing resentment of television's intrusions into their family life, and despite their considerable guilt at not being able to control their children's viewing, parents don't take steps to extricate themselves from television's domination. They can no longer cope without it.

—Marie Winn, *The Plug-In Drug*

EXERCISE 4-9

Working individually or with a peer-response group, decide what rhetorical strategies are used in each paragraph. Choose from any one or combination of narrative, description, process, examples, definition, analysis, classification, comparison and contrast, analogy, and cause and effect. For help, consult 4i.

A.   Another way to think about *metamessages* is that they frame a conversation, much as a picture frame provides a context for the images in the picture. Metamessages let you know how to interpret

47 what someone is saying by identifying the activity that is going on. Is this an argument or a chat? Is it helping, advising, or scolding? At the same time, they let you know what position the speaker is assuming in the activity, and what position you are being assigned.

—Deborah Tannen, *You Just Don't Understand*

B.

48 I retain only one confused impression from my earliest years: it's all red, and black, and warm. Our apartment was red: the upholstery was of red moquette, the Renaissance dining-room was red, the figured silk hangings over the stained-glass doors were red, and the velvet curtains in Papa's study were red too. The furniture in this awful sanctum was made of black pear wood; I used to creep into the kneehole under the desk and envelop myself in its dusty glooms; it was dark and warm, and the red of the carpet rejoiced my eyes. That is how I seem to have passed the early days of infancy. Safely ensconced, I watched, I touched, I took stock of the world.

—Simone de Beauvoir, *Memoirs of a Dutiful Daughter*

C.

49 In the case of wool, very hot water can actually cause some structural changes within the fiber, but the resulting shrinkage is minor. The fundamental cause of shrinkage in wool is felting, in which the fibers scrunch together in a tighter bunch, and the yarn, fabric, and garment follow suit. Wool fibers are curly and rough-surfaced, and when squished together under the lubricating influence of water, the fibers wind around each other, like two springs interlocking. Because of their rough surfaces, they stick together and can't be pulled apart.

—James Gorman, "Gadgets"

D.

50 After our lunch, we drove to the Liverpool public library, where I was scheduled to read. By then, we were forty-five minutes late, and on arrival we saw five middle-aged white women heading away toward an old car across the street. When they recognized me, the women came over and apologized: They were really sorry, they said, but they had to leave or they'd get in trouble on the job. I looked at them. Every one of them was wearing an inexpensive, faded housedress and, over that, a cheap and shapeless cardigan sweater. I felt honored by their open-mindedness in having wanted to come and listen to my poetry. I thought and I said that it was I who should apologize: I was late. It was I who felt, moreover, unprepared: What in my work, to date, deserves the open-minded attention of blue-collar white women terrified by the prospect of overstaying a union-guaranteed hour for lunch?

—June Jordan, "Waiting for a Taxi"

E.

51 Lacking access to a year-round supermarket, the many species—from ants to wolves—that in the course of evolution have learned the advantages of hoarding must devote a lot of energy and ingenuity to protecting their stashes from marauders. Creatures like beavers and honeybees, for example, hoard food to get them through cold winters.

Others, like desert rodents that face food scarcities throughout the year, must take advantage of the short-lived harvests that follow occasional rains. For animals like burying beetles that dine on mice hundreds of times their size, a habit of biting off more than they can chew at the moment forces them to store their leftovers. Still others, like the male MacGregor's bowerbird, stockpile goodies during mating season so they can concentrate on wooing females and defending their arena d'amour.

—Jane Brody, "A Hoarder's Life: Filling the Cache—and Finding It"

EXERCISE 4-10

Working individually or with a peer-response group, reread the paragraphs in Exercise 4-7 and determine the rhetorical strategy (or strategies) being used in each.

4j What is a transitional paragraph?

Transitional paragraphs are found in long essays. These paragraphs form a bridge between one long discussion on a single topic that requires a number of paragraphs and another discussion, usually lengthy, of another topic. Paragraph 52 is an example of a *transition paragraph* that allows the writer to move from a long discussion of people's gestures to a long discussion of people's eating habits.

52 Like gestures, eating habits are personality indicators, and even food preferences and attitudes toward food reveal the inner self. Food plays an important role in the lives of most people beyond its obvious one as a necessity.

—Jean Rosenbaum, M.D., *Is Your Volkswagen a Sex Symbol?*

4k How can I write effective concluding paragraphs?

A **concluding paragraph** ends the discussion smoothly by following logically from the essay's introductory paragraph (4b) containing a THESIS STATEMENT and from the essay's body paragraphs (4c). Always integrate a concluding device into the final paragraph so that the discussion does not end abruptly. A conclusion that is hurriedly tacked on is a missed opportunity to provide a sense of completion and a finishing touch that adds to the whole essay. Box 30 lists some strategies for concluding your essay as well as some strategies to avoid.

The same writers who wait to write their introductory paragraph until they've drafted their body paragraphs often also wait to write their concluding paragraph until they've drafted their introduction. They do this to coordinate the beginning and end so that they can make sure they don't repeat the same strategy in both places.

 Concluding paragraphs 30

Strategies to Try

- A strategy adapted from those used for introductory paragraphs (4b)—but be careful to choose a different strategy for your introduction and conclusion:
  - Relating a brief concluding interesting story or anecdote
  - Giving one or more pertinent—perhaps surprising—concluding statistics
  - Asking one or more provocative questions for further thought
  - Using an appropriate quotation to sum up the thesis statement
  - Redefining a key term for emphasis
- An ANALOGY that summarizes the thesis statement
- A SUMMARY of the main points, but only if the piece of writing is longer than three to four pages
- A statement that urges awareness by the readers
- A statement that looks ahead to the future
- A call to readers

Strategies to Avoid

- Introducing new ideas or facts that belong in the body of the essay
- Rewording your introduction
- Announcing what you've discussed, as in "In this paper, I have explained why oil prices have dropped."
- Making absolute claims, as in "I have proved that oil prices don't always affect gasoline prices."
- Apologizing, as in "Even though I'm not an expert, I feel my position is correct."

Paragraph 53 is a concluding paragraph from an essay on the history of pizza and its modern appeal. It summarizes the main points of the essay.

53 For a food that is traced to Neolithic beginnings, like Mexico's tortillas, Armenia's lahmejoun, Scottish oatcakes, and even matzos, pizza has remained fresh and vibrant. Whether it's galettes, the latest thin-crusted invasion from France with bacon and onion toppings, or a plain slice of a cheese pie, the varieties of pizza are clearly limited only by one's imagination.

—Lisa Pratt, "A Slice of History"

Paragraph 54 is a concluding paragraph from an essay on the risks of genetic engineering. It looks ahead to the future and calls for action.

54 I am not advocating that we stop the development of the new biology. I believe that we can achieve wonderful and important results with it. But we do need to ensure that its application is both peaceful and safe. We have to learn from the history of nuclear physics and organic chemistry. Indeed, I believe we have no real choice. We can't afford to develop the new biological technologies without controlling them.

—Susan Wright, "Genetic Engineering: The Risks"

EXERCISE 4-11

Working individually or in a peer-response group, return to Exercise 4-1, in which you wrote introductory paragraphs for three informally outlined essays. Now, write a concluding paragraph for each.

5 CRITICAL THINKING, READING, AND WRITING

The processes I show you in this chapter can help as you participate in exchanges of ideas and opinions that develop as a result of getting a college education and living a reflective life. I discuss critical thinking as a concept (5a) and as an activity (5b); critical reading as a concept (5c) and as an activity (5d and 5e); writing critically (5f); and reasoning critically (5g through 5j).

5a What is critical thinking?

Thinking isn't something you choose to do, any more than a fish chooses to live in water. To be human is to think. But while thinking may come naturally, awareness of how you think doesn't. Thinking about thinking is the key to critical thinking.

Critical thinking means taking control of your conscious thought processes. If you don't take control of those processes, you risk being controlled by the ideas of others. The word *critical* here has a neutral meaning. It doesn't mean taking a negative view or finding fault, as when someone criticizes another person for doing something wrong.

Critical thinking is an attitude as much as an activity. If you face life with curiosity and a desire to dig beneath the surface, you're a critical thinker. The essence of critical thinking is thinking beyond the obvious— beyond the flash of visual images on a television screen, the alluring promises of glossy advertisements, the evasive statements by some people in the news, the half-truths of propaganda, the manipulations of slanted language and faulty reasoning.

5b How do I engage in critical thinking?

To engage in critical thinking, you want to become fully aware of an idea or an action, to reflect on it, and ultimately to react to it. You engage in this process numerous times every day. For example, you're thinking critically when you meet someone new and decide whether you like the person, when you read a book and form an opinion of it, and when you interview for a job and then evaluate its requirements and your ability to fulfill them. Box 31 describes the general process of critical thinking in academic settings. This same process applies as well to reading critically (5c and 5d) and writing critically (5f).

◉ Steps in the critical thinking process   31

1. **S = Summarize**   Extract and restate the material's main message or central point. Use only what you see on the page. Add nothing.

2. **A = Analyze**   Examine the material by breaking it into its component parts. By seeing each part of the whole as a distinct unit, you discover how the parts interrelate. Consider the line of reasoning as shown by the EVIDENCE offered (5i) and logic used (5j). Read "between the lines" to draw INFERENCES (5c.2), gaining information that's implied but not stated. When reading or listening, notice how the reading or speaking style and the choice of words work together to create a TONE (1e).

3. **S = Synthesize**   Pull together what you've summarized and analyzed by connecting it to your own experiences, such as reading, talking with others, watching television and films, using the Internet, and so on. In this way, you create a new whole that reflects your newly acquired knowledge and insights combined with your prior knowledge.

4. **E = Evaluate**   Judge the quality of the material now that you've become informed through the activities of SUMMARY, ANALYSIS, and SYNTHESIS. Resist the very common urge to evaluate before you summarize, analyze, and synthesize.

The steps in the critical thinking process are somewhat fluid, just as they are in the writing process (2a). Expect sometimes to combine steps, reverse their order, and return to parts of the process you thought you had completed. As you do so, remember that synthesis and evaluation are two different mental activities: *Synthesis* calls for making connections; *evaluation* calls for making judgments.

👁 **ALERT:** The distinctions between summary and synthesis need your close attention. Often, students confuse the two or think they're the same. Never think your summary of material is a synthesis.●

5c What is the reading process?

Reading is an active process—a dynamic, meaning-making interaction between the page and your brain. Understanding the **reading process** helps people become critical thinkers.

Making **predictions** is a major activity in the reading process. Your mind is constantly guessing what's coming next. When it sees what comes next, it either confirms or revises its prediction and moves on. For example, suppose you're glancing through a magazine and come upon the title "The Heartbeat." Your mind begins guessing: Is this a love story? Is this about how the heart pumps blood? Maybe, you say to yourself, it's a story about someone who had a heart attack. Then, as you read the first few sentences, your mind confirms which guess was correct. If you see words like *electrical impulse, muscle fibers,* and *contraction,* you know instantly that you're in the realm of physiology. In a few more sentences, you narrow your prediction to either "the heart as pump" or "the heart suffering an attack."

To make predictions efficiently, consciously decide the purpose you have for reading the material. People generally read for two reasons—for relaxation or to learn something. Reading a popular novel helps you relax. Reading for college courses calls for you to understand material and remember it. When you read to learn, you usually have to reread. One encounter with new material is rarely enough to understand it fully. Reading for college courses calls for you to understand and remember the material.

The speed at which you read depends on your purpose for reading. When you're hunting for a particular fact, you can skim the page until you come to what you want. When you read about a subject you know well, you might read somewhat rapidly, slowing down when you come to new material. When you're unfamiliar with the subject, you need to work slowly because your mind needs time to absorb the new material.

The reading process involves your thinking on three levels, which is another reason why college work calls for much rereading, as described in Box 32.

 Steps in the reading process   **32**

1. **Reading for literal meaning:** Read "on the lines" to see what's stated (5c.1).
2. **Reading to draw inferences:** Read "between the lines" to see what's not stated but implied (5c.2).
3. **Reading to evaluate:** Read "beyond the lines" to form your own opinion about the material (5c.3).

5c.1 Reading for literal meaning

Reading for **literal meaning** is reading for comprehension. Your goal is to discover the main ideas, the supporting details, or, in a work of fiction, the central details of plot and character.

Reading for literal meaning is not as easy as it might sound. When you come across a new concept, think it through. Rushing through material to "cover" it rather than to understand it takes more time in the end. If the author's writing style is complex, "unpack" the sentences: Break them into smaller units or reword them in a simpler style. Also, see Box 33 for specific suggestions about ways to improve your reading comprehension.

 Ways to help your reading comprehension   **33**

- **Make associations.** Link new material to what you already know, especially when you're reading about an unfamiliar subject. You may even find it helpful to read an easier book on the subject first in order to build your knowledge base.

- **Make it easy for you to focus.** If your mind wanders, be fiercely determined to concentrate. Do whatever it takes: Arrange for silence or music, for being alone or in the library with others who are studying. Try to read at your best time of day (some people concentrate better in the morning, others in the evening).

- **Allot the time you need.** To comprehend new material, you must allow sufficient time to read, reflect, reread, and study. Discipline yourself to balance classes, working, socializing, and family activities. Reading and studying take time. Nothing prevents success in college as much as poor time management.

- **Master the vocabulary.** If you don't understand the key terms in your reading, you can't fully understand the concepts. As you encounter new words, first try to figure out their meanings from context clues (21e). Also, many textbooks list key terms and their definitions (called a *glossary*) at the end of each chapter or the book. Of course, nothing replaces having a good dictionary at hand.

5c.2 Reading to draw inferences

When you read for **inferences,** you're reading to understand what's suggested or implied but not stated. Often, you have to infer the author's PURPOSE. Here's an example.

How to tell the difference between modern art and junk puzzles many people, although few are willing to admit it. The owner of an art gallery in Chicago had a prospective buyer for two sculptures made of discarded metal and put them outside his warehouse to clean them up. Unfortunately, some junk dealers, who apparently didn't recognize abstract expressionism when they saw it, hauled the two 300-pound pieces away.

—Ora Gygi, "Things Are Seldom What They Seem"

The literal meaning of the Gygi paragraph is that some people can't tell the difference between art and junk. A good summary would say that two abstract metal sculptures were carted away as junk when an art dealer set them outside a warehouse to clean them. However, looking at the inferential meaning reveals that the paragraph explains that few people will admit it when they don't know the difference between art and junk. Further, the paragraph implies that people often don't want to appear uneducated or show themselves lacking in good taste because something called "art" looks like "junk" to them. The word *apparently*—a good word for writing inferences—uses IRONY (21d) to seem tactful but is just the opposite. Therefore, the art dealer doesn't end up feeling embarrassed because he left the sculptures outdoors unattended. If we are laughing, it is at the junk dealers—although the ultimate laugh is on the whole art world.

Drawing inferences takes practice. Box 34 lists questions to help you read "between the lines." A discussion of each point follows the box.

 Checklist for drawing inferences during reading   **34**

- Is the **tone** of the material appropriate?
- Can I detect **prejudice** or **bias** in the material?
- Is the separation of **fact** and **opinion** clear or muddy?

Tone

Tone (1e) is communicated by many aspects of writing, but especially word choice (21e). Tone in writing can be described the same way as tone in speaking: friendly, pompous, sarcastic, cautious, and so on. If you read exclusively for literal meaning (5c.1), you'll likely miss the tone and possibly the point of the whole piece.

For example, as a critical reader, be suspicious of a highly emotional tone in writing. If you find it, chances are the writer is trying to manipulate the audience. Resist this. Also as a writer, if you find your tone growing emotional, step back and rethink the situation. No matter what point you want to make, your chance of communicating successfully to an audience depends on your using a moderate, reasonable tone. For instance, the exaggerations below in the NO example (*robbing treasures, politicians are murderers*) might hint at the truth of a few cases, but they're too extreme to be taken seriously. The language of the YES version is far more likely to deliver its intended message.

> **NO**   Urban renewal must be stopped. Urban redevelopment is ruining this country, and money-hungry capitalists are robbing treasures from law-abiding citizens. Corrupt politicians are murderers, caring nothing about people being thrown out of their homes into the streets.

> **YES**   Urban renewal is revitalizing our cities, but it has caused some serious problems. While investors are trying to replace slums with decent housing, they must also remember that they're displacing people who don't want to leave their familiar neighborhoods. Surely, a cooperative effort between government and the private sector can lead to creative solutions.

Prejudice or bias

Another role for inferential reading is to detect **prejudice** or **bias.** This goes further than the concept that every writer has a point of view in presenting information or in trying to persuade readers. When material is distorted by hatred or dislike of individuals, groups of people, or ideas, you want to suspect its accuracy and fairness. Of course, prejudice and bias can be worded in positive language, so don't be deceived by such a tactic. Also, writers usually imply their prejudices and bias rather than state them outright. For example, suppose you read, "Poor people like living in crowded conditions because they're used to such surroundings" or "Women are so wonderfully nurturing that they can't succeed in business." Right away, you can detect the prejudice. Always question any material that rests on a weak foundation.

Fact versus opinion

Another skill in reading inferentially is the ability to differentiate **fact** from **opinion.** *Facts* are statements that can be verified. *Opinions* are statements of personal beliefs. Facts can be verified by observation, research, or experimentation, but opinions are open to debate. A problem arises when a writer intentionally blurs the distinction between fact and opinion. Critical readers know the difference.

For example, here are two statements, one a fact, and one an opinion.

1. Women can never make good mathematicians.
2. Although fear of math isn't purely a female phenomenon, girls tend to drop out of math classes sooner than boys, and some adult women have an aversion to math and math-related activity that is akin to anxiety.

Reading inferentially, we can see that statement 1 clearly is an opinion. Is it worthy of consideration? Perhaps it could be open to debate, but the word *never* implies that the writer is unwilling to allow for even one exception. Conversely, statement 2 at least seems to be factual, though research would be necessary to confirm or deny the position.

As a reader, when you can "consider the source"—that is, find out who made a statement—you have an advantage in trying to distinguish between fact and opinion. For example, you would probably read an essay for or against capital punishment differently if you knew the writer was an inmate on death row rather than a disinterested party who held an opinion. To illustrate, statement 1 above is from a male Russian mathematician, as reported by David K. Shipler, a well-respected veteran reporter on Russian affairs for the *New York Times*. Statement 2 is from a book called *Overcoming Math Anxiety* by Sheila Tobias, a university professor who has extensively studied why many people dislike math. Her credentials can help her statement be accepted by readers as true. If, however, someone known for belittling women had made statement 2, our reaction would be quite different.

To differentiate between fact and opinion, reflect on the material and think beyond the obvious. For example, is the statement "Strenuous exercise is good for your health" a fact? It has the ring of truth, but it definitely isn't a fact. Some people with severe arthritis or heart trouble should avoid some forms of exercise. Also, what does *strenuous* mean—a dozen push-ups, jogging, aerobics, or tennis?

EXERCISE 5-1

Working individually or with a peer-response group, decide which statements are facts and which are opinions. When the author and source are provided, explain how that information influenced your judgment. For help, consult 5c.2.

1. The life of people on earth is better now than it has ever been—certainly much better than it was 500 years ago.

    —Peggy Noonan, "Why Are We So Unhappy When We Have It So Good?"

2. Every three minutes a woman in the United States learns she has breast cancer.

3. Every journey into the past is complicated by delusions, false memories, false naming of real events.

    —Adrienne Rich, poet, *Of Woman Born*

4. A mind is a terrible thing to waste.

—United Negro College Fund

5. History is the branch of knowledge that deals systematically with the past.

—*Webster's New World College Dictionary,* Third Edition

6. In 1927, F. E. Tylcote, an English physician, reported in the medical journal *Lancet* that in almost every case of lung cancer he had seen or known about, the patient smoked.

—William Ecenbarger, "The Strange History of Tobacco"

7. The earth's temperature is gradually rising.

8. You can, Honest Abe notwithstanding, fool most of the people all of the time.

—Stephen Jay Gould, "The Creation Myths of Cooperstown"

9. You change laws by changing lawmakers.

—Sissy Farenthold, political activist, *Bakersfield Californian*

10. The Internet is ruining the morals of young people.

EXERCISE 5-2

Read the following passages, and then (1) list all literal information, (2) list all implied information, and (3) list the opinions stated. Refer to sections 5c.1 and 5c.2 for help.

EXAMPLE   The study found many complaints against the lawyers were not investigated, seemingly out of a "desire to avoid difficult cases."

—Norman F. Dacey

Literal information: Few complaints against lawyers are investigated.

Implied information: The words *difficult cases* imply a cover-up: Lawyers, or others in power, hesitate to criticize lawyers for fear of being sued or for fear of a public outcry if the truth about abuses and errors were revealed.

Opinions: No opinions. It reports on a study.

A.   It is the first of February, and everyone is talking about starlings. Starlings came to this country on a passenger liner from Europe. One hundred of them were deliberately released in Central Park, and from those hundred descended all of our countless millions of starlings today. According to Edwin Way Teale, "Their coming was the result of one man's fancy. That man was Eugene Schieffelin, a wealthy New York drug manufacturer. His curious hobby was the introduction into America of all the birds mentioned in William Shakespeare." The birds adapted to their new country splendidly.

—Annie Dillard, *Terror at Tinker Creek*

B.   The kind of constitution and government Gandhi envisaged for an independent India was spelled out at the forty-fifth convention of the All-India Congress, which began at Karachi on March 27, 1931. It was a party political convention the like of which I had not seen before— nor seen since—with its ringing revolutionary proclamations acclaimed by some 350 leaders, men and women, just out of jail, squatting in the heat under a tent in a semicircle at Gandhi's feet, all of them, like Gandhi, spinning away like children playing with toys as they talked. They made up the so-called Subjects Committee, selected from the five thousand delegates to do the real work of the convention, though in reality, it was Gandhi alone who dominated the proceedings, writing most of the resolutions and moving their adoption with his customary eloquence and surprising firmness.

—William L. Shirer, *Gandhi: A Memoir*

5c.3 Reading to evaluate

When you **read to evaluate,** you're judging the writer's work. Evaluative reading comes after you have summarized, analyzed, and synthesized the material (Box 31). Reading "between the lines" is usually concerned with recognizing tone, detecting prejudice, and differentiating fact from opinion. Reading to evaluate, "beyond the lines," requires an overall assessment of the soundness of the writer's reasoning, evidence, or observations and the fairness and perceptiveness the writer shows, from accuracy of word choice and tone to the writer's respect for the reader.

5d How do I engage in critical reading?

Critical reading is a parallel process to critical thinking (5a and 5b). To read critically is to think about what you're reading while you're reading it. It means that words don't merely drift by as your eyes scan the lines. To prevent that, use approaches such as reading systematically (5d.1) and reading closely and actively (5d.2).

5d.1 Reading systematically

To **read systematically** is to use a structured plan: *preview, read,* and *review.* Reading systematically closely parallels the writing process. Like PLANNING in writing, *previewing* gets you ready and keeps you from reading inefficiently. Like DRAFTING in writing, *reading* means moving through the material so that you come to understand and remember it. Like REVISION in writing, *reviewing* takes you back over the material to clarify, fine-tune, and make it thoroughly your own. Here are techniques for reading systematically.

1. **Preview:** Before you begin reading, look ahead. Glance at the pages you intend to read so that your mind can start making predictions (5c). As you look over the material, ask yourself questions. Don't expect to answer all the questions at this point; their purpose is to focus your thoughts.

   ■ To preview a chapter in a textbook, first look at the table of contents. How does this chapter fit into the whole book? What topics come before? Which come after? Now turn to the chapter you're assigned and read all the headings, large and small. Note the boldfaced words (in darker print), and all visuals and their captions, including photographs, drawings, figures, tables, and boxes. If there's a glossary at the end of the chapter, scan it for words you do and do not know.

   ■ To preview a book or material in a book that has few or no headings, again, begin with the table of contents and ask questions about the chapter titles. If the book has a preface or introduction, skim it. Check for introductory notes about the author and head notes, which often precede individual works in collections of essays or short stories. Read pivotal paragraphs, such as the opening paragraphs and (unless you're reading for suspense) the last few paragraphs.

2. **Read:** Read the material closely and actively (5d.2). Seek the full meaning at all three levels of reading: *literal, inferential,* and *evaluative* (5c). Most of all, expect to reread. Rarely can anyone fully understand and absorb college-level material in one reading. When you read, always set aside time to allow for more than one rereading.

3. **Review:** Go back to the spots you looked at when you previewed the material. Also, go back to other important places you discovered as you were reading. Ask yourself the same sorts of questions as when you previewed, this time answering as fully as possible. If you can't come up with answers, reread. For best success, review in *chunks*—small sections that you can capture comfortably. Don't try to cover too much material at one time.

   ■ To help you concentrate as you read, keep in mind that you intend to review—and then do it: Review immediately after you read. Review again the next day and again about a week later. Each time you review, add new knowledge to refine your understanding of the material. As much as time permits, review at intervals during a course. The more reinforcement, the better.

   ■ Collaborative learning can reinforce what you learn from reading. Ask a friend or classmate to discuss the material with you and quiz you. Conversely, offer to teach the material to someone; you'll quickly discover whether you've mastered it well enough to communicate it.

5d.2 Reading closely and actively

The secret to **reading closely** and **actively** is to annotate as you read. *Annotating* means writing notes to yourself in a book's margins and using asterisks and other codes to alert you to special material. Some readers start annotating right away, while others wait to annotate after they've previewed the material and read it once. Experiment to find what works best for you. I recommend your using two different ink colors, one for close reading (blue in the example below) and one for active reading (black in the example below).

Close reading means annotating for content. You might, for example, number and briefly list the steps in a process or summarize major points in the margin. When you review, your marginal notes help you glance over the material and quickly recall what it's about.

Active reading means annotating to make connections between the material and what you already know or have experienced. This is your chance to converse on paper with the writer. Consider yourself a partner in the making of meaning, a full participant in the exchange of ideas that characterizes a college education.

Doesn't matter who wins, but tactics and prowess can be admired.

Although I like to play, and sometimes like to watch, I cannot see what possible difference it makes which team beats which. The tactics are sometimes interesting, and certainly the prowess of the players deserves applause—but most men seem to use commercial sports as a kind of (narcotic,) shutting out reality, rather than heightening it.

Sports talk is boring.

There is nothing more boring, in my view, than a prolonged discussion by laymen of yesterday's game. These dreary conversations are a form of social alcoholism, enabling them to achieve a (dubious rapport) without ever once having to come to grips with a subject worthy of a grown man's concern.

Other examples include soap operas and sitcoms.

When my son and husband watch together, the rapport is very real.

It is easy to see the (opiate) quality of sports in our society when tens of millions of men will spend a splendid Saturday or Sunday fall afternoon sitting (stupefied) in front of the TV, watching a "big game," when they might be out exercising their own flaccid muscles and stimulating their lethargic corpuscles.

Instead of watching men should exercise.

Annotations of an excerpt from the essay shown in Exercise 5-3, using blue for content (close reading) and black for synthesis (active reading)

S. Harris essay, "Sports Only"

content	connections I make
⊕1 H. likes sports and exercise. He even built a tennis court for his summer home.	H. isn't "everyman." It takes big bucks to build one's own tennis court.
⊕2 H. thinks the average American male is obsessed with sports.	That "average" (if there is such a thing) male sounds a lot like my husband.
⊕3 Athletics/Sports are one strand, not the web, of society.	It's worth thinking why sports have such a major hold on men. And why not women, on "average"? (This might be a topic for a paper someday.)

Double-entry notebook excerpt, based on the first three paragraphs of the essay in Exercise 5-3. The left column deals with content (close reading), and the right covers synthesis (active reading).

If you feel uncomfortable writing in a book—even though the practice of annotating texts dates back to the Middle Ages—create a *double-entry notebook.* Draw a line down the center of your notebook page. On one side, write content notes (close reading). On the other, write synthesis notes (active reading). Be sure to write down exactly where in the reading you're referring to. Illustrated above is a short example from a double-entry notebook (the symbol ⊕ stands for "paragraph").

EXERCISE 5-3

The following essay was published as a newspaper column. Annotate the entire essay, using one color of ink for your notes about content and another for your notes that synthesize as you connect the material to your knowledge and experience. Use the annotated excerpt on page 115 as a model.

Sports Only Exercise Our Eyes

Sydney J. Harris

Before I proceed a line further, let me make it clear that I enjoy physical exercise and sport as much as any man. I like to bat a baseball, dribble a basketball, kick a soccer ball and, most of all, swat a tennis ball. A man who scorned physical activity would hardly build a tennis court on his summerhouse grounds, or use it every day.

Having made this obeisance, let me now confess that I am puzzled and upset—and have been for many years—by the almost obsessive interest in sports taken by the average American male.

Athletics is one strand in life, and even the ancient Greek philosophers recognized its importance. But it is by no means the whole web, as it seems to be in our society. If American men are not talking business, they're talking sports, or they're not talking at all.

This strikes me as an enormously adolescent, not to say retarded, attitude on the part of presumed adults. Especially when most of the passion and enthusiasm center on professional teams, which bear no indigenous relation to the city they play for, and consist of mercenaries who will wear any town's insignia if the price is right.

Although I like to play, and sometimes like to watch, I cannot see what possible difference it makes which team beats which. The tactics are sometimes interesting, and certainly the prowess of the players deserves applause—but most men seem to use commercial sports as a kind of narcotic, shutting out reality, rather than heightening it.

There is nothing more boring, in my view, than a prolonged discussion by laymen of yesterday's game. These dreary conversations are a form of social alcoholism, enabling them to achieve a dubious rapport without ever once having to come to grips with a subject worthy of a grown man's concern.

It is easy to see the opiate quality of sports in our society when tens of millions of men will spend a splendid Saturday or Sunday fall afternoon sitting stupefied in front of the TV, watching a "big game," when they might be out exercising their own flaccid muscles and stimulating their lethargic corpuscles.

Ironically, our obsession with professional athletics not only makes us mentally limited and conversationally dull, it also keeps us physically inert—thus violating the very reason men began engaging in athletic competitions. Isn't it tempting to call this national malaise of "spectatoritis" childish? Except children have more sense, and would rather run out and play themselves.

117

5e How do I tell the difference between summary and synthesis?

Distinguishing between summary and synthesis is crucial in critical thinking, critical reading, and critical writing. **Summary** comes before synthesis (Box 31, in section 5b) in the critical thinking process. To *summarize* is to extract the main message or central point and restate it in a sentence or two. A summary doesn't include supporting evidence or details. It is the gist, the hub, the seed of what the author is saying. It isn't your personal reaction to what the author says. (For help in writing a summary, see Box 131, in section 31e.)

Synthesis comes after summary in the critical thinking process (Box 31, in section 5b). To *synthesize* is to weave together material from several sources, including your personal prior knowledge, to create a new whole. Unsynthesized ideas and information are like separate spools of thread, neatly lined up, possibly coordinated but not integrated. Synthesized ideas and information are threads woven into a tapestry—a new whole that shows relationships.

We synthesize unconsciously all the time—interpreting and combining ideas from various sources to create new patterns. These thought processes are mirrored in the rhetorical strategies used in writing (see section 4i). To synthesize, we consciously apply those strategies. We can, for instance, compare ideas in sources, contrast ideas in sources, create definitions that combine and extend definitions in individual sources, apply examples or descriptions from one source to illustrate ideas in another, and find causes and effects described in one source that explain another.

EXERCISE 5-4

Individually or in a peer-response group, reread the explanations of "summary" and "synthesis." Then, choose any sample paragraph in Chapter 4 or 5 of this handbook, and write a summary of it. Next, collect at least two other definitions or explanations of the two terms by consulting sources such as dictionaries (pay particular attention to the word history and the meanings of prefixes, suffixes, and roots), Internet search engines, and other resources, including the glossaries of other textbooks. Finally, write a synthesis by comparison and contrast of the two concepts, either by enlarging the explanations of the two concepts or by writing why you think the ones in this handbook are sufficient.

Now, let's examine two different examples of synthesis. Their sources are the essay by Sydney J. Harris in Exercise 5-3 and the following excerpt from a long essay by Robert Lipsyte. (Lipsyte, a sports columnist for the *New York Times*, was writing in the spring of 1995 at the end of a nine-month U.S. baseball strike. Lipsyte argues that sports have become too commercialized and therefore no longer inspire loyalty, teach good sportsmanship, or provide young people with admirable role models.)

> Baseball has done us a favor. It's about time we understood that staged competitive sports events—and baseball can stand for all the games—are no longer the testing ground of our country's manhood and the theater of its once seemingly limitless energy and power.
>
> As a mirror of our culture, sports now show us spoiled fools as role models, cities and colleges held hostage and games that exist only to hawk products.
>
> The pathetic posturing of in-your-face macho has replaced a once self-confident masculinity.
>
> —Robert Lipsyte, "The Emasculation of Sports"

SYNTHESIS BY COMPARISON AND CONTRAST

Both Harris and Lipsyte criticize professional sports, but for different reasons. In part, Harris thinks that people who passively watch sports on TV and rarely exercise are ruining their health. Lipsyte sees a less obvious but potentially more sinister effect of sports: the destruction of traditional values by athletes who are puppets of "big business."

SYNTHESIS BY DEFINITION

The omission of women from each writer's discussion seems a very loud silence. Considered together, these essays define sports only in terms of males. Harris criticizes men for their inability to think and talk beyond sports and business, an insulting and exaggerated description made even less valid by the absence of women. Lipsyte, despite the numbers of women excelling both in team and individual sports, claims that sports have lost a "once self-confident masculinity." An extended definition would include women, even though they might prefer to avoid the negative portraits of Harris and Lipsyte.

Each synthesis belongs to the person who made the connections. Someone else might make entirely different connections. Use the following techniques to help you recall prior knowledge and synthesize several sources. (The CRITICAL RESPONSE essay by a student, Anna Lozanov, in section 5f, is an excellent example of making connections between reading and personal experience.)

- Use MAPPING (2j) to discover relationships between sources and your prior knowledge.
- Use your powers of play. Mentally toss ideas around, even if you make connections that seem outrageous. Try opposites (for example, read about athletes and think about the most nonathletic person you know). Try turning an idea upside down (for example, list

the benefits of being a bad sport). Try visualizing what you're reading about, and then tinker with the mental picture (for example, picture two people playing tennis and substitute dogs playing Frisbee or seals playing table tennis). The possibilities are endless—make word associations, think up song lyrics, draft a TV advertisement. The goal is to jump-start your thinking so that you can see ideas in new ways.

■ Discuss your reading with someone else. Summarize its content, and elicit the other person's opinions and ideas. Deliberately debate that opinion or challenge those ideas. Discussions and debates are good ways to get your mind moving.

EXERCISE 5-5

Here is another excerpt from the essay by Robert Lipsyte. First, summarize the excerpt. Then, annotate it for its content and for the connections you make between Lipsyte's ideas and your prior knowledge. Finally, write a synthesis of this excerpt and the Sydney J. Harris essay in Exercise 5-3. (Words in brackets supply background information some readers might need.)

> We have come to see that [basketball star Michael] Jordan, [football star] Troy Aikman and [baseball star] Ken Griffey have nothing to offer us beyond the gorgeous, breathtaking mechanics of what they do. And it's not enough, now that there's no longer a dependable emotional return beyond the sensation of the moment itself. The changes in sports—the moving of franchises, free agency—have made it impossible to count on a player, a team, and an entire league still being around for next year's comeback. The connection between player and fan has been irrevocably destabilized, for love and loyalty demand a future. Along the way, those many virtues of self-discipline, responsibility, altruism, and dedication seem to have been deleted from the athletic contract with America.
>
> —Robert Lipsyte, "The Emasculation of Sports"

5f   How do I write a critical response?

A **critical response** essay has two missions: to summarize a source's central point or main idea and to respond to the main idea based on your *synthesis* (5b and 5e).

A well-written critical response accomplishes these two missions with style and grace. That is, it doesn't say, "My summary is . . . " and "Now, here's what I think. . . ." The two parts should be well integrated. A critical response essay may be short or somewhat long, depending on whether you're asked to respond to a single passage or to an entire work. Box 35 gives general guidelines for writing a critical response.

⊙ **Guidelines for writing a critical response**   **35**

1. Write a SUMMARY of the main idea or central point of the material you're responding to.
2. Write a smooth TRANSITION between that summary and what comes next: your response. This *transitional statement*, which bridges the two parts, need not be a formal THESIS STATEMENT (2q), but it needs to signal clearly the beginning of your response.
3. Respond to the source based on your prior knowledge and experience.
4. Fulfill all DOCUMENTATION requirements. See Chapters 35–37 for coverage of five DOCUMENTATION STYLES (MLA, APA, CM, CBE, and COS). Ask your instructor which to use.

Here's a critical response essay written by Anna Lozanov, a student at a state university. Her assignment was to read and respond to the short essay "Sports Only Exercise Our Eyes" by Sydney J. Harris, shown in Exercise 5-3. Lozanov's transitional statement from summary to response comes at the beginning of her third paragraph: "Just this weekend, however, I had an occasion to reconsider the value of sports." The essay uses MLA STYLE documentation (Chapter 35). In the essay, the numbers in parentheses tell the pages in the cited work where the quoted words are found. The work itself is cited at the essay's end.

```
          Critical Response by Anna Lozanov
     to "Sports Only Exercise Our Eyes" by Sydney J. Harris
          Except for a brief period in high school when I was
wild about a certain basketball player, I never gave
sports much thought. I went to games because my friends
went, not because I cared about football or baseball or
track. I certainly never expected to defend sports, and
when I first read Sydney Harris's essay "Sports Only
Exercise Our Eyes," I thoroughly agreed with him. Like
Harris, I believed that men who live and breathe sports
are "mentally limited and conversationally dull" (111).
```

→

For the entire thirteen years of my marriage, I have complained about the amount of time my husband, John, spends watching televised sports. Of course, I've tried to get him to take an interest in something else. There was the time as a newlywed when I flamboyantly interrupted the sixth game of the World Series--wearing only a transparent nightie. Then, in 1978, I had the further audacity to go into labor with our first child--right in the middle of the Super Bowl. Even the child tried to help me cure my husband of what Harris calls an "obsession" (111). Some months after the fateful Super Bowl, the kid thoroughly soaked his father, who was concentrating so intently on the Tigers' struggle for the American League pennant that he didn't even notice! Only a commercial brought the dazed sports fan back into the living room from Tiger Stadium.

Just this weekend, however, I had an occasion to reconsider the value of sports. Having just read the Harris essay, I found myself paying closer attention to my husband and sons' Saturday afternoon television routine. I was surprised to discover that they didn't just "vegetate" in front of the TV; during the course of the afternoon, they actually discussed ethics, priorities, commitments, and the consequences of abusing one's body. When one of the commentators raised issues like point shaving and using steroids, John and the kids talked about cheating and using steroids. When another commentator brought up the issue of skipping one's senior year to go straight to the pros, John explained the importance of a college education and discussed the short career of most professional football players.

Then, I started to think about all the times I've gone to the basement and found my husband and sons performing exercise routines as they watched a game on TV. Even our seven-year-old, who loathes exercise, pedals vigorously on the exercise bike while the others do sit-ups and curls. Believe it or not, there are times when they're all exercising more than just their eyes.

→

```
        I still agree with Harris that many people spend
   too much time watching televised sports, but after this
   weekend, I certainly can't say that all of that time is
   wasted--at least not at my house. Anything that can turn
   my couch potatoes into thinking, talking, active human
   beings can't be all bad. Next weekend, instead of putting
   on a nightie, I think I'll join my family on the couch.

                        Work Cited
   Harris, Sydney J. "Sports Only Exercise Our Eyes." The Best
        of Sydney J. Harris. Boston: Houghton, 1975. 111-12.
```

5g How do I assess evidence critically?

The cornerstone of all reasoning is evidence. **Evidence** consists of facts, statistical information, examples, and opinions of experts. As a reader, you expect writers to provide solid evidence for any claim made or conclusion reached. As a writer, you want to use evidence well to support your claims and conclusions. To assess evidence, you want to evaluate it (5g.1) and know the difference between primary and secondary sources (5g.2).

5g.1 Evaluating evidence

You can evaluate evidence by asking questions to guide your judgment.

- **Is the evidence sufficient?** To be sufficient, evidence can't be skimpy. As a rule, the more evidence, the better. Readers have more confidence in the results of a survey that draws on a hundred respondents rather than on ten. As a writer, you may convince your reader that violence is a serious problem in high schools on the basis of only two examples, but you'll be more convincing with additional examples—or, better still, if you also report statistics for a school district, a city, or a nation.

- **Is the evidence representative?** Evidence is representative if it is typical. As a reader, assess the objectivity and fairness of evidence. Don't trust a claim or conclusion about a group based on only a few members rather than on a truly typical sample. A pollster surveying national political views would not get representative evidence by interviewing people only in Austin, Texas, because that group doesn't represent the regional, racial, political, and ethnic makeup of the entire U.S. electorate. As a writer, the evidence you offer should represent your claim fairly; don't base your point on an exception.

123

- **Is the evidence relevant?** Relevant evidence is directly related to the conclusion you're drawing. Determining relevance often demands subtle thinking. Suppose you read that one hundred students who had watched television for more than two hours a day throughout high school earned significantly lower scores on a college entrance exam than one hundred students who had not. Can you conclude that students who watch less television perform better on college entrance exams? Not necessarily. Other differences between the two groups could account for the different scores: geographical region, family background, socioeconomic group, or the quality of schools attended. The evidence on TV watching and college entrance exams would be relevant only if both groups were identical except for the amount of time they watch television.

- **Is the evidence accurate?** Accurate evidence is correct and complete. Inaccurate evidence is useless. Evidence must come from a reliable source, whether it is primary or secondary (5g.2). Equally important, evidence must be presented honestly, not misrepresented or distorted.

- **Is the evidence qualified?** Reasonable evidence doesn't make extreme claims. Claims that use words such as *all, always, never,* or *certainly* are disqualified if even one exception is found. Conclusions are more sensible and believable when qualified with words such as *some, many, may, possibly, often,* and *usually.* Remember that today's "facts" may be revised as time passes and knowledge grows.

5g.2 Recognizing primary versus secondary sources as evidence

Primary sources are firsthand evidence. They're based on your own or someone else's original work or direct observation. Because there's no one to distort the meaning of the original work, firsthand evidence has the greatest impact on a reader. Here's an eyewitness account, a solid example of a primary source.

> Poverty is dirt. . . . Let me explain about housekeeping with no money. For breakfast, I give my children grits with no oleo or cornbread without eggs and oleo. This doesn't use up many dishes. What dishes there are, I wash in cold water and with no soap. Even the cheapest soap has to be saved for the baby's diapers. Look at my hands, so cracked and red. Once I saved for two months to buy a jar of Vaseline for my hands and the baby's diaper rash. When I had saved enough, I went to buy it and the price had gone up two cents. The baby and I suffered on. I have to decide every day if I can bear to put my cracked sore hands into the cold water and strong soap. But you ask, why not hot water? Fuel costs

money. If you've a wood fire, it costs money. If you burn electricity, it costs money. Hot water is a luxury. I do not have luxuries. . . .

—Jo Goodwin Parker, "What's Poverty?"

What in Parker's account makes the reader trust what she says? She is specific, and she is authoritative. She is therefore reliable.

Of course, not all eyewitnesses are reliable, so you must judge which ones to believe. Few people will ever see the surface of the moon or the top of Mount Everest. People rely, therefore, on the first-hand observation of astronauts and mountain climbers who've been there. Indeed, much of what we learn of history depends on letters, diaries, and journals—the reports of eyewitnesses who saw events unfold. They help the reader "see," beyond the everyday sense of the word. For example, Parker could look at her hands. So too can the audience by reading her work.

Surveys, polls, and experiments extend everyone's powers of observation. After all, who can see the attitude of the American public toward marriage, or a presidential candidate, or inflation? For evidence on such matters, polls or surveys constitute primary evidence if the data are carefully controlled and measured.

Secondary sources report, describe, comment on, or analyze the experiences or work of others. As evidence, a secondary source is at least once removed from the primary source. It reports on the original work, the direct observation, or the firsthand experience. Still, secondary evidence can have great value and impact if it meets the evaluation criteria in 5g.1. Here's a secondhand report of an observation.

> The immediate causes of death from nuclear attack are the blast wave, which can flatten heavily reinforced buildings many kilometers away, the firestorm, the gamma rays, and the neutrons, which effectively fry the insides of passersby. A schoolgirl who survived the American nuclear attack on Hiroshima, the event that ended the Second World War, wrote this firsthand account:
>
>> Through a darkness like the bottom of hell, I could hear the voices of the other students calling for their mothers. And at the base of the bridge, inside a big cistern that had been dug out there, was a mother weeping, holding above her head a naked baby that was burned bright red all over its body. . . . But every single person who passed was wounded, all of them, and there was no one, there was no one to turn to for help. And the singed hair on the heads of the people was frizzled and whitish and covered with dust. They did not appear to be human, not creatures of this world.
>
> —Carl Sagan, *Cosmos*

The value of a secondhand account hinges on the reliability of the reporter. And that reliability comes from how specific, accurate, and authoritative the observations are. An expert's reputation comes from some special experience (the parents of many children could be considered "experts" on child rearing) or special training (an accountant could be an expert on taxes). Because Carl Sagan, author of the sample paragraph on page 125, was a respected scientist, scholar, and writer, readers can be quite confident that he has fully and fairly represented what the schoolgirl said. But no one can be sure of that without seeing her original account.

In college, you often depend on secondary sources (for example, most textbooks), but sometimes you're expected to use primary sources (for example, a published diary, scientists' journal articles reporting their research, works of literature). Box 36 gives guidelines for evaluating a secondary source.

Checklist for evaluating a secondary source   36

- **Is the source authoritative?** Did an expert or a person you can expect to write credibly on the subject write it?
- **Is the source reliable?** Does the material appear in a reputable publication—a book published by an established publisher, a respected journal or magazine—or on a reliable Internet site?
- **Is the source well known?** Is the source cited elsewhere as you read about the subject? (If so, the authority of the source is probably widely accepted.)
- **Is the information well supported?** Is the source based on primary evidence? If the source is based on secondary evidence, is the evidence authoritative and reliable?
- **Is the tone balanced?** Is the language relatively objective (and therefore more likely reliable), or is it slanted (probably not reliable)?
- **Is the source current?** Is the material up to date (and therefore more likely reliable), or has later authoritative and reliable research made it outdated? ("Old" isn't necessarily unreliable. In many fields, classic works of research remain authoritative for decades or even centuries.)

COMPUTER TIP: Use the guidelines in Box 36 to evaluate electronic sources. Don't assume that because the material is on the Internet, it is accurate. The Web site of a liar or bigot can "look" as nice as any legitimate Web site. For more specifics about evaluating online sources, see the extended discussion in 34f. ▣

EXERCISE 5-6

Indicate for each passage whether it constitutes primary or secondary evidence. Then, decide whether the evidence is reliable or not, and explain why or why not. Refer to section 5g for help.

A.   I went one morning to a place along the banks of the Madeira River where the railroad ran, alongside rapids impassable to river traffic, and I searched for any marks it may have left on the land. But there was nothing except a clearing where swarms of insects hovered over the dead black hen and other items spread out on a red cloth as an offering to the gods of macumba, or black magic. This strain of African origins in Brazil's ethnic character is strong in the Northwest Region.
—William S. Ellis, "Brazil's Imperiled Rain Forest"

B.   Most climatologists believe that the world will eventually slip back into an ice age in 10,000 to 20,000 years. The Earth has been unusually cold for the last two to three million years, and we are just lucky to be living during one of the warm spells. But the concern of most weather watchers looking at the next century is with fire rather than ice. By burning fossil fuels and chopping down forests, humans have measurably increased the amount of carbon dioxide in the atmosphere. From somewhere around 300 parts per million at the turn of the century, this level has risen to 340 parts per million today. If the use of fossil fuels continues to increase, carbon dioxide could reach 600 parts per million during the next century.
—Steve Olson, "Computing Climate"

C.   Marriages on the frontier were often made before a girl was half through her adolescent years, and some diaries record casualness in the manner such decisions were reached. Mrs. John Kirkwood recounts:

The night before Christmas, John Kirkwood . . . the pathfinder, stayed at our house over night. I had met him before and when he heard the discussion about my brother Jasper's wedding, he suggested that he and I also get married. I was nearly fifteen years old and I thought it was high time that I got married so I consented.
—Lillian Schlissel, *Women's Diaries of the Westward Journey*

EXERCISE 5-7

Individually or with a peer-response group, choose one thesis statement below and list the kinds of primary and secondary sources you might likely consult to support the thesis (guess intelligently, but you need not be certain the sources exist). Then, decide which sources would be considered primary and which secondary.

Thesis statement 1: The history of this college is very straightforward.
Thesis statement 2: The history of this college is complicated.

5h How do I assess cause and effect critically?

Some evidence has to rely on the accuracy of a cause-and-effect relationship. **Cause and effect** describes the relationship between one event (cause) and another event that happens (effect). The relationship also works in reverse: One event (effect) results from another event (cause). Whether you begin with a cause or with an effect, you're using the same basic pattern.

Cause A ⟶ produces ⟶ effect B

You may seek to understand the effects of a known cause:

More studying ⟶ produces ⟶ ?

Or you may seek to determine the cause or causes of a known effect:

? ⟶ produces ⟶ recurrent headaches

Be careful not to take cause and effect statements at face value. Think through the relationship between cause A and effect B. Sometimes, the relationship is exactly the opposite of what's being claimed. Consult the guidelines in Box 37.

Checklist for assessing cause and effect   37

- **Is there a clear relationship between events?** Related causes and effects happen in sequence: A cause occurs before an effect. First the wind blows; then a door slams; then a pane of glass in the door breaks. But CHRONOLOGICAL ORDER merely implies a cause-and-effect relationship. Perhaps someone slammed the door shut. Perhaps someone threw a baseball through the glass pane. A cause-and-effect relationship must be linked by more than chronological sequence. The fact that B happens after A doesn't prove that A causes B.

- **Is there a pattern of repetition?** Scientific proof depends on a pattern of repetition. To establish that A causes B, every time A is present, B must occur. Or, put another way, B never occurs unless A is present. The need for repetition explains why the U.S. Food and Drug Administration (FDA) runs thousands of clinical trials before approving a new medicine.

- **Are there multiple causes and/or effects?** Avoid oversimplification. The basic pattern of cause and effect—single cause, single effect (A causes B)—rarely represents the full picture. Multiple causes and/or effects are more typical of real

⟶

> ### Checklist for assessing cause and effect *(continued)* 37
>
> life. For example, it would be oversimplification to assume that
> a lower crime rate is strictly due to high employment rates.
> Similarly, one cause can produce multiple effects. For example,
> advertisements for a liquid diet drink focus on the drink's most
> appealing effect, rapid weight loss, ignoring less desirable effects
> such as lost nutrients and a tendency to regain the weight.

5i How do I assess reasoning processes critically?

To think, read, and write critically, you need to distinguish *sound reasoning* from *faulty reasoning*. **Induction** and **deduction** are the two basic reasoning processes. They're natural thought patterns used every day to help people think through ideas and make decisions. The two processes are summarized in Box 38.

> ⊙ ### Comparison of inductive and deductive reasoning 38
>
> | | Inductive Reasoning | Deductive Reasoning |
> |---|---|---|
> | Argument begins | with specific evidence | with a general claim |
> | Argument concludes | with a general statement | with a specific statement |
> | Conclusion is | reliable or unreliable | true or false |
> | Purpose is | to discover something new | to apply what's known |

5i.1 Recognizing and using inductive reasoning

Inductive reasoning moves from particular facts or instances to general principles. Suppose you go to the Registry of Motor Vehicles to renew your driver's license and have to stand in line for two hours. A few months later you return to get new license plates, and once again you have to stand in line for two hours. You mention your annoyance to a couple of friends who say they had exactly the same experience. You conclude that the registry is inefficient and indifferent to the needs of its patrons. You've arrived at this conclusion by means of induction. Box 39 shows the features of inductive reasoning.

◎ **Summary of inductive reasoning** 39

- **Inductive reasoning moves from the specific to the general.** It begins with specific evidence—facts, observations, or experiences—and moves to a general conclusion.

- *Inductive conclusions are considered reliable or unreliable, not true or false.* Because inductive thinking is based on a sampling of facts, an inductive conclusion indicates probability, the degree to which the conclusion is likely to be true—not certainty.

- An inductive conclusion is held to be reliable or unreliable in relation to the quantity and quality of the evidence (5g) on which it's based.

- Induction leads to new "truths." It can support statements about the unknown based on what's known.

5i.2 Recognizing and using deductive reasoning

Deductive reasoning is the process of reasoning from general claims to a specific instance. If several visits to the Registry of Motor Vehicles convince you that the registry is indifferent to the needs of its patrons, you'll not be happy the next time you must go there. Your reasoning might go something like this:

> The registry wastes people's time.
> I have to go to the registry tomorrow.
> Therefore, tomorrow my time will be wasted.

You reached the conclusion—"Therefore, tomorrow my time will be wasted"—by means of deduction.

Deductive arguments have three parts: two **premises** and a **conclusion.** This three-part structure is known as a **syllogism.** The first premise of a deductive argument may be a fact or an assumption. The second premise may also be a fact or an assumption.

Whether or not an argument is **valid** has to do with its form or structure. Here the word *valid* isn't the general term people use in conversation to mean "acceptable" or "well grounded." In the context of reading and writing logical arguments, the word *valid* has a very specific meaning. A deductive argument is *valid* when the conclusion logically follows from the premises; a deductive argument is *invalid* when the conclusion doesn't logically follow from the premises. For example:

VALID

PREMISE 1	When it snows, the streets get wet. [fact]
PREMISE 2	It is snowing. [fact]
CONCLUSION	Therefore, the streets are getting wet.

INVALID

PREMISE 1	When it snows, the streets get wet. [fact]
PREMISE 2	The streets are getting wet. [fact]
CONCLUSION	Therefore, it is snowing.

The invalid argument has acceptable premises because the premises are facts. The argument's conclusion, however, is wrong. It ignores other reasons why the streets may be wet. The street could be wet from rain, from street-cleaning trucks that spray water, or from people washing their cars. Because the conclusion doesn't follow logically from the premises, the argument is invalid.

Here's another invalid argument because its conclusion doesn't follow from the premises (after all, many things other than a dead battery can stop a car from starting).

INVALID

PREMISE 1	When the battery is dead, a car will not start. [fact]
PREMISE 2	My car will not start. [fact]
CONCLUSION	My battery is dead.

In any deductive argument, beware of premises that are implied but not stated—called **unstated assumptions.** Remember that an argument can be logically valid even though it is based on wrong assumptions. The response to such an argument is to attack the assumptions as wrong, not the conclusion. For example, suppose a corporation argues that it can't install pollution-control devices because the cost would cut deeply into its profits. This argument rests on the unstated assumption that no corporation should do something that would lower its profits. That assumption is wrong, and so is the argument. But it can be shown to be wrong only when the assumptions are challenged.

Similarly, if a person says that certain information is correct because it is in the newspaper, that person's deductive reasoning is flawed. Here, the unstated assumption is that everything in a newspaper is correct—which isn't true. Whenever there's an unstated assumption, supply it and then check to be sure it is true. Deductive reasoning is summarized in Box 40.

Summary of deductive reasoning 40

- **Deductive reasoning moves from the general to the specific.** The three-part structure that makes up a deductive argument, or SYLLOGISM, includes two premises and a conclusion drawn from them.

- A deductive argument is VALID if the conclusion logically follows from the premises.

- *A deductive conclusion may be judged true or false.* If both premises are true, the conclusion is true. If the argument contains an assumption, the writer must prove the truth of the assumption to establish the truth of the argument.

- Deductive reasoning applies what the writer already knows. Though it doesn't yield new information, it builds stronger arguments than inductive reasoning because it offers the certainty that a conclusion is either true or false.

EXERCISE 5-8

Working individually or with a peer-response group, determine whether each conclusion here is valid or invalid. Be ready to explain your answers. For help, consult 5i.

1. Faddish clothes are expensive.
   This shirt is expensive.
   This shirt must be part of a fad.

2. When a storm is threatening, small-craft warnings are issued.
   A storm is threatening.
   Small-craft warnings will be issued.

3. The Pulitzer Prize is awarded to outstanding literary works.
   The Great Gatsby never won a Pulitzer Prize.
   The Great Gatsby isn't an outstanding literary work.

4. All states send representatives to the United States Congress.
   Puerto Rico sends a representative to the United States Congress.
   Puerto Rico is a state.

5. All risks are frightening.
   Taking a new job is a risk.
   Taking a new job is frightening.

6. Before a new home can be occupied, it must be inspected.
   That new home is occupied.
   That new home has been inspected.
7. Most weekly newsmagazines are published on Mondays.
   This is a weekly newsmagazine.
   This newsmagazine is published on Monday.
8. Science fiction novels are usually violent.
   This is a science fiction novel.
   This novel is obviously violent.
9. All veterans are entitled to education benefits.
   Elaine is a veteran.
   Elaine is entitled to education benefits.
10. Midwestern universities produce great college basketball teams.
    Elmstown has a great college basketball team.
    Elmstown is a Midwestern university.

5j How can I recognize and avoid logical fallacies?

Logical fallacies are flaws in reasoning that lead to illogical statements. Though logical fallacies tend to occur when ideas are being argued, they can be found in all types of writing. Most logical fallacies masquerade as reasonable statements, but they're in fact attempts to manipulate readers by appealing to their emotions instead of their intellects, their hearts rather than their heads. The names by which logical fallacies are known indicate the way that thinking has gone wrong.

Hasty generalization

A hasty generalization draws conclusions from inadequate evidence. Suppose someone says, "My hometown is the best place in the state to live." And the person gives only two examples to support the opinion. That's not enough. And others might not feel the same way, perhaps for many reasons. Therefore, the person who makes such a statement is indulging in a hasty generalization. **Stereotyping** is another kind of hasty generalization. It happens, for example, when someone says, "Everyone from country X is dishonest." Such a sweeping claim about all members of a particular ethnic, religious, racial, or political group is stereotyping. Yet another kind of stereotyping is **sexism,** which occurs when someone discriminates against another person based on gender (21g). For example, when an observer of a minor traffic accident involving women makes negative comments about all "women drivers," the person is guilty of a combination of stereotyping and sexism—both components of hasty generalization.

False analogy

A false analogy draws a comparison in which the differences outweigh the similarities or the similarities are irrelevant. For example, "Old Joe Smith would never make a good president because an old dog can't learn new tricks" is a false analogy. Joe Smith isn't a dog. Also, learning the role of a president cannot be compared to a dog's learning tricks. Homespun analogies like this have an air of wisdom about them but tend to fall apart when examined closely.

Begging the question

Begging the question tries to offer proof by simply using another version of the argument itself. This is also called *circular reasoning.* For example, "Wrestling is a dangerous sport because it is unsafe" begs the question. *Unsafe* is a synonym for *dangerous,* so the statement goes around in a circle, getting nowhere. Evidence of the claimed danger is missing. Here's another example with a different twist: "Wrestling is a dangerous sport because wrestlers get injured." Here, the support for the second part of the statement is the argument in the first part of the statement. Obviously, since wrestling is a popular sport, it can be safe when undertaken with proper training and practice. And here's yet another example: "Wrestlers love danger." This time, the problem is the unstated assumption that wrestling's supposed danger, not the sport, is what attracts wrestlers. Yet the audience can't be assumed to share the opinion that wrestling is dangerous.

Irrelevant argument

An irrelevant argument reaches a conclusion that doesn't follow from the premises. It's also called a *non sequitur* (Latin for "it does not follow"). This happens when a conclusion doesn't follow from the premises. Here's an example: "Jane Jones is a forceful speaker, so she'll make a good mayor." What does speaking ability have to do with being a good mayor?

False cause

A false cause assumes that because two events are related in time, the first caused the second. It's also known as *post hoc, ergo propter hoc* (Latin for "after this, therefore because of this"). For example, if someone claims that a new weather satellite launched last week has caused the rain that's been falling ever since, that person is connecting two events that have no causal relationship to each other.

Self-contradiction

Self-contradiction uses two premises that can't both be true at the same time. Here's an example: "Only when nuclear weapons have finally destroyed us will we be convinced of the need to control them." This is self-contradictory because no one would be around to be convinced if everyone had been destroyed.

Red herring

A red herring tries to distract attention from one issue by introducing a second that's unrelated to the first. It's sometimes called *ignoring the question.* Here's an example: "Why worry about pandas becoming extinct when we haven't solved the plight of the homeless?" What do homeless people have to do with pandas? If the point is that money spent to prevent the extinction of pandas should go to the homeless, then that's what should be said. By using an irrelevant issue, a person hopes to distract the audience, just as putting a herring in the path of a bloodhound would distract it from the scent it has been told to follow.

Argument to the person

An argument to the person means attacking the person making the argument rather than the argument itself. It's also known as the *ad hominem* (Latin for "to the man") attack. When a person's appearance, habits, or character is criticized instead of the merits of that person's argument, the attack is a fallacy. Here's an example: "We'd take her position on child abuse seriously if she were not so nasty to her husband." What does nastiness to an adult, though it isn't nice, have to do with child abuse?

Guilt by association

Guilt by association means that a person's arguments, ideas, or opinions lack merit because of that person's activities, interests, or companions. For example, here's the fallacy in operation: "Jack belongs to the International Hill Climbers Association, which declared bankruptcy last month. This makes him unfit to be mayor of our city." The fact that the group that declared bankruptcy has Jack as a member has nothing to do with his ability to be the mayor.

Jumping on the bandwagon

Jumping on the bandwagon means something is right or permissible because "everyone does it." It's also called *ad populum* (Latin for "to the people"). This fallacy operates in statements such as "How could smoking be unhealthy if millions of people smoke?"

False or irrelevant authority

Using false or irrelevant authority means citing the opinion of someone who has no expertise in the subject at hand. This fallacy attempts to transfer prestige from one area to another. Many television commercials rely on this tactic—a famous tennis player praising a brand of motor oil or a popular movie star lauding a brand of cheese.

Card-stacking

Card-stacking ignores evidence on the other side of a question. It's also known as *special pleading*. From all the available facts, only those that will build the best (or worst) possible case are used. Many television commercials use this strategy. When three slim, happy consumers praise a diet plan, only at the very end of the ad does the announcer—in a very low and speedy voice—say that results vary, and even that language seems to have been chosen to be vague and noninformative.

The either-or fallacy

The either-or fallacy offers only two alternatives when more exist. This fallacy is also called *false dilemma*. Such fallacies tend to touch on emotional issues and can therefore seem accurate until analyzed. For example, "Either go to college or forget about getting a job" is an example of an either-or fallacy. Obviously, many jobs don't require a college education.

Taking something out of context

Taking something out of context deliberately distorts an idea or a fact by removing it from its previously surrounding material. For example, suppose that a newspaper movie critic writes, "The plot was predictable and boring, but the music was sparkling." And the next day, an ad for the movie claims "critics call it 'sparkling.'" This is an example of the critic's words having been taken out of context and thereby a distortion of the original.

Appeal to ignorance

Appeal to ignorance tries to make an incorrect argument based on its never having been shown to be false—or, the reverse, an incorrect argument based on its not yet having been proven true. Such appeals can be very persuasive because they prey on people's superstitions or lack of knowledge. Such appeals are often stated in the fuzzy language of double negatives. Here's an example: "Because it hasn't been proven that eating food X does *not* cause cancer, we can assume that it does." In truth, the absence of opposing evidence proves nothing.

Ambiguity and equivocation

Ambiguity and equivocation are statements that can be interpreted in more than one way, thus concealing the truth. For example, suppose a person is asked, "Is she doing a good job?" and the person answers with "She's performing as expected." Such an answer is open to positive or negative interpretation. A similar example of this fallacy is when the question "Have you made any progress?" is answered by "We've held some meetings."

EXERCISE 5-9

Working individually or with a peer-response group, identify the kind of fallacy in each item. Then explain why it's a fallacy. If there's no logical flaw in a statement, explain why it isn't a fallacy.

EXAMPLE   Seat belts are the only hope for reducing the death rate from automobile accidents. [This is an either-or fallacy because it assumes that nothing but seat belts can reduce the number of fatalities from car accidents.]

1. Joanna Hayes should write a book about the Central Intelligence Agency. She has starred in three films that show the inner workings of the agency.
2. It is ridiculous to have spent thousands of dollars to rescue those two whales trapped in the Arctic ice. Why, look at all of the people trapped in jobs that they don't like.
3. Every time my roommate has a math test, she becomes extremely nervous. Clearly, she isn't good at math.
4. Plagiarism is deceitful because it is dishonest.
5. The local political coalition to protect the environment would get my support if its leaders did not drive cars that are such gas hogs.
6. UFOs must exist because no reputable studies have proved conclusively that they don't.
7. Water fluoridation affects the brain. Citywide, students' test scores began to drop five months after fluoridation began.
8. Learning to manage a corporation is exactly like learning to ride a bicycle: Once you learn the skills, you never forget how, and you never fall.
9. Medicare is free; the government pays for it from taxes.
10. Reading good literature is the one way to appreciate culture.

6 WRITING ARGUMENT

6a What is a written argument?

When you write an **argument,** you attempt to convince a reader to agree with you on a topic open to debate. You support your position with evidence, reasons, and examples—factual, logical data, not opinions. The terms *argument writing* and *persuasive writing* (1c) are often used interchangeably. When a distinction is made between them, persuasive writing is the broader term. It includes advertisements, letters to editors, emotionally charged speeches and writing, and formal written arguments. The focus of this chapter is formal written argument as usually assigned in college courses.

Taking and defending a position in a written argument is an engaging intellectual process, especially when it involves a topic of substance. The ability to think critically (Box 31, section 5b, page 106) is central to writing argument. In fact, before you can choose a position and convincingly defend it, you must critically examine all sides of the issue.

Written argument is completely different from the arguing people do in everyday life. Verbal arguments often originate in anger and involve bursts of temper or unpleasant emotional confrontations. Written argument, in contrast, is constructive, setting forth a debatable position calmly and respectfully. The passion that underlies a writer's position comes not from angry words but from the force of a balanced, well-developed, clearly written presentation.

You'll learn three patterns for written argument—Rogerian, classical, and Toulmin. The ability to argue reasonably and effectively is an important skill not only in college but also throughout life—in family relationships, with friends, and in the business world. And as you become experienced with written arguments, you can apply the same techniques to oral arguments.

Before you start writing arguments, please know that what I explain in this chapter depends on your knowing what I discuss in Chapters 1 through 5 of this handbook. If you take a few minutes to review those chapters, you'll have a richer context for writing.

6b How do I choose a topic for an argument?

When you choose a topic for written argument, be sure that it's open to debate. Don't confuse matters of information (facts) with matters of debate. An essay becomes an argument when it *takes a position* on a fact or other type of information.

FACT	Students at Deitmer College are required to take physical education.
ONE SIDE: **OPEN TO DEBATE**	Students at Deitmer College should not be required to take physical education.
OTHER SIDE: **OPEN TO DEBATE**	Students at Deitmer College should be required to take physical education.

Your written argument can defend either one of the sides listed above by stating the side it takes and defending it. Still, you'd want to keep the opposite side in mind because, at some point in the essay (6e), a solid written argument always mentions opposing views and systematically refutes them. If you do not mention opposing views, your readers could be justified in assuming you aren't well informed, or fair-minded, or disciplined as a thinker.

Assignments in written argument take various forms. One major type states both the topic and the position to take on that topic. In such cases, you're expected to fulfill the assignment whether or not you agree with the given point of view. Your readers look at your ability to marshal a defense of the assigned position and to reason logically about it. Another major type is relatively unstructured, thereby requiring you to choose a debatable topic as well as your position on it. In this case, the topic you choose should be suitable for college writing, not trivial (for example, not "the best way to chew gum"). Your readers look at your ability to choose a debatable topic of substance, to take an intelligent, defensible position on that topic, and to support that position reasonably and convincingly.

If you think that all sides of a debatable topic have merit, choose one anyway. Don't stall out from indecision. You're not making a lifetime commitment. Concentrate on the merits of one position, and argue that position as effectively as possible.

The two student essays at the end of this chapter (6k) were written in response to an assignment about the commercialization of holidays. One student, Lindsey, argued that holidays are indeed too commercialized. The other student, Daniel, argued the opposite position—that commercialization of holidays is a good development.

6c How do I develop an assertion and a thesis statement for my argument?

An **assertion** is a statement that expresses a point of view on a debatable topic. It can be supported by evidence, reasons, and examples (including facts, statistics, names, experiences, and experts). The exact wording of the assertion rarely finds its way into the essay, but the assertion serves as a focus for your thinking. And later, it serves as the basis for developing your thesis statement.

TOPIC	The commercialization of holidays.
ASSERTION	Holidays have become too commercialized.
ASSERTION	Holidays have not become too commercialized.

Before you decide on an assertion—the position you want to argue—explore the topic. Don't rush into deciding on your assertion. Consider all sides. Remember that **what mainly separates most good writing from bad is the writer's ability to move back and forth between general statements and specific details.** Use the RENNS formula (4f) to check yourself to see whether you can marshal sufficient details to support your generalizations.

Even if you know immediately what assertion you want to argue, don't stop there. The more thoroughly you think about all sides of the topic, the broader the perspective you'll bring to your writing. After all, a solid argument at some point mentions opposing positions on the topic and refutes them (6e). Another reason to think through your position in some detail is to allow you to keep an open mind. When you take sides, your choice will be informed. Beware, however, of switching sides at the last minute; you'll be wasting your valuable time.

To stimulate your thinking about the topic and the assertion of your position, use the techniques for planning discussed in Chapter 2. Also, list all points you can think of for each of the contrasting points of view (*pro* and *con; agree* and *disagree; for* and *against*). If you find there are more than two sides to a topic, use whatever labels represent them. This list of all points on all sides becomes a checklist for you to make sure you've covered not only the important points in your argument but also refuted the main points in the opposing position.

If time allows—and if your instructor approves students' doing so—use the library and the Internet to research your topic (1g) so that your essay has additional depth. Also—again, if permitted by your instructor—talk with other people for help in expanding your thinking. Of course, because your goal in any conversation is to further your understanding of opposing points of view, interview other people rather than argue with them.

Now you can use your assertion as a basis for composing your essay's THESIS STATEMENT (2q). Here's how Daniel progressed from assertion to thesis statement for his essay on the benefits of holiday commercialism (6k):

- I think holiday commercialism is a good thing. [This assertion is a start.]
- All commercial uses of holidays are very good for our economy and people's spirits. [This is a preliminary thesis because it gives reason—economic and emotional benefits—but the word *all* is misleading, and "very good" is too vague.]
- In spite of what some people think, commercial uses of holidays benefit the nation's economy and people's spirits. [This thesis statement is better, but "what some people think" veers off the topic. Also, the wording *benefit . . . people's spirits* is awkward.]
- Commercial uses of holidays benefit the nation's economy and lift people's spirits. [This is the final version of Casey's thesis statement—though he later added the transitional words *After all* to connect the thesis statement to his introduction. This final version meets the requirements for a thesis statement given in Box 12, section 2q, page 37.]

EXERCISE 6-1

Working individually or with a peer response group, develop an assertion and a thesis statement for each of the listed topics. You may choose any defensible position. For help, consult 6a through 6c.

EXAMPLE   *Topic:* Book censorship in high school

Assertion: Books should not be censored in high school.

Thesis statement: When books are taken off high school library shelves or are dropped from high school curricula, students are denied an open exchange of ideas.

1. watching television many hours a day
2. taking many kinds of vitamins
3. prison sentences for nonviolent crimes
4. giving grades in school

6d What part does audience play in my argument?

The PURPOSE of written argument is to convince your readers—the AUDIENCE—to be influenced by your position on a debatable topic. Consult section 1d for ways to think about the audience for your writing in all kinds of situations. However, in writing an argument, you want to consider one additional factor: the degree of agreement you can expect from the reader. Will the audience be hostile in the face of what you say? Will your audience be open-minded and perhaps ready to adopt your point of view? What other reactions might you expect?

The more emotionally charged a topic is, the greater the chance that any position argued will elicit either strong agreement or strong disagreement. For example, abortion, capital punishment, and gun control are emotionally loaded topics because they touch on matters of personal belief, including individual rights and religion. A topic such as the commercialization of holidays, given to the two students whose essays appear at the end of this chapter, is less emotionally loaded. A topic that likely is even less emotionally loaded, yet still open to debate, would be whether computer X is better than computer Y.

The degree to which an audience might be friendly or hostile needs to influence your choice of strategies to use for trying to reach and convince it. For example, if you anticipate that many readers will disagree with you, consider using **Rogerian argument.** Rogerian argument is based on the principles of communication developed by psychologist Carl Rogers. According to Rogers, communication is eased when people find *common ground* in their points of view. The common ground in a debate over capital punishment might be that serious crimes are increasing in numbers and viciousness. Once both sides agree on the problem, they might be more willing to consider opposing opinions on whether capital punishment is a deterrent to crime.

6e What is the structure of a classical argument?

The structure of a **classical argument** is based on a six-part plan developed by the ancient Greeks and Romans. Lindsey's essay in section 6k uses the classical pattern; Daniel's essay in section 6k uses a modified form of that pattern. Box 41 describes six parts of a classical argument.

◎ **Elements in a persuasive essay:**   **41**
      Classical argument

1. **Introductory paragraph:** sets the stage for the position that is argued in the essay (4b).
2. **Thesis statement:** states the position being argued (2q). In a short essay, the thesis statement often appears at the end of the introductory paragraph.
3. **Background information:** gives the reader basic information needed for understanding the position being argued. This information can be part of the introductory paragraph (as in Daniel's essay in 6k) or can appear in its own paragraph (as in Lindsey's essay in 6k).

→

Elements in a persuasive essay: **41**
Classical argument *(continued)*

4. **Reasons or evidence:** the support offered for the position being argued. *This is the core of the essay.* You want your reasoning to be logical (5h through 5j), and your evidence to meet critical standards (5g). Each reason or piece of evidence usually consists of a general statement backed up with specific details or examples. Depending on the length of the essay, one or two paragraphs are devoted to each reason or type of evidence. Often, but not always, the most familiar reason and evidence are presented first, saving the most unfamiliar for last. Writers might choose this CLIMACTIC ORDER because it usually holds an audience's attention and has the greatest impact. (Consult 4h for help with alternate ways to arrange details in paragraphs.)

5. **Objections and responses to them:** discusses reasons and evidence that the opposing position likely holds and offers rebuttal to them. This "refutation," which can be lengthy or brief according to the overall length of the essay, appears in its own paragraph or paragraphs, usually immediately before the concluding paragraph (as in Lindsey's essay, 6k). In a modified pattern of classical argument, the refutation immediately follows the introductory paragraph, as a bridge to the rest of the essay. The thesis statement then falls at the end of the introductory paragraph or at the end of the refutation paragraph (as in Daniel's essay, 6k). In yet another modification, each paragraph that presents a type of evidence or reason (item 4 on this list) also mentions and responds to the opposing position.

6. **Concluding paragraph:** ends the essay logically and gracefully— never abruptly (4k).

EXERCISE 6-2

Individually or with a peer-response group, practice working with the activity "objections and responses to them." Choose a debatable topic (choose one or use a topic being written about by a volunteer in your class). Brainstorm a list of points, some pro and some con. If you're part of a group, work together to assign the pro and con positions to different sets of students. Then, conduct a brief debate on which side has more merit, with the pro and con sides taking turns. At the end, your group can vote for the side that is more convincing.

6f What is the Toulmin model for argument?

The **Toulmin model** for argument has been gaining in popularity among teachers and students. This model defines three essential elements in an effective argument: the claim, the support, and the warrants. Though these terms may be new to you, they describe concepts that you've encountered before, as Box 42 explains.

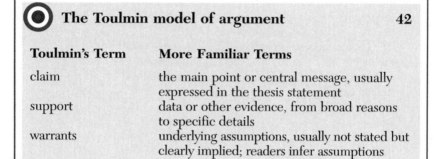

	The Toulmin model of argument	42

Toulmin's Term	More Familiar Terms
claim	the main point or central message, usually expressed in the thesis statement
support	data or other evidence, from broad reasons to specific details
warrants	underlying assumptions, usually not stated but clearly implied; readers infer assumptions

Analyzed in Toulmin's terms, here's the argument in Daniel's essay (6k).

- **Claim:** Commercial uses of holidays benefit the nation's economy and lift people's spirits.

- **Support:** (1) Economic prosperity circulates money, which in turn creates jobs. (2) Holidays are festive times that cheer people up with decorations, costumes, gift giving, and a friendly atmosphere. (3) Successful businesses improve everyone's quality of life by sponsoring charitable causes, parades, fireworks displays, and cultural events.

- **Warrants:** (1) Strengthening the nation's economy benefits everyone. (2) The spiritual aspects of holidays are not paramount.

To understand the concept of *warrant,* think about the concept of *inferences,* which are key components of reading critically (5c). Inferences are implications written "between the lines." Warrants are implied, "between the lines" assumptions to be inferred from the argument.

Warrants fall into three categories: (1) Warrants based on **authority** rest on respect for the credibility and trustworthiness of the person. (2) Warrants based on **substance** rest on the reliability of factual evidence. (3) Warrants based on **motivation** rest on the values and beliefs of the writer and audience. Daniel's first warrant is based on authority because it reports a view supported by economists and citizens alike.

Daniel's second warrant is based on motivation because it is based on the writer's valuing of economic prosperity over spiritual considerations.

The concepts in the Toulmin model can help you not only write but also read arguments with a critical eye. They're equally useful whether you're using Rogerian, classical, or Toulmin argument. However, as you read and revise your written argument, you can benefit from applying Toulmin's concepts to what you are saying. If you can't identify the claim, support, and warrants, you likely have to assume that your argument needs work.

EXERCISE 6-3

Individually or with a peer-response group, discuss these arguments and determine how to make the connection between the claim and the support.

EXAMPLE   *Claim:* Some college students cheat on exams. Therefore, if we want to reduce cheating on exams, we should establish an honor code at this school.

Warrant: Schools that want to reduce cheating on exams should establish an honor code.

1. Parking is scarce at this college. Therefore, the college should build more parking lots.
2. Faculty members who teach later than first period can't find parking spaces on campus. Therefore, the college should set aside reserved parking for the faculty.
3. Students at this college need part-time jobs. Therefore, the college should open a job referral office.

6g How do I define key terms in an argument?

Words become **key terms** when they're central to the message you want to communicate. While the meaning of some key terms is readily evident, others may be open to interpretation. For example, abstract words such as *love, freedom,* and *democracy* have different meanings in different contexts.

Daniel starts his essay (6k) with the key term *signs of commercialism,* an expression that many think is open to interpretation. Therefore, he provides examples to show exactly how he has used the term. Similarly, when Daniel uses *economy,* a word with many meanings, in the TOPIC SENTENCE of the third paragraph of his essay, he defines it as the "ongoing circulation of money." And in the rest of that paragraph, he explains how circulation of money operates. Therefore, he makes clear that he isn't referring to any of the other meanings of economy, such as managing finances, avoiding waste, or using resources efficiently.

Many students ask whether they should use dictionary definitions in an essay. Looking words up in a dictionary to understand precise meanings is certainly recommended, but quoting a dictionary definition can be risky. It's an overused strategy and, for college writing, often considered an "easy way out." However, if the meaning of a word is complex or easily misinterpreted so that you decide to give the dictionary definition, never identify it as "from *Webster's*." Give the complete title of the dictionary you're citing: for example, *Webster's New World College Dictionary,* Third Edition.

6h How do I reason effectively in an argument?

In many instances, of course, you can't actually expect to change your reader's mind. The basis for a debatable position is often personal opinion or belief, both of which are strongly held. Therefore, your goal is to convince your reader that your point of view has merit. People often "agree to disagree" in the best spirit of intellectual exchange. In this case, your audience wants to see how effectively you've reasoned and presented your position.

The opposite positions that Lindsey and Daniel take on the issue of commercializing holiday times originate with their personal beliefs and perceptions of the world. Lindsey feels that commercialism ruins the holidays; Daniel thinks commercialism is beneficial. The chance of either person convincing the other is slight, but if they write solid arguments, at the least they can come to respect the soundness of the other's argument.

A sound argument relies on three types of **appeals to reason:** logical, emotional, and ethical. Box 43 summarizes how to use the three appeals.

⊙ **Guidelines for reasoning effectively**   43
in written argument

- **Be logical:** Use sound reasoning.
- **Enlist the emotions of the reader:** Appeal to the values and beliefs of the reader by arousing the reader's "better self."
- **Establish credibility:** Show that you as the writer can be relied on as a knowledgeable person with good sense.

The **logical appeal,** called *logos* by the ancient Greeks, is the most widely used appeal in arguments. The logic is based on sound reasoning

(5g). It analyzes cause and effect correctly (5h). Also, it uses appropriate patterns of inductive reasoning and deductive reasoning (5i), and it distinguishes clearly between fact and opinion (5c.2). Finally, sound reasoning means it avoids logical fallacies (5j).

Emotional appeals, called *pathos* by the ancient Greeks, can be effective when used in conjunction with logical appeals. The word *emotional* has a specific meaning in this context: "arousing and enlisting the emotions of the reader." Used honestly and with restraint, emotional appeals arouse the audience's "better self" by eliciting sympathy, civic pride, or similar feelings based on values and beliefs. Effective emotional appeals use description and examples to stir emotions; they do not rely on sentimentality or biased, SLANTED LANGUAGE (21h) designed to exploit human feelings and thereby manipulate them.

In his essay (6k), Daniel uses an emotional appeal well in his fifth paragraph. He mentions that stores give toys to children in hospitals. But he doesn't overdo it. Nowhere does he use language such as *feeling pity for these sweet children who suffer from dreadful illnesses that ravage their tiny bodies.* Had he indulged in such excesses, the audience would likely realize it's being manipulated. Such realizations close minds rather than open them. In her essay (6k), Lindsey appeals to the emotions well in her second paragraph about the origins of the holiday spirit. She uses restraint by simply pointing out facts that support the logic of her argument and that might also stir the reader's pride in country and heritage. She doesn't attempt to lecture the audience about how they "should" feel.

Ethical appeals, called *ethos* by the ancient Greeks, establish the credibility of the writer. Audiences judge writers as ethical or unethical by the use of facts, evidence, and logic. Audiences don't trust a writer who states opinions as fact, distorts evidence, or makes claims that can't be supported. For example, had Lindsey used the statement *A child who doesn't get gifts for Christmas carries an emotional scar throughout life,* it would be an opinion as well as an exaggeration. It has no place in written argument. Ethical appeals can't take the place of logical appeals, but the two work well together.

One effective way to make an ethical appeal is to draw on your personal experience. (Some college instructors don't want students to write in the first person, so check with your instructor before you try this technique.) If you use personal experience, be sure that it relates directly to the generalization you're supporting. Also, be aware that a personal experience can say as much about the writer as about the experience. For example, if Daniel had been a volunteer at a hospital when gifts from a local business were distributed, the story of the experience not only would have supported his claim in his fifth paragraph; it also would have illustrated his good character.

6i How do I establish a reasonable tone in an argument?

A reasonable TONE (1e) tells your audience that you're being fair-minded. When in writing an argument you anticipate opposing positions and refute them with balanced language and emphasis, you demonstrate that you respect the other side. No matter how strongly you disagree with opposing arguments, never insult the other side. Name-calling reflects poor judgment and a lack of self-control. Similarly, your choice of words establishes your tone. The saying "It isn't *what* you say but *how* you say it" needs to be on your mind at all times as you write an argument. Avoid exaggerating, and don't show anger. The more emotionally loaded a topic (for example, abortion or capital punishment), the more tempted you might be to use careless, harsh words. For example, calling the opposing position "stupid" would say more about you than it would about the issue. As much as possible, use appropriate FIGURATIVE LANGUAGE, such as a well-chosen SIMILE or METAPHOR (21d), to enhance, rather than distort, your point.

6j How did two students draft and revise their arguments?

As you know, Lindsey argued that holidays have become too commercialized. Daniel chose the opposite position, saying the commercialization of holidays has advantages. The final draft of each essay appears at the end of this chapter. The marginal annotations identify the elements of a classical argument (6e). These annotations are for your guidance only; do not use them in your final draft.

In an early draft, Lindsey wrote an introduction that included the background information on the holidays. When she revised, she moved that information to a separate paragraph because she saw that the introductory paragraph was too long and the thesis statement was overshadowed. Also, she felt that a separate paragraph on background information would give her space to use an emotional appeal (6h). An early draft of Lindsey's third paragraph consisted only of the topic sentence and the last three sentences of the final draft. When she revised, she realized that she needed more examples to support the topic sentence, so she added the material about greeting cards and about time and stress.

Daniel wrote a DISCOVERY DRAFT (3a) to explore the ideas he had discovered and compiled using the techniques discussed in Chapter 2. As he wrote his draft, he discovered, for example, that he needed to define the expression *signs of commercialism* by giving specific examples. Also, he had thought of only two reasons that would support his thesis: an improved economy and an enhanced spirit. He needed at least one more reason. He decided to interview friends who worked in a shopping mall about their views. Some mentioned that their stores reach out to the community and collect gifts or food for the needy. That gave him a third reason. Finally, in an early draft, Daniel's second paragraph was the next to last. When he revised, he realized that paragraph would be a nice bridge between the introduction and his thesis statement, so he moved it.

As these two students revised, they consulted the revision checklists in section 3c.5 (see pages 56–57). Also, they referred to the special checklist for written argument in Box 44.

 Revision checklist for written arguments   **44**

- Is the thesis statement about a debatable topic (6c)?
- Do the reasons or evidence support the thesis statement? Are the generalizations supported by specific details (6c)?
- Is the opposing position stated and refuted (6e)?
- Are key terms defined (6g)?
- Does the argument appeal chiefly to reason? Is it supported by an ethical appeal? If it uses an emotional appeal, is the appeal restrained (6h)?
- Is the tone reasonable (6i)?

EXERCISE 6-4

Working individually or with a peer-response group, choose a topic from this list and plan an essay that argues a debatable position on the topic. Apply all the principles you've learned in this chapter.

1. animal experimentation
2. surrogate mothers
3. value of the space program
4. prayers in public schools
5. celebrity endorsements
6. highway speed limits

6k Final drafts of argument essays by two students

Lindsey Black

Professor Gregory

English 101

April 10, 2001

Commercialism Is Ruining the Holidays

Introduction: identification of the situation Holidays should be special occasions that have religious, historical, and cultural significance. Increasingly, however, holidays in the United States are turning into little more than business opportunities. From coast to coast, the jingles and beeps of cash registers drown out the traditional sounds of holiday observance. **Thesis statement** The spirit of the holidays is being destroyed by commercialism.

Background: origins and significance The origins of the holiday spirit are varied in the United States. Thanksgiving reminds Americans to be grateful for their blessings, and the Fourth of July stimulates pride in the founding of the nation. Labor Day is a tribute to workers. Memorial Day honors soldiers who died in defense of the country, and Veterans Day honors all veterans of the armed forces. Christmas and Easter have great religious significance to Christians. Holidays used to be occasions for people to come together and celebrate their heritages. Today, however, the overriding message of the holidays is "spend money."

Evidence: one type The most visible evidence that commercialism now dominates holidays is the unfortunate emphasis on spending money in preparation for religious holidays. For example, buying and mailing Christmas

→

cards has become standard practice for individuals,
families, and industry. How many people can ignore
the social and business pressures to mail cards?
The commitment of money and time for this activity
is not small. The gift situation is equally
stressful. Although exchanging gifts on Christmas or
Hanukkah was always part of the celebration, the
thought behind the present used to be the point.
Today, however, advertising--particularly on
television--sets a high standard of expectations.
Can home-baked cookies compare to a microwave oven?
Can hand-drawn, handwritten cards be as impressive
as elaborate greeting cards that play music?

Evidence: another type   Other evidence that commercialism is ruining
holidays is the emphasis on shopping for bargains
rather than on activities related to cultural
history. Huge sales held before holidays, and often
on the holiday itself, are advertised heavily in
newspapers, on television, and on radio. Veterans
Day has become the day to buy fall and winter
clothing at reduced prices, and Memorial Day
means specially lowered prices on products for
the coming summer. Parades and ceremonies on Labor
Day honoring the workers of America get less
attention than back-to-school sales. The image
of the family gathering on Thanksgiving Day is
being replaced with the image of the family
shopping the day after Thanksgiving, when stores
are more crowded than on any other day except the
day before Christmas.

Possible objections and responses   In spite of all this, not all people are
troubled by the spirit of commercialism on holidays.
Many people enjoy the festivity of exchanging cards
and gifts. Some people feel that the chance to buy

→

at sales helps them stay within their budgets and therefore enjoy life more. What these people do not realize is that the festive spirit of giving can quickly turn sour when large amounts of money are suddenly not available for necessities. Also, these people do not realize that holiday sales tend to lure shoppers into spending more money than they had planned, often for things that they did not think they needed until they saw them "on sale."

Conclusion: call for awareness   Holiday celebrations in the United States today have more to do with the wallet than the spirit. Some people refuse to participate in the frenzy of a commercial interpretation of holidays, of course. But for too many people, holidays are becoming stressful rather than joyful, upsetting rather than uplifting.

Daniel Casey
Professor Gregory
English 101
April 10, 2001

   Commercialism at Holiday Time Benefits the Nation

Introduction: gives background   Signs of commercialism at holiday time are easy to see in the United States. Christmas decorations begin their call to consumers in October. Memorial Day and Labor Day remind shoppers to prepare for the seasonal change in clothing fashions. Halloween and Easter mean children can make toll calls to the Great Pumpkin or the Easter Bunny.

→

Presentation
and refutation
of opposite
view

Some people disapprove of these commercial uses of holidays in the United States. These people feel that the meaning of a holiday gets lost when television is blaring news of the latest holiday sale or expensive gift item. Many people also feel that the proliferation of gifts and greeting cards creates stressful pressure on budgets and ruins any pleasure derived from giving and receiving. No one, however, has to forget the meaning of a holiday simply because commerce is involved. In fact, commercialism can increase people's enjoyment of the

Thesis
statement

holidays. After all, commercial uses of holidays benefit the nation's economy and lift people's spirits.

Reason:
one effect

Commerce at holiday time in the United States enriches the economy. Prosperity in the United States is based on the ongoing circulation of money, which holidays encourage. When people spend money on gifts and holiday products, jobs are created. The jobs are in many sectors of the economy: manufacturing, distribution, advertising, and retailing. Jobs help people support their families. Profits help business and industry grow. Salaries and profits bring about tax revenues that support schools, police, hospitals, and other government services.

Reason:
second
effect

In addition to economic benefits, commercial activity enhances the spirit of holidays. Most people feel more cheerful at holiday time. Everyone takes part in one big party. Advertising related to holidays, along with stores filled with holiday products, creates an atmosphere of festivity across the nation. Being able to say "Happy Thanksgiving" or "Merry Christmas" to strangers while shopping

→

breaks down barriers and helps everyone feel part of one big family. The festivity on the streets, in malls, and in stores is infectious. Giving and getting gifts and greeting cards helps people stay in touch with each other and express their feelings. Children look forward all year to wearing a store-bought costume for Halloween, sitting on Santa's lap in a department store, and talking to the Easter Bunny at the local shopping mall.

Reason: third effect   The holiday activities that help businesses prosper also inspire many businesses to improve everyone's quality of life. Many companies, for example, organize collections of clothing and preparation of hot meals for needy people at holiday time. Toy stores often give away toys for Christmas and Hanukkah to children in hospitals and in caretaking homes. Macy's department store annually delights people of all ages with its Thanksgiving Day Parade in New York City. The entire nation is invited to enjoy the parade in person or on television. In small towns and large cities, many businesses sponsor fireworks, mounted and displayed safely by professionals, to celebrate the Fourth of July. Goodwill and good business go together to everyone's benefit at holiday time.

Conclusion: summary of main points   The United States is a nation blessed with economic strength and resourceful people. Although commercialism can detract from the true meaning of a holiday, it does not have to. People can discipline themselves to balance the spiritual with the commercial. Americans recognize that the advantages of a stimulated economy and a collective festive spirit are worth the effort of such self-discipline.

www.prenhall.com/troyka

Visit the Troyka Web site for information on:

- Using the parts of speech
- Avoiding comma splices and run-on sentences
- Correcting misplaced and dangling modifiers

You'll also find access to the *Guide to Grammar and Writing*, written by Charles Darling, at <cctc2.commnet.edu/grammar/>. This site, offered by Capital Community College, provides definitions, examples, and quizzes on sentence parts, fragments, and modifier placement, among other grammar topics.

PART TWO

UNDERSTANDING GRAMMAR AND WRITING CORRECT SENTENCES

7 PARTS OF SPEECH AND SENTENCE STRUCTURES

PARTS OF SPEECH

7a Why learn the parts of speech?

Knowing the names and definitions of parts of speech gives you a vocabulary for identifying words and understanding how language works to create meaning. No part of speech exists in a vacuum. To identify a word's part of speech correctly, you need to see how the word functions in a sentence. Sometimes the same word functions differently in different sentences, so check the part of speech used in each instance.

We ate **fish.** [*Fish* is a noun. It names a thing.]

We **fish** on weekends. [*Fish* is a verb. It names an action.]

7b What is a noun?

A **noun** names a person, place, thing, or idea: *student, college, textbook, education.* Box 45 lists different kinds of nouns.

◉ Nouns		45
PROPER	names specific people, places, or things (first letter is always capitalized)	*Garth Brooks, Paris, Buick*
COMMON	names general groups, places, people, or things	*singer, city, automobile*

→

Nouns *(continued)*		45
CONCRETE	names things experienced through the senses: sight, hearing, taste, smell, and touch	*landscape, pizza, thunder*
ABSTRACT	names things not knowable through the senses	*freedom, shyness*
COLLECTIVE	names groups	*family, team*
NONCOUNT OR MASS	names "uncountable" things	*water, time*
COUNT	names countable items	*lake, minute*

✦ **ESL NOTES:** (1) Nouns often appear with words that tell *how much* or *how many, whose, which one,* and similar information. These words include ARTICLES* (*a, an, the*) and other DETERMINERS or LIMITING ADJECTIVES; see 7f and Chapter 46. (2) Words with these suffixes (word endings) are usually nouns: *-ness, -ence, -ance, -ty,* and *-ment;* see sections 20 and 22d.✦

7c What is a pronoun?

A **pronoun** takes the place of a NOUN. The words or word that a pronoun replaces is called the pronoun's ANTECEDENT. See Box 46 for a list of different kinds of pronouns. For information on how to use pronouns correctly, see Chapters 9 and 10.

David is an accountant. [noun]
He is an accountant. [pronoun]
The finance committee needs to consult **him.** [The pronoun *him* refers to its antecedent *David.*]

⊙ Pronouns		46
PERSONAL *I, you, its, her, they, ours,* and others	refers to people or things	**I** saw **her** take a book to **them**.
		→

*Find the definition of any word in small capital letters (such as VERB) in the Terms Glossary at the back of this book, directly before the Index.

Pronouns *(continued)* **46**

RELATIVE *who, which, that*	introduces certain NOUN CLAUSES and ADJECTIVE CLAUSES	The book **that** I lost was valuable.
INTERROGATIVE *that, which, who, whose,* and others	introduces a question	**Who** called?
DEMONSTRATIVE *this, that, these, those*	points out the ANTECEDENT	Whose books are **these**?
REFLEXIVE OR INTENSIVE *myself, themselves,* and other *-self* or *-selves* words	reflects back to the antecedent; intensifies the antecedent	They claim to support **themselves**. I **myself** doubt it.
RECIPROCAL *each other, one another*	refers to individual parts of a plural antecedent	We respect **each other**.
INDEFINITE *all, anyone, each,* and others	refers to nonspecific persons or things	**Everyone** is welcome here.

EXERCISE 7-1

Underline and label all nouns (N) and pronouns (P). Refer to sections 7a, 7b, and 7c for help.

EXAMPLE   Treadmills can be a way to fitness and rehabilitation.

1. Not only humans use them.
2. Scientists conduct experiments by placing lobsters on treadmills.
3. Scientists can study a lobster when it is fitted with a small mask.
4. The mask allows researchers to monitor the crustacean's heartbeat.
5. The lobster may reach speeds of a half-mile or more an hour.

7d What is a verb?

Main verbs express action, occurrence, or state of being. For information on how to use verbs correctly, see Chapter 8.

I **dance.** [action]

The audience **became** silent. [occurrence]

Your dancing **was** excellent. [state of being]

👁 **ALERT:** If you're not sure whether a word is a verb, try substituting a different TENSE (8g to 8k) for the word. If the sentence still makes sense, the word is a verb. ●

> **NO** He is a **changed** man. He is a **will change** man. [*Changed* isn't a verb because the sentence doesn't make sense when *change* is substituted.]

> **YES** The man **changed** his profession. The man **will change** his profession. [*Changed* is a verb because the sentence makes sense when the verb *will change* is substituted.]

EXERCISE 7-2

Underline all verbs. Refer to section 7d for help.

EXAMPLE   The history of eyeglasses <u>reveals</u> a long road to a simple design.

1. People used a magnifying lens as a reading glass about A.D. 1000.
2. An Italian invented the first eyeglasses in 1284.
3. For centuries, people held eyeglasses to their eyes with their hands or nose.
4. In the 1700s, a French optician added three-inch wires on both sides of the glasses.
5. Finally, in the eighteenth century, an English optician lengthened the wires to the ears.

7e What is a verbal?

Verbals are verb parts functioning as NOUNS, ADJECTIVES, or ADVERBS. Box 47 lists the three different kinds of verbals.

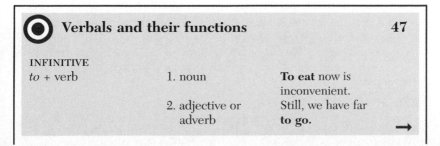

⊙ **Verbals and their functions**		**47**
INFINITIVE		
to + verb	1. noun	**To eat** now is inconvenient.
	2. adjective or adverb	Still, we have far **to go.**

→

Verbals and their functions *(continued)* 47

PAST PARTICIPLE *-ed* form of REGULAR VERB or equivalent in IRREGULAR VERB	adjective	**Boiled, filtered** water is safe.
PRESENT PARTICIPLE *-ing* form of verb	1. noun (called a GERUND) 2. adjective	**Eating** in diners on the road is an adventure. **Running** water may not be safe.

ESL NOTE: For information about correctly using the verbals called INFINITIVES and GERUNDS as objects, see Chapter 49.

7f What is an adjective?

Adjectives modify—that is, they describe or limit—NOUNS, PRONOUNS, and word groups that function as nouns. For information on how to use adjectives correctly, see Chapter 11.

> I saw a **green** tree. [*Green* modifies the noun *tree.*]
>
> It was **leafy.** [*Leafy* modifies the pronoun *it.*]
>
> The flowering trees were **beautiful.** [*Beautiful* modifies the NOUN PHRASE *the flowering trees.*]

ESL NOTE: You can identify some kinds of adjectives by looking at their endings. Usually, words with the SUFFIXES *-ful, -ish, -less,* and *-like* are adjectives (20 and 22d.)

Determiners, frequently called **limiting adjectives,** tell whether a noun is general (*a* tree) or specific (*the* tree). Determiners also tell which one (*this* tree), how many (*twelve* trees), whose (*our* tree), and similar information.

The determiners *a, an,* and *the* are almost always called **articles.** *The* is a **definite article.** Before a noun, *the* conveys that the noun refers to a specific item (*the* plan). *A* and *an* are **indefinite articles.** They convey that a noun refers to an item in a nonspecific or general way (*a* plan).

SPELLING ALERT: Use *a* when the word following it starts with a consonant: *a carrot,* a *broken egg,* a *hip.* Also, use *a* when the word following starts with an *h* that is sounded: *a historical event, a home.* Use *an* when the word following starts with a vowel sound: *an honor, an old bag, an egg.* ●

⊕ **ESL NOTE:** For information about using articles with COUNT and NON-COUNT NOUNS, and about articles with PROPER NOUNS and GERUNDS, see Chapter 46. ⊕

Box 48 lists kinds of determiners. Please note, however, that some words in Box 48 function also as PRONOUNS. To identify a word's part of speech, always check to see how it functions in each particular sentence.

That car belongs to Harold. [*That* is a demonstrative adjective.]

That is Harold's car. [*That* is a demonstrative pronoun.]

⬤ **Determiners (or Limiting adjectives)** 48

ARTICLES
a, an, the   **The** news reporter used **a** cell phone to report **an** assignment.

DEMONSTRATIVE
this, these, that, those   **Those** students rent **that** house.

INDEFINITE
any, each, few, other,   **Few** films today have complex plots.
some, and others

INTERROGATIVE
what, which, whose   **What** answer did you give?

NUMERICAL
one, first, two, second,   The **fifth** question was tricky.
and others

POSSESSIVE
my, your, their, and others   **My** violin is older than **your** cello.

RELATIVE
what, which, whose,   We do not know **which** road to take.
whatever, and others

7g What is an adverb?

Adverbs modify—that is, adverbs describe or limit—VERBS, ADJECTIVES, other adverbs, and CLAUSES. For information on how to use adverbs correctly, see Chapter 11.

Chefs plan meals **carefully.** [*Carefully* modifies the verb *plan*.]

Vegetables provide **very** important vitamins. [*Very* modifies the adjective *important*.]

Those potato chips are **too** heavily salted. [*Too* modifies the adverb *heavily*.]

Fortunately, people are learning that salt can be harmful. [*Fortunately* modifies the rest of the sentence, an INDEPENDENT CLAUSE.]

Descriptive adverbs show levels of intensity, usually by adding *more* (or *less*) and *most* (or *least*): *more* happily, *least* clearly (see section 11e). Many descriptive adverbs are formed by adding *–ly* to adjectives: *sadly, loudly, normally.* But many adverbs do not end in *–ly: very, always, not, yesterday,* and *well* are a few. Some adjectives look like adverbs but are not: *brotherly, lonely, lovely.*

Relative adverbs are words such as *where, why,* and *when.* They are used to introduce ADJECTIVE CLAUSES (7p.2).

Conjunctive adverbs modify—that is, conjunctive adverbs describe or limit—by creating logical connections to give words meaning. Conjunctive adverbs can appear anywhere in a sentence: at the start, in the middle, or at the end. Box 49 lists the kinds of relationships that conjunctive adverbs can show.

However, we consider Isaac Newton an even more important scientist.

We consider Isaac Newton, **however,** an even more important scientist.

We consider Isaac Newton an even more important scientist, **however.**

⊙ **Conjunctive adverbs and relationships they express**   49

Relationship	Words
ADDITION	*also, furthermore, moreover, besides,*
CONTRAST	*however, still, nevertheless, conversely, nonetheless, instead, otherwise,*
COMPARISON	*similarly, likewise,*
RESULT OR SUMMARY	*therefore, thus, consequently, accordingly, hence, then,*
TIME	*next, then, meanwhile, finally, subsequently,*
EMPHASIS	*indeed, certainly,*

EXERCISE 7-3

Underline and label all adjectives (ADJ) and adverbs (ADV). For help, consult 7e, 7f, and 7g.

                ADJ   ADJ
EXAMPLE   Scientific evidence shows that massage therapy can

              ADV   ADJ
          dramatically improve people's health.

1. Premature babies who are massaged gently gain 47 percent more weight than babies who do not receive touch treatment.
2. Frequently, massaged premature babies go home from the hospital sooner, saving an average of $10,000 per baby.
3. Also, daily massage helps many people with stomach problems digest their food easily because important hormones are released during the rubdown.
4. People with the HIV virus find their weakened immune system significantly improved by targeted massage.
5. In addition, massage treatments have helped people with asthma breathe more freely.

7h What is a preposition?

Prepositions are words that convey relationships, usually in time or space. Common prepositions include *in, under, by, after, to, on, over,* and *since.* A PREPOSITIONAL PHRASE (7o) consists of a preposition and the words it modifies.

In the fall, we will hear a concert **by our favorite tenor.**
After the concert, he will fly **to San Francisco.**

⊕ **ESL NOTE:** For a list of prepositions and the IDIOMS they create, see Chapter 48.⊕

7i What is a conjunction?

A **conjunction** connects words, PHRASES, or CLAUSES. **Coordinating conjunctions** join two or more grammatically equal words, phrases, or clauses. Box 50 lists the coordinating conjunctions and the relationships they express.

We hike **and** camp every summer. [*And* joins two words.]
We hike along scenic trails **or** in the wilderness. [*Or* joins two phrases.]
I love the outdoors, **but** my family does not. [*But* joins two INDEPENDENT CLAUSES.]

163

⊙ **Coordinating conjunctions**   **50**
    and relationships they express

Relationship	Words
ADDITION	*and*
CONTRAST	*but, yet*
RESULT OR EFFECT	*so*
REASON OR CAUSE	*for*
CHOICE	*or*
NEGATIVE CHOICE	*nor*

Correlative conjunctions are two conjunctions that work in pairs: *both . . . and, either . . . or, neither . . . nor, not only . . . but (also), whether . . . or,* and *not . . . so much as.*

> **Both** English **and** Spanish are spoken in many homes in the United States.

> **Not only** students **but also** businesspeople should study a second language.

Subordinating conjunctions introduce DEPENDENT CLAUSES (7p.2). Subordinating conjunctions express relationships making the dependent clause in a sentence grammatically less important than the independent clause (7p.1) in the sentence. Box 51 lists the most common subordinating conjunctions. For information about how to use them correctly, see 17e through 17h.

> **Because** it snowed, school was canceled.

> Many people were happy **after** they heard the news.

⊙ **Subordinating conjunctions**   **51**
    and relationships they express

Relationship	Words
TIME	*after, before, once, since, until, when, whenever, while*

→

Subordinating conjunctions	**51**
and relationships they express *(continued)*	

REASON OR CAUSE	*as, because, since*
RESULT OR EFFECT	*in order that, so, so that, that*
CONDITION	*if, even if, provided that, unless*
CONTRAST	*although, even though, though, whereas*
LOCATION	*where, wherever*
CHOICE	*than, whether*

7j What is an interjection?

An **interjection** is a word or expression that conveys surprise or a strong emotion. Alone, an interjection is usually punctuated with an exclamation point (!). As part of a sentence, an interjection is usually set off by one or more commas.

Hooray! I won the race.

Oh, my friends missed seeing the finish.

EXERCISE 7-4

Identify the part of speech of each numbered and underlined word. Choose from noun, pronoun, verb, adjective, adverb, preposition, coordinating conjunction, correlative conjunction, and subordinating conjunction. For help, consult 7b through 7i.

    1   2   3
Although few people realize that coffee is drunk by more people

              4   5   6
than any other beverage, it is actually the second best-selling item of

    7   8   9
international commerce. Petroleum is the first item. People in the

                              10
United States consume 1.5 million tons of coffee beans per year.

                              11
That is more coffee than the entire world drank only fifty years ago.

12   13   14
Nevertheless, the Swedish are the world's heaviest coffee consumers.

15   16
In an average year, each Swede consumes nearly 30 pounds of coffee,

17   18   19   20   ▼   21   ▼
and this consumption is slowly rising. Therefore, if both Americans and

Swedes continue to consume coffee at this rate, coffee may

22   23 24   25
eventually equal or surpass petroleum as the largest item of

international commerce.

SENTENCE STRUCTURES

7k How is a sentence defined?

A **sentence** is defined in several ways: On a strictly mechanical level, a sentence starts with a capital letter and finishes with a period, question mark, or exclamation point. Grammatically, a sentence consists of an INDEPENDENT CLAUSE: *Skydiving is dangerous.* You might hear a sentence described as a "complete thought," but that definition is too vague to help much. From the perspective of its purpose, a sentence is defined as listed in Box 52.

⊙   **Sentences and their purposes**   52

- **A declarative sentence**
  makes a statement: Skydiving is dangerous.

- An **interrogative sentence**
  asks a question: Is skydiving dangerous?

- An **imperative sentence**
  gives a command: Be careful when you skydive.

- An **exclamatory sentence**
  expresses strong feeling: How I love skydiving!

---

71 What is a subject and a predicate in a sentence?

The **subject** and **predicate** of a sentence are its two essential parts. Without both, a group of words isn't a sentence. Box 53 shows the sentence pattern with both. Terms used in the box are defined after it.

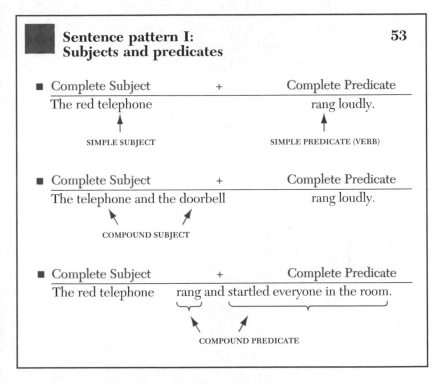

Sentence pattern I: Subjects and predicates 53

The **simple subject** is the word or group of words that acts, is described, or is acted upon.

The **telephone** rang. [Simple subject, *telephone*, acts.]

The **telephone** is red. [Simple subject, *telephone*, is described.]

The **telephone** was being connected. [Simple subject, *telephone*, is acted upon.]

The **complete subject** is the simple subject and its MODIFIERS.

The red telephone rang.

A **compound subject** consists of two or more NOUNS or PRONOUNS and their modifiers.

The telephone and the doorbell rang.

The **predicate** contains the VERB in the sentence. The predicate tells what the subject is doing or experiencing or what is being done to the subject.

The telephone **rang.** [*Rang* tells what the subject, *telephone,* did.]

The telephone **is** red. [*Is* tells what the subject, *telephone,* experiences.]

The telephone **was being connected.** [*Was being connected* tells what was being done to the subject, *telephone.*]

A **simple predicate** contains only the verb.

The lawyer **listened.**

A **complete predicate** contains the verb and its modifiers.

The lawyer **listened carefully.**

A **compound predicate** contains two or more verbs.

The lawyer **listened and waited.**

🌐 **ESL NOTES:** (1) The subject of a declarative sentence usually comes before the predicate, but there are exceptions (19e). In sentences that ask a question, part of the predicate usually comes before the subject. For more information about word order in English sentences, see Chapter 47. (2) In English, don't add a PERSONAL PRONOUN to repeat the stated noun.

> **NO** My **grandfather he** lived to be eighty-seven. [The personal pronoun, *he,* repeats the stated noun, *grandfather.*]

> **YES** My **grandfather** lived to be eighty-seven.

> **NO** **Winter storms** that bring ice, sleet, and snow **they** can cause traffic problems. [The personal pronoun, *they,* repeats the stated noun, *winter storms.*]

> **YES** **Winter storms** that bring ice, sleet, and snow can cause traffic problems. 🌐

EXERCISE 7-5

Use a slash to separate the complete subject from the complete predicate. For help, consult 7l.

EXAMPLE   The Panama Canal in Central America / provides a water route between the Atlantic and Pacific Oceans.

1. Ships sailed an extra 3,000 to 5,000 miles around South America before the construction of the Panama Canal.

2. Over 800,000 ships have traveled the 50 miles of the Panama Canal.
3. The United States built the canal and then operated it for 86 years at a cost of $3 billion.
4. The United States has collected about $2 billion from canal operations.
5. Panama was awarded total ownership of the Panama Canal by the United States on December 31, 1999.

7m What are direct and indirect objects?

A **direct object** is a noun, pronoun, or group of words acting as a noun that receives the action of a TRANSITIVE VERB (8f). To check for a direct object, make up a *whom?* or *what?* question about the verb.

An **indirect object** is a noun, pronoun, or group of words acting as a noun that tells *to whom* or *for whom* the action expressed by a transitive verb was done. To check for an indirect object, make up a **to whom?** **for whom?** **to what?** or **for what?** question about the verb.

Direct objects and indirect objects always fall in the PREDICATE of a sentence. Box 54 shows how direct and indirect objects function in sentences.

Sentence pattern II: **54**
Direct and indirect objects

- Complete Subject   +   Complete Predicate
  The caller   offered   money.
                  VERB   DIRECT OBJECT

- Complete Subject   +   Complete Predicate
  The caller   offered the lawyer money.
        VERB   INDIRECT   DIRECT
                OBJECT   OBJECT

- Complete Subject   +   Complete Predicate
  The client   sent the lawyer a retainer.
        VERB   INDIRECT   DIRECT
                OBJECT   OBJECT

🌐 **ESL NOTES:** (1) In sentences with indirect objects followed by the word *to* or *for*, put the direct object before the indirect object.

> **NO**   Please give **to John** this letter.
>
> **YES**   Please give this letter **to John.**

(2) When a pronoun is used as an indirect object, some verbs require *to* or *for* before the pronoun, and others don't.

> **NO**   Please explain **me** the rule.
>
> **YES**   Please explain the rule **to me.** [*Explain* requires *to* before an indirect object.]
>
> **NO**   Please give **to me** the letter.
>
> **YES**   Please give **me** the letter. [*Give* does not require *to* before an indirect object.]

In some sentence constructions, some verbs don't require *to* before an indirect object: *Our daughter helped our son [to] write his name.* Still, you can use *to* if you prefer, as long as you put the direct object before the indirect object.

> **YES**   Please give the letter **to me.**🌐

EXERCISE 7-6

Draw a single line under all direct objects and a double line under all indirect objects. For help, consult 7m.

EXAMPLE   Toni Morrison's award-winning novels give <u>readers</u> the <u>gifts</u> of wisdom, inspiration, and pleasure.

1. Literary critics gave high praise to Toni Morrison for her first novel, *The Bluest Eye,* but the general public showed little interest.
2. *Song of Solomon* won Morrison the National Book Critics Circle Award in 1977, and *Beloved* won her the Pulitzer Prize in 1988.
3. A literary panel awarded Toni Morrison the 1993 Nobel Prize in Literature, the highest honor a writer can receive.
4. Her 1998 novel, *Paradise,* traces for readers the tragic lives of a rejected group of former slaves.
5. Twenty-five years after *The Bluest Eye* was published, Oprah Winfrey selected it for her reader's list, and it immediately became a bestseller.

7n   What are complements, modifiers, and appositives?

7n.1 Recognizing complements

A **complement** renames or describes a SUBJECT or an OBJECT. It appears in the PREDICATE of a sentence.

A **subject complement** is a NOUN, PRONOUN, or ADJECTIVE that follows a LINKING VERB (Box 60, section 8a, page 183). **Predicate nominative** is another term for a noun used as a subject complement, and **predicate adjective** is another term for an adjective used as a subject complement.

An **object complement** follows a DIRECT OBJECT and either describes or renames the direct object. Box 55 shows how subject and object complements function in a sentence.

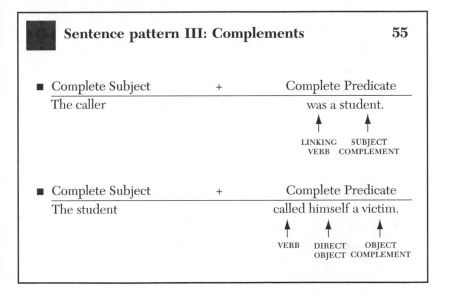

Sentence pattern III: Complements   **55**

- Complete Subject   +   Complete Predicate

  The caller   was a student.

                                    LINKING   SUBJECT
                                     VERB   COMPLEMENT

- Complete Subject   +   Complete Predicate

  The student   called himself a victim.

                                VERB   DIRECT   OBJECT
                                     OBJECT COMPLEMENT

EXERCISE 7-7

Underline all complements and identify each as a subject complement (SUB) or an object complement (OB).

EXAMPLE   The Native American Shawnee of Tennessee called their main

                  OB
       food <u>rockahominie</u>.

1. Many people know this food today as hominy.
2. Hominy is whole dried corn kernels cooked until the skins come off.
3. The process of turning dried corn into hominy is inexpensive but time-consuming.
4. In the southern United States, many people consider hominy a breakfast treat.
5. Fried patties of hominy grits, which are ground kernels rather than whole ones, taste delicious.

7n.2 Recognizing modifiers

A **modifier** is a word or group of words that describes or limits other words. Modifiers appear in the SUBJECT or the PREDICATE of a sentence.

The **large red** telephone rang. [The adjectives *large* and *red* modify the noun *telephone*.]

The lawyer answered **quickly.** [The adverb *quickly* modifies the verb *answered*.]

The person **on the telephone** was **extremely** upset. [The PREPOSITIONAL PHRASE *on the telephone* modifies the noun *person;* the adverb *extremely* modifies the adjective *upset*.]

Therefore, the lawyer spoke **gently.** [The adverb *therefore* modifies the INDEPENDENT CLAUSE *the lawyer spoke gently;* the adverb *gently* modifies the verb *spoke*.]

Because the lawyer's voice was calm, the caller felt reassured. [The ADVERB CLAUSE *because the lawyer's voice was calm* modifies the independent clause *the caller felt reassured*.]

7n.3 Recognizing appositives

An **appositive** is a word or group of words that renames the NOUN or PRONOUN preceding it.

The student's story, **a tale of broken promises,** was complicated. [The appositive *a tale of broken promises* renames the noun *story*.]

The lawyer consulted an expert, **her law professor.** [The appositive *her law professor* renames the noun *expert*.]

The student, **Joe Jones,** asked to speak to his lawyer. [The appositive *Joe Jones* renames the noun *student*.]

👁 **PUNCTUATION ALERT:** When an appositive is not essential for identifying what it renames (that is, when it is NONRESTRICTIVE), use a comma or commas to set off the appositive from the rest of the sentence; see section 24g). ●

7o What is a phrase?

A **phrase** is a group of words that does not contain both a SUBJECT and PREDICATE and therefore cannot stand alone as an independent unit.

Noun phrase

A **noun phrase** functions as a NOUN in a sentence.

The modern census dates back to the seventeenth century.

Verb phrase

A **verb phrase** functions as a VERB in a sentence.

Two military censuses **are mentioned** in the Bible.

Prepositional phrase

A **prepositional phrase** always starts with a PREPOSITION and functions as a MODIFIER.

William the Conqueror conducted a census **of landowners in newly conquered England in 1086.** [three prepositional phrases in a row, beginning with *of, in, in*]

Absolute phrase

An **absolute phrase** usually contains a noun or PRONOUN and a PRESENT or PAST PARTICIPLE. An absolute phrase modifies the entire sentence that it's in.

Censuses being the fashion, Quebec and Nova Scotia took sixteen counts between 1665 and 1754.

Eighteenth-century Sweden and Denmark had complete records of their populations, **each adult and child having been counted.**

Verbal phrase

A **verbal phrase** contains a verb part that functions not as a verb, but as a noun or an ADJECTIVE. Such cases are INFINITIVES, present participles, and past participles.

In 1624, Virginia began **to count its citizens** in a census. [*To count its citizens* is an INFINITIVE PHRASE.]

Going from door to door, census takers interview millions of people. [*Going from door to door* is a PRESENT PARTICIPIAL PHRASE.]

Amazed by some people's answers, census takers always listen carefully. [*Amazed by some people's answers* is a PAST PARTICIPIAL PHRASE.]

Gerund phrase

A **gerund phrase** functions as a noun. Telling the difference between a gerund phrase and a present participial phrase can be tricky because both use the *-ing* verb form. The key is to determine how the phrase functions in the sentence: A gerund phrase functions only as a noun, and a participial phrase functions only as a modifier.

Including each person in the census was important. [This is a gerund phrase because it functions as a noun, which is the subject of the sentence.]

Including each person in the census, Abby spent many hours on the crowded city block. [This is a present participial phrase because it functions as a modifier, namely, an adjective describing Abby.]

EXERCISE 7-8

Combine each set of sentences into a single sentence by converting one sentence into a phrase—either an absolute phrase, noun phrase, verb phrase, prepositional phrase, participial phrase, or gerund phrase. You can omit, add, or change words. Identify which type of phrase you created.

You can combine most sets in several correct ways, but make sure the meaning of your finished sentence is clear. For help, consult 7o.

EXAMPLE   Stress is an increasing burden to businesspeople. Because of this, everyone looks for ways to lessen the pressures of work.

With stress an increasing burden for businesspeople, everyone looks for ways to lessen the pressures of work. (prepositional phrase)

1. Stress levels among businesspeople are increasing. This increase is caused by companies that are cutting their expenses by downsizing.
2. Researchers have spent years studying stress in the workplace. They have developed many techniques to prevent and reduce stress.
3. Management psychologist John H. Howard began studying stress in 1971. He compiled a list of symptoms of stress and the most common causes.
4. According to Dr. Howard, uncertainty and feeling overworked are the most common causes of work-related stress. These feelings result from increasing competition in the marketplace.
5. Dr. Howard discovered simple ways to combat stress. His techniques include exercising, deep breathing, and visualizing.
6. Dr. Salvatore R. Maddi believes stress levels fall when business-people deal effectively with change. Successful businesspeople see change as a challenge, not a threat.
7. According to Dr. Maddi, businesspeople with a strong sense of commitment and control cope best with change. They cope by examining the reasons for change and focusing on self-improvement.
8. Dr. Maddi calls his technique *compensatory self-improvement.* Consciously practicing this technique can bring a renewed sense of accomplishment and self-esteem.
9. Techniques for reducing stress are valuable. They enable business-people to overcome anxiety and escape the pressures of work.
10. Feeling less stressed on the job leads to more relaxed time away from work. In this newfound personal time, businesspeople may discover new interests that lead to more enjoyable jobs.

7p What is a clause?

A **clause** is a group of words with both a SUBJECT and a PREDICATE. Clauses can be either *independent clauses,* also called *main clauses,* or *dependent clauses,* also called *subordinate clauses.*

7p.1 Recognizing independent clauses

An **independent clause** contains a subject and a predicate and can stand alone as a sentence. Box 56 shows the basic pattern.

 Sentence pattern IV: Independent clauses   **56**

Independent Clause

■ Complete Subject   +   Complete Predicate

  The telephone   rang.

7p.2 Recognizing dependent clauses

A **dependent clause** contains a subject and a predicate but cannot stand alone as a sentence. To be part of a complete sentence, a dependent clause must be joined to an independent clause (7p.1). Dependent clauses are either *adverb clauses* or *adjective clauses.*

Adverb clauses

An **adverb clause,** also called a *subordinate clause,* starts with a SUB-ORDINATING CONJUNCTION, such as *although, because, when,* or *until.* A subordinating conjunction expresses a relationship between a dependent clause and an independent clause; see Box 51 in section 7i. Adverb clauses usually answer some question about the independent clause: *How? Why? When? Under what circumstances?*

> **If the bond issue passes,** the city will install sewers. [The adverb clause modifies the verb *install;* it explains under what circumstances.]
>
> They are drawing up plans **as quickly as they can.** [The adverb clause modifies the verb *drawing up;* it explains how.]
>
> The homeowners feel happier **because they know the flooding will soon be better controlled.** [The adverb clause modifies the entire independent clause; it explains why.]

175

👁 **ALERT:** When you write an adverb clause before an independent clause, separate the clauses with a comma; see section 24b.1. ●

Adjective clauses

An **adjective clause,** also called a *relative clause,* starts with a RELATIVE PRONOUN, such as *who, which,* or *that.* Or an adjective clause can start with a RELATIVE ADVERB, such as *when* or *where.* An adjective clause modifies the NOUN or PRONOUN that it follows. Box 57 shows how adverb and adjective clauses function in sentences.

> The car **that Jack bought** is practical. [The adjective clause describes the noun *car; that* is a relative pronoun referring to *car.*]
>
> The day **when I can buy my own car** is getting closer. [The adjective clause modifies the noun *day; when* is a relative adverb referring to *day.*]

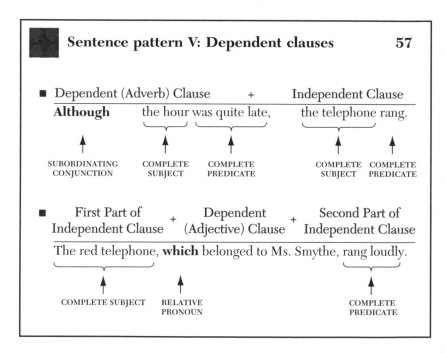

Sentence pattern V: Dependent clauses   57

■ Dependent (Adverb) Clause   +   Independent Clause

Although	the hour	was quite late,	the telephone	rang.
SUBORDINATING CONJUNCTION	COMPLETE SUBJECT	COMPLETE PREDICATE	COMPLETE SUBJECT	COMPLETE PREDICATE

■ First Part of Independent Clause + Dependent (Adjective) Clause + Second Part of Independent Clause

The red telephone,	**which**	belonged to Ms. Smythe,	rang loudly.
COMPLETE SUBJECT	RELATIVE PRONOUN		COMPLETE PREDICATE

Use *who, whom, whoever, whomever,* and *whose* when an adjective clause refers to a person or to an animal with a name.

> The Smythes, **who collect cars,** are wealthy.
>
> Their dog Bowser, **who is large and loud,** has been spoiled.

Use *which* or *that* when an adjective clause refers to a thing or to an animal that isn't a pet.

👁 **PUNCTUATION ALERT:** When an adjective clause is NONRESTRICTIVE, use *which* and set it off from the independent clause with commas. Don't use commas with *that* in a RESTRICTIVE CLAUSE; see section 9s.

My car, **which** I bought used, needs major repairs. [The adjective clause is nonrestrictive, so it begins with *which* and is set off with commas.]

The car **that** I want to buy has a CD player. [The adjective clause uses *that* and is restrictive, so it is not set off with commas.] ●

Sometimes, writers omit *that* from an adjective clause. For grammatical analysis, however, consider the omitted *that* to be implied and, therefore, present.

EXERCISE 7-9

Underline the dependent clause in each sentence, and label it an ADJ or an ADV clause. For help, consult 7p.2.

                    ADV
EXAMPLE   <u>When umbrellas were invented</u>, people used them for sun protection.

1. Eighteenth-century ladies carried fancy umbrellas as a fashion statement while strolling down the street.
2. Although umbrellas are mostly used today in the rain, they have many more uses.
3. Gentlemen in England carry sturdy umbrellas, which make convenient walking sticks.
4. One company makes a "sporting umbrella" that unfolds into a seat.
5. Marketing consultants, who receive requests for moveable advertising, suggest umbrellas can be mini-billboards when they are decorated with the company's name and logo.

Noun clauses

Noun clauses function as nouns. Noun clauses can begin with many of the same words that begin adjective clauses: *that, who, which,* and their derivatives, as well as *when, where, whether, why,* and *how.*

Promises are not always dependable. [noun]
What politicians promise is not always dependable. [noun clause]

The electorate often cannot figure out the **truth.** [noun]
The electorate often cannot know **that the truth is being manipulated.** [noun clause]

Because they start with similar words, noun clauses and adjective clauses are sometimes confused with each other. The way to tell is that the word starting an adjective clause has an ANTECEDENT, while the word starting a noun clause doesn't.

177

Good politicians understand **whom they must please.** [Noun clause; *whom* does not have an antecedent.]

Good politicians **who make promises** know all cannot be kept. [Adjective clause modifies *politicians,* which is the antecedent of *who.*]

⊕ **ESL NOTE:** Noun clauses in INDIRECT QUESTIONS are phrased as statements, not questions: *Kara asked why we needed the purple dye.* Don't phrase a noun clause this way: *Kara asked why did* [or *do*] *we need the purple dye?* If you prefer to change to a DIRECT QUESTION, usually VERB TENSE, PRONOUN, and other changes are necessary; see section 15e.⊕

Elliptical clauses

In an **elliptical clause,** one or more words are deliberately left out to make the clause more concise (Chapter 16). An elliptical clause delivers its meaning clearly only if the message of the clause makes sense without the missing words.

Engineering is one of the majors [**that**] **she considered.** [*that,* functioning as a relative pronoun, omitted from adjective clause]

She decided [**that**] **she would rather major in management.** [*that,* functioning as a conjunction, omitted between clauses]

After [**he takes**] **a refresher course,** he will be eligible for a raise. [subject and verb omitted from adverb clause]

Broiled fish tastes better **than boiled fish** [**tastes**]. [second half of the comparison omitted]

EXERCISE 7-10

Use subordinate conjunctions and relative pronouns from the list below to combine each pair of sentences. You may use the words more than once, but try to use as many different ones as possible. Some sentence pairs may be combined in several ways. Create at least one elliptical construction. For help, consult 7p.

who	that	although	because	if	when
which	after	since	even though	as	unless

EXAMPLE   The fighting in the Pacific was reaching its peak during World War II. U.S. and Japanese forces began to pick up strange radio messages.

As the Pacific fighting was reaching its peak during World War II, U.S. and Japanese forces began to pick up strange radio messages.

1. Most U.S. military personnel thought that the unintelligible messages were some strange Japanese code. The U.S. military personnel overheard the messages.

2. The Japanese were listening in. They could not understand the messages either.
3. A few members of the U.S. forces understood what the messages said. Those members of the U.S. forces were Navajo speakers.
4. The overheard messages were in a code. This code was based on the Navajo language.
5. Only Navajo Marines sent and received these messages. The Navajo Marines were specially recruited for this assignment.
6. The messages conveyed meaning by tone of voice as well as vocabulary. Decoding techniques using only written words could not break the code.
7. Were any Navajos living in Japan? The mystery of the messages was never explained.
8. Navajo is an extraordinarily complex language. The Japanese were never able to break the code.
9. The Navajo code talkers conveyed important messages. The messages affected critical battles on Saipan, Guadalcanal, and Iwo Jima.
10. The Navajos were asked to avoid publicity after the war in case the code was needed again. Ultimately, their achievement was widely recognized.

7q What are the four sentence types?

There are four **sentence types:** simple, compound, complex, and compound-complex. A **simple sentence** is composed of a single INDEPENDENT CLAUSE and no DEPENDENT CLAUSES.

Charlie Chaplin was born in London on April 16, 1889.

A **compound sentence** is composed of two or more independent clauses. These clauses may be connected by a COORDINATING CONJUNCTION (*and, but, for, or, nor, yet, so*), a semicolon alone, or a CONJUNCTIVE ADVERB.

His father died early, **and** his mother, with whom he was very close, spent time in mental hospitals.
Many people enjoy Chaplin films; others do not.
Many people enjoy Chaplin films**; however,** others do not.

A **complex sentence** is composed of one independent clause and one or more dependent clauses.

When times were bad, Chaplin lived in the streets. [dependent clause starting *when;* independent clause starting *Chaplin*]
When Chaplin was performing with a troupe that was touring the United States, he was hired by Mack Sennett, **who owned the Keystone Company.** [dependent clause starting *when;* dependent clause starting *that;* independent clause starting *he;* dependent clause starting *who*]

A **compound-complex sentence** integrates a compound sentence and a complex sentence. It contains two or more independent clauses and one or more dependent clauses.

> Chaplin's comedies were immediately successful, **and** he became rich **because of the enormous popularity of his character,** the Little Tramp, **who was famous for his tiny mustache, baggy trousers, big shoes, and trick derby.** [independent clause starting *Chaplin's;* independent clause starting *he;* dependent clause starting *because;* dependent clause starting *who*]

> **When studios could no longer afford him,** Chaplin co-founded United Artists, **and** then he produced and distributed his own films. [dependent clause starting *when;* independent clause starting *Chaplin;* independent clause starting *then*]

◉ **PUNCTUATION ALERTS:** (1) Use a comma before a coordinating conjunction connecting two independent clauses; see 24b. (2) When independent clauses are long or contain commas, use a subordinating conjunction—or use a semicolon to connect the sentences; see 25d and 25b. ●

EXERCISE 7-11

Decide whether each sentence is simple, compound, complex, or compound-complex. For help, consult 7q.

EXAMPLE   Doctors fight a constant battle against harmful bacteria.
         (*simple*)

1. When bacteria develop a resistance to an antibiotic drug, that drug can no longer fight those bacteria.
2. A simple experiment shows this resistance in action.
3. In the morning, a researcher puts a single bacterial cell into a glass dish that is known as a petri dish.
4. Bacteria multiply rapidly, so this one cell will increase to 10 million bacterial cells by midafternoon.
5. In the petri dish, these 10 million bacteria look like a heap of salt to the naked eye.
6. Then the researcher puts an antibiotic drug into the petri dish, and the drug begins killing off the bacteria.
7. The heap of bacteria disappears quickly, but a few bacteria always survive contact with the antibiotic.
8. These surviving bacteria are immune to that antibiotic, and they are very dangerous because they pass on this immunity to all their descendants.
9. The bacteria once again multiply, and in a few hours, they build up another heap that looks just like the first one.
10. This time, however, the researcher finds that the antibiotic will not kill the growing pile of bacteria in the petri dish.

8 VERBS

8a What do verbs do?

A **verb** expresses an action, an occurrence, or a state of being. Verbs also reveal when something occurs—in the present, the past, or the future. Verbs convey other information as well; see Box 58. For types of verbs, see Box 59.

Many people **overeat** on Thanksgiving. [action]
Mother's Day **fell** early this year. [occurrence]
Memorial Day **is** tomorrow. [state of being]

◉ Information that verbs convey 58

PERSON	Who or what acts or experiences an action—*first person* (the one speaking), *second person* (the one being spoken to), or *third person* (the person or thing being spoken about)
NUMBER	How many SUBJECTS act or experience an action—*singular* (one) or *plural* (more than one)
TENSE	When an action occurs—*past, present,* or *future* (see 8g–8k)
MOOD	What attitude is expressed toward the action—*indicative, imperative,* or *subjunctive* (see 8l and 8m)
VOICE	Whether the subject acts or is acted upon—*active voice* or *passive voice* (see 8n–8p)

Types of verbs 59

MAIN

A verb expressing action, occurrence, or state of being

She **talked** to the group.

LINKING

A main verb that conveys a state of being (*is*), relates to the senses (*taste*), or indicates a condition (*grow*) and that joins a subject to a word or words that rename or describe it (8a)

She **was** happy about speaking.

AUXILIARY

A verb that combines with a main verb to tell about TENSE (8g), MOOD (8l), or VOICE (8n) (also called *helping verb*)

She **has** talked to them before.

MODAL AUXILIARY

Verbs that add shades of meaning such as ability or possibility to other verbs; there are nine modals: *can, could, will, would, shall, should, may, might, must* (8e and Chapter 50)

She **might** talk to them again.

TRANSITIVE

A verb that must be followed by a DIRECT OBJECT—a NOUN or PRONOUN that completes the verb's message (8f)

She **spoke French** to them.

INTRANSITIVE

A verb that does not have a direct object completing its message (8f)

She **talked** slowly.

Linking verbs

Linking verbs are main verbs that indicate a state of being or a condition. They link a SUBJECT with one or more words that rename or describe the subject, which is called a SUBJECT COMPLEMENT. A linking verb works like an equal sign between a subject and its complement. Box 60 shows how linking verbs function in sentences.

⊙ **Linking verbs**   **60**

■ Linking verbs may be forms of the verb *be* (*am, is, was, were;* see
  section 8e for a complete list).

George Washington   **was**   president.
⌣⌣⌣⌣⌣⌣⌣⌣⌣   ⌣⌣   ⌣⌣⌣⌣⌣⌣⌣⌣⌣
SUBJECT   LINKING   COMPLEMENT (PREDICATE
                          VERB   NOMINATIVE: RENAMES SUBJECT)

■ Linking verbs may deal with the senses (*look, smell, taste, sound,*
  feel).

George Washington   **sounded**   confident.
⌣⌣⌣⌣⌣⌣⌣⌣⌣   ⌣⌣⌣⌣⌣   ⌣⌣⌣⌣⌣⌣⌣
SUBJECT   LINKING   COMPLEMENT (PREDICATE
                          VERB   ADJECTIVE: DESCRIBES SUBJECT)

■ Certain other verbs that convey a sense of existing or becoming—
  appear, seem, become, get, grow, turn, remain, stay, and *prove,*
  for example—can be linking verbs.

George Washington   **grew**   old.
⌣⌣⌣⌣⌣⌣⌣⌣⌣   ⌣⌣⌣   ⌣⌣
SUBJECT   LINKING   COMPLEMENT (PREDICATE
                          VERB   ADJECTIVE: DESCRIBES SUBJECT)

■ To test whether a verb other than a form of *be* is functioning as
  a linking verb, substitute *was* (for a singular subject) or *were*
  (for a plural subject) for the original verb. If the sentence
  makes sense, the original verb is functioning as a linking verb.

> **NO**   George Washington **grew** a beard ➤ George Washington
> **was** a beard. [*Grew* is not functioning as a linking verb.]

> **YES**   George Washington **grew** old ➤ George Washington **was**
> old. [*Grew* is functioning as a linking verb.]

VERB FORMS

8b **What are the forms of main verbs?**

A **main verb** names an action (*People* **dance**), an occurrence
(*Christmas* **comes** *once a year*), or a state of being (*It* **will be** *warm*
tomorrow). Every main verb has five forms.

- The **simple form** conveys an action, occurrence, or state of being taking place in the present (*I laugh*) or, with an AUXILIARY VERB, in the future (*I will laugh*).

- The **past-tense form** is the basis for conveying an action, occurrence, or state completed in the past (*I laughed*). REGULAR VERBS add *-ed* or *-d* to the simple form. IRREGULAR VERBS vary (see Box 61).

- The **past participle form** in regular verbs uses the same form as the past tense. Irregular verbs vary; see Box 61. To function as a verb, a past participle must combine with a SUBJECT and one or more auxiliary verbs (*I have laughed*). Otherwise, past participles function as ADJECTIVES (*crumbled cookies*).

- The **present participle form** adds *-ing* to the simple form (*laughing*). To function as a verb, a present participle combines with a subject and one or more auxiliary verbs (*I was laughing*). Otherwise, present participles function as adjectives (*my laughing friends*) or as NOUNS (*Laughing is healthy*).

- The **infinitive** usually consists of *to* and the simple form following *to* (*I started to laugh at his joke*); see 9k. The infinitive functions as a noun or an adjective, not a verb.

⊕ ESL NOTE: When verbs function as other parts of speech, they are called VERBALS (7e): INFINITIVES, PRESENT PARTICIPLES, PAST PARTICIPLES. When present participles function as nouns, they're called GERUNDS (7o). For information about using gerunds and infinitives as OBJECTS after certain verbs, see Chapter 49.⊕

8c What are the *-s* forms of verbs?

The **-s form of a verb** is the third-person singular in the PRESENT TENSE. The ending *-s* (or *-es*) is added to the verb's SIMPLE FORM (*smell* becomes *smells*, as in *The bread smells delicious*).

Be and *have* are irregular verbs. For the third-person singular, present tense, *be* uses *is* and *have* uses *has*.

The cheesecake **is** popular.

The éclair **has** chocolate icing.

If you tend to drop the *-s* or *-es* ending when you speak, always use it when you write. Proofread carefully to make sure you've not omitted any *-s* forms.

◎ ALERT: In informal speech, the LINKING, or *copula*, VERB *to be* sometimes doesn't change forms in the present tense. However, ACADEMIC WRITING requires you to use standard third-person singular forms in the present tense.

He **is** (not *be*) hungry.

The bakery **has** (not *have*) fresh bread. ●

EXERCISE 8-1

Rewrite each sentence, changing the subject to the word or words given in parentheses. Change the form of the verb shown in italics to match this new subject. Keep all sentences in the present tense.

EXAMPLE   The song of a bird *represents* different things to different
listeners. (The songs of birds)

The songs of birds represent different things to different
listeners.

1. A poet *imagines* a songbird as a fellow poet creating beautiful art.
(Poets)
2. To a biologist, however, singing birds *communicate* practical
information. (a singing bird)
3. A male sparrow that *whistles* one melody to attract a mate *sings* a
different tune to warn off other male sparrows. (Male sparrows)
4. Female redwing blackbirds usually *distinguish* a male redwing's song
from a mockingbird's imitation, but a male redwing almost never *hears*
the difference. (A female redwing blackbird) (male redwings)
5. Nevertheless, in experiments, female birds *are* sometimes fooled by a
carved wooden male and a recorded mating song. (a female bird)

8d What is the difference between regular and irregular verbs?

A **regular verb** forms its PAST TENSE and PAST PARTICIPLE by adding *-ed* or *-d* to the SIMPLE FORM: *type, typed; cook, cooked; work, worked.* Most verbs in English are regular.

In informal speech, some people skip over the *-ed* sound, pronouncing it softly or not at all. In ACADEMIC WRITING, however, you are required to use it. If you're not used to hearing or pronouncing this sound, proofread carefully to see that you have all needed *-ed* endings in your writing.

> **NO**   The cake was **suppose** to be tasty.
>
> **YES**   The cake was **supposed** to be tasty.

Irregular verbs, in contrast, do not consistently add *-ed* or *-d* to form the past tense and past participle. Some irregular verbs change an internal vowel to make past tense and past participle: *sing, sang, sung.* Some change an internal vowel and add an ending other than *-ed* or *-d*: *grow, grew, grown.* Some use the simple form throughout: *cost, cost,*

cost. Unfortunately, a verb's simple form doesn't provide a clue about whether the verb is irregular or regular.

Although you can always look up the principal parts of any verb, memorizing any you don't know solidly is much more efficient in the long run. About two hundred verbs in English are irregular. Box 61 lists the most frequently used irregular verbs.

◎ Common irregular verbs   **61**

SIMPLE FORM	PAST TENSE	PAST PARTICIPLE
arise	arose	arisen
awake	awoke *or* awaked	awaked *or* awoken
be (is, am, are)	was, were	been
bear	bore	borne *or* born
beat	beat	beaten
become	became	become
begin	began	begun
bend	bent	bent
bet	bet	bet
bid ("to offer")	bid	bid
bid ("to command")	bade	bidden
bind	bound	bound
bite	bit	bitten *or* bit
blow	blew	blown
break	broke	broken
bring	brought	brought
build	built	built
burst	burst	burst
buy	bought	bought
cast	cast	cast
catch	caught	caught
choose	chose	chosen
cling	clung	clung
come	came	come
cost	cost	cost
creep	crept	crept
cut	cut	cut
deal	dealt	dealt
dig	dug	dug
dive	dived *or* dove	dived
do	did	done

→

Common irregular verbs *(continued)* 61

SIMPLE FORM	PAST TENSE	PAST PARTICIPLE
draw	drew	drawn
drink	drank	drunk
drive	drove	driven
eat	ate	eaten
fall	fell	fallen
feed	fed	fed
feel	felt	felt
fight	fought	fought
find	found	found
flee	fled	fled
fling	flung	flung
fly	flew	flown
forbid	forbade *or* forbad	forbidden
forget	forgot	forgotten *or* forgot
forgive	forgave	forgiven
forsake	forsook	forsaken
freeze	froze	frozen
get	got	got *or* gotten
give	gave	given
go	went	gone
grow	grew	grown
hang ("to suspend")*	hung	hung
have	had	had
hear	heard	heard
hide	hid	hidden
hit	hit	hit
hurt	hurt	hurt
keep	kept	kept
know	knew	known
lay	laid	laid
lead	led	led
leave	left	left
lend	lent	lent
let	let	let
lie	lay	lain
light	lighted *or* lit	lighted *or* lit
lose	lost	lost
make	made	made

* When it means "to execute by hanging," *hang* is a regular verb: *In wartime, some armies routinely **hanged** deserters.*

→

Common irregular verbs *(continued)*   61

SIMPLE FORM	PAST TENSE	PAST PARTICIPLE
mean	meant	meant
pay	paid	paid
prove	proved	proved *or* proven
quit	quit	quit
read	read	read
rid	rid	rid
ride	rode	ridden
ring	rang	rung
rise	rose	risen
run	ran	run
say	said	said
see	saw	seen
seek	sought	sought
send	sent	sent
set	set	set
shake	shook	shaken
shine ("to glow")*	shone	shone
shoot	shot	shot
show	showed	shown *or* showed
shrink	shrank	shrunk
sing	sang	sung
sink	sank *or* sunk	sunk
sit	sat	sat
slay	slew	slain
sleep	slept	slept
sling	slung	slung
speak	spoke	spoken
spend	spent	spent
spin	spun	spun
spring	sprang *or* sprung	sprung
stand	stood	stood
steal	stole	stolen
sting	stung	stung
stink	stank *or* stunk	stunk
stride	strode	stridden
strike	struck	struck
strive	strove	striven
swear	swore	sworn

* When it means "to polish," *shine* is a regular verb: We **shined** our shoes.

→

Common irregular verbs *(continued)*   61

SIMPLE FORM	PAST TENSE	PAST PARTICIPLE
sweep	swept	swept
swim	swam	swum
swing	swung	swung
take	took	taken
teach	taught	taught
tear	tore	torn
tell	told	told
think	thought	thought
throw	threw	thrown
understand	understood	understood
wake	woke *or* waked	waked *or* woken
wear	wore	worn
wring	wrung	wrung
write	wrote	written

SPELLING ALERT: For information about *y* being changed to an *i*, or about whether to double a final consonant before adding the *-ed* ending, see 22c. ●

EXERCISE 8-2

Write the correct past-tense form of the regular verbs given in parentheses. For help, consult 8d.

EXAMPLE Psychologists often (wonder) <u>wondered</u> about the saying that people's emotions are contagious.

(1) Researchers (report) _____ that people looking at pictures of smiling or angry faces unconsciously (imitate) _____ the same expressions. (2) The subjects who (display) _____ these facial expressions (experience) _____ the feelings that go with them. (3) People who (copy) _____ each other's gestures when talking also (transmit) _____ emotions to one another. (4) The researchers (describe) _____ the entire process in medical terms. (5) According to the researchers, the people in the study ("catch") _____ an "emotional virus," which (seem) _____ to make it easier for them to get along.

EXERCISE 8-3

Write the correct past-tense form of the irregular verbs given in parentheses. For help, consult Box 61 in 8d.

EXAMPLE   Ben Johnson (think) <u>thought</u> as he (speak) <u>spoke</u> to prison
                    inmates that his story might help them.

    (1) At age 33, Ben Johnson (become) _____ the youngest chief of
pediatric neurosurgery in the United States at one of the top hospitals, Baltimore's Johns Hopkins. (2) This accomplishment seemed
impossible for a young African American youth who (grow) _____ up
in run-down apartments in Boston and Detroit. (3) In fifth grade, he
(get) _____ Fs and Ds on his report card. (4) His mother, with only a
third-grade education herself, (teach) _____ Ben to care about his education. (5) Ben and his older brother, Curtis, (write) _____ two book
reports each week and watched no more than three TV shows a week.
(6) By seventh grade, Ben (be) _____ at the top of his class at Wilson
Junior High. (7) However, excelling in an interracial sports center
(come) _____ with problems. (8) His most humiliating experience
(begin) _____ when Ben (win) _____ the Outstanding Athlete award,
and his white coach (make) _____ insulting comments to Ben's white
teammates because they had let a black athlete (beat) _____ them.
(9) Also, Ben had a terrible temper and (break) _____ a classmate's
nose with a rock and (cut) _____ another with a padlock. (10) The
turning point for Ben (come) _____ when he (be) _____ fourteen and
(draw) _____ a knife on a friend. (11) Fortunately, the friend's belt
buckle (keep) _____ the knife from entering his stomach. (12) Ben
(run) _____ home horrified and (spend) _____ several hours alone
thinking. (13) This experience changed him because he now (know)
_____ that if people could make him angry they could control him.
(14) He (swear) _____ never to give anyone else power over his life.

8e What are auxiliary verbs?

    Auxiliary verbs, also called *helping verbs,* combine with MAIN VERBS
to make VERB PHRASES. Box 62 shows how auxiliary verbs work.

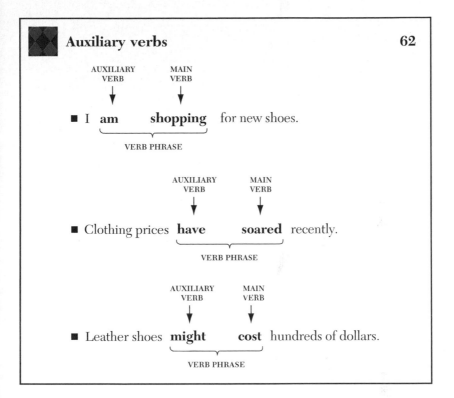

Auxiliary verbs   62

AUXILIARY VERB   MAIN VERB

■ I **am shopping** for new shoes.

VERB PHRASE

AUXILIARY VERB   MAIN VERB

■ Clothing prices **have soared** recently.

VERB PHRASE

AUXILIARY VERB   MAIN VERB

■ Leather shoes **might cost** hundreds of dollars.

VERB PHRASE

be, do, have

The three most common auxiliary verbs are *be, do,* and *have.* These three verbs can also be main verbs. Their forms vary more than most irregular verbs, as Boxes 63 and 64 show.

Forms of the verb *be*   63

SIMPLE FORM	be
-s FORM	is
PAST TENSE	was, were
PRESENT PARTICIPLE	being
PAST PARTICIPLE	been

→

191

Forms of the verb *be* (continued)   63

Person	Present Tense	Past Tense
I	am	was
you (singular)	are	were
he, she, it	is	was
we	are	were
you (plural)	are	were
they	are	were

◉ Forms of the verbs *do* and *have*   64

SIMPLE FORM	do	have
PAST TENSE	did	had
PAST PARTICIPLE	done	had
-s FORM	does	has
PRESENT PARTICIPLE	doing	having

👁 **ALERT:** In ACADEMIC WRITING, always use the standard forms for *be, do,* and *have,* as shown in Boxes 63 and 64.

The gym **is** [not *be*] a busy place.

The gym **is** [not *be*] filling with spectators. ●

🌐 **ESL NOTE:** When *be, do,* and *have* function as auxiliary verbs, change their form to agree with a third-person singular subject—and don't add *-s* to the main verb.

   NO   **Does** the library **closes** at 6:00?

   YES   **Does** the library **close** at 6:00? 🌐

Modal auxiliary verbs

Can, could, shall, should, will, would, may, might, and *must* are the nine modal auxiliary verbs. **Modal auxiliary verbs** communicate ability, permission, obligation, advisability, necessity, or possibility. They never change form.

Exercise **can lengthen** lives. [possibility]
She **can jog** for five miles. [ability]
The exercise **must occur** regularly. [necessity, obligation]
People **should protect** their bodies. [advisability]
May I exercise? [permission]

🌐 **ESL NOTE:** For more about modal auxiliary verbs and the meanings they communicate, see Chapter 50. 🌐

EXERCISE 8-4

Using the auxiliary verbs in the list below, fill in the blanks. Use each auxiliary verb only once, even though some would be a correct answer in more than one sentence. For help, consult section 8e.

are   may   should   can   has   do

EXAMPLE   It ~~may~~ come as a surprise to discover that perfumes, hair sprays, and smelly soaps attract bears.

(1) Many people who camp in the wild know that the smell of food _____ often brought a hungry bear to a campsite. (2) Fewer people realize that curious bears _____ sometimes attracted to campsites that smell of perfume, hair spray, or soap. (3) Therefore, if you go camping in the woods or the mountains, you _____ avoid smelly cosmetics and put away all your food and garbage. (4) If you ever _____ meet a bear in the wild, stay calm and do not try to protect your food. (5) Talking to the animal in a quiet voice while backing off slowly is a better strategy than running away, because an excited bear _____ run as fast as a racehorse.

8f What are intransitive and transitive verbs?

A verb is **intransitive** when an OBJECT is not required to complete its meaning: *I sing.* A verb is **transitive** when an object is necessary to complete its meaning: *I need a guitar.* Many verbs have both transitive and intransitive meanings. Some verbs are transitive only: *need, have, like, owe, remember.* Only transitive verbs function in the PASSIVE VOICE. Dictionaries label verbs as transitive *(vt)* or intransitive *(vi)*. Box 65 shows how transitive and intransitive verbs operate in sentences.

Comparison of intransitive and transitive verbs 65

INTRANSITIVE (OBJECT NOT NEEDED)

They **sat** together quietly. [*Together* and *quietly* are not DIRECT OBJECTS; they are MODIFIERS.]

The cat **sees** in the dark. [*In the dark* is not a direct object; it is a modifier.]

I can **hear** well. [*Well* is not a direct object; it is a modifier.]

TRANSITIVE (OBJECT NEEDED)

They **sent** a birthday card to me. [*Birthday card* is a direct object.]

The cat **sees** the dog. [*Dog* is a direct object.]

I can **hear** you. [*You* is a direct object.]

The verbs *lie* and *lay* are particularly confusing. *Lie* means "to recline, to place oneself down, or to remain." *Lie* is intransitive (it cannot be followed by an object). *Lay* means "to put something down." *Lay* is transitive (it must be followed by an object). As you can see in Box 66, the word *lay* is both the past tense of *lie* and the present-tense simple form of *lay*. That makes things difficult. My best advice is memorize them. Yet truthfully, each time I use *lie* and *lay*, I need to pause, think, and recite the list to myself.

 Using *lie* and *lay* 66

	lie	lay
SIMPLE FORM	lie	lay
PAST TENSE	lay	laid
PAST PARTICIPLE	lain	laid
-*s* FORM	lies	lays
PRESENT PARTICIPLE	lying	laying

Intransitive Forms

PRESENT TENSE	The hikers **lie** down to rest.
PAST TENSE	The hikers **lay** down to rest.

→

Using *lie* and *lay* (continued) 66

Transitive Forms

PRESENT TENSE The hikers **lay** their backpacks on a rock.
[*Backpacks* is a direct object.]

PAST TENSE The hikers **laid** their backpacks on a rock.
[*Backpacks* is a direct object.]

Two other verb pairs tend to confuse people because of their intransitive and transitive forms: *raise* and *rise* and *set* and *sit*.

Raise and *set* are transitive (they must be followed by an object). *Rise* and *sit* are intransitive (they cannot be followed by an object). Fortunately, although each word has a meaning different from the other words, they don't share any forms: *raise, raised, raised; rise, rose, risen;* and *set, set, set; sit, sat, sat.*

EXERCISE 8-5

Underline the correct word of each pair in parentheses. For help, consult 8f.

EXAMPLE Whenever I come home, I always check to see where my cat is (laying, lying).

(1) Coming home from jogging one morning, I (laid, lay) my keys on the counter and saw my cat, Andy, (laying, lying) in a patch of sunlight on the living room floor. (2) When I (sat, set) down beside him, he (raised, rose) up on his toes, stretched, and then (laid, lay) down a few feet away. (3) (Sitting, Setting) there, I reached out to Andy, and my contrary cat jumped up onto the couch. As he landed, I heard a clinking noise. (4) I (raised, rose) the bottom of the slipcover, and there (laid, lay) my favorite earrings, the ones I thought I had lost last week. Deciding he had earned a special privilege, Andy curled up on a red silk pillow in the corner of the couch. (5) Since the earrings now (laid, lay) safely in my pocket, I let him (lay, lie) there undisturbed.

VERB TENSE

8g What is verb tense?

Verb tense conveys time. Verbs show tense (time) by changing form. English has six verb tenses, divided into *simple* and *perfect* groups. The three **simple tenses** divide time into present, past, and future. The **present simple tense** describes what happens regularly, what takes place in the present, and what is consistently or generally true. The **past simple tense** tells of an action completed or a condition ended. The **future simple tense** indicates action yet to be taken or a condition not yet experienced.

Rick **wants** to speak Spanish fluently. [present simple tense]

Rick **wanted** to improve rapidly. [past simple tense]

Rick **will want** to progress even further next year. [future simple tense]

The three **perfect tenses** also divide time into present, past, and future. They show more complex time relationships than the simple tenses. For information on using the perfect tenses, see section 8i.

The three simple tenses and the three perfect tenses also have **progressive forms.** These forms indicate that whatever the verb describes is ongoing or continuing. For information on using progressive forms, see section 8j. Box 67 summarizes verb tenses and progressive forms.

⊙ **Summary of tenses: Simple, perfect,   67
   and progressive**

Simple Tenses

	REGULAR VERB	IRREGULAR VERB	PROGRESSIVE FORM
PRESENT	I talk	I eat	I am talking; I am eating
PAST	I talked	I ate	I was talking; I was eating
FUTURE	I will talk	I will eat	I will be talking; I will be eating

Perfect Tenses

	REGULAR VERB	IRREGULAR VERB	PROGRESSIVE FORM
PRESENT PERFECT	I have talked	I have eaten	I have been talking; I have been eating
PAST PERFECT	I had talked	I had eaten	I had been talking; I had been eating
FUTURE PERFECT	I will have talked	I will have eaten	I will have been talking; I will have been eating

🌐 **ESL NOTE:** Box 67 shows that most verb tenses are formed by combining one or more AUXILIARY VERBS with the SIMPLE FORM, the PRESENT PARTICIPLE, or the PAST PARTICIPLE of a MAIN VERB. Auxiliary verbs are necessary in the formation of most tenses, so be sure not to omit them.

NO   I **talking** to you.

YES   I **am talking** to you. 🌐

8h How do I use the simple present tense?

The **simple present tense** uses the SIMPLE FORM of the verb (see 8b). It describes what happens regularly, what takes place in the present, and what is generally or consistently true. Also, it can convey a future occurrence with verbs like *start, stop, begin, end, arrive,* and *depart.*

Calculus class **meets** every morning. [regularly occurring action]

Mastering calculus **takes** time. [general truth]

The course **ends** in eight weeks. [specific future event]

👁 **VERB ALERT FOR LITERATURE:** To describe or discuss the action in a work of literature, always use the present tense. This holds true no matter how old the work.

In Shakespeare's *Romeo and Juliet,* Juliet's father **wants** her to marry Paris, but Juliet **loves** Romeo. ●

8i How do I form and use the perfect tenses?

The **perfect tenses** generally describe actions or occurrences that are still having an effect at the time or are having an effect until a specified time. The perfect tenses are composed of an AUXILIARY VERB and a main verb's PAST PARTICIPLE (see 8b).

For the **present perfect tense** (see Box 67), use *has* only for the THIRD-PERSON SINGULAR and *have* for all other subjects. For the **past perfect,** use *had* with the past participle. For the **future perfect,** use *will have* with the past participle.

PRESENT PERFECT	Our government **has offered** to help. [having effect now]
PRESENT PERFECT	The drought **has created** terrible hardship. [having effect until a specified time—when the rains come]
PAST PERFECT	As soon as the tornado **had passed,** the heavy rain started. [Both events occurred in the past; the tornado occurred before the rain, so the earlier event uses *had.*]
FUTURE PERFECT	Our chickens' egg production **will have reached** five hundred per day by next year. [The event will occur before a specified time.]

197

8j How do I form and use progressive forms?

Progressive forms describe an ongoing action or condition. They also express habitual or recurring actions or conditions. The **present progressive** uses the present-tense form of *be* that agrees with the subject in PERSON and NUMBER, plus the *-ing* form (PRESENT PARTICIPLE) of the main verb. The **past progressive** uses *was* or *were* to agree with the subject in person and number, plus the present participle of the main verb. The **future progressive** uses *will be* plus the present participle. The **present perfect progressive** uses *have been* or *has been* to agree with the subject, plus the *-ing* form of the main verb. The **past perfect progressive** uses *had been* and the *-ing* form of the main verb. The **future perfect progressive** uses *will have been* plus the PRESENT PARTICIPLE (see 8b).

PRESENT PROGRESSIVE	The smog **is stinging** everyone's eyes. [event taking place now]
PAST PROGRESSIVE	Eye drops **were selling** well last week. [event ongoing in the past within stated limits]
FUTURE PROGRESSIVE	We **will be ordering** more eye drops than usual this month. [recurring event that will take place in the future]
PRESENT PERFECT PROGRESSIVE	Scientists **have been warning** us about air pollution for years. [recurring event that took place in the past and may still take place]
PAST PERFECT PROGRESSIVE	We **had been ordering** three cases of eye drops a month until the smog worsened. [recurring past event that has now ended]
FUTURE PERFECT PROGRESSIVE	By May, we **will have been selling** eye drops for eight months. [ongoing condition to be completed at a specific time in the future]

EXERCISE 8-6

Underline the correct verb in each pair of parentheses. If more than one answer is possible, be prepared to explain the differences in meaning between the choices. For help, consult 8g through 8j.

EXAMPLE   Every eleven years planet Earth (<u>experiences</u>, will be experiencing) a dramatic attack.

1. A huge magnetic force, called a "solar maximum," (is racing, races) every eleven years from the sun toward the earth at two million miles per hour.

2. The magnetic force (is, was) 30 times more concentrated than the normal force that (will reach, reaches) the earth.

3. A less violent "solar wind," of one million miles per hour, (hits, will have hit) the earth now and then between the solar maximums.

4. While these occurrences (had, were having) little effect in previous years, advances in technology today (had made, have made) us vulnerable to the sun's shifting winds.

5. Since 1996, solar winds occasionally (had been wiping, have wiped) out cell phones, pagers, and pay-at-the-pump gasoline services.

6. A solar maximum suddenly (knocked, was knocking) out electrical power to six million people in the U.S. Northeast in 1989.

7. Such communication disruptions (cost, have been costing) over $100 million a year in repairs and lost business, which (affects, has affected) government offices, private companies, and individual citizens.

8. Fortunately, no astronaut (has been orbiting, orbited) the earth when a solar wind (will be occurring, has occurred).

9. Currently, government space scientists (are collecting, will be collecting) data and soon (are evaluating, will evaluate) the effects of solar maximums on satellites, airplanes, power lines, oil and gas pipelines, and spacecraft.

10. Space experts at NASA, the National Aeronautics and Space Administration, (hope, were hoping) the new "Living with a Star" program (will be telling, will tell) them how the next solar maximum in 2011 (will affect, was affecting) us.

8k How do I use tense sequences accurately?

Verb **tense sequences** show time relationships correctly. They help you deliver messages about actions, occurrences, or states that take place at different times. Box 68 shows how tense in the same sentence can vary depending on when actions (or occurrences or states) occur.

◉ **Summary of tense sequences**   **68**

■ If your independent clause contains a simple-present-tense verb, then in your dependent clause, you can

• Use PRESENT TENSE to show same-time action:

  The director **says** that the movie **is** a tribute to Chaplin.
  I **avoid** shellfish because I **am** allergic to it.

• Use PAST TENSE to show earlier action:

  I **am** sure that I **deposited** the check.
                                                                    →

Summary of tense sequences *(continued)* 68

- Use the PRESENT PERFECT TENSE to show (1) a period of time extending from some point in the past to the present or (2) an indefinite past time:

    They **say** that they **have lived** in Canada since 1979.
    I **believe** that I **have seen** that movie before.

- Use the FUTURE TENSE for action to come:

    The book **is** open because I **will be reading** it later.

■ If your independent clause contains a past-tense verb, then in your dependent clause you can

- Use the PAST PERFECT TENSE to show earlier action:

    The sprinter **knew** that she **had broken** the record.

- Use the present tense to state a general truth:

    Christopher Columbus **discovered** that the world is round.

■ If your independent clause contains a present-perfect or past-perfect-tense verb, then in your dependent clause you can

- Use the past tense:

    The bread **has become** moldy since I **purchased** it.
    Sugar prices **had** already **declined** when artificial sweeteners first **appeared.**

■ If your independent clause contains a future-tense verb, then in your dependent clause you can

- Use the present tense to show action happening at the same time:

    You **will be** rich if you **win** the prize.

- Use the past tense to show earlier action:

    You **will** surely **win** the prize if you **remembered** to mail the entry form.

- Use the present perfect tense to show future action earlier than the action of the independent-clause verb:

    The river **will flood** again next year unless we **have built** a better dam by then.

→

Summary of tense sequences *(continued)* 68

- If your independent clause contains a future-perfect tense verb, then in your dependent clause verb you can

  - Use either the present tense or the present perfect tense:

    Dr. Chang **will have delivered** five thousand babies by the time she **retires.**

    Dr. Chang **will have delivered** five thousand babies by the time she **has retired.**

👁 **ALERT:** Don't use a future-tense verb in a dependent clause when the verb in the independent clause is in the future tense. Use a present-tense verb in the independent clause.

NO The river **will flood** us unless we **will prepare** our defense.

YES The river **will flood** us unless we **prepare** our defense. [Prepare is a present-tense verb.]

YES The river **will flood** us unless we **have prepared** our defense. [*Have prepared* is a present perfect verb.]●

Also, tense sequences may include INFINITIVES and PARTICIPLES. To name or describe an activity or occurrence coming either at the same time or after the time expressed in the MAIN VERB, use the **present infinitive.**

I **hope to buy** a used car. [*To buy* comes at a future time. *Hope* is the main verb, and its action is now.]

I **hoped to buy** a used car. [*Hoped* is the main verb, and its action is over.]

I **had hoped to buy** a used car. [*Had hoped* is the main verb, and its action is over.]

The PRESENT PARTICIPLE (a verb's *-ing* form) can describe action happening at the same time.

Driving his new car, the man **smiled.** [The driving and the smiling happened at the same time.]

To describe an action that occurs before the action in the main verb, use the **perfect infinitive** (*to have gone, to have smiled*), the PAST PARTICIPLE, or the **present perfect participle** (*having gone, having smiled*).

201

Candida **claimed to have written** fifty short stories in college.
[*Claimed* is the main verb, and *to have written* happened first.]

Pleased with the short story, Candida **mailed** it to several magazines.
[*Mailed* is the main verb, and *pleased* happened first.]

Having sold one short story, Candida **invested** in a computer.
[*Invested* is the main verb, and *having sold* happened first.]

EXERCISE 8-7

Underline the correct verb in each pair of parentheses that best suits the sequence of tenses. Be ready to explain your choices. For help, consult 8k.

EXAMPLE When he (is, was) seven years old, Yo-Yo Ma, possibly the world's greatest living cellist, (moves, moved) to the United States with his family.

1. Yo-Yo Ma, who (had been born, was born) in France to Chinese parents, (lived, lives) in Boston, Massachusetts, today and (toured, tours) as one of the world's greatest cellists.

2. Years from now, after Mr. Ma has given his last concert, music lovers still (treasure, will treasure) his many fine recordings.

3. Mr. Ma's older sister, Dr. Yeou-Cheng Ma, was nearly the person with the concert career. She had been training to become a concert violinist until her brother's musical genius (began, had begun) to be noticed.

4. Even though Dr. Ma eventually (becomes, became) a physician, she still (had been playing, plays) the violin.

5. The family interest in music (continues, was continuing), for Mr. Ma's children (take, had taken) piano lessons.

6. Although most people today (knew, know) Mr. Ma as a brilliant cellist, he (was making, has made) films as well.

7. One year, while he (had been traveling, was traveling) in the Kalahari Desert, he (films, filmed) dances of southern Africa's Bush people.

8. Mr. Ma first (becomes, became) interested in the Kalahari people when he (had studied, studied) anthropology as an undergraduate at Harvard University.

9. When he shows visitors around Boston now, Mr. Ma has been known to point out the Harvard University library where, he claims, he (fell asleep, was falling asleep) in the stacks when he (had been, was) a student.

10. Indicating another building, Mr. Ma admits that in one of its classrooms he almost (failed, had failed) German.

MOOD

8l What is mood in verbs?

Mood in verbs conveys an attitude toward the action in a sentence. English has three moods: *indicative, imperative,* and *subjunctive.* Use the **indicative mood** to make statements about real things, about highly likely things, and for questions about fact.

INDICATIVE   The door to the tutoring center opened. [real]

She seemed to be looking for someone. [highly likely]

Do you want to see a tutor? [question about a fact]

The **imperative mood** expresses commands and direct requests. Often the subject is omitted in an imperative sentence, but nevertheless the subject is implied to be either *you* or one of the indefinite pronouns such as *anybody, somebody,* or *everybody.*

👁 **PUNCTUATION ALERT:** Use an exclamation point after a strong command; use a period after a mild command or a request (23e, 23a).

IMPERATIVE   Please shut the door.

Watch out! That screw is loose. ●

The **subjunctive mood** expresses speculation, other unreal conditions, conjectures, wishes, recommendations, indirect requests, and demands. The words that often signal the subjunctive mood are *if, as if, as though,* and *unless.* In speaking, subjunctive verb forms were once used frequently in English, but they're heard far less today. Nevertheless, in ACADEMIC WRITING, you need to use the subjunctive mood.

SUBJUNCTIVE   If **I were** you, I would ask for a tutor.

8m What are correct subjunctive forms?

For the **present subjunctive,** always use the SIMPLE FORM of the verb for all PERSONS and NUMBERS.

The prosecutor asks that she **testify** [not *testifies*] again.

It is important that they **be** [not *are*] allowed to testify.

For the **past subjunctive,** use the simple past tense: *I wish that I **had** a car.* The one exception is for the past subjunctive of *be:* Use *were* for all forms.

I wish that I **were** [not *was*] leaving on vacation today.

They asked if she **were** [not *was*] leaving on vacation today.

8m.1 Using the subjunctive in *if, as if, as though,* and *unless* clauses

In dependent clauses introduced by *if* and sometimes by *unless,* the subjunctive describes speculations or conditions contrary to fact.

> If it **were** [not *was*] to rain, attendance at the race would be disappointing. [speculation]
>
> The runner looked as if he **were** [not was] winded, but he said he wasn't. [a condition contrary to fact]

In an *unless* clause, the subjunctive signals that what the clause says is highly unlikely.

> Unless rain **were** [not was] to create floods, the race will be held this Sunday. [Floods are highly unlikely.]

Not every clause introduced by *if, unless, as if,* or *as though* requires the subjunctive. Use the subjunctive only when the dependent clause describes speculation or a condition contrary to fact.

> INDICATIVE   If she **is** going to leave late, I will drive her to the race. [Her leaving late is highly likely.]
>
> SUBJUNCTIVE   If she **were** going to leave late, I would drive her to the race. [Her leaving late is a speculation.]

8m.2 Using the subjunctive in *that* clauses for wishes, indirect requests, demands, and recommendations

When *that* clauses describe wishes, requests, demands, or recommendations, the subjunctive can convey the message.

> I wish that this race **were** [not *was*] over. [a wish about something happening now]
>
> He wishes that he **had seen** [not *saw*] the race. [a wish about something that is past]
>
> The judges are demanding that the doctor **examine** [not *examines*] the runners. [a demand for something to happen in the future]

Also, MODAL AUXILIARY VERBS *would, could, might,* and *should* can convey speculations and conditions contrary to fact.

> If the runner **were** [not *was*] faster, we **would** see a better race. [*Would* is a modal auxiliary verb.]

The issue here is that when an INDEPENDENT CLAUSE expresses a conditional statement using a modal auxiliary verb, you want to be sure that in the DEPENDENT CLAUSE, you don't use another modal auxiliary verb.

NO   If I **would have trained** for the race, I **might have** won.

YES   If I **had trained** for the race, I **might have** won.

EXERCISE 8-8

Fill in the blanks with the form of the verb given in parentheses. For help, consult 8l to 8m.

EXAMPLE   Imagining the possibility of brain transplants requires that we (to be) <u>be</u> open-minded.

(1) If almost any organ other than the brain (to be) _____ the candidate for a swap, we would probably give our consent. (2) If the brain (to be) _____ to hold whatever impulses form our personalities, few people would want to risk a transplant. (3) Many popular movies have asked that we (to suspend) _____ disbelief and imagine the consequences should a personality actually (to be) _____ transferred to another body. (4) In real life, however, the complexities of a successful brain transplant require that not-yet-developed surgical techniques (to be) _____ used. (5) For example, it would be essential that during the actual transplant each one of the 500 trillion nerve connections within the brain (to continue) _____ to function as though the brain (to be) _____ lying undisturbed in a living human body.

VOICE

8n What is voice in verbs?

Voice in a verb tells whether a SUBJECT acts or is acted upon. English has two voices: *active and passive*. A subject in the **active voice** performs the action.

Most clams **live** in salt water. [The subject *clams* does the acting: Clams *live*.]

They **burrow** into the sandy bottoms of shallow waters. [The subject *they* does the acting: They *burrow*.]

A subject in the **passive voice** is acted upon. The person or thing doing the acting often appears in a PHRASE that starts with *by*. Verbs in the passive voice use forms of *be, have,* and *will* as AUXILIARY VERBS with the PAST PARTICIPLE of the MAIN VERB.

Clams **are considered** a delicacy by many people. [The subject *clams* is acted upon *by many people*.]

Some types of clams **are** highly **valued** by seashell collectors. [The subject *types* is acted upon *by seashell collectors*.]

8o How do I write in the active, not passive, voice?

Because the ACTIVE VOICE emphasizes the doer of an action, active constructions are more direct and dramatic. Active constructions usually require fewer words than passive constructions, which makes for greater conciseness (see 16c). Most sentences in the PASSIVE VOICE can be converted to active voice.

PASSIVE African tribal masks are often imitated by Western sculptors.

ACTIVE Western sculptors often imitate African tribal masks.

8p What are proper uses of the passive voice?

Although the active voice is usually best, in special circumstances you need to use the passive voice.

8p.1 Using passive voice when the doer of the action is unknown or unimportant

When no one knows who or what did something or when the doer of an action isn't important, writers use the passive voice.

The lock **was broken** sometime after four o'clock. [Who broke the lock is unknown.]

In 1899, the year I was born, a peace conference **was held** at The Hague. [The doers of the action—holders of the conference—aren't important.]

—E. B. White, "Unity"

8p.2 Using passive voice to focus on the action, not the doer of the action

Sometimes the action in the sentence is more important than the doer of the action. For example, if you want to focus on historical discoveries in a narrative, use the passive voice. Conversely, if you want to emphasize the people making the discoveries, use the active voice.

ACTIVE **Joseph Priestley discovered** oxygen in 1774. [*Joseph Priestley* is the subject.]

PASSIVE **Oxygen was discovered** in 1774 by Joseph Priestley. [*Oxygen* is the subject.]

ACTIVE **The postal clerk sent** the unsigned letter before I could retrieve it from the mailroom. [The emphasis is on the person, *the postal clerk,* rather than the action, *sent.*]

PASSIVE The unsigned letter **was sent** before it **could be retrieved** from the postal clerk. [The emphasis is on the events, *was sent* and *could be retrieved,* not on the doer of the action, the unknown sender and *the postal clerk.*]

8p.3 Using passive or active voice in the social and natural sciences

In the past, the social sciences and natural sciences preferred the passive voice (Chapter 41). Very recently, the style manuals for these disciplines have been advising writers to use the active voice whenever possible. "Verbs are vigorous, direct communicators," point out the editors of the *Publication Manual of the American Psychological Association.* "Use the active rather than the passive voice," they say.*

EXERCISE 8-9

First, determine which sentences are in the active voice and which the passive voice. Second, rewrite the sentence in the other voice, and then decide which voice better suits the meaning. Be ready to explain your choice. For help, consult 8n through 8p.

EXAMPLE   In the West African country of Ghana, a few woodcarvers are creating coffins that reflect their occupants' special interests. (*active; change to passive*)

In the West African country of Ghana, *coffins that reflect their occupants' special interests are being created by a few woodcarvers.*

1. A coffin in the shape of a green onion was chosen by a farmer.
2. A hunter's family buried him in a wooden coffin shaped like a leopard.
3. A dead chief was carried through his fishing village by friends and relatives bearing his body in a large, pink, wooden replica of a fish.
4. Woodcarver Paa Joe can turn out about ten coffins a year.
5. Although a few of these fantasy coffins have been displayed in museums, most of them end up buried in the ground.

*American Psychological Association, *Publication Manual of the American Psychological Association,* 4th ed. (Washington: APA, 1994) 32.

Focus on Revising

Here are two case studies of writers revising. Now's the time to apply all you've learned from Chapter 8 about verbs. In the Observation section, you see a student writer revising. In the Participation section, you are invited to revise another student's writing.

Observation

A student wrote the following draft for a course called Family Financial Planning. The assignment was to explain a basic method of investing.

An easy way for people to diversify their investments is provided by mutual funds. A mutual fund may hold one, two, or all three of the following financial assets: stocks, bonds, and money market instruments. Within these categories, a fund manager is selecting a wide variety of holdings. Usually, no single holding was more than 5 percent of the fund's total worth. If one holding was to lose money, the fund as a whole could still be profitable. In a prospectus, the fund manager is suppose to reveal the goals and potential risks of the fund to investors. A lower return is generally earned by funds with a lower investment risk. While funds with a higher investment risk may earn a higher return, they may also lose more money. Fund managers hope their mutual funds have earned investors a profit by the end of the year. The U.S. government's program, the FDIC (Federal Deposit Insurance Corporation), will not have insured mutual funds, so investors need to be careful when choosing where to put their money.

Annotations:

Unneeded passive voice: 8p

Present progressive used; needs present: 8h

Past tense used; needs present: 8h

Subjunctive needed for *if* clause: 8m.1

-ed missing: 8d

Unneeded passive voice: 8p

Present perfect used; needs future perfect: 8i

Future perfect used; needs present: 8h

Observation: Revised by Student

Mutual funds provide an easy way for people to diversify their investments. A mutual fund may hold one, two, or three of the following financial assets: stocks, bonds, and money market instruments. Within these categories, a fund manager selects a wide variety of holdings. Usually, no single holding is more than 5 percent of the fund's total worth. If one holding were to lose money, the fund as a whole could still be profitable. In a prospectus, the fund manager is supposed to reveal the goals and potential risks of the fund to investors. Funds with a lower investment risk generally earn a lower return. While funds with a higher investment risk may earn a higher return, they may also lose more money. Fund managers hope their mutual funds will have earned investors a profit by the end of the year. The U.S. government's program, the FDIC (Federal Deposit Insurance Corporation), does not insure mutual funds, so investors need to be careful when choosing where to put their money.

Participation

A student wrote the following draft for a course called Geriatric Nursing. The assignment was to shed new light on a health concern for elderly people. Its information is well organized and useful, but the draft suffers from verb errors. Find and correct the errors, and revise in other ways you think would improve the draft.

Forgetting where a person lay a pair of glasses yesterday is not cause for concern. However, this type of experience often worrying people in their sixties, seventies, and beyond. They are concern about their ability to stay mentally alert as brain cells begin to die. However, the fact that the human brain can continue to form new cells for more than 90 years is shown by new research.

Scientists also, recently will have found a correlation between people's physical health and their mental alertness. Generally, the more physically fit a person is the more mentally alert that person will be. A slowdown in their ability to recall information or to work on several tasks at once is experienced by many older people. This is a normal part of the aging process and should not cause anxiety.

As long as people do not have Alzheimer's or other diseases that were affecting the mind, they can continue to learn new skills and to analyze difficult concepts throughout their lives.

9 PRONOUNS: CASE AND REFERENCE

PRONOUN CASE

9a What does case mean?

Case refers to different forms that PRONOUNS—and NOUNS, but only sometimes—take when they relate to other words in a sentence. Pronouns have three cases: **subjective, objective,** and **possessive.** In contrast, nouns take case only in the possessive: that is, only when an apostrophe is needed (Chapter 27).

9b What are personal pronouns?

Personal pronouns refer to persons or things. As Box 69 shows, they have SINGULAR and PLURAL forms for all three cases: subjective, objective, and possessive.

	Case for personal pronouns					69
	Subjective		**Objective**		**Possessive**	
Person*	SING.	PLUR.	SING.	PLUR.	SING.	PLUR.
FIRST	I	we	me	us	my/mine	our/ours
SECOND	you	you	you	you	your/yours	your/yours
THIRD	he	they	him	them	his	their/theirs
	she		her		her/hers	
	it		it		its	

* For more about the concepts of *person* and *number* (singular and plural), see Box 73 in section 10b, pages 227–228.

9c How do pronouns operate in the subjective case?

Pronouns in the **subjective case** function as SUBJECTS.

We were going to get married. [*We* is the subject.]

John and **I** wanted an inexpensive band for our wedding. [*I* is part of the compound subject *John and I.*]

He and I found an affordable one-person band. [*He and I* is the compound subject.]

9d How do pronouns operate in the objective case?

Pronouns in the **objective case** function as OBJECTS.

We saw **him** perform in a public park. [*Him* is the DIRECT OBJECT.]

We showed **him** our budget. [*Him* is the INDIRECT OBJECT.]

He wrote down what we wanted and shook hands with **us**. [*Us* is the object of the preposition *with.*]

9e How do pronouns and nouns operate in the possessive case?

Pronouns and nouns in the **possessive case** indicate ownership. (Special rules apply to use of the possessive case before *–ing* words; see 9l. Also, *who, whoever, whom,* and *whomever* require special attention; see 9i.)

The **musician's** contract was in the mail the next day. [*Musician's,* a noun in the possessive case, indicates ownership.]

The first signature on the contract was **mine**. [*Mine,* a pronoun in the possessive case, indicates ownership and refers to the noun *signature.*]

John signed **his** name next to **mine**. [*His* and *mine,* pronouns in the possessive case, indicate ownership and refer to the noun *name.*]

👁 **PUNCTUATION ALERT:** Don't use an apostrophe in personal pronouns: *its, ours, yours, hers, his,* and *theirs* (27c).●

9f How do pronouns operate in compound constructions?

A **compound construction** contains more than one SUBJECT or OBJECT.

He saw the eclipse of the sun. [single subject]
He and I saw the eclipse of the sun. [compound subject]
The eclipse astonished **us.** [single object]
The eclipse astonished **him and me.** [compound object]

Compound constructions use the same pronoun-case rules as do single constructions. A compound subject uses the SUBJECTIVE CASE, and a compound object uses the OBJECTIVE CASE. Be careful not to switch cases when you use compound constructions. If you're not sure which case to use, try the **Drop Test.** To do this, drop all words from the compound construction except the pronoun in question, as explained in Box 70.

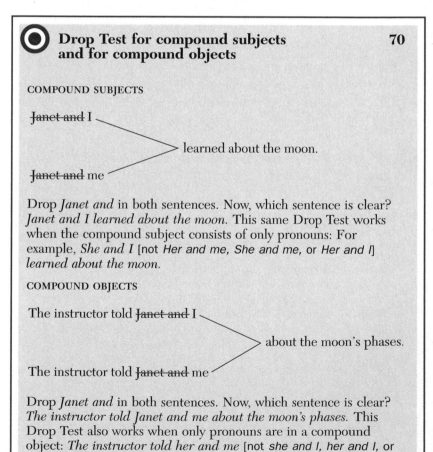

Drop Test for compound subjects and for compound objects   70

COMPOUND SUBJECTS

~~Janet and~~ I

> learned about the moon.

~~Janet and~~ me

Drop *Janet and* in both sentences. Now, which sentence is clear? *Janet and I learned about the moon.* This same Drop Test works when the compound subject consists of only pronouns: For example, *She and I* [not *Her and me, She and me,* or *Her and I*] *learned about the moon.*

COMPOUND OBJECTS

The instructor told ~~Janet and~~ I

> about the moon's phases.

The instructor told ~~Janet and~~ me

Drop *Janet and* in both sentences. Now, which sentence is clear? *The instructor told Janet and me about the moon's phases.* This Drop Test also works when only pronouns are in a compound object: *The instructor told her and me* [not *she and I, her and I,* or *she and me*] *about the moon's phases.*

When you use two pronouns in a compound, the rules in Box 70 apply, no matter which pronoun comes first. That is, what holds for *her and me* also holds for *me and her.*

Also, when you use two pronouns in a compound, don't mix pronouns in the subjective case with pronouns in the objective case. Keep both pronouns in the same case. For example, use *he and I* (both subjective), not *him and I* (not, as here, objective mixed with subjective); similarly, use *she and I* (both objective), not *her and I* (not, as here, objective mixed with subjective).

When pronouns are in a PREPOSITIONAL PHRASE, the pronouns are always in the objective case. That is, a pronoun is always the OBJECT of the preposition. This rule holds whether the pronouns are singular or plural. You can also use the Drop Test in Box 70 to check what is correct.

NO The instructor gave an assignment *to* **Sam and I.** [*To* is a preposition; *I* is in the subjective case, so *I* is an error after a preposition.]

YES The instructor gave an assignment *to* **Sam and me.** [*To* is a preposition; *me* is in the objective case, so *me* is correct.]

NO The instructor spoke *with* **he and I.** [*With* is a preposition; *he and I* are in the subjective case, so *he and I* is an error after a preposition.]

NO The instructor spoke *with* **him and I.** [*With* is a preposition; *him* is in the objective case, so *him* is correct. However, *I* is in the subjective case, so *I* is an error after a preposition.]

YES The instructor spoke *with* **him and me.** [*With* is a preposition; *him and me* are both in the objective case, so *him and me* is correct.]

Between is one preposition that often leads to errors. Like all pronouns, *between* is followed by the objective case.

NO The instructor divided the work *between* **Sam and I.** [*Between* is a preposition; *I* is in the subjective case, so *I* is an error after a preposition.]

YES The instructor divided the work *between* **Sam and me.** [*Between* is a preposition; *me* is in the objective case, so *me* is correct after a preposition.]

EXERCISE 9-1

Underline the correct pronoun from each pair in parentheses. For help, consult 9e and 9f.

EXAMPLE Bill and (I, me) noticed two young swimmers being pulled out to sea.

(1) The two teenagers caught in the rip current waved and hollered at Bill and (I, me). (2) The harder (they, them) both swam toward shore, the further away the undercurrent pulled them from the beach. (3) The yellow banners had warned Bill and (I, me) that a dangerous rip current ran beneath the water. (4) I yelled at Bill, "Between you and (I, me), (we, us) have to save them!" (5) (He and I, Him and me) both ran and dove into the crashing waves. (6) As former lifeguards, Bill and (I, me) knew what to do. (7) (We, us) two remembered the rule for surviving a rip current is to swim across the current. (8) Only when swimmers are safely away from the current should they swim toward shore. (9) I reached the teenage girl, who cried, "My boyfriend and (I, me) are drowning." (10) Bill rescued the frightened teenage boy, and when they were safely on shore, the boy looked at (he and I, him and me) and gasped, "Thanks. The two of (we, us) know you saved our lives."

9g How does case operate in appositives?

An APPOSITIVE renames a PRONOUN or a NOUN: *The crowd cheered when **she, Venus Williams,** won the match* [*Venus Williams* renames *she*]. Appositives obey the same rules as in 9c and 9d: Stay in the same case, either all in the subjective case or all in the objective case. Again, you can use the Drop Test in Box 70 to see what is correct.

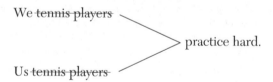

Drop *tennis players.* Now, which sentence is clear? Because *We practice hard* is correct, *We tennis players practice hard* is also correct.

The Drop Test in Box 70 also works when pronouns, without nouns, are in an appositive: *The winners, **she and I** [not her and me], advanced to the finals.* Similarly, the Drop Test works when nouns and pronouns are together in the objective case: *The crowd cheered the winners, **Venus and me** [not Venus and I].*

9h How does case operate after linking verbs?

A LINKING VERB connects a SUBJECT to a word that renames the subject. The renamed word can be an ADJECTIVE, noun, or pronoun (Box 60, 8a, page 183). Here is an example: *The contest winner was **I.*** [*I* renames *the contest winner,* which is the noun-subject, so the subjective case is correct.] Similarly: *The ones who will benefit are **they and I.*** [*They and I* renames the *ones who will benefit,* which is the pronoun-subject, so the subjective case is correct.]

Although in informal speech and writing, people sometimes use the objective case even though the subjective case is correct, in ACADEMIC WRITING always use the subjective case when it is grammatically correct.

EXERCISE 9-2

Underline the correct pronoun of each pair in parentheses. For help, consult 9c through 9h.

EXAMPLE   Dad, because your wedding anniversary is next week, (we, us) sisters decided to get you and Mother a gift you will never forget.

(1) Anne and (me, I) have given this a great deal of thought, especially in light of the conversations you and Mom have had with us about stress at work. (2) You and Mom have always insisted that (we, us) children save money for special occasions, and Anne asked (me, I) if she and I could use our savings for a weekend getaway for you as the perfect anniversary gift. (3) It is (she and I, she and me) who most worry about how (you and her, you and she) are doing, so Anne and (I, me) think this trip will benefit everyone. (4) In fact, Dad, Mom mentioned to Anne last week how much she'd love for you and (she, her) to spend more time together. (5) It would make Anne and (me, I) feel great to do something nice for you two. (6) So, Dad, you and Mom start packing for a weekend at your favorite bed and breakfast, a time you and (her, she) desperately need and deserve. (7) Anne and (I, me) will be waiting when you two come home rested and free of stress.

9i What cases are correct for *who, whoever, whom,* and *whomever?*

The pronouns *who* and *whoever* are in the subjective case. The pronouns *whom* and *whomever* are in the objective case.

9i.1 Using *who, whoever, whom,* and *whomever* in dependent clauses

When DEPENDENT CLAUSES start with the pronouns *who, whoever, whom,* or *whomever,* be careful to use the correct pronoun case. To determine which case is correct, see whether the pronoun is functioning as a SUBJECT or an OBJECT.

Because informal spoken English tends to blur distinctions between *who* and *whom,* and between *whom* and *whomever,* don't rely entirely on what sounds right. Instead, adapt the Drop Test in Box 71. As it shows, temporarily drop everything in the sentence up to the pronoun in question, and then make substitutions. Remember that *he, she, they, who,* and *whoever* are subjects; and *him, her, them, whom,* and *whomever* (the -*m* forms and *her*) are objects.

 Drop Test: *who* or *whom* in the   **71**
subjective case and objective case

Subjective Case for *who* and *whom*

EXAMPLE   The newspapers predicted (**who, whom**) would vote.

1. DROP   *The newspapers predicted*
2. TEST   Temporarily substitute *he and him* (or *she and her*) to get ***He*** would *vote* and ***Him*** would vote.
3. ANSWER   ***He*** *would vote.* Therefore, because both *he* and *who* are in the subjective case, the correct choice is *The newspapers predicted **who** would vote.*

This same Drop Test works for *whoever: Voter registration drives try to enroll **whoever** is eligible to vote.* Temporarily substitute for *whoever* the words *he* and *him.* The correct choice is *He* (not *Him*) *is eligible to vote,* which proves that *whoever,* the subjective case, is needed.

Objective Case for *who* and *whom*

EXAMPLE   Volunteers go to senior citizen centers hoping to enroll people (**who, whom**) others have ignored.

1. DROP   *Volunteers go to senior citizen centers hoping to enroll people*
2. TEST   Temporarily put *they* and *them* after *others have ignored* to get *Others have ignored **they*** or *Others have ignored **them.***
3. ANSWER   *Others have ignored **them.*** Therefore, because *them* and *whom* are in the objective case, the correct choice is *Volunteers go to senior citizen centers hoping to enroll people **whom** others have ignored.*

This same Drop Test works for *whomever: The senior citizens can vote for **whomever** they wish.* Temporarily substitute for *whomever* the words *he* and *him.* The correct choice is *they wish to vote for **him*** (*not **he***), which proves that *whomever,* the objective case, is needed.

9i.2 Using *who* and *whom* in questions

At the beginning of questions, use *who* if the question is about the subject, and use *whom* if the question is about the object. If you want to test for correct case, recast the question into a statement, temporarily substituting *he* or *she* (subjective case) or *him* or *her* (objective case).

> **Who** watched the space shuttle lift off? [*He* (not *Him*) *watched the space shuttle lift off* uses the subjective case, so *who* is correct.]
>
> Ann admires **whom**? [*Ann admires him* (not *he*) uses the objective case, so *whom* is correct.]
>
> **Whom** does Ann admire? [*Ann admires him* (not *he*) uses the objective case, so *whom* is correct.]
>
> To **whom** does Ann speak about becoming an astronaut? [*Ann speaks to her* (not *she*) about becoming an astronaut, so *whom* is correct.]

◉ **ALERT:** Grammatically, *whom* in the *"to whom"* example above is a pronoun coming after a preposition (*to*). The rule in operation is "Pronouns in a prepositional phrase are always in the objective case." ●

EXERCISE 9-3

Underline the correct pronoun of each pair in parentheses. For help, consult 9i.

EXAMPLE   (Whoever, Whomever) has been dragged out of bed by the urge for a peanut butter sandwich can join millions of other people with similar cravings.

(1) There isn't anything strange about a person (who, whom) experiences late-night cravings for favorite snacks. (2) (Whoever, Whomever) has worried about such habits can take comfort from a Canadian researcher. (3) Among the one thousand college students (who, whom) he studied, a large majority admitted that they craved specific foods. (4) Women (who, whom) these cravings strike tend to desire chocolate and sweets; men usually crave high-protein foods like meat. (5) Few people (who, whom) are told about this difference are very surprised. (6) What may be surprising is that researchers have not found many pregnant women (who, whom) crave dill pickles. (7) Nevertheless, (whoever, whomever) researchers ask about cravings, the pickle myth is bound to come up.

9j What is the appropriate pronoun case after *than* or *as*?

When *than* or *as* is part of a sentence of comparison, the sentence sometimes doesn't include words to complete the comparison outright. Rather, by omitting certain words, the sentence implies the comparison.

For example, *My two-month-old Saint Bernard is larger **than** most full-grown dogs [are]* doesn't need the final word *are.*

When a pronoun follows *than* or *as,* the meaning of the sentence depends entirely on whether the pronoun is in the subjective case or the objective case. Here are two sentences that convey two very different messages, depending on whether the subjective case (*I*) or the objective case (*me*) is used.

1. My sister loved that dog more **than** I.
2. My sister loved that dog more **than** me.

In sentence 1, because *I* is in the subjective case, the sentence means *My sister loved that dog more than **I** [loved it].* In sentence 2, because *me* is in the objective case, the sentence means *My sister loved that dog more than [she loved] **me.*** In both situations, you can check whether you're using the correct case by supplying the implied words to see if they make sense.

9k How do pronouns operate before infinitives?

Most INFINITIVES consist of the SIMPLE FORMS of verbs that follow *to:* for example, *to laugh, to sing, to jump, to dance.* (A few exceptions occur when the *to* is optional: *My aunt helped the elderly man [to] cross the street;* and when the *to* is awkward: *My aunt watched the elderly man [to] get on the bus.*) For both the SUBJECTS of infinitives and the OBJECTS of infinitives, use the objective case.

Our tennis coach expects **me** *to serve.* [Because the word *me* is the subject of the infinitive *to serve,* the objective-case pronoun is correct.]

Our tennis coach expects **him** *to beat* me. [Because the word *him* is the subject of the infinitive *to beat,* and *me* is the object of the infinitive, the objective-case pronoun is correct.]

9l How do pronouns operate with *-ing* words?

When a verb's *-ing* form functions as a NOUN, it's called a GERUND: *Brisk **walking** is excellent exercise.* When a noun or PRONOUN comes before a gerund, the POSSESSIVE CASE is required: ***His** brisk **walking** built up his stamina.* In contrast, when a verb's *-ing* form functions as a MODIFIER, it requires the subjective case for the pronoun, not the possessive case: ***He, walking** briskly, caught up to me.*

Here are two sentences that convey different messages, depending entirely on whether a possessive comes before the *-ing* word.

1. The detective noticed the **man *staggering.***
2. The detective noticed the **man's *staggering.***

Sentence 1 means that the detective noticed the *man;* sentence 2 means that the detective noticed the *staggering.* The same distinction applies to pronouns: When *the man* is replaced by either *him* or *his,* the meaning is the same as in sentences 1 and 2.

3. The detective noticed **him** *staggering.*
4. The detective noticed **his** *staggering.*

In conversation, such distinctions are often ignored, but use them in ACADEMIC WRITING.

EXERCISE 9-4

Underline the correct pronoun of each pair in parentheses. For help, consult 9i through 9l.

EXAMPLE   When the Hewlett-Packard Company decided not to manufacture a personal computer designed by young Steve Wozniak, the rejection motivated (him, <u>his</u>) starting the Apple Computer Company.

(1) Few people in Steve Wozniak's world of personal computers have had careers as rewarding as (he, him) and his friend Steve Jobs. (2) Their story begins with (them, their) selling a van and a calculator to get (they, them) enough cash to make a prototype computer. (3) Many people with an idea like Wozniak and Jobs's are less willing than (them, they) to take risks. (4) Apple's early spectacular success as a company came from (it, its) making computers easy for individuals to own and use. (5) Because their idea made both Wozniak and Jobs multimillionaires before age thirty, the notion of (them, their) leaving the business world seemed to interest (they, them). (6) Wozniak went back to college but eventually returned to Apple, which continued to want (his, him) inventing and engineering computers for it. Meanwhile, Jobs's decision to start a new computer company led him to gamble once again on his talent and business skill, which eventually took him back to Apple.

PRONOUN REFERENCE

9m What is pronoun reference?

Pronoun reference means the relationship between a PRONOUN and its ANTECEDENT (the NOUN or other pronoun to which a pronoun refers). To communicate clearly, each pronoun in your writing must refer to a single, nearby antecedent. Here are examples in which each pronoun has a clear antecedent.

Facts do not cease to exist just because **they** are ignored.

—Aldous Huxley

> I knew a **woman,** lovely in **her** bones / When small **birds** sighed, **she** would sigh back at **them.**
>
> —Theodore Roethke, "I Knew a Woman"

9n What makes pronoun reference clear?

Pronoun reference is clear when your readers know immediately to whom each pronoun refers. Box 72 lists guidelines for using pronouns clearly, and the section in parentheses is where each is explained.

◉ Guidelines for clear pronoun reference   72

- Place pronouns close to their ANTECEDENTS (9o).
- Make a pronoun refer to a specific antecedent (9q).
- Do not overuse *it* (see 9q), and reserve *you* only for DIRECT ADDRESS (9r).
- Use *that, which,* and *who* correctly (9s).

9o How do pronouns refer clearly to a single antecedent?

Every pronoun needs to refer to a specific, nearby ANTECEDENT. If the same pronoun in your writing has to refer to more than one antecedent, replace some pronouns with nouns. In this way, all the remaining pronouns can clearly refer to a single antecedent.

NO   In 1911, **Roald Amundsen** reached the South Pole just thirty-five days before **Robert F. Scott** arrived. **He** [who? Amundsen or Scott?] had told people that **he** [who? Amundsen or Scott?] was going to sail for the Arctic, but **he** [who? Amundsen or Scott?] was concealing **his** [whose? Amundsen's or Scott's?] plan. Soon, **he** [who? Amundsen or Scott?] turned south for the Antarctic. On the journey home, **he** [who? Amundsen or Scott?] and **his** [whose? Amundsen's or Scott's?] party froze to death just a few miles from safety.

YES   In 1911, **Roald Amundsen** reached the South Pole just thirty-five days before **Robert F. Scott** arrived. **Amundsen** had told people that **he** was going to sail for the Arctic, but **he** was concealing **his** plan. Soon, **Amundsen** turned south for the Antarctic. Meanwhile, on **their** journey home, **Scott** and **his** **party** froze to death just a few miles from safety.

Be careful with the VERBS *said* and *told* in sentences that contain pronoun reference. To maintain clarity, use quotation marks and slightly reword each sentence to make the meaning clear.

NO   **Her** mother told **her she** was going to visit **her** grandmother.

YES   **Her** mother told **her,** "**You** are going to visit your grandmother."

YES   **Her** mother told **her,** "**I** am going to visit your grandmother."

9p Why should pronouns be close to their antecedents?

If too many words come between a PRONOUN and its ANTECEDENT, even though the words are logically related, your pronoun reference is unclear.

NO   **Alfred Wegener** was a highly trained German meteorologist and professor of geophysics and meteorology at the University of Graz in Austria. **He** was the first to suggest that all the continents on earth were originally part of one large landmass. According to **his** theory, the super continent broke up long ago, and the fragments drifted apart. **He** named the super continent Pangaea. [Although *he* and *his* can refer only to *Wegener,* too much material intervenes between the pronouns and their antecedent, *Wegener.*]

YES   **Alfred Wegener** was a highly trained German meteorologist and professor of geophysics and meteorology at the University of Graz in Austria. **He** was the first to suggest that all the continents on earth were originally part of one large landmass. According to **Wegener's** theory, the super continent broke up long ago, and the fragments drifted apart. **He** named the super continent Pangaea.

When you start a new paragraph in a piece of writing, be cautious about beginning it with a pronoun whose antecedent is in a prior paragraph. You're better off repeating the name.

⊕ ESL NOTE: Many languages omit a pronoun as a subject because the verb delivers the needed information. English, however, requires the use of the pronoun as a subject. For example, don't omit *it* in the following: *Political science is an important academic subject.* **It** *is studied all over the world.* ⊕

EXERCISE 9-5

Revise so that each pronoun refers clearly to its antecedent. Either replace pronouns with nouns or restructure the material to clarify pronoun reference. For help, consult 9p.

EXAMPLE   People who return to work after years away from the corporate world often discover that business practices have changed. They may find fiercer competition in the workplace, but they may also discover that they are more flexible than before.

Here is one possible revision: *People who return to work after years away from the corporate world often discover that business practices have changed. Those people may find fiercer competition in the workplace, but they may also discover that business practices are more flexible than before.*

Most companies used to frown on employees who became involved in office romances. They often considered them to be using company time for their own enjoyment. Now, however, managers realize that happy employees are productive employees. With more women than ever before in the workforce and with people working longer hours, they have begun to see that male and female employees want and need to socialize. They are also dropping their opposition to having married couples on the payroll. They no longer automatically believe that they will bring family matters into the workplace or stick up for one another at the company's expense.

One departmental manager had doubts when a systems analyst for research named Laura announced that she had become engaged to Peter, who worked as a technician in the same department. She told her that either one or the other might have to transfer out of the research department. After listening to her plea that they be allowed to work together on a trial basis, the manager reconsidered. She decided to give Laura and Peter a chance to prove that their relationship would not affect their work. The decision paid off. They demonstrated that they could work as an effective research team, right through their engagement and subsequent marriage. Two years later, when Laura was promoted to assistant manager of a different department and after he asked to move also, she enthusiastically recommended that Peter follow Laura to her new department.

9q How can I avoid vague pronoun reference?

Vague pronoun reference means it isn't clear what ANTECEDENT the pronoun is referring to. The result is unclear and confusing writing.

9q.1 Making *it, that, this,* and *which* refer to a specific antecedent

The pronouns *it, that, this,* and *which* are sometimes used too loosely for the reader to be sure of the antecedent. Sometimes the problem is that the antecedent is implied. For clarity, explicitly state the antecedent.

NO Comets usually fly by the earth at 100,000 mph, whereas asteroids sometimes collide with the earth. **This** interests scientists. [Does *this* refer to the speed of the comets, to comets flying by the earth, or to asteroids colliding with the earth?]

YES Comets usually fly by the earth at 100,000 mph, whereas asteroids sometimes collide with the earth. **This difference** interests scientists. [Adding a noun after *this* or *that* clarifies the meaning.]

NO I told my friends that I was going to major in geology, **which** made my parents happy. [Does *which* refer to telling your friends or to majoring in geology?]

YES My parents were happy **because I discussed my major with my friends.**

YES My parents were happy **because I chose to major in geology.**

Also, the title of any piece of writing stands on its own. In your introductory paragraph, don't refer to your title with *this* or *that*. For example, if an essay's title is "Geophysics as a Major," the following holds for the first sentence:

NO **This subject** unites the sciences of physics, biology, and paleontology.

YES **Geophysics** unites the sciences of physics, biology, and paleontology.

9q.2 Using *they* and *it* precisely

The expression *they say* cannot take the place of stating precisely who is doing the saying. Your credibility as a writer depends on your mentioning a source precisely, and so avoiding *they* as an authority improves your writing.

NO **They say** that earthquakes are becoming more frequent. [*They* doesn't identify the authority who made the statement.]

YES **Seismologists** say that earthquakes are becoming more frequent.

The expressions *it said* and *it is said that* reflect imprecise thinking. Also, they're wordy. Revising such expressions improves your writing.

NO **It said** in the newspaper that California has minor earthquakes almost daily. [*It said in the newspaper that* is wordy.]

YES **The newspaper reported** that California has minor earthquakes almost daily.

9q.3 Using *it* to suit the situation

The word *it* has three different uses in English. Here are examples of correct uses of *it*.

1. PERSONAL PRONOUN: Ryan wants to visit the 18-inch Schmidt telescope, but **it** is on Mount Palomar.

2. EXPLETIVE (sometimes called a *subject filler*, it delays the subject): **It** is interesting to observe the stars.

3. IDIOMATIC EXPRESSION (words that depart from normal use, such as using *it* as the sentence subject when writing about weather, time, distance, and environmental conditions): **It** is sunny. **It** is midnight. **It** is not far to the hotel. **It** is very hilly.

All three uses listed above are correct, but avoid combining them in the same sentence. The result can be an unclear and confusing sentence.

> **NO** Because our car was overheating, **it** came as no surprise that **it** broke down just as **it** began to rain. [*It* is overused here, even though all three uses—2, 1, and 3 on the above list, respectively—are acceptable.]

> **YES** **It** came as no surprise that our overheating car broke down just as the rain began. [The word order is revised so that *it* is used once.]

ESL NOTE: In some languages, *it* in an expletive is not used. In English, always use *it*.

> **NO** Is a lovely day.
> **YES** **It** is a lovely day.

9r Why use *you* only for direct address?

You is not a substitute for specific words that refer to people, situations, and occurrences. For example, I use *you* in this handbook only to address you, the student. Except for direct address, use the exact words needed instead of *you*.

> **NO** In many states, **you** have **your** prisons with few rehabilitation programs. [Do *you*, the reader of this handbook, have few rehabilitation programs? Also, are the prisons *yours*?]

> **YES** In many states, **prisons** have few rehabilitation programs.

NO	In Russia, **you** usually have to stand in long lines to buy groceries. [Are *you*, the reader, planning to do your grocery shopping in Russia?]
YES	**Russian consumers** usually have to stand in long lines to buy groceries.

EXERCISE 9-6

Revise these sentences so that all pronoun references are clear. If a sentence is correct, circle its number. For help, consult 9q and 9r.

EXAMPLE By collecting data on animal species around the world, you gain insight into the ways animals communicate.

By collecting data on animal species around the world, researchers gain insight into the ways animals communicate. [Revision changes PERSON from *you* not used for direct address to third person, the noun *researchers*.]

1. Researchers find that animal communication is more complex and more varied than you might expect.
2. Throughout the animal kingdom, they use low-pitched noises to convey aggression and high-pitched noises to convey fear.
3. They say that dogs bark for many reasons: to ask for food, to alert a family to danger, to convey excitement.
4. Elephants send messages to herds three miles away using sounds too low for you to hear.
5. In the water, damselfish emit squeaks and dolphins send out clicks and whistles. This interests marine biologists.
6. Elk males have rutting contests to prove which male is stronger, with the one that ruts louder and longer proving his dominance.
7. They do not communicate only by using sounds: lobsters use chemical signals, lizards use head bobs, fireflies use light signals.
8. You can teach chimps to use sign language to communicate in simple sentences, such as "Give JoJo banana."

9s How do I use *that, which,* and *who* correctly?

To use the pronouns *that* and *which* correctly, you want to check the context of the sentence you're writing. *Which* and *that* refer to animals and things. Only sometimes do they refer to anonymous or collective groups of people.

To decide whether to use *that* or *which*, determine whether the CLAUSE it's to be attached to is either a RESTRICTIVE CLAUSE (a clause that adds essential information to a sentence) or a NONRESTRICTIVE CLAUSE (a clause that can be omitted from a sentence without changing its basic message); for help, see 24f. Many professional writers reserve *which* for nonrestrictive clauses and *that* for restrictive clauses. Other writers have begun to use *that* and *which* interchangeably. Current practice allows the use of either as long as you are consistent in each piece of writing. However, for ACADEMIC WRITING, your instructor might expect you to maintain the distinction.

> The zoos **that most delight children** display newborn animals as well as their parents. [*That* starts information essential for understanding which zoos are being referred to; *that most delight children* is a restrictive clause.]

> Zoos, **which delight most children,** attract more visitors each year. [*Which* starts information that can be omitted from the sentence without changing its basic message; *which delight most children* is a nonrestrictive clause.]

Who refers to people or to animals with names or special talents. *Who* works for restrictive and nonrestrictive clauses alike.

> **Theodore Roosevelt, who** was the twenty-sixth U.S. president, inspired the creation of the stuffed animal known as the teddy bear. [*Theodore Roosevelt* was a person.]

> **Lassie, who** was known for her intelligence and courage, was actually played by a series of male collies. [*Lassie* is an animal with special talents.]

◉ **COMMA ALERT:** Use commas before and after a nonrestrictive clause. Don't use commas before and after a restrictive clause; see 24k.4. ●

EXERCISE 9-7

Fill in the blanks with *that, which,* or *who.* For help, consult 9s.

EXAMPLE   People who find their U.S. dollar bills eaten by mice, charred by fire, or rotting in a puddle of water can usually rescue the money.

1. As a free public service, the U.S. Department of the Treasury redeems U.S. paper money _____ has been badly damaged.
2. "Mutilated currency," _____ the Treasury defines as paper money _____ is less than 50 percent intact or of doubtful value, can be turned in at an office in Washington.
3. A "mutilated currency examiner," _____ inspects the damaged bills to determine their value, authorizes the payment _____ is to be made to their owners.
4. People _____ prefer to save their damaged money would never think of using this service.
5. This group of people, _____ includes many collectors of various odds and ends, values unusual objects more than a check from the U.S. Treasury Department.

www.prenhall.com/troyka

10 AGREEMENT

10a What is agreement?

In everyday speech, agreement indicates that people hold the same ideas. Grammatical **agreement** is also based on sameness. Specifically this means you need to match SUBJECTS and VERBS, and you also need to match PRONOUNS and ANTECEDENTS. The rules for grammatical agreement can be tricky, so do what most people do when they're unsure: Consult a handbook for writers, like the one you're now reading.

SUBJECT-VERB AGREEMENT

10b What is subject-verb agreement?

Subject-verb agreement means that a SUBJECT and its VERB match in NUMBER (singular or plural) and PERSON (first, second, or third person). Box 73 presents the major concepts in grammatical agreement.

The **firefly glows.** [*Firefly* is a singular subject in the third person; *glows* is a singular verb in the third person.]

Fireflies glow. [*Fireflies* is a plural subject in the third person; *glow* is a plural verb in the third person.]

🎯 **Major concepts in grammatical agreement**   73

■ **Number,** as a concept in grammar, refers to *singular* (one) and *plural* (more than one).

■ The **first person** is the speaker or writer. *I* (singular) and *we* (plural) are the only subjects that occur in the first person.

   SINGULAR   **I see** a field of fireflies.

    PLURAL   **We see** a field of fireflies.

→

Major concepts in grammatical agreement   73
(*continued*)

- The **second person** is the person spoken or written to. *You* (for both singular and plural) is the only subject that occurs in the second person.

  SINGULAR   **You see** a shower of sparks.

  PLURAL   **You see** a shower of sparks.

- The **third person** is the person or thing being spoken or written about. *He, she, it* (singular) and *they* (plural) are the third-person subject forms. Most rules for subject-verb agreement involve the third person.

  SINGULAR   The **scientist sees** a cloud of cosmic dust.

  PLURAL   The **scientists see** a cloud of cosmic dust.

10c Why is a final -s or -es in a subject or verb so important?

SUBJECT-VERB AGREEMENT often involves one letter: *s* or its form *es* when added to words that themselves end in *-s* and in a few other situations (22c). For verbs, you depend entirely on the *-s* or *-es* ending to signal a singular verb (ends with an *-s* or *-es*) or a plural verb (does not end with an *-s* or *-es*). For subjects, you depend entirely on an *-s* or *-es* ending to signal a singular subject (does not end with an *-s* or *-es*) or a plural subject (ends with an *-s* or *-es*).

For verbs in the present tense, you form the SIMPLE FORM of THIRD-PERSON SINGULAR by adding *-s* or *-es: laugh, laughs; kiss, kisses*. Major exceptions are the verbs *be* (*is*), *have* (*has*) and *do* (*does*); see 8c. Yet, even they end in *-s*.

That **student agrees** that **young teenagers watch** too much television.

Those **young teenagers are** taking valuable time from studying.

That **student has** a part-time job for ten or twenty hours a week.

Still, that **student does** well in college.

For a subject to become plural, you add *-s* or *-es* to its end: *lip, lips; princess, princesses*. Major exceptions include most pronouns (*they, it*) and a few nouns that for singular and plural either don't change (*deer, deer*) or change internally (*mouse, mice*). Box 74 shows you how to visualize the basic pattern for agreement using *-s* or *-es*.

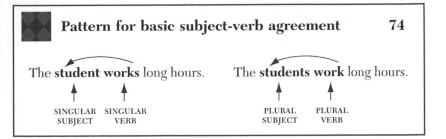

Here's a visual memory device for how agreement works for most subject-verb agreement. Note that the final *-s* or *-es* can take only one path at a time—to the end of the verb or to the end of the subject.

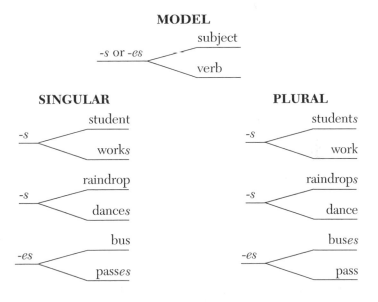

👁 **ALERT:** When you use an AUXILIARY VERB, also called a *helping verb* (such as *be, do, can, might, must,* or *would;* see 8e), with a main verb, don't add *-s* or *-es* to the main verb: *The coach **can walk*** [not *can walks*] *to campus. The coach **does like*** [not *does likes*] *his job.* ●

EXERCISE 10-1

Use the subject and verb in each set to write two complete sentences—one with a singular subject and one with a plural subject. Keep all verbs in the present tense. For help, consult 10c.

229

EXAMPLE climber, increase

> Singular subject: Without proper equipment, a mountain *climber increases* the risk of falling.
>
> Plural subject: Without proper equipment, mountain *climbers increase* the risk of falling.

1. dog, bark
2. flower, bloom
3. team, compete
4. planet, rotate

5. author, write
6. tornado, demolish
7. jet, depart
8. professor, might quiz

10d Can I ignore words between a subject and its verb?

Words between a SUBJECT and its VERB don't affect agreement. Ignore all intervening words between the subject and its verb. Focus strictly on the subject and its verb. Box 75 shows you how to visualize this pattern.

NO **Winners** of the state contest **goes** to the national finals. [*Winners* is the subject; the verb must agree with it. Ignore the intervening words *of the state contest*.]

YES **Winners** of the state contest **go** to the national finals.

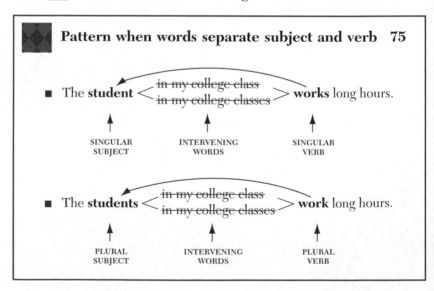

Pattern when words separate subject and verb   75

- The **student** < ~~in my college class~~ / ~~in my college classes~~ > **works** long hours.

  ↑ SINGULAR SUBJECT   ↑ INTERVENING WORDS   ↑ SINGULAR VERB

- The **students** < ~~in my college class~~ / ~~in my college classes~~ > **work** long hours.

  ↑ PLURAL SUBJECT   ↑ INTERVENING WORDS   ↑ PLURAL VERB

The words *one of the . . .* often require a second look. Use a singular verb to agree with the word *one.* Don't be distracted by the plural noun that comes after *of the.* Looking at the same issue a different way, *one of the* . . . is a PREPOSITIONAL PHRASE, which is always ignored when identifying a sentence's subject and its verb. (For information on the phrase *one of the . . . who,* see 10k.)

NO   **One** of the problems **are** funds for traveling to the national finals.

YES   **One** of the problems **is** funds for traveling to the national finals.

Similarly, eliminate all intervening word groups starting with *including, together with, along with, accompanied by, in addition to, except,* and *as well as.*

NO   The **moon,** *as well as* Venus, **are** visible in the night sky. [*Moon* is the subject. The verb must agree with it. Ignore the intervening words *as well as Venus.*]

YES   The **moon,** as well as Venus, **is** visible in the night sky.

10e How do verbs operate when subjects are connected by *and*?

When two SUBJECTS are connected by *and,* they create a single COMPOUND SUBJECT. A compound subject calls for a plural verb. Box 76 shows you how to visualize this pattern. (For related material on PRONOUNS and ANTECEDENTS, see 10o.)

The Cascade Diner *and* **the Wayside Diner** *have* [not has] fried catfish today. [These are two different diners.]

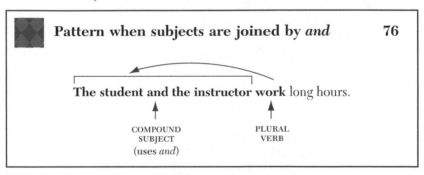

Pattern when subjects are joined by *and*   **76**

The student and the instructor work long hours.

COMPOUND   PLURAL
SUBJECT   VERB
(uses *and*)

The one exception comes when *and* joins subjects that refer to a single thing or person.

My friend *and* **neighbor** *makes* [not *make*] excellent chili. [In this sentence, the friend is the same person as the neighbor. If they were two different people, *makes* would become *make.*]

Macaroni *and* **cheese** *contains* [not *contain*] carbohydrates, protein, and many calories. [*Macaroni and cheese* is one dish, not two separate dishes, so it requires a singular verb.]

each, every

The words *each* and *every* are singular even if they refer to a compound subject. Therefore, they take a singular verb.

> **Each human hand and foot *makes*** [not *make*] a distinctive print.

> To identify lawbreakers, **every police chief, sheriff, and federal marshal *depends*** [not *depend*] on such prints.

 ALERT: Use one word, either *each* or *every*, not both at the same time. **Each** [not *Each and every*] *robber has been caught.* (For more information about pronoun agreement for *each* and *every*, see 10h and 10q.) ●

10f How do verbs operate when subjects are connected by *or*?

When SUBJECTS are joined by *or*, *either . . . or*, *neither . . . nor*, or *not only . . . but (also)*, the verb must agree with the subject closest to it. Ignore everything before the last-mentioned noun or pronoun. Box 77 shows this pattern with *or*. (For related material on pronouns and antecedents, see 10p.)

> ~~Neither~~ spiders ~~nor~~ **flies** **upset** me.

> ~~Not only~~ spiders **but also** ~~all other~~ **arachnids have** four pairs of legs.

> ~~A dinner of six clam fritters, four blue crabs,~~ **or** ~~one steamed~~ **lobster sounds** good.

Pattern when subjects are joined by *or*   77

- ~~Either the instructor or~~
  ~~Either the instructors or~~ ⟩ the **student knows** the answer.

  SINGULAR SUBJECT   SINGULAR VERB

- ~~Either the instructor or~~
  ~~Either the instructors or~~ ⟩ the **students know** the answer.

  PLURAL SUBJECT   PLURAL VERB

10g How do verbs operate with inverted word order?

In English, the SUBJECT normally comes before its VERB: *Astronomy is interesting.* **Inverted word order** reverses the typical subject-verb pattern by putting the verb first. For example, most questions use inverted word order: *Is astronomy interesting?* Whether you use normal or inverted word order, check that you're using the correct verb by finding the subject first and seeing whether the verb form is correct with that subject.

Into deep space **shoot** probing **satellites.** [The plural verb *shoot* agrees with the inverted plural subject *satellites.*]

On the television screen **appears** an **image** of Saturn. [The singular verb *appears* agrees with the inverted singular subject *image.*]

👁 **ALERT:** If your sentence begins with *there* followed by a form of the verb *be* (*is, are, was, were*), you're using a construction that writers sometimes need for effect, although it isn't concise (Chapter 16). When you use it, check after the *there* to find the subject, and then choose the right form of *be* to agree with the subject. If your sentence begins with *it,* always use the singular form of *be* (*is, was*).

There *are* nine **planets** in our solar system. [The verb *are* agrees with the subject *planets.*]

There *is* probably no **life** on eight of them. [The verb *is* agrees with the subject *life.*]

It *is* the property owners who are seeking changes in the tax laws. [The verb *is* agrees with *it,* not with *property owners.*]●

EXERCISE 10-2

Supply the correct present-tense form of the verb in parentheses. For help, consult 10c through 10g.

EXAMPLE   Detectives and teachers (to know) <u>know</u> experienced liars can fool almost anybody, but a new computer can tell who is telling the truth.

1.   Police officers and teachers often (to wish) _____ they could "read" people's facial expressions.
2.   Trained police officers or a smart teacher (to know) _____ facial tics and nervous mannerisms (to show) _____ someone is lying.

3. However, a truly gifted liar, along with well-coached eyewitnesses, (to reveal) _____ very little through expressions or behavior.

4. There (to be) _____ forty-six muscle movements in the human face which create all facial expressions.

5. Neuroscientist Terrence Seinowski, accompanied by a team of researchers, (to be) _____ developing a computer program to recognize even slight facial movements made by the most expert liars.

10h How do verbs operate with indefinite pronouns?

INDEFINITE PRONOUNS usually refer to unknown persons, things, quantities, or ideas. The unknown aspect is why these pronouns are labeled "indefinite." As part of a sentence, however, the indefinite pronoun is usually clear from the meaning.

Most indefinite pronouns are singular and require a singular verb for agreement. Yet, others are always plural, and a few can be singular *or* plural. Box 78 clarifies this situation by listing indefinite pronouns according to what verb form they require. (For related material on pronouns and antecedents, see 10q.)

ALERT: The rules for indefinite pronouns often collide with practices of avoiding sexist language. For suggestions, see sections 10r and 21g. ●

◉ Common indefinite pronouns 78

Always Plural

both	many

Always Singular

another	every	no one
anybody	everybody	nothing
anyone	everyone	one
anything	everything	somebody
each	neither	someone
either	nobody	something

Singular *or* Plural, Depending on Context

all	more	none
any	most	some

Here are example sentences:

SINGULAR INDEFINITE PRONOUNS

Everything about that intersection **is** dangerous.

But whenever **anyone says** anything, **nothing is** done.

Each of us **has** [not *have*] to shovel snow; **each is** [not *are*] expected to help.

Every snowstorm of the past two years **has** [not *have*] been severe.

Every one of them **has** [not *have*] caused massive traffic jams.

SINGULAR *OR* PLURAL INDEFINITE PRONOUNS

Some of our streams **are** polluted. [*Some* refers to the plural noun *streams*, so the plural verb *are* is correct.]

Some pollution **is** reversible, but **all** pollution **threatens** the balance of nature. [*Some* and *all* refer to the singular noun *pollution*, so the singular verbs *is* and *threatens* are correct.]

All that environmentalists ask **is** to give nature a chance. [*All* has the meaning here of "everything" or "the only thing," so the singular verb *is* is correct.]

Winter has driven the birds south; **all have** left. [*All* refers to the plural noun *birds*, so the plural verb *have* is correct.]

👁 **ALERT:** Don't mix singular and plural with *this, that, these,* and *those* when used with *kind* and *type. This* and *that* are singular, as are *kind* and *type; these* and *those* are plural, as are *kinds* and *types:* **This** [not *These*] **kind** of rainwear is waterproof. **These** [not *This*] **kinds** of sweaters keep me warm. ●

10i How do verbs operate with collective nouns?

COLLECTIVE NOUNS name groups of people or things: *family, audience, class, number, committee, team, group,* and the like. When the group of people or things is acting as one unit, use a singular verb. When members of the group are acting individually, use a plural verb. As you're writing, be careful not to shift back and forth between a singular and a plural verb for the same noun.

The senior **class** nervously **awaits** final exams. [The *class* is acting as a single unit, so the verb is singular.]

The senior **class were fitted** for their graduation robes today. [Each member (of the class) was fitted individually, so the verb is plural.]

👁 **ALERT:** For collective nouns, the plural verb usually sounds better to people used to U.S. English; however, rely on the rule, not the sound, to be correct. ●

10j Does the linking verb agree with the subject or the subject complement?

Even though a linking verb connects a sentence's SUBJECT to its subject complement (7n), the linking verb must agree with the subject. It must not agree with the subject complement; therefore, for purposes of agreement, ignore the subject complement. See the examples below to understand the terms and rule.

NO The worst **part** of owning a car *are* the bills. [The subject is the singular *part*, so the plural verb *are* is wrong. The subject complement is the plural *bills* and doesn't affect agreement.]

YES The worst **part** of owning a car *is* the bills. [The singular subject *part* agrees with the singular verb *is*. The subject complement doesn't affect agreement.]

10k What verbs agree with *who, which,* and *that?*

If the ANTECEDENT of *who, which,* or *that* is singular, use a singular verb. If the antecedent is plural, use a plural verb.

The scientist will share the prize with the **researchers *who* work** with her. [*Who* refers to *researchers,* so the plural verb *work* is used.]

George Jones is the **student *who* works** in the science lab. [*Who* refers to *student,* so the singular verb *works* is used.]

If you use phrases including *one of the* or *the only one of the* immediately before *who, which,* or *that* in a sentence, be careful about the verb you use. *Who, which,* or *that* always refers to the plural word immediately following *one of the,* so the verb must be plural. Although *the only one of* is also always followed by a plural word, *who, which,* or *that* must be singular to agree with the singular *one.*

Tracy is ***one of the*** students ***who* talk** in class. [*Who* refers to *students,* so the verb *talk* is plural. *Tracy* is pointed out, but the talking is still done by all the students.]

Jim is ***the only one of the*** students ***who* talks** in class. [*Who* refers to *one,* so the verb *talks* is singular. *Jim* is the single person who is talking.]

EXERCISE 10-3

Supply the correct present-tense form of the verb in parentheses. For help, consult 10g through 10k for help.

EXAMPLE   Everybody on a class trip to the coastal waters of the Pacific Ocean (to enjoy) <u>enjoys</u> an opportunity to study dolphins in their natural habitat.

1. A class of college students in marine biology (to take) _____ notes individually while watching dolphins feed off the California coast.
2. Everyone in the class (to listen) _____ as a team of dolphin experts (to explain) _____ some of the mammals' characteristics.
3. A group of dolphins, called a pod, usually (to consist) _____ of 10,000 to 30,000 members.
4. One unique characteristic of dolphins' brains (to be) _____ the sleep patterns that (to keep) _____ one-half of the brain awake at all times.
5. All (to need) _____ to stay awake to breathe or else they would drown.

101 How do verbs operate with amounts, fields of study, and other special nouns?

Amounts

SUBJECTS that refer to time, sums of money, distance, or measurement are singular. They take singular verbs.

Two hours *is* not enough time to finish. [time]
Three hundred dollars *is* what we must pay. [sum of money]
Two miles *is* a short sprint for some serious joggers. [distance]
Three-quarters of an inch *is* needed for a perfect fit. [measurement]

Fields of study

When you refer to a field of study, it's singular even though it appears to be plural: *economics, mathematics, physics,* and *statistics.*

***Statistics* is required** of science majors. [*Statistics* is a course of study, so the singular verb *is* is correct.]
***Statistics* show** that a teacher shortage is coming. [*Statistics* isn't used here as a field of study, so the plural verb *show* is correct.]

Special nouns

Athletics, news, ethics, and *measles* are singular despite their plural appearance. Also, *United States of America* is singular: It is one nation. However, *politics* and *sports* take singular or plural verbs, depending on the meaning of the sentence.

The ***news* gets** better each day. [*News* is a singular noun, so the singular verb *gets* is correct.]
***Sports* is** a good way to build physical stamina. [*Sports* is one general activity, so the singular verb *is* is correct.]

237

Three ***sports* are offered** at the recreation center. [*Sports* are separate activities, so the plural verb *are offered* is correct.]

Jeans, pants, scissors, clippers, tweezers, eyeglasses, thanks, and *riches* are among words that require a plural verb, even though they refer to one thing. However, if you use *pair* with *jeans, pants, scissors, clippers, tweezers,* or *eyeglasses,* use a singular verb for agreement.

Those ***slacks* need** pressing. [plural]

That ***pair*** of slacks **needs** pressing. [singular]

Series and *means* can be singular or plural, according to the meaning you intend.

Two new TV ***series* are** big hits. [*Series* refers to several individual items (two different series), so the plural verb *are* is correct.]

A ***series*** of disasters **is** plaguing our production. [*Series* refers to a whole group (the whole series of disasters), so the singular verb *is* is correct.]

10m How do verbs operate with titles of written works, company names, and words as themselves?

A title itself refers to one work or entity (even when plural and compound NOUNS are in the title), so a singular verb is correct.

Breathing Lessons by Anne Tyler **is** a prize-winning novel.

Many companies have plural words in their names. However, a company should always be treated as a singular unit, requiring a singular verb.

***Cohn Brothers* boxes** and **delivers** fine art.

Whenever you write about words as themselves to call attention to those words, use a singular verb, even if more than one word is involved.

We implies that everyone is included.

During the Vietnam War, ***protective reaction strikes* was** a euphemism for *bombing*.

EXERCISE 10-4

Supply the correct present-tense form of the verb in parentheses. For help, consult 10h through 10m.

EXAMPLE   Everyone (to use) <u>uses</u> phrases involving color in daily conversation, as when they say that someone "has the blues" or was "caught red-handed."

1. Hardly anyone (to realize) _____ that in such phrases, *red-handed* or *the blues* has a significant and generally unknown meaning.
2. Explanations about the origins of phrases like *red-letter day* (to be) _____ often a surprise.
3. An assortment of language experts (to agree) _____ that because special dates, such as national holidays, were often printed in red on calendars, people started to use *red letter* to refer to any special day.
4. There are many other curious uses of such color words; one (to be) _____ *greenroom,* a waiting room for guests who are going to appear on a television talk show.
5. People rarely meet an individual who (to know) _____ that the term *greenroom* originated in the nineteenth century, when theaters always used green paint for an actor's dressing room.

EXERCISE 10-5

This is an exercise covering all of subject-verb agreement (10b through 10m). Supply the correct form of the verb in parentheses.

EXAMPLE   Of the thirty thousand plant species on earth, the rose (to be) is the most universally known.

1. Each plant species (to invite) _____ much discussion about origins and meanings, and when talk turns to flowers, the rose is usually the first mentioned.
2. More fragrant and colorful (to be) _____ other types of flowers, yet roses (to remain) _____ the most popular worldwide.
3. Each of the types of roses (to symbolize) _____ beauty, love, romance, and secrecy.
4. There (to be) _____ over two hundred pure species of roses and thousands of mixed species, thirty-five of which (to flourish) _____ in the soil of North America.
5. It's impossible to determine exactly where or when the first rose (to be) _____ domesticated, because roses have existed for so many centuries; one of the earliest references dates back to 3000 B.C.
6. One such myth from Greek mythology (to suggest) _____ that the rose first appeared with the birth of the goddess Aphrodite.
7. Another myth, which focuses on the rose's thorns, (to say) _____ that an angry god shot arrows into the stem to curse the rose forever with arrow-shaped thorns.

239

8. While theories of this kind (to explain) _____ the significance and evolution of the rose, few people can explain the flower's enduring popularity.

9. Even today, a couple (to demonstrate) _____ love by exchanging red roses.

10. Of all flowers, the bestseller (to remain) _____ the rose.

PRONOUN-ANTECEDENT AGREEMENT

10n What is pronoun-antecedent agreement?

Pronoun-antecedent agreement means that a PRONOUN matches its ANTECEDENT in NUMBER (singular or plural) and PERSON (first, second, or third person). Box 79 shows you how to visualize this pattern of grammatical agreement. You might also want to consult Box 73 in section 10b for explanations and examples of the concepts *number* and *person*.

The **firefly** glows when **it** emerges from **its** nest at night. [The singular pronouns *it* and *its* match their singular antecedent, *firefly*.]

Fireflies glow when **they** emerge from **their** nests at night. [The plural pronouns *they* and *their* match their plural antecedent, *fireflies*.]

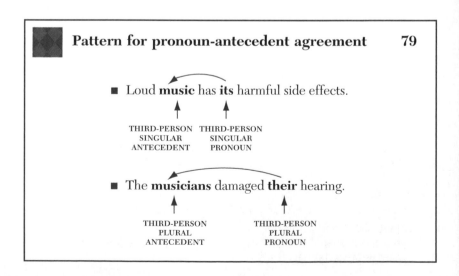

Pattern for pronoun-antecedent agreement   79

- Loud **music** has **its** harmful side effects.

THIRD-PERSON SINGULAR ANTECEDENT   THIRD-PERSON SINGULAR PRONOUN

- The **musicians** damaged **their** hearing.

THIRD-PERSON PLURAL ANTECEDENT   THIRD-PERSON PLURAL PRONOUN

10o How do pronouns operate with antecedents connected by *and*?

When *and* connects two or more ANTECEDENTS, they require a plural pronoun. This rule applies even if each separate antecedent is singular. (For related material on subjects and verbs, see 10e.)

The Cascade Diner *and* the Wayside Diner closed for New Year's Eve to give **their** [not *its*] employees the night off. [Two separate diners require a plural pronoun.]

When *and* joins singular nouns that nevertheless refer to a single person or thing, use a singular pronoun.

My friend *and* neighbor makes **his** [not *their*] excellent chili every Saturday. [The friend is the same person as the neighbor, so the singular *his* (or *her*) is correct. If two different people were involved, the correct pronoun would be *their,* and *make* would be the correct verb.]

each, every

The words *each* and *every* are singular, even when they refer to two or more antecedents joined by *and.* The same rule applies when *each* or *every* is used alone (10h). (For related material on subjects and verbs, see 10e.)

***Each* human hand *and* foot** leaves **its** [not *their*] distinctive print.

The rule still applies when the construction *one of the* follows *each* or *every.*

***Each one of the* robbers** left **his** [not *their*] fingerprints at the scene.

10p How do pronouns operate when antecedents are connected by *or*?

When ANTECEDENTS are joined by *or* or by CORRELATIVE CONJUNCTIONS such as *either . . . or, neither . . . nor,* or *not only . . . but (also),* the antecedents might mix singulars and plurals. For the purposes of agreement, ignore everything before the final antecedent. Box 80 shows you how to visualize this pattern. (For related material on subject-verb agreement, see 10f.)

~~After the restaurant closes, *either*~~ the resident mice ~~*or*~~ the owner's **cat** gets **itself** a meal.

~~After the restaurant closes, *either*~~ the owner's cat ~~*or*~~ the resident **mice** get **themselves** a meal.

241

> ### Pattern when antecedents are joined by *or*   80
>
> ■ ~~Either the loudspeakers or~~ **the microphone** needs **its** electric
> cord repaired.
>
>   SINGULAR   SINGULAR
>   ANTECEDENT   PRONOUN
>
> ■ ~~Either the microphone or~~ **the loudspeakers** need **their** electric
> cords repaired.
>
>   PLURAL   PLURAL
>   ANTECEDENT   PRONOUN

10q How do pronouns operate with indefinite-pronoun antecedents?

INDEFINITE PRONOUNS usually refer to unknown persons, things, quantities, or ideas. The unknown aspect is why these pronouns are labeled "indefinite." But in a sentence, context gives an indefinite pronoun a clear meaning, even if the pronoun doesn't have a specific antecedent. Most indefinite pronouns are singular. Two indefinite pronouns, *both* and *many,* are plural. A few indefinite pronouns can be singular or plural, depending on the meaning of the sentence.

For a list of indefinite pronouns, grouped as singular or plural, see Box 78 in section 10h. For more information about avoiding sexist language, especially when using indefinite pronouns, see 10r and 21g. (For related material on subjects and verbs, see 10e.)

SINGULAR INDEFINITE PRONOUNS

Everyone taking this course hopes to get **his or her** [not *their*] college degree within a year.

Anybody wanting to wear a cap and gown at graduation must have **his or her** [not *their*] measurements taken.

Each of the students handed in **his or her** [not *their*] final term paper.

SINGULAR *OR* PLURAL INDEFINITE PRONOUNS

When winter break arrives for students, **most** leave **their** dormitories for home. [*Most* refers to *students,* so the plural pronoun *their* is correct.]

As for the luggage, **most is** already on **its** way to the airport. [*Most* refers to *luggage,* so the singular pronoun *its* is correct.]

None thinks that **he or she** will miss graduation. [*None* is singular as used in this sentence, so the singular pronoun *he or she* is correct.]

None of the students has paid **his or her** [not *their*] graduation fee yet. [*None* is singular as used in this sentence, so the singular pronoun *his or her* is correct.]

None are so proud as **they** who graduate. [*None* is plural as used in this sentence, so the plural pronoun *they* is correct.]

10r How can I use nonsexist pronouns correctly?

The term *nonsexist* refers to gender-free language. It has become standard style to use **nonsexist pronouns** where gender-free language is appropriate. In the past, concerning pronouns, it was grammatically correct to use only masculine pronouns to refer to INDEFINITE PRONOUNS: "*Everyone* open **his** book." Today, however, people know that the pronouns *he, his, him,* and *himself* exclude women, who make up over half the population. Box 81 shows three ways to avoid using masculine pronouns when referring to males and females together. For more information on gender-neutral language, see 21g.

Questions often arise concerning the use of *he or she* and *his and her*. In general, writers find these gender-free pronoun constructions awkward. To avoid them, many writers make the antecedents plural. Doing this becomes problematic when the subject is a SINGULAR INDEFINITE PRONOUN (Box 78 in section 10h). In the popular press (such as newspapers and magazines), the use of the plural pronoun *they* or *them* with a singular antecedent has been gaining favor. Indeed, some experts find that the history of English supports this use. In ACADEMIC WRITING, however, it is better for you not to follow the practice of the popular press. Language practice changes, however, so what I say here is my best advice as I write this book.

⊙ **Ways to avoid using only the masculine pronoun 81 to refer to males and females together**

- ■ **Solution 1:** Use a pair of pronouns—*he or she*. However, avoid using a pair more than once in a sentence or in many sentences in a row. A *he or she* construction acts as a singular pronoun.

  Everyone hopes that **he or she** will win a scholarship.

  A **doctor** usually has time to keep up to date only in **his or her** specialty.

  ➡

243

**Ways to avoid using only the masculine pronoun   81
to refer to males and females together** *(continued)*

- **Solution 2:** Revise into the plural.
  Many students hope that **they** will win a scholarship.
  Most doctors have time to keep up to date only in **their** specialties.

- **Solution 3:** Recast the sentence.
  Everyone hopes to win a scholarship.
  Few specialists have time for general reading.

10s How do pronouns operate when antecedents are collective nouns?

A COLLECTIVE NOUN names a group of people or things, such as *family, group, audience, class, number, committee,* and *team.* When the group acts as one unit, use a singular pronoun to refer to it. When the members of the group act individually, use a plural pronoun. In the latter case, if the sentence is awkward, substitute a plural noun for the collective noun. (For related material on subjects and verbs, see 10i.)

> The **audience** was cheering as **it** stood to applaud the performers. [The *audience* was acting as one unit, so the singular pronoun *it* is correct.]
>
> The **audience** put on **their** coats and walked out. [The members of the audience were acting as individuals, so all actions become plural; therefore, the plural pronoun *their* is correct.]
>
> The **family** is spending **its** vacation in Rockport, Maine. [All the family members went to one place together.]

The parallel sentence to the last example above would be *The **family** are spending **their** vacations in Maine, Hawaii, and Rome,* which might mean that each family member is going to a different place. But such a sentence is awkward. Therefore, revise the sentence.

> The **family members** are spending **their** vacations in Maine, Hawaii, and Rome. [Substituting a plural noun *family members* for the collective noun *family* sounds more natural.]

EXERCISE 10-6

Underline the correct pronoun in parentheses. For help, consult 10n through 10s.

EXAMPLE   Many people wonder what gives certain leaders (his or her, their) spark and magnetic personal appeal.

1. The cluster of personal traits that produces star quality is called *charisma,* a state that bestows special power on (its, their) bearers.
2. Charisma is the quality that allows an individual to empower (himself, herself, himself or herself, themselves) and others.
3. Power and authority alone don't guarantee charisma; (it, they) must be combined with passion and strong purpose.
4. A charismatic leader has the ability to draw other people into (his, her, his or her, their) dream or vision.
5. (He, She, He or she, They) can inspire followers to believe that the leader's goals are the same as (his, her, his or her, their) own.
6. Not all leaders who possess charisma enjoy having this ability to attract and influence (his, his or her, their) followers.
7. Charismatic leaders are often creative, especially in (his, her, his or her, their) capacity for solving problems in original ways.
8. Today, a number of major corporations offer (its, their) employees charisma-training courses to enhance leadership qualities.
9. Usually, it's not the quiet, low-profile manager but rather the charismatic manager with strong leadership qualities who convinces others that (his, her, his or her, their) best interests are served by the course of action (he, she, he or she, they) is/are proposing.
10. Charisma trainers advise would-be leaders to start by bringing order to (his, her, his or her, their) activities; in stressful times, anyone who appears to have some part of (his, her, his or her, their) life under control makes others relax and perform (his, her, his or her, their) responsibilities better.

www.prenhall.com/troyka

11 ADJECTIVES AND ADVERBS

11a What are the differences between adjectives and adverbs?

The differences between adjectives and adverbs relate to how they function. **Adjectives** modify NOUNS and PRONOUNS. **Adverbs** modify VERBS, adjectives, and other adverbs. What's the same about adjective and adverbs is that they are both MODIFIERS—that is, words or groups of words that describe other words. Box 82 compares adjectives and adverbs in action.

ADJECTIVE   The **brisk** *wind* blew. [Adjective *brisk* modifies noun *wind*.]

ADVERB   The wind *blew* **briskly.** [Adverb *briskly* modifies verb *blew*.]

 Differences between adjectives and adverbs   82

WHAT ADJECTIVES MODIFY	EXAMPLES
nouns	The **busy** *lawyer* took a **quick** *look* at her schedule.
pronouns	*She* felt **triumphant**, for *they* were **attentive**.

WHAT ADVERBS MODIFY	EXAMPLES
verbs	The lawyer *spoke* **quickly** and **well.**
adverbs	The lawyer spoke **very** *quickly.*
adjectives	The lawyer was **extremely** *busy.*
independent clauses	**Therefore,** *the lawyer rested.*

Some people think that all adverbs end in *-ly*. But this isn't correct. While many adverbs do end in *-ly* (eat *swiftly*, eat *frequently*, eat *hungrily*), some do not (eat *fast*, eat *often*, eat *seldom*). To complicate matters further, some adjectives end in *-ly* (*lovely* flower, *friendly* dog). Use meaning, not an *-ly* ending, to identify adverbs.

ESL NOTE: (1) In English, the adjective is always singular, even if a noun is plural: *The **hot** [not hots] drinks warmed us up.* (2) Word order in English calls for special attention to the placement of adjective and adverbs. Here is an example using the adverb *carefully: Thomas closed* [don't place *carefully* here] *the window **carefully*** (see 47b, 47c).

EXERCISE 11-1

Underline and label all adjectives (ADJ) and adverbs (ADV). Then, draw an arrow from each adjective and adverb to the word or words it modifies. For help, consult 11a.

ADJ   ADV   ADJ

EXAMPLE Leaky faucets are unexpectedly leading to genuine romance

ADJ   ADJ

in super-sized hardware stores.

1. While shopping for new faucets and drills, today's singles also carefully look for possible mates at discount home improvement stores across the country.
2. Understandably, many people find these stores a healthy alternative to dark bars and blind dates.
3. Recently, an employee in the flooring department quietly confided that the best nights for singles are Wednesdays and Thursdays, while weekends generally attract families.
4. A young single mom returns home excitedly because a quick trip to the lumber department for a new door resulted in a date for Saturday night.
5. A lonely widower in his fifties jokingly says he wishes he had developed earlier an interest in wallpapering and gardening.

11b When should I use adverbs, not adjectives, as modifiers?

Adverbs MODIFY verbs, adjectives, and other adverbs. Don't use adjectives as adverbs.

NO   The candidate inspired us **great.** [Adjective *great* cannot modify verb *inspired.*]

YES   The candidate inspired us **greatly.** [Adverb *greatly* can modify verb *inspired.*]

NO   The candidate felt **unusual** energetic. [Adjective *unusual* cannot modify adjective *energetic.*]

YES   The candidate felt **unusually** energetic. [Adverb *unusually* can modify adjective *energetic.*]

NO   The candidate spoke **exceptional** forcefully. [Adjective *exceptional* cannot modify adverb *forcefully.*]

YES   The candidate spoke **exceptionally** forcefully. [Adverb *exceptionally* modifies adverb *forcefully.*]

11c How can I avoid double negatives?

A **double negative** is a statement with two negative MODIFIERS, the second of which repeats the message of the first. Negative modifiers include *no, never, not, none, nothing, hardly, scarcely,* and *barely.*

NO   The factory workers will **never** vote for **no** strike.

YES   The factory workers will **never** vote for **a** strike.

NO   The union members did **not** have **no** money in reserve.

YES   The union members did **not** have **any** money in reserve.

YES   The union members had **no** money in reserve.

Take special care to avoid double negatives with contractions of *not: isn't, don't, didn't, haven't,* and the like (27d). The contraction containing *not* serves as the only negative in a sentence. Don't add a second negative.

NO   He **didn't** hear **nothing.**

YES   He **didn't** hear **anything.**

NO   They **haven't** had **no** meetings.

YES   They **haven't** had **any** meetings.

Similarly, be careful to avoid double negatives when you use *nor.* The word *nor* is correct only after *neither* (7i). Use the word *or* after any other negative.

NO   Stewart **didn't** eat dinner **nor** watch television last night.

YES   Stewart **didn't** eat dinner **or** watch television last night.

YES   Stewart **neither** ate dinner **nor** watched television last night.

11d Do adjectives or adverbs come after linking verbs?

LINKING VERBS (8a) connect a SUBJECT to a COMPLEMENT (7n.1). Always use an adjective, not an adverb, as the complement.

> The *guests* **looked** happy. [Verb *looked* links subject *guests* to adjective *happy*.]

The words *look, feel, smell, taste, sound,* and *grow* are usually linking verbs, but sometimes they're simply verbs. Check how any of these verbs is functioning in a sentence.

> Zora *looks* **happy.** [*Looks* functions as a linking verb, so the adjective *happy* is correct.]

> Zora *looks* **happily** at the sunset. [*Looks* doesn't function as a linking verb, so the adverb *happily* is correct.]

bad, badly

The words *bad* (adjective) and *badly* (adverb) are particularly prone to misuse with linking verbs.

> **NO**   The students felt **badly.** [This means the students used their fingers badly.]
>
> **YES**   The student felt **bad.** [This means the student had a bad feeling about something.]
>
> **NO**   The food smelled **badly.** [This means the food had a bad ability to smell.]
>
> **YES**   The food smelled **bad.** [This means the food had a bad smell to it.]

good, well

When the word *well* refers to health, it is an adjective; at all other times, *well* is an adverb. The word *good* is always an adjective.

> Evander looks **well.** [This means that Evander seems to be in good health, so the adjective *well* is correct.]

> Evander writes **well.** [This means that Evander writes skillfully, so the adverb *well* is correct.]

Use *good* as an adjective, except when you refer to health.

> **NO**   She sings **good.** [*Sings* isn't a linking verb, so it calls for an adverb, not the adjective *good*.]
>
> **YES**   She sings **well.** [*Sings* isn't a linking verb, so the adverb *well* is correct.]

EXERCISE 11-2

Underline the correct uses of negatives, adjectives, and adverbs by selecting between the choices in parentheses. For help, consult sections 11a through 11d.

EXAMPLE   Because she was only five when her father died, Bernice King, Martin Luther King's youngest child, (<u>barely</u>, bare) remembers the details of her father's (solemnly, <u>solemn</u>) funeral, yet her father's image lives (strong, <u>strongly</u>) within her.

1. Although she did feel (badly, bad) about her father's death when she was younger, King's daughter has managed to put his influence on her to good use by speaking (passionately, passionate) about issues her father first introduced.

2. In her (widely, wide) acclaimed book of sermons and speeches, titled *Hard Questions, Hard Answers,* Bernice King strives to deal with the (intensely, intense) topic of race relations.

3. Bernice King believes, as did her father, that all people must connect (genuinely, genuine), or they won't (never, ever) manage to coexist.

4. Bernice King decided to enter the ministry after she heard a (deeply, deep) voice within her directing her to this (extremely, extreme) (spiritually, spiritual) profession.

5. Bernice King entered the public eye in 1993, when she gave a (locally, local) televised Martin Luther King Day sermon at her father's church, and since then she has lived (happily, happy) in her home in Atlanta with memories of her father that are (peacefully, peaceful) recollections.

11e How do I correctly use comparative and superlative forms of adjectives and adverbs?

When you write about comparisons, ADJECTIVES and ADVERBS often carry the message. The adjective and adverbs also communicate degrees of intensity. When a comparison is between two things, a **comparative** form is used. When a comparison is made about three or more things, a **superlative** form is used.

11e.1 Using correct forms of comparison for regular adjectives and adverbs

Most adjectives and adverbs are regular (section 11e.2 explains when they're irregular). They communicate degrees of intensity in one of two ways: either by adding -*er* and -*est* endings or by adding the words *more, most, less,* and *least* (see Box 83).

> ⊙ **Forms of comparison for regular**   83
> **adjectives and adverbs**
>
> POSITIVE   Use when nothing is being compared.
>
> COMPARATIVE   Use when two things are being compared. Add
> the ending -er or the word *more* or *less.*
>
> SUPERLATIVE   Use to compare three or more things. Add the
> ending -est or the word *most* or *least.*
>
> | POSITIVE | COMPARATIVE | SUPERLATIVE |
> |---|---|---|
> | green | greener | greenest |
> | happy | happier | happiest |
> | selfish | less selfish | least selfish |
> | beautiful | more beautiful | most beautiful |
>
> That tree is **green.**
> That tree is **greener** than this tree.
> That tree is the **greenest** tree on the block.

The number of syllables in the adjective or adverb usually determines whether to use -er, -est or *more, most* and *less, least.*

- **One-syllable words** usually take -er and -est endings: *large, larger, largest* (adjectives); *far, farther, farthest* (adverbs).
- **Adjectives of two syllables** vary. If the word ends in -y, change the y to i and add -er, -est endings: *pretty, prettier, prettiest.* Otherwise, some two-syllable adjectives take -er, -est endings: *yellow, yellower, yellowest.* Others take *more, most* and *less, least: more tangled, most tangled; less tangled, least tangled.*
- **Adverbs of two syllables** take *more, most* and *less, least: easily, more easily, most easily; less easily, least easily.*
- **Three-syllable words** take *more, most* and *less, least: more/most dignified, less/least dignified* (adjective); *more/most carefully, less/least carefully* (adverb).

⊚ **ALERT:** Be careful not to use a double comparative or double superlative. Use either the -er and -est ending or *more, most* or *less, least.* Don't use both.

He was **younger** [not *more younger*] than his brother.
Her music was the **loudest** [not *most loudest*] on the stereo.
Children are **more easily** [not *more easier*] influenced than adults. ●

11e.2 Using correct forms of comparison for irregular adjectives and adverbs

A few comparative and superlative forms are irregular. Box 84 gives you the list. I suggest that you memorize them so they come to mind easily.

◉ **Irregular comparatives and superlatives**   84

POSITIVE [1]	COMPARATIVE [2]	SUPERLATIVE [3+]
good (*adjective*)	better	best
well (*adjective* and *adverb*)	better	best
bad (*adjective*)	worse	worst
badly (*adverb*)	worse	worst
many	more	most
much	more	most
some	more	most
little	less	least

The Wallaces saw a **good** movie.

The Wallaces saw a **better** movie than the **Pascals** did.

The Wallaces saw the **best** movie they had ever seen.

The Millers had **little** trouble finding jobs.

The Millers had **less** trouble finding jobs than the Smiths did.

The Millers had the **least** trouble finding jobs of everyone.

◉ **ALERT:** (1) Be aware of the difference between *less* and *fewer.* They aren't interchangeable. Use *less* with NONCOUNT NOUNS, either items or values: *The sugar substitute has less* **aftertaste.** Use *fewer* with numbers or COUNT NOUNS: *The sugar substitute has fewer* **calories.** (2) Don't use *more, most* or *less, least* with **absolute adjectives,** that is, adjectives that communicate a noncomparable quality or state, such as *unique* or *perfect.* Something either *is,* or *is not,* one of a kind. No degrees of intensity are involved: *This teapot is* **unique** (not *the most unique*); *The artisanship is* **perfect** (not *the most perfect*). ●

EXERCISE 11-3

Complete the chart that follows. Then, write a sentence for each word in the completed chart. For help, consult 11e.

EXAMPLE *funny, funnier, funniest:* My brother has a *funny* laugh; he thinks Mom has a *funnier* laugh; the person who has the *funniest* laugh in our family is uncle Dominic.

POSITIVE	COMPARATIVE	SUPERLATIVE
little	_____	_____
_____	greedier	_____
_____	_____	most complete
gladly	_____	_____
_____	_____	fewest
_____	thicker	_____
some	_____	_____

11f How do I avoid a string of too many nouns as modifiers?

NOUNS sometimes MODIFY other nouns: *truck driver, train track, security system.* Usually, these terms create no problems. However, try hard not to use several nouns in a row as modifiers. A string of too many nouns makes it difficult for your reader to figure out which nouns are being modified and which nouns are doing the modifying. You can revise such sentences in several ways.

REWRITE THE SENTENCE

NO   I asked my adviser to write **two college recommendation letters** for me.

YES   I asked my adviser to write *letters of recommendation to two colleges* for me.

CHANGE ONE NOUN TO A POSSESSIVE AND ANOTHER TO AN ADJECTIVE

NO   He will take the **United States Navy examination** for **navy engineer** training.

YES   He will take the *United States Navy's examination* for *naval engineer training.*

CHANGE ONE NOUN TO A PREPOSITIONAL PHRASE

NO   Our **student adviser training program** has won many awards.

YES   Our *training program for student advisers* has won many awards. [This change requires a change from the singular *adviser* to the plural *advisers.*]

253

EXERCISE 11-4

Underline the better choice in parentheses. For help, consult this entire chapter.

EXAMPLE   Stunt work is a visual art that (frequent, <u>frequently</u>) involves physical risk to the performer.

1. The first stunt performers were (most likely, likeliest) the Roman gladiators, who entertained crowds with chariot races and sword fights.
2. Actors in the early silent movies sustained (many, more) injuries during filming because they used no doubles for their stunts.
3. In a 1916 movie about the Civil War, no (fewer, less) than sixty-seven extras suffered injuries during the filming of one scene.
4. Today, more than two hundred (high, highly) trained stunt performers, ranging in age from ten to eighty-two, work (regular, regularly) in Hollywood movies.
5. In a single year, stunt performer Harry Madsen was beaten, knifed, shot, set on fire, and thrown out a fourth-floor window. He was paid (good, well) and had a (good, well) time, too.

12 SENTENCE FRAGMENTS

12a What is a sentence fragment?

A **sentence fragment** looks like a sentence, but it's actually only part of a sentence. That is, even though a sentence fragment begins with a capital letter (see 30a) and ends with a period (or question mark or exclamation point; see Chapter 23), it doesn't contain an INDEPENDENT CLAUSE. Fragments are merely unattached PHRASES or DEPENDENT CLAUSES.

FRAGMENT	The telephone with redial capacity. [NO VERB]
CORRECT	The telephone has redial capacity.
FRAGMENT	Rang loudly for ten minutes. [no SUBJECT]
CORRECT	The telephone rang loudly for ten minutes.
FRAGMENT	At midnight. [a phrase without a verb or subject]
CORRECT	The telephone rang at midnight.
FRAGMENT	Because the telephone rang loudly. [Dependent clause starting with SUBORDINATING CONJUNCTION *because*]
CORRECT	Because the telephone rang loudly, the family was awakened in the middle of the night.
FRAGMENT	Which really annoyed me. [dependent clause with RELATIVE PRONOUN *which* but without a verb in the INDEPENDENT CLAUSE]
CORRECT	The telephone call was a wrong number, which really annoyed me.

Sentence fragments can ruin the clarity of your writing. Moreover, in ACADEMIC WRITING and BUSINESS WRITING, sentence fragments imply that you don't know basic sentence structure or that you're a careless proofreader.

NO	The lawyer was angry. When she returned from court. She found the key witness waiting in her office. [Was the lawyer angry when she returned from court, or when she found the witness in her office?]

255

> **YES**   The lawyer was angry when she returned from court. She found the key witness waiting in her office.
>
> **YES**   The lawyer was angry. When she returned from court, she found the key witness waiting in her office.

Let's go beyond the grammatical terms to a more practical approach to recognizing sentence fragments, so that you avoid them in your writing. (Remember that any words in small capital letters in this handbook are defined, usually with examples, in the Terms Glossary, starting on page 821.) To learn to recognize sentence fragments, see 12b; to learn several ways to correct sentence fragments, see 12c and 12d.

Many writers wait until the REVISING and EDITING stages of the WRITING PROCESS to check for sentence fragments. During DRAFTING, the goal is to get ideas down on paper or disk. As you draft, if you suspect that you've written a sentence fragment, simply underline or highlight it in boldface or italics and move on. Later, you can easily find it to check and correct.

12b How can I recognize a sentence fragment?

If you tend to write sentence fragments, you want a system for recognizing them. Box 85 shows you a Sentence Test for checking that you haven't written a sentence fragment. Then, following Box 85, I discuss each question in more detail in sections 12b.1 through 12b.3.

◉ **Sentence Test to identify sentence fragments   85**

Question 1: Is the word group a dependent clause?

A DEPENDENT CLAUSE is a word group that has a subject and a verb but starts with a word that creates dependence—either a SUBORDINATING CONJUNCTION or a RELATIVE PRONOUN.

FRAGMENT	**When** winter comes early. [starts with *when,* a word that creates dependence]
CORRECT	**When** winter comes early, **ships often rescue the stranded whales.** [adds independent clause]
FRAGMENT	**Which** can happen quickly. [starts with *which,* a word that creates dependence]
CORRECT	**Whales cannot breathe through the ice and drown, which** can happen quickly. [adds an independent clause]

→

Sentence Test to identify sentence fragments   **85**
(continued)

Question 2: Is there a verb?

FRAGMENT   Thousands of whales in the Arctic Ocean. [Because a
VERB is missing, it's a PHRASE, not a sentence.]

CORRECT   Thousands of whales **live** in the Arctic Ocean. [adds a
verb to create a sentence]

Question 3: Is there a subject?

FRAGMENT   Stranded in the Arctic Ocean. [Because a SUBJECT is missing, it's a phrase, not a sentence.]

CORRECT   **Many whales *were*** stranded in the Arctic Ocean [adds a
subject (and the verb *were* to *stranded*) to create a sentence]

12b.1   Question 1: Is the word group a dependent clause?

If you answer yes to question 1, you're looking at a SENTENCE FRAG-
MENT. A DEPENDENT CLAUSE is a word group that has a subject and a
verb but starts with a word that creates dependence. The only words that
create dependence are SUBORDINATING CONJUNCTIONS or RELATIVE PRO-
NOUNS. Such a word before an INDEPENDENT CLAUSE creates a dependent clause. A dependent clause can't stand alone as a sentence, so it's a
sentence fragment. To become a complete sentence, the fragment needs
either to be joined to an independent clause or rewritten as one.

Fragments with subordinating conjunctions

A complete list of subordinating conjunctions appears in Box 51 (see 7i,
pages 164–165). Some frequently used ones are *after, although, because,
before, if, unless,* and *when.*

FRAGMENT   **Because** she returned my books. [*Because,* a subordinating
conjunction, creates a dependent clause.]

CORRECT   **Because** she returned my books, ***I can study.*** [A comma
and the independent clause *I can study* is added, and the sentence becomes complete.]

FRAGMENT   **Unless** I study. [*Unless,* a subordinating conjunction, creates a
dependent clause.]

CORRECT   ***I won't pass the test*** **unless** I study. [The independent
clause *I won't pass the test* is added, and the sentence
becomes complete.]

◉ When a dependent clause starts with a subordinating conjunction and comes before its independent clause, use a comma to separate the clauses (24c). ●

Fragments with relative pronouns

Relative pronouns are *that, which, who, whom,* and *whose.*

FRAGMENT   **That** we had studied for all week. [*That,* a relative pronoun, creates a dependent clause here.]

CORRECT   *We passed our midterm exam* **that** we had studied for all week. [The independent clause *We passed our midterm exam* is added, and the sentence becomes complete.]

When *which, who,* and *whose* begin questions, they function as INTERROGATIVE PRONOUNS, not relative pronouns. Questions are complete sentences, not fragments: *Who* is your professor? *Whose* book is that? *Which* class are you taking?

12b.2 Question 2: Is there a verb?

If you answer no to question 2, you're looking at a sentence fragment. When a VERB is missing from a word group, the result is a PHRASE, not a sentence. You can figure out if a word is a verb by seeing if it can change in TENSE. Verbs have tenses to tell what *is* happening, what *has* happened, or what *will* happen.

Now the telephone **rings.** [present tense]
Yesterday, the telephone **rang.** [past tense]

When you check for verbs, remember that VERBALS are not verbs. Verbals might look like verbs, but verbals don't function as verbs (see 7e).

FRAGMENT   Yesterday, the students **registering** for classes. [*Registering* is a verbal called a PRESENT PARTICIPLE, which isn't a verb.]

CORRECT   Yesterday, the students **were registering** for classes. [Adding the AUXILIARY VERB *were* to the present participle *registering* creates a verb.]

FRAGMENT   They **informed** that the course was not being offered. [*Informed* is a verbal called a PAST PARTICIPLE, which isn't a verb.]

CORRECT   They **had been informed** that the course was not being offered. [Adding the auxiliary verbs *had been* to past participle *informed* creates a verb.]

FRAGMENT   Now the students **to register** for classes. [*To register* is a verbal called an INFINITIVE, which isn't verb.]

CORRECT   Now the students **want to register** for classes. [Adding the verb *want* to the infinitive *to register* creates a verb.]

12b.3 Question 3: Is there a subject?

If you answer no to question 3, you're looking at a sentence fragment. When a SUBJECT is missing from a word group, the result is a PHRASE, not a sentence. To see if a word is a subject, ask "Who?" or "What?" performs the action.

FRAGMENT   Studied hard for class. [*Who* studied hard for class? unknown]

CORRECT   The students studied hard for class. [*Who* studied hard for class? *The students* is the answer, so a subject makes the sentence complete.]

FRAGMENT   Contained some difficult questions. [*What* contained some difficult questions? unknown]

CORRECT   The test contained some difficult questions. [*What* contained some difficult questions? *The test* is the answer, so a subject makes the sentence complete.]

Be especially careful with COMPOUND PREDICATES—for example, *We **took** the bus to the movie **and walked** home.* If you were to place a period after *movie,* the second part of the compound predicate would be a sentence fragment. Every sentence needs its own subject. To check for this kind of sentence fragment, ask the question "Who?" or "What?" of each verb.

NO   A few students organized a study group to prepare for midterm exams. **Decided to study together for the rest of the course.** [*Who* decided to study together? The answer is *The students* (who formed the group), but this subject is missing.]

YES   A few students organized a study group to prepare for midterm exams. ***The students* decided to study together for the rest of the course.**

IMPERATIVE SENTENCES—commands and some requests—may appear at first glance to be fragments caused by missing subjects. They're not fragments, however. Imperative sentences are complete sentences because their subjects are implied. An implied subject can be *you, anybody, somebody,* or *everybody,* and other INDEFINITE PRONOUNS.

Run! [This sentence implies the pronoun *you.* The complete sentence would be *You run!*]

Return all library books to the front desk. [This sentence implies the indefinite pronoun *everyone.* The complete sentence would be *Everyone (should) return all library books to the front desk.*]

EXERCISE 12-1

Identify each word group as either a complete sentence or a fragment. If the word group is a sentence, circle its number. If it's a fragment, tell why it's incomplete. For help, see Box 85 in 12b and sections 12b.1 through 12b.3.

EXAMPLE Because gold is shiny, flexible, and scarce. [Starts with a subordinating conjunction (*because*), creating dependence, and lacks an independent clause to complete the thought; see Box 85 and section 12c.1]

1. Making gold ideal for a variety of uses.
2. Since gold does not easily tarnish, corrode, or rust.
3. Provides brilliance to coins, jewelry, and artwork.
4. Because gold combines easily to strengthen copper, silver, or nickel.
5. Weighs twice as much as a square inch of lead.
6. One ounce of gold can be rolled out to a 300-square-foot sheet.
7. Or can be pulled into a 40-mile-long wire.
8. The melting point of gold is 1,945 degrees Fahrenheit.
9. Although tons of gold lie under the oceans.
10. The value of gold being less than the cost of mining gold from ocean floors.

12c What are major ways of correcting fragments?

Once you've identified a SENTENCE FRAGMENT (12b), you're ready to correct it. You can do this in one of two ways: by joining it to an independent clause (12c.1) or by rewriting it (12c.2).

12c.1 Correcting a sentence fragment by joining it to an independent clause

Each of the three kinds of sentence fragments listed in Box 85 in 12b can be corrected by being joined to an INDEPENDENT CLAUSE—that is, a complete sentence. The first two examples below deal with dependent-clause fragments; the examples on pages 261–262 following the ALERT examine fragments with missing subjects and/or verbs.

FRAGMENT **Because** the ice was thick. [Although this word group has a SUBJECT (*ice*) and VERB (*was*), it starts with the SUBORDINATING CONJUNCTION *because*.]

CORRECT **Because** the ice was thick, *icebreakers were required to serve as rescue ships.* [By adding a comma and joining the fragment to the independent clause *icebreakers were required to serve as rescue ships,* a complete sentence is created.]

CORRECT *Icebreakers were required to serve as rescue ships* **because** the ice was thick. [By joining the fragment to the independent clause *Icebreakers were required to serve as rescue ships,* a complete sentence is created.]

FRAGMENT Who feared the whales would panic. [starts with the RELATIVE PRONOUN *who*]

CORRECT *The noisy motors of the ships worried the crews,* who feared the whales would panic. [By joining the fragment to the independent clause *The noisy motors of the ships worried the crews,* a complete sentence is created.]

👁 **ALERT:** Be careful with words that indicate time, such as *after, before, since,* and *until.* They aren't always subordinating conjunctions. Sometimes they function as ADVERBS—especially if they begin a complete sentence. At other times, they function as PREPOSITIONS. When you see one of these words that indicate time, realize that you aren't necessarily looking at a dependent-clause fragment.

Before, the whales had responded to classical music. [A complete sentence in which *Before* is an adverb that modifies the independent clause *the whales had responded to classical music.*]
Before the whales had responded to classical music, some crewmembers tried rock and roll music. [If the word group before the comma stood on its own, it would be a sentence fragment because it starts with *Before* functioning as a subordinating conjunction.]●

FRAGMENT To announce new programs for crime prevention. [*To announce* starts an INFINITIVE PHRASE, not a sentence.]

CORRECT *The mayor called a news conference last week* to announce new programs for crime prevention. [Infinitive phrase starting with *to announce* is joined with an independent clause.]

FRAGMENT Hoping for strong public support. [*Hoping* starts a PRESENT-PARTICIPLE phrase, not a sentence.]

CORRECT Hoping for strong public support, *she gave examples of problems throughout the city.* [Present-participle phrase starting with *Hoping* is joined with the independent clause.]

FRAGMENT Introduced by her assistant. [*Introduced* starts a PAST-PARTICIPLE PHRASE, not a sentence.]

CORRECT Introduced by her assistant, *the mayor began with an opening statement.* [Past-participle phrase starting with *Introduced* is joined with an independent clause.]

FRAGMENT During the long news conference. [*During* functions as a preposition—starting a PREPOSITIONAL PHRASE—not a sentence.]

CORRECT *Cigarette smoke made the conference room seem airless* during the long news conference. [The prepositional phrase starting with *during* is joined with an independent clause.]

FRAGMENT	**A politician with fresh ideas.** [*A politician* starts an APPOSITIVE PHRASE, not a sentence.]
CORRECT	*Most people respected the mayor,* **a politician** with fresh ideas. [The appositive phrase starting with *a politician* is joined with an independent clause.]

EXERCISE 12-2

Find and correct any sentence fragments. If a sentence is correct, circle its number. For help, consult sections 12a through 12c.

EXAMPLE   Kwanzaa is an African American holiday. That is observed from December 25 to January 1.

Kwanzaa is an African American *holiday that* is observed from December 25 to January 1.

1. Kwanzaa was created in 1966 by Maulana Karenga, an African American teacher. Who wanted to teach people about their African heritage.
2. The word *Kwanzaa* comes from the Swahili phrase *ya kwanza.* Which means "first."
3. Although Kwanzaa allows African Americans to honor the history of black people.
4. The holiday also gives other North Americans a chance to learn African traditions.
5. Although Christmas and Hanukkah are religious holidays. Kwanzaa is a cultural holiday.
6. The festival, which lasts seven days, celebrates seven principles. That are called the *nguzo saba* in Swahili.
7. The seven principles, which are unity, self-determination, collective responsibility, cooperative economics, purpose, creativity, and faith.
8. Each evening during the seven days of Kwanzaa, observers light one of the candles in the *kinara.* Which is a seven-cup candleholder.
9. When they discuss how the principle of the day affects their lives.
10. When family and friends gather on the final night, they celebrate the feast known as the *Karamu.*

12c.2 Correcting a sentence fragment by rewriting it

Each of the three kinds of SENTENCE FRAGMENTS listed in Box 85 in 12b can be corrected by being rewritten as an INDEPENDENT CLAUSE—that is, a complete sentence. The first two examples below deal with dependent-clause fragments; the others examine fragments with missing subjects and/or verbs.

FRAGMENT	**Because** the ice was thick. [Although this word group has a SUBJECT (*ice*) and VERB (*was*), it starts with the SUBORDINATING CONJUNCTION *because*.]
CORRECT	The ice was thick. [Fragment starting with *Because* rewritten to become a complete sentence.]
FRAGMENT	**Who** feared the whales would panic. [starts with RELATIVE PRONOUN *who*]
CORRECT	*The crew* feared the whales would panic. [Fragment starting with *Who* rewritten to become a complete sentence.]
FRAGMENT	**To announce** new programs for crime prevention. [*To announce* starts an INFINITIVE PHRASE, not a sentence.]
CORRECT	*The mayor called a news conference last week because she wanted* to announce new programs for crime prevention. [Infinitive phrase starting with *To announce* rewritten to become a complete sentence.]
FRAGMENT	**Hoping** for strong public support. [*Hoping* starts a PRESENT-PARTICIPLE phrase, not a sentence.]
CORRECT	*She was* hoping for strong public support. [Present-participle phrase starting with *Hoping* rewritten to become a complete sentence.]
FRAGMENT	**Introduced** by her assistant. [*Introduced* starts a PAST-PARTICIPLE PHRASE, not a sentence.]
CORRECT	**Introduced** by her assistant**, *the mayor began with an opening statement.*** [Past-participle phrase starting with *Introduced* rewritten to become a complete sentence.]
FRAGMENT	**During** the long news conference. [*During* functions as a preposition that starts a PREPOSITIONAL PHRASE, not a sentence.]
CORRECT	*It was hard to breathe* **during** the long news conference. [The prepositional phrase starting with *During* rewritten to become a complete sentence.]
FRAGMENT	**A politician** with fresh ideas. [*A politician* starts an APPOSITIVE PHRASE, not a sentence.]
CORRECT	*She seemed to be* a politician with fresh ideas. [Appositive phrase rewritten to become a complete sentence.]

12d How can I correct a fragment that is an incomplete compound predicate?

A COMPOUND PREDICATE contains two or more VERBS. When the second half of a compound predicate is punctuated as a separate sentence, it becomes a sentence fragment.

FRAGMENT	The reporters asked the mayor many questions about the new program. **And then discussed her answers among themselves.** [*And then discussed* starts a compound predicate fragment, not a sentence.]
CORRECT	The reporters asked the mayor many questions about the new program and then discussed her answers among themselves. [Compound predicate fragment starting with *and then discussed* rejoined to the independent clause.]
CORRECT	The reporters asked the mayor many questions about the new program. ***Then the reporters* discussed** her answers among themselves. [Compound predicate fragment starting with *And then discussed* is rewritten as a complete sentence.]

EXERCISE 12-3

Go back to Exercise 12-1 and revise the sentence fragments into complete sentences. In some cases, you may be able to combine two fragments into one complete sentence.

12e What are the two special fragment problems?

Two special fragment problems sometimes come up when people write lists and examples. Lists and examples must be part of a complete sentence, unless they are formatted as a column.

You can connect a list fragment by attaching it to the preceding independent clause using a colon (Chapter 26) or dash (Chapter 29). You can correct an example fragment by attaching it to an independent clause (with or without punctuation, depending on the meaning) or by rewriting it as a complete sentence.

FRAGMENT	You have a choice of desserts. **Carrot cake, chocolate silk pie, apple pie, or peppermint ice cream.** [The list cannot stand on its own as a sentence.]
CORRECT	You have a choice of desserts: carrot cake, chocolate silk pie, apple pie, or peppermint ice cream. [Colon joins the sentence and the list.]
CORRECT	You have a choice of desserts—carrot cake, chocolate silk pie, apple pie, or peppermint ice cream. [Dash joins the sentence and the list.]
FRAGMENT	There are several good places to go for brunch. **For example, the restaurants Sign of the Dove and Blue Yonder.** [Examples can't stand on their own as a sentence.]

| CORRECT | There are several good places to go for brunch— **for example,** the restaurants Sign of the Dove and Blue Yonder. |
| CORRECT | There are several good places to go for brunch. **For example,** *there's* the restaurants Sign of the Dove and Blue Yonder. |

12f How can I recognize intentional fragments?

Professional writers sometimes intentionally use fragments for emphasis and effect.

> But in the main, I feel like a brown bag of miscellany propped against a wall. Pour out the contents, and there is discovered a jumble of small things priceless and worthless. **A first-water diamond, an empty spool, bits of broken glass, lengths of string, a key to a door long since crumbled away, a rusty knife-blade, old shoes saved for a road that never was and never will be, a nail bent under the weight of things too heavy for any nail, a dried flower or two still a little fragrant.**
>
> —Zora Neale Hurston, *How It Feels to Be Colored Me*

Being able to judge the difference between an acceptable and unacceptable sentence fragment comes from years of reading the work of skilled writers. For ACADEMIC WRITING, most instructors don't accept sentence fragments in student writing until a student demonstrates a consistent ability to write well-constructed, complete sentences. As a rule, avoid sentence fragments in academic writing.

EXERCISE 12-4

Revise this paragraph to eliminate all sentence fragments. In some cases, you can combine word groups to create complete sentences; in other cases, you must supply missing elements to rewrite. Some sentences may not require revision. In your final version, check not only the individual sentences but also the clarity of the whole paragraph. For help, consult 12a through 12d.

EXAMPLE Although many people considered him crazy. George Ferris decided to build a "Great Wheel" in 1892.

Although many people considered him *crazy, George* Ferris decided to build a "Great Wheel" in 1892.

(1) The 1893 Columbian World Exposition Committee contacted George Ferris. Because the members knew he was a creative designer.

(2) The Columbian World Exposition received its name from Christopher Columbus. Who had discovered what he called the "New World" 400 years earlier. (3) The Chicago Exposition Committee wanted a more dramatic structure than the Eiffel Tower. Which the French had built for the Paris Exposition of 1889. (4) George Ferris, who was an architect and bridge-builder with a vision, proposed a gigantic rotating wheel that people could ride on safely. (5) Since he designed a wheel that was 250 feet in diameter and held 36 cars, each 27 feet long and 13 feet wide. (6) Many people, including the Exposition director Daniel Burnham, doubted that Ferris could build a large steel structure. That could carry 2,160 passengers each ride. (7) Ferris built his giant wheel, and people paid fifty cents for a twenty-minute ride. Even though most other rides only cost five cents. (8) At night, 3,000 incandescent bulbs lit the rotating wheel. Which fascinated the people who stared in amazement. (9) William Sullivan, who was also a bridge-builder, later designed a smaller, more practical wheel. Sullivan's company has made over 1,300 Ferris Wheels since 1906 and continuing today. (10) George Ferris, the "crackpot" with wheels in his head, built an extraordinarily creative moving structure. That remains today a sentimental favorite at carnivals and amusement parks.

EXERCISE 12-5

Revise this paragraph to eliminate all sentence fragments. In some cases, you can combine word groups to create complete sentences; in other cases, you must supply missing elements to revise word groups. Some sentences may not require revision. In your final version, check not only the individual sentences but also the clarity of the whole paragraph. Refer to sections 12a through 12e for help.

(1) Your car shuddering and jolting. (2) As a hubcap flies off one of the tires and clatters across the road. (3) Have just hit a pothole in the pavement. (4) Potholes, typically formed when water seeps into cracks in the road surface, freeze, and then melt. (5) Are usually found in northern regions. (6) However, can also be a problem in warmer climates. (7) Where heat and frequent rain may cause the pavement to collapse. (8) A research laboratory that has counted sixteen million potholes. (9) Scarring the roads in the United States. (10) Each one a source of grief to countless drivers. (11) Because potholes bring expense and even danger. (12) Cities are finding ingenious ways of dealing with them. (12) Including a scheme in San Antonio, Texas, for volunteers to adopt a pothole. (14) And pay for its repair by buying an adoption certificate. (15) In return, the city gives the adopted pothole's "parents" a promise. (16) To have the hole fixed within a few days.

Focus on Revising

Here are two case studies of writers revising. Now's the time to apply all you've learned from Chapter 12 about sentence fragments. In the Observation section, you see a student writer revising. In the Participation section, you're invited to revise another student's writing.

Observation

A student wrote the following draft for a course called Introduction to Marketing. The assignment was to explain a marketing term. Read through the draft. The sentence fragments are highlighted. Before you look at the student's revision, revise the material yourself. Then, compare your revision with the student's.

Millions of dollars are gained or lost based on how a company markets its products. Therefore, many companies hire a marketing director. To develop a marketing strategy. Which begins with identifying and analyzing a target market. This step includes listing common characteristics of the group of people the seller wants to reach. For example, a company selling colorful pocket folders to elementary school children. Wants to start a marketing campaign. The marketing director compiles a list of popular children's television shows, musical artists, and sports figures. For pictures to put on the folders. The company also determines color and design preferences of six- to twelve-year-olds. Next, the marketing director works to define and update a marketing mix. Consisting of the product, the distribution of the product, ways to promote the product, and the price of the product. Usually, a marketing manager works with artists to design the folders. And decides which stores

Dependent clause with relative pronoun punctuated as a sentence: 12b.1

Fragment without a subject punctuated as a sentence: 12b.3

Partial phrase punctuated as a sentence: 12c, 12e

Infinitive phrase punctuated as a sentence: 12c

Fragment with a verbal but no verb, punctuated as a sentence: 12b.2

Prepositional phrase punctuated as a sentence: 12c

One-half of a compound predicate punctuated as a sentence: 12d

Dependent clause punctuated as a sentence: 12b.1 —— to stock, what kind of advertising to use, and how much to charge. When a marketing plan persuades the target group of consumers to purchase the product. The selling strategy is a success.

Observation: Revised by Student

Millions of dollars are gained or lost based on how a company markets its products. Therefore, many companies hire a marketing director to develop a marketing strategy. The process begins with identifying and analyzing a target market. This step includes listing common characteristics of the group of people the seller wants to reach. For example, a company selling colorful pocket folders to elementary school children wants to start a marketing campaign. The marketing director compiles a list of popular children's television shows, musical artists, and sports figures for pictures to put on the folders. The company also determines color and design preferences of six- to twelve-year-olds. Next, the marketing director works to define and update a marketing mix, consisting of the product, the distribution of the product, ways to promote the product, and the price of the product. Usually, a marketing manager works with artists to design the folders and decides which stores to stock, what kind of advertising to use, and how much to charge. When a marketing plan persuades the target group of consumers to purchase the product, the selling strategy is a success.

Participation

A student wrote the following draft for a course called Introduction to Fiction. The assignment was to provide background information about what led a major short story writer to write one of his or her stories.

Read through the draft. Then revise it to eliminate the sentence fragments. Also, make any additional changes that you think would improve the content, organization, and style of the material.

"The Lottery" by Shirley Jackson has both horrified and intrigued readers. Since it first appeared in the June 28, 1948, edition of The New Yorker magazine. The story's matter-of-fact tone creates a sense of reality. Readers assume nothing is strange. Until Mrs. Hutchison's neighbors begin hurling stones at her.

At first, the author, Shirley Jackson, refused to answer questions or to explain the significance of this modern-day stoning ritual. After pressure from editors and readers. Jackson finally gave some background. How she came to write the story and what it meant.

The setting was Jackson's hometown of Bennington, New York. Making some people think the story's characters were residents of that town. Because the story is about a fertility ritual. She wanted to match the date in the story to the date of the summer solstice, June 22. But an editor persuaded her to set the date in the story. For a few days after the June issue would appear. The timing helped prompt the biggest response to a story The New Yorker had ever received.

Jackson explained that she wanted "to shock the story's readers with a graphic dramatization of the pointless violence and general inhumanity in their own lives." She succeeded. In shocking most people. Others thought the stoning really happened. And wanted to know where so they could go and watch.

13 COMMA SPLICES AND RUN-ON SENTENCES

13a What are comma splices and run-on sentences?

Comma splices and run-on sentences are somewhat similar errors: One has a comma by itself between two complete sentences, and one has no punctuation at all between two complete sentences.

A **comma splice,** also called a *comma fault,* occurs when a comma, rather than a period, is used incorrectly between complete sentences. The word *splice* means "to fasten ends together," which is a handy procedure, except when splicing has anything to do with sentences.

A **run-on sentence,** also called a *fused sentence* and a *run-together sentence,* occurs when two complete sentences run into each other without any punctuation. Comma splices and run-on sentences create confusion because readers can't tell where one thought ends and another begins.

COMMA SPLICE	The icebergs broke off from the **glacier, they** drifted into the sea.
RUN-ON SENTENCE	The icebergs broke off from the **glacier they** drifted into the sea.
CORRECT	The icebergs broke off from the **glacier. They** drifted into the sea.

There is one exception. You can use a comma between two independent clauses, but only if the comma is followed by one of the seven COORDINATING CONJUNCTIONS: *and, but, for, or, nor, yet, so.* A comma in this construction is correct; see Chapter 24.

CORRECT	The iceberg broke off from the glacier, **and** it drifted into the sea.

◎ **PUNCTUATION ALERT:** Occasionally, when your meaning allows it, you can use a colon (Chapter 26) or a dash (Chapter 29) to join two independent clauses. ●

Many writers wait until the REVISING and EDITING stages of the WRITING PROCESS to check for comma splices and/or run-on sentences. During DRAFTING, the goal is to put ideas down on paper or disk. As you draft, if you suspect that you've written a comma splice or a run-on sentence, simply underline or highlight it in boldface or italics, and move on. Later, you can easily find it to check and correct.

13b How can I recognize comma splices and run-on sentences?

When you know how to recognize an INDEPENDENT CLAUSE, you'll know how to recognize COMMA SPLICES and RUN-ON SENTENCES. An independent clause can stand alone as a complete sentence. An independent clause contains a SUBJECT and a PREDICATE. Also, an independent clause doesn't begin with a word that creates dependence—that is, it doesn't begin with a SUBORDINATING CONJUNCTION or a RELATIVE PRONOUN.

Interestingly, almost all comma splices and run-on sentences are caused by only four patterns. If you become familiar with these four patterns, listed in Box 86, you'll more easily locate them in your writing.

Patterns that create comma splices   **86**
and run-on sentences

- Watch out for a PRONOUN starting the second independent clause.

  NO   The physicist Marie Curie discovered **radium, she** won two Nobel Prizes.

  YES   The physicist Marie Curie discovered **radium. She** won two Nobel Prizes.

- Watch out for a CONJUNCTIVE ADVERB (such as *furthermore, however, similarly, therefore,* and *then;* see Box 49, section 7g, page 162, for a complete list) starting the second independent clause.

  NO   Marie Curie and her husband, Pierre, worked together at **first, however,** he died tragically at age forty-seven.

  YES   Marie Curie and her husband, Pierre, worked together at **first. However,** he died tragically at age forty-seven.

- Watch out for a TRANSITIONAL EXPRESSION (such as *in addition, for example, in contrast, of course,* and *meanwhile;* see Box 26, section 4g.1, page 84, for a reference list) starting the second independent clause.

➡

Patterns that create comma splices 86
and run-on sentences *(continued)*

> **NO** Marie Curie and her husband won a Nobel Prize for the
> discovery of **radium, in addition, Marie** herself won
> another Nobel Prize for her work on the atomic weight of
> radium.

> **YES** Marie Curie and her husband won a Nobel Prize for the
> discovery of **radium; in addition, Marie** herself won
> another Nobel Prize for her work on the atomic weight of
> radium.

■ Watch out for a second independent clause that explains, says
more about, contrasts with, or gives an example of what's said in
the first independent clause.

> **NO** Marie Curie died of leukemia in **1934, exposure** to
> radioactivity killed her.

> **YES** Marie Curie died of leukemia in **1934. Exposure** to
> radioactivity killed her.

👁 **PROOFREADING ALERT:** To proofread for comma splices, cover all words
on one side of the comma and see if the words remaining form an independent clause. If they do, next cover all words you left uncovered, on the
other side of the comma. If the second side of the comma is also an independent clause, you're looking at a comma splice. (This technique doesn't
work for run-on sentences because a comma isn't present.) ●

Experienced writers sometimes use a comma to join very short
independent clauses, especially if one independent clause is negative
and the other is positive: *Mosquitos don't* **bite, they** *stab.* In ACA-
DEMIC WRITING, however, many instructors consider this an error, so
you'll be safe if you use a period. (Another option is a semicolon, if the
two independent clauses are closely related in meaning: *Mosquitos
don't* **bite; they** *stab.*

13c How can I correct comma splices and run-on sentences?

Once you have identified a COMMA SPLICE or a RUN-ON SENTENCE,
you're ready to correct it. You can do this in one of four ways, as shown
in Box 87 and discussed further in the sections in parentheses.

> ◉ **Ways to correct comma splices**   87
>   **and run-on sentences**
>
> ■ Use a period between the INDEPENDENT CLAUSES (13c.1).
> ■ Use a semicolon between the independent clauses (13c.2).
> ■ Use a comma together with a COORDINATING CONJUNCTION (13c.3).
> ■ Revise one independent clause into a DEPENDENT CLAUSE (13c.4).

13c.1 Using a period to correct comma splices and run-on sentences

You can use a period to correct comma splices and run-on sentences by placing the period between the two sentences. For the sake of sentence variety and emphasis (see Chapter 19), however, you want to choose other options as well, such as those shown in sections 13c.3 and 13c.4. Strings of short sentences rarely establish relationships and levels of importance among ideas.

COMMA SPLICE   A shark is all **cartilage, it** doesn't have a bone in its body.

RUN-ON SENTENCE   A shark is all **cartilage it** doesn't have a bone in its body.

CORRECT   A shark is all **cartilage. It** doesn't have a bone in its body. [A period separates the independent clauses.]

COMMA SPLICE   Sharks can smell blood from a quarter mile **away, they** then swim toward the source like a guided missile.

RUN-ON SENTENCE   Sharks can smell blood from a quarter mile **away they** then swim toward the source like a guided missile.

CORRECT   Sharks can smell blood from a quarter mile **away.** **They** swim toward the source like a guided missile. [A period separates the independent clauses.]

13c.2 Using a semicolon to correct comma splices and run-on sentences

You can use a semicolon to correct comma splices and run-on sentences by placing the semicolon between the two sentences. Use a semicolon only when the separate sentences are closely related in meaning. For the sake of sentence variety and emphasis, however, you'll want to choose other options, such as those shown in sections 13c.1, 13c.3, and 13c.4; for correct semicolon use, see Chapter 25.

COMMA SPLICE The great white shark supposedly eats **humans, research** shows that most white sharks spit them out after the first bite.

RUN-ON SENTENCE The great white shark supposedly eats **humans research** shows that most white sharks spit them out after the first bite.

CORRECT The great white shark supposedly eats **humans; research** shows that most white sharks like to spit them out after the first bite. [A semicolon separates two independent clauses that are close in meaning.]

13c.3 Using a comma together with a coordinating conjunction to correct comma splices and run-on sentences

You can connect independent clauses with a comma together with a coordinating conjunction (*and, but, or, nor, for, so, yet*) to correct a comma splice. You can also correct a run-on sentence by inserting a comma followed by a coordinating conjunction.

PUNCTUATION ALERT: Use a comma before a coordinating conjunction that links independent clauses (24b). ●

When you use a coordinating conjunction, be sure that your choice fits the meaning of the material. *And* signals addition; *but* and *yet* signal contrast; *for* and *so* signal cause; and *or* and *nor* signal alternatives.

COMMA SPLICE Every living creature gives off a weak electrical charge in the **water, special** pores on a shark's skin can detect these signals.

RUN-ON SENTENCE Every living creature gives off a weak electrical charge in the **water special** pores on a shark's skin can detect these signals.

CORRECT Every living creature gives off a weak electrical charge in the **water, *and* special** pores on a shark's skin can detect these signals.

EXERCISE 13-1

Revise the comma splices and run-on sentences by using a period, a semicolon, or a comma and coordinating conjunction. For help, consult sections 13c.1 through 13c.3.

EXAMPLE Artists in Santa Fe, New Mexico, are proudly reviving interest in ancient Hispanic crafts the artists display their handmade items during the annual Traditional Spanish Market in July.

Artists in Santa Fe, New Mexico, are proudly reviving interest in ancient Hispanic *crafts. The* artists display their handmade items during the annual Traditional Spanish Market in July.

1. Every summer Santa Fe holds the country's oldest and largest open market for traditional Hispanic work, however, few people know how respected and valuable the artistry is.
2. Some artists sell small items such as silver jewelry and prayer books covered in buffalo hide other artists offer detailed altarpieces and Spanish colonial furniture.
3. Members of the Lopez family never use commercial dyes they go to nearby caves to gather plants for brewing into natural colors.
4. Teenagers of the Rodriguez family create straw appliqué crucifixes, they take tiny pieces of flattened straw, rub them until shiny, and lay them delicately into wood.
5. Market visitors admire the colorful blankets Mr. Irwin Trujillo weaves to his own designs he rarely mentions that one of his blankets was purchased by the famous Smithsonian Institution, a museum in Washington, D.C.

13c.4 Revising one independent clause into a dependent clause to correct comma splices and run-on sentences

You can revise a comma splice or run-on sentence by revising one of the two independent clauses into a dependent clause. This method is suitable only when one idea can logically be SUBORDINATED (17e) to the other. Also, be careful never to end the dependent clause with a period or semicolon. If you do, you've created the error of a SENTENCE FRAGMENT.

Create dependent clauses with subordinating conjunctions

One way to create a dependent clause is to insert a SUBORDINATING CONJUNCTION (such as *because, although, when,* and *if*—see Box 51, section 7i, pages 164–165, for a complete list). Always choose a subordinating conjunction that fits the meaning of each particular sentence: *because* and *since* signal cause; *although* signals contrast; *when* signals time; and *if* signals condition. Dependent clauses that begin with a subordinating conjunction are called ADVERB CLAUSES.

COMMA SPLICE Homer and Langley Collyer had packed their house from top to bottom with **junk, police** could not open the front door to investigate a reported smell.

RUN-ON SENTENCE	Homer and Langley Collyer had packed their house from top to bottom with **junk police** could not open the front door to investigate a reported smell.
CORRECT	**Because** Homer and Langley Collyer had packed their house from top to bottom with **junk, police** could not open the front door to investigate a reported smell. [*Because* starts a dependent clause that is joined by a comma with the independent clause starting with *police*.]
COMMA SPLICE	Old newspapers and car parts filled every room to the **ceiling, enough** space remained for fourteen pianos.
RUN-ON SENTENCE	Old newspapers and car parts filled every room to the **ceiling enough** space remained for fourteen pianos.
CORRECT	**Although** old newspapers and car parts filled every room to the **ceiling, enough** space remained for fourteen pianos. [The subordinating conjunction *although* starts a dependent clause that is joined by a comma with the independent clause starting with *enough*.]

👁 **PUNCTUATION ALERT:** Place a comma between an introductory dependent clause and the independent clause that follows (24c). ●

Create dependent clauses with relative pronouns

You can create a dependent clause with a RELATIVE PRONOUN (*who, whom, whose, which, that*). Dependent clauses with a relative pronoun are called ADJECTIVE CLAUSES.

COMMA SPLICE	The Collyers had been crushed under a pile of **newspapers, the newspapers** had toppled onto the brothers.
RUN-ON SENTENCE	The Collyers had been crushed under a pile of **newspapers the newspapers** had toppled onto the brothers.
CORRECT	The Collyers had been crushed under a pile of **newspapers *that* had toppled** onto the brothers. [The relative pronoun *that* starts a dependent clause that is joined with the independent clause starting with *had toppled*.]

👁 **PUNCTUATION ALERT:** Sometimes you need commas to set off an adjective clause from the rest of the sentence. This happens only when the adjective is NONRESTRICTIVE (nonessential), so check carefully (see 24f). ●

EXERCISE 13-2

Identify and then revise the comma splices and run-on sentences. Circle the numbers of correct sentences. For help, consult sections 13b through 13c.4.

(1) Drug dealers sentenced to Rikers Island Detention Center in New York City listen carefully, they like the thought of making $200,000 a year legally. (2) Speaking to them is a 33-year-old self-made millionaire he knows firsthand about gangs and drugs. (3) Fernando Mateo dropped out of school in the tenth grade, however, he learned how to be a carpet layer. (4) Mateo's bosses showed him no respect therefore, he started his own business with a $2,000 loan from his father. (5) Thirteen years later, he owns two big stores, his business brings in $3 million per year. (6) Mateo now pays for and supervises a program, it trains young prison inmates to lay carpet. (7) The young men usually install carpet in office buildings they are grateful that Mateo's clients fully support this project. (8) Business people see the value in helping these inmates. (9) Mateo knows many young men serve their time and walk out unprepared to hold an honest job instead, his trainees leave the Detention Center with a trade. (10) One former drug peddler said, "I don't have to worry about watching my back or getting shot, and my mom knows I won't end up dead or in jail."

13d How can I correctly use a conjunctive adverb or other transitional expression between independent clauses?

CONJUNCTIVE ADVERBS and other TRANSITIONAL EXPRESSIONS link ideas between sentences. When these words fall between sentences, a period or semicolon must immediately precede them—and a comma usually immediately follows them.

Conjunctive adverbs include such words as *however, therefore, also, next, then, thus, furthermore,* and *nevertheless* (see Box 49, section 7g, page 162, for a complete list). Be careful to remember that conjunctive adverbs are not COORDINATING CONJUNCTIONS (*and, but,* and so on; see 13c.3).

COMMA SPLICE	Buying or leasing a car is a matter of individual preference, **however,** it's wise to consider several points before making a decision.
RUN-ON SENTENCE	Buying or leasing a car is a matter of individual preference **however** it's wise to consider several points before making a decision.
CORRECT	Buying or leasing a car is a matter of individual preference. **However,** it's wise to consider several points before making a decision.
CORRECT	Buying or leasing a car is a matter of individual preference**; however,** it's wise to consider several points before making a decision.

Transitional expressions include *for example, for instance, in addition, in fact, of course,* and *on the one hand/on the other hand* (see Box 26, section 4g.1, page 184, for a complete list).

COMMA SPLICE	Car leasing requires a smaller down payment**, for example,** in many cases, you need only $1,000 or $2,000 and the first monthly payment.
RUN-ON SENTENCE	Car leasing requires a smaller down payment **for example** in many cases, you need only $1,000 or $2,000 and the first monthly payment.
CORRECT	Car leasing requires a smaller down payment**. For example,** in many cases, you need only $1,000 or $2,000 and the first monthly payment.
CORRECT	Car leasing requires a smaller down payment**; for example,** in many cases, you need only $1,000 or $2,000 and the first monthly payment.

👁 **PUNCTUATION ALERT:** A conjunctive adverb or a transitional expression is usually followed by a comma when it starts a sentence (24g). ●

EXERCISE 13-3

Revise comma splices or run-on sentences caused by incorrectly punctuated conjunctive adverbs or other transitional expressions. If an item is correct, circle its number. For help, see 13d.

EXAMPLE   African American cowboys in the 1800s made up 25 percent of the cowboy population unfortunately, their contributions were not included in old history books and early western movies.

African American cowboys in the 1800s made up 25 percent of the cowboy *population. Unfortunately,* their contributions were not included in old history books and early western movies.

1. During the nineteenth century, over 2,500 black cowboys and cowgirls herded cattle in the West however, few people are familiar with their accomplishments.
2. Many former Texas slaves had become expert riders and cattle hand-lers, therefore, ranchers hired them to round up five to six million loose cattle after the Civil War.
3. Black cowboys often guarded the railroad boss and his cash payroll for example, the black cowhand Bose Ikard often guarded up to $20,000 and "never lost a dime."
4. Stagecoach Mary battled blizzards, rain, and heat as she delivered the U.S. mail to isolated cabins in Montana, in addition, this elderly black woman managed to fight off thieves and wolves along the way.

5. Paul W. Stewart spent eleven years collecting information and artifacts about African Americans in the West as a result, everyone can see the displays at the Black American West Museum in Denver, Colorado.

EXERCISE 13-4

Revise all comma splices and run-on sentences, using as many different methods of correction as you can.

(1) For many years, the women of a village in northwestern India have walked five miles to do their laundry they do this once a week. (2) Their destination is the edge of a small canal, they can spread their wash and beat it rhythmically. (3) When they're done, they bind up the sheets and clothes then they walk the five miles back to their homes. (4) Foreign aid workers who came to help the villagers believed that five miles was too far to walk with all that laundry they built a place for washing nearer the village. (5) The women praised the washing place, which was designed for them to do their laundry in the traditional way still, they refused to use it. (6) The women's refusal to use the new washing place was a mystery the aid workers asked an anthropologist to visit the village to study the problem. (7) She gained the women's confidence she learned that the village women are seldom allowed to go outside their homes. (8) They spend most of their lives inside their families' mud castles they look forward to their weekly excursion to the canal five miles away. (9) Laundry day got them out of the village therefore, it was their one opportunity to see their friends, to laugh, and to share stories.

Focus on Revising

Here are two case studies of writers revising. Now's the time to apply all you've learned from Chapter 13 about comma splices and run-on sentences. In the Observation section, you see a student writer revising. In the Participation section, you're invited to revise another student's writing.

Observation

A student wrote the following draft for a course called Environmental Biology. The assignment was to write about a successful environmental program or project. The draft contains well-described facts and good development, but it suffers from comma splices and run-on sentences.

Read through the draft. The errors are highlighted and explained. Before you look at the student's revision, revise the material yourself. Then, compare your revision with the student's.

The Mississippi River provides North America with a water route, fish, and beautiful scenery. Sadly, garbage being dumped into the river creates major problems it poisons marine life, pollutes the water, and creates hazards for boats.

> Run-on with pronoun *it*: Box 87

Chad Pregracke decided to take action, therefore, in the summer of 1997, he started removing garbage from a 100-mile section of the river.

> Comma splice with conjunctive adverb *therefore*: Box 87

Chad was pleased, in one summer he removed 45,000 pounds of trash. Each summer vacation from college, Chad returned to clean up the river. Four years later, he had removed nearly 200 refrigerators, over 100 containers of pesticide, 4 motorcycles, and 7 lawnmowers.

> Comma splice with second independent clause that explains the first independent clause: Box 87

Pregracke started the river cleanup project alone however, soon he inspired others to help him. At present, several students spend their summers on Chad's barges they help him pull up such items as tires, Porta Potties, and lawn ornaments, then load them on a barge, and dispose of them properly. The hardworking crew can clean 900 miles of river in a summer. Chad's enthusiasm is contagious, he has inspired river cleanup festivals in towns all along the Mississippi. Impressed with his accomplishments, companies like Cargill and O'Douls have contributed badly needed money to run the operation. To ensure that the river stays clean, Chad started the Adopt a Mississippi Mile program, it recruits communities along the Mississippi to take responsibility for a section of the river.

> Run-on with conjunctive adverb *however*: Box 87

> Run-on with pronoun *they*: Box 87

> Comma splice with pronoun *he*: Box 87

> Comma splice with pronoun *it*: Box 87

One person's desire for a clean river has made the Mississippi a safer, healthier, and more beautiful river.

Observation: Revised by Student

The Mississippi River provides North America with a water route, fish, and beautiful scenery. Sadly, garbage being dumped into the river creates major problems. It poisons marine life, pollutes the water, and creates hazards for boats.

Chad Pregracke decided to take action; therefore, in the summer of 1997, he started removing garbage from a 100-mile section of the river. Chad was pleased that in one summer he removed 45,000 pounds of trash. Each summer vacation from college, Chad returned to clean up the river. Four years later, he had removed nearly 200 refrigerators, over 100 containers of pesticide, 4 motorcycles, and 7 lawnmowers.

Pregracke started the river cleanup project alone; however, soon he inspired others to help him. At present, several students spend their summers on Chad's barges. They help him pull up such items as tires, Porta Potties, and lawn ornaments, then load them on a barge, and dispose of them properly. The hardworking crew can clean 900 miles of river in a summer. Chad's enthusiasm is contagious. He has inspired river cleanup festivals in towns all along the Mississippi. Impressed with his accomplishments, companies like Cargill and O'Douls have contributed badly needed money to run the operation. To ensure that the river stays clean, Chad started the Adopt a Mississippi Mile program. It recruits communities along the Mississippi to take responsibility for a section of the river.

One person's desire for a clean river has made the Mississippi a safer, healthier, and more beautiful river.

Participation

A student wrote the following draft for a course entitled Introduction to Film. The assignment was to write about a significant person in the early history of film.

Read through the draft. Then, revise it to eliminate the comma splices and run-on sentences. Also, make any additional changes that you think would improve the content, organization, and style of the material.

The first motion picture camera was invented in 1904 it was used only to capture people or other objects moving. The following year, a young secretary named Alice Guy was working for Leon Gaumont, a photographer in Paris, France, he had patented one of the first motion picture cameras. Guy asked Gaumont if she could film a few of her friends in a short skit. In 1906, Guy filmed *The Cabbage Fairy*, a 90-second fairy tale. Gaumont saw the entertainment value of the production, therefore he encouraged Guy to direct and produce more films.

Over the next eleven years, Guy made nearly 400 films and pioneered numerous filming techniques for example, she was the first to use close-ups and fade-outs. Audiences marveled at her reverse filming technique, it showed a house being destroyed and then rebuilt. Guy was the first person to use sound film and color film, she also used special effects to film explosions, car chases, and crashes.

Guy and her husband moved to the United States in 1907. Within three years, she opened her own studio called Solax Company in Fort Lee, New Jersey. Using the most modern equipment available at the time, she made 300 more films.

With all her accomplishments, people may wonder why Alice Guy's name is not better known. Unfortunately, Guy's story has a sad ending, her husband took over the studio, caused it to go bankrupt, and then left for Hollywood with another woman. Guy was then in her fifties with two children and no money she was unable to resurrect her career. To make matters worse, her name was removed from her films and replaced with names of male assistants.

14 MISPLACED AND DANGLING MODIFIERS

MISPLACED MODIFIERS

14a What is a misplaced modifier?

A MODIFIER is a word or group of words that describes or limits another word or group of words. A **misplaced modifier** is positioned incorrectly in a sentence, which means, therefore, that it describes the wrong word and changes the writer's meaning. Always place a modifier as close as possible to what it describes.

14a.1 Avoiding squinting modifiers

A **squinting modifier** is misplaced because it modifies both the word that comes before it and the word that follows it. Check that your modifiers are placed so that they communicate the meaning you intend.

NO The football player being recruited **eagerly** believed each successive offer would be better. [What was *eager*? The recruitment or the player's belief?]

YES The football player being recruited believed **eagerly** that each successive offer would be better.

YES The football player being **eagerly** recruited believed that each successive offer would be better.

14a.2 Placing limiting words carefully

Words such as *only, not only, just, not just, almost, hardly, nearly, even, exactly, merely, scarcely,* and *simply* serve to limit the meaning of a word according to where they are placed. When you use such words, position them precisely. Consider how moving the placement of the word *only* changes the meaning of this sentence: *Professional coaches say that high salaries motivate players.*

283

Only professional coaches say that high salaries motivate players.
[No one else says this.]

Professional coaches **only** say that high salaries motivate players.
[The coaches probably do not mean what they say.]

Professional coaches say **only** that high salaries motivate players.
[The coaches say nothing else.]

Professional coaches say that **only** high salaries motivate players.
[Nothing except high salaries motivates players.]

Professional coaches say that high salaries **only** motivate players.
[High salaries do nothing other than motivate players.]

Professional coaches say that high salaries motivate **only** players.
[High salaries do motivate the players but not the coaches and managers.]

14b How can I avoid split infinitives?

An INFINITIVE is a VERB form that starts with *to: to motivate, to convince, to create* are examples (7e). A **split infinitive** occurs when a word or words are placed between the word *to* and its verb. The effect is awkward.

NO Orson Welles's radio drama "War of the Worlds" managed *to, in October 1938, convince* listeners that they were hearing an invasion by Martians. [*In October 1938* is misplaced because the words come between *to* and *convince.*]

YES **In October 1938,** Orson Welles's radio drama "War of the Worlds" managed *to convince* listeners that they were hearing an invasion by Martians.

Often, the word that splits an infinitive is an ADVERB ending in *-ly.* In general, place adverbs either before or after the infinitive.

NO People feared that they would no longer be able **to *happily live*** in peace.

YES People feared that they would no longer be able **to live *happily*** in peace.

The rule about split infinitives has been changing recently. Current usage says that sometimes the best placement for a single adverb is actually between *to* and the verb.

Welles wanted **to *realistically* portray** a Martian invasion for the radio audience.

If you want to avoid splitting infinitives in your ACADEMIC WRITING, revise to avoid the split:

Welles wanted his "Martian invasion" **to sound *realistic*** for the radio audience. [The adverb *realistically* was changed to the adjective *realistic.*]

14c How can I avoid other splits in my sentences?

When too many words split—that is, come between—a SUBJECT and its VERB or between a verb and its OBJECT, the result is a sentence that lurches rather than flows from beginning to end.

NO The **announcer,** because the script, which Welles himself wrote, called for perfect imitations of emergency announcements, **opened** with a warning that included a description of the "invasion." [The subject *announcer* is placed too far away from the verb *opened,* so this split is too large.]

YES Because the script, which Welles himself wrote, called for perfect imitations of emergency announcements, the **announcer opened** with a warning that included a description of the "invasion." [The subject and verb, *announcer opened,* aren't split.]

NO Many churches **held** for their frightened communities **"end of the world" prayer services.** [The verb *held* is placed too far away from the object *"end of the world" prayer services,* so this split is too large.]

YES Many churches **held "end of the world" prayer services** for their frightened communities. [The subject and object, *held "end of the world" prayer services,* aren't split.]

EXERCISE 14-1

Revise these sentences to correct misplaced modifiers, split infinitives, and other splits. If a sentence is correct, circle its number. For help, consult 14a through 14c.

EXAMPLE Barrow, Alaska, is closer to the North Pole located on the Arctic Ocean than any other U.S. city.

Located on the Arctic Ocean, Barrow, Alaska, is closer to the North Pole than any other U.S. city.

1. The 4,400 residents of Barrow, Alaska, in a region where wind chills can go down to 100 degrees Fahrenheit below zero, not only survive but thrive.
2. These hardy residents adjust their lives to 24-hour nights in winter and 24-hour days in summer, 64 percent of whom are original natives.
3. The mayor of Barrow rides over the hard-packed snow his bike to work every day.
4. Businesses provide electric plug-in stations so customers while they shop can keep their cars running and heated.
5. Fran Tate runs Pepe's North of the Border, the Mexican restaurant closest to the North Pole, and she asks customers to every time they visit sign her guest book.

285

6. Fran nearly sends Christmas cards and a personal note to the 7,000 people on her list, including psychologist Dr. Joyce Brothers and basketball legend Karl Malone.

7. At Ipalook Elementary School's enormous indoor playground, students who are playing happily go outside whenever the weather is above 20 degrees Fahrenheit below zero.

8. Barrow has no roads connecting it with the outside world, which means the residents rely on airplanes for supplies and mail.

9. The airport for one of Alaska's largest corporations, which is a fuel and construction business owned by the Inupiat natives, is essential.

10. Residents, because they have no mall or movie theater, read, talk with friends in town, chat on the Internet, and enjoy the peace and quiet of the open tundra.

EXERCISE 14-2

Using each list of words, create all the possible logical sentences. Insert commas as needed. Explain differences in meaning among the alternatives you create. For help, consult 14a through 14c.

EXAMPLE   exchange students
learned to speak French
while in Paris
last summer

a. Last summer / exchange students / learned to speak French / while in Paris.

b. While in Paris, / exchange students / learned to speak French / last summer.

c. Exchange students / learned to speak French / while in Paris / last summer.

d. Exchange students / learned to speak French / last summer / while in Paris.

1. chicken soup
according to folklore
helps
cure colds

2. tadpoles
instinctively
swim
toward
their genetic relatives

3. the young driver
while driving
in the snow
skidded
carelessly

4. climbed
the limber teenager
a tall palm tree
to pick a ripe coconut
quickly

286

5. and cause mini-avalanches
   ski patrollers
   set explosives
   often
   to prevent big avalanches

DANGLING MODIFIERS

14d How can I avoid dangling modifiers?

A **dangling modifier** describes or limits a word or words that do not actually appear in the sentence. Aware of the intended meaning, the writer unconsciously supplies the missing words, but the reader gets confused. To correct a dangling modifier, state clearly your intended SUBJECT in the sentence.

NO   **Having read Faulkner's short story "A Rose for Emily,"** *the ending* surprised us. [This sentence says the *ending* was *reading the story*, which is impossible.]

YES   Having read Faulkner's short story "A Rose for Emily," **we were surprised by the ending.** [Second half of sentence is rewritten to include the subject *we*.]

YES   **We** read Faulkner's short story "A Rose for Emily" **and were surprised by** the ending. [Sentence is rewritten to include the subject *We*.]

NO   **When courting Emily,** *the townspeople* gossiped about her. [This sentence says the *townspeople* were *courting Emily*, which isn't true.]

YES   **When Emily was being courted** *by Homer Barron,* the townspeople gossiped about her. [First half of sentence is rewritten to include the name of the person doing the courting: *Homer Barron.*]

A major cause of dangling modifiers is the unnecessary use of the PASSIVE VOICE. Whenever possible, use the ACTIVE VOICE (8n–8p).

NO   **To earn money, china-painting lessons** were offered by Emily to wealthy young women. [*China-painting lessons* cannot *earn money. Were offered by Emily* is in the passive voice.]

YES   **To earn money, Emily** offered china-painting lessons to wealthy young women. [Change to the active voice; *Emily offered* corrects the problem.]

EXERCISE 14-3

Identify and correct any dangling modifiers in these sentences. If a sentence is correct, circle its number. For help, consult 14d.

EXAMPLE   Starting out as a short-order cook, the work can be confusing to a trainee.

Starting out as a short-order cook, *a trainee can find the work confusing.*

1. Cooking in a busy coffee shop or diner, a quick pair of hands is a necessity for a short-order cook.
2. To do a good job, the ability to concentrate is also a must for a short-order cook.
3. Especially at lunchtime, customers expect their meals yesterday morning.
4. While preparing several orders at once, kitchen utensils and ingredients have to be located at a moment's notice.
5. To keep the kitchen running smoothly, a long list of orders and recipes must be remembered by the cook.
6. When first learning the job, orders like "wreck two" and "cowboy" may be puzzling.
7. After catching on to the diner staff's slang, "wreck two" for an order of two scrambled eggs and "cowboy" for a Western omelet will make sense.
8. Crammed with food and utensils, an inexperienced cook may see a diner's small kitchen as a stressful place to work.
9. The pressures of the job can begin to become manageable, however, by learning how to plan ahead for the busy times.
10. Along with the diner's other workers, the opportunity also exists to enjoy the funny slang, the joking conversations, and even the hectic pace.

14e How can I proofread for misplaced and dangling modifiers?

Sentence errors like MISPLACED MODIFIERS and DANGLING MODIFIERS are hard to spot because of the way the human brain works. Writers know what they mean to say when they write. When they PROOFREAD, however, they often misread what they've written for what they intended to write. The mind unconsciously adjusts for the error. In contrast, readers see only what's on the paper or screen. I suggest that you, or someone else while you're listening, read your writing aloud to proofread it for these kinds of problems.

15 SHIFTING AND MIXED SENTENCES

SHIFTING SENTENCES

15a What is a shifting sentence?

A **shift** within a sentence is an unnecessary abrupt change in PERSON, NUMBER, SUBJECT, VOICE, TENSE, MOOD, or DIRECT or INDIRECT DISCOURSE. These shifts blur meaning. Sometimes a shift occurs between two or more sentences in a paragraph. If you set out on one track (writing in FIRST PERSON, for example), your readers expect you to stay on that same track (don't unnecessarily shift to THIRD PERSON, for example). When you do not, you have written a shifting sentence or paragraph.

15b How can I avoid shifts in person and number?

Who or what performs or receives an action is defined by the term *person.* FIRST PERSON (*I, we*) is the speaker or writer; SECOND PERSON (*you*) is the one being spoken or written *to;* and THIRD PERSON (*he, she, it, they*) is the person or thing being spoken or written *about.*

The essential point is that SHIFTS are incorrect unless the meaning in a particular context makes them necessary.

> **NO**   **I** enjoy reading financial forecasts of the future, but **you** wonder which will turn out to be correct. [The first person *I* shifts to the second person *you.*]

> **YES**   **I** enjoy reading financial forecasts of the future, but **I** wonder which will turn out to be correct.

NUMBER refers to whether words are *singular* (one) or *plural* (more than one) in meaning. Do not start to write in one number and then shift for no reason to the other number.

NO   Because **people** are living longer, **an employee** in the twenty-first century will retire later. [The plural *people* shifts to the singular *employee*.]

YES   Because **people** are living longer, **employees** in the twenty-first century will retire later.

In ACADEMIC WRITING, reserve *you* for addressing the reader directly. Use the third person for general statements.

NO   **I** like my job in customer service because **you** get to solve people's problems. [*I* is in the first person, so a shift to the second person *you* is incorrect.]

YES   **I** like my job in customer service because **I** get to solve people's problems.

NO   **People** enjoy feeling productive, so when a job is unsatisfying, **you** usually become depressed. [*People* is in the third person, so a shift to the second person *you* is incorrect.]

YES   **People** enjoy feeling productive, but when a job is unsatisfying, **they** usually become depressed.

Be careful with words in the singular (usually NOUNS) used in a general sense, such as *employee, student, consumer, neighbor,* or *someone.* These words are always third-person singular. The only ANTECEDENTS in the third-person singular are *he, she,* and *it.* Remember that *they* is plural, so the word *they* can't be used with singular nouns.

NO   When **an employee** is treated with respect, **they** are more motivated to do a good job. [*Employee* is third-person singular, so the shift to the third person plural *they* is incorrect.]

YES   When **an employee** is treated with respect, **he or she** is more motivated to do a good job.

YES   When **employees** are treated with respect, **they** are more motivated to do a good job.

YES   **An employee** who is treated with respect is more motivated to do a good job.

YES   **Employees** who are treated with respect are more motivated to do a good job.

👁 **ALERT:** When you use INDEFINITE PRONOUNS (such as *someone, everyone,* or *anyone*), you want to use GENDER-NEUTRAL LANGUAGE. For advice, see 10r and 21g. ●

EXERCISE 15-1

Eliminate shifts in person and number between, as well as within, sentences. Some sentences may not need revision. For help, consult 15b.

(1) According to some experts, snobbery is measured by your mental attitude, not the extent of your worldly goods. (2) Because a snob is unsure of his or her social position, snobs are driven by what others think of them. (3) You tend to be too dependent on buying status symbols to define your place in the world, and snobs look down on others. (4) You can trace the origin of this word to the British Isles. (5) The term *snob*—from the same root, meaning "cut," as *snip* and *snub*—was originally applied to the local cobbler. (6) Some of these shoemakers tended to take on the airs of his or her wealthy customers. (7) Students at Cambridge University would taunt social climbers for "acting like a snob." (8) The students helped turn the word *snob* into our most common term for persons aspiring to a higher social level.

15c How can I avoid shifts in subject and voice?

A SHIFT in SUBJECT is rarely justified when it is accompanied by a shift in VOICE. The voice of a sentence is either *active* (*People expect changes*) or *passive* (*Changes are expected*). Some subject shifts, however, are justified by the meaning of a passage: for example, *People look forward to the future, but the future holds many secrets.*

NO Most **people expect** major improvements in the future, but some **hardships are** also **anticipated.** [The subject shifts from *people* to *hardships,* and the voice shifts from active to passive.]

YES Most **people expect** major improvements in the future, but **they** also **anticipate** some hardships.

YES Most **people expect** major improvements in the future but also **anticipate** some hardships.

15d How can I avoid shifts in tense and mood?

TENSE refers to the time in which the action of a VERB takes place—past, present, or future: *We **will go** to the movies after we **finish** dinner.* An unnecessary tense SHIFT within or between sentences can make the statement confusing or illogical.

NO A campaign to clean up movies in the United States **began** in the 1920s as civic and religious groups **try** to ban sex and violence from the screen. [The tense incorrectly shifts from the past *began* to the present *try.*]

YES A campaign to clean up movies in the United States **began** in the 1920s as civic and religious groups **tried** to ban sex and violence from the screen.

NO   Film producers and distributors **created** the Production Code in the 1930s. At first, violating its guidelines **carried** no penalty. Eventually, however, films that **fail** to get the board's seal of approval **do not receive** wide distribution. [This shift occurs between sentences—the past tense *created* and *carried* shift to the present tense *fail* and *do not receive*.]

YES   Film producers and distributors **created** the Production Code in the 1930s. At first, violating its guidelines **carried** no penalty. Eventually, however, films that **failed** to get the board's seal of approval **did not receive** wide distribution.

MOOD indicates whether a sentence is a statement or question (INDICATIVE MOOD), a command or request (IMPERATIVE MOOD), or a conditional or other-than-real statement (SUBJUNCTIVE MOOD). A shift in mood creates an awkward construction and can cause confusion.

NO   The Production Code included two guidelines on violence: **Do not show** the details of brutal killings, and movies **should not be** explicit about how to commit crimes. [The verbs shift from the imperative mood *do not show* to the indicative mood *movies should not be.*]

YES   The Production Code included two guidelines on violence: **Do not show** the details of brutal killings, and **do not show** explicitly how to commit crimes. [This revision uses the imperative mood for both guidelines.]

YES   The Production Code included two guidelines on violence: Movies **were not to show** the details of brutal killings or explicit ways to commit crimes.

NO   The code's writers worried that **if a crime were to be** accurately **depicted** in a movie, **copycat crimes will follow.** [The sentence shifts from the subjunctive mood *if a crime were to be depicted* to the indicative mood *copycat crimes will follow.*]

YES   The code's writers worried that **if a crime were to be** accurately **depicted** in a movie, **copycat crimes would follow.**

15e How can I avoid shifts between indirect and direct discourse?

Indirect discourse is not enclosed in quotation marks because it reports, rather than quotes, something that someone said. In contrast, **direct discourse** is enclosed in quotation marks because it quotes exactly the words that someone said. It's incorrect to write direct discourse and omit the quotation marks. Also, it's incorrect to write sentences that mix indirect and direct discourse. Such SHIFT errors confuse readers who can't tell what was said and what is being merely reported.

NO A critic said that board members were acting as censors and **what you are doing is unconstitutional.** [*Said that* sets up indirect discourse, but *what you are doing is unconstitutional* is direct discourse; it also lacks quotation marks and the changes in language that distinguish reported words from spoken words.]

YES A critic said that board members were acting as censors and **that what they were doing was unconstitutional.** [This revision uses indirect discourse consistently.]

YES A critic in stating, that board members were acting as censors added, **"What you are doing is unconstitutional."** [This revision uses discourse correctly, with quotation marks and other changes in language to distinguish reported words from actual spoken words.]

Whenever you change your writing from direct discourse to indirect discourse (when you decide to paraphrase rather than quote someone directly, for example), you need to make changes in VERB TENSE and other grammatical features. Simply removing the quotation marks is not enough.

NO He asked **did we enjoy the movie?** [This version has the verb form needed for direct discourse, but the pronoun *we* is wrong and quotation punctuation is missing.]

YES He asked **whether we enjoyed the movie.** [This version is entirely indirect discourse, and the verb has changed from *enjoy* to *enjoyed*.]

YES He asked, **"Did you enjoy the movie?"** [This version is direct discourse. It repeats the original speech exactly, with correct quotation punctuation.]

EXERCISE 15-2

Revise these sentences to eliminate incorrect shifts within sentences. Some sentences can be revised in several ways. For help, consult 15b through 15e.

EXAMPLE   In 1942, the United States government is faced with arresting five million people for not paying their federal income taxes.

In 1942, the United States government *was faced* with arresting five million people for not paying their federal income taxes.

1. Congress needed money to pay for U.S. participation in World War II, so a new tax system was proposed.
2. Tax payments were due on March 15, not April 15 as it is today.
3. For the first time, Congress taxed millions of lower-income citizens. Most people do not save enough to pay the amount of taxes due.
4. When a scientific poll showed lawmakers that only one in seven Americans had saved enough money, he became worried.

EXERCISE 15-3

Revise this paragraph to eliminate incorrect shifts between sentences and within sentences. For help, consult 15a through 15e.

(1) When people think positively, your chances of success really do seem to go up. (2) A psychologist in Kansas confirms that optimists hold an advantage over a less hopeful person. (3) He finds that an optimist often does better than expected in school and could handle stress at work more easily than other people. (4) Other researchers praise the benefits of optimism in her study of patients who must cope with severe illnesses. (5) These psychologists designed a "hope scale" that ranks people according to their level of hopefulness and is used to place them among either the optimistic crowd or the less optimistic crowd. (6) The psychologists contend that optimists are not simply someone who thinks, "I'm a winner," and therefore says that things always turn out right for me in the end. (7) Rather, a true optimist combines confidence in his or her problem-solving abilities with the readiness to seek advice from friends. (8) True optimists also had to be willing to motivate yourself so that important goals can be accomplished.

MIXED SENTENCES

15f What is a mixed sentence?

A mixed sentence has two or more parts, with the first part starting in one direction, but the rest of the parts going off in another. This mixing of sentence parts leads to unclear meaning. To avoid this error, as you write each sentence, remember how you started it and make sure that whatever comes next in the sentence relates grammatically and logically to the start.

NO Because our side lost the contest eventually motivated us to do better. [*Because our side lost the contest* starts the sentence in one direction, but *eventually motivated us to do better* goes off in another direction.]

YES Because our side lost the contest, **we** eventually became motivated to do better.

YES Our side lost the contest, **which** eventually motivated us to do better.

NO Because television's first transmissions in the 1920s included news programs quickly became popular with the public. [The opening DEPENDENT CLAUSE starts off on one track (and is not correctly punctuated), but the INDEPENDENT CLAUSE goes off in another direction. What does the writer want to emphasize, the first transmissions or the popularity of news programs?]

> **YES** Because television's first transmissions in the 1920s included news, programs became popular with the public. [The revision helps but is partial: the dependent clause talks about the news, but the independent clause goes off in another direction by talking about the popularity of the programs in general.]

> **YES** Television's first transmissions in the 1920s included news programs, **which were** popular with the public. [Dropping *because* and adding *which were* solves the problem by keeping the focus on news programs throughout.]

> **NO** By increasing the time for network news to thirty minutes increased the prestige of network news programs. [A PREPOSITIONAL PHRASE, such as *by increasing,* can't be the subject of a sentence.]

> **YES** Increasing the time for network news to thirty minutes increased the prestige of network news programs. [Dropping the preposition *by* clears up the problem.]

> **YES** By increasing the time for network news to thirty minutes, **the network executives** increased the prestige of network news programs. [Inserting a logical subject, *the network executives,* clears up the problem.]

The phrase *the fact that* lacks CONCISENESS (Chapter 16), and it also tends to cause a mixed sentence.

> **NO** The fact that quiz show scandals in the 1950s prompted the networks to produce even more news shows.

> **YES** The fact **is** that quiz show scandals in the 1950s prompted the networks to produce even more news shows. [Adding *is* clarifies the meaning.]

> **YES** Quiz show scandals in the 1950s prompted the networks to produce even more news shows. [Dropping *the fact that* clarifies the meaning.]

15g How can I correct a mixed sentence with faulty predication?

Faulty predication, sometimes called *illogical predication,* occurs when a SUBJECT and its PREDICATE don't make sense together.

> **NO** The purpose of television was invented to entertain people. [A *purpose* cannot be *invented.*]

> **YES** The purpose of television was to entertain people.

> **YES** Television was invented to entertain people.

Faulty predication often results from a lost connection between a subject and its SUBJECT COMPLEMENT.

295

NO   Walter Cronkite's outstanding **characteristic** as a newscaster **was credible.** [The subject complement *credible* could logically describe *Walter Cronkite,* but *Walter Cronkite* is not the sentence's subject. Rather, the sentence's subject is his *characteristic.* Therefore, the sentence lacks a subject complement that would name a *characteristic* of *Walter Cronkite as a newscaster.*]

YES   Walter Cronkite's outstanding **characteristic** as a newscaster **was credibility.** [When *credibility* is substituted for *credible,* the sentence is correct.]

YES   Walter Cronkite was credible as a newscaster. [When *Walter Cronkite* becomes the sentence's subject, *credible* is correct.]

In ACADEMIC WRITING, avoid nonstandard constructions such as *is when* or *is where.* They should be avoided not only because they are nonstandard, but also because they usually lead to faulty predication.

NO   A disaster **is when** TV news shows get some of their highest ratings.

YES   TV news shows get some of their highest ratings during a disaster.

In academic writing, avoid constructions such as *the reason . . . is because.* By using both *reason* and *because,* the construction is redundant (it says the same thing twice). Instead, use either *the reason . . . is that* or *because* alone.

NO   One **reason** that TV news captured national attention in the 1960s **is because** it covered the Vietnam War thoroughly.

YES   One **reason** TV news captured national attention in the 1960s **is that** it covered the Vietnam War thoroughly.

YES   TV news captured national attention in the 1960s **because** it covered the Vietnam War thoroughly.

EXERCISE 15-4

Revise the mixed sentences so that the beginning of each sentence fits logically with its end. If a sentence is correct, circle its number. For help, consult 15f and 15g.

EXAMPLE   The reason women and men sometimes behave differently is because their brains operate differently.

Women and men sometimes behave differently because their brains operate differently.

1. By studying brain scans has provided researchers with pictures of neuron activity in the human brain.

2. The reason that a man's brain is 10 to 15 percent larger than a woman's brain is because men's bodies are generally 10 to 15 percent larger than women's.

3. The fact that women use both sides of the brain and more readily see relationships among objects or ideas.
4. One theory focuses on whether women have more brain neurons that control difficult intellectual functions such as language is being studied.
5. Whether walking or doing complicated math, women activate neurons in several areas of the brain at the same time.
6. The reason most men are able to focus more intently on an activity is because their neural action stays only in one area of the brain.
7. Because of a woman's ability to think simultaneously about a variety of topics enables her to read or sew while watching television.
8. While reading a map is usually when differences in brain activity show up on the scans.
9. Neurologists are interested in men's ability to look at maps and mentally rotate positions on them.
10. Even though women perform better on a memory test are three times as likely as men to develop Alzheimer's disease.

15h How can I write correct elliptical constructions?

An **elliptical construction** deliberately leaves out one or more words in a sentence to avoid repeating them.

> Victor has his book and Joan's. [This means *Victor has his book and Joan's book.* The second *book* is left out deliberately.]

For an elliptical construction to be correct, the one or more words you leave out need to be identical to those appearing in the sentence. For instance, the example sentence above about Victor and Joan would have an incorrect elliptical construction if the writer's intended meaning were *Victor has his book and Joan has her own book.*

> **NO** During the 1920s in Chicago, the cornetist Manuel Perez **was leading** one outstanding jazz group, and Tommy and Jimmy Dorsey another. [The words *was leading* cannot take the place of *were leading*, which is required after *Tommy and Jimmy Dorsey.*]

> **YES** During the 1920s in Chicago, the cornetist Manuel Perez **was leading** one outstanding jazz group, and Tommy and Jimmy Dorsey **were leading** another.

> **YES** During the 1920s in Chicago, the cornetist Manuel Perez **led** one outstanding jazz group, and Tommy and Jimmy Dorsey another. [*Led* is correct with both *Manuel Perez* and *Tommy and Jimmy Dorsey*, so *led* can be omitted after *Dorsey.*]

15i How can I write correct comparisons?

When you write a sentence in which you want to compare two or more things, make sure that no important words are omitted.

> **NO** Individuals driven to achieve make **better** business executives. [*Better* is a word of comparison (11e), but no comparison is stated.]

> **YES** Individuals driven to achieve make **better** business executives **than do people not interested in personal accomplishments.**

> **NO** Most personnel officers value high achievers **more than risk takers.** [*More* is a word of comparison, but it's unclear whether the sentence says *personnel officers value high achievers over risk takers* or *personnel officers value high achievers more than risk takers value them.*]

> **YES** Most personnel officers value high achievers **more than they value** risk takers.

> **YES** Most personnel officers value high achievers **more than** risk takers **do.**

15j How can I proofread for little words I omit unintentionally?

If you're rushing or distracted as you write, you might unintentionally omit little words, such as ARTICLES, PRONOUNS, CONJUNCTIONS, and PREPOSITIONS. I do, unfortunately. My only solution is to read my writing aloud, word by word; or, better still, I ask someone else to read it aloud because I tend to fill in any missing words in my own work.

> **NO** On May 2, 1808, citizens Madrid rioted against French soldiers and were shot.

> **YES** On May 2, 1808, citizens **of** Madrid rioted against French soldiers and were shot.

> **NO** The Spanish painter Francisco Goya recorded both the riot the execution in a pair of pictures painted 1814.

> **YES** The Spanish painter Francisco Goya recorded both the riot **and** the execution in a pair of pictures painted in 1814.

EXERCISE 15-5

Revise this paragraph to create correct elliptical constructions, to complete comparisons, and to insert any missing words. For help, see 15h though 15j.

(1) A giant tsunami is as destructive and even larger than a tidal wave. (2) The word *tsunami* is Japanese for "harbor wave," for this kind wave appears suddenly in harbor or bay. (3) A tsunami begins

with rapid shift in ocean floor caused by an undersea earthquake or volcano. (4) The wave this produces in the open sea is less than three feet high, but it can grow to a height of a hundred feet as it rushes and strikes against the shore. (5) For this reason, tsunamis are much more dangerous to seaside towns than ships on the open sea. (6) In 1960, a huge tsunami that struck coasts of Chile, Hawaii, and Japan killed total of 590 people.

Focus on Revising

Here are two case studies of writers revising. Now's the time to apply all you've learned from Chapter 14 about misplaced modifiers (14a) and dangling modifiers (14d). Also watch for omitted words and for shifting and mixed sentences (Chapter 15). In the Observation section, you see a student writer revising. In the Participation section, you're invited to revise another student's writing.

Observation

A student wrote the early draft below for a course called Freshman Composition. The assignment was to compose a narrative of a personal experience with which other students in the class might identify. This draft explains the experience clearly, uses specific examples effectively, and uses tone well to convey how the writer felt. Unfortunately, misplaced modifiers and dangling modifiers detract from the overall effectiveness. The errors are highlighted and explained. Before you look at the student's revision, try your hand at revising. Then, compare your revision with the student's.

Dangling modifier: 14d

Moving to a different part of the United States was one of the most difficult experiences of my life. Looking forward to my senior year in high school, my father's company informed him that he had been transferred from Boston to Colorado Springs, and would we be ready to move in a month? Boston was less liked by my father than by me, so I was not thrilled about having to leave. But after days of arguing and talking to my parents, I knew that the decision was final.

Shift from direct to indirect discourse: 15e

Shift in subject and voice: 15c

Incorrect elliptical construction: 15h

Unnecessary shift in person and number: 15b

Mixed construction: 15f

Misplaced modifier: 14a

Omitted word: 15j

Misplaced modifier; awkward placement: 14a

Misplaced modifier: 14a

Unnecessary shift in tense: 15d

Dangling modifier: 14d

Dangling modifier: 14d

Misplaced modifier; ambiguous placement: 14a

Misplaced modifier; ambiguous placement: 14a

Incorrect elliptical construction: 15h

When our family arrived in Colorado Springs, I was depressed. Our house was comfortable, about twice the size of our Boston apartment, but you had the feeling that it was in the middle of nowhere. I couldn't go without a car anywhere. In Boston, all I have to do is hop on the "T" to get wherever I wanted. Also, by discovering that the expressions for some everyday things were different than in Boston. When I asked for a "submarine," a thick sandwich on a long roll, the convenience store clerk said she didn't have kits for making model ships with a confused look. Calling them "heros," the city didn't feel like home to me. When shopping in Colorado Springs, salespeople offered me what they called a "sack" instead of a bag to carry my purchases. As far as I knew, *sack* meant a quarterback had been tackled in football game.

Slowly, however, I began to realize that in Colorado even they have movies, fast-food restaurants, and shopping malls. Mostly, the people made the big difference for me. It didn't happily take long for me to get to know some students in my high school and to, much to my surprise, find that many were eager to make me feel at home. By now, I can't imagine a better place to live than Colorado Springs.

Observation: Revised by Student

Moving to a different part of the United States was one of the most difficult experiences of my life. I was looking forward to my senior year in high school when my father's company informed him that he had been transferred from Boston to Colorado Springs and asked him if we could be ready to move in a month? I liked Boston, and my friends were unhappy I had to leave. Sadly, I knew the decision was final.

When our family arrived in Colorado Springs, I was depressed. Our house was comfortable, about twice the size of our Boston apartment, but I felt it was in the middle of nowhere. I couldn't go anywhere without a car. In Boston, all I had to do was hop on the "T" to get wherever I wanted.

Also, expressions for some everyday things were different than in Boston. When I asked for a "submarine," a thick sandwich on a long roll, the convenience store clerk said with a confused look she didn't have kits for making model ships. By calling them "heros," I didn't feel at home in the city. When shopping in Colorado Springs, I was offered a "sack" instead of a "bag" to carry my purchases. As far as I knew, *sack* meant a quarterback had been tackled in a football game.

Slowly, however, I began to realize that even in Colorado they have movies, fast-food restaurants, and shopping malls. Mostly, the people made the big difference for me. Happily, it didn't take long for me to get to know some students in my high school and, much to my surprise, to find that many were eager to make me feel at home. By now, I can't imagine a better place to live than in Colorado Springs.

Participation

A student working in the college peer-counseling program for job hunters wrote the draft that begins below for an article in the campus newspaper. This draft shows a very good awareness of audience, and it contains well-organized and useful information. But misplaced modifiers, dangling modifiers, omitted words, and shifting and mixed sentences detract from its effectiveness.

Read through the draft. Then, revise it to eliminate the errors. Also, make any additional revisions that you think would improve the content, organization, and style of the material.

Most job hunters enter business world through a door labeled "Job Interviews." Regardless of training and experience, the interview is the occasion when an employer gets an impression of the candidate. What can a person do so that you perform successfully at what is likely to be a fifteen- to thirty-minute interview?

Understanding the objectives of the interview, the time can be used to best advantage. Applicants who familiarize themselves usually with the companies are most successful. Most businesses with a position to fill interview with three basic questions in mind: Is this applicant qualified to do the job? Will this applicant perform if hired? Will you fit into the work environment?

An applicant can use a well-prepared resume to present information about work experience and training. At the interview, applicants should be prepared to talk about courses taken, jobs held, and capabilities demonstrated. Probing for specific details, the applicant's abilities will be judged by the employer. Even though most job applicants know that personal questions about marital status or plans to have children are illegal, they might be raised by some interviewers anyway. By preparing a polite answer such as "I make it a rule never to let my personal life interfere with business," the employer will be impressed with the applicant's tact and strength.

A major concern of an interviewer focuses on whether nicely the applicant would fit into the company. An applicant who plays merely a role to impress an interviewer is making a mistake, particularly if you are offered a job that you are not suited for. Present a natural image. Use the interview to find out how the company's work environment will fit your personal style.

www.prenhall.com/troyka

Visit the Troyka Web site for information on:

- Using concise writing
- Using variety and emphasis
- Spelling and hyphenating

You'll also find access to *The UVic Writer's Guide* at <www.clearcf.uvic.ca/writersguide/ Pages/WordsTOC.html>. Sponsored by the Department of English at the University of Victoria, this site includes extra coverage of word usage, spelling, and gender-inclusive language. (This site uses Canadian spelling.)

PART THREE

WRITING EFFECTIVE SENTENCES AND USING EFFECTIVE WORDS

www.prenhall.com/troyka

16 CONCISENESS

16a What is conciseness?

Conciseness is desirable in writing; it requires that you craft sentences that are direct and to the point. Its opposite, **wordiness,** is undesirable because sentences are filled with empty words and phrases that increase the word count but contribute nothing to meaning. Wordy writing is padded with deadwood, forcing readers to clear away the branches and overgrowth—an annoying waste of time that implies the writer isn't focused. Usually, the best time to work on making your writing more concise is while you are REVISING.*

WORDY   ~~As a matter of fact,~~ ʈhe ∧ television station ~~which is situated in the local area~~ has won ~~a great~~ many awards ~~in the final analysis~~ because of its ~~type of~~ coverage of ~~all kinds of~~ controversial issues.

(above WORDY: T local)

CONCISE   The local television station has won many awards because of its coverage of controversial issues.

16b What common expressions reduce conciseness?

Many common expressions we use in informal speech are not concise. Box 88 lists some and shows you how to eliminate them.

---

* You can find the definition of a word printed in small capital letters (such as REVISING) in the Terms Glossary toward the back of this handbook.

◉ Cutting unnecessary words and phrases   88

EMPTY WORD OR PHRASE	WORDY EXAMPLE REVISED
as a matter of fact	Many marriages, ~~as a matter of fact,~~ end in divorce.
at the present time	The proposed law is being debated ∧now ~~at the present time.~~
because of the fact that, in light of the fact that, due to the fact that	Because ~~of the fact that~~ the museum has a special exhibit, it stays open late.
by means of	We traveled by ~~means of a~~ car.
factor	The project's final cost was the essential ∧consideration. ~~factor to consider.~~
for the purpose of	Work crews arrived ~~for the purpose of~~ ∧to ~~fixing~~ the potholes.
have a tendency to	The team ~~has a tendency~~ ∧tends to lose home games.
in a very real sense	~~In a very real sense,~~ All fire fighters are heroes.
in the case of	~~In the case of~~ The election, ~~it~~ will be close.
in the event that	~~In the event that~~ ∧If you're late, I will buy our tickets.
in the final analysis	~~In the final analysis,~~ No two eyewitnesses agreed on what they saw.
in the process of	We are ~~in the process of~~ reviewing the proposal.
it seems that	~~It seems that~~ The union struck over health benefits.

→

305

Cutting unnecessary words and phrases 88
(*continued*)

EMPTY WORD OR PHRASE	WORDY EXAMPLE REVISED
manner	The child spoke ∧in a reluctant manner. *reluctantly.*
nature	The movie review was of a sarcastic nature∧.
that exists	The crime rate that exists is unacceptable.
the point I am trying to make	The point I am trying to make is television reporters invade our privacy. (T)
type of, kind of	Gordon took a relaxing type of vacation.
What I mean to say	What I mean to say is I love you.

EXERCISE 16-1

Working individually or with a group, revise each sentence to eliminate words or phrases that are not concise. For help, consult 16a and 16b.

EXAMPLE   Folk wisdom has a tendency to be untrue.

Folk wisdom *is often* untrue.

1. As a matter of fact, it seems as though a great many folk beliefs that are popular are, in a very real sense, totally wrong.
2. For example, the American Academy of Ophthalmology makes the statement that reading in the dark will not have the effect of ruining a person's eyes.
3. In the case of spicy foods, specialists have proved that foods of this sort are not necessarily bad for the stomach, even for people who have been treated as ulcer patients.
4. What about our mothers' warning that exists about catching colds when we are in the process of becoming chilled?
5. It is certainly quite true that more people have a tendency to get sick in winter than people do in summer.
6. It seems that lower temperatures are not the factor that deserves the blame, however.
7. In view of the fact that cold weather often has a tendency to drive people indoors and to bring people together inside, this

factor has the appearance of increasing our odds of infecting one another.

8. Finally, there has been a long-standing tradition that states that the full moon has the effect on people of making them crazy.

9. Investigations that were made by researchers who were tireless and careful came to the ultimate conclusion that there is no such relationship in existence.

10. Research does show, however, that some people become highly agitated and short-tempered when the moon is full.

16c What sentence structures usually work against conciseness?

Two sentence structures, although appropriate in some contexts, often work against CONCISENESS because they can lead to WORDINESS: writing EXPLETIVE constructions and writing in the PASSIVE VOICE.

Avoiding expletive constructions

An expletive construction starts with *it* or *there* followed by a form of the VERB *be*. When you cut the expletive construction and revise, the sentence becomes more direct.

~~It is necessary for~~ $\overset{S}{}$ students ~~to~~ $\overset{must}{\wedge}$ fill in both questionnaires.

~~There are~~ $\overset{T}{}$ three majors $\overset{are}{\wedge}$ offered by the computer science department.

🌐 **ESL NOTES:** (1) *It* in an expletive construction is not a PRONOUN referring to a specific ANTECEDENT. *It* is an "empty" word that fills the SUBJECT position in the sentence but does not function as the subject. The actual subject appears after the expletive construction: ***It was the teacher*** *who answered the question.* If concise, the sentence would be *The teacher answered the question.* (2) *There* in an expletive construction does not indicate a place. Rather, *there* is an "empty" word that fills the subject position in the sentence but does not function as the subject. The actual subject appears after the expletive construction: ***There are many teachers*** *who can answer the question.* If concise, the sentence would be *Many teachers can answer the question.* 🌐

Avoiding the passive voice

In general, the passive voice is less concise—as well as less lively—than the ACTIVE VOICE. In the active voice, the subject of a sentence does the action named by the verb.

ACTIVE   Professor Higgins teaches public speaking. [*Professor Higgins* is the subject, and he does the action: He *teaches*.]

In the passive voice, the subject of a sentence receives the action named by the verb.

PASSIVE   Public speaking is taught by Professor Higgins. [*Public speaking* is the subject, and it receives the action *taught*.]

Unless your meaning justifies using the passive voice, choose the active voice (8n–8p).

PASSIVE   Volunteer work was done by students for credit in sociology. [The passive phrase *was done by students* is unnecessary for the intended meaning. *Students,* not *volunteer work,* are doing the action and should get the action of the verb.]

ACTIVE   **The students did** volunteer work for credit in sociology.

ACTIVE   **Volunteer work earned** students credit in sociology. [Since the verb has changed to *earned, volunteer work* performs the action of the verb.]

By mistakenly believing the passive voice sounds "mature" or "academic," student writers sometimes deliberately use it. The result is wordy, overblown sentences that suggest a writer's lack of skill.

NO   One very important quality developed by individuals during their first job is self-reliance. This strength was gained by me when I was allowed by my supervisor to set up and conduct a survey project on my own.

YES   Many individuals develop the important quality of self-reliance during their first job. I gained this strength when my supervisor allowed me to set up and conduct my own survey project.

YES   During their first job, many people develop self-reliance, as I did when my supervisor let me set up and conduct my own survey project.

16d How else can I revise for conciseness?

Four other techniques can help you revise your writing for CONCISENESS and crisp wording: eliminating unplanned repetition (16d.1); combining sentences (16d.2); shortening CLAUSES (16d.3); and shortening PHRASES and cutting words (16d.4). These techniques involve matters of judgment. If you develop your writing style well (Chapters 17, 18, and 19), you want to keep its good features and cut only its redundancies.

16d.1 Revising to eliminate unplanned repetition

Unplanned repetition lacks conciseness because it delivers the same message more than once, usually in slightly different words. Unplanned repetition, or redundancy, implies that the writer lacks focus and judgment. (Its opposite, planned repetition, reflects both focus and judgment, as it creates a powerful rhythmic effect; see 19h). As you revise, check that every word you've written is necessary for delivering your message.

NO	Bringing **the project** to **final completion** three weeks early, the supervisor of **the project** earned our **respectful regard.** [*Completion* implies *bringing to final*; *project* is used twice in one sentence; and *regard* implies *respect.*]
YES	Completing the project three weeks early, the supervisor earned our respect. [eighteen words reduced to eleven by cutting all redundancies]
NO	The package, **rectangular in shape,** lay on the counter. [*Rectangular* is a shape, so *shape* is redundant.]
YES	The **rectangular** package lay on the counter.
NO	**Astonished,** the architect **circled around** the building **in amazement.**
YES	**Astonished,** the architect **circled** the building.
YES	The architect **circled** the building **in amazement**.

🌐 **ESL NOTE:** In all languages, words often carry an unspoken message. This implied meaning is assumed by native speakers of the language. In English, some implied meanings can cause redundancy in writing. For example, *I sent an e-mail by computer* is redundant. In American English, *to send an e-mail* implies *by computer.* As you become more familiar with American English, you'll begin to notice such redundancies.🌐

16d.2 Revising by combining sentences

Look at sets of sentences in your writing to see if you can fit information contained in one sentence into another sentence. For more about combining sentences, see Chapter 17, particularly section 17i.

TWO SENTENCES	The *Titanic* was discovered seventy-three years after being sunk by an iceberg. The wreck was located in the Atlantic Ocean by a team of French and American scientists.
SENTENCES COMBINED	Seventy-three years after being sunk by an iceberg, the *Titanic* was located in the Atlantic Ocean by a team of French and American scientists.
TWO SENTENCES	The stern of the ship was missing, and external damage to the hull was visible. Otherwise, the *Titanic* seemed to be in excellent condition.
SENTENCES COMBINED	Aside from a missing stern and external damage to its hull, the *Titanic* seemed to be in excellent condition.

16d.3   Revising by shortening clauses

Look at clauses in your writing to see if you can more concisely convey the same information. For example, sometimes you can cut a RELATIVE PRONOUN and its verb:

WORDY   The *Titanic*, **which was** a huge ocean liner, sank in 1912.

CONCISE   The *Titanic*, a huge ocean liner, sank in 1912.

Sometimes you can reduce a clause to a word.

WORDY   The scientists held a memorial service for the passengers and crew **who had drowned.**

CONCISE   The scientists held a memorial service for the **drowned** passengers and crew.

Sometimes ELLIPTICAL CONSTRUCTIONS (7p.2 and 15h) can shorten clauses. If you use this technique, be sure that any omitted word is implied clearly.

WORDY   **When they were** confronted with disaster, some passengers behaved heroically, **while** others **behaved** selfishly.

CONCISE   Confronted with disaster, some passengers behaved heroically, others selfishly.

16d.4   Revising by shortening phrases and cutting words

Sometimes you can reduce a phrase or redundant word pair to a single word. Redundant word pairs include *each and every, one and only, forever and ever, final and conclusive, perfectly clear, few* (or *many*) *in number, consensus of opinion,* and *reason . . . is because.*

NO   **Each and every** person was hungry.

YES   **Every** person was hungry after the movie.

YES   **Each** person was hungry after the movie.

NO   The **consensus of opinion** was that the movie was disappointing.

YES   The **consensus** was that the movie was disappointing.

YES   **Everyone agreed** that the movie was disappointing.

WORDY   More than fifteen hundred **travelers on that voyage** died in the shipwreck.

CONCISE   More than fifteen hundred **passengers** died in the shipwreck.

Sometimes you can rearrange words so that others can be deleted.

WORDY   **Objects** found inside the ship included **unbroken** bottles of wine and expensive **undamaged** china.

CONCISE   Found **undamaged** inside the ship were bottles of wine and expensive china.

16e How do verbs affect conciseness?

ACTION VERBS are strong verbs. *Be* and *have* are weak verbs that lead to wordy sentences. When you revise weak verbs to strong ones, you can both increase the impact of your writing and reduce the number of words in your sentences.

WEAK VERB	The plan before the city council **has to do with** tax rebates.
STRONG VERB	The plan before the city council **proposes** tax rebates.
WEAK VERB	The board members **were of the opinion** that the changes in the rules **were changes they would not accept.**
STRONG VERB	The board members **said** that **they would not accept** the changes in the rules.

Strong verbs come into play when you revise your writing to reduce PHRASES and to change NOUNS to verbs.

Replacing a phrase with a verb

Phrases such as *be aware of, be capable of, be supportive of* can often be replaced with one-word verbs.

I **envy** [not *am envious of*] your mathematical ability.

I **appreciate** [not *am appreciative of*] your modesty.

Your skill **illustrates** [not *is illustrative of*] how hard you studied.

Revising nouns into verbs

Many nouns are derived from verbs. They usually end with *-ance, -ment,* and *-tion* (*toler**ance**, enforce**ment**, narra**tion***). When you turn such wordy nouns back into verbs, your writing is more concise.

NO	The **accumulation of** paper lasted thirty years.
YES	The paper **accumulated** for thirty years.
NO	We **arranged for the establishment of** a student advisory committee.
YES	We **established** a student advisory committee.
NO	The building **had the appearance of** having been neglected.
YES	The building **appeared** to have been neglected.

311

EXERCISE 16-2

Consulting sections 16c through 16e, combine each set of sentences to eliminate wordy constructions.

EXAMPLE   A creative idea, says psychologist Robert Epstein, can be like a rabbit. The rabbit runs by fast. We glimpse only the rabbit's ears or tail.

A creative idea, says psychologist Robert Epstein, can be like a rabbit that runs by so fast that we glimpse only its ears or tail.

1. There is evidence that suggests that there is only one difference between creative people and the rest of us. It is creative people who are always poised to capture the new ideas we might not catch right away.
2. Creative thinking has to do with seizing opportunities. Creative thinking has to do with staying alert. Creative thinking has to do with seeking challenges and pushing boundaries.
3. The goal is that the idea be caught first and that the idea be evaluated later. A fleeting thought is captured by the alert person by writing it down at once. The goal is not to worry whether the thought will have eventual value.
4. There is an important part of creativity, and that is daydreaming, which is an activity allowing thoughts to bubble up spontaneously. These creative thoughts surprise us with their freshness.
5. Creativity can be unlocked in us by our trying something different. It is possible to turn pictures sideways or upside down to see them in new ways. We can mold clay while we think about a writing problem that is difficult.
6. It is stressed by the psychologist Robert Epstein that there are many exciting advances in everything. The advances are in fields from astrophysics to car design to dance. The advances creatively combine ideas that are from widely different sources.
7. Epstein gave his students the assignment of a problem. The problem called for the retrieval of a Ping-Pong ball. It was located at the bottom of a vertical drainpipe that was sealed at the bottom.
8. Some of the tools that the students had been given by Epstein were too short to reach the ball. Other tools that the students had been given were too wide to fit into the pipe.
9. The students were stumped at first. The students tried unsuccessfully to capture the ball with the tools. Then, the students stepped back from the immediate situation. The students saw the big picture and began thinking creatively.
10. Water was poured down the drainpipe by the students. The ball achieved flotation and rose to the top. The ball was retrieved by the students there.

EXERCISE 16-3

Working individually or with a group, revise this paragraph to make it more concise. For help, consult all sections of this chapter.

EXAMPLE   More North American companies that are based in the United States are entering global markets around the world.

More U.S.–based companies are entering global markets.

(1) One such firm is the Campbell Soup Company, whose goal is to expand from a U.S. soup company into a global food force extending beyond the fifty states. (2) Eventually, Campbell hopes to receive half its revenues from foreign consumers in other countries. (3) The primary and most important strategy for this change from the existing position is expansion, and Campbell products are now being shipped from the United States to Asia, where the people consume large quantities of soup. (4) Campbell is also reworking its recipes, such as the recipes for its *flaki* soup that it ships to Poland and for its watercress and duck-gizzard soup that it ships to China, in order to make the soups appeal to specific ethnic groups around the world.

17 COORDINATION AND SUBORDINATION

Used well, **coordination** and **subordination** in sentences enhance writing style. These structuring methods reflect the relationships between ideas that a writer seeks to express. Some writers enlist coordination and subordination while they DRAFT, but often writers wait until they REVISE to check for good opportunities to use these two techniques.

TWO SENTENCES	The sky turned dark gray. The wind died down.
USING COORDINATION	The sky turned dark gray**, and** the wind died down.
USING SUBORDINATION	**As** the sky turned dark gray, the wind died down. [Here, the wind is the focus.]
SUBORDINATED VERSION 2	**As** the wind died down, the sky turned dark gray. [Here, the sky is the focus.]

COORDINATION

17a What is coordination of sentences?

Coordination of sentences is a grammatical strategy to communicate that the ideas in two or more INDEPENDENT CLAUSES are equivalent or balanced. Coordination can produce harmony by bringing related elements together. Whenever you use the technique of coordination of sentences, make sure that it works well with the meaning you want to communicate.

The sky turned **brighter, and** people emerged from buildings.

The sky turned **brighter; the** people emerged from buildings.

17b What is the structure of a coordinate sentence?

A **coordinate sentence,** also known as a *compound sentence,* consists of two or more INDEPENDENT CLAUSES joined by either a semicolon or by a comma working in concert with a COORDINATING CONJUNCTION (*and, but, for, or, nor, yet, so*). Box 89 shows patterns for coordination of sentences.

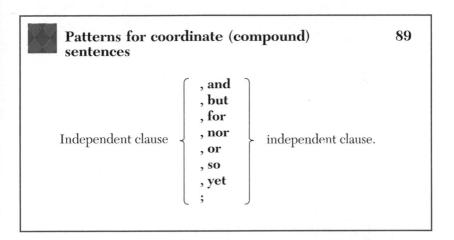

Patterns for coordinate (compound) sentences   89

Independent clause { , and / , but / , for / , nor / , or / , so / , yet / ; } independent clause.

17c What meaning does each coordinating conjunction convey?

Each COORDINATING CONJUNCTION has its own meaning. When you choose one, be sure that its meaning accurately expresses the relationship between the equivalent ideas that you want to convey.

- **and** means addition
- **but** and **yet** mean contrast
- **so** means result or effect
- **for** means reason or choice
- **or** means choice
- **nor** means negative choice

◉ Always use a comma before a coordinating conjunction that joins two INDEPENDENT CLAUSES (24b). ●

17d What are two major misuses of coordination?

One major misuse of COORDINATION occurs when unrelated or non-equivalent ideas, each in its own INDEPENDENT CLAUSE, are coordinated. The result looks like a coordinated sentence, but the ideas are unrelated.

> **NO** Computers came into common use in the 1970s, and they sometimes make costly errors. [The statement in each independent clause is true, but the ideas are not related or equivalent.]

> **YES** Computers came into common use in the 1970s, and now they are indispensable business tools.

A second major misuse of coordination occurs when it's overused. Simply stringing sentences together with COORDINATING CONJUNCTIONS makes relationships among ideas unclear—and it lacks style.

> **NO** Dinosaurs could have disappeared for many reasons, **and** one theory holds meteors and asteroids hit the earth, **so** the impact created a huge dust cloud that caused a false winter. The winter lasted for years, and the dinosaurs died.

> **YES** Dinosaurs could have disappeared for many reasons. One theory holds that the climate suddenly became cold, and another suggests that a sudden shower of meteors and asteroids hit the earth. The impact created a huge dust cloud that caused a false winter. The winter lasted for years, killing the dinosaurs.

EXERCISE 17-1

Working individually or with a group, revise these sentences to eliminate illogical or overused coordination. If you think a sentence needs no revision, explain why. For help, consult 17a through 17d.

EXAMPLE   Fencing, once a form of combat, has become a competitive sport worldwide, and today's fencers disapprove of those who identify fencing with fighting.

Fencing, once a form of combat, has become a competitive sport worldwide, *but* today's fencers disapprove of those who identify fencing with fighting.

1. As depicted in movies, fencing sometimes appears to be reckless swordplay, and fencing requires precision, coordination, and strategy.

2. The first fencing competitions in the fourteenth century were small, and because it was very popular, fencing was one of the few sports included in the first modern Olympic Games in 1896, and fencing has been part of the Olympics ever since then.

3. Fencing equipment includes a mask, a padded jacket, a glove, and one of three weapons—a foil, épée, or saber—and a fencer's technique and targets differ depending on the weapon used and the fencer's experience.
4. Generally, a fencer specializes in one of the three weapons, but some competitors are equally skilled with all three.
5. The object of fencing is to be the first to touch the opponent five times, and a "president," who is sometimes assisted by a number of judges, officiates at competitions.

SUBORDINATION

17e What is subordination in sentences?

Subordination is a grammatical strategy to communicate that one idea in a sentence is more important than another idea in the same sentence. Using the technique of subordination in a sentence, you place the more important idea in an INDEPENDENT CLAUSE and the less important—the subordinate—idea in a DEPENDENT CLAUSE. The information you choose to subordinate depends on the meaning you want to deliver.

INDEPENDENT CLAUSE   DEPENDENT

Two cowboys fought a dangerous Colorado snowstorm **while they**

CLAUSE   DEPENDENT CLAUSE

were looking for cattle. When they came to a canyon,

INDEPENDENT CLAUSE

they saw outlines of buildings through the blizzard.

To illustrate the difference in writing style when you use subordination, here's a passage with the same message as the example above, but without subordination.

Two cowboys fought a dangerous Colorado snowstorm. They were looking for cattle. They came to a canyon. They saw outlines of buildings through the blizzard.

17f What is the structure of a subordinate sentence?

To use SUBORDINATION in your sentences, start the DEPENDENT CLAUSE with either a SUBORDINATING CONJUNCTION, listed in Box 91 (in 17n), or a RELATIVE PRONOUN (*which, that, who, whom, whose*).

If they are very lucky, the passengers may glimpse dolphins breaking water playfully near the ship.

—Elizabeth Gray, student

Pandas are solitary animals, **which** means they are difficult to protect from extinction.

—Jose Santos, student

Patterns of subordination with dependent clauses are shown in Box 90. Dependent clauses are of two types: ADVERB CLAUSES and ADJECTIVE CLAUSES. An adverb clause starts with a subordinating conjunction. Each subordinating conjunction has a specific meaning that expresses a relationship between the dependent clause and the INDEPENDENT CLAUSE. An adjective clause starts with a relative pronoun.

 Subordination patterns 90

Sentences with Adverb Clauses

- **Adverb clause,** independent clause.
  - **After the sky grew dark,** the wind died suddenly.
- Independent clause, **adverb clause.**
  - Birds stopped singing, **as they do during an eclipse.**
- Independent clause, **adverb clause.**
  - The stores closed **before the storm began.**

Sentences with Adjective Clauses

- Independent clause **restrictive (essential)* adjective clause.**
  - Weather forecasts warned of a storm **that might bring a thirty-inch snowfall.**
- Independent clause, **nonrestrictive (nonessential)* adjective clause.**
  - Spring is the season for tornadoes, **which may have wind speeds over 220 miles an hour.**
- Beginning of independent clause **restrictive (essential)* adjective clause** end of independent clause.
  - Anyone **who lives through a tornado** remembers the experience.
- Beginning of independent clause, **nonrestrictive (nonessential)* adjective clause,** end of independent clause.
  - The sky, **which had been clear,** turned greenish black.

* For an explanation of RESTRICTIVE and NONRESTRICTIVE ELEMENTS see (24f).

318

17g What meaning does each subordinating conjunction convey?

Each SUBORDINATING CONJUNCTION has its own meaning. When you choose one, be sure that its meaning accurately expresses the relationship between the ideas that you want to convey. Box 91 lists subordinating conjunctions according to their different meanings.

⊙ Subordinating conjunctions and their meanings   91

TIME
after, before, once, since, until, when, whenever, while

- **After** you have handed in your report, you cannot revise it.

REASON OR CAUSE
as, because, since

- **Because** you have handed in your report, you cannot revise it.

PURPOSE OR RESULT
in order that, so that, that

- I want to read your report **so that** I can evaluate it.

CONDITION
if even, if, provided that, unless

- **Unless** you have handed in your report, you can revise it.

CONTRAST
although, even though, though, whereas, while

- **Although** you have handed in your report, you can ask to revise it.

CHOICE
than, whether

- You took more time to revise **than** I did before the lab report deadline.

PLACE OR LOCATION
where, wherever

- **Wherever** you say, I'll find it to hand in my report.

319

EXERCISE 17-2

Working individually or with a group, combine each pair of sentences, using an adverb clause to subordinate one idea. Then, revise each sentence so that the adverb clause becomes the independent clause. For help, see 17e through 17g, especially Box 90.

EXAMPLE   The U.S. Mint produces new coins. The U.S. Bureau of Engraving and Printing makes $1, $5, $10, $20, and $100 bills.

      a. *While the U.S. Mint produces new coins, the U.S. Bureau of Engraving and Printing makes $1, $5, $10, $20, and $100 bills.*

      b. *While the U.S. Bureau of Engraving and Printing makes $1, $5, $10, $20, and $100 bills, the U.S. Mint produces new coins.*

1. The U.S. Mint can produce more than 50 million coins a day. The U.S. Bureau of Engraving and Printing can produce 20 million notes a day.
2. The Federal Reserve Banks are responsible for both destroying old money and ordering new coins and notes. They must keep the right amount of money in circulation.
3. Coins can stay in circulation for decades. People let them accumulate in jars and drawers in their homes.
4. A $1 bill lasts about fifteen to eighteen months. It reaches its average life span.
5. The U.S. Federal Reserve Banks destroy dirty, worn, and torn bills. The Federal Reserve Banks are destroying more than $40 billion worth of money a year.

EXERCISE 17-3

Working individually or with a group, combine each pair of sentences, using an adjective clause to subordinate one idea to the other. Then, revise each sentence so that the adjective clause becomes the independent clause. Use the relative pronoun given in parentheses. For help, consult 17e through 17g, especially Box 90.

EXAMPLE   Aristides was an ancient Greek politician famous for his honesty and judgment. He was known as Aristides the Just. (who)

      a. *Aristides, who was an ancient Greek politician famous for his honesty and judgment, was known as Aristides the Just.*

      b. *Aristides, who was known as Aristides the Just, was an ancient Greek politician famous for his honesty and judgment.*

1. An ancient Greek law allowed voters to banish politicians from their city. It asked citizens to write the name of an unpopular politician on their ballots. (that)
2. A voter was filling out a ballot when Aristides the Just walked by. The voter needed help in spelling *Aristides.* (who)
3. Aristides knew the voter did not recognize him. He asked why the voter wanted to banish that particular politician. (who)
4. The voter said he resented hearing someone called "the Just" all the time. He handed Aristides his ballot. (who)
5. Aristides' reaction demonstrated that the nickname "the Just" was well deserved. His reaction was to write his own name on the voter's ballot even though that person's vote helped banish Aristides. (which)

17h What are two major misuses of subordination?

One major misuse of SUBORDINATION occurs when a SUBORDINATING CONJUNCTION doesn't communicate a sensible relationship between the INDEPENDENT CLAUSE and the DEPENDENT CLAUSE. Box 91 (17g) lists subordinating conjunctions and their different meanings.

> **NO** Because Beethoven was deaf when he wrote them, his final symphonies were masterpieces. [*Because* is illogical here; it says the masterpieces resulted from the deafness.]

> **YES** Although Beethoven was deaf when he wrote them, his final symphonies were masterpieces. [*Although* is logical here; it says Beethoven wrote masterpieces in spite of his being deaf.]

A second major misuse of subordination occurs when it's overused, resulting in too many images or ideas crowded together in one sentence. This causes readers to lose track of the message. Whenever you write a sentence with two or more dependent clauses, check that your message is clear. If it isn't, you've likely overused subordination.

> **NO** A new technique for eye surgery, **which is supposed to correct nearsightedness, which previously could be corrected only by glasses,** has been developed, **although many eye doctors do not approve of the new technique because it can create unstable vision, which includes intense glare from headlights on cars and many other light sources.** [The base sentence *A new technique for eye surgery has been developed* is crowded with five dependent clauses attached to it.]

> **YES** A new technique for eye surgery, **which is supposed to correct nearsightedness,** has been developed. Previously, only glasses could correct nearsightedness. Many doctors do

not approve of the new technique **because it can create unstable vision.** The problems include intense glare from car headlights and many other sources of light. [In this revision, one long sentence has been broken into four sentences, making the material easier to read and the relationships among ideas clearer. Two dependent clauses remain, which balance well with the other sentence constructions. Some words have been moved to new positions.]

ESL NOTE: If you're told that your sentences are too long and complex, limit the number of words in each sentence. The advice of many ESL teachers is to revise any sentence containing a total of more than three independent and dependent clauses.

EXERCISE 17-4

Working individually or with a group, correct illogical or excessive subordination in this paragraph. As you revise according to the message you want to deliver, use some dependent clauses as well as some short sentences. (Also, if you wish, apply the principles of coordination discussed in sections 17a through 17d.) For help, consult 17h.

Although people in the United States think of hot dogs as their traditional food, this American favorite originated in Germany in 1852 when butchers in Frankfurt, Germany, stuffed meat into a long casing, which in honor of the town, they called their creation a "frankfurter." Because one butcher noticed that the frankfurter resembled the shape of his dog, a dachshund, he decided to name the meat roll a "dachshund sausage," a name which caught on in Germany. When Germans brought dachshund sausages to the United States, peddlers sold them on the street, although the dachshund sausages were so hot that people often burned their fingers because they had trouble holding the meat. When one clever peddler put the sausage in a bun, a *New York Times* cartoonist decided to draw a picture of hot dachshund sausages in buns, although he called them "hot dogs" because he didn't know how to spell *dachshund*.

17i How do I effectively use coordination and subordination together?

Your writing style improves when you use a logical and pleasing variety of SENTENCE TYPES, utilizing COORDINATION and SUBORDINATION to improve CONCISENESS and the flow of ideas. Here's a paragraph that demonstrates a good balance in the use of coordination and subordination.

When I was growing up, I lived on a farm just across the field from my grandmother. My parents were busy trying to raise six children and to establish their struggling dairy farm. It was nice to have Grandma so close. While my parents were providing the necessities of life, my patient grandmother gave her time to her shy, young granddaughter. I always enjoyed going with Grandma and collecting the eggs that her chickens had just laid. Usually, she knew which chickens would peck, and she was careful to let me gather the eggs from the less hostile ones.

—Patricia Mapes, student

When you use both coordination and subordination, avoid using in one sentence both a COORDINATE CONJUNCTION and a SUBORDINATE CONJUNCTION to express one relationship.

NO   **Although** the story was well written, **but** it was too illogical.
[The subordinating conjunction *although* expresses the contrast, so also using *but* is incorrect.]

YES   **Although** the story was well written, it was too illogical.

YES   The story was well written, **but** it was too illogical.

EXERCISE 17-5

Working individually or in a group, use subordination and coordination to combine these sets of short, choppy sentences. For help, consult all sections of this chapter.

EXAMPLE   Owls cannot digest the bones and fur of the mice and birds they eat. They cough up a furry pellet every day.

         Because owls cannot digest the bones and fur of the mice and birds they *eat, they* cough up a furry pellet every day.

1. Owl pellets are the latest teaching tool in biology classrooms around the country. The pellets provide an alternative to dissecting frogs and other animals.

2. Inside the pellet are the remains of the owl's nightly meal. They include beautifully cleaned hummingbird skulls, rat skeletons, and lots of bird feathers.

3. The owl-pellet market has been cornered by companies in New York, California, and Washington. These companies distribute pellets to thousands of biology classrooms all over the world.

4. Company workers scour barns and the ground under trees where owls nest to pick up the pellets. The pellets sell for $1 each.

5. The owl-pellet business may have a short future. The rural areas of the United States are vanishing. Old barns are being bulldozed. All the barns are torn down. The owls will be gone, too.

EXERCISE 17-6

Working individually or with a group, revise this paragraph to be more effective by using coordination and subordination. For help, consult all sections of this chapter.

Thirst is the body's way of surviving. Every cell in the body needs water. People can die by losing as little as 15 to 20 percent of their water requirements. Blood contains 83 percent water. Blood provides indispensable nutrients for the cells. Blood carries water to the cells. Blood carries waste away from the cells. Insufficient water means cells cannot be fueled or cleaned. The body becomes sluggish. The body can survive eleven days without water. Bodily functions are seriously disrupted by a lack of water for more than one day. The body loses water. The blood thickens. The heart must pump harder. Thickened blood is harder to pump through the heart. Some drinks replace the body's need for fluids. Alcohol or caffeine in drinks leads to dehydration. People know they should drink water often. They can become moderately dehydrated before they even begin to develop a thirst.

18 PARALLELISM

18a What is parallelism?

When you write words, PHRASES, or CLAUSES within a sentence to match in their grammatical forms, the result is **parallelism.** Parallelism serves to emphasize information or ideas in writing. The technique relates to the concept of parallel lines in geometry, lines that run alongside each other and never meet. Parallelism delivers grace, rhythm, and impact.

> The deer often come to eat their grain, the wolves to destroy their sheep, the bears to kill their hogs, and the foxes to catch their poultry. [The message of the multiple, accumulating assaults is echoed by the parallel structures.]
>
> —J. Hector St. Jean de Crèvecoeur, *Letters from an American Farmer*

You gain several advantages in using parallel structures:

- You can express ideas of equal weight in your writing;
- You can emphasize important information or ideas;
- You can add rhythm and grace to your writing style.

Many writers attend to parallelism when they are REVISING. If you think while you're DRAFTING that your parallelism is faulty or that you can enhance your writing style by using parallelism, underline or highlight the material and keep moving forward. When you revise, you can return to the places you've marked.

18b What is a balanced sentence?

A **balanced sentence** is a type of parallelism in which contrasting content is delivered. The two parallel structures are usually, but not always, INDEPENDENT CLAUSES. A balanced sentence uses COORDINATION (see 17a through 17d). The two coordinate structures are characterized by opposites in meaning, sometimes with one structure cast in the negative.

Mosquitos don't bite; they stab.

By night, the litter and desperation disappeared as the city's glittering lights came on; by day, the filth and despair reappeared as the sun rose.

—Jennifer Kirk, student

👁 **PUNCTUATION ALERT:** Authorities differ about using a comma or a semicolon between the parts of a balanced sentence. In ACADEMIC WRITING, to avoid appearing to make the error of a COMMA SPLICE (see Chapter 13), use a semicolon (or revise in some other way). ●

18c How do words, phrases, and clauses work in parallel form?

When you put words, PHRASES, and CLAUSES into parallel form, you enhance your writing style with balance and grace.

PARALLEL WORDS   Recommended exercise includes running, swimming, and cycling.

PARALLEL PHRASES   Exercise helps people maintain healthy bodies and handle mental pressures.

PARALLEL CLAUSES   Many people exercise because they want to look healthy, because they need to increase stamina, and because they hope to live longer.

18d How does parallelism deliver impact?

Parallel structures serve to emphasize the meaning that sentences deliver. Deliberate, rhythmic repetition of parallel forms creates an effect of balance (18b), reinforcing the impact of a message.

Go back to Mississippi, go back to Alabama, go back to South Carolina, go back to Georgia, go back to Louisiana, go back to the slums and ghettos of our northern cities, knowing that somehow this situation can and will be changed.

—Martin Luther King Jr., "I Have a Dream"

If King had not used PARALLELISM, his message would have made less of an impact on his listeners. His structures reinforce the power of his message. A sentence without parallelism could have carried his message, but with far less effect: *Return to your homes in Mississippi, Alabama,*

South Carolina, Georgia, Louisiana, or the cities, and know that the situation will be changed.

Here's a longer passage in which parallel structures, concepts, and rhythms echo the intensity of the message.

> You ask me what is **poverty**? Listen to me. Here I am, dirty, **smelly,** and with no "proper" underwear on and with the stench of my rotting teeth near you. I will tell you. Listen to me. Listen without pity. I cannot use your pity. Listen with understanding. Put yourself in my dirty, worn-out, ill-fitting shoes, and hear me.
>
> **Poverty** is getting up every morning from a dirt- and illness-stained mattress. The sheets have long since been used for diapers. **Poverty** is living in a **smell** that never leaves. This is a **smell** of urine, sour milk, and spoiling food sometimes joined with the strong **smell** of long-cooked onions. Onions are cheap. If you have **smelled** this **smell,** you did not know how it came. It is **the smell** of the outdoor privy. It is **the smell** of young children who cannot walk the long dark way in the night. It is **the smell** of the mattresses where years of "accidents" have happened. It is **the smell** of the milk that has gone sour because the refrigerator long has not worked, and it costs money to get it fixed. It is **the smell** of rotting garbage. I could bury it, but where is the shovel? Shovels cost money.

> —Jo Goodwin Parker, "What Is Poverty?"

EXERCISE 18-1

Working individually or with a group, highlight all the parallel elements of the Jo Goodwin Parker passage in addition to those shown above in boldface.

18e How can I avoid faulty parallelism?

Faulty parallelism usually results when you join nonmatching grammatical forms with COORDINATING CONJUNCTIONS (18e.1), with CORRELATIVE CONJUNCTIONS (18e.2), with the words *than* and *as* (18e.3), or with function words (18e.4).

18e.1 Using parallelism correctly with coordinating conjunctions

The coordinating conjunctions are *and, but, or, nor, for, yet,* and *so* (for the relationship each expresses, see section 7i or 17c). To avoid faulty parallelism, write the words that accompany coordinating conjunctions in matching grammatical forms.

> **NO** Love *and* being married go together.
>
> **YES** Love *and* marriage go together.
>
> **YES** Being in love *and* being married go together.

18e.2 Using parallelism correctly with correlative conjunctions

Correlative conjunctions are paired words such as *not only . . . but (also), either . . . or,* and *both . . . and.* To avoid faulty parallelism, write the words joined by correlative conjunctions in matching grammatical forms.

> **NO** Differing expectations for marriage *not only* **can lead to disappointment** *but also* **makes the couple angry.**

> **YES** Differing expectations for marriage *not only* **can lead to disappointment** *but also* **can make the couple angry.**

18e.3 Using parallelism correctly with *than* and *as*

To avoid faulty parallelism when you use *than* and *as* for comparisons, write the elements of comparison in matching grammatical forms.

> **NO** **Having a solid marriage** can be more satisfying *than* **the acquisition of wealth.**

> **YES** **Having a solid marriage** can be more satisfying *than* **acquiring wealth.**

> **YES** **A solid marriage** can be more satisfying *than* **wealth.**

18e.4 Using parallelism correctly with function words

Function words include ARTICLES (*the, a, an*); the *to* of the INFINITIVE (*to* love); PREPOSITIONS (for example, *of, in, about*); and sometimes RELATIVE PRONOUNS. When you write a series of parallel structures, be consistent in the second and successive structures about repeating or omitting a function word. In making judgments about the benefits of repeating function words for the sake of parallelism, do so only if you think that repeating such words clarifies your meaning or highlights the parallelism that you intend. Some instructors, however, prefer that function words never be repeated, so check before you do.

> **NO** **To assign** unanswered letters their proper weight, **free** us from the expectations of others, **to give** us back to ourselves— here lies the great, singular power of self-respect.

> **YES** **To assign** unanswered letters their proper weight, **to free** us from the expectations of others, **to give** us back to ourselves— here lies **the great, the singular** power of self-respect.
>
> —Joan Didion, "On Self-Respect"

I have in my own life a precious friend, a woman of 65 **who has** lived very hard, **who is** wise, **who listens** well, **who has been** where I am and can help me understand it, and **who represents** not only an ultimate ideal mother to me but also the person I'd like to be when I grow up.

—Judith Viorst, "Friends, Good Friends—and Such Good Friends"

We looked into the bus, which **was** painted blue with orange daisies, **had** picnic benches instead of seats, and **showed** yellow curtains billowing out its windows.

—Kerric Falk, student

EXERCISE 18-2

Working individually or with a group, revise these sentences by putting appropriate information in parallel structures. For help, consult 18a through 18e.

EXAMPLE   Difficult bosses affect not only their employees' performances but their private lives are affected as well.

Difficult bosses affect not only their employees' performances *but their private lives as well.*

1. According to psychologist Harry Levinson, the five main types of bad boss are the workaholic, the kind of person you would describe as bullying, a person who communicates badly, the jellyfish type, and someone who insists on perfection.
2. As a way of getting ahead, to keep their self-respect, and for simple survival, wise employees handle problem bosses with a variety of strategies.
3. To cope with a bad-tempered employer, workers can both stand up for themselves and reasoning with a bullying boss.
4. Often, bad bosses communicate poorly or fail to calculate the impact of their personality on others; being a careful listener and sensitivity to others' responses are qualities that good bosses possess.
5. Employees who take the trouble to understand what makes their boss tick, engage in some self-analysis, and staying flexible are better prepared to cope with a difficult job environment than suffering in silence like some employees.

EXERCISE 18-3

Consulting sections 18a through 18e, combine the sentences in each numbered item, using techniques of parallelism.

EXAMPLE   College scholarships are awarded not only for academic and athletic ability, but there are also scholarships that recognize unusual talents. Other scholarships even award accidents of birth, like left-handedness.

College scholarships are awarded not only for academic and athletic ability *but also for unusual talents and even for accidents of birth, like left-handedness.*

1. A married couple met at Juniata College in Huntingdon, Pennsylvania. They are both left-handed, and they have set up a scholarship for needy left-handed students attending Juniata.

2. Writers who specialize in humor bankroll a student humor writer at the University of Southern California in Los Angeles. A horse-racing association sponsors a student sportswriter. The student sportswriter must attend Vanderbilt University in Nashville, Tennessee.

3. The Rochester Institute of Technology in New York State is choosing 150 students born on June 12, 1979. Each one is to receive a grant of $1,500 per year. These awards are to be given to select students to honor the school's 150th anniversary, which was celebrated on June 12, 1979.

4. The College of Wooster in Ohio grants generous scholarships to students if they play the bagpipes, a musical instrument native to Scotland. Students playing the traditional Scottish drums and those who excel in Scottish folk dancing also qualify.

5. In return for their scholarships, Wooster's bagpipers must pipe for the school's football team. The terms of the scholarships also require the drummers to drum for the team. The dancers have to cheer the athletes from the sidelines.

EXERCISE 18-4

Working alone or with a group, find the parallel elements in these three passages. Next, imitate the parallelism in the examples, using a different topic of your choice for each.

A.   Our earth is but a small star in a great universe. Yet of it we can make, if we choose, a planet unvexed by war, untroubled by hunger or fear, undivided by senseless distinctions of race, color, or theory.
                                                    —Stephen Vincent Benét

B.   Some would recover [from polio] almost entirely. Some would die. Some would come through unable to move their legs, or unable to move arms and legs; some could move nothing but an arm, or nothing but a few fingers and their eyes. Some would leave the hospital with a cane, some with crutches, crutches and steel leg braces, or in wheelchairs—white-faced, shrunken, with frightened eyes, light blankets over their legs. Some would remain in an iron lung—a great, eighteen-hundred-pound, casket-like contraption, like the one in which the woman in the magic show (her head and feet sticking out of either end) is sawed in half.
                                        —Charles L. Mee Jr., "The Summer Before Salk"

C.   I am lonely only when I am overtired, when I have worked too long without a break, when for the time being I feel empty and need filling up. And I am lonely sometimes when I come back home after a lecture trip, when I have seen a lot of people and talked a lot, and am full to the brim with experience that needs to be sorted out.

—May Sarton, "The Rewards of a Solitary Life"

18f How does parallelism operate in outlines and lists?

All items in formal OUTLINES and lists must be parallel in grammar and structure. (For more about outline format and outline development, see 2r.)

OUTLINE

NO

Reducing Traffic Fatalities
I. Stricter laws
    A. Top speed should be 55 mph on highways.
    B. Higher fines
    C. Requiring jail sentences for repeat offenders
II. The use of safety devices should be mandated by law.

YES

Reducing Traffic Fatalities
I. Passing stricter speed laws
    A. Making 55 mph the top speed on highways
    B. Raising fines for speeding
    C. Requiring jail sentences for repeat offenders
II. Mandating by law the use of safety devices

LISTS

NO   Workaholics share these characteristics:
1. They are intense and driven.
2. Strong self-doubters
3. Labor is preferred to leisure by workaholics.

YES   Workaholics share these characteristics:
1. They are intense and driven.
2. They have strong self-doubts.
3. They prefer labor to leisure.

EXERCISE 18-5

Working individually or with a group, revise this outline into parallel form. For help, consult 18f.

Reducing Traffic Fatalities

I. Stricter laws needed
   A. Legislating top speed of 55 mph for highways
   B. Higher fines
   C. Repeat offenders sentenced to jail
II. Legislating uses of safety devices
   A. All passengers, back and front, should be required to have safety belts.
   B. Drivers must be held responsible when passengers are not wearing seat belts.
   C. Forcing car manufacturers to offer side and front airbags in all cars.

19 VARIETY AND EMPHASIS

19a What are variety and emphasis in writing?

Achieving variety and emphasis moves your writing beyond correctness to the pleasures of style and grace. When you write sentences of various lengths and structures (7k to 7q) within a paragraph or longer piece of writing, you create **sentence variety.** Working in concert with sentence variety, **emphasis** allows you to add weight to ideas of special importance.

Using techniques of variety and emphasis, you help readers distinguish between major and minor points; recognize TONE (1e, 5c.2), which gives depth to your message; and enjoy a pleasing writing style. Usually, the best time to apply the principles of variety and emphasis is while you are REVISING.

19b How do different sentence lengths create variety and emphasis?

To emphasize one idea among many others, you can express it in a sentence noticeably different in length from the sentences surrounding it. In the following example, a four-word sentence between two longer sentences carries the key message of the passage.

> Today is one of those excellent January partly cloudies in which light chooses an unexpected landscape to trick out in gilt, and then shadow sweeps it away. **You know you're alive.** You take huge steps, trying to feel the planet's roundness arc between your feet.
>
> —Annie Dillard, *Pilgrim at Tinker Creek*

Sometimes a string of short sentences create impact and emphasis. Yet, at other times, a string of short sentences can be dull to read.

NO   There is a problem. It is widely known as sick-building syndrome. It comes from indoor air pollution. It causes office workers to suffer. They have trouble breathing. They have painful rashes. Their heads ache. Their eyes burn.

YES   Widely known as sick-building syndrome, indoor air pollution causes office workers to suffer. They have trouble breathing. They have painful rashes. Their heads ache. Their eyes burn. [Many revisions are possible. This uses a long sentence to mention indoor air pollution and its victims; next, this retains the series of short sentences to emphasize each problem. Also, the CONCISENESS of the revised version reduces 38 words to 28.]

Similarly, a string of COMPOUND SENTENCES—INDEPENDENT CLAUSES connected with coordinating conjunctions (*and, but, for, nor, or, yet, so*) without balance or well-considered COORDINATION—can be monotonous to read and don't communicate relationships among ideas.

NO   Science fiction writers are often thinkers, **and** they are often dreamers, **and** they let their imaginations wander. Jules Verne was such a writer, **and** he predicted space ships, **and** he forecast atomic submarines, **but** most people did not believe airplanes were possible.

YES   Science fiction writers are often thinkers and dreamers who let their imaginations wander. Jules Verne was one such writer. He predicted space ships and atomic submarines before most people believed airplanes were possible.

EXERCISE 19-1

Working individually or with a group, revise these sets of sentences to vary the sentence lengths effectively. For help, consult 19a and 19b.

1.   Biometeorology is a science. It examines the study of weather's unseen power over living things. The science concentrates on the effects of weather patterns on human behavior and health. Many researchers study these effects. They are attempting to find a connection between the two. One such researcher is William Ferdinand Peterson. He has spent the past twenty years collecting statistics and anecdotes. He wrote the book *The Patient and the Weather*. His research focuses on the invisible elements of air. These elements include passing fronts. These elements include falling barometric pressure. The elements include shifting wind directions.

2.   Feared winds and all their variations—from katabatic to chinook to Santa Ana—are frequently considered the cause of every illness that can be imagined by many people in every country. In Russia, high winds and the frequency of strokes seem related, and in Italy, southern winds and heart attacks seem connected, and in Japan, researchers have noticed an increase in asthma attacks whenever the wind changes direction.

19c How does an occasional question, mild command, or exclamation create variety and emphasis?

The majority of sentences in English are DECLARATIVE—they declare something by making a statement. Declarative sentences offer an almost infinite variety of structures and patterns. For variety and emphasis, you might want occasionally to use three alternative types of sentences.

A sentence that asks a question is called INTERROGATIVE. Occasional questions, placed appropriately, tend to involve readers. A sentence that issues a mild or strong command is called IMPERATIVE. Occasional mild commands, appropriately used, gently urge your reader to think along with you. A sentence that makes an exclamation is called EXCLAMATORY. An occasional exclamatory sentence, appropriate to the context, can enliven writing, although this sentence type tends to occur only rarely in ACADEMIC WRITING.

PUNCTUATION ALERT: A declarative sentence ends with a period (Chapter 23)—or semicolon (Chapter 25) or colon (Chapter 26). A mild command ends with a period. A strong command and an exclamation end with an exclamation mark (Chapter 23). ●

Here's a paragraph with declarative, interrogative, and imperative sentences. (No exclamatory sentence occurs here, although the final sentence could have been treated as one.)

> Imagine what people ate during the winter as little as seventy-five years ago. They ate food that was local, long-lasting, and dull, like acorn squash, turnips, and cabbage. Walk into an American supermarket in February and the world lies before you: grapes, melons, artichokes, fennel, lettuce, peppers, pistachios, dates, even strawberries, to say nothing of ice cream. Have you ever considered what a triumph of civilization it is to be able to buy a pound of chicken livers? If you lived on a farm and had to kill a chicken when you wanted to eat one, you wouldn't ever accumulate a pound of chicken livers.
> —Phyllis Rose, "Shopping and Other Spiritual Adventures in America Today"

EXERCISE 19-2

Working individually or with a group, write an imitation of the paragraph below. This paragraph varies sentence lengths and uses a question and a command effectively. The result emphasizes the key points. Choose your own topic, but follow the style of the paragraph closely. For help, consult section 19c.

> Why do most Americans spend $95 a year to operate their clothes dryers when nature provides free energy for the same task? Consider

the humble clothesline and clothespins. They cost about $30 for a lifetime, and solar power is free, unlike an electric dryer, which can cost as much as $500. In an increasingly mechanized indoor life, people who hang their clothes on the line are obliged to notice the weather. Today is a perfect morning for drying, they think. Or will it rain this afternoon? Another line in the basement or spare room works well in rainy weather and in winter. Indoor drying has the further benefit of humidifying the house; twenty pounds of wet wash contributes about one gallon of water to the air.

19d How can modifiers create variety and emphasis?

MODIFIERS can expand sentences to add richness to your writing and create a pleasing mixture of variety and emphasis. Your choice of where to place modifiers to expand your sentences depends on the focus you want each sentence to communicate—on its own and in concert with its surrounding sentences. Be careful, however, where you place modifiers because you don't want to introduce the error known as a MISPLACED MODIFIER (14a).

BASIC SENTENCE	The river rose.
ADJECTIVE	The **swollen** river rose.
ADVERB	The river rose **dangerously.**
PREPOSITIONAL PHRASE	The river rose **above its banks.**
PARTICIPIAL PHRASE	**Swelled by melting snow,** the river rose.
ABSOLUTE PHRASE	**Uprooted trees swirling away in the current,** the river rose.
ADVERB CLAUSE	**Because the snows had been heavy that winter,** the river rose.
ADJECTIVE CLAUSE	The river, **which runs through vital farmland,** rose.

EXERCISE 19-3

Working individually or with a group, expand each sentence by adding each kind of modifier illustrated in 19d.

1. We bought a house.
2. The roof leaked.
3. I remodeled the kitchen.
4. Neighbors brought food.
5. Everyone enjoyed the barbeque.

19e How does a change in word order create variety and emphasis?

Standard word order in English places the SUBJECT before the VERB.

The **mayor *walked*** into the room. [*Mayor* is the subject, which comes before the verb *walked*.]

Because the above word order is standard, any variation from it creates emphasis. For example, **inverted word order** places the verb before the subject.

Into the room ***walked*** the **mayor**. [*Mayor* is the subject, which comes after the verb *walked*.]

19f How does changing a sentence's subject create emphasis?

The SUBJECT of a sentence establishes the focus for that sentence. To create the emphasis you want, you can vary each sentence's subject. All the example sentences below express the same information, but the focus changes in each according to the subject (and its corresponding verb).

Our study *showed* that 25 percent of college students' time is spent eating or sleeping. [Focus is on the study.]

College students *eat or sleep* 25 percent of the time, according to our study. [Focus is on the students.]

Eating or sleeping *occupies* 25 percent of college students' time, according to our study. [Focus is on eating and sleeping.]

Twenty-five percent of college students' time *is spent* in eating or sleeping, according to our study. [Focus is on the percentage of time.]

19g How can a periodic sentence among cumulative sentences create variety and emphasis?

The **cumulative sentence** is the most common sentence structure in English. Its name reflects the way information accumulates in the sentence until it reaches a period. Its structure starts with a SUBJECT and VERB and continues with modifiers. Another term for a cumulative sentence is *loose sentence* because it lacks a tightly planned structure.

For greater impact, you might occasionally use a **periodic sentence,** also called a *climactic sentence*, which reserves the main idea for the end of the sentence. This structure tends to draw in the reader as it moves toward the period. If overused, however, periodic sentences lose their punch.

CUMULATIVE	A car hit a shoulder and turned over at midnight last night on the road from Las Vegas to Death Valley Junction.
PERIODIC	At midnight last night, on the road from Las Vegas to Death Valley Junction, a car hit a shoulder and turned over.

—Joan Didion, "On Morality"

19h How does repetition affect variety and emphasis?

When your message is suitable, you can repeat one or more words that express a main idea. This technique creates a rhythm that focuses attention on the main idea. Here's an example that uses deliberate repetition along with a variety of sentence lengths to deliver its meaning.

Coal is **black** and it warms your house and cooks your food. The night is **black,** which has a moon, and a million stars, and is beautiful. Sleep is **black,** which gives you rest, so you wake up feeling **good.** I am **black.** I feel very **good** this evening.

—Langston Hughes, "That Word *Black*"

At the same time, don't confuse deliberate repetition with a lack of vocabulary variety.

NO An insurance agent can be an excellent adviser when you want to buy a car. An insurance agent has complete records on most cars. An insurance agent knows which car models are prone to have accidents. An insurance agent can tell you which car models are the most expensive to repair if they are in a collision. An insurance agent can tell you which models are most likely to be stolen. [Although only a few synonyms exist for *insurance agent, car,* and *model,* some do and should be used. Also, the sentence structure here lacks variety.]

YES If you are thinking of buying a new car, an insurance agent, who usually has complete records on most cars, can be an excellent adviser. Any professional insurance broker knows which automobile models are prone to have accidents. Did you know that some cars suffer more damage than others in a collision? If you want to know which vehicles crumple more than others and which are least expensive to repair, ask an insurance agent. Similarly, some car models are more likely to be stolen, so find out from the person who specializes in dealing with car insurance claims.

EXERCISE 19-4

Working individually or with a group, apply techniques of variety and emphasis discussed in this chapter to revise the following paragraph. Revisions will vary, of course. Use different kinds of modifiers (19d). You can reduce or increase the number of words and of sentences. Try to include at least one question or exclamation. Also, try to vary the word order at least once.

Huge caves known collectively as the Carlsbad Caverns are hidden beneath the sands of New Mexico. The caverns contain a mysterious underground world. More than 20 miles of caves have been discovered. Miles more are found each year. Some of the caves contain mysterious underground lakes. Others are huge chambers, and their ceilings rise 200 feet. Electric lights illuminate the caves for visitors. The lights create a dramatic effect. The lights reveal unusual rock formations. Spikes of rock hang from the ceiling. Tall, pointy rocks rise from the floor. Delicate sheets of thin rock are hanging like drapery. The slow drip of minerals through the caves' limestone roof formed them all. The caves echo with watery noises and glimmer with reflected light. The desert is above. In the desert, the sun shines, and winds blow, and birds sing, and coyotes howl. Below in the caverns, no daylight penetrates. The air is cold and still. There are no winds or animal sounds. Such sounds do not disturb the silence. It is amazing to see the contrast between the desert and the caves. Not many people would have guessed that these caves beneath the desert originated as a coral reef in an ancient sea.

20 USAGE GLOSSARY

A usage glossary presents the customary manner of using particular words and phrases. "Customary manner," however, is not as firm in practice as the term implies. Usage standards change. If you think a word's usage might differ from what you read here, consult a dictionary published more recently than the current edition of this handbook.

The meaning of *informal* or *colloquial* in the definition of a word or phrase is that it's found in everyday or conversational speech, but should be avoided in academic writing. Another term, *nonstandard*, indicates that the word or phrase, although widely understood in speech, shouldn't be used in standard spoken or written English.

All terms of grammar and writing in this Usage Glossary are defined in the Terms Glossary, which begins directly before the Index.

a, an Use *a* before words that begin with a consonant (**a** *dog*, **a** *grade*, **a** *hole*) or a consonant sound (**a** *one-day sale*, **a** *European*). Use *an* before words or acronyms that begin with a vowel sound or a silent *h* (**an** *owl*; **an** *hour*; **an** *MRI*, because the *M* is sounded *em*). American English uses *a*, not *an*, before words starting with a pronounced *h*: **a** (not *an*) *historical event*.

accept, except The verb *accept* means "agree to; receive." As a preposition, *except* means "leaving out." As a verb, *except* means "exclude, leave out."

- The workers wanted to **accept** [verb] management's offer **except** [preposition] for one detail: They wanted the limit on overtime **excepted** [verb] from the contract.

advice, advise *Advice*, a noun, means "recommendation." *Advise*, a verb, means "recommend; give advice."

- I **advise** [verb] you to follow your car mechanic's **advice** [noun].

affect, effect As a verb, *affect* means "cause a change in; influence." (*Affect* is a noun in psychology.) As a noun, *effect* means "result or conclusion"; as a verb, *effect* means "bring about."

- Loud music **affects** people's hearing for life, so some bands have **effected** changes to lower the volume. Many fans, however, don't care about the harmful **effects** of high-decibel levels.

aggravate, irritate *Aggravate* is used colloquially to mean "irritate." In academic writing, use *aggravate* only to mean "intensify; make worse." Use *irritate* to mean "annoy; make impatient."

- The coach was **irritated** by reduced time for practice, which **aggravated** the team's difficulties with concentration.

ain't *Ain't* is a nonstandard contraction. Use *am not, is not,* or *are not* for standard spoken and written English.

all ready, already *All ready* means "completely prepared." *Already* means "before; by this time."

- The team was **all ready** to play, but the coach was **already** in a bad mood.

all right *All right* is always written as two words, never one (never *alright*).

all together, altogether *All together* means "in a group, in unison." *Altogether* means "entirely, thoroughly."

- The jurors told the judge that it was **altogether** absurd for them to stay **all together** in a single hotel room.

allude, elude *Allude* means "refer to indirectly." *Elude* means "escape notice."

- The detectives **alluded** to budget cuts by saying that "conditions beyond their control allowed the suspect to **elude** us."

allusion, illusion An *allusion* is an indirect reference to something. An *illusion* is a false impression or idea.

- The couple's casual **allusions** to European tourist sites created the **illusion** that they had visited them.

a lot *A lot* is informal for *a great deal* or *a great many.* Avoid using it in academic writing. If you must use it, write it as two words (never *alot*).

a.m., p.m. Use these abbreviations only with numbers, not as substitutes for the words *morning, afternoon,* or *evening.* Some editors consider capital letters wrong for these abbreviations, yet many editors and dictionaries allow both. Whichever you choose, be consistent in each piece of writing.

- We will arrive in the **evening** [not *p.m.*], and we must leave by **8:00 a.m.**

among, amongst, between Use *among* for three or more items. Use *between* for two items. American English prefers *among* to *amongst*.

- My three housemates discussed **among** [not *between* or *amongst*] themselves the choice **between** staying in college and getting full-time jobs.

amoral, immoral *Amoral* means "neither moral [conforming to standards of rightness] nor immoral [the opposite of *moral*]." *Amoral* also means "without any sense of what's moral or immoral." *Immoral* means "morally wrong."

- Although many people consider birth control an **amoral** issue, the Catholic Church considers it **immoral.**

amount, number Use *amount* for uncountable things (wealth, work, corn, happiness). Use *number* for countable items.

- The **amount** of rice to cook depends on the **number** of dinner guests.

an See *a, an.*

and/or This term is appropriate in business and legal writing when either or both of the two items can apply: *Sending messages is quicker by e-mail **and/or** fax.* In the humanities, writers usually express the alternatives in words: *Sending messages is quicker by e-mail, fax, or both.*

anymore Use *anymore* with the meaning "now, any longer" only in negations or questions. In positive statements, instead of *anymore,* use an adverb such as *now.*

- No one knits **anymore.** Summers are so hot **now** [not *anymore*] that we drink huge amounts of water.

anyone, any one *Anyone* is a singular indefinite pronoun meaning "any person at all." *Any one* (two words), an adjective that modifies a pronoun, means "a member of a group."

- **Anyone** could test-drive **any one** of the display vehicles.

anyplace *Anyplace* is informal. Use *any place* or *anywhere* instead.

anyways, anywheres *Anyways* and *anywheres* are nonstandard for *anyway* and *anywhere.*

apt, likely, liable *Apt* and *likely* are used interchangeably. Strictly, *apt* indicates a tendency or inclination. *Likely* indicates a reasonable expectation or greater certainty than *apt. Liable* denotes legal responsibility or implies unpleasant consequences.

- Evander is **apt** to prefer a movie to Shona's party, so I'll **likely** go without him. She's **liable** to be hurt unless one of us shows up.

as, as if, as though, like Use *as, as if,* or *as though,* but not *like,* when the words coming after include a verb.

- This hamburger tastes good, **as** [not *like*] a hamburger should. It tastes **as if** [or *as though,* not *like*] it was barbequed over charcoal, not gas.

In comparisons, both *as* and *like* can function as prepositions. However, use *as* to indicate equivalence between two nouns or pronouns, and use *like* to indicate similarity but not equivalence.

- Joshua acted **as** [not *like*] peacemaker. After all, Russia, **like** [not *as*] China, belongs to the United Nations.

assure, ensure, insure *Assure* means "promise, convince." *Ensure* and *insure* both mean "make certain or secure," but *insure* is reserved for financial or legal matters.

- The insurance agent **assured** me that he could **insure** my car, but only I could **ensure** that I would drive safely.

as to *As to* is nonstandard for *about.*

awful, awfully *Awful* is an adjective meaning "to inspire awe" and "to create fear." *Awfully* is an adverb meaning "in a way to inspire awe" and "terrifying." Only colloquially are *awful* or *awfully* used to mean "very," or "extremely."

- I was **extremely** [not *awfully*] tired yesterday.

a while, awhile As two words, *a while* (an article and a noun) can function as a subject or object. As one word, *awhile* is an adverb. In a prepositional phrase, the correct form is *for a while, in a while,* or *after a while.*

- It took **a while** [article and noun] to drive to the zoo, where we saw the seals bask **awhile** [adverb modifying verb *bask*] in the sun after romping **for a while** [prepositional phrase] in the water.

backup, back up As a noun, *backup* means "a replacement, fill-in, surrogate; a copy of computer files." As an adjective, *backup* means "alternate, alternative." As a verb, *back up* (two words) means "to serve as a substitute or support"; "to accumulate, as from a stoppage"; and "to make a backup copy of a computer disk or hard drive."

- I'll need a **backup** [noun] of your hard drive if I'm going to serve as your **backup** [adjective] computer consultant. I **back up** [verb] all computer disks and drives when I work with them.

bad, badly *Bad* is an adjective only after linking verbs (*look, feel, smell, taste, sound;* these verbs can function as either linking verbs or action verbs depending on the context.) *Badly* is an adverb; it's nonstandard after linking verbs.

■ Farmers feel **bad** [*feel* in a linking verb, so *bad* is the adjective] because a **bad** [adjective] drought has **badly** [adverb] damaged their crops.

been, being *Been* is the past participle of the verb *be. Being* is the present participle of *be.* As main verbs, *being* and *been* must always be used with auxiliary verbs.

■ You *are* **being** [not *being* alone] silly if you think I believe you *have* **been** [not *been* alone] to Sumatra.

being as, being that *Being as* and *being that* are nonstandard for *because* or *since.*

■ We had to forfeit the game **because** [not *being as* or *being that*] our goalie was badly injured.

beside, besides As prepositions, *beside* means "next to, by the side of," and *besides* means "other than, in addition to." As an adverb, *besides* means "also, moreover."

■ She stood **beside** the new car, insisting that she would drive. No one **besides** her had a driver's license. **Besides,** she owned the car.

better, had better *Better* is informal for *had better.*

■ We **had better** [not *better* alone] be careful of the ice.

between See *among, amongst, between.*

bias, biased As a noun, *bias* means "a mental leaning for or against something or someone." As a verb, *bias* means "to be prejudiced." The past tense of this verb is *biased.* As an adjective, *biased* means "prejudiced."

■ Horace's **bias** [noun] against federal-level politicians grew from his disapproval of their **biased** [adjective] attitudes toward certain foreign countries. Beverly was **biased** [verb] against all politicians, no matter their level.

breath, breathe *Breath* is a noun; *breathe* is a verb.

■ Take a deep **breath** [noun] before you start so that you can **breathe** [verb] normally afterward.

bring, take *Bring* indicates movement from a distant place to a near place. *Take* indicates movement from a near to a distant place.

■ If you **bring** over sandwiches, we'll have time to **take** [not *bring*] the dog to the vet.

but, however, yet Use *but, however,* or *yet* alone, not in combination with each other.

- The economy is strong, **but** [not *but yet* or *but however*] unemployment is high.

calculate, figure, reckon These are colloquial terms for *estimate, imagine, expect, think,* and the like.

can, may *Can* signifies ability or capacity. *May* requests or grants permission. In negative expressions, *can* is acceptable for *may.*

- When you **can** [not *may*] get here on time, you **may** [not *can*] be excused early. However, if you are *not* on time, you **cannot** [or *may not*] expect privileges.

can't hardly, can't scarcely These double negatives are nonstandard for *can hardly* and *can scarcely.*

capitol, capital *Capitol* means "a building in which legislators meet." *Capital* means a city (Denver, the *capital* of Colorado), wealth, or "most important" (a *capital* offense).

- If the governor can find enough **capital,** the state legislature will agree to build a new **capitol** for the twenty-first century.

censor, censure The verb *censor* means "delete objectionable material; judge." The verb *censure* means "condemn or reprimand officially."

- The town council **censured** the mayor for trying to **censor** a report.

chairman, chairperson, chair Many writers and speakers prefer the gender-neutral terms *chairperson* and *chair* to *chairman.* In general, *chair* is used more than *chairperson.*

choose, chose *Choose* is the simple form of the verb. *Chose* is the past-tense form of the verb.

- I **chose** a movie last week, so you **choose** one tonight.

cite, site The verb *cite* means "quote by way of example, authority, or proof." The noun *site* means "a particular place or location."

- The private investigator **cited** evidence from the crime **site** and the defendant's Web **site.**

cloth, clothe *Cloth* is a noun meaning "fabric." *Clothe* is a verb meaning "dress with garments or fabric."

- "**Clothe** me in red velvet," proclaimed the king, and the royal tailors ran to gather samples of **cloth** to show him.

complement, compliment   As a noun, *complement* means "something that goes well with or completes." As a noun, *compliment* means "praise, flattery." As a verb, *complement* means "brings to perfection, goes well with; completes." As a verb, *compliment* means "praise, flatter."

- The dean's **compliment** was a perfect **complement** to the thrill of my graduating. My parents felt proud when she **complimented** me publicly, an honor that **complemented** their joy.

conscience, conscious   The noun *conscience* means "a sense of right and wrong." The adjective *conscious* means "being aware or awake."

- Always be **conscious** of what your **conscience** is telling you.

consensus of opinion   This phrase is redundant; use *consensus* only.

- The legislature reached **consensus** on the issue of campaign reform.

continual(ly), continuous(ly)   *Continual* means "occurring repeatedly." *Continuous* means "going on without interruption."

- Larry needed intravenous fluids **continuously** for days, so the nurses **continually** monitored him.

could care less   *Could care less* is nonstandard for *could not care less.*

could of   *Could of* is nonstandard for *could have.*

couple, a couple of   These terms are nonstandard for *a few* or *several.*

- Rest here for **a few** [not *a couple* or *a couple of*] minutes.

criteria, criterion   A *criterion* is "a standard of judgment." *Criteria* is the plural of *criterion.*

- A sense of history is an important **criterion** for judging political candidates, but voters must consider other **criteria** as well.

data   *Data* is the plural of *datum,* a word rarely used today. Informally, *data* is used as a singular noun that takes a singular verb. In academic or professional writing, *data* is considered plural and takes a plural verb (although this usage is currently viewed as overly formal by some).

- The **data** suggest [not *suggests*] some people are addicted to e-mail.

different from, different than   In academic and professional writing, use *different from* even though *different than* is common in informal speech.

- Please advise us if your research yields data **different from** past results.

disinterested, uninterested   The preferred use of *disinterested* means "impartial, unbiased." Colloquially, *disinterested* can mean "not interested, indifferent," but in more formal contexts, *uninterested* is preferred for "not interested, indifferent."

- Jurors must be **disinterested** in hearing evidence, but never **uninterested.**

don't *Don't* is a contraction for *do not,* never for *does not,* (its contraction is *doesn't*).

- She **doesn't** [not *don't*] like crowds.

effect See *affect, effect.*

elude See *allude, elude.*

elicit, illicit The verb *elicit* means "draw forth or bring out." The adjective *illicit* means "illegal."

- The senator's **illicit** conduct **elicited** a mass outcry from her constituents.

emigrate (from), immigrate (to) *Emigrate* means "leave one country to live in another." *Immigrate* means "enter a country to live there."

- My great-grandmother **emigrated** from Kiev, Russia, to London, England, in 1890. Then, she **immigrated** to Toronto, Canada, in 1892.

enclose, inclose; enclosure, inclosure In American English, *enclose* and *enclosure* are the preferred spellings.

ensure See *assure, ensure, insure.*

enthused *Enthused* is nonstandard for *enthusiastic.*

- Adam was **enthusiastic** [not *enthused*] about the college he chose.

etc. *Etc.* is the abbreviation for the Latin *et cetera,* meaning "and the rest." For writing in the humanities, avoid using *etc.* Acceptable substitutes are *and the like, and so on,* or *and so forth.*

everyday, every day The adjective *everyday* means "daily." *Every day* (two words) is an adjective with a noun that can function as a subject or an object.

- Being late for work has become an **everyday** [adjective] occurrence for me. **Every day** [subject] brings me closer to being fired. I worry about it **every day** [object].

everyone, every one *Everyone* is a singular, indefinite pronoun. *Every one* (two words) is an adjective with a pronoun meaning "each member in a group."

- **Everyone** enjoyed **every one** of the comedy skits.

347

everywheres Nonstandard for *everywhere.*

except See *accept, except.*

explicit, implicit *Explicit* means "directly stated or expressed." *Implicit* means "implied, suggested."

- The warning on cigarette packs is **explicit:** "Smoking is dangerous to health." The **implicit** message is, "Don't smoke."

farther, further Although many writers reserve *farther* for geographical distances and *further* for all other cases, current usage treats them as interchangeable.

fewer, less Use *fewer* for anything that can be counted (that is, with count nouns): *fewer* dollars, *fewer* fleas, *fewer* haircuts. Use *less* with collective (or other noncount nouns): *less* money, *less* scratching, *less* hair.

finalize In academic and professional writing, choose *complete* or *make final* instead of *finalize.*

- The two nations **completed** [not *finalized*] a peace treaty.

firstly, secondly, thirdly These are from British English. In American English, use *first, second,* and *third.*

former, latter When two items are referred to, *former* signifies the first item and *latter* signifies the second item. Never use *former* and *latter* when referring to more than two items.

- Brazil and Ecuador are South American countries. Portuguese is the official language in the **former,** Spanish in the **latter.**

go, say All forms of *go* are nonstandard when used in place of all forms of *say.*

- While stepping on my hand, Frank **says** [not *goes*], "Your hand is in my way."

gone, went *Gone* is the past participle of *go; went* is the past tense of *go.*

- They **went** [not *gone*] to the concert after Ira **had gone** [not *had went*] home.

good and *Good and* is a nonstandard intensifier. Instead, use more precise words.

- They were **exhausted** [not *good and tired*].

good, well *Good* is an adjective. As an adverb, *good* is nonstandard. Instead, use *well.*

- **Good** [adjective] maintenance helps cars run **well** [adverb; not *good*].

got, have *Got* is nonstandard for *have.*

- What do we **have** [not *got*] for supper?

hardly Use *hardly* with *can*, never with *can't.*

have, of Use *have*, not *of*, after such verbs as *could, should, would, might*, and *must.*

- You **should** have [not *should of*] called first.

have got, have to, have got to Avoid using *have got* when *have* alone delivers your meaning. Also, avoid using *have to* or *have got to* for *must.*

- I **have** [not *have got*] several more sources to read. I **must** [not *have got to*] finish my reading today.

he/she, s/he, his/her When using gender-neutral language, write out *he or she* or *his or her* instead of using and/or constructions. To be more concise switch to plural pronouns and antecedents. (For more about gender-neutral language, see 21g.)

- **Everyone** bowed **his or her** head. [**Everyone** bowed **his** head is considered sexist language if women were present when the heads were bowed.]
- The **people** bowed **their** heads.

hopefully *Hopefully* is an adverb meaning "with hope, in a hopeful manner," so as an adverb, it can modify a verb, an adjective, or another adverb. However, *hopefully* is nonstandard as a sentence modifier meaning "we hope"; therefore, in academic writing, avoid this usage.

- They waited **hopefully** [adverb] for the crippled airplane to land. **We hope** [not *Hopefully,*] it will land safely.

humanity, humankind, humans, mankind To use gender-neutral language, choose *humanity, humankind,* or *humans* instead of *mankind.*

- Some think that the computer has helped **humanity** more than any other twentieth-century invention.

i.e. This abbreviation refers to the Latin term *id est.* In academic writing, use the English translation, *that is.*

if, whether At the start of a noun clause that expresses speculation or unknown conditions, you can use either *if* or *whether.* However, in such conditional clauses use only *whether* (or *whether or not*) when alternatives are expressed or implied. In a conditional clause that does not express or imply alternatives, use only *if.*

- **If** [not *whether*] you promise not to step on my feet, I might dance with you. Still, I'm not sure **if** [or *whether*] I want to dance with you. Once I decide, I'll dance with you **whether or not** [not *if*] I like the music or **whether** [not *if*] the next song is fast or slow.

illicit   See *elicit, illicit.*

illusion   See *allusion, illusion.*

immigrate   See *emigrate, immigrate.*

immoral   See *amoral, immoral.*

imply, infer   *Imply* means "hint at or suggest." *Infer* means "draw a conclusion." A writer or speaker *implies;* a reader or listener *infers.*
- When the governor **implied** that she wouldn't seek reelection, reporters **inferred** that she was planning to run for vice president.

in regard to, with regard to, as regards, regarding   Use *about, concerning,* and *for* in place of these wordy phrases. Also, avoid the nonstandard *as regards to.*
- **Concerning** [not *in regard to, with regard to, as regards,* or *regarding*] your question, we can now confirm that your payment was received.

incredible, incredulous   *Incredible* means "extraordinary; not believable." *Incredulous* means "unable or unwilling to believe."
- Listeners were **incredulous** as the freed hostages described the **incredible** hardships they had experienced.

inside of, outside of   These phrases are nonstandard when used to mean *inside* or *outside.* When writing about time, never use *inside of* to mean "in less than."
- She waited **outside** [not *outside of*] the apartment house. He changed to clothes that were more informal in **less than** [not *inside of*] ten minutes.

insure   See *assure, ensure, insure.*

irregardless   *Irregardless* is nonstandard for *regardless.*

is when, is where   Never use these constructions when you define something. Instead, use active verbs.
- Defensive driving **involves staying** [not *is when* you *stay*] alert.

its, it's   *Its* is a personal pronoun in the possessive case. *It's* is a contraction of *it is.*
- The dog buried **its** bone today. **It's** hot today, which makes the dog restless.

kind, sort Combine *kind* and *sort* with *this* or *that* when referring to singular nouns, but combine them with *these* or *those* when referring to plural nouns. Also, never use *a* or *an* after *kind of* or *sort of*.

- To stay cool, drink **these kinds** of fluids [not *this kind*] for **this sort of** day [not *this sort of a*].

kind of, sort of These phrases are colloquial adverbs. In academic writing, use *somewhat*.

- The campers were **somewhat** [not *kind of*] dehydrated after the hike.

later, latter Later means "after some time; subsequently." *Latter* refers to the second of two items.

- The college library stays open **later** than the town library; also, the **latter** is closed on weekends.

lay, lie The verb *lay* (**lay,** *laid, laid, laying*) means "place or put something, usually on something else" and needs a direct object. The verb *lie* (**lie,** *lay, lain, lying*), meaning "recline," doesn't need a direct object. Substituting *lay* for *lie*, or the opposite, is nonstandard.

- *Lay* [not *lie*] down the blanket [direct object], and then place the baby to **lie** [not *lay*] in the shade.

leave, let *Leave* means "depart." *Leave* is nonstandard for *let*. *Let* means "allow, permit."

- Could you **let** [not *leave*] me use your car tonight?

less See *fewer, less*.

lie See *lay, lie*.

like See *as, as if, as though, like*.

likely See *apt, likely, liable*.

lots, lots of, a lot of These are colloquial constructions. Instead, use *many, much,* or *a great deal*.

mankind See *humanity, humankind, humans, mankind*.

may See *can, may*.

maybe, may be *Maybe* is an adverb; *may be* (two words) is a verb phrase.

- **Maybe** [adverb] we can win, but our team **may be** [verb phrase] too tired.

may of, might of   *May of* and *might of* are nonstandard for *may have* and *might have.*

media   *Media* is the plural of *medium,* yet colloquial usage pairs it with a singular verb.

- The **media** *offend* [plural verb] me by exploiting helpless people just to get a story.

morale, moral   *Morale* is a noun meaning "a mental state relating to courage, confidence, or enthusiasm." As a noun, *moral* means an "ethical lesson implied or taught by a story or event." As an adjective, *moral* means "ethical."

- One **moral** of the story is that many people who suffer from low **morale** still abide by high **moral** standards.

most   *Most* is nonstandard for *almost.* Also, *most* is the superlative form of an adjective (*some words, more words,* **most** *words*) and of adverbs (*most* suddenly).

- **Almost** [not *Most*] all writers agree that Shakespeare penned the **most** [adjective] brilliant plays ever written.

Ms.   *Ms.* is a woman's title free of reference to marital status, equivalent to *Mr.* for men. Generally, use *Ms.* unless a woman requests *Miss* or *Mrs.*

must of   *Must of* is nonstandard for *must have.*

nowheres   *Nowheres* is nonstandard for *nowhere.*

number   See *amount, number.*

of   Use *have,* not *of,* after modal auxiliary verbs (*could, may, might, must, should, would*). See also, *could of; may of, might of; must of; should of; would of.*

off of   *Off of* is nonstandard for *off.*

- Don't fall **off** [not *off of*] the stage.

OK, O.K., okay   These three forms are informal. In academic writing, choose words that express more specific meanings. If you must use the term, choose the full word *okay.*

- The weather was **suitable** [not *okay*] for a picnic.

on account of, owing to the fact that   Use *because* or *because* of in place of these wordy phrases.

- **Because of the rain** [not *On account of the rain* or *Owing to the fact that it rained*], the picnic was cancelled.

outside of See *inside of, outside of.*

percent, percentage Use *percent* with specific numbers: two *percent*, 95 *percent*. Use *percentage* to refer to portions of a whole in general terms.

■ Of the eligible U.S. population, **35 percent** votes regularly in national elections. In local elections, **the percentage** [not *the percent*] is much lower.

pixel, pixelation, pixilated *Pixel*, a relatively new word created from "picture/pix" and "element," is the name for a small dot on a video screen. The number of *pixels* on a screen determines its clarity (computer screens usually have 640 *pixels* across and 480 *pixels* down, while large-screen televisions often have 800 *pixels* per inch). *Pixelation* (with an *e*, as in *pixel*) is a noun meaning "a film technique that makes people appear to move faster than they are." *Pixilated* (with an *i*), a verb unrelated to *pixels*, derives from *pixie*, meaning "a mischievous elf," and now describes someone who is slightly drunk.

plus *Plus* is nonstandard for *and, also, in addition,* and *moreover.*

■ The band booked three concerts in Hungary, **and** [not *plus*] it will tour Poland for a month. **In addition,** [not *Plus,*] it may perform once in Austria.

precede, proceed *Precede* means "go before." *Proceed* means "to advance, go on, undertake, carry on."

■ **Preceded** by elephants and music, the ringmaster **proceeded** into the main tent.

pretty *Pretty* is informal for *rather, quite, somewhat,* or *very.*

■ The flu epidemic was **quite** [not *pretty*] severe.

principal, principle *Principle* means "a basic truth or rule." As a noun, *principal* means "chief person and main or original amount." As an adjective, *principal* means "most important."

■ During the assembly, the **principal** said, "A **principal** value in our democracy is the **principle** of free speech."

proceed See *precede, proceed.*

quotation, quote *Quotation* is a noun, and *quote* is a verb. Don't use *quote* as a noun.

■ One newspaper reporter **quoted** [verb] the U.S. President, and soon the **quotations** [noun—not *quotes*, which is a verb] were widely broadcast.

raise, rise *Raise* is a verb (***raise,*** *raised, raising*) which means "lift," or "construct" and needs a direct object. *Rise* (***rise,*** *rose, risen, rising*) means "go upward," and doesn't need a direct object. Substituting *rise* for *raise,* or the opposite, is nonstandard.

- When the soldiers **rise** [not *raise*] early, they **raise** [not *rise* or *rise up*] the flag of liberty.

real, really These are nonstandard for *very* and *extremely.*

reason is because This phrase is redundant. To be concise and correct, use *reason is that.*

- One **reason** we moved **is that** [not *is because*] our factory was relocated.

reason why This phrase is redundant. To be concise and correct, use *reason* or *why.*

- I don't know **why** [not *the reason why*] they left home.

regarding See *in regard to, with regard to, as regards, regarding.*

regardless See *irregardless.*

respectful, respectfully As an adjective, *respectful* means "marked by, shows regard for, or gives honor to." *Respectfully* is the adverb form of *respectful.* Be careful not to confuse them with *respective* and *respectively* (see next entry).

- The child listened **respectfully** [adverb] to the lecture about **respectful** [adjective] behavior.

respective, respectively *Respective,* a noun, refers to two or more individual persons or things. *Respectively,* an adverb, refers back to two or more individuals or things in the same sequence that they were originally mentioned. Be careful not to confuse them with *respectful* and *respectfully* (see above entry).

- After the fire drill, Dr. Daniel Eagle and Dr. Jessica Chess returned to their **respective** offices [that is, he returned to his office, and she returned to her office] on the second and third floors, **respectively** [his office is on the second floor, and her office is on the third floor].

right *Right* is colloquial for *quite, very, extremely,* or similar intensifiers.

- You did **very** [not *right*] well on the quiz.

rise See *raise, rise.*

scarcely Use *scarcely* with *can,* never with *can't.*

secondly See *firstly, secondly, thirdly.*

seen *Seen* is the past participle of the verb *see* (*see, saw,* **seen,** *seeing*). *Seen* is nonstandard for *saw,* a verb in the past tense. Always use *seen* with an auxiliary verb.

- Last night, I **saw** [not *seen*] the movie that you ***had* seen** [not *seen*] last week.

set, sit The verb *set* (**set,** *setting*) means "put in place, position, put down" and needs a direct object. The verb *sit* (**sit,** *sat, sitting*) means "be seated" and doesn't need a direct object. Substituting *set* for *sit,* and the opposite, is nonstandard.

- Susan **set** [not *sat*] the sandwiches beside the salad, made Spot **sit** [not *set*] down, and then **sat** [not *set*] on the sofa.

shall, will, should *Shall* was once used with *I* and *we* for future-tense verbs, and *will* was used for all other persons. Today, *shall* is considered highly formal, and *will* is more widely used. Similarly, distinctions were once made between *shall* and *should,* but today *should* is preferred. However, in questions, *should* is used about as often as *shall.*

- We **will** [or *shall*] depart on Monday, but he **will** [never *shall*] wait until Thursday to depart. **Should** [or *Shall*] I telephone ahead to reserve a suite at the hotel?

should of *Should of* is nonstandard for *should have.*

sit See *set, sit.*

site See *cite, site.*

sometime, sometimes, some time The adverb *sometime* means "at an unspecified time." The adverb *sometimes* means "now and then." *Some time* (two words) is an adjective with a noun that means "an amount or span of time."

- **Sometime** [adverb for "at an unspecified time"] next year, I must take my qualifying exams. I **sometimes** [adverb for "now and then"] worry whether I'll find **some time** [adjective with a noun] to study for them.

sort of See *kind of, sort of.*

stationary, stationery *Stationary* means "not moving, unchanging." *Stationery* refers to paper and related writing products.

- Johnson's medical condition became **stationary,** so Zelda took out her **stationery** to write his parents that the medical situation was unchanged.

such *Such* is informal for intensifiers such as *very* and *extremely*. However, *such* is acceptable to mean "of the same or similar kind."

- The play got **very** [not *such*] bad reviews. The playwright was embarrassed by **such** strong criticism.

supposed to, used to The final -*d* is essential in both phrases.

- We were **supposed to** [not *suppose to*] leave early. I **used to** [not *use to*] wake up before the alarm rang.

sure *Sure* is nonstandard for *surely* or *certainly*.

- I was **certainly** [not *sure*] surprised at the results.

sure and, try and Both phrases are nonstandard for *sure to* and *try to*.

- Please **try to** [not *try and*] reach my doctor.

than, then *Than* indicates comparison; *then* relates to time.

- Please put on your gloves, and **then** your hat. It's colder outside **than** you think.

that there, them there, this here, these here These phrases are nonstandard for *that, them, this, these,* respectively.

that, which Use *that* with restrictive (essential) clauses only. You can use *which* with both restrictive and nonrestrictive (nonessential) clauses; however, many people reserve *which* to use only with nonrestrictive clauses.

- The house **that** [or *which*] Jack built is on Beanstalk Street, **which** [not *that*] runs past the reservoir.

their, there, they're *Their* is a possessive pronoun. *There* means "in that place" or is part of an expletive construction. *They're* is a contraction of *they are*.

- **They're** going to **their** accounting class in the building over **there** near the library. Do you know that **there** are twelve sections of Accounting 101?

theirself, theirselves, themself These words are nonstandard for *themselves*.

them Use *them* as an object pronoun only. Do not use *them* in place of the adjectives *these* and *those*.

- Let's buy **those** [not *them*] delicious looking strawberries.

then See *than, then*.

thirdly See *firstly, secondly, thirdly*.

thusly *Thusly* is nonstandard for *thus*.

till, until Both are acceptable, although *until* is preferred for academic writing.

to, too, two *To* is a preposition. *Too* is an adverb meaning "also; more than enough." *Two* is a number.

- When you go **to** Chicago, visit the Art Institute. Try **to** visit Harry Caray's for dinner, **too.** It won't be **too** expensive because **two** people can share a meal.

toward, towards Although both are acceptable, writers of American English generally prefer *toward*.

try and, sure and See *sure and, try and*.

type *Type* is nonstandard when used to mean *type of*.

- I recommend that you use only that **type of** [not *type*] glue on plastic.

unique Never combine *unique* with *more, most*, or other qualifiers.

- Solar heating is **unique** [not *somewhat unique*] in the Northeast. One **unique** [not *very unique*] heating system in a Vermont house uses hydrogen for fuel.

uninterested See *disinterested, uninterested*.

used to See *supposed to, used to*.

utilize *Utilize* is considered an overblown word for *use* in academic writing.

- The team **used** [not *utilized*] all its players to win the game.

wait on *Wait on* is an informal substitute for *wait for*. *Wait on* is appropriate only when people give service to others.

- I had to **wait for** [not *wait on*] half an hour for the hotel desk clerk to **wait on** me.

way, ways When referring to distance, use *way* rather than *ways*.

- He is a long **way** [not *ways*] from home.

well See *good, well*.

where *Where* is nonstandard for *that* used as a subordinating conjunction.

- I read **that** [not *where*] salt raises blood pressure.

where . . . at This phrase is redundant; use only *where*.

- *Where* is your house? [not *Where is your house **at**?*]

whether See *if, whether.*

which See *that, which.*

who, whom Use *who* as a subject or a subject complement; use *whom* as an object see (9i.1).

who's, whose *Who's* is the contraction of *who is. Whose* is a possessive pronoun.

- **Who's** willing to drive? **Whose** truck should we take?

will See *shall, will*

-wise The suffix *-wise* means "in a manner, direction, or position." Never attach *-wise* indiscriminately to create new words. Instead, choose words that already exist; when in doubt, consult a dictionary to see if the *-wise* word you have in mind is acceptable.

would of *Would of* is nonstandard for *would have.*

your, you're *Your* is a possessive. *You're* is the contraction of *you are.*

- **You're** kind to volunteer **your** time at the senior center.

21 THE IMPACT OF WORDS

21a What is American English?

Evolving over centuries into a rich language, **American English** is the variation of English spoken in the United States. It demonstrates that many cultures have created the U.S. "melting pot" society. Food names, for example, reflect that Africans brought the words *okra, gumbo,* and *goober* (peanut); Spanish and Latin American peoples contributed *tortilla, taco, burrito,* and *enchilada.* Greek speakers gave us *pita,* Cantonese speakers *chow,* and Japanese speakers *sushi.*

The meanings of some words change with time. For example, W. Nelson Francis points out in *The English Language* (New York: W. W. Norton, 1965) that the word *nice* "has been used at one time or another in its 700-year history to mean: *foolish, wanton, strange, lazy, coy, modest, fastidious, refined, precise, subtle, slender, critical, attentive, minutely accurate, dainty, appetizing, agreeable.*"

21b What are levels of formality in language?

Levels of formality in DICTION (word choice; 21e) and SENTENCE VARIETY (19a) can be divided into three grades: highly informal (an e-mail or a letter to a friend); highly formal (the language of ceremony, written and often spoken); and medium or semiformal (ACADEMIC WRITING). A medium or semiformal level is expected in college writing, because its TONE is reasonable and evenhanded, its writing style clear and efficient, and its word choice appropriate for an academic audience.

INFORMAL	Stars? Wow! They're, like, made of gas!
MEDIUM OR SEMIFORMAL	Gas clouds slowly transformed into stars.
FORMAL	The condensations of gas spun their slow gravitational pirouettes, slowly transmogrifying gas cloud into star.

—Carl Sagan, "Starfolk: A Fable"

In the informal example, the writer's attitude toward the subject is playful and humorous, so it's appropriate when writing a close friend or in a journal. In the medium or semiformal example, the writer's attitude toward the subject is straightforward, so it's appropriate for most academic and professional situations. In the formal example, the writer's words are appropriate for readers who know about scientific phenomena and understand FIGURATIVE LANGUAGE.

21c What is edited American English?

Edited American English, also known as STANDARD ENGLISH, are the standards of the written language expected of a textbook; these standards apply in magazines such as *U.S. News and World Report* and *National Geographic;* in newspapers such as the *Washington Post* and the *Wall Street Journal;* and in most nonfiction books. With edited American English, you can achieve the medium or semiformal language level required in ACADEMIC WRITING.

Edited American English isn't a special or fancy dialect for elite groups. Rather, it's a form of the language used by educated people to standardize communication in the larger world. Edited American English conforms to widely established rules of grammar, sentence structure, punctuation, and spelling—as covered in this handbook.

Nonstandard English is legitimately spoken by some groups in our society. With its own grammar and usage customs, it communicates clearly to other speakers of nonstandard English. Yet, one thing is certain: Speakers of nonstandard English often benefit when they can switch, either temporarily or permanently, to the medium or semiformal level of language (21b) required in academic writing. This means that speakers of nonstandard English never need to reject their preferred or home language. Indeed, it's the right of all individuals to decide what works for them in various situations in their lives, and the ability to "code switch" gives them options.

Also, advertising language and other writing intended for a large, diverse audience might ignore the conventions of edited American English. Such published, nonstandard departures from edited American English are not appropriate in academic writing.

21d What is figurative language?

Figurative language uses words for more than their literal meanings. Such words aren't merely decorative or pretentious (21h). Figurative language greatly enhances meaning. It makes comparisons and connections that draw on one idea or image to explain another. Box 92 explains the different types of figurative language.

Types of figurative language 92

ANALOGY

A comparison of similar traits between dissimilar things (An analogy can range from one sentence to a paragraph to an entire essay; see 4i.9.)

A cheetah sprinting across the dry plains after its prey, the base runner dashed for home plate.

IRONY

The use of words to suggest the opposite of their usual sense

Told that the car repair would cost $2,000 and take at least two weeks, she said, "Oh, that's just great."

METAPHOR

A comparison between otherwise dissimilar things without using the word *like* or *as* (Avoid the error of a mixed metaphor, explained in the text.)

The rush-hour traffic bled out of all the city's major arteries.

OVERSTATEMENT (HYPERBOLE)

Deliberate exaggeration for emphasis

The poet Andrew Marvell said that praising his love's eyes and forehead could take one hundred years.

PERSONIFICATION

The assignment of a human trait to a nonhuman thing

The book begged to be read.

SIMILE

A direct comparison between otherwise dissimilar things, using the word *like* or *as*

Langston Hughes said that a deferred dream dries up like a raisin in the sun.

UNDERSTATEMENT

Deliberate restraint for emphasis

It gets a little warm when the temperature reaches 105 degrees.

Avoiding mixed metaphors

A **mixed metaphor** blends images that make no sense together. Avoid them.

NO The violence of the hurricane reminded me of driving a truck.

YES The violence of the hurricane reminded me of a train crashing into a huge tractor trailer repeatedly.

EXERCISE 21-1

Working individually or with a group, identify each figure of speech. Also, revise any mixed metaphors. For help, consult 21d.

1. We stand with one foot in the twentieth century while we set sail on the sea of a new era in the twenty-first.
2. Having spent the whole day on the beach, he came home as red as a lobster.
3. If I eat one more bite of that chocolate cake, I'll explode.
4. What I love best about you is that you use all the hot water every time you take a shower.
5. The daisies nodded their heads in the hot sun.
6. Beginning to testify in the courtroom, the defendant was as nervous as a long-tailed cat in a roomful of rocking chairs.
7. Think of the environment as a human body, where small problems in one part do not much affect other parts, any more than a paper cut causes most of us more than an instant's pain and a heartfelt "Ouch!" Problems throughout a system like the air or the oceans, however—say, pollution building up beyond the system's ability to cleanse itself—can kill the entire organism just as surely as cholesterol building up in arteries can kill you or me.
8. The actor displayed the entire range of human emotions from A to B.
9. My heart stopped when I opened the gift my parents gave me.
10. Our supervisor said that reorganizing the department according to our recommendations would be trading a headache for an upset stomach.

21e Why should I use exact diction in my writing?

Diction, the term for choice of words, affects the clarity and impact of any writing you do. Your best chance of delivering the message you intend to your readers is to choose words that fit exactly with each piece of writing. Wrong word choice is an error that students tend to make before they become more experienced with writing and speaking in college. To choose words correctly—that is to have good diction—you need to understand the concepts of *denotation* and *connotation* in words. Connotations are never completely fixed, for they can vary with different contexts.

21e.1 What is denotation in words?

The **denotation** of a word is its exact, literal meaning. It's the meaning you find when you look up the word in a dictionary. Readers expect words to be used according to their established meanings for their established functions.

Using dictionaries

A dictionary is your ultimate authority for a word's denotation—that is, its definition. The reference section in most college libraries includes one or more kinds of dictionaries for general use and for specialized areas.

- An **unabridged dictionary** contains the most extensive, complete, and scholarly entries. *Unabridged* means "not shortened." Such dictionaries include all infrequently used words that abridged dictionaries often omit. The most comprehensive, authoritative unabridged dictionary of English is the *Oxford English Dictionary (OED)*, which traces each word's history and gives quotations to illustrate changes in meaning and spelling over the life of the word.

- An **abridged dictionary** contains most commonly used words. *Abridged* means "shortened." When an abridged dictionary serves the needs of most college students, the dictionaries are referred to as "college editions." Typical of these is *Merriam-Webster's Collegiate Dictionary* (at <http://www.m-w.com/netdict.htm> online and and also in print) *The New American Webster Handy College Dictionary.*

- A **specialized dictionary** focuses on a single area of language. You can find dictionaries of slang (for example, *Dictionary of Slang and Unconventional English,* ed. Eric Partridge); word origins (for example, *Dictionary of Word and Phrase Origins,* ed. William Morris and Mary Morris); synonyms (for example, *Roget's 21st Century Thesaurus*); usage (for example, *Modern American Usage: A Guide,* ed. Jacques Barzun); idioms (for example, *A Dictionary of American Idioms,* by Adam Makkai); regionalisms (for example, *Dictionary of American Regional English,* edited by Frederic Cassidy); and many others.

⊕ **ESL NOTE:** The *Dictionary of American English* (Boston: Heinle & Heinle, distributed by Berlitz, 2000) is particularly useful for students who speak English as a second (or third, etc.) language. ⊕

21e.2 What is connotation in words?

Connotation refers to ideas implied by a word. Connotations involve associations and emotional overtones that go beyond a word's definition. For example, *home* usually evokes more emotion than its denotation "a dwelling place" or its synonym *house*. *Home* carries the connotation, for some, of the pleasures of warmth, security, and love of family. For others, however, *home* may carry unpleasant connotations, such as abusive experiences or the impersonality of an institution to house the elderly.

Using a thesaurus

Sometimes a good college dictionary explains the small differences among synonyms, but a thesaurus is devoted entirely to providing synonyms for words. In distinguishing among **synonyms**—the other words close in meaning to a word—a thesaurus demonstrates connotation in operation. As you use a thesaurus, remain very alert to the subtle shades of meanings that create distinctions among words. For instance, using *notorious* to describe a person famous for praiseworthy achievements in public life is wrong. Although *notorious* means "well-known" and "publicly discussed"—which is true of famous people—the connotation of the word is "unfavorably known or talked about." George Washington is famous, not notorious. Al Capone, by contrast, is notorious.

Here's another example with the word *obdurate*, which means "not easily moved to pity or sympathy." Its synonyms include *inflexible, obstinate, stubborn,* and *hardened.*

NO   Footprints showed in the **obdurate** concrete. [*Hardened* would be correct.]

YES   The supervisor remained **obdurate** in refusing to accept excuses.

YES   My **obdurate** roommates won't let my pet boa constrictor live in the bathtub.

COMPUTER TIP: Most word processing programs include a thesaurus. But be cautious in using it. Unless you know the exact meaning of an offered synonym, as well as its part of speech, you may choose a wrong word or introduce a grammatical error into your writing. For example, one word processing program's thesaurus offers these synonyms for *deep* in the sense of "low (down, inside)": *low, below, beneath,* and *subterranean.* None of these words could replace *deep* in sentences such as *The crater is too deep* [not *too low, too below, too beneath,* or *too subterranean*] *to be filled with sand or rocks.*

EXERCISE 21-2

Working individually or with a group, look at each list of words, and divide the words among three headings: "Positive" (good connotations); "Negative" (bad connotations); and "Neutral" (no connotations). If you think that a word belongs under more than one heading, you can assign it more than once, but be ready to explain your thinking. For help, consult a good dictionary and section 21e.2.

EXAMPLE   grand, big, bulky, significant, oversized

> Positive: *grand, significant;* Negative: *bulky, oversized;*
> Neutral: *big*

1. harmony, sound, racket, shriek, melody, music, noise, pitch, voice
2. talkative, articulate, chattering, eloquent, vocal, verbose, gossipy, fluent, gabby
3. decorative, beautiful, modern, ornate, overelaborate, dazzling, flashy, elegant, sparkling
4. long, lingering, enduring, continued, drawn-out, stretched, never-ending, unbreakable, incessant
5. calculating, shrewd, crafty, ingenious, keen, sensible, sly, smooth, underhanded

21f Why should I mix specific, concrete language with general, abstract language?

Specific words identify individual items in a group (*Buick, Honda, Ford*). **General words** relate to an overall group (*car*). **Concrete words** identify what can be perceived by the senses, by being seen, heard, tasted, felt, smelled (*black padded leather dashboard*) and carry specific images and details. **Abstract words** denote qualities (*kind*), concepts (*speed*), relationships (*friends*), acts (*cooking*), conditions (*bad weather*), and ideas (*transportation*) and are more general.

Usually, specific and concrete words bring life to general and abstract words. Therefore, whenever you use general and abstract words, try to supply enough specific, concrete details and examples to illustrate them. Here are sentences with general words that come to life when revised with specific words.

GENERAL	His car gets good gas mileage.
SPECIFIC	His Slurpo gets about 35 mpg on the highway and 30 mpg in the city.
GENERAL	Her car is comfortable and easy to drive.
SPECIFIC	When she drives her new Cushia on a five-hour trip, she arrives refreshed, and does not need a long nap to recover, as she did when she drove her ten-year-old Upushme.

What separates most good writing from bad is the writer's ability to move back and forth between the general and abstract and the specific and concrete. Consider these sentences that effectively use a combination of general and specific words to compare cars:

GENERAL   SPECIFIC   SPECIFIC CONCRETE   SPECIFIC
My car, a 220-horsepower Trans Am, accelerates from 0 to 50 miles per

        SPECIFIC   SPECIFIC
hour in 6 seconds but gets only 18 miles per gallon. In contrast, the

        SPECIFIC   ABSTRACT   GENERAL   SPECIFIC
Dodge Lancer gets very good gas mileage, about 35 mpg in

        GENERAL   SPECIFIC   CONCRETE ABSTRACT
highway driving and 30 mpg in stop-and-go traffic.

EXERCISE 21-3

Revise this paragraph by providing specific and concrete words and
phrases to explain and enliven the ideas presented here in general and
abstract language. You may revise the sentences to accommodate your
changes in language. For help, consult 21f.

> The house for rent was exactly what I wanted. It had trees on the
> lawn and a driveway for my car. It had a porch, and flowers grew near
> the doorway. I was thrilled that the rent was even less money than I
> had hoped to spend. The real estate broker said I could move in that
> very day. I called a friend, who owned a truck, and asked him to help
> me move in. We got started that afternoon and almost finished
> unpacking all the boxes by that evening.

21g   What is gender-neutral language?

Gender-neutral language is the opposite of *sexist language;* it does
not assign men and women certain roles or positions in society. Gender-
neutral language represents men and women fairly (for example, in replacing *policeman* with *police officer* or *doctors' wives* with *doctors' spouses*).

Sexist language assigns roles or characteristics to people based on
their sex and gender. Most women and men today feel that sexist language
unfairly discriminates against both sexes. It inaccurately assumes that
every nurse and homemaker is female (and therefore referred to as "she"),
and that every physician and stockbroker is male (and therefore referred
to as "he"). Indeed, one widespread instance of sexist language occurs
when the pronoun *he* is used to refer to someone whose sex is unknown or
irrelevant. Although tradition holds that *he* is correct in such situations,
many men and women find it offensive. Using only masculine pronouns to
represent all humans excludes women and thereby distorts reality.

Gender-neutral language rejects demeaning STEREOTYPES or outdated assumptions, such as "women are bad drivers," "men can't cook," and
"all children have two parents." Don't describe women's looks, clothes,
or age unless you do the same for men. Don't use a title for one spouse
and the first name for the other spouse: *Phil Miller* [not *Mr. Miller*] and

his wife, Jeannette, travel on separate planes; or *Jeannette and Phil Miller* live in Idaho. Box 93 gives you guidelines for using gender-neutral language.

◉ How to avoid sexist language   93

- Avoid using only the masculine pronoun to refer to males and females together. The *he or she* and *his or hers* constructions act as SINGULAR PRONOUNS, and they therefore call for SINGULAR VERBS. Try to avoid using *he or she* constructions, especially more than once in a sentence or in consecutive sentences. A better solution is revising to the plural. You can also revise to omit the gender-specific pronoun.

  NO   A **doctor** has little time to read outside **his** specialty.

  YES   A **doctor** has little time to read outside **his or her** specialty.

  NO   A successful **stockbroker** knows **he** has to work long hours.

  YES   Successful **stockbrokers** know **they** have to work long hours.

  NO   **Everyone** hopes that **he or she** will win the scholarship.

  YES   **Everyone** hopes to win the scholarship.

- Avoid using *man* when both men and women are intended.

  NO   **Man** is a social animal.

  YES   **People** are social animals.

  NO   The history of **mankind** is predominately violent.

  YES   **Human** history is predominately violent.

  NO   Dogs are **men's** best friends.

  YES   Dogs are **people's** best friends.

- Avoid stereotyping jobs and roles by gender when both men and women are included.

NO	YES
chairman	chair, chairperson
policeman	police officer
businessman	businessperson, business executive
statesman	statesperson, diplomat
teacher . . . she	teachers . . . they
principal . . . he	principals . . . they

→

How to avoid sexist language *(continued)* 93

- Avoid expressions that seem to exclude one sex.

NO	YES
mankind	humanity
the common man	the average person
man-sized sandwich	huge sandwich
old wives' tale	superstition

- Avoid using demeaning and patronizing labels.

NO	YES
male nurse	nurse
gal Friday	assistant
coed	student
My girl can help.	My secretary can help (or better still, Ida Morea can help).

EXERCISE 21-4

Working individually or with a group, revise these sentences by changing sexist language to gender-neutral language. For help, consult 21g.

1. Many of man's most important inventions are found not in scientific laboratories but in the home.
2. Among these inventions are the many home appliances that were designed in the early 1900s to simplify women's housework.
3. Every housewife should be grateful to the inventors of labor-saving appliances such as vacuum cleaners, washing machines, and water heaters.
4. Before such appliances became available, a family was fortunate if the husband could afford to hire a cleaning lady or a maid to help with the housework.
5. Otherwise, each family member had tasks to do that could include washing his clothes by hand or carrying hot water for bathing up or down the stairs.
6. Once family members were freed from these difficult duties early in the twentieth century, women had more time to spend with their children.
7. Also, now everyone in the household had more time for his favorite pastimes and hobbies.
8. None of the inventors of modern home appliances could have guessed what far-reaching effects his inventions would have on our society.

9. Every worker, from laborer to businessman, could return each day to a house where there was not nearly as much heavy housework waiting to be done.

10. Even more important, with less housework to do, women could now leave the home to take jobs as office girls and sometimes even lady doctors and lawyers.

21h What other types of language should I avoid in academic writing?

Language that distorts or tries to manipulate a reader needs to be avoided in ACADEMIC WRITING. These and other types of language to avoid in an academic LEVEL OF FORMALITY are listed, with examples, in Box 94.

◎ Language to avoid in academic writing 94

■ Don't use **slanted language,** also called *loaded language;* readers feel manipulated by the overly emotional TONE and DICTION.

NO Our senator is a deceitful, crooked thug.

YES Our senator lies to the public and demands bribes.

NO Why do labs employ Frankensteins to maim helpless kittens and puppies?

YES Why do labs employ uncaring technicians that harm kittens and puppies?

■ Don't use **pretentious language;** readers realize you're showing off.

NO As I alighted from my vehicle, my clothing became besmirched with filth.

YES My coat got muddy as I got out of my car.

NO He has a penchant for ostentatiously flaunting recently acquired haberdashery accoutrements.

YES He tends to show off his new clothes shamelessly.

■ Don't use **sarcastic language;** readers realize you're being nasty.

NO He was a regular Albert Einstein with my questions. [This is sarcastic if you mean the opposite.]

YES He had trouble understanding many of my questions.

→

Language to avoid in academic writing *(continued)*   **94**

■ Don't use **colloquial language;** readers sense you're being overly casual and conversational.

  NO   Christina flunked chemistry.

  YES   Christina failed chemistry.

■ Don't use **euphemisms,** also called *doublespeak;* your readers realize you're hiding the truth (more in 21l).

  NO   Our company will **downsize** to meet efficiency standards.

  YES   Our company has to cut jobs to maintain our profits.

  NO   We consider our hostages as **foreign guests** being guarded by **hosts.**

  YES   We consider our hostages as enemies to be guarded closely.

■ Don't use SEXIST LANGUAGE or STEREOTYPES (more in 21g and 5j).

■ Don't use **regional language** (more in 21i and 5j).

■ Don't use CLICHÉS (more in 21j).

■ Don't use unnecessary JARGON (more in 21k).

■ Don't use NONSTANDARD LANGUAGE (more in 21c).

■ Don't use **bureaucratic language** (more in 21m).

21i What is regional language?

Regional language, also called *dialectal language,* is specific to certain geographical areas. For example, a *dragonfly* is a *snake feeder* in parts of Delaware, a *darning needle* in parts of Michigan, and a *snake doctor* or an *ear sewer* in parts of the southern United States. Using a dialect in writing for the general reading public tends to shut some people out of the communication. Except when dialect is the topic of the writing, ACADEMIC WRITING rarely accommodates dialect well. Avoid it in academic assignments.

21j What are clichés?

A **cliché** is a worn-out expression that has lost its capacity to communicate effectively because of overuse. Many clichés are SIMILES or METAPHORS, once clever but now flat. For example, these are clichés: *dead as a doornail, gentle as a lamb,* and *straight as an arrow.*

If you've heard certain expressions repeatedly, so has your reader. Instead of a cliché, use descriptive language that isn't worn out. If you can't think of a way to rephrase a cliché, drop the words entirely.

Interestingly, however, English is full of frequently used word groups that aren't clichés: for example, *up and down* and *from place to place.* These common word groups aren't considered clichés, so you can use them freely. If you're not sure of how to tell the difference between a cliché and a common word group, remember that a cliché often—but not always—contains an image (*busy as a bee* and *strong as an ox*).

EXERCISE 21-5

Working individually or with a group, revise these clichés. Use the idea in each cliché for a sentence of your own in plain English. For help, consult 21j.

1. The bottom line is that Carl either raises his grade point average or finds himself in hot water.
2. Carl's grandfather says, "When the going gets tough, the tough get going."
3. Carl may not be the most brilliant engineering major who ever came down the pike, but he has plenty of get-up-and-go.
4. When they were handing out persistence, Carl was first in line.
5. The $64,000 question is, Will Carl make it safe and sound, or will the college drop him like a hot potato?

21k When is jargon unnecessary?

Jargon is the specialized vocabulary of a particular group. Jargon uses words that people outside that group might not understand. Specialized language exists in every field: professions, academic disciplines, business, various industries, government departments, hobbies, and so on.

Reserve jargon for a specialist AUDIENCE (1d.3). As you write, keep your audience in mind as you decide whether a word is jargon in the context of your material. For example, a football fan easily understands a sportswriter's use of words such as *punt* and *safety,* but they are jargon words to people unfamiliar with American-style football. Avoid using jargon unnecessarily. When you must use jargon for a nonspecialist audience, be sure to explain any special meanings.

This example shows specialized language used appropriately; it's taken from a college textbook. The authors can assume that students know the meaning of *eutrophicates, terrestrial,* and *eutrophic.*

As the lake eutrophicates, it gradually fills until the entire lake will be converted into a terrestrial community. Eutrophic changes (or eutrophication) are the nutritional enrichment of the water, promoting the growth of aquatic plants.

—Davis and Solomon, *The World of Biology*

21l What are euphemisms?

Euphemisms attempt to avoid the harsh reality of truth by using more pleasant, "tactful" words. Good manners dictate that euphemisms sometimes be used in social situations: For example, in U.S. culture, *passed away* is in some situations thought to be gentler than *died*. Many such uses of euphemisms are acceptable.

In other situations, however, euphemisms drain meaning from truthful writing. Unnecessary euphemisms might describe socially unacceptable behavior (for example, *Johnny has a wonderfully vivid imagination* instead of *Johnny lies*). They also might try to hide unpleasant facts (for example, *She is between assignments* instead of *She's lost her job*). Avoid unnecessary euphemisms.

21m What is bureaucratic language?

Bureaucratic language uses words that are stuffy and overblown. Bureaucratic language (or *bureaucratese,* a word created to describe the style) is marked by unnecessary complexity. This kind of language can take on a formality that complicates the message and makes readers feel left out.

NO   In reference to the above captioned, you can include a page that additionally contains an Include instruction under the herein stated circumstances. The page including the Include instruction is included when you paginate the document, but the included text referred to in its Include instruction is not included. [This message is meaningless, but the writer seems to understand the message. Anyone who doesn't is clearly uninformed or unable to read intelligently.]

—From instructions for compiling a user's manual

(By the way, in response to earlier editions of this handbook, I've been asked to give a YES alternative for this example. I regret that I can't understand enough of the NO example to do that. If you, gentle reader, can help, please use my contact information in the Preface.)

EXERCISE 21-6

Working individually or with a group, revise these examples of pretentious language, jargon, euphemism, and bureaucratic language. For help, consult 21h and 21k through 21m.

What Is Bureaucratic Language?

1. In-house employee interaction of a nonbusiness nature is disallowed.
2. Shortly after Mrs. Harriman went to her reward, Mr. Harriman moved to Florida to be near his son and daughter-in-law and their bundle of joy.
3. Your dearest, closest acquaintance, it has been circulated through rumor, is entering into matrimony with her current beloved.
4. My male sibling concocted a tale that was entirely fallacious.
5. An individual's cognitive and affective domains are at the center of his or her personality.
6. When the finalization of this negotiation comes through, it will clarify our position in a positive manner.
7. The refuse has accumulated because the sanitation engineers were on strike last month.
8. Employees who are employed by the company for no less than five years in a full-time capacity fulfill the eligibility requirements for participation in the company's savings program.

22 SPELLING AND HYPHENATION

22a What makes a good speller?

You might be surprised to hear that good spellers don't know how to spell and hyphenate every word they write. What they do know, however, is to check if they're not sure of a word's spelling. If your inner voice questions a spelling, do what good spellers do—consult a dictionary.

What do you do if even the first few letters of a word seem mysterious? This is a common dilemma among writers. My best advice is that you think of an easy-to-spell SYNONYM for the word you need; look up that synonym in a thesaurus; and among the synonyms, find the word you need to spell. Every once in a while, a book for "poor spellers" is published, claiming that by using it writers can look up the wrong spelling to find the correct spelling. Unfortunately, such books rarely succeed because they never have the wrong spelling that matches *yours*.

Many people, surveys show, believe incorrectly that only naturally skilled spellers can write well. The truth is, correct spelling matters a great deal in final drafts, but *not* in earlier drafts. The best time to check spellings you doubt is when you're EDITING. Good writers know that their most important abilities involve having first-rate ideas (Chapters 1–6), a graceful style of writing (Chapters 17–19), precise word choice (Chapters 16, 20, and 21), and correct grammar (Chapters 7–15).

The various origins and ways that English-speaking people around the world pronounce words make it almost impossible to rely solely on pronunciation to spell a word. What you can rely on, however, are the proofreading hints and spelling rules explained in this chapter.

COMPUTER TIP: Word processing software usually includes a spell-check program, which claims to spot spelling errors because the words typed in don't match the spellings in the software's dictionary. Each program operates a little differently, but most allow you to "ask" for a spelling check; some will underline in color when a word you've typed seems incorrectly spelled. Such programs alert you to a wrong spelling or mistyping (called a *typo*), but they have one major drawback. The pro-

374

grams can't detect that you've spelled a wrong word if what you've typed is a legitimate spelling, on its own, of a word. For example, if you mean *top* but have typed *too,* or if you mean *from* and type *form,* no spell-check program "sees" what you've typed in error as a mistake. In these and other similar cases, only the human eye (that is, a reader) can discover the errors. ▣

22b How can I proofread for errors in spelling and hyphen use?

Many spelling and hyphenation errors are the result of illegible hand-writing, slips of the pen, or typographical mistakes. Catching these "typos" requires especially careful proofreading, using the techniques in Box 95.

◉ **Proofreading for errors in spelling**   **95**
and hyphen use

- Slow down your reading speed to allow yourself to concentrate on the individual letters of words rather than on the meaning of the words.
- Stay within your "visual span," the number of letters you can identify with a single glance (for most people, about six letters).
- Put a ruler or large index card under each line as you proofread, to focus your vision and concentration.
- Read each paragraph in reverse, from the last sentence to the first. This method can keep you from being distracted by the meaning of the material.

SPELLING

22c How are plurals spelled?

In American English, plurals take many forms. The most common form adds an *s* or *es* at the end of the word. The list below covers all variations of creating plurals.

- **Adding -s** or **-es:** Plurals of most words are formed by adding an *s,* including words that end in "hard" *-ch* (sounding like *k*): *leg, leg**s**; shoe, shoe**s**; stomach, stomach**s**.* Words ending in *-s, -sh, -x, -z,* or "soft" *-ch* (as in *beach*) are formed by adding *-es* to the singular: *len**s**, lens**es**; tax, tax**es**; bea**ch**, bea**ch**es.*

- **Words ending in -o:** Add -s if the -o is preceded by a vowel: *radio, radios; cameo, cameos.* Add -es if the -o is preceded by a consonant: *potato, potatoes.* With a few words, you can choose the -s or es plural form, but current practice generally supports adding -es: *cargo, cargoes; tornado, tornadoes; zero, zeros* or *zeroes.*

- **Words ending in -f or -fe:** Some final f and fe words are made plural by adding an s: *belief, beliefs.* Others require changing -f or -fe to -ves: *life, lives; leaf, leaves.* Words ending in -ff or -ffe simply add -s: *staff, staffs; giraffe, giraffes.*

- **Compound words:** For most compound words, add an s or es at the end of the last word: *checkbooks, player-coaches.* In a few cases, the first word is made plural: *sister-in-law, sisters-in-law; miles per hour.* (For information about hyphens in compound words, see 22j.)

- **Internal changes and endings other than -s:** A few words change internally or add endings other than an s to become plural: *foot, feet; man, men; crisis, crises; child, children.*

- **Foreign words:** The best advice is to check your dictionary. In general, many Latin words ending in -um form the plural by changing -um to -a: *curriculum, curricula; datum, data; medium, media.* Also, Latin words that end in -us usually form the plural by changing -us to -i: *alumnus, alumni; syllabus, syllabi.* Additionally, Greek words that end in -on usually form the plural by changing -on to -a: *criterion, criteria; phenomenon, phenomena.*

- **One-form words:** Some words have the same form in both the singular and plural: *deer, elk, fish.* You need to use modifiers, as necessary, to indicate which form you mean: *one deer, nine deer.*

EXERCISE 22-1

Write the correct plural form of these words. For help, consult 22c.

1. yourself
2. sheep
3. photo
4. woman
5. appendix
6. millennium
7. lamp
8. runner-up
9. criterion
10. lunch
11. echo
12. syllabus
13. wife
14. get-together
15. crisis

22d How are suffixes spelled?

A **suffix** is an ending added to a word that changes the word's meaning or its grammatical function. For example, adding the suffix -able to the VERB *depend* creates the ADJECTIVE *dependable.*

■ **-y words:** If the letter before a final *y* is a consonant, change the *y* to *i* and add the suffix: *try, tries, tried.* In the case of *trying* and similar words, the following rule applies: Keep the *y* when the suffix begins with *i* (*apply, applying*). If the letter before the final *y* is a vowel, keep the final *y*: *employ, employed, employing.* These rules don't apply to IRREGULAR VERBS (see list, Box 61, Chapter 8, pages 186–189).

■ **-e words:** Drop a final *e* when the suffix begins with a vowel, unless doing this would cause confusion: for example, *be + ing* can't be written *bing,* but *require* does become *requiring; like* does become *liking.* Keep the final *e* when the suffix begins with a consonant: *require, requirement; like, likely.* Exceptions include *argue, argument; judge, judgment; true, truly.*

■ **Words that double a final letter:** If the final letter is a consonant, double it *only* if it passes these three tests: (1) its last two letters are a vowel followed by a consonant; (2) it has one syllable or is accented on the last syllable; (3) the suffix begins with a vowel: *drop, dropped; begin, beginning; forget, forgettable.*

■ **-cede, -ceed, -sede words:** Only one word in the English language ends in *-sede: supersede.* Only three words end in *-ceed: exceed, proceed, succeed.* All other words with endings that sound like "seed" end in *-cede: concede, intercede, precede.*

■ **-ally and -ly words:** The suffixes *-ally* and *-ly* turn words into adverbs. For words ending in *-ic,* add *-ally: logically, statistically.* Otherwise, add *-ly: quickly, sharply.*

■ **-ance, -ence, and -ible, -able:** No consistent rules govern words with these suffixes. The best advice is when in doubt, look the word up.

22e What is the *ie, ei* rule?

The famous three-line, rhymed rule for using *ie* and *ei* is usually true:

I before *e* [bel**ie**ve, f**ie**ld, gr**ie**f],

Except after *c* [c**ei**ling, conc**ei**t],

Or when sounded like "ay"—

As in n**ei**ghbor and w**ei**gh [**ei**ght, v**ei**n].

There are major exceptions (sorry!) to the *ie, ei* rule, listed here. My best advice is that you memorize them.

■ *ie:* consc**ie**nce, financ**ie**r, sc**ie**nce, spec**ie**s

■ *ei:* **ei**ther, n**ei**ther, l**ei**sure, s**ei**ze, counterf**ei**t, for**ei**gn, forf**ei**t, sl**ei**gh, sl**ei**ght (as in *sleight of hand*), w**ei**rd

EXERCISE 22-2

Follow the directions for each group of words. For help, consult 22d and 22e.

1. Add -*able* or -*ible:* (a) profit; (b) reproduce; (c) control; (d) coerce; (e) recognize.
2. Add -*ance* or -*ence:* (a) luxuri_____; (b) prud_____; (c) devi_____; (d) resist_____; (e) independ_____.
3. Drop the final *e* as needed: (a) true + ly; (b) joke + ing; (c) fortunate + ly; (d) appease + ing; (e) appease + ment.
4. Change the final *y* to *i,* as needed: (a) happy + ness; (b) pry + ed; (c) pry + ing; (d) dry+ ly; (e) beautify + ing.
5. Double the final consonant, as needed: (a) commit + ed; (b) commit + ment; (c) drop + ed; (d) occur + ed; (e) regret + ful.
6. Insert *ie* or *ei* correctly: (a) rel_____f; (b) ach_____ve; (c) w_____rd; (d) n_____ce; (e) dec_____ve.

22f How are homonyms and other frequently confused words spelled?

Homonyms are words that sound exactly like other words: *to, too, two; no, know.* The different spellings of homonyms tend to confuse many writers. The same holds for words that sound almost alike (*accept, except; conscience, conscious*).

Another reason for spelling problems is so-called swallowed pronunciation, which means one or more letters at the end of a word aren't pronounced clearly. For example, the -*d* ending in *used to* or *prejudiced* or the -*ten* ending in *written* are often swallowed rather than pronounced. When writers spell as they mispronounce, spelling errors result.

For more information about word usage that affects spelling, see Chapter 20, which contains an extensive Usage Glossary. For example, some misspellings arise when two words are incorrectly combined into one—as in *all right* (not *alright*); *a while* (not *awhile*). Box 96 lists homonyms and other words that can be confused and lead to misspellings.

Homonyms and other frequently confused words   96

■ ACCEPT	to receive
EXCEPT	with the exclusion of
■ ADVICE	recommendation
ADVISE	to recommend

→

Homonyms and other frequently confused words *(continued)*   96

■ **AFFECT**   to influence [verb]; emotion [noun]
   EFFECT   result [noun]; to bring about or cause [verb]

■ **AISLE**   space between rows
   ISLE   island

■ **ALLUDE**   to make indirect reference to
   ELUDE   to avoid

■ **ALLUSION**   indirect reference
   ILLUSION   false idea, misleading appearance

■ **ALREADY**   by this time
   ALL READY   fully prepared

■ **ALTAR**   sacred platform or place
   ALTER   to change

■ **ALTOGETHER**   thoroughly
   ALL TOGETHER   everyone or everything in one place

■ **ARE**   PLURAL form of *to be*
   HOUR   sixty minutes
   OUR   plural form of *my*

■ **ASCENT**   the act of rising or climbing
   ASSENT   consent [noun]; to consent [verb]

■ **ASSISTANCE**   help
   ASSISTANTS   helpers

■ **BARE**   nude, unadorned
   BEAR   to carry; an animal

■ **BOARD**   piece of wood
   BORED   uninterested

■ **BRAKE**   device for stopping
   BREAK   to destroy, make into pieces

■ **BREATH**   air taken in
   BREATHE   to take in air

■ **BUY**   to purchase
   BY   next to, through the agency of

■ **CAPITAL**   major city; money
   CAPITOL   government building

■ **CHOOSE**   to pick
   CHOSE   PAST TENSE of *choose*

■ **CITE**   to point out
   SIGHT   vision
   SITE   a place

→

Homonyms and other frequently confused words *(continued)* 96

■	CLOTHES	garments
	CLOTHS	pieces of fabric
■	COARSE	rough
	COURSE	path; series of lectures
■	COMPLEMENT	something that completes
	COMPLIMENT	praise, flattery
■	CONSCIENCE	sense of morality
	CONSCIOUS	awake, aware
■	COUNCIL	governing body
	COUNSEL	advice [noun]; to advise [verb]
■	DAIRY	place associated with milk production
	DIARY	personal journal
■	DESCENT	downward movement
	DISSENT	disagreement
■	DESERT	to abandon [verb]; dry, usually sandy area [noun]
	DESSERT	final, sweet course in a meal
■	DEVICE	a plan; an implement
	DEVISE	to create
■	DIE	to lose life (dying) [verb]; one of a pair of dice [noun]
	DYE	to change the color of something (dyeing)
■	DOMINANT	commanding, controlling
	DOMINATE	to control
■	ELICIT	to draw out
	ILLICIT	illegal
■	EMINENT	prominent
	IMMANENT	living within; inherent
	IMMINENT	about to happen
■	ENVELOP	to surround
	ENVELOPE	container for a letter or other papers
■	FAIR	light-skinned; just, honest
	FARE	money for transportation; food
■	FORMALLY	conventionally, with ceremony
	FORMERLY	previously
■	FORTH	forward
	FOURTH	number four in a series
■	GORILLA	animal in ape family
	GUERRILLA	soldier conducting surprise attacks

→

Homonyms and other frequently confused words *(continued)*

■	HEAR	to sense sound by ear
	HERE	in this place
■	HOLE	opening
	WHOLE	complete; an entire thing
■	HUMAN	relating to the species *Homo sapiens*
	HUMANE	compassionate
■	INSURE	buy or give insurance
	ENSURE	guarantee, protect
■	ITS	POSSESSIVE form of *it*
	IT'S	CONTRACTION for *it is*
■	KNOW	to comprehend
	NO	negative
■	LATER	after a time
	LATTER	second one of two things
■	LEAD	heavy metal substance [noun]; to guide [verb]
	LED	past tense of *lead*
■	LIGHTNING	storm-related electricity
	LIGHTENING	making lighter
■	LOOSE	unbound, not tightly fastened
	LOSE	to misplace
■	MAYBE	perhaps [adverb]
	MAY BE	might be [verb]
■	MEAT	animal flesh
	MEET	to encounter
■	MINER	a person who works in a mine
	MINOR	underage
■	MORAL	distinguishing right from wrong; the lesson of a fable, story, or event
	MORALE	attitude or outlook, usually of a group
■	OF	PREPOSITION indicating origin
	OFF	away from; not on
■	PASSED	past tense of *pass*
	PAST	at a previous time
■	PATIENCE	forbearance
	PATIENTS	people under medical care
■	PEACE	absence of fighting
	PIECE	part of a whole; musical arrangement

→

Homonyms and other frequently confused words *(continued)* 96

- **PERSONAL**   intimate
  PERSONNEL   employees
- **PLAIN**   simple, unadorned
  PLANE   to shave wood; aircraft
- **PRECEDE**   to come before
  PROCEED   to continue
- **PRESENCE**   being at hand; attendance at a place or in something
  PRESENTS   gifts
- **PRINCIPAL**   foremost [ADJECTIVE]; school head [noun]
  PRINCIPLE   moral conviction, basic truth
- **QUIET**   silent, calm
  QUITE   very
- **RAIN**   water that falls to earth [noun]; to fall like rain [verb]
  REIGN   to rule
  REIN   strap to guide or control an animal [noun]; to guide or control [verb]
- **RAISE**   to lift up
  RAZE   to tear down
- **RESPECTFULLY**   with respect
  RESPECTIVELY   in that order
- **RIGHT**   correct; opposite of *left*
  RITE   ritual
  WRITE   to put words on paper
- **ROAD**   path
  RODE   past tense of *ride*
- **SCENE**   place of an action; segment of a play
  SEEN   viewed
- **SENSE**   perception, understanding
  SINCE   measurement of past time; because
- **STATIONARY**   standing still
  STATIONERY   writing paper
- **THAN**   in comparison with; besides
  THEN   at that time; next; therefore
- **THEIR**   possessive form of *they*
  THERE   in that place
  THEY'RE   contraction of *they are*

→

Homonyms and other frequently confused words *(continued)* 96

■	THROUGH	finished; into and out of
	THREW	past tense of *throw*
	THOROUGH	complete
■	TO	toward
	TOO	also; indicates degree (*too much*)
	TWO	number following *one*
■	WAIST	midsection of the body
	WASTE	discarded material [noun]; to squander, to fail to use up [verb]
■	WEAK	not strong
	WEEK	seven days
■	WEATHER	climatic condition
	WHETHER	if, when alternatives are expressed or implied
■	WHERE	in which place
	WERE	past tense of *be*
■	WHICH	one of a group
	WITCH	female sorcerer
■	WHOSE	possessive form of *who*
	WHO'S	contraction of *who is*
■	YOUR	possessive form of *you*
	YOU'RE	contraction for *you are*
	YORE	long past

EXERCISE 22-3

Circle the correct homonym or commonly confused word of each group in parentheses.

Imagine that you (are, our) standing in the middle of a busy sidewalk, with a worried look on (your, you're, yore) face. In your hand (your, you're, yore) holding a map, (which, witch) you are puzzling over. If that happened in (real, reel) life, (its, it's) almost certain that within (to, too, two) or three minutes a passerby would ask if you (where, were) lost and would offer you (assistance, assistants). That helpful passerby, (buy, by) taking a (personal, personnel) interest in your problem, is displaying a quality known as empathy—the ability (to, too, two) put yourself in another person's place. Some researchers claim that empathy is an instinct that (human, humane) beings share with many other animals. Other scientists wonder (weather, whether) empathy is instead a (conscience, conscious) (moral, morale) choice that people make. Whatever explanation for the origin (of, off) empathy is (right, rite, write), such empathy generally has a positive (affect, effect)—especially if (your, you're, yore) a person who (maybe, may be) (to, too, two) lost to (know, no) (where, were) (to, too, two) turn.

HYPHENS

22g What is the role of the hyphen?

A **hyphen** serves to divide words at the end of a line, to combine words into compounds, to communicate numbers, and to help writers deliver their messages with spelling that's as clear as possible.

22h When do I use a hyphen at the end of a line?

Generally, try not to divide a word with a hyphen at the end of a line. It makes reading easier. (In printed books, hyphens are acceptable because of the strict limits on line length.) If you must divide a word, try hard not to divide the last word on the first line of a paper, the last word in a paragraph, or the last word on a page.

When you cannot help using hyphens at the end of a line, break the word only between syllables. If you aren't sure about the syllables in a word, consult a dictionary. Box 97 lists guidelines for end-of-line word breaks.

⊙ **Guidelines for hyphens in end-of-line**   **97**
    word breaks

■ Divide words only between syllables.

    NO   ent-ertain   proc-eed

    YES   enter-tain   pro-ceed

■ Never divide words that are short, of one syllable, or pronounced as one syllable.

    NO   we-alth   en-vy   scream-ed

    YES   wealth   envy   screamed

→

Guidelines for hyphens in end-of-line   **97**
word breaks *(continued)*

■ Never divide a word when only one or two letters would be left
or carried over.

    NO   a-live   touch-y   he-licopter   helicopt-er

    YES   alive   touchy   heli-copter   helicop-ter

■ Divide between two consonants according to pronunciation.

    NO   ful-lness   omitt-ing   asp-halt

    YES   full-ness   omit-ting   as-phalt

22i   How do I use a hyphen with prefixes and suffixes?

    Prefixes are syllables in front of a **root**—a word's core, which carries
the origin or meaning. Prefixes modify meanings. **Suffixes** also have
modifying power, but they follow roots; see 22d. Some prefixes and suffixes are attached to root words with hyphens, but others are not. Box 98
shows you how to decide.

◉   **Guidelines for hyphens with prefixes**   **98**
     and suffixes

■ Use hyphens after the prefixes *all-*, *ex-*, *quasi-*, and *self-*.

    YES   all-inclusive   self-reliant

■ Never use a hyphen when *self* is a root word, not a prefix.

    NO   self-ishness   self-less

    YES   selfishness   selfless

■ Use a hyphen to avoid a distracting string of letters.

    NO   antiintellectual   belllike   prooutsourcing

    YES   anti-intellectual   bell-like   pro-outsourcing

                                                   →

Guidelines for hyphens with prefixes   **98**
and suffixes *(continued)*

■ Use a hyphen to add a prefix or suffix to a numeral or a word that starts with a capital letter.

  NO   post1950s   proAmerican   Rembrandtlike
  YES   post-1950   pro-American   Rembrandt-like

■ Use a hyphen before the suffix *-elect*.

  NO   presidentelect
  YES   president-elect

■ Use a hyphen to prevent confusion in meaning or pronunciation.

  YES   re-dress (means *dress again*)   redress (means *set right*)
  YES   un-ionize (means *remove the ions*)   unionize (means *form a union*)

■ Use a hyphen when two or more prefixes apply to one root word.

  YES   pre- and post-war eras   two-, three-, or four-year program

---

22j How do I use hyphens with compound words?

A **compound word** puts two or more words together to express one concept. Compound words come in three forms: an *open-compound word,* as in *night shift,* hyphenated words, as in *tractor-trailer,* and a *closed-compound word,* as in *handbook.* Box 99 lists basic guidelines for positioning hyphens in compound words.

◉ **Guidelines for hyphens with compound**   **99**
words

■ Divide a compound word already containing a hyphen only after that hyphen, if possible. Also, divide a closed-compound word only between the two complete words, if possible.

  NO   self-con-scious   sis-ter-in-law   mas-terpiece
  YES   self-conscious   sister-in-law   master-piece

→

Guidelines for hyphens with compound words *(continued)*   99

- Use a hyphen between a prefix and an open-compound word.

  NO   antigun control [*gun control* is an open-compound word]

  YES   anti-gun control

- Use a hyphen for most compound words that precede a noun. Don't use a hyphen for most compound words that follow a noun.

  YES   well-researched report   report is well researched

  YES   two-inch clearance   clearance of two inches

- Never use a hyphen when a compound modifier starts with an *-ly* adverb.

  NO   happily-married couple   loosely-tied package

  YES   happily married couple   loosely tied package

- Never use a hyphen with COMPARATIVE (*-er, more, less*) and SUPERLATIVE (*-est, most, least*) compound forms.

  NO   better-fitting shoes [*better* is a comparative adjective]

  YES   better fitting shoes

  NO   least-significant factors [*least* is a superlative adverb]

  YES   least significant factors

- Never use a hyphen when a compound modifier is a foreign phrase.

  YES   *post hoc* fallacies

- Never use a hyphen with a possessive compound.

  NO   a full-week's work   eight-hours' pay

  YES   a full week's work   eight hours' pay

22k How do I use hyphens with spelled-out numbers?

A **spelled-out number** uses words, not numerals. Box 100 gives you guidelines. (For information about when to spell out a number and when to write it in numerals, see 30o.)

⊙ **Guidelines for hyphens with spelled-out numbers**   **100**

- Use a hyphen between two-word numbers from twenty-one through ninety-nine. Don't use a hyphen with numbers over one hundred.

  YES   thirty-five   two hundred thirty-five

- Use a hyphen in a compound-word modifier formed from a number and a word, whether or not the number is in words or numerals.

  YES   fifty-minute class [*also* 50-minute class]

  YES   three-to-one odds [*also* 3-to-1 odds]

- Use a hyphen between the numerator and the denominator of two-word fractions.

  YES   one-half   two-fifths   seven-tenths

- Use a hyphen between compound nouns joining two units of measure.

  YES   light-years   kilowatt-hours

👁 **ALERT:** Use numerals rather than words for a fraction that has to be written in more than two words. If your context limits you from using numerals, use hyphens only between the words of the numerator and only between the words of the denominator—but never between the numerator and the denominator: two one-hundredths (*2/100*), thirty-three ten-thousandths (*33/10,000*). ●

EXERCISE 22-4

Provide the correct form of the words in parentheses, according to the rules in sections 22g through 22k. Explain your reasoning for each.

1. The tiger is (all powerful) _____ in the cat family.
2. (Comparison and contrast) _____ studies of tigers and lions show that the tiger is the (more agile) _____ and powerful.
3. The tiger's body is a (boldly striped) _____ yellow, with a white (under body) _____ .
4. The tiger's maximum length is about (eleven feet) _____, about (one quarter) _____ of which is accounted for by its tail, and its maximum weight is up to (five hundred) _____ pounds.

5. The Bengal tiger, the largest of the family, is aggressive and (self confident) _____.

6. In India, where the Bengal tiger is called a (village destroyer) _____, it goes (in to) _____ villages to hunt for food.

7. Entire villages have been temporarily abandoned by (terror stricken) _____ people who have seen a Bengal tiger nearby.

8. Villagers seek to protect their homes by destroying tigers with traps, (spring loaded) _____ guns, and (poisoned arrows) _____.

9. Bengal tigers are also called (cattle killers) _____, although they attack domestic animals only when they cannot find wild ones.

10. Many people who do not live near a zoo get to see tigers only in (animal shows) _____, although (pro animal) _____ activists try to prevent tigers being used this way.

Visit the Troyka Web site for information on:

- Using end punctuation
- Using other punctuation marks
- Capitalizing, italicizing, abbreviating, and numbering

You'll also find access to *LEO: Literacy Education Online* at <leo.stcloudstate.edu/>. This site includes additional information on commas, number usage, and quotation marks, as well as other pertinent grammar topics.

PART **FOUR**

USING PUNCTUATION AND MECHANICS

www.prenhall.com/troyka

23 PERIODS, QUESTION MARKS, AND EXCLAMATION POINTS

Periods, question marks, and **exclamation points** are collectively called *end punctuation* because they occur at the ends of sentences.

I love you**.** Do you love me**?** I love you**!**

PERIODS

23a When does a period end a sentence?

A **period** ends a statement, a mild command, or an INDIRECT QUESTION.* Don't use a period to end a DIRECT QUESTION, a strong command, or an emphatic declaration.

END OF A STATEMENT
A journey of a thousand miles must begin with a single step.
—Lao-tsu, *The Way of Lao-tsu*

MILD COMMAND
Put a gram of boldness into everything you do.
—Baltasar Gracian

INDIRECT QUESTION
I asked if they wanted to climb Mt. Everest. [As an indirect question, this sentence reports that a question was asked. If it were a direct question, it would end with a question mark: *I asked, "Do you want to climb Mt. Everest?"*]

23b How do I use periods with abbreviations?

Most **abbreviations,** though not all, call for periods. Typical abbreviations with periods include *Mt., St., Dr., Mr., Ms., Mrs., Fri., Feb.,*

---

* You can find the definition of a word printed in small capital letters (such as INDIRECT QUESTION) in the Terms Glossary toward the back of this handbook.

R.N., *a.m.*, and *p.m.* (For more about *a.m.* and *p.m.*, see Chapter 20 and section 30k; for more about abbreviations, see 30j through 30n.)

◉ **ALERT:** Spell out the word *professor* in ACADEMIC WRITING; don't abbreviate it. ●

Abbreviations without periods include the names of states (for example, IL, CO) and some organizations and government agencies (for example, CBS and NASA).

Ms. Yuan, who works at **NASA,** lectured to **Dr.** Garcia's physics class at 9:30 **a.m.**

◉ **PUNCTUATION ALERT:** When the period of an abbreviation falls at the end of a sentence that calls for a period, the period of the abbreviation serves also to end the sentence. If, however, your sentence ends in a question mark or an exclamation point, put it after the period of the abbreviation.

The phone rang at 4:00 **a.m.**

It's upsetting to answer a wrong number call at 4:00 **a.m.!**

Who would call at 4:00 **a.m.?** ●

QUESTION MARKS

23c When do I use a question mark?

A **question mark** ends a **direct question,** one that quotes the exact words the speaker used. (In contrast, an **indirect question** reports a question and ends with a period.)

How many attempts have been made to climb Mt. Everest? [An indirect question would end with a period: *She wants to know how many attempts have been made to climb Mt. Everest.*]

◉ **PUNCTUATION ALERT:** Don't use a question mark with any other punctuation.

NO She asked, "How are you**?.**"

YES She asked, "How are you**?**" ●

Questions in a series are each followed by a question mark, whether or not each question is a complete sentence.

After the fierce storm, the mountain climbers debated what to do next. Turn back**?** Move on**?** Rest for a while**?**

◉ **ALERT:** When questions in a series are not complete sentences (as in the above example), you can choose whether or not to capitalize the first letter, but be consistent in each piece of writing. ●

Sometimes a statement or mild command is phrased as a question to be polite. In such cases, a question mark is optional, but be consistent in each piece of writing.

Would you please send me a copy**.**

23d When can I use a question mark in parentheses?

The only time to use a question mark in parentheses (?) is if a date or other number is unknown or doubtful. Never use (?) to communicate that you're unsure of information.

Mary Astell, a British writer of pamphlets on women's rights, was born in 1666 **(?)** and died in 1731.

The word *about* is often a more graceful substitute for (?): *Mary Astell was born* **about** *1666.*

Also, never use (?) to communicate IRONY or sarcasm. Choose words to deliver your message.

> **NO** Having altitude sickness is a pleasant **(?)** experience.
>
> **YES** Having altitude sickness is **as** pleasant **as having a bad case of the flu.**

EXCLAMATION POINTS

23e When do I use an exclamation point?

An **exclamation point** ends a strong command or an emphatic declaration. A strong command is a firm and direct order: *Look out behind you!* An emphatic declaration is a shocking or surprising statement: *There's been an accident!*

👁 **PUNCTUATION ALERT:** Don't combine an exclamation point with any other punctuation.

> **NO** "There's been an accident**!,**" she shouted.
>
> **YES** "There's been an accident**!**" she shouted. ●

23f What is considered overuse of exclamation points?

In ACADEMIC WRITING, words, not exclamation points, need to communicate the intensity of your message. Reserve exclamation points for an emphatic declaration within a longer passage.

When we were in Nepal, we tried each day to see Mt. Everest. But each day we failed. **Clouds defeated us!** The summit never emerged from a heavy overcast.

Also, using exclamation points too frequently suggests an exaggerated sense of urgency.

> **NO** Mountain climbing can be dangerous. You must know correct procedures! You must have the proper equipment! Otherwise, you could die!

> **YES** Mountain climbing can be dangerous. You must know correct procedures. You must have the proper equipment. Otherwise, you could die!

Never use (!) to communicate amazement or sarcasm. Choose words to deliver your message.

> **NO** At 29,141 feet (!), Mt. Everest is the world's highest mountain. Yet, Chris (!) wants to climb it.

> **YES** At **a majestic** 29,141 feet, Mt. Everest is the world's highest mountain. Yet, Chris, **amazingly,** wants to climb it.

EXERCISE 23-1

Insert any needed periods, question marks, and exclamation points and delete any unneeded ones. For help, consult all sections of this chapter.

EXAMPLE   Have you ever crossed a wide river or a deep canyon on a suspension bridge that sways in the wind.

Have you ever crossed a wide river or a deep canyon on a suspension bridge that sways in the wind**?**

1. The first (?) modern bridge was built over the Severn River in England in 1781.
2. Engineers considered it modern (?) because it was built with cast-iron girders
3. Earlier bridges had been built from wood or stone!
4. The Severn Bridge used cast-iron girders because iron was a lightweight (!) substitute for stone.
5. "Why would anyone prefer lightweight materials for building a sturdy bridge" is a question you may ask?
6 Strong but light building materials require fewer bridge supports, a technique that looks graceful and keeps costs down!
7. By the 1930s, as bridges grew longer and narrower, people wondered if they were safe because they often swayed in the wind!

8. Few (?) were surprised when the Tacoma Narrows Bridge in Washington State began to twist in a windstorm.
9. Nevertheless, everyone was shocked when the wind ripped the bridge apart in just a few minutes (!).
10. Today, engineers use superior building materials and technologically advanced techniques to assure that bridges are safe?

EXERCISE 23-2

Insert needed periods, question marks, and exclamation points. For help, consult all sections of this chapter.

Bill Gates, the billionaire founder of Microsoft Corp, expanded his empire by buying time itself He completed the deal when he purchased the 16 million images of the Bettmann Archive, a company that controls the largest collection of historical photographs in existence Otto Bettmann started the company that bears his name with some of his father's photographs The elder Bettmann had been a surgeon in Germany who over time put together a small file of scientific illustrations and X-rays When the son was forced to flee Germany in the 1930s, he packed the photographs in two trunks and brought them to the United States with him How did this modest, unpromising file of scientific images grow into the world's largest collection of photographs Over the years, Otto took some photos himself, but he also bought the pictures of retiring photographers and other collectors In this way, he built a library of images that constitutes a photographic history of the twentieth century Bill Gates's purchase of this collection thus puts him in a unique position: He now owns the past

24 COMMAS

24a What is the role of the comma?

Commas are the most frequently used marks of punctuation, occurring twice as often as all other punctuation marks combined. A comma must be used in certain places, it must not be used in other places, and it's optional in still other places. This chapter helps you sort through the various rules.

For quick access to most answers when you have a comma question, consult Box 101. The sections in parentheses indicate where you can find fuller explanations.

 Key uses of commas   101

COMMAS WITH COORDINATING CONJUNCTIONS LINKING INDEPENDENT CLAUSES (24b)

- Postcards are ideal for brief greetings, **and** they can also be miniature works of art.

COMMAS AFTER INTRODUCTORY ELEMENTS (24c)

- **Although most postcards cost only a dime,** one recently sold for thousands of dollars. [clause]
- **On postcard racks,** several designs are usually available. [phrase]
- **For example,** animals are timeless favorites. [transitional expression]
- **However,** most cards show local landmarks. [word]

COMMAS WITH ITEMS IN SERIES (24d)

- **Places, paintings, and people** appear on postcards.
  [*and* between last two items]

→

397

> ### Key uses of commas *(continued)*   **101**
>
> - **Places, paintings, people, animals** occupy dozens of display racks. [no *and* between last two items]
>
> COMMAS WITH COORDINATE ADJECTIVES (24e)
>
> - Some postcards feature **appealing, dramatic** scenes.
>
> NO COMMAS WITH CUMULATIVE ADJECTIVES (24e)
>
> - Other postcards feature **famous historical** scenes.
>
> COMMAS WITH NONRESTRICTIVE ELEMENTS (24f)
>
> - **Four years after the first postcard appeared,** the U.S. government began to issue prestamped postcards. [nonrestrictive element introduces independent clause]
>
> - The Golden Age of postcards, **which lasted from about 1900 to 1929,** yielded many especially valuable cards. [nonrestrictive element interrupts independent clause]
>
> - Collectors attend postcard shows, **which are similar to baseball-card shows.** [nonrestrictive element ends independent clause]
>
> NO COMMAS WITH RESTRICTIVE ELEMENTS (24f)
>
> - Collectors **who attend these shows** may specialize in a particular kind of postcard. [restrictive clause]
>
> COMMAS WITH QUOTED WORKS (24h.5)
>
> - One collector told me, "Attending a show is like digging for buried treasure." [quoted words at end of sentence]
>
> - "I always expect to find a priceless postcard," he said. [quoted words at start of sentence]
>
> - "Everyone there," he joked, "believes a million-dollar card is hidden in the next stack." [quoted words interrupted mid-sentence]

24b How does a comma operate with a coordinating conjunction that links independent clauses?

When a coordinating conjunction (*and, but, for, or, nor, so, yet*) links two (or more) INDEPENDENT CLAUSES, place a comma before the coordinating conjunction. Box 102 shows this pattern.

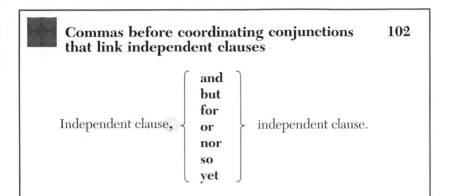

**Commas before coordinating conjunctions 102
that link independent clauses**

$$\text{Independent clause,} \left\{ \begin{array}{l} \textbf{and} \\ \textbf{but} \\ \textbf{for} \\ \textbf{or} \\ \textbf{nor} \\ \textbf{so} \\ \textbf{yet} \end{array} \right\} \text{independent clause.}$$

The sky turned dark gray, **and** the wind died suddenly.

The November morning had just begun, **but** it looked like dusk.

Shopkeepers closed their stores early, **for** they wanted to get home.

Soon high winds would start, **or** thick snow would begin silently.

Farmers could not continue harvesting, **nor** could they round up their animals in distant fields.

The firehouse whistle blew four times, **so** everyone knew a blizzard was closing in.

People on the road tried to reach safety, **yet** a few unlucky ones were stranded.

Exceptions

- When two independent clauses are very short, and they contrast with each other, you can link them with a comma without using a coordinating conjunction: *Mosquitos don't bite, they stab.* Some instructors consider this an error, so in ACADEMIC WRITING, you'll never be wrong if you use a period or semicolon (Chapter 25) instead of a comma.

- When one or both independent clauses linked by a coordinating conjunction happen to contain other commas, drop the coordinating conjunction and use a semicolon instead of the comma. This can help clarify meaning.

  With temperatures below freezing, the snow did not melt; ~~and~~ **people** wondered, gazing at the white landscape, when they would see grass again.

👁 **ALERTS:** (1) Don't put a comma *after* a coordinating conjunction that joins independent clauses.

NO	A house is renovated in two weeks **but,** an apartment takes a week.
YES	A house is renovated in two weeks**,** **but** an apartment takes a week.

(2) Don't use a comma when a coordinating conjunction links only two words, two PHRASES, or two DEPENDENT CLAUSES.

NO	Habitat for Humanity depends on volunteers for **workers, and donations** to help with its construction projects. [*Workers* and *donations* are only two words; the conjunction alone explains their relationship.]
YES	Habitat for Humanity depends on volunteers for **workers and donations** to help with its construction projects.
NO	Each language has **a beauty of its own, and forms of expression** that are duplicated nowhere else. [A *beauty of its own* and *forms of expression* are only two phrases.]
YES	Each language has **a beauty of its own and forms of expression** that are duplicated nowhere else.

—Margaret Mead, "Unispeak"

(3) Don't use a comma alone between independent clauses, or you'll create a COMMA SPLICE (Chapter 13).

NO	Five inches of snow fell in two hours, driving was hazardous.
YES	Five inches of snow fell in two hours**, and** driving was hazardous.●

EXERCISE 24-1

Combine each pair of sentences using the coordinating conjunction shown in parentheses. Rearrange words when necessary. For help, consult 24b.

EXAMPLE Almonds originated in China. They are now the top export crop from the United States. (but)

Almonds originated in China**,** *but* they are now the top export crop from the United States.

1. California's 6,000 almond growers produce over 70 percent of the world's almonds. This crop is worth nearly $800 million a year. (and)
2. Central California provides ideal growing conditions for almonds. The flat land is rich in nutrients. (for)
3. Almonds and peaches are genetically related. A small almond cutting can be spliced to a peach pit root to make the almond tree sturdier. (so)
4. Almond trees cannot self-pollinate. Growers depend on bees from over one million beehives to pollinate the pale pink blossoms. (so)

5. Bees will not fly when the temperature is below 54 degrees. Bees will not fly when it rains. (nor)
6. Picking almonds from the trees takes too long. Shaking the trees makes most nuts fall to the ground. (but)
7. Workers used to shake the branches with long poles. Mechanical shaking machines make harvesting the nuts much easier today. (but)
8. Machines blow and rake the nuts to areas between the trees. Another machine lifts the almonds into a wagon. (and)
9. The nuts are hulled and shelled by machine. Many nuts remain flawless and demand a high price. (yet)
10. Chipped nuts are bought by companies that make candy bars. The nuts are purchased to package for baking. (or)

24c How does a comma operate with introductory clauses, phrases, and words?

A comma follows any introductory element that comes before an INDEPENDENT CLAUSE. An introductory element can be a CLAUSE, PHRASE, or words. Because these elements are not sentences by themselves, you need to join them to independent clauses. Box 103 shows this pattern.

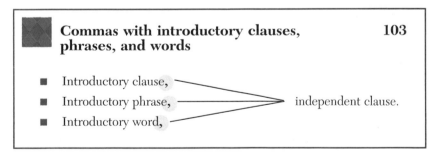

Commas with introductory clauses, phrases, and words   **103**

- Introductory clause,
- Introductory phrase,   → independent clause.
- Introductory word,

When the topic is dieting, many people say sugar craving is their worst problem. [introductory DEPENDENT CLAUSE]

Between 1544 and 1689, sugar refineries appeared in London and New York. [introductory PREPOSITIONAL PHRASE]

Beginning in infancy, we develop lifelong tastes for sweet foods. [introductory PARTICIPIAL PHRASE]

Sweets being a temptation for many adults, most parents avoid commercial baby foods that contain sugar. [introductory ABSOLUTE PHRASE]

For example, fructose comes from fruit, but it's still sugar.
[introductory TRANSITIONAL EXPRESSION]

Nevertheless, many people think fructose isn't harmful.
[introductory CONJUNCTIVE ADVERB]

To satisfy a craving for ice cream, even timid people sometimes brave midnight streets. [introductory INFINITIVE PHRASE]

Exception

When an introductory element is short, and the sentence can be understood easily, some writers omit the comma. However, in ACADEMIC WRITING, you'll never be wrong if you use the comma.

> **YES**   In 1992, the Americans with Disabilities Act was passed. [preferred]

> **YES**   In 1992 the Americans with Disabilities Act was passed.

An **interjection** is an introductory word that conveys surprise or other emotions. Use a comma after an interjection at the beginning of a sentence: **Oh,** *we didn't realize that you're allergic to cats.* **Yes,** *your sneezing worries me.*

◉ **PUNCTUATION ALERT:** Use a comma before (if it does not begin the sentence) and after (if it does not end the sentence) a transitional expression in a sentence.

By the way, the parade begins at noon. [introductory transitional expression with comma after it]

The parade, **by the way,** begins at noon. [transitional expression with comma before and after it, in middle of sentence]

The parade begins at noon, **by the way.** [transitional expression with comma before it, at end of sentence]

However, our float isn't finished. [introductory conjunctive adverb with comma after it]

Our float, **however,** isn't finished. [conjunctive adverb with comma before and after it, in middle of sentence]

Our float isn't finished, **however.** [conjunctive adverb with comma before it, at end of sentence] ●

EXERCISE 24-2

Using a comma after the introductory element, combine each set of sentences into one sentence according to the directions in parentheses. You can add, delete, and rearrange words as needed. Refer to 24c for help.

EXAMPLE   Several magicians have revealed their secrets. They have revealed their secrets recently. (begin with *recently*)

Recently, several magicians have revealed their secrets.

1. One famous trick involves sawing a woman in half. This trick actually uses two women. (begin with *for example*)
2. The magician opens the lid to a large rectangular box. The magician shows the audience it's empty. (begin with *first*)
3. The brave female assistant lies down in the box. The opened box lid faces away from the audience. (begin with *when*)
4. The assistant puts her head outside one end of the box. She seems to put her wiggling feet out the other end. (begin with *locked inside*)
5. Observers watch in astonishment. The magician pushes a saw through the middle of the box. (begin with *in astonishment*)
6. This illusion seems impossible. This illusion is safely performed with two women participating. (begin with *although*)
7. The first assistant walks behind the box. This assistant lies down in the box and pulls her knees up to her chest. (begin with *walking*)
8. The first woman now occupies only one side. And the other woman hidden under the box's false bottom emerges to get into position on the second side. (begin with *in the closed box*)
9. The second woman folds her body by bending forward at the waist. She puts her feet out the holes at her end of the box (begin with *to create the illusion*)
10. Each woman is positioned in different ends of the box. The magician can safely make a grand show of sawing a woman in half. (begin with *because*)

24d How does a comma operate with items in a series?

A **series** is a group of three or more elements—words, PHRASES, or CLAUSES—that match in grammatical form and are of equal importance in a sentence. Box 104 shows this pattern.

 Commas in a series 104

- word, word, and word
- phrase, phrase, and phrase
- clause, clause, and clause

- word, word, word
- phrase, phrase, phrase
- clause, clause, clause

Marriage requires **sexual, financial, and emotional** discipline.

—Anne Roiphe, "Why Marriages Fail"   403

Culture is a way of **thinking, feeling, believing.**

—Clyde Kluckhohn, *Mirror for Man*

My love of flying goes back to those early days **of roller skates, of swings, and of bicycles.**

—Tresa Wiggins, student

We have been taught **that children develop by ages and stages, that the steps are pretty much the same for everybody, and that to grow out of the limited behavior of childhood, we must climb them all.**

—Gail Sheehy, *Passages*

Some publications omit the comma between the last item of a series and the coordinating conjunction. Recently, practice is changing even in ACADEMIC WRITING, which means that some instructors require the use of a comma here and others don't. Check with the instructors of your writing classes to find out what each requires.

> **NO** The sweater comes in **blue, green, pink and black.** [Do the sweaters come in three or four colors?]

> **YES** The sweater comes in **blue, green, pink, and black.** [The comma before *and* clarifies that the sweaters come in four colors.]

When items in a series contain commas or other punctuation, separate them with semicolons instead of commas (25e).

If it's a bakery, they have to sell cake; if it's a photography shop, they have to develop film; and if it's a dry-goods store, they have to sell warm underwear.

—Art Buchwald, "Birth Control for Banks"

Numbered or lettered lists within a sentence are considered items in a series. With three or more items, use commas (or semicolons if the items themselves contain commas) to separate them.

To file your insurance claim, please enclose (1) a letter requesting payment, (2) a police report about the robbery, **and** (3) proof of purchase of the items you say are missing.

⊘ **PUNCTUATION ALERT:** In a series, don't use a comma before the first item or after the last item, unless a different rule makes it necessary.

> **NO** Many **artists, writers, and composers, have indulged** in daydreaming. [comma separates compound subject from the VERB (24k.6)]

> **YES** Many artists, writers, and composers have indulged in daydreaming.

NO Such dreamers include**,** Miró, Debussy, Dostoevsky, and Dickinson.

YES Such dreamers include Miró, Debussy, Dostoevsky, and Dickinson.

YES Such dreamers include**, of course,** Miró, Debussy, Dostoevsky, and Dickinson. [As a TRANSITIONAL EXPRESSION, *of course* is set off from the rest of the sentence by commas before and after it (24c).]●

EXERCISE 24-3

Insert commas to separate the items in a series. If a sentence needs no commas, explain why. For help, consult 24d.

EXAMPLE   In the fertile Kentucky mountain country of the late 1700s, deer elk and black bears were abundant.

In the fertile Kentucky mountain country of the late 1700s**,** *deer**,** elk**,** and black bears* were abundant.

1. Rabbits squirrels raccoons and other small game were so common that they were simply taken for granted by the Shawnees Cherokees and European pioneers who settled there.
2. An alert observer noted that wild turkeys were so fat that the branches of trees could not hold their weight buffalo tracks were as wide as highways and everybody wore a cap made of raccoon skin.
3. The farmers followed closely on the heels of the hunters trappers and scouts despite the difficulties of making their way through a wilderness of vertical mountains overgrown forests and lush meadows.
4. The year 1788 marked the beginning of a mass migration of farmers from Virginia North Carolina Pennsylvania and other long-settled areas over the mountains to Kentucky.
5. Kentucky had so many new inhabitants in five short years that it became the first "western" state to be admitted to the Union.

24e   How does a comma operate with coordinate adjectives?

Coordinate adjectives are two or more ADJECTIVES of equal weight that describe—that is, modify—a NOUN. In contrast, **cumulative adjectives** build meaning from word to word, as they move toward the noun. Box 105 shows the pattern for coordinate adjectives. The key to applying this rule is your ability to recognize when adjectives are coordinate and when they aren't. Box 106 tells you how.

Commas with coordinate adjectives 105

coordinate adjective, coordinate adjective noun

Tests for coordinate and comulative adjectives 106

If either one of these tests works, the adjectives are coordinate and require a comma between them.

- Can the order of the adjectives be reversed without changing the meaning or creating nonsense? If yes, use a comma.

  NO The concert featured **new several** bands. [*New several* makes no sense.]

  YES The **huge, restless** crowd waited for the concert to begin. [*Restless, huge* still carries the same meaning so these are coordinate adjectives.]

- Can *and* be sensibly inserted between the adjectives? If yes, use a comma.

  NO The concert featured **several and new** bands. [*Several and new* makes no sense.]

  YES The **huge and restless** crowd waited. [Modifier *huge and restless* makes sense, so these are coordinate adjectives.]

The audience cheered when the **pulsating, rhythmic** music filled the stadium. [*Pulsating* and *rhythmic* are coordinate adjectives.]

Each band had a **distinctive musical** style. [*Distinctive* and *musical* aren't coordinate adjectives.]

PUNCTUATION ALERT: Don't put a comma between a final coordinate adjective and the noun it modifies.

  NO Hundreds of **roaring, cheering, yelling, fans** filled the stadium.

  YES Hundreds of **roaring, cheering, yelling fans** filled the stadium. ●

EXERCISE 24-4

Insert commas to separate coordinate adjectives. If a sentence needs no commas, explain why. For help, consult 24e.

EXAMPLE   Only corn grown for popcorn pops consistently because all
other kinds of corn lack tough enamel-like shells.

Only corn grown for popcorn pops consistently because all
other kinds of corn lack *tough,* *enamel-like* shells.

1. The outside of an unpopped popcorn kernel is a hard plasticlike coating.
2. Inside an unpopped kernel is a soft starchy substance combined with water.
3. Applying heat causes the water molecules to expand until the pressure pops the dark yellow kernel.
4. The popped kernel turns itself inside out and absorbs air into its white pulpy matter.
5. The thinner softer shells of nonpopcorn corn don't allow water to heat to the high popping temperature.

24f How do commas operate with nonrestrictive elements?

A **restrictive element** contains information (a descriptive word, clause, or phrase) that's essential for a sentence to deliver its message; thus, it is often called an *essential element.* A **nonrestrictive element** contains information that's *not* essential for a sentence to deliver its meaning, and therefore, you will often see the term *nonessential element.* The key is in recognizing what's essential (restrictive) and what's nonessential (nonrestrictive) in a sentence. Box 107 defines and explains the difference in the meaning of these terms.

 Restrictive **and** *nonrestrictive* **defined**   **107**

Restrictive

A restrictive element contains information essential for the sentence to deliver its message. By being essential, the words in the element limit—that is, "restrict"—the meaning in some way. Don't use commas with restrictive elements.

Many U.S. states retest drivers **who are over sixty-five** to check their driving competency.

→

Restrictive and nonrestrictive defined (continued)   107

The information *who are over sixty-five* is essential to understanding the sentence because it limits or restricts the meaning of *drivers* to only those over the age of sixty-five. Drivers *under* sixty-five are not included. To check whether an element is essential, drop it and read the sentence. If the meaning of the sentence changes, then the information element is essential in delivering the message intended in the sentence. This means the element is restrictive (essential), and <u>commas are not used</u>.

Nonrestrictive

A nonrestrictive element contains information that's *not* essential for the sentence to deliver its message. By being nonessential, the words in the element don't limit—or "restrict"—the meaning in some way. Use commas with nonrestrictive (nonessential) elements.

My parents**, who are both over sixty-five,** took a defensive driving course.

The information *who are both over sixty-five* is not essential because the words *my parents* carry the sentence's message so that we know which parents took a defensive driving course. (Information about their age is "extra" to this message, so <u>commas are required</u>.)

Box 108 shows the pattern for comma use with nonrestrictive elements. The pattern for restrictive elements calls for no commas.

Commas with nonrestrictive elements   108

- ■ **Nonrestrictive element,** independent clause.
- ■ Beginning of independent clause, **nonrestrictive element,** end of independent clause.
- ■ Independent clause, **nonrestrictive element.**

Restrictive and nonrestrictive elements can fall at the beginning, in the middle, or at the end of a sentence. To test whether an element is nonrestrictive, read the sentence without the element. If the meaning of the sentence does not change, the element is nonrestrictive.

MORE EXAMPLES OF RESTRICTIVE ELEMENTS

Some people **in my neighborhood** enjoy jogging. [The reader needs the information *in my neighborhood* to know which people enjoy jogging. The information is essential, so no commas are used.]

Some people **who are in excellent physical condition** enjoy jogging. [The reader needs the information *who are in excellent physical condition* to know which people enjoy jogging. The information is essential, so no commas are used.]

The agricultural scientist **Wendy Singh** has developed a new fertilization technique. [*Wendy Singh* is essential to identify exactly which agricultural scientist developed the new technique, so no commas are used.]

MORE EXAMPLES OF NONRESTRICTIVE ELEMENTS

An energetic person, Anna Hom enjoys jogging. [Without knowing that Anna Hom is *an energetic person,* the reader can understand that she enjoys jogging. The information is nonessential, so commas are used.]

Anna Hom**, who is in excellent physical condition,** enjoys jogging. [Without knowing Anna Hom's *physical condition,* the reader can understand that Anna Hom enjoys jogging. The information is nonessential, so commas are used.]

Anna Hom enjoys jogging**, which is also Adam's favorite pastime.** [Without knowing about *Adam's favorite pastime,* the reader can understand that Anna Hom enjoys jogging. The information is nonessential, so commas are used.]

The agricultural scientist**, a new breed of farmer,** explains how to control a farming environment. [Without knowing that the scientist is *a new breed of farmer,* the reader can understand that the agricultural scientist explains how to control a farming environment. The information is nonessential, so commas are used.]

EXERCISE 24-5

Using your knowledge of restrictive and nonrestrictive elements, insert commas as needed. If a sentence is correct, explain why. For help, consult 24f.

EXAMPLE   Many features of suburban homes including front doors imitate parts of the aristocratic mansions of past centuries.

Many features of suburban homes**,** *including front doors***,** imitate parts of the aristocratic mansions of past centuries.

1. The design of ordinary North American homes includes features that originated with the wealthy who often had different uses for them.
2. Large front doors often approached by a set of stairs allowed noble families to show off as they walked in and out of their houses.
3. Wide indoor staircases which originated in the palaces of fifteenth-century Italy are now found in many large suburban homes.

4. In Italian palaces, wide staircases led to the ballrooms and dining rooms of the second floor called the "noble floor" because only the upper classes used it.

5. People today who select the latest entertainment features such as 48-inch television screens are following the lead of the ultra-wealthy in earlier times.

6. The two silent film stars who built Pickfair a Hollywood mansion of the 1920s created a sensation by including the first-ever private movie theater in their new home.

7. The typical family today who owns a stereo system of some kind and a VCR outdoes Pickfair in the quality and variety of its home entertainment.

8. Although today's homes often imitate the wealthy mansions of the past, one important exception is the family kitchen unknown in the aristocratic home.

9. In wealthy households of old, the kitchen a drab working room was used only by the servants for cooking.

10. Today, the kitchen the main gathering place in many homes is used by both rich and poor families for cooking as well as for eating and conversing.

24g How do commas operate to set off transitional and parenthetical expressions, contrasts, words of direct address, and tag sentences?

TRANSITIONAL EXPRESSIONS move the reader from one idea to another. For a list of transitional expressions, see Box 26 in 4g.1, page 84. CONJUNCTIVE ADVERBS are a subcategory of transitional expressions. For a list of conjunctive adverbs, see Box 49 in 7g, page 162. Use commas to set them off.

California and Florida, **for example,** are important food producers. [transitional expression]

Therefore, the American Midwest is considered the world's breadbasket. [conjunctive adverb]

Parenthetical expressions are "asides." They add information but aren't necessary for understanding the message of a sentence. Set them off with parentheses or commas.

American farmers **(according to U.S. government figures)** export more wheat than they sell at home.

A major drought, **sad to say,** wiped out this year's wheat crop.

Expressions of contrast state what is *not* the case. Set them off with commas.

Feeding the world's population is **a serious, though not impossible,** problem.

We must work against world hunger continuously, **not only when famines strike.**

Words of direct address name the person or group being spoken to (addressed). Set them off with commas.

Join me, **brothers and sisters,** to end hunger.

Your contribution to the Relief Fund, **Steve,** will help us greatly.

A **tag sentence** is a normal sentence that ends with a "tag," an attached phrase or question. Set off a tag with a comma. When the tag is a question, the sentence ends with a question mark. This holds whether or not the **tag question** is formed with a CONTRACTION.

People will give blood regularly, **I hope.**

The response to the blood drive was impressive, **wasn't it?**

EXERCISE 24-6

Add commas to set off any transitional, parenthetical, and contrasting elements, words of direct address, and tag sentences. Adjust end punctuation as necessary. For help, consult 24g.

EXAMPLE   Writer's block it seems to me is a misunderstood phenomenon.

Writer's block, *it seems to me,* is a misunderstood phenomenon.

1. An inability to write some say stems from lack of discipline and a tendency to procrastinate.
2. In other words the only way to overcome writer's block is to exert more willpower.
3. But writer's block is a complex psychological event that happens to conscientious people not just procrastinators.
4. Strange as it may seem such people are often unconsciously rebelling against their own self-tyranny and rigid standards of perfection.
5. If I told you my fellow writer that all it takes to start writing again is to quit punishing yourself, you would think I was crazy wouldn't you?

24h How do commas operate to set off quoted words from explanatory words?

Explanatory words are words such as *said, stated, declared,* and others that introduce DIRECT DISCOURSE. When they fall in the same sentence, quoted words are set off from explanatory words. Box 109 shows this pattern.

 Commas with quoted words   **109**

- Explanatory words, "Quoted words."
- "Quoted words," explanatory words.
- "Quoted words begin," explanatory words, "quoted words continue."

Speaking of ideal love, the poet William Blake wrote, "Love seeketh not itself to please."

"My love is a fever," said William Shakespeare about love's passion.

"I love no love," proclaimed poet Mary Coleridge, "but thee."

Exception

When the quoted words are blended into the grammatical structure of your sentence, don't use commas to set them off. These are instances of INDIRECT DISCOURSE, usually occurring with *as* and *that*.

The duke describes the duchess **as** "too soon made glad."

The duchess insists **that** "appearing glad often is but a deception."

PUNCTUATION ALERT: When the quoted words end with an exclamation point or a question mark, retain that original punctuation, even if explanatory words follow.

QUOTED WORDS	*"O Romeo! Romeo!"*
NO	"O Romeo! Romeo!," whispered Juliet from her window.
NO	"O Romeo! Romeo," whispered Juliet from her window.
YES	"O Romeo! Romeo!" whispered Juliet from her window.
QUOTED WORDS	*"Wherefore art thou Romeo?"*
NO	"Wherefore art thou Romeo?," Juliet urgently said.
NO	"Wherefore art thou Romeo," Juliet urgently said.
YES	"Wherefore art thou Romeo?" Juliet urgently said.

EXERCISE 24-7

Punctuate the following dialogue correctly. If a sentence is correct, explain why. For help, consult 24h.

EXAMPLE   "Can you tell me just one thing?," asked the tourist.

"Can you tell me just one thing**?"** asked the tourist.

1. "I'm happy to answer any questions you have" said the rancher to the tourist.
2. "Well, then" said the tourist "I'd like to know how you make ends meet on such a tiny ranch."
3. "Do you see that man leaning against the shed over there?" asked the rancher.
4. The rancher continued "He works for me, but I don't pay him any money. Instead, I have promised him that after two years of work, he will own the ranch."
5. "Then, I'll work for him, and in two more years, the ranch will be mine again!," said the rancher with a smile.

24i How do commas operate in dates, names, addresses, correspondence, and numbers?

When you write dates, names, addresses, correspondence, and numbers, use commas according to accepted practice. Boxes 110 through 113 explain.

⊙ Commas with dates   110

- Use a comma between the date and the year: *July 20, 1969.*
- Use a comma between the day and the date: *Sunday, July 20.*
- Within a sentence, use a comma on both sides of the year in a full date: *Everyone planned to be near a TV set on July 20, 1969, to watch the lunar landing.*
- Don't use a comma when only the month and year, or the month and day, are given. Also, don't use a comma between the season and year.

    YES People knew that one day in **July 1969** would change the world.

    YES News coverage was especially heavy on **July 21.**

    YES In **summer 1969** a man walked on the moon.

    →

Commas with dates *(continued)* 110

- Don't use a comma in an inverted date, a form used in the U.S. military and throughout the world except in the United States.

  YES People stayed near their televisions on **20 July 1969** to watch the moon landing.

⦿ **Commas with names, places, and addresses** 111

- When an abbreviated academic degree (*M.D., Ph.D.*) comes after a person's name, use a comma between the name and the title (*Angie Eng, M.D.*), and also after the title if other words follow in the sentence: *The jury listened closely to the expert testimony of* **Angie Eng, M.D., last week.**
- When an indicator of birth order or succession (*Jr., Sr., III, IV*) follows a name, don't use a comma: *Martin Luther* **King Jr.** or *Henry* **Ford II**
- When you invert a person's name, use a comma to separate the last name from the first: **Troyka, David**
- When city and state names are written together, use a comma to separate them: **Philadelphia, Pennsylvania.** If the city and state fall within a sentence, use a comma after the state as well: *My family settled in* **Philadelphia, Pennsylvania,** *before I was born.*
- When a complete address is part of a sentence, use a comma to separate all the items, except the state and zip code: *I wrote to* **Ms. Vivian Garcia, 1001 Rule Road, Upper Saddle River, NJ 07458,** *for more information about the comma.*

⦿ **Commas in correspondence** 112

- For the opening of an informal letter, use a comma: *Dear Betty,*
- For the opening of a business or formal letter, use a colon: *Dear Ms. Carpenter:*
- For the close of a letter, use a comma: Sincerely yours, Best regards, Love,

Commas with numbers 113

- Counting from right to left, put a comma after every three digits in numbers with more than four digits.

  72,867   156,567,066

- A comma is optional in most four-digit numbers. Be consistent within each piece of writing.

$1776	$1,776
1776 miles	1,776 miles
1776 potatoes	1,776 potatoes

- Don't use a comma in a four-digit year: *1990* (*Note:* If the year has five digits or more, do use a comma: *25,000 B.C.*)
- Don't use a comma in an address of four digits or more: *12161 Dean Drive*
- Don't use a comma in a page number of four digits or more: *see page 1338*
- Use a comma to separate related measurements written as words: *five feet, four inches*
- Use a comma to separate a scene from an act in a play: *act II, scene iv* (or *act 2, scene 4*)
- Use a comma to separate references to a page and a line: *page 10, line 6*

EXERCISE 24-8

Insert commas where they are needed. For help, consult 24i.

EXAMPLE   On June 1 1984 the small German-French production company released a feature film called *Paris Texas.*

On June 1, 1984, the small German-French production company released a feature film called *Paris, Texas.*

1. Made by the noted German director Wim Wenders, *Paris Texas* was set in an actual town in Lamar County Texas with a population of 24699.
2. The movie's title was clearly intended to play off the slightly more famous Paris in France.
3. The custom of naming little towns in the United States after cosmopolitan urban centers in the Old World has resulted in such places as Athens Georgia and St. Petersburg Florida.

4. As of July 31 1999 the American St. Petersburg had 234647 citizens and the American Athens had 140372.

5. By comparison, St. Petersburg Russia and Athens Greece have populations of approximately 4 million and 1 million, respectively.

24j How do commas clarify meaning?

A comma is sometimes needed to clarify the meaning of a sentence, even though no rule calls for one. The best solution is to revise the sentence.

> **NO** Of the gymnastic team's twenty five were injured.
>
> **YES** Of the gymnastic team's **twenty, five** were injured.
>
> **YES** Of **twenty on** the gymnastic team, five were injured.
> [preferred]

> **NO** Those who can practice many hours a day.
>
> **YES** **Those who can,** practice many hours a day.
>
> **YES** **They** practice many hours a day **when they can.**
> [preferred]

> **NO** George dressed and performed for the sellout crowd.
>
> **YES** **George dressed,** and performed for the sellout crowd.
>
> **YES** **After** George dressed, **he** performed for the sellout crowd.
> [preferred]

EXERCISE 24-9

Insert commas to prevent misreading. For help, consult, 24j.

EXAMPLE   When hunting owls use both vision and hearing.

When hunting, owls use both vision and hearing.

1. Flying at night owls consult a mental "map" of their surroundings.

2. During the daylight hours, healthy owls who can fly over their territories and create a map using their eyes and ears.

3. A team of scientists gave owls distorting eyeglasses to make the birds relearn their mental maps.

4. The bespectacled owl scientists found wears its glasses as contentedly as humans.

5. In a short time after they have produced a new mental map using their glasses the owls once again can spot and chase small rodents across the ground.

24k How can I avoid misusing the comma?

Throughout this chapter, ⊚ ALERTS remind you about comma misuses, as they relate to each comma rule. Most of these misuses are overuses—inserting a comma where one is unnecessary. This section summarizes the Alert notes and lists other frequent misuses of the comma.

When advice against overusing a comma clashes with a rule requiring one, follow the rule that requires the comma.

> The town of Kitty Hawk, North Carolina, attracts thousands of tourists each year. [Even though the comma after *North Carolina* separates the subject and its verb (which it normally shouldn't), the comma is required here because of the rule that calls for a comma within a sentence when the name of a state follows the name of a city (24i).]

24k.1 Avoiding misuse of commas with coordinating conjunctions

Don't use a comma after a COORDINATING CONJUNCTION that joins two INDEPENDENT CLAUSES, unless another rule makes it necessary (24b). Also, don't use a comma to separate two items joined with a coordinating conjunction—there must be at least three (see 24d).

NO   The sky was dark gray **and,** it looked like dusk.

YES   The sky was dark gray**, and** it looked like dusk.

NO   **The moon, and the stars** were shining last night.

YES   **The moon and the stars** were shining last night.

24k.2 Avoiding misuse of commas with subordinating conjunctions and prepositions

Don't put a comma after a SUBORDINATING CONJUNCTION (17e–17g) or a PREPOSITION (7h, 48a) unless another rule makes it necessary.

NO   **Although,** the storm brought high winds, it did no damage.

YES   **Although the storm brought high winds,** it did no damage. [comma follows full subordinated DEPENDENT CLAUSE, not the subordinate conjunction that begins it]

NO   The storm did no damage **although,** it brought high winds.

YES   The storm did no damage **although it brought high winds.** [no comma when subordinate clause follows the INDEPENDENT CLAUSE]

NO People expected worse **between,** the high winds and the heavy downpour.

YES People expected worse **between the high winds and the heavy downpour.** [preposition begins sentence element that needs no comma before or after]

24k.3 Avoiding misuse of commas in a series

Don't use a comma before the first, or after the last, item in a series, unless another rule makes it necessary (24d).

NO The gymnasium was decorated **with, red, white, and blue** ribbons for the Fourth of July.

NO The gymnasium was decorated with **red, white, and blue,** **ribbons** for the Fourth of July.

YES The gymnasium was decorated with **red, white, and blue** ribbons for the Fourth of July.

Don't put a comma between a final COORDINATE ADJECTIVE and the NOUN that the adjectives modify. Also, don't use a comma between adjectives that are not coordinate (24e).

NO He wore an **old, baggy, sweater.**

YES He wore an **old, baggy sweater.** [coordinate adjectives]

NO He has **several, new sweaters.**

YES He has **several new sweaters.** [noncoordinate or cumulative adjectives]

24k.4 Avoiding misuse of commas with restrictive elements

Don't use a comma to set off a RESTRICTIVE (essential) element from the rest of a sentence (24f).

NO **Vegetables, stir-fried in a wok,** are crisp and flavorful. [The words *stir-fried in a wok* are essential, so they are not set off with commas.]

YES **Vegetables stir-fried in a wok** are crisp and flavorful.

24k.5 Avoiding misuse of commas with quotations

Don't use a comma to set off INDIRECT DISCOURSE; use a comma only with DIRECT DISCOURSE (24h).

NO Jon said **that, he likes** stir-fried vegetables.

YES Jon said **that he likes** stir-fried vegetables.

YES **Jon said, "I like** stir-fried vegetables."

24k.6 Avoiding a comma that separates a subject from its verb, a verb from its object, or a preposition from its object

A comma does not make sense between these elements, though in some cases another comma rule might supersede this guideline (as in the first example in section 24k).

NO   **The brothers Wright, made** their first successful airplane flights on December 17, 1903. [As a rule, a comma doesn't separate a subject from its verb.]

YES   **The brothers Wright made** their first successful airplane flights on December 17, 1903.

NO   These inventors enthusiastically **tackled, the problems** of powered flight and aerodynamics. [As a rule, a comma doesn't separate a verb from its OBJECT.]

YES   These inventors enthusiastically **tackled the problems** of powered flight and aerodynamics.

NO   Airplane hobbyists visit Kitty Hawk's flight museum **from, all over the world.** [As a rule, a comma doesn't separate a PREPOSITION from its object.]

YES   Airplane hobbyists visit Kitty Hawk's flight museum **from all over the world.**

EXERCISE 24-10

Some commas have been deliberately misused in these sentences. Delete misused commas. If a sentence is correct, explain why. For help, consult all parts of this chapter, especially 24j and 24k.

EXAMPLE   Large U.S. cities experienced a cultural flowering during the 1920s, and nurtured a diversity of cultures.

> Large U.S. cities *experienced* a cultural flowering during the 1920s *and nurtured* a diversity of cultures.

1. In the 1920s, the Harlem Renaissance, was not confined to New York City; Harlem was only one of several, African American urban districts where the arts flourished during this decade.

2. Black urban singers began to attract a national audience and, Harlem surpassed Broadway in the originality of its musical revues, poetry, and fiction.

3. One of the leading poets of the Harlem Renaissance, was Claude McKay, who arrived in the United States from Jamaica in 1912 at age twenty-three.

4. He studied briefly at Booker T. Washington's, famous Tuskegee Institute in Alabama.

5. In 1917, he moved to Harlem, where he published his first poem.
6. McKay said that, poetry was his vehicle of protest.
7. He wrote his 1919 poem "If We Must Die" in response to, the race riots of that year.
8. Marcus Garvey, and his Universal Negro Improvement Association sought to transport blacks to, a new and better life in Africa.
9. Garvey, who was born in Jamaica like Claude McKay, was one of the first people, who taught African Americans that black is beautiful.
10. The Harlem Renaissance continued through 1945, when writers from Langston Hughes and Richard Wright to Zora Neale Hurston and Margaret Walker launched their great literary careers.

241 How can I avoid comma errors?

You can avoid most comma errors with these two bits of advice:

■ As you write or reread what you've written, don't insert a comma simply because you happen to pause to think or take a breath before moving on. Pausing isn't a reliable guide for writers, although the myth continues to thrive. Throughout the United States, and indeed the world, people's breathing rhythms, accents, and thinking patterns vary greatly.

■ As you're writing, if you're unsure about a comma, insert it and circle the spot. Later, when you're EDITING, check this handbook for the rule that applies.

www.prenhall.com/troyka

25 SEMICOLONS

25a What are the uses of a semicolon?

While a period signals the complete separation of INDEPENDENT CLAUSES, a **semicolon** indicates only a partial ("semi") separation. Use a semicolon in only two situations. A semicolon can replace a period between sentences that are closely related in meaning (25b and 25c). Also, a semicolon belongs between sentence structures that already contain one or more commas (25d) and with certain lists (25e).

25b When can I use a semicolon, instead of a period, between independent clauses?

The choice between a period and a semicolon for separating independent clauses depends on whether your meaning is better communicated by a complete separation (period) or a partial separation (semicolon). Box 114 shows this pattern for using semicolons.

> **Semicolon pattern I**   **114**
>
> Independent clause; independent clause.

The desert known as Death Valley became a U.S. National Park in 1994; it used to be a U.S. National Monument.

This is my husband's second marriage; it's the first for me.

—Ruth Sidel, "Marion Deluca"

👁 **PUNCTUATION ALERT:** Never use a comma alone between independent clauses—this rule will prevent you from creating a comma splice (Chapter 13). ●

25c When else can I use a semicolon between independent clauses?

When the second of a set of independent clauses closely related in meaning starts with a CONJUNCTIVE ADVERB or with a TRANSITIONAL EXPRESSION, you can choose to separate the clauses with a semicolon instead of a period. Also, insert a comma following a conjunctive adverb or transitional expression that starts an independent clause. Although some professional writers today omit the comma after short words (*then, next, soon*), the rule remains for most ACADEMIC WRITING. Box 115 shows this pattern for using semicolons.

 Semicolon pattern II   **115**

- Independent clause**;** conjunctive adverb, independent clause.
- Independent clause**;** transitional expression, independent clause.

The average annual rainfall in Death Valley is about two inches**; nevertheless,** hundreds of plant and animal species survive and even thrive there. [conjunctive adverb]

Photographers have spent years recording desert life cycles**; as a result,** we can watch bare sand flower after a spring storm. [transitional expression]

👁 **PUNCTUATION ALERT:** Never use only a comma between independent clauses that are connected by a conjunctive adverb or words of transition—this rule will prevent you from creating a comma splice (13d). ●

25d How do semicolons operate with coordinating conjunctions?

As a general rule, when INDEPENDENT CLAUSES are linked by a coordinating conjunction (*and, but, or, nor, for, so, yet*), good practice calls for a comma, not a period or semicolon, before the coordinating conjunction (24b). However, when one or more of the independent clauses already contain a comma, you can link the independent clauses by substituting a semicolon for the period. This can help your reader see the relationship between the ideas more clearly. Box 116 shows the various combinations of this pattern.

 Semicolon pattern III 116

- Independent clause, one that contains a comma; coordinating conjunction followed by independent clause.

- Independent clause; coordinating conjunction followed by independent clause, one that contains a comma.

- Independent clause, one that contains a comma; coordinating conjunction followed by independent clause, one that contains a comma.

When the peacock has presented his back, the spectator will usually begin to walk around him to get a front view; **but** the peacock will continue to turn so that no front view is possible.
—Flannery O'Connor, "The King of the Birds"

Our Constitution is in actual operation; everything appears to promise that it will last; **but** in this world, nothing is certain but death and taxes.
—Benjamin Franklin, in a 1789 letter

For anything worth having, one must pay the price; **and** the price is always work, patience, love, self-sacrifice.
—John Burroughs

25e When should I use semicolons between items in a series?

When a sentence contains a series of items that are long or that already contain one or more commas, separate the items with semicolons. Punctuating this way groups the elements, so that your reader can see where one item ends and the next begins. Box 117 shows this pattern for semicolons.

Semicolon pattern IV	**117**

Independent clause containing a series of items, any of which contain a comma; another item in the series; and another item in the series.

The assistant chefs chopped onions, green peppers, and parsley; sliced chicken and duck breasts into strips; started a broth simmering; **and** filled a large, shallow copper pan with oil.

25f How do I avoid misusing the semicolon?

Not using a semicolon after an introductory phrase

If you use a semicolon after an introductory PHRASE, you create the error known as a SENTENCE FRAGMENT (Chapter 12).

> **NO** **Open until midnight;** the computer lab is well used. [Using a semicolon turns an introductory phrase into a sentence fragment.]

> **YES** Open until midnight, the computer lab is well used.

Not using a semicolon after a dependent clause

If you use a semicolon after a DEPENDENT CLAUSE, you create the error known as a sentence fragment (Chapter 12).

> **NO** **Although the new dorms have computer facilities;** many students still prefer to go to the computer lab. [Using a semicolon turns a dependent clause into a sentence fragment.]

> **YES** Although the new dorms have computer facilities, many students still prefer to go to the computer lab.

Not using a semicolon to introduce a list

When the words that introduce a list form an independent clause, use a colon, never a semicolon (26b).

> **NO** **The newscast featured three major stories;** the latest pictures of Uranus, a speech by the president, and dangerous brush fires in Nevada. [*The newscast featured three major stories* is an INDEPENDENT CLAUSE, so the punctuation before the list should be a colon, not a semicolon.]

> **YES** The newscast featured three major stories: the latest pictures of Uranus, a speech by the president, and dangerous brush fires in Nevada.

👁 **PUNCTUATION ALERT:** If the words introducing the list do not form an INDEPENDENT CLAUSE, use no punctuation at all to introduce the list (26b and 26e).

> **NO** **The newscast was about:** the latest pictures of Uranus, a speech by the president, and dangerous brush fires in Nevada. [The words before the colon are not an independent clause, so no punctuation is needed.]

> **YES** The newscast was about the latest pictures of Uranus, a speech by the president, and dangerous brush fires in Nevada. ●

EXERCISE 25-1

Insert semicolons as needed in these items. Also, fix any incorrectly used semicolons. If a sentence is correct, explain why. For help, consult all sections of this chapter.

EXAMPLE   When writers at a magazine wondered whether people are honest today; they designed an experiment to find out.

         When writers at a magazine wondered whether people are honest today, they designed an experiment to find out.

1. If you find a lost wallet, you may consider yourself lucky, if you return the wallet along with all the cash in it, you are acting honestly.
2. Writers at a magazine tested people's honesty by pretending to lose their wallets, people who returned a wallet with all the money in it passed the test.
3. The writers tried this experiment in many different neighborhoods, all in all, they left 120 wallets in twelve cities, towns, and suburbs across the country.
4. One writer would stop in a public place and tie a shoelace while intentionally letting the wallet slip out of a pocket, meanwhile, a colleague kept watch from a distance.
5. Every wallet contained the following items; $50 cash, business cards, and grocery lists to make the wallet look authentic, photographs, and an identification card with a phone number, so that the person who found the wallet could phone the owner and return it.
6. Many people called that telephone number or handed in the wallet to police; although others simply walked off with the money.
7. In a run-down part of one town, a man quickly scooped up the wallet he found on a sidewalk, putting it into his pocket, but the man, who looked as if he could use the money, went straight to the nearest police station with the wallet.
8. A well-dressed, middle-aged woman in a wealthy suburb spotted one wallet, examined its contents, and got into her Cadillac, she kept the wallet.

425

9. Wallets were returned with all the money in them 67 percent of the time; small towns had more returns than cities or suburbs.

10. People interviewed by the magazine often expected younger people to be less honest than their elders, however, younger people in the wallet test had the same "honesty score" as older people—exactly 67 percent.

EXERCISE 25-2

Combine each set of sentences into one sentence so that it contains two independent clauses. Use a semicolon correctly between the two clauses. You may add, omit, revise, and rearrange words. Try to use all the patterns in this chapter and explain the reasoning behind your decisions. More than one revision may be correct. For help, consult all sections of this chapter.

EXAMPLE   Rosa Parks's refusal to move to the back of a bus in Montgomery, Alabama, in 1955 sparked the modern civil rights movement. Her action led to the greatest social revolution in U.S. history.

Rosa Parks's refusal to move to the back of a bus in Montgomery, Alabama, in 1955 sparked the modern civil rights movement; *her* action led to the greatest social revolution in U.S. history.

1. This defiant stand against bigotry by a single African American woman made Parks one of the most respected civil rights leaders of the 1950s. Now in her eighties, she has not lost her pep.

2. Parks remains active in the quest for improved race relations. She frequently travels to advocate equality. She devotes much of her time to an organization that she helped found. And she has written two autobiographical books.

3. Parks neither sought nor expected the attention that her act of defiance brought her. Nevertheless, she is pleased that people consider her the "mother of the civil rights movement."

4. Parks continues to spread her message to the people of the world, as she did when she embarked on a 381-day tour throughout the United States and many foreign countries in 1996. She advises her audiences to coexist peacefully. She tells them to live as one.

5. The message from 1955 reverberates strongly today because of one enthusiastic, honored, and respected woman. The message Rosa Parks has brought to the world is sure to outlast each generation that hears it.

26 COLONS

26a What are the uses of a colon?

A **colon** is a full stop that draws attention to the words that follow. In sentences, a colon—which can only be placed at the end of an INDEPENDENT CLAUSE—introduces a list, an APPOSITIVE, or a QUOTATION. In a variation on this, a colon comes after an independent clause that introduces yet another independent clause. Also, colons play a role in standard formats.

26b When can a colon introduce a list, an appositive, or a quotation?

When a COMPLETE SENTENCE—that is, an INDEPENDENT CLAUSE—introduces a list, an APPOSITIVE, or a QUOTATION, you can place a colon before the words being introduced. In these cases, the words being introduced don't have to form an independent clause themselves. Box 118 shows this pattern for using a colon.

Colon sentence pattern I   118

- Independent clause: list.
- Independent clause: appositive.
- Independent clause: "Quoted words."

Introducing listed items

Lists are often included within sentences and are not separated by punctuation, but when a complete sentence introduces a list, you can use a colon.

If you really want to lose weight, you must do three things:
eat smaller portions, exercise, and drink lots of water. [The required
independent clause comes before the listed items.]

When the lead-in words at the end of an independent clause are *such
as, including, like,* and *consists of,* don't use a colon. In contrast, if the
lead-in words at the end of an independent clause are *the following* or *as
follows,* do use a colon.

The students demanded improvements *such as* an expanded menu
in the cafeteria, improved janitorial services, and more up-to-date
textbooks.

The students demanded *the following:* an expanded menu in the
cafeteria, improved janitorial services, and more up-to-date textbooks.

Introducing appositives

An APPOSITIVE is a word or words that rename a NOUN or PRONOUN.
When an appositive is introduced by an independent clause, you can use
a colon.

**Only cats would likely approve of one old-fashioned remedy for
cuts:** a lotion of catnip, butter, and sugar. [The required independent
clause comes before the appositive: *a lotion of catnip, butter, and sugar*
renames *old-fashioned remedy.*]

Introducing quotations

When an independent clause introduces a quotation, you can use a
colon after it. (If the words introducing a quotation don't form an independent clause, use a comma.)

The little boy in E.T. did say something neat: "How do you explain
school to a higher intelligence?" [The required independent clause comes
before the quotation.]

—George F. Will, "Well, I Don't Love You, E.T."

26c When can I use a colon between two independent clauses?

When a second INDEPENDENT CLAUSE explains or summarizes a first
independent clause, you can use a colon to separate them. Box 119
shows this pattern for using a colon.

Colon sentence pattern II	119

Independent clause**:** Independent clause that explains or summarizes the prior independent clause.

👁 **ALERT:** You can choose to use a capital letter or a lowercase letter for the first word of an independent clause that follows a colon. Whichever you choose, be consistent in a piece of writing. I use a capital letter in this handbook.

> We will never forget the first time we made dinner together**: He** got stomach poisoning and was too sick to go to work for four days.
>
> —Lisa Baladendrum, student ●

26d What standard formats require a colon?

A variety of standard formats in American English require a colon. (Also, colons are used in many DOCUMENTATION STYLES, as shown in Chapters 35, 36, and 37.)

TITLE AND SUBTITLE
A Brief History of Time: From the Big Bang to Black Holes

HOURS, MINUTES, AND SECONDS
The plane took off at 7:15 p.m.

The track star passed the halfway point at 1:23.02.

👁 **ALERT:** In the military, hours and minutes are written without colons and with four digits on a 24-hour clock: *The staff meeting originally scheduled for Tuesday at* **0930** *will be held Tuesday at* **1430** *instead.* ●

REFERENCES TO BIBLE CHAPTERS AND VERSES
Psalms 23:1–3

Luke 3:13

MEMOS
To: Dean Kristen Olivero

From: Professor Daniel Black

Re: Student Work-Study Program

SALUTATION IN A BUSINESS LETTER
Dear Dr. Jewell:

26e When is a colon wrong?

Independent clauses

As discussed in section 26b, a colon can introduce a list, an APPOSI-TIVE, or a QUOTATION, but only when an INDEPENDENT CLAUSE does the introducing. Similarly, as shown in 26c, a colon can be used between two independent clauses when the second summarizes or explains the first. Be sure that you are dealing with independent clauses, not other word groups.

NO The cook bought: eggs, milk, cheese, and bread. [*The cook bought* isn't an independent clause.]

YES The cook bought eggs, milk, cheese, and bread.

Never use a colon to separate a PHRASE or DEPENDENT CLAUSE from an independent clause. Otherwise, you'll create a SENTENCE FRAGMENT (see 12b.1).

NO Day after day: the drought dragged on. [*Day after day* is a phrase, not an independent clause.]

YES Day after day, the drought dragged on.

NO After the drought ended: the farmers celebrated. [*After the drought ended* is a dependent clause, not an independent clause.]

YES After the drought ended, the farmers celebrated.

Lead-in words

As shown in section 26b, never use a colon after the lead-in words *such as, including, like,* and *consists of.*

NO The health board discussed many problems **such as:** poor water quality, aging sewage treatment systems, and the lack of alternate water supplies. [A colon is incorrect after *such as.*]

YES The health board discussed poor water quality, aging sewage treatment systems, and the lack of alternate water supplies. [*Such as* is dropped and the sentence slightly revised.]

YES The health board discussed many problems, **such as** poor water quality, an aging sewage treatment system, and the lack of alternate water supplies. [Comma before *such as* tells the reader that the list coming up is nonrestrictive (nonessential)—it illustrates *problems.*]

YES The health board discussed many problems: poor water quality, aging sewage treatment systems, and the lack of an alternate water supplies. [If such as is dropped and the independent clause no longer ends with it, the colon is correct.]

EXERCISE 26-1

Insert colons where needed and delete any not needed. If a sentence is correct, explain why. For help, consult all sections of this chapter.

EXAMPLE   The twentieth century saw a flowering of Irish literature, W. B. Yeats, G. B. Shaw, Samuel Beckett, and Seamus Heaney all won the Nobel Prize in Literature.

The twentieth century saw a flowering of Irish literature: W. B. Yeats, G. B. Shaw, Samuel Beckett, and Seamus Heaney all won the Nobel Prize in Literature.

1. People who work the night shift are typically deprived of essential sleep, an average of nine hours a week.
2. The Iroquois of the Great Lakes region lived in fortified villages and cultivated: corn, beans, and squash.
3. Five nations originally formed the Iroquois Confederacy: the Mohawk, the Oneida, the Onondaga, the Cayuga, and the Seneca.
4. Later, these five Iroquois nations were joined by: the Tuscarora.
5. Shouting: "Come back!" Adam watched the vehicle speed down the highway.
6. When a runner breaks through that unavoidable wall of exhaustion, a very different feeling sets in; an intense sense of well-being known as the "runner's high."
7. However: the "runner's high" soon disappears.
8. Two new nations were born on the same day in 1947, India and Pakistan achieved their independence from Britain at midnight on August 15.
9. To   English 101 Instructors
   From   Dean of Instruction
   Re   Classroom Assignments
10. Only a hurricane could have kept Lisa from meeting Nathaniel at 800 p.m.; unfortunately, that night a hurricane hit.
11. George's interests were typical of a sixteen-year-old, cars, music videos, and dating.
12. Like many people who have never learned to read or write, the woman who told her life story in *Aman; The Story of a Somali Girl* was able to remember an astonishing number of events in precise detail.
13. The Greek philosopher Socrates took these words as his motto, "The unexamined life is not worth living."
14. Socrates was executed after being found guilty of: teaching young people new ideas.
15. The voice coming from the radio could belong to only one person; the great jazz singer Ella Fitzgerald.

431

27 APOSTROPHES

27a What is the role of the apostrophe?

The **apostrophe** plays four roles in writing: It creates the POSSESSIVE CASE of NOUNS, forms the possessive case of INDEFINITE PRONOUNS, stands for one or more omitted letters in a word (a CONTRACTION), and can help form plurals of letters and numerals. Here are two roles the apostrophe doesn't play: It doesn't belong with plurals of nouns, and it doesn't form the plural of PERSONAL PRONOUNS in the possessive case.

27b How do I use an apostrophe to show a possessive noun?

An apostrophe works with a NOUN to form the POSSESSIVE CASE, which shows ownership or a close relationship.

OWNERSHIP	the **writer's** pen
CLOSE RELATIONSHIP	the **novel's** plot

Possession in nouns can be communicated in two ways: by a PHRASE starting with *of* (*comments **of** the instructor; comments **of** Professor Furman*) or by an apostrophe and the letter *s* (*the instructor's comments; Professor Furman's comments*). Here's a list of specific rules governing usage of *'s*.

■ **Add 's to nouns not ending in s:**

She felt a **parent's** joy. [*Parent* is a singular noun not ending in *s*.]
They care about their **children's** education. [*Children* is a plural noun not ending in *s*.]

■ **Add 's to singular nouns ending in s:**
You can add *'s* or the apostrophe alone to show possession when a singular noun ends in *s*. In this handbook, I use *'s* to clearly mark

432

singular-noun possessives, no matter what letter ends the noun. Whichever rule variation you choose, be consistent in each piece of writing.

The **bus's** (or **bus'**) air conditioning is out of order.
Chris's (or **Chris'**) ordeal ended.

If you encounter a tongue-twisting pronunciation (*Charles* **Dickens's** *novel*), you may decide not to add the additional *s* (*Charles* **Dickens'** *novel*). You must, however, be consistent in each piece of writing.

- **Add only an apostrophe to a plural noun ending in *s*:**

The **boys'** statements were taken seriously.
Three **months'** maternity leave is in the **workers'** contract.

- **Add 's to the last word in compound words and phrases:**

His **mother-in-law's** corporation has bought out a competitor.
The **tennis player's** strategy was brilliant.
We want to hear the **caseworker's** recommendation.

- **Add 's to each noun in individual possession:**

Shirley's and **Kayla's** houses are next to each other. [Shirley and Kayla each own a house; they don't own the houses jointly.]

- **Add 's to only the last noun in joint or group possession:**

Kareem and Brina's house has a screened porch. [Kareem and Brina own one house.]
Avram and Justin's houses always have nice lawns. [Avram and Justin jointly own more than one house.]

27c How do I use an apostrophe with *hers, his, its, ours, yours,* and *theirs*?

When a POSSESSIVE PRONOUN ends with the letter *s* (*hers, his, its, ours, yours,* and *theirs*), never add an apostrophe. Here's a list of PERSONAL PRONOUNS and their possessive forms.

PERSONAL PRONOUNS	POSSESSIVE FORMS
I	my, mine
you	your, yours
he	his
she	her, hers
it	its
we	our, ours
they	their, theirs
who	whose

433

27d How do I use an apostrophe with contractions?

In a **contraction,** an apostrophe takes the place of one or more omitted letters. Be careful not to confuse a contraction with a POSSESSIVE PRONOUN. Doing so is a common spelling error, one that many people—including employers—consider evidence of a poor education. Whether or not that's fair, it's usually true.

it's (contraction for *it is*)	**its** (possessive pronoun)
they're (contraction for *they are*)	**their** (possessive pronoun)
who's (contraction for *who is*)	**whose** (possessive form of *who*)
you're (contraction for *you are*)	**your** (possessive pronoun)

NO	The government has to balance **it's** budget.
YES	The government has to balance **its** budget.
NO	The professor **who's** class was canceled is ill.
YES	The professor **whose** class was canceled is ill.

In choosing whether or not to use a contraction or a full form, consider that many instructors think contractions aren't appropriate in ACADEMIC WRITING. Nevertheless, the *MLA Handbook* accepts contractions, including *'90s* for *the 1990s.* In this handbook, I use contractions because I'm addressing you, the student. I suggest, however, that before you use contractions in your academic writing, check with your instructor. Here's a list of common contractions.

COMMON CONTRACTIONS

aren't	= *are not*		she's	= *she is*
can't	= *cannot*		there's	= *there is*
didn't	= *did not*		they're	= *they are*
don't	= *do not*		wasn't	= *was not*
he's	= *he is*		we're	= *we are*
it's	= *it is*		weren't	= *were not*
I'd	= *I would, I had*		we've	= *we have*
I'm	= *I am*		who's	= *who is*
isn't	= *is not*		won't	= *will not*
let's	= *let us*		you're	= *you are*

⊚ **ALERT:** One contraction that is required in all writing is *o'clock* (which stands for *of the clock,* an expression used long ago). ●

27e How do I use an apostrophe to show a possessive indefinite pronoun?

An apostrophe works with a PRONOUN to form the POSSESSIVE CASE, which shows ownership or a close relationship.

OWNERSHIP	everyone's pen
CLOSE RELATIONSHIP	something's qualities

Possession in INDEFINITE PRONOUNS can be communicated in two ways: by a PHRASE starting with *of* (comments *of* everyone) or by an apostrophe and the letter *s* (everyone's comments).

27f How does *s* or *'s* form the plural of a letter, numeral, symbol, and word as a word?

To form the plural of a letter, numeral, symbol, and word as a word, you can choose to add either *'s* or *s*. Either style is acceptable, as long as you are consistent in a piece of writing. In this handbook, I use *s* alone, rather than *'s*. In all cases, use italics (or use underlining or quotation marks) for the item, but don't use italics (or use underlining or quotation marks) for the added *'s* or *s*.

SINGULAR LETTER AS WORD	Printing *M* is hard for kindergarteners.
PLURAL LETTERS AS WORD	Printing *Ms* (or *M's*) is hard for kindergarteners.
SINGULAR NUMERAL AS NOUN	The URL contains a *6*.
PLURAL NUMERALS AS NOUN	The URL contains three *6s* (or *6's*).
PLURAL YEAR OR YEARS	The trend lasted through the *1990s* (or *1990's*).
PLURAL OF SYMBOLS	What do those *&'s* mean?
SINGULAR WORD AS WORD	Words like *if* imply a conditional situation.
PLURAL WORDS AS WORD	I didn't feel safe accepting the offer because there were too many *ifs* (or *if's*) involved.

27g When is an apostrophe wrong?

If you're a writer who makes the same apostrophe errors repeatedly, memorize the rules you need (some you likely know almost without thought) so that you won't be annoyed by "that crooked little mark," a nickname popular with students who wish it would go away. Box 120 lists the major apostrophe errors.

Leading causes of apostrophe errors **120**

- Never use an apostrophe with the PRESENT-TENSE VERB.

  Cholesterol **plays** [not **play's**] an important role in how long we live.

- Always use an apostrophe after the *s* in a POSSESSIVE plural of a noun.

  Patients's [or **Patients'**—but not **Patients**] questions seek detailed answers.

- Never add an apostrophe at the end of a nonpossessive noun ending in *s*.

  Medical **studies** [not **studies'** or **study's**] show this to be true.

- Never use an apostrophe to form a nonpossessive plural.

  Teams [not **Team's**] of doctors have studied the effects of cholesterol.

EXERCISE 27-1

Rewrite these sentences to insert *'s* or an apostrophe alone to make the words in parentheses show possession. (Delete the parentheses.) For help, consult 27b and 27e.

EXAMPLE   All boxes, cans, and bottles on a (supermarket) shelves are designed to appeal to (people) emotions.

               All boxes, cans, and bottles on a *supermarket's* shelves are designed to appeal to *people's* emotions.

1. A (product) manufacturer designs packaging to appeal to (consumers) emotions through color and design.
2. Marketing specialists know that (people) beliefs about a (product) quality are influenced by their emotional response to the design of its package.
3. Circles and ovals appearing on a (box) design supposedly increase a (product user) feelings of comfort, while bold patterns and colors attract a (shopper) attention.
4. Using both circles and bold designs in (Arm & Hammer) and (Tide) packaging produces both effects in consumers.
5. (Heinz) familiar ketchup bottle and (Coca-Cola) famous label achieve the same effects by combining a bright color with an old-fashioned, "comfortable" design.

6. Often, a (company) marketing consultants will custom-design products to appeal to the supposedly "typical" (adult female) emotions or to (adult males), (children), or (teenagers) feelings.
7. One of the (marketing business) leading consultants, Stan Gross, tests (consumers) emotional reactions to (companies) products and their packages by asking consumers to associate products with well-known personalities.
8. Thus, (test takers) responses to (Gross) questions might reveal that a particular laundry detergent has (Sylvester Stallone) toughness, (Oprah Winfrey) determination, or (someone else) sparkling personality.
9. Manufacturing (companies) products are not the only ones relying on (Gross) and other corporate (image makers) advice.
10. (Sports teams) owners also use marketing specialists to design their (teams) images, as anyone who has seen the angry bull logo of the Chicago Bulls basketball team will agree.

EXERCISE 27-2

Rewrite these sentences so that each contains a possessive noun. For help, consult 27b and 27e.

EXAMPLE   Early visitors to Greenland wrote about an unusual custom of the native people of that island.

Early visitors to Greenland wrote about an unusual custom of *the island's native people.*

1. The native people of Greenland used to settle disputes by insulting each other in public.
2. Two individuals involved in a dispute sang insulting songs about the faults of each other.
3. Other members of the tribe joined in the singing and decided whose insults were the funniest and the most embarrassing.
4. After the decision of the tribe members was given, the winner and the loser forgot the dispute.
5. Similar customs, intended to keep the peace among all members of the community, were found in medieval Europe and early China.

28 QUOTATION MARKS

28a What is the role of quotation marks?

Quotation marks are used most often to enclose **direct quotations**—the exact spoken or written words of a speaker or writer. Quotation marks also set off some titles, and quotation marks call attention to words used in a special sense.

Double quotation marks (" ") are standard. In most computer fonts, the opening marks differ slightly in appearance from the closing marks. The opening marks look like tiny 6s, the closing marks like tiny 9s. In some computer fonts, the opening and closing marks look the same (" "). Single quotation marks (' ') are used for quotations within quotations: *Gregory said,* **"I heard the man shout 'help me' but could not reach him in time."** Quotation marks operate only in pairs: to open and to close. When you proofread your writing, check carefully that you've inserted the closing mark.

Please note, before you continue reading this chapter, that I use MLA STYLE to format the examples here and in other chapters. This affects the documentation features and the lengths of "short" and "long" quotations. These factors vary with different documentation styles. For MLA style, used in most English courses, see Chapter 35. For APA STYLE, see Chapter 36.

28b How do I use quotation marks with short direct quotations?

A DIRECT QUOTATION is any exact words from a print or nonprint source. In MLA STYLE, a quotation is considered *short* if it occupies no more than four typed lines. Use double quotation marks at the start and finish of a short quotation. Give DOCUMENTATION information after a short quotation, before the sentence's ending period.

SHORT QUOTATIONS

```
Gardner has suggested the possibility of a ninth
intelligence: existential, "the proclivity to pose
(and ponder) questions about life, death, and ultimate
realities" (72).
```

```
Susana Urbina, who surveyed many studies about
intelligence, found that intelligence "is such a
multifaceted concept that no single quality can define
it . . ." (1130).
```

28c Are quotation marks used with long quotations?

No. With a long DIRECT QUOTATION, don't use quotation marks. In MLA STYLE, a quotation is *long* if it occupies more than four typed lines. Instead of quotation marks with a long quotation, you indent all its lines as a block (that is, the quotation is "set off" or "displayed"). This format makes quotation marks unnecessary. Give DOCUMENTATION information after the long quotation and after the period that ends the quotation.

LONG QUOTATIONS

```
Gardner uses criteria by which to judge whether an
ability deserves to be categorized as an "intelligence."
Each must confer
            a set of skills of problem solving--enabling
        the individual to resolve genuine problems or
        difficulties [author's emphasis] that he or she
        encounters and laying the groundwork for the
        acquisition of new knowledge. (Frames 60-61)
```

In the Gardner example above, note that a capital letter is *not* used to start the quotation. The lead-in words (*Each must confer*) are an incomplete sentence, so they need the quotation to complete the sentence.

```
Goleman also emphasizes a close interaction of the
emotional and rational states with the other
intelligences that Gardner has identified:
            These two minds, the emotional and the
        rational, operate in tight harmony for the most
        part, intertwining their very different ways of
        knowing to guide us through the world.
```

> Ordinarily there is a balance between emotional
> and rational minds, with emotion feeding into
> and informing the operations of the rational
> mind, and the rational mind refining and
> sometimes vetoing the inputs of the
> emotions. (9)

In the Goleman example above, note that a capital letter starts the quotation because the lead-in words are a complete sentence. (A colon can—but isn't required to—end the lead-in sentence because it's an independent clause; see 26b.)

◉ **ALERT:** Whether a quotation is one word or occupies many lines, you are always required to DOCUMENT its SOURCE (Chapters 31 through 37). Also, when you quote material, be very careful to record the words exactly as they appear in the original.●

28d How do I use quotation marks for quotations within quotations?

In MLA STYLE, practice varies between short and long quotations when a quotation contains internal quotation marks. In short quotations of poetry, use single quotation marks for any internal quotation marks, and use double quotation marks for the entire quotation. Give DOCUMENTATION information after the entire quotation, before the sentence's ending period.

In long quotations of poetry—those that are displayed (set off in a block) and not enclosed in quotation marks—keep the double quotation marks as they appear in the original. Give DOCUMENTATION information after the long quotation and after the period that ends the quotation.

Short quotations: Use single within double quotation marks

With short quotations, the double quotation marks show the beginning and end of words taken from the source; the single quotation marks replace double marks used in the source.

ORIGINAL SOURCE

Most scientists concede that they don't really know what "intelligence" is. Whatever it might be, paper and pencil tests aren't the tenth of it.

—Brent Staples, "The IQ Cult," p. 293

STUDENT'S USE OF THE SOURCE

Brent Staples argues in his essay about IQ as object of
reverence: "Most scientists concede that they don't

```
really know what 'intelligence' is. Whatever it might be,
paper and pencil tests aren't the tenth of it" (293).
```

Long quotations: Use quotation marks as in source

All long quotations must be set off (displayed) without being enclosed in quotation marks. Therefore, you will show any double and single quotation marks exactly as the source does.

28e How do I use quotation marks for quotations of poetry and dialogue?

Poetry

A quotation of poetry is *short* if it includes three lines or fewer of the poem. As with prose quotations (28d), use double quotation marks to enclose the material. If the poetry lines have internal double quotation marks, change them to single quotation marks. To show when a line of poetry breaks to the next line, use a slash (/) with one space on each side. Give DOCUMENTATION information after a short poetry quotation, before the period that ends the sentence.

As Auden wittily defined personal space, "some thirty inches from my nose / The frontier of my person goes" (*Complete*, 205).

A quotation of poetry is *long* if it includes more than three lines of the poem. As with prose quotations (28d), indent all lines as a block, without quotation marks to enclose the material. Start new lines exactly as they appear in your source. Give documentation information after the long quotation and after the period that ends the quotation.

ALERT: When you quote lines of poetry, follow the capitalization of your source.●

Dialogue

Dialogue, also called DIRECT DISCOURSE, presents a speaker's exact words. Enclose direct discourse in quotation marks. In contrast, INDIRECT DISCOURSE reports what a speaker said. Don't enclose indirect discourse in quotation marks. In addition to these differences in punctuation, PRONOUN use and VERB TENSES also differ for these two types of discourse.

DIRECT DISCOURSE   The mayor said, **"I intend** to veto that bill.**"**
INDIRECT DISCOURSE   The mayor said that **he intended** to veto that bill.

Whether you're reporting the words of a real speaker or making up dialogue in a short story, use double quotation marks at the beginning and end of a speaker's words. This tells your reader which words are the speaker's. Also, start a new paragraph each time the speaker changes.

> "I don't know how you can see to drive," she said.
> "Maybe you should put on your glasses."
> "Putting on my glasses would help you to see?"
> "Not me; you," Macon said. "You're focused on the windshield instead of the road."
>
> —Anne Tyler, *The Accidental Tourist*

In American English, if two or more paragraphs are needed for a single speaker's words, use double opening quotation marks at the start of each paragraph, but save the closing double quotation marks until the end of the last quoted paragraph.

EXERCISE 28-1

Decide whether each sentence below is direct or indirect discourse and then rewrite each sentence in the other form. Make any changes needed for grammatical correctness. With direct discourse, put the speaker's words wherever you think they belong in the sentence. For help, consult 28b through 28e.

EXAMPLE   A medical doctor told some newspaper reporters that he was called into a television studio one day to treat a sick actor.

> *A medical doctor told some newspaper reporters, "I was called into a television studio one day to treat a sick actor."*

1. The doctor was told that he would find his patient on the set of *Side Effects,* a new television series that takes place in a hospital.
2. On his arrival at the television studio, the doctor announced, "I'm Dr. Gatley, and I'm looking for *Side Effects."*
3. The studio security guard asked him if he meant to say that he was auditioning for the part of Dr. Gatley in *Side Effects.*
4. The visitor insisted that he really was Dr. Gatley.
5. The security guard whispered, "I like your attitude. With such self-confidence, you're sure to go far in television."

28f   How do quotation marks operate with titles of short works?

When you refer to certain short works by their titles, enclose the titles in quotation marks (other works, usually longer, need to be in italics or underlined; see 30g). Short works include short stories, essays, poems, articles from periodicals, pamphlets, brochures, songs, and individual episodes of a series on television or radio.

◎ **ALERT:** When placing the title of your own piece of writing on a title page or at the top of a page, never use quotation marks. ●

> What is the rhyme scheme of Andrew Marvell's "Delight in Disorder"?
> [poem]
> Have you read "The Lottery"? [short story]
> The best source I found is "The Myth of Political Consultants."
> [magazine article]
> "Shooting an Elephant" describes George Orwell's experiences in
> Burma. [essay]

Titles of some other works are neither enclosed in quotation marks nor written in italics or underlined. For guidelines, see Box 121 in 30e and Box 122 in 30g.

🖳 **COMPUTER TIP:** Most computer word processing programs allow you to use italics, or to underline, whichever words you indicate. Choose italics or underlining consistently in a piece of writing. (If handwriting or using a typewriter, underlining is the equivalent of italics.)◧

EXERCISE 28-2

Correct any misuses of quotation marks. If you think a sentence is correct, explain why. For help, consult 28f.

1. In her short story The Lady from Lucknow, Bharati Mukherjee describes a visitor from India who resents being treated as an exotic object.

2. Although his poem The Red Wheelbarrow contains only sixteen words, William Carlos Williams creates in it both a strong visual image and a sense of mystery.

3. With her soulful singing and relaxed gestures, Billie Holiday gave a bare television studio the atmosphere of a smoky jazz club in The Sound of Jazz. The program was broadcast in 1957 as part of the television series *The Seven Lively Arts.*

4. Woody Guthrie wrote This Land Is Your Land as both a hymn to a vast continent and a song of protest against the selfish misuse of its resources.

5. In her essay "The Imagination of Disaster, Susan Sontag writes that viewers of disaster movies like to see how these movies succeed in "making a mess"—especially if the mess includes the make-believe destruction of a big city.

28g How do I use quotation marks for words used in special senses?

When you refer to a word as a word, you can choose to either enclose it in quotation marks or put it in italics (or use underlining). Whichever you choose, be consistent throughout each piece of writing.

NO Many people confuse affect and effect.

YES Many people confuse "affect" and "effect."

YES Many people confuse *affect* and *effect*.

Always put quotation marks around the English translation of a word or PHRASE. Also, use italics (or underlining) for the word or phrase in the other language.

My grandfather usually ended arguments with *de gustibus non disputandum est* ("there is no disputing about tastes").

Many writers use quotation marks around words or phrases meant ironically or in other nonliteral ways.

The proposed tax "reform" is actually a tax increase.

Some writers put technical terms in quotation marks and define them—but only the first time they appear. Don't use quotation marks after the terms have been introduced and defined.

"Plagiarism"—the undocumented use of another person's words or ideas—can result in expulsion. Plagiarism is a serious offense.

At times, writers put quotation marks around words that they sense might be inappropriate for ACADEMIC WRITING, such as a SLANG term or a CLICHÉ used intentionally to make a point. If possible, use different language—not quotation marks—in these cases. Take the time to think of accurate, appropriate, and fresh words instead. If you prefer to stick with the slang or cliché, use quotation marks.

They "eat like birds" in public, but they "stuff their faces" in private.

They **eat almost nothing** in public, but they **eat hefty heaps of food** in private.

A nickname doesn't call for quotation marks, unless you use the nickname along with the full name. When a person's nickname is widely known, you do not have to give both the nickname and the full name. For example, use *Senator Ted Kennedy* or *Senator Edward Kennedy*, whichever is appropriate in context. Because he's well known, don't use *Senator Edward "Ted" Kennedy*.

EXERCISE 28-3

Correct any misuses of quotation marks. If you think a sentence is correct, explain why. For help, consult 28g.

EXAMPLE   *Bossa nova,* Portuguese for new wave, is the name of both a dance and a musical style originating in Brazil.

Bossa nova, Portuguese for "new wave," is the name of both a dance and a musical style originating in Brazil.

1. To Freud, the "superego" is the part of the personality that makes moral demands on a person. The "superego" is the third of Freud's three elements of personality.
2. Although many people believe the old adage "Where there's a will, there's a way," psychologists say that to get results, willingness must be combined with ability and effort.
3. "Observation" and "empathy" are two of the chief qualities that mark the work of the Dutch painter Rembrandt.
4. *Casbah,* an Arabic word meaning fortress, is the name given to the oldest part of many North African cities.
5. "Flammable" and *inflammable* are a curious pair of words that once had the same meaning but today are often considered opposites.

28h How do quotation marks operate with other punctuation?

Commas and periods with quotation marks

A comma or period that is grammatically necessary is always placed inside the closing quotation mark.

Jessica enjoyed F. Scott Fitzgerald's story "The Freshest Boy," so she was eager to read his novels. [comma before closing quotation mark]

Max said, "Don't stand so far away from me." [comma before opening quotation mark (24j.5); period before closing quotation mark]

Edward T. Hall coined the word "proxemia." [period before closing quotation mark]

Semicolons and colons with quotation marks

A semicolon or colon is placed outside the closing quotation mark, unless it is part of the quotation.

Computers offer businesses "opportunities that never existed before"; some workers disagree. [semicolon after closing quotation mark]

We have to know each culture's standard for "how close is close": No one wants to offend. [colon after closing quotation mark]

Question marks, exclamation points, and dashes with quotation marks

If the punctuation marks belong to the words enclosed in quotation marks, put them inside the quotation marks.

"Did I Hear You Call My Name?" was the winning song.

"I've won the lottery!" Arielle shouted.

"Who's there? Why don't you ans—"

If a question mark, an exclamation point, or a dash doesn't belong to the material being quoted, put the punctuation outside the quotation marks.

Have you read Nikki Giovanni's poem "Knoxville, Tennessee"?

If only I could write a story like David Wallace's "Girl with Curious Hair"!

Weak excuses—a classic is "I have to visit my grandparents"—change little.

When you use quotation marks and want to know how they work with capital letters, see 30d; with brackets, 29c; with ellipsis points, 29d; and with the slash, 29e.

28i When are quotation marks wrong?

Don't enclose a word in quotation marks to call attention to it, to intensify it, or to be sarcastic.

NO I'm "very" happy about the news.

YES I'm very happy about the news.

Don't enclose the title of your paper in quotation marks (nor underline it). However, if the title of your paper contains another title that requires quotation marks, use them only for the included title.

NO "The Elderly in Nursing Homes: A Case Study"

YES The Elderly in Nursing Homes: A Case Study

NO Character Development in Shirley Jackson's Story The Lottery

YES Character Development in Shirley Jackson's Story "The Lottery"

EXERCISE 28-4

Correct any errors in the use of quotation marks and other punctuation with quotation marks. If you think a sentence is correct, explain why. For help, consult 28e through 28i.

1. Dying in a shabby hotel room, the witty writer Oscar Wilde supposedly said, "Either that wallpaper goes, or I do".

2. Was it the Russian novelist Tolstoy who wrote, "All happy families resemble one another, but each unhappy family is unhappy in its own way?"

3. In his poem A Supermarket in California, Allen Ginsberg addresses the dead poet Walt Whitman, asking, Where are we going, Walt Whitman? The doors close / in an hour. Which way does your beard point tonight?

4. Toni Morrison made this reply to the claim that "art that has a political message cannot be good art:" She said that "the best art is political" and that her aim was to create art that was "unquestionably political" and beautiful at the same time.

5. Benjamin Franklin's strange question—"What is the use of a newborn child?—" was his response to someone who doubted the usefulness of new inventions.

29 OTHER PUNCTUATION MARKS

This chapter explains the uses of the **dash, parentheses, brackets, ellipsis points,** and the **slash.** These punctuation marks aren't used often, but each serves a purpose and gives you options with your writing style.

DASH

29a When can I use a dash in my writing?

The **dash,** or a pair of dashes, lets you interrupt a sentence to add information. Such interruptions can fall in the middle or at the end of a sentence. To make a dash, hit the hyphen key twice (--). Do not put a space before, between, or after the hyphens. Some word processing programs automatically convert two hyphens into a dash; either form is correct. In print, the dash appears as an unbroken line approximately the length of two hyphens joined together (—). If you handwrite, make the dash at least twice as long as a hyphen.

29a.1 Using a dash or dashes for special emphasis

If you want to emphasize an example, a definition, an APPOSITIVE, or a contrast, you can use a dash or dashes. Some call a dash "a pregnant pause"—that is, take note, something special is coming. Use dashes sparingly so that you don't dilute their impact.

EXAMPLE

The care-takers—those who are helpers, nurturers, teachers, mothers—are still systematically devalued.

—Ellen Goodman, "Just Woman's Work?"

DEFINITION

Although the emphasis at the school was mainly language—speaking, reading, writing—the lessons always began with an exercise in politeness.

—Elizabeth Wong, *Fifth Chinese Daughter*

APPOSITIVE

Two of the strongest animals in the jungle are vegetarians—the elephant and the gorilla.

—Dick Gregory, *The Shadow That Scares Me*

CONTRAST

Fire cooks food—and burns down forests.

—Smokey the Bear

Place what you emphasize with dashes next to or nearby the material it refers to so that what you want to accomplish with your emphasis is not lost.

NO   The current **argument is**—one that faculty, students, and coaches debate fiercely—whether to hold athletes to the same academic standards as others face.

YES   The current **argument**—one that faculty, students, and coaches debate fiercely—**is** whether to hold athletes to the same academic standards as others face.

29a.2 Using a dash or dashes to emphasize an aside

An **aside** is a writer's comment, often the writer's personal views, on what's been written. Generally, this technique isn't appropriate for ACADEMIC WRITING, so before you insert an aside, carefully consider your writing PURPOSE and your AUDIENCE.

Television showed us the war. It showed us the war in a way that was—if you chose to watch television, at least—unavoidable.

—Nora Ephron, *Scribble Scribble*

👁 **ALERTS:** (1) If the words within a pair of dashes require a question mark or an exclamation point, place it before the second dash: *A first date—do you remember?—stays in the memory forever.* (2) Never use commas, semicolons, or periods next to dashes. If such a need arises, revise your writing. (3) Don't enclose quotation marks in dashes except when the meaning requires them. These two examples show that, when required, the dash stops before or after the quotation marks; the two punctuation marks do not overlap: *Many of George Orwell's essays—"A Hanging," for example—draw on his experiences as a civil servant. "Shooting an Elephant"—another Orwell essay—appears in many anthologies.* ●

EXERCISE 29-1

Write a sentence about each topic, shown in italics. Use dashes to set off what is asked for, shown in roman, in each sentence, For help, consult 29a.

EXAMPLE *health,* a definition

> *Anorexia nervosa—an eating disorder characterized by an obsession with losing weight—*is common among young gymnasts and ballet dancers.

1. *television program,* a contrast
2. *politician,* an appositive
3. *food,* an aside
4. *music,* an example
5. *a sport,* a definition
6. *a fact,* an example

PARENTHESES

29b When can I use parentheses in my writing?

Parentheses let you interrupt a sentence to add various kinds of information. Parentheses are like dashes (29a) in that they set off extra or interrupting words—but unlike dashes which emphasize material, parentheses de-emphasize what they enclose. Use parentheses sparingly because overusing them can make your writing lurch, not flow. Also, they tend to be very distracting for readers.

29b.1 Using parentheses to enclose interrupting words

EXPLANATION

After they've finished with the pantry, the medicine cabinet, and the attic, they will throw out the red geranium (too many leaves), sell the dog (too many fleas), and send the children off to boarding school (too many scuffmarks on the hardwood floors).

—Suzanne Britt, "Neat People vs. Sloppy People"

EXAMPLE

Though other cities (Dresden, for instance) had been utterly destroyed in World War II, never before had a single weapon been responsible for such destruction.

—Laurence Behrens and Leonard J. Rosen,
Writing and Reading Across the Curriculum

ASIDE

The older girls (non-graduates, of course) were assigned the task of making refreshments for the night's festivities.

—Maya Angelou, *I Know Why the Caged Bird Sings*

The sheer decibel level of the noise around us is not enough to make us cranky, irritable, or aggressive. (It can, however, affect our mental and physical health, which is another matter.)

—Carol Tavris, *Anger: The Misunderstood Emotion*

29b.2 Using parentheses for listed items

When you number listed items within a sentence, enclose the numbers (or letters) in parentheses.

Four items are on the agenda for tonight's meeting: (1) current membership figures, (2) current treasury figures, (3) the budget for renovations, and (4) the campaign for soliciting additional public contributions.

👁 **PUNCTUATION ALERTS:** For listed items that fall within a sentence, (1) use a colon before a list only if the list is preceded by an INDEPENDENT CLAUSE (see 26b and 26e), and (2) use commas or semicolons to separate the items, but be consistent within a piece of writing. If, however, if any item contains punctuation itself, use a semicolon to separate the items. ●

In legal writing and in some BUSINESS WRITING, you can use parentheses to enclose a numeral that repeats a spelled-out number.

The monthly rent is three hundred fifty dollars ($350).
Your order of fifteen (15) gross was shipped today.

In ACADEMIC WRITING, especially in subjects in which the use of figures or measurements is frequent, enclose alternative or comparative forms of the same number in parentheses, as in *2 mi (3.2 km).*

29b.3 Using other punctuation with parentheses

When a complete sentence enclosed in parentheses stands alone, start it with a capital letter and end it with a period. When a sentence in parentheses falls within another sentence, don't start with a capital or end with a period.

NO   Looking for his car keys (He had left them at my sister's house.) wasted an entire hour.

YES   Looking for his car keys (he had left them at my sister's house) wasted an entire hour.

YES   Looking for his car keys wasted an entire hour. (He had left them at my sister's house.)

Never put a comma before an opening parenthesis. If the material before the parenthetical material requires a comma, place that comma after the closing parenthesis.

NO   Although clearly different from my favorite film, (*The Wizard of Oz*) *Gone with the Wind* is also outstanding.

YES   Although clearly different from my favorite film (*The Wizard of Oz*), *Gone with the Wind* is also outstanding.

You can use a question mark or an exclamation point within parentheses that occur in a sentence.

Looking for clues (what did we expect to find?) wasted four days.

Never use quotation marks around parentheses that come before or after any quoted words.

NO   Alberta Hunter "(Down Hearted Blues)" is known for singing jazz.

YES   Alberta Hunter ("Down Hearted Blues") is known for singing jazz.

BRACKETS

29c When should I use brackets in my writing?

Brackets allow you to enclose words you need to insert into quotations, but only in the specific cases discussed below.

29c.1 Adjusting a quotation with brackets

When you use a quotation, you might need to either change the form of a word (a verb's tense, for example), add a brief definition, or fit the quotation into the grammatical structure of your sentence. In such cases, enclose the material you have inserted into the quotation in brackets. (These examples use MLA STYLE for PARENTHETICAL REFERENCES; 35b.)

ORIGINAL SOURCE

Current research shows that successful learning takes place in an active environment.

—Deborah Moore, "Facilities and Learning Styles," p. 22

QUOTATION WITH BRACKETS

Deborah Moore supports a student-centered curriculum and agrees with "current research [which] shows that successful learning takes place in an active environment."

ORIGINAL SOURCE

The logic of the mind is *associative;* it takes elements that symbolize a reality, or trigger a memory of it, to be the same as that reality.

—Daniel Goleman, *Emotional Intelligence,* p. 294

QUOTATION WITH BRACKETS

The kinds of intelligence are based in the way the mind functions: "The logic of the mind is *associative* [one idea connects with another]; it takes elements that symbolize a reality, or trigger a memory of it, to be the same as that reality" (Goleman 294).

29c.2 Using brackets to point out an error in a source or to add information within parentheses

In words you want to quote, sometimes page-makeup technicians or authors make a mistake without realizing it—a wrong date, a misspelled word, or an error of fact. You fix that mistake by putting your correction in brackets, without changing the words you want to quote. This tells your readers that the error was in the original work and not made by you.

[*sic*]

Insert *sic* in italics, enclosed in brackets, to show your readers that you've quoted an error accurately. *Sic* is a Latin word that means "so," or "thus," which says "It is so (or thus) in the original."

ERROR

A journalist wrote, "The judge accepted an [*sic*] plea of not guilty.

MISSPELLING

The building inspector wrote about the consequence of doubling the apartment's floor space: "With that much extra room per person, the tennants [*sic*] would sublet."

Very brief parenthetical material inside parentheses

Use brackets to insert information within a parentheses.

That expression (first used in *A Fable for Critics* [1848] by James R. Lowell) was popularized in the early twentieth century by Ella Wheeler Wilcox.

ELLIPSIS POINTS

29d How should I use ellipsis points in my writing?

The word *ellipsis* means "omission." **Ellipsis points** in writing are a series of three spaced dots (use the period key on the keyboard). You're required to use ellipsis points to indicate you've intentionally omitted words—perhaps even a sentence or more—from the source you're quoting. These rules apply to both prose and poetry.

The *MLA Handbook* no longer recommends that ellipsis points you have inserted be enclosed in brackets to make it clear to your reader that the omission is yours. See the insert at the end of this book for more information.

29d.1 Using ellipsis points with prose

ORIGINAL SOURCE

These two minds, the emotional and the rational, operate in tight harmony for the most part, intertwining their very different ways of knowing to guide us through the world. Ordinarily, there is a balance between emotional and rational minds, with emotion feeding into and informing the operations of the rational mind, and the rational mind refining and sometimes vetoing the inputs of the emotions. Still, the emotional and rational minds are semi-independent faculties, each, as we shall see, reflecting the operation of distinct, but interconnected, circuitry in the brain.

—Daniel Goleman, *Emotional Intelligence,* p. 9

QUOTATION OF SELECTED WORDS, NO ELLIPSIS NEEDED

Goleman explains that the "two minds, the emotional and the rational" usually provide "a balance" in our daily observations and decision making (9).

QUOTATION WITH ELLIPSIS MID-SENTENCE

Goleman emphasizes the connections between parts of the mind: "Still, the emotional and rational minds are semi-independent faculties, each . . . reflecting the operation of distinct, but interconnected, circuitry in the brain (9).

QUOTATION WITH ELLIPSIS AND PARENTHETICAL REFERENCE

Goleman emphasizes that "These two minds, the emotional and the rational, operate in tight harmony for the most part . . ." (9). [*Note:* In MLA-style, place a sentence-ending period after the parenthetical reference.]

QUOTATION WITH ELLIPSIS ENDING THE SENTENCE

On page 9, Goleman states: "These two minds, the emotional and the rational, operate in tight harmony for the most part. . . ."

QUOTATION WITH SENTENCE OMITTED

Goleman explains that "These two minds, the emotional and the rational, operate in tight harmony for the most part.

```
. . . Still, the emotional and rational minds are
semi-independent faculties" (9).
```

**QUOTATION WITH WORDS OMITTED FROM THE MIDDLE OF ONE SENTENCE
TO THE MIDDLE OF ANOTHER**

```
Goleman states: "Ordinarily, there is a balance between
emotional and rational minds . . . reflecting the
operation of distinct, but interconnected, circuitry in
the brain" (9).
```

**QUOTATION WITH WORDS OMITTED FROM THE MIDDLE OF ONE SENTENCE
TO A COMPLETE OTHER SENTENCE**

```
Goleman explains: "These two minds, the emotional and the
rational, operate in tight harmony. . . . Still, the
emotional and rational minds are semi-independent faculties,
each, as we shall see, reflecting the operation of distinct,
but interconnected, circuitry in the brain" (9).
```

When you omit words from a quotation, you also omit punctuation related to those words, unless the punctuation keeps the sentence correct.

```
Goleman explains: "These two minds . . . operate in tight
harmony" (9). [comma in original source omitted after minds]
```

```
Goleman explains that the emotional and rational minds work
together while, "Still, . . . each, as we shall see,
[reflects] the operation of distinct, but interconnected,
circuitry in the brain" (9). [comma kept after Still because it's an
introductory word; form of reflecting changed for sense of sentence, as in 29c.1]
```

29d.2 Using ellipsis points with poetry

When you omit one or more words from a line of poetry, follow the rules for prose, above. However, when you omit a full line or more from poetry, use a full line of spaced dots.

ORIGINAL SOURCE

Hush-a-bye baby,
Upon the tree top,
When the wind blows
The cradle will rock;
When the bough breaks,
The cradle will fall,
And down will come baby,
Cradle and all.

QUOTATION WITH LINES OMITTED

Hush-a-bye baby,
Upon the tree top,
. . . .
And down will come baby,
Cradle and all.

SLASH

29e When can I use a slash in my writing?

The **slash** (/), also called a *virgule* or *solidus*, is a diagonal line that separates or joins in special circumstances.

29e.1 Using a slash to separate quoted lines of poetry

When you quote more than three lines of a poem, no slash is involved; you merely follow the rules in 29d. When you quote three lines or fewer, enclose them in quotation marks and run them into your sentence—and use a slash to divide one line from the next. Leave a space on each side of the slash.

> One of my mottos comes from the beginning of Anne Sexton's poem "Words": "Be careful of words, **/** even the miraculous ones."

Capitalize and punctuate each line of poetry as in the original—but even if the quoted line of poetry doesn't have a period, use one to end your sentence. If your quotation ends before the line of poetry ends, use ellipsis points (29d).

29e.2 Using a slash for numerical fractions in typed manuscripts

To type numerical fractions, use a slash (with no space before or after the slash) to separate the numerator and denominator. In mixed numbers—that is, whole numbers with fractions—leave a space between the whole number and its fraction: 1 2/3, 3 7/8. (For information about using spelled-out and numerical forms of numbers, see 30o.)

29e.3 Using a slash for *and/or*

When writing in the humanities, try not to use word combinations connected with a slash, such as *and/or*. In academic disciplines in which such combinations are acceptable, separate the words with a slash. Leave no space before or after the slash. In the humanities, listing both alternatives in normal sentence structure is usually better than separating choices with a slash.

NO The best quality of reproduction comes from 35-mm slides/direct-positive films.

YES The best quality of reproduction comes from 35-mm slides **or** direct-positive films.

EXERCISE 29-2

Supply needed dashes, parentheses, brackets, ellipsis points, and slashes. If a sentence is correct as written, circle its number. In some sentences, when you can use either dashes or parentheses, explain your choice. For help, consult all sections of this chapter.

EXAMPLE   Two tiny islands in the English Channel Jersey and Guernsey have breeds of cows named after them.

Two tiny islands in the English Channel—Jersey and Guernsey—have breeds of cows named after them.

1. In *The Color Purple* a successful movie as well as a novel, Alice Walker explores the relationships between women and men in traditional African American culture.
2. W. C. Fields offered two pieces of advice on job hunting: 1 never show up for an interview in bare feet, and 2 don't read your prospective employer's mail while he is questioning you about your qualifications.
3. A series of resolutions was passed 11–0 with one council member abstaining calling on the mayor and the district attorney to improve safety conditions and step up law enforcement on city buses.
4. All the interesting desserts ice cream, chocolate fudge cake, pumpkin pie with whipped cream are fattening, unfortunately.
5. Thunder is caused when the flash of lightning heats the air around it to temperatures up to 30,000°F 16,666°C.
6. Christina Rossetti wonders if the end of a life also means the end of love in a poem that opens with these two lines: "When I am dead, my dearest, Sing no sad songs for me."
7. After the internationally famous racehorse Dan Patch died suddenly from a weak heart, his devoted owner, Will Savage, died of the same condition a mere 32 1/2 hours later.
8. In his famous letter from the Birmingham jail on April 16, 1963, Martin Luther King Jr. wrote: "You the eight clergymen who had urged him not to hold a protest deplore the demonstrations taking place in Birmingham."
9. The world's most expensive doll house sold for $256,000 at a London auction contains sixteen rooms, a working chamber organ, and a silver clothes press but no toilet.
10. The person renting this apartment agrees to pay seven hundred fifty dollars $750 per month in rent.

11. Railroad entrepreneur George Francis Train his real name! dreamed of creating a chain of great cities across the United States, all connected by his Union Pacific Railroad.

12. Patients who pretend to have ailments are known to doctors as "Munchausens" after Baron Karl Friedrich Hieronymus von Münchhausen he was a German army officer who had a reputation for wild and unbelievable tales.

EXERCISE 29-3

Follow the directions for each item. For help, consult all sections of this chapter.

EXAMPLE   Write a sentence about getting something right using dashes.

> *I tried and failed, I tried and failed again—and then I did it.*

1. Write a sentence that quotes only three lines of the following sonnet by William Shakespeare:

> Let me not to the marriage of true minds
> Admit impediments. Love is not love
> Which alters when it alteration finds,
> Or bends with the remover to remove.
> O, no! it is an ever-fixèd mark
> That looks on tempests and is never shaken;
> It is the star to every wand'ring bark,
> Whose worth's unknown, although his height be taken.
> Love's not Time's fool, though rosy lips and cheeks
> Within his bending sickle's compass come;
> Love alters not with his brief hours and weeks,
> But bears it out even to the edge of doom.
>   If this be error, and upon me proved,
>   I never writ, nor no man ever loved.

2. Write a sentence using parentheses to enclose a brief example.

3. Write a sentence using dashes to set off a definition.

4. Write a sentence that includes four numbered items in a list.

5. Quote a few sentences from any source you choose. Omit words without losing meaning or use brackets to insert words to maintain meaning or grammatical structure. Use ellipsis points to indicate the omission, and place the parenthetical reference where it belongs.

30 CAPITALS, ITALICS, ABBREVIATIONS, AND NUMBERS

CAPITALS

30a When do I capitalize a "first" word?

First word in a sentence

Always capitalize the first letter of the first word in a sentence.

Four inches of snow fell last winter.

A series of questions

If questions in a series are complete sentences, start each with a capital letter. If, however, the questions aren't complete sentences, you can choose to capitalize or not. Whatever your choice, be consistent in each piece of writing. In this handbook, I use capitals for a series of questions.

What facial feature would most people like to change? **E**yes? **E**ars? **N**ose?

What facial feature would most people like to change? **e**yes? **e**ars? **n**ose?

Small words in titles or headings

Capitalize small words (*the, a, an* and short PREPOSITIONS, such as *with, of, to*) in a title or heading only when they begin the title or when the source capitalizes these small words.

Always capitalize *I*, no matter where it falls in a sentence or group of words: ***I** love you now, although **I** didn't used to.* The same holds for *O*, the INTERJECTION: *You are, **O** my fair love, a burning fever; **O my** gentle love, embrace me.* In contrast, never capitalize the interjection *oh*, unless it starts a sentence or is capitalized in words you're quoting.

After a colon

When a complete sentence follows a colon, you can choose to start that sentence with either a capital or a lowercase letter, but be consistent in each piece of writing. When the words after a colon are not a complete sentence, do not capitalize.

She reacted instantly: **S**he picked up the ice cream and pushed it back into her cone.

She reacted instantly: **s**he picked up the ice cream and pushed it back into her cone.

She bought four pints of ice cream: **v**anilla, chocolate, strawberry, and butter pecan.

👁 **ALERT:** A colon can follow only a complete sentence (an INDEPEN-DENT CLAUSE; see 26a). ●

Formal outline

In a formal outline (2r), start each item with a capital letter. Use a period only when the item is a complete sentence.

30b When do I use capitals with listed items?

A list run into a sentence

If run-in listed items (see below) are complete sentences, start each with a capital and end each with a period (or question mark or exclamation point). If the run-in listed items are incomplete sentences, start each with a lowercase letter and end each with a comma—unless the items already contain commas, in which case use semicolons. If you list three or more items that are incomplete sentences, use *and* before the last item.

YES We found three reasons for the delay: (1) **B**ad weather held up delivery of materials. (2) **P**oor scheduling created confusion. (3) **I**mproper machine maintenance caused an equipment failure**.**

YES The reasons for the delay were (1) **b**ad weather**,** (2) **p**oor scheduling**, and** (3) **e**quipment failure.

YES The reasons for the delay were (1) **b**ad weather, which had been predicted**;** (2) **p**oor scheduling, which is the airline's responsibility**; and** (3) **e**quipment failure, which no one can predict**.**

A displayed list

In a displayed list, each item starts on a new line. If the items are sentences, capitalize the first letter and end with a period (or question mark or exclamation point). If the items are not sentences, you can use a capital letter or not. Whichever you choose, be consistent in each piece of writing. Punctuate a displayed list as you would a run-in list.

YES We found three reasons for the delay:
(1) **B**ad weather held up delivery of materials**.**
(2) **P**oor scheduling created confusion**.**
(3) **I**mproper machine maintenance caused an equipment failure**.**

YES The reasons for the delay were
(1) **b**ad weather**,**
(2) **p**oor scheduling**, and**
(3) **e**quipment failure**.**

◉ **ALERTS:** (1) If a complete sentence leads into a displayed list, you can end the sentence with a colon. However, if an incomplete sentence leads into a displayed list, use no punctuation. (2) Use PARALLELISM for items in a list. For example, if one item is a sentence, use sentences for all the items (18f); or if one item starts with a VERB, start all items with a verb in the same TENSE; and so on.●

30c When do I use capitals with sentences in parentheses?

When you write a complete sentence within parentheses that falls within another sentence, don't start with a capital or end with a period—but do use a question mark or exclamation point, if needed. When you write a sentence within parentheses that doesn't fall within another sentence, capitalize the first word and end with a period (or question mark or explanation point).

I did not know till years later that they called it the Cuban Missile Crisis. But I remember Castro. (**W**e called him Castor Oil and were awed by his beard**.**) We might not have worried so much (**w**hat would the communists want with our small New Hampshire town**?**) except we lived 10 miles from a U.S. air base.
—Joyce Maynard, "An 18-Year-Old Looks Back on Life"

30d When do I use capitals with quotations?

If a quotation within your sentence is itself less than a complete sentence, don't capitalize the first quoted word. If the quotation you have used in your sentence is itself a complete sentence, capitalize the first word.

Mrs. Enriquez says that students who are learning a new language should visit that country and "absorb a good accent with the food."
Mrs. Enriquez likes to point out that when students live in a new country, "**T**hey'll absorb a good accent with the food."

When you write DIRECT DISCOURSE—which you introduce with verbs such as *said, stated, reported,* and others (see 31f) followed by a comma (see 24h)—capitalize the first letter of the quoted words only if it's capitalized in the original. However, don't capitalize a partial quotation, and don't capitalize the continuation of a one-sentence quotation within your sentence.

> Mrs. Enriquez said, "**S**tudents who are learning a new language should visit that country. They'll absorb a good accent with the food."

> Mrs. Enriquez told me that the best way to "**a**bsorb a good accent" in a language is to visit the country and eat its food.

> "Of course," she continued with a smile, "**t**he accent lasts longer than the food."

30e   When do I capitalize nouns and adjectives?

Capitalize PROPER NOUNS (nouns that name specific people, places, and things): *Abraham Lincoln, Mexico, World Wide Web.* Also, capitalize **proper adjectives** (adjectives formed from proper nouns): *a Mexican entrepreneur, a Web address.* Don't capitalize ARTICLES (*the, a, an*) that accompany proper nouns and proper adjectives, unless they start a sentence.

When a proper noun or adjective loses its very specific "proper" association, it also loses its capital letter: *french fries, pasteurized.* When you turn a common noun (*lake*) into a proper noun (*Lake Mead*), capitalize all words.

Expect sometimes that you'll see capitalized words that this handbook says not to capitalize. For example, a corporation's written communications usually capitalize their own entities (*our Board of Directors* or *this Company*), even though the rule calls for lowercase (*the board of directors, the company*). Similarly, the administrators of your school might write *the Faculty* and *the College* (or *the University*), even though the rule calls for a lowercase *f, c,* and *u.* How writers capitalize can depend on AUDIENCE and PURPOSE in each specific context.

Box 121 is a capitalization guide. If you don't find what you need, locate an item in it (or in Box 122) that's close to what you want, and use it as a model.

⊙ **Capitalization guide**		121
	CAPITALS	**LOWERCASE LETTERS**
NAMES	Mother Teresa (*also,* used as names: Mother, Dad, Mom, Pa)	my mother [relationship]
	Doc Holliday	the doctor [role] →

Capitalization guide *(continued)* 121

	CAPITALS	LOWERCASE LETTERS
TITLES	President Truman	the president
	Democrat [party member]	democrat [believer in democracy]
	Representative Patsy Mink	the congressional representative
	Senator Edward M. Kennedy	a senator
	Queen Elizabeth II	the queen
PEOPLE	Caucasian [race]	white (*also* White)
	African American, Hispanic, Latino [ethnic group]	black (*also* Black)
	Irish, Korean, Lakota [nationality]	
	Jew, Catholic, Protestant, Buddhist [religious affiliation]	
ORGANIZATIONS	Department of State	the department
	the Ohio State Supreme Court	the state supreme court
	the Republican Party	the party
	Ford Motor Company	the company
	Los Angeles Lakers	basketball team
	American Medical Association	professional group
	Sigma Chi	fraternity
	Alcoholics Anonymous	self-help group
PLACES	Dallas	the city
	the South [region]	turn south [direction]
	the West Coast	the coast
	Main Street	the street
	Atlantic Ocean	the ocean
	the Black Hills	the hills

→

Capitalization guide *(continued)* 121

	CAPITALS	LOWERCASE LETTERS
BUILDINGS	the Capitol (in Washington, DC) Ace High School Front Road Café Highland Hospital	the state capitol [building] a high school a restaurant a hospital
SCIENTIFIC TERMS	Earth [as one of nine planets] the Milky Way, the Galaxy [as name] *Streptococcus aureus* Gresham's law	the earth [otherwise] our galaxy, the moon a streptococcal infection the theory of relativity
LANGUAGES	Spanish, Chinese	
SCHOOL COURSES	Chemistry 342 English 111 Introduction to Photography	a chemistry course my English class a photography course
NAMES OF SPECIFIC THINGS	Black Parrot tulip Purdue University Heinz ketchup a Toyota Camry Twelfth Dynasty	climbing rose the university ketchup, sauce a car the dynasty
TIMES	Monday, Fri. September, February	today, the eighteenth century a month
SEASONS	Christmas season	spring, summer, autumn, winter, the fall semester
HOLIDAYS	Kwanzaa, New Year's Day Passover, Ramadan	feast day, the holiday religious holiday (*or* observance)

→

Capitalization guide *(continued)* 121

	CAPITALS	LOWERCASE LETTERS
HISTORICAL EVENTS AND DOCUMENTS	World War II	the war
	Battle of the Bulge	the battle
	the Roaring Twenties	the decade
	the Great Depression (of the 1930s)	the depression [any serious economic downturn]
	the Reformation	cultural movement
	Paleozoic	era or age, prehistory
	the Civil Rights Movement (of the 1960s)	a civil rights activist
	the Bill of Rights	fifth-century manuscripts
RELIGIOUS TERMS	God, Athena	a god, a goddess
	Islam	a religion
	the Torah, the Koran, the Bible,	a holy book
		biblical
	Scripture	scriptural
LETTER PARTS	Dear Ms. Carpenter:	
	Sincerely,	
	Yours truly,	
PUBLISHED AND RELEASED MATERIAL	"The Lottery"	[Capitalize first letter of first word and all other major words]
	A History of the United States to 1877	
	Jazz on Ice	the show, a performance
	Nixon Papers	the archives
	Mass in B Minor	the B minor mass
ACRONYMS AND INITIALISMS	NASA	
	NATO	
	AFL-CIO	

→

Capitalization guide *(continued)*   121

	CAPITALS	LOWERCASE LETTERS
COMPUTER TERMS	Gateway, Dell	high-tech company
	Microsoft Word, WordPerfect	software program [capitalize name per its manual]
	World Wide Web, the Web	
	the Internet	online
	Web site, Web page	a home page, a link
	America Online	a server
	LISTSERV (trademark software)	electronic mailing list
	Google	a search engine
		e-mail
	CD-ROM	
	COBOL	a computer language
	Netscape	a browser
		software (*or* computer) tool
PROPER ADJECTIVES	Victorian	southern
	Midwestern	transatlantic
	Indo-European	alpine

EXERCISE 30-1

Add capital letters as needed. See 30a through 30e for help.

1. When the philosopher Bertrand Russell was asked if he'd be willing to die for his beliefs, he replied, "of course not. After all, i may be wrong."
2. "Please hurry," pleaded Rebecca, "or we'll be late for the opening curtain of the san francisco ballet company."
3. The fine art course taught by professor Sanzio accepts only students who already have credits in fine art 101 and Renaissance studies 211.
4. Let's go, a series of guidebooks (they advise travelers about less touristy places), are found in thousands of backpacks and suitcases every summer.
5. Lovers of Mexican american food know there's far more to that cuisine than tacos and enchiladas.

6. At one point in the action, the script calls for the "assembled multitudes" to break into shouts of "hail, o merciful queen Tanya!"
7. How should we think of the start of the french revolution? Was it the best of times? the worst of times? a time of indecision, perhaps?
8. In the chapter "the making of a new world," among those credited with the european discovery of the americas before Columbus are (1) the vikings, (2) groups of fishers and whalers from europe, and (3) peoples who crossed the Bering strait to alaska in prehistoric times.
9. People sometimes forget that the bible was not originally written in english.
10. The organization of african unity (oau) was founded in 1962, when many african nations were winning their independence.

ITALICS

30f What are italics?

Italics is the name of the typeface (letter style) that slants to the right (*hello there*). In contrast, **roman** typeface is the most common type variant in print (you're looking at it right now). If you are handwriting or your word processing program doesn't give you the option of italics, underline instead. Italics and underlining mean the same thing in student writing.

ROMAN	your writing
ITALICS	*your writing*
UNDERLINED	your writing

30g How do I choose between using italics and quotation marks?

As a rule, use italics for titles of long works (*West Side Story*, a movie) or for works that contain subsections (*Twilight Zone*, a television show). Generally, use quotation marks for titles of shorter works ("I Wanna Hold Your Hand," a song) and for titles of subsections within a longer work (Chapter 1, "Loomings").

Box 122 is a guide for using italics, quotation marks, or nothing. If you don't find what you need, locate an item that is as much like what you want as possible and use it as a model.

Italics, quotation marks, or nothing   **122**

Titles

ITALICS	**QUOTATION MARKS OR NOTHING**
Sense and Sensibility [a novel]	Title of Student Essay
Death of a Salesman [a play]	act 2 [part of play]
The African Queen [a film]	the Epilogue [part of film or book]
Midwives	"The Last Leaf " [story in book]
Structured Reading [textbook]	"Darkness at Noon" [essay in book]
The Iliad [book-length poem]	"Whittling" [short poem]
Scientific American [a magazine]	"The Molecules of Life" [article in
Time magazine [title only]	magazine]
Symphonie Fantastique	Concerto in B-flat Minor [a musical
[long musical work]	work identified by form, number,
	and key]
The Best of Bob Dylan [a CD]	"Mr. Tambourine Man" [a song]
Kids Count [Web site title]	Excel [software program]
the *Los Angeles Times*	
[a newspaper]*	

Other Words

ITALICS	**QUOTATION MARKS OR NOTHING**
the *Intrepid* [a ship]	an aircraft carrier
H.M.S. *Pinafore* [only name,	
not preceding initials]	
Voyager 2 [specific name of	Boeing 747 [type of aircraft]
a spacecraft]	
summa cum laude [term from	burrito, chutzpah [commonly
another language]	understood non-English terms]
What does *odd* mean? [a word	"left out; different" [definitions or
referred to as a word]	translations]
the *ABCs*; confusing *3s* and *8s*	
[only letters and numbers	
referred to as themselves]	

* Even if *The* is part of a newspaper title, don't capitalize or italicize it. [In MLA-style and CM-style documentation, omit *The*. In APA-style, CO-style, and CBE-style documentation, keep *The*.]

30h Does documentation require underlining instead of italics?

For student papers DOCUMENTATION styles generally use only underlining, even if the rules usually call for italics (30f and 30g). This guideline holds for MLA (Chapter 35) and CM (*Chicago Manual of Style*, Chapter 37) documentation styles. APA style requires italics rather than underlining, unless your word processor does not easily produce italic typeface or your instructor requires underlining. For CSE-STYLE documentation (Council of Science Editors, Chapter 37), use neither underlining nor italics. For COS documentation (*Columbia Guide to Online Style*, Chapter 37), use italics since underlining typically indicates links in hypertext.

Note in MLA STYLE that the underline stops before any punctuation, whereas in APA STYLE underlining includes any punctuation. When using other documentation styles, check Chapter 37 or the respective style manuals. These guides are the *MLA Handbook for Writers of Research Papers* by Joseph Gibaldi (5th ed., 2000); *Publication Manual of the American Psychological Association* (5th ed., 2001); *The Chicago Manual of Style* (14th ed., 1993); *The CBE Manual for Authors, Editors, and Publishers* (6th ed., 1994), and *The Columbia Guide to Online Style* by Janice R. Walker and Todd Taylor (1998).

30i Can I use italics for special emphasis?

Some professional writers, especially writers of nonfiction and self-help material, occasionally use italics to clarify a meaning or stress a point. In ACADEMIC WRITING, however, you're expected to convey special emphasis through your choice of words and sentence structure (Chapter 19), not with italics (or underlining). If your message absolutely calls for it, use italics sparingly—and only after you are sure nothing else will do.

> Many people we *think* are powerful turn out on closer examination to be merely frightened and anxious.
>
> —Michael Korda, *Power!*

💻 **COMPUTER TIP:** In e-mail and other online communications, if you can't use italics or underlining, you can type an underscore before the first letter and after the last letter of the word(s) involved.▣

EXERCISE 30-2

Edit these sentences for correct use of italics (or underlining), quotation marks, and capitals. For help, consult 30a through 30i.

1. The article "the Banjo" in the Encyclopaedia Britannica calls the Banjo "America's only national instrument" because it combines the

traditional mbanza (a Bantu word native to certain southern areas of africa) and some European string instruments.

2. The writer of a humor column at a newspaper called The "Globe and Mail" has described an imaginary newspaper called The mop and pail, where things are more ridiculous than in Real Life.

3. "Porgy and Bess," a Folk Opera by George and ira Gershwin and Du Bose Heyward, introduced the beautiful, haunting song *Summertime*.

4. Marlon Brando persuaded the Director of *The Godfather* to cast him as the Elderly don Corleone by auditioning with cotton-stuffed cheeks and mumbling hoarsely.

5. When the name of a Small Business begins with the letter a repeated many times, as in AAAAAbc "Auto Body," we know its marketing plan includes being listed First in the telephone directory.

ABBREVIATIONS

30j What are standard practices for using abbreviations?

Some abbreviations are standard in all writing circumstances (*Mr.*, not *Mister*, in a name; *St.* Louis, the city, not *Saint* Louis). In some situations, you may have a choice about whether or not to abbreviate or spell out a word. Choose what seems suited to your PURPOSE for writing and your AUDIENCE, and be consistent in each piece of writing.

NO The great painter Vincent Van Gogh was **b.** in Holland in 1853, but he lived most of his life and died in **Fr.**

YES The great painter Vincent Van Gogh was **born** in Holland in 1853, but he lived most of his life and died in **France.**

NO Our field hockey team left after Casey's **psych** class on **Tues., Oct.** 10, but the flight had to make an unexpected stop (in **Chi.**) before reaching **L.A.**

YES Our field hockey team left after Casey's **psychology** class on **Tuesday, October** 10, but the flight had to make an unexpected stop (in **Chicago**) before reaching **Los Angeles.**

NO Please confirm in writing your order for one **doz.** helmets in **lg** and **x-lg.**

YES Please confirm in writing your order for one **dozen** helmets in **large** and **extra large.**

 ALERTS: (1) Most abbreviations call for periods: *Mrs., R.N., A.M.* (2) Acronyms (pronounceable words formed from the initials of a name) generally have no periods: *NASA* (National Aeronautics and Space Administration) and *AIDS* (*a*cquired *i*mmuno *d*eficiency *s*yndrome).

(3) Postal abbreviations for states have no periods (see Box 123, in 30l).
(4) When the final period of an abbreviation falls at the end of a sentence, that period serves also to end the sentence. ●

30k How do I use abbreviations with times and symbols?

Time

The abbreviations *a.m.* (or *A.M.*) and *p.m.* (or *P.M.*) can be used only with exact times: *7:15 a.m.; 3:47 p.m.* (Some style books for periodical publications [the *New York Times* and the Associated Press, for example] require capital letters for A.M. and P.M. In ACADEMIC WRITING, you'll never be wrong if you use capitals. In this handbook, I have used the lowercase style.)

👁 **ALERT:** Use *a.m.* (*A.M.*) and *p.m.* (*P.M.*) only with numbers indicating exact times. Don't use them in place of the words *morning, evening,* and *night* (Chapter 20; 30p). ●

Use capital letters, each followed by a period, in abbreviations for eras.

B.C. (Latin for "before Christ") comes after the year: *12 B.C.*

B.C.E. ("before the common era," a more contemporary term some writers prefer) comes after the year: *12 B.C.E.* [C.E., for "of the common era," also follows the year; it can replace *A.D.*]

A.D. (Latin for *anno Domini,* "in the year of our Lord") comes before the year: *A.D. 977*

Symbols

Symbols are rarely used in ACADEMIC WRITING in the humanities, except for special situations such as charts or tables. In the sciences, symbols are expected, particularly in writing on technical topics: *v* for velocity; *m* for mass.

In the humanities, spell out the words *percent* and *cent;* don't use symbols. You can, however, use a dollar sign, but never in place of the word *money* and only when writing a specific dollar amount: *$23 billion, $7.85.*

30l How do I use abbreviations for titles, names and terms, and addresses?

Titles

Use either a title of address before a name (***Dr.*** *Daniel Klausner*) or an academic degree after a name (*Daniel Klausner,* ***Ph.D.***), not both.

However, because *Jr., Sr., II, III,* and so forth are part of a birth name, you can use both titles of address and academic degree abbreviations: **Dr.** *Martin Luther King* **Jr.;** *Gavin Alexander* **III, M.D.**

◎ **ALERT:** Insert a comma both before and after an academic degree that follows a person's name, unless it falls at the end of a sentence: *Joshua Coleman,* **LL.D.,** *is our guest speaker.* or *Our guest speaker is Joshua Coleman,* **LL.D.** ●

Names and terms

If you use a term frequently in a piece of writing, follow these guidelines: The first time you use the term, spell it out completely and then put its abbreviation in parentheses immediately after. In later references, you can use the abbreviation alone.

Spain voted to continue as a member of the **North Atlantic Treaty Organization** (**NATO**), to the surprise of other **NATO** members.

You can abbreviate *U.S.* as a modifier before a noun (*the* **U.S.** *ski team*), but spell out *United States* when you use it as a noun (*We're all amazed by the ski team from the* **United States.**)

Addresses

If you include a full address in a piece of writing, use the postal abbreviation for the state name, as listed in Box 123. For any other combination of a city and a state, or a state by itself, spell out the state name; don't abbreviate it. MLA, APA, CM, CBE documentation styles also use these abbreviations, where needed.

⊙ **Postal abbreviations**   123

AL	Alabama	**MT**	Montana
AK	Alaska	**NE**	Nebraska
AZ	Arizona	**NV**	Nevada
AR	Arkansas	**NH**	New Hampshire
CA	California	**NJ**	New Jersey
CO	Colorado	**NM**	New Mexico
CT	Connecticut	**NY**	New York
DE	Delaware	**NC**	North Carolina
DC	District of Columbia	**ND**	North Dakota

→

<table>
<tr><td colspan="4">**Postal abbreviations** *(continued)*   **123**</td></tr>
</table>

FL	Florida	**OH**	Ohio
GA	Georgia	**OK**	Oklahoma
HI	Hawaii	**OR**	Oregon
ID	Idaho	**PA**	Pennsylvania
IL	Illinois	**RI**	Rhode Island
IN	Indiana	**SC**	South Carolina
IA	Iowa	**SD**	South Dakota
KS	Kansas	**TN**	Tennessee
KY	Kentucky	**TX**	Texas
LA	Louisiana	**UT**	Utah
ME	Maine	**VT**	Vermont
MD	Maryland	**VA**	Virginia
MA	Massachusetts	**WA**	Washington [state]
MI	Michigan	**WV**	West Virginia
MN	Minnesota	**WI**	Wisconsin
MS	Mississippi	**WY**	Wyoming
MO	Missouri		

👁 **PUNCTUATION ALERT:** When you write a city and state within a sentence, use a comma before and after the state. If you include a zip code, however, don't use a comma after the state—instead, place the comma after the zip code. ●

NO   Portland, Oregon is much larger than Portland, Maine.

YES   Portland, Oregon, is much larger than Portland, Maine.

30m What abbreviations are common in MLA-style documentation?

DOCUMENTATION is the acknowledgement of each source that you quote (see 31c), paraphrase (see 31d), or summarize (see 31e). Styles—specific formats— of documentation in APA, CM, CBE, and COS can be found in Chapters 36 and 37. Boxes 124 and 125 list scholarly and month abbreviations required in MLA STYLE for your use as you research and write.

⊚ **Major scholarly abbreviations—MLA-style** 124

anon.	anonymous	**i.e.**	that is
b.	born	**ms., mss.**	manuscript, manuscripts
c. *or* ©	copyright	**NB**	note well (*nota bene*)
c. *or* **ca.**	circa *or* about [with dates]	**n.d.**	no date (of publication)
cf.	compare		
col., cols.	column, columns	**p., pp.**	page, pages
d.	died	**par.**	paragraph
ed., eds.	edition, edited by, editor(s)	**pref.**	preface
		rept.	report, reported by
e.g.	for example	**rev.**	review, reviewed by; revised
esp.	especially	**sec., secs.**	section, sections
et al.	and others	**v.** *or* **vs.**	versus [*v* in legal cases]
ff.	and the following pages	**vol., vols.**	volume, volumes

⊚ **Month abbreviations—MLA-style** 125

Jan.	January	**May**	(none)	**Sept.**	September
Feb.	February	**June**	(none)	**Oct.**	October
Mar.	March	**July**	(none)	**Nov.**	November
Apr.	April	**Aug.**	August	**Dec.**	December

30n When can I use *etc.*?

The abbreviation *etc.* comes from the Latin *et cetera,* meaning "and the rest." In ACADEMIC WRITING, don't use *etc.* Accepted substitutes include *and the like, and so on, and so forth,* among others. A more concrete description would be even better.

NO We took paper plates, plastic forks, **etc.,** to the picnic.

YES We took paper plates, plastic forks, **and other disposable items** to the picnic.

👁 **PUNCTUATION ALERT:** If you do write *etc.*, always put a comma after it; you do not use a comma after any of its substitutes. (For example, an acceptable use of *etc.* is in tables and charts, where space is limited.)●

EXERCISE 30-3

Revise these sentences for correct use of abbreviations. For help, consult 30j through 30n.

1. A college prof. has compiled a list of bks. that she thinks every educated person in the U.S. should read.

2. Although Ian Ryan Fleming junior hoped that one day he'd live at 1 Broadway, Dallas, T.X., an even bigger dream came true when he and his fam. moved to 1600 Pennsylvania Ave., Washington D.C.

3. Police officer Adam Furman knew from Lucinda's accent that she came from S. America and couldn't possibly have been b. in SD, as she claimed.

4. Dozens of hrs. and thousands of $ later, the contractors finally finished their work at three in the P.M., having extended the driveway to the main rd., just about four ft. away.

5. In Aug., the pres. of the apt. owners' assoc. addressed a 12-p. letter to the attn. of every tenant who had a cracked window.

NUMBERS

30o When do I use spelled-out numbers?

Your decision to write a number as a word or as a numeral depends on what you are refering to and how often numbers occur in your piece of writing. The guidelines I give in this handbook are for MLA STYLE, which focuses on writing in the humanities. For other disciplines, follow the guidelines in their style manuals (30h). If you're unsure of the guidelines to follow, ask your instructor.

In each piece of writing, you might decide to reserve numerals for some categories of numbers and spelled-out words for other categories. Be careful not to mix spelled-out numbers and numerals for a particular category.

> **NO** In **four** days, our volunteers increased from **five** to **eight** to **17** to **233.**

> **YES** In **four** days, our volunteers increased from **5** to **8** to **17** to **233.**
> [All the numbers referring to volunteers are given in numerals, while *four* is spelled out because it refers to a different category: days.]

👁 **ALERT:** When you write a two-word number, use a hyphen between the spelled-out words, starting with *twenty-one* and continuing through *ninety-nine* (22b).●

If you use numbers frequently in a piece of writing, spell out numbers *one* to *nine* but use numerals for *10* and above.

When you write in MLA style for courses in the humanities, never start a sentence with a numeral. Spell out the number—or better still, revise the sentence so that the number doesn't need to fall at the beginning. For practices in other disciplines, consult their manuals.

> **NO**   **$375 dollars** for each credit is the tuition rate for nonresidents.
>
> **YES**   **Three hundred seventy-five dollars** for each credit is the tuition rate for nonresidents.
>
> **YES**   The tuition rate for nonresidents is **$375** for each credit.

If you're using specific numbers often in a piece of writing (temperatures when writing about climate, percentages in an economics essay, or other specific measurements of time, distance, and other quantities), use numerals. If you give only an approximation, spell out the numbers: *About twelve inches of snow fell.* In the humanities, the names of centuries are always spelled out: *the eighteenth century.*

30p What are standard practices for using numbers?

Box 126 shows standard practices for writing numbers. Use it as a basic guide, and rely on the style books mentioned in section 30h for answers to other questions you may have.

⊙ **Specific numbers in writing**   **126**

DATES	August 6, 1941
	1732–1845
	from 34 B.C. to A.D. 230
ADDRESSES	10 Downing Street
	237 North 8th Street
	Export Falls, MN 92025
TIMES	8:09 a.m. (*or* A.M.), 6:00 p.m. (*or* P.M.)
	six o'clock [not *6 o'clock*]
	four in the afternoon *or* 4 p.m. [not *four p.m.*]
DECIMALS	0.01 12 1/4
AND FRACTIONS	98.6 a sixth
	3.1416 three-quarters [not *3-quarters*]
	7/8 one-half

→

Specific numbers in writing *(continued)*   126

CHAPTERS AND PAGES	Chapter 27, page 2 p. 1023 *or* pp. 660–62 [MLA style]
SCORES AND STATISTICS	a 6–0 score a 5 to 1 ratio (*and* a ratio of 5:1) 29 percent a one percent change (*and* at the 1 percent level)
IDENTIFICATION NUMBERS	94.4 on the FM dial please call (012) 345-6789
MEASUREMENTS	67.8 miles per hour 2 feet 2 level teaspoons 1.5 gallons a 700-word essay 14 liters 8-1/2-by-11-inch paper [MLA style]
ACT, SCENE, AND LINE	act 2, scene 2 (*or* act II, scene ii) lines 75–79
TEMPERATURES	40°F *or* −5°F 20° Celsius
MONEY	$1.2 billion 25 cents $3.41 $10,000

EXERCISE 30-4

Revise these sentences so that the numbers are in correct form, either spelled out or in numerals. For help, consult 30o and 30p.

1. At five fifteen p.m., the nearly empty city streets filled with 1000's of commuters.
2. A tarantula spider can survive without food for about two years and 3 months.
3. By the end of act one, scene five, Romeo and Juliet are in love and at the mercy of their unhappy fate.
4. Sound travels through air at a speed of 1,089 feet per second, but in water it travels four hundred and fifty percent faster, at four thousand, eight hundred fifty-nine feet per second.
5. 21 years old and unhappily married, Cleopatra met middle-aged Julius Caesar in forty-eight B.C.E.
6. An adult blue whale, which can weigh one hundred tons, the combined weight of 30 elephants, has gained over seven-point-five pounds an hour since infancy.

7. On the morning of August thirteen, nineteen hundred thirty, 3 huge meteorites smashed into the Amazon jungle.

8. 2 out of every 5 people who have ever lived on earth are alive today, according to 1 estimate.

9. The house at six hundred and fifty-three Oak Street—the 1 that children think is haunted—has been empty for 8 years waiting for a buyer willing to pay its price of $ six million, forty-nine thousand dollars.

10. The 1912 sinking of the *Titanic,* in which one thousand five hundred and three people drowned, is widely known, but few people remember that more than three thousand people lost their lives aboard the ferryboat *Doña Paz* when it hit an oil tanker in the Philippines in nineteen eighty-seven.

Visit the Troyka Web site for information on:

- **Researching your paper**
- **Using MLA, APA, CM, CBE, and COS documentation styles**
- **Designing documents**

You'll also find access to the *Online Writing Lab (OWL)* at <owl.english.purdue.edu/handouts/index2.html#research>. Hosted by Purdue University, this site offers advice on researching, citing resources, and avoiding plagiarism.

PART FIVE

WRITING RESEARCH

31 USING SOURCES AND AVOIDING PLAGIARISM

In the most basic sense, **research writing** today is the same as it has always been—a process. The process involves conducting research, understanding and evaluating the results of your research, and writing a properly documented paper. But today, new technology is revolutionizing research writing. The Internet gives researchers immediate access to seemingly unbounded information. The advantages are tremendous, but the wise researcher will keep certain cautions in mind.

This handbook teaches you the fundamentals of research—from formulating a research question, compiling a WORKING BIBLIOGRAPHY,* and avoiding PLAGIARISM to DRAFTING, REVISING, and using a DOCUMENTATION STYLE correctly in your paper. You will also learn how to use today's powerful new tools in research while avoiding their pitfalls. Beginning in this chapter, too, you will observe a real student, Lisa Laver, as she moves through the research process.

When instructors speak of research, they often allude to *outside sources*. Outside sources are materials apart from (or "outside") your own knowledge or thinking that provide information and from which you often learn something you did not know before. SOURCES include books, articles, interviews with people, television and radio programs, maps, online databases, and others. Research paper assignments require you to use CRITICAL THINKING to ANALYZE, SUMMARIZE, and, mostly, SYNTHESIZE (5e) one or more sources. Using outside sources effectively and efficiently takes practice, so allow yourself time to become familiar with what is involved. The more you follow the guidelines in Box 127, the more you will succeed.

---

* You can find the definition of a word printed in small capital letters (such as WORKING BIBLIOGRAPHY) in the Terms Glossary toward the back of this handbook.

⊙ ■ **Guidelines for using outside sources**   **127**
      in your writing

1. Apply the concepts and skills of thinking critically (5a–5b), reading critically (5c–5e), and writing critically (5f–5j).
2. Avoid plagiarism by always crediting the source for any ideas and words not your own.
3. Use documentation (Chapters 35–37) to credit sources accurately and completely.
4. Know how and when to use the following techniques for incorporating material from sources into your own writing:

- **Quotation:** the exact words of a source set off in quotation marks (31c)
- **Paraphrase:** a detailed restatement of someone else's statement expressed in your own words and your own sentence structures (31d)
- **Summary:** a condensed statement of the main points of someone else's passage expressed in your own words and your own sentence structures (31e)

31a How can I avoid plagiarism?

To **plagiarize** is to present another person's words or ideas as if they were your own. Plagiarism is a kind of stealing. The word *plagiarize* comes from the Latin word for kidnapper and literary thief. It is a serious offense that can be grounds for failing a course or expulsion from college. Plagiarism can be intentional, as it is when you submit as your own work a paper you did not write. Plagiarism is also intentional when you deliberately incorporate the work of other people into your writing without using documentation to acknowledge those sources. Plagiarism can also be unintentional—but no less serious an offense—if you are unaware of what must be acknowledged and how to do so correctly with DOCUMENTATION.

31a.1 Knowing what not to document

When you write a paper that draws on outside sources, you are not expected to document common knowledge (if there is any on your topic) or your own thinking about the subject.

Common knowledge

You do not have to document **common knowledge.** Common knowledge is information that most educated people know, although they might need to remind themselves of certain facts by checking information in a reference book. For example, it is common knowledge that the U.S. space program included moon landings. Even though you might have to look in a reference book to recall that Neil Armstrong was the first person to set foot on the moon on July 20, 1969, those facts are common knowledge and do not have to be documented.

You move into the realm of research and the need to document as soon as you get into less commonly known details about the moon landing: the duration of the stay on the moon, the size and capabilities of the spaceship, what the astronauts ate during their journey, and similar details. If you feel that you are walking a thin line between knowledge held in common and knowledge learned from research, be safe and document. Sometimes, of course, a research paper does not happen to contain common knowledge. For example, Lisa Laver, whose research paper appears in Chapter 35, had only very general common knowledge about the broad topic of intelligence. She had even less knowledge of her narrowed topic, "newer theories for defining intelligence." Laver's research paper consists of a little of her common knowledge and much more of what she summarizes and synthesizes from outside sources. The third and very important component of her paper is her own thinking based on what she learned from her research.

Your own thinking

You do not have to document **your own thinking** about your subject. As you conduct your research, you learn new material by building on your prior knowledge—what you already know. You are expected to think about that new material, using the sequence for CRITICAL THINKING explained in Chapter 5, especially Box 31, page 106. When you synthesize what you have learned from outside sources, you are engaging in your own thinking. Carefully watch the line: When in doubt, document.

Be particularly careful not to allow PLAGIARISM to slip into your research paper's THESIS STATEMENT or TOPIC SENTENCES. It is plagiarism to put a source's main idea into your words and pass that off as yours in your thesis statement or topic sentences. Similarly, it is plagiarism to combine the main ideas of several sources, put them into your own words, and pass that off as your own idea. Your thesis statement and topic sentences must reflect your synthesis of what you have learned from outside sources. Notice how Lisa Laver relied on synthesis and her own thinking in her research paper, presented in Chapter 35.

EXAMPLES OF LAVER'S OWN THINKING

- The thesis statement: paragraph 1
- Synthesis used for most topic sentences (which start all paragraphs except 1 and 9)
- Comments or opinion: opening sentence of paragraph 4 and entire concluding paragraph
- Transitional sentences: opening sentences of paragraphs 2, 3, 8, and 9
- Conclusion: paragraph 9

31a.2 Knowing what to document

What should you document? Document everything that is not common knowledge or your own thinking (31a.1). Document any material from an outside source that you quote (31c), paraphrase (31d), or summarize (31e). Never forget that writing the exact words of others or the ideas of others in your own words means that you must document.

Careful notetaking is the key to preventing PLAGIARISM. As you conduct research using outside sources, apply these widely used techniques that help researchers avoid plagiarism.

PREVENTING PLAGIARISM WHILE TAKING NOTES

- **Record complete documentation information.** Become entirely familiar with the DOCUMENTATION STYLE you will need in your paper (31b). If you are not sure which style to use, ask your instructor.

  Next, make a master guide for the specific information your documentation style requires for each type of source. You can easily create a master guide by photocopying the summary box for your documentation style: Use Box 150 for MLA style, Box 151 for APA style, Box 152 for CM style, Box 153 for CBE style, and Box 154 for CO style. Having the specifics for your documentation style always at hand will save you time and minimize your chances of inadvertent plagiarism.

  Web pages used in your paper require the same level of DOCUMENTATION as a book or a professional journal; they are a SOURCE. The thoughts and ideas of the author are presented on the Web page and must be acknowledged as another person's work even if the format is less formal than that of traditional sources.

  Because many Web pages are actually self-published and have no editor to ensure quality control or to insist on a standard format, you may have to look throughout an entire Web site to find and identify all the components needed for proper documentation. If all the elements of the needed documentation cannot be found, you may have to reconsider whether the particular Web page meets the criteria for a good research source (see Boxes 148 and 149 in section 34f, pages 557–559). If it does not, it may have to be discarded or other sources may have to be used to verify the information.

An additional risk with using questionable sources on the Web is that the source itself may be plagiarized. If you unintentionally use such a source, it nonetheless constitutes plagiarism on your part. To become as familiar as you can with your Internet sources, be sure you can answer questions such as those in Box 149.

Drawing on your master guide, write a BIBLIOGRAPHY card for each source. Record all the information for the type of source. Also, record any information you need to locate the source again.

- **Record documentation information as you go along.** Be sure to write down complete, detailed documentation facts. Use your clearest, most readable handwriting. When you write a research paper, your chances of unintentional plagiarism decrease sharply if you can easily figure out from your notes the exact source and its information. Do not expect to relocate a source later—it may be unavailable, or you may not be able to recall where you found it.

- **Use a consistent notetaking system.** Do not expect to reconstruct from memory what came from the source and what is the result of your own thinking. Try using different colors of ink or a clear coding system to keep three things separate: (1) paraphrased or summarized source material, (2) quotations from a source, and (3) your own thoughts. For quotations, many professional writers use oversized quotation marks so that they are certain they will see them later.

31b How can I understand the concept of documentation?

Documentation means acknowledging your sources. It is a two-part process: You mark the exact place in a paper where you have quoted, paraphrased, or summarized a source, and you provide the BIBLIO-GRAPHIC information necessary for your reader to locate this same source. The root word *biblio-* means "book," and traditionally, the bibliographic information referred to a book's title, author, publisher, and place and year of publication. Today, researchers use both print and electronic sources, but the concept remains the same: Acknowledge where you have used someone else's ideas and provide all the information your reader needs to locate that same source.

A **documentation style** refers to a specific system for providing information on sources used in a research paper. Documentation styles vary among the disciplines. This handbook presents five documentation styles, as shown in Box 128.

Where to find the MLA, APA, CM, CBE, and COS information you need   128

MLA Style: Red Bar, Chapter 35, Pages 561–617

- MLA parenthetical citations: 35b–35c
- Guidelines for compiling an MLA-style Works Cited list (Box 150): 35d
- Directory of MLA Works Cited list models: 35d.1
- Content or other notes with MLA parenthetical documentation: 35d.2

APA Style: Blue Bar, Chapter 36, Pages 618–653

- APA in-text style, parenthetical citations: 36b–36c
- Guidelines for compiling an APA-style References list (Box 151): 36f
- Directory of APA References list models: 36g
- Abstracts and content notes: 36d–36e

CM Style: Green Bar, Chapter 37, Pages 654–667

- Guidelines for compiling CM-style bibliographic notes (Box 152): 37a
- Directory of CM-style bibliographic note models: 37b

CBE Style: Gray Bar, Chapter 37, Pages 667–674

- Guidelines for compiling a CBE-style Cited References list (Box 153): 37c
- Directory of CBE-style list of references models: 37d

CO Style: Yellow Bar, Chapter 37, Pages 675–686

- COS parenthetical citations: 37e.1
- Differences between print and online publication in CO-style bibliographic notes: 37e.2
- Guidelines for compiling a COS Works Cited list (Box 154): 37e.2
- Directory of COS Works Cited list models: 37f

Before you begin searching for sources, know which documentation style you need to use. (If your assignment does not specify a documentation style, ask your instructor.) Then, as you take notes on each source, you can record accurately and fully all the information your documentation style requires. It is extremely inefficient and frustrating to have to track down a source because you don't have complete information.

31c How can I use quotations effectively?

Quotations are the exact words of a source set off in quotation marks (28a). Quotations are not PARAPHRASES (31d) or SUMMARIES (31e), techniques to use when you present your sources' ideas in your own words. One advantage to quotations is that they allow your reader to encounter your source's words directly. Consult Box 129 for guidelines when using quotations.

⊚ **Guidelines for using quotations** 129

1. Use quotations from authorities on your subject to support what you say. Do not use quotations as either your THESIS STATEMENT or TOPIC SENTENCES.
2. Select quotations that fit your message.
3. Choose a quotation only if one or more of the following apply:
   - Its language is particularly appropriate or distinctive;
   - Its idea is particularly hard to paraphrase accurately;
   - The authority of the source is especially important to support your material;
   - The source's words are open to more than one interpretation, so your reader needs to see the original.
4. Do not use quotations in more than a quarter of your paper; rely mostly on paraphrase and summary.
5. Quote accurately.
6. Integrate quotations smoothly into your prose (31c.4), paying special attention to the verbs you use (31f).
7. **Avoid plagiarism** (31a). Always document your source. Enclose quotations of four lines or fewer in quotation marks (28b). Even if you use a small part of a longer quotation in your paper, use quotation marks to signal that all the words enclosed in them are words quoted directly from a source. (See 28c for formatting quotations of five or more lines.)

Two conflicting demands confront you when you use quotations in your writing. Along with using quotations for effect and support, you also need to make your writing coherent and readable. You might seem to gain authority by quoting experts on your topic, but if you use too many quotations, you lose coherence as well as control of your own paper. If more than a quarter of your paper consists of quotations, you may have written what is called a "Scotch tape special." Having too many quotations gives readers—including instructors—the impression that you have not synthesized (see 5e) what your sources say. You are letting others speak for you. Therefore, use quotations sparingly. When you draw on support from an authority, rely mostly on paraphrase (31d) and summary (31e).

31c.1 Quoting accurately

When using quotations, be very careful to quote each source exactly. Always check your quotations against the originals—and then recheck. Mistakes are extremely easy to make when you are copying from a source, especially in transferring from your notes into your paper. When practical, photocopy a source's words you think you might want to quote. Mark on the copy the exact place that caught your attention as a possible quotation; otherwise, you might forget your impressions and waste time trying to reconstruct your thought processes.

Often, you have to add a word or words to a quotation so that it fits grammatically with your prose or so that the reader will understand the quote which is no longer in its own context: Always put those added words in brackets (29c.1). Also, make sure your added words do not distort the original meaning of the quotation. The following quotation is taken from original material shown in section 31e.2. The bracketed material explains what *these minds* refer to in the original quotation; this helps the reader understand what was clear in the context of the original source but is not clear when quoted in isolation. The bracketed information supplies words to clarify the material.

> "In many or most moments, these minds [emotional and rational] are exquisitely coordinated; feelings are essential to thought, thought to feeling" (Goleman 9).*

If you delete a portion of a quotation, indicate the omission with ellipsis points (in MLA-style, bracketed ellipsis points; see 29d). When using ellipsis points, make sure that the remaining words accurately reflect the source's meaning. Also, check that your omission does not create an awkward sentence structure.

ORIGINAL

These two minds, the emotional and the rational, operate in tight harmony for the most part, intertwining their very different ways of knowing to guide us through the world. Ordinarily there is a balance between emotional and rational minds, with emotion feeding into and informing the operations of the rational mind, and the rational mind refining and sometimes vetoing the inputs of the emotions. Still, the emotional and rational minds are semi-independent faculties, each, as

---

* Source information is in MLA style throughout this chapter.

we shall see, reflecting the operation of distinct, but interconnected circuitry of the brain (Goleman 9).

QUOTATION WITH ELLIPSES

Goleman explains: "These two minds, the emotional and the rational, operate in tight harmony for the most part, intertwining their very different ways of knowing to guide us through the world. . . . Still, the emotional and rational minds are semi-independent faculties . . ." (Goleman 9). [First ellipsis indicates an entire sentence has been omitted; second ellipsis indicates words from one sentence have been omitted.]

31c.2 Selecting quotations from accepted authorities that fit your meaning

Quotations from authorities on your subject can bring credibility to your discussion. However, you must be able to justify every quotation you decide to use. If you are unsure whether to quote, follow the criteria in item 4 of Box 127 at the beginning of this chapter. If you decide not to quote, either paraphrase (31d) or summarize (31e) the material. For example, Lisa Laver, author of the student research paper in Chapter 35 about definitions of intelligence, quoted Daniel Goleman because he is an accepted authority on her topic. (See Box 142 in section 33k, page 543.)

Equally important, use a quotation only if its words fit your context. Never force a quotation to fit your material because most readers can quickly discern the manipulation. Also, if you have to hunt for a quotation simply because you want to include a particular authority's words, chances are that the quotation will seem forced or tacked on.

31c.3 Keeping long quotations to a minimum

When you use a QUOTATION, your purpose is to supply evidence or support for your paper. Do not use a quotation to reconstruct someone else's argument. When a quotation is very long, you might be making this error. Also, if you need to present a complicated argument in detail and thus quote long passages, make absolutely sure every word in the quotation counts. Edit out irrelevant parts (using ellipsis points to indicate deleted material; see 31c.1 and 29d). Otherwise, your readers may skip over the long quotation—and your instructor will assume that you did not want to take the time to PARAPHRASE or SUMMARIZE the material.

ALERT: For instructions on how to format the layout of a prose quotation more than four lines long (or more than three quoted lines of poetry) in MLA style, see sections 28c and 28e, pages 439–440 and 441–442. For formatting more than forty quoted words in APA style, see section 36h, page 641.

31c.4 Integrating quotations smoothly into your prose

When you use quotations, you must integrate them smoothly into your writing to avoid choppy, incoherent sentences. Quotations should mesh with the grammar, style, and logic of your prose. Consider this example based on the original material in section 31c.1.

> **NO** Goleman explains how the emotional and rational minds "intertwining their very different ways of knowing to guide us through the world" (9). [grammar problem]

> **YES** Goleman explains how the emotional and rational minds work together by "intertwining their very different ways of knowing to guide us through the world" (9).

Perhaps the biggest complaint instructors have about student research papers is that sometimes quotations are simply stuck in, with no apparent reason. Without context-setting information, the reader cannot know how the writer connects the quotation with its surroundings. When words are placed between quotation marks, they take on special significance for your message as well as your language.

Always make sure your readers know who said the quoted words; otherwise, you have used a *disembodied quotation* (some instructors call these "ghost quotations"). Quotation marks set off someone else's words, but they tell the reader nothing about who is being quoted and why. Your prose and documentation must do that.

A quotation should almost never begin a paragraph. Rely on your own TOPIC SENTENCE to start or set up the paragraph. Then, you can use the quotation if it supports or extends what you have said.

Citing the author's name and the title of the work as you introduce a quotation helps create a context for the quotation. Moreover, if the author is noteworthy, you give additional authority to your message by referring to his or her credentials as part of this introduction. Consider the following treatments of source material.

SOURCE

Gardner, Howard. *The Disciplined Mind: What All Students Should Understand.* New York: Simon & Schuster, 1999.

ORIGINAL MATERIAL

While we all possess all of the intelligences, perhaps no two persons—not even identical twins—exhibit them in the same combination of strengths.

QUOTATION USING AUTHOR'S NAME

```
Howard Gardner explains, "While we all possess all
of the intelligences, perhaps no two persons--not even
identical twins--exhibit them in the same combination of
strengths" (72).
```

QUOTATION USING AUTHOR'S NAME AND SOURCE TITLE

```
Howard Gardner explains in The Disciplined Mind: What All
Students Should Understand: "While we all possess all
of the intelligences, perhaps no two persons--not even
identical twins--exhibit them in the same combination of
strengths" (72).
```

QUOTATION USING AUTHOR'S NAME, CREDENTIALS, AND SOURCE TITLE

```
Howard Gardner, a psychologist and author of fifteen
books on the human mind, states in The Disciplined Mind:
What All Students Should Understand, "While we all
possess all of the intelligences, perhaps no two
persons--not even identical twins--exhibit them in the
same combination of strengths" (72).
```

Sometimes quotations speak for themselves, but at times they do not. For example, you may understand how a quotation fits your paper because you know how it was used in the original material. If you think your reader may puzzle over why you included the quotation, add a brief introductory remark to provide the needed information.

QUOTATION USING AUTHOR'S NAME AND INTRODUCTORY ANALYSIS

```
Psychologist Howard Gardner claims that humans possess
nine intelligences, but he notes: "While we all possess
all of the intelligences, perhaps no two persons--not
even identical twins--exhibit them in the same
combination of strengths" (72).
```

You can also integrate a quotation into your own writing by interrupting the quotation with your own words. (Remember that if you insert your own words *within* the quotation, you must put those words between brackets; see 29c.)

```
"While we all possess all of the intelligences," Howard
Gardner explains, "perhaps no two persons--not even
identical twins--exhibit them in the same combination of
strengths" (72).
```

 ALERT: After using an author's full name in the first reference, you can use only the author's last name in subsequent references, unless another source has that same last name.●

EXERCISE 31-1

Read the following original material, from "Avoiding the Hazards of Drowsy Driving" by Jane E. Brody in the *New York Times*, December 21, 1994, page C10. Then, read items 1 through 5 below and explain why each is an incorrect use of a quotation. Revise the numbered sentences. Each quotation should end with this MLA parenthetical reference: (Brody C10).

ORIGINAL MATERIAL

It may lack the drama of drunken driving, but drowsy driving is even more common and can be just as deadly. Mix it with even one alcoholic drink and you have an asleep-at-the-wheel cocktail in the making.

With holiday preparations and celebrations prompting millions to cheat on sleep and then drive, often after a drink, the risk of dozing off behind the wheel is greater than ever. Even at quieter and more sober times, about 40 percent of adults are shortchanged on sleep and in danger of being lulled into slumber by humming tires on a dark road. Compounding the problem is a growing fear of stopping to nap at highway rest areas, which in some states have become high-crime areas. In many states, rest areas are too small or too far apart to meet the needs of all the sleepy drivers.

UNACCEPTABLE USES OF QUOTATIONS

1. Many hazards on the road are caused by sleepy drivers. "The risk of dozing off behind the wheel is greater than ever" (Brody C10).

2. Researchers have determined that "it may lack the drama of drunken driving, but drowsy driving can be just as deadly" (Brody C10).

3. With studies showing that fully 40 percent of all adults suffer from a lack of sleep at all times, "being lulled into slumber by humming tires on a dark road" (Brody C10).

4. In 1994, a researcher cited drivers' reluctance to stop at rest areas, which at that time "in some states have become high-crime areas" (Brody C10).

5. But even when drivers consider rest stops to be safe, often such areas are "just too small or far apart to meet the needs of all the sleepy drivers" (Brody C10).

EXERCISE 31-2

1. For a paper on mental concentration and what enables some people to focus while others have difficulty, write a two- to three-sentence passage that includes your own words and a quotation from the material below. After the quoted words, use this parenthetical reference: (Tolson 40).

Many athletes speak of choking as a failure to be "in the zone." That state is not unlike the "flow" defined by the Hungarian-American psychologist Mihaly Csikszentmihalyi. He began his career-long interest in the early 1960s studying a group of artists for his thesis on creativity. Struck by how so many became oblivious to their surroundings while they worked, he went on to investigate whether other activities and even jobs produced such absorption, such flow. What he found was that any pursuit was an "autotelic activity" if the doing and not the goal was the end in itself and if it involved such things as intense concentration, clarity of goals, quick feedback, and a fine balance of skills and challenges.

—Jay Tolson, "Into the Zone"

2. For a paper arguing that biologists need more funding to speed up our understanding of the earth's living creatures before many more of them become extinct, quote from the Wilson material in Exercise 31-6 (see page 499). Be sure to include at least one numerical statistic in your quotation. (For documentation purposes, keep in mind that Wilson's article appears on pages 29–30. The last words on the bottom of page 29 of this article are "Four species of mammals, for example," and page 30 begins "have recently.")

3. Write a two- to three-sentence passage that includes your own words and a quotation from a source you are using for a paper assigned in one of your courses. If you have no such assignment, choose any material suitable for a college-level paper. Your instructor might request a photocopy of the material from which you are quoting.

31d How can I paraphrase accurately?

When you **paraphrase,** you precisely restate in your own words a passage written (or spoken) by another person. A paraphrase is more detailed and longer than a SUMMARY (31e). A paraphrase is a parallel text, one that corresponds to or follows faithfully an original writing. Your paraphrases offer an account of what an authority says, not in the original words but in yours.

As a bonus, the process of writing a paraphrase can help you untangle difficult passages and come to understand them. Paraphrasing forces you to read closely and to extract precise meaning from complex passages. Consult the guidelines for writing a paraphrase in Box 130.

⊙ **Guidelines for writing a paraphrase**   **130**

1. Say what the source says, but no more.
2. Emphasize what the source emphasizes.
3. Use your own words, phrasing, and sentence structure to restate the message. If certain synonyms are awkward, quote the material—but resort to quotation only occasionally.

→

> **Guidelines for writing a paraphrase** *(continued)* **130**
>
> 4. Read over your sentences to make sure that they do not distort the source's meaning.
> 5. Expect your material to be as long as, and possibly longer than, the original.
> 6. Use verbs effectively to help you integrate paraphrases smoothly into your prose (see 31f).
> 7. **Avoid plagiarism** (see 31a).
> 8. As you take notes, record all DOCUMENTATION facts about your source so that you can acknowledge your source accurately and avoid plagiarism.

31d.1 Restating material completely using your own words

When you PARAPHRASE, restate the material—and no more. Do not skip points. Do not guess at meaning. Do not insert your own opinions or interpretations. If the source's words trigger your own thinking, preserve your thought right away because you might not recall it later. But beware: Make sure your thoughts are visually separate from your paraphrase—in the margin, in a different color ink, circled, or clearly differentiated in some other way.

As you paraphrase, use your own words; otherwise you will be quoting. Use your own sentence structures. You can use synonyms, but sometimes synonyms or substitute phrases are not advisable. Consider how each synonym fits into the flow of your sentence. For example, for a basic concept such as *people,* the use of *Homo sapiens* might seem strained. In paraphrasing, the further you get from the original phrasing, the more likely you are to sound like yourself. Don't be surprised to find that when you change language and sentence structure, you might also have to change punctuation, VERB TENSE, and VOICE. When you finish, read over your paraphrase to check that it makes sense and does not distort the meaning of the source.

31d.2 Avoiding plagiarism when you paraphrase

You must avoid PLAGIARISM (31a) when you paraphrase. Even though a paraphrase is not a direct quotation, you must use DOCUMENTATION to credit your source. Also, you must reword your source material, not merely change a few words. Compare the following passages.

SOURCE

Goleman, Daniel. *Emotional Intelligence.* New York: Bantam, 1995. 9.

ORIGINAL

These two minds, the emotional and the rational, operate in tight harmony for the most part, intertwining their very different ways of knowing to guide us through the world. Ordinarily there is a balance between emotional and rational minds, with emotion feeding into and informing the operations of the rational mind, and the rational mind refining and sometimes vetoing the inputs of the emotions. Still, the emotional and rational minds are semi-independent faculties, each, as we shall see, reflecting the operation of distinct, but interconnected circuitry of the brain.

In many or most moments, these minds are exquisitely coordinated; feelings are essential to thought, thought to feeling. But when passions surge, the balance tips: it is the emotional mind that captures the upper hand, swamping the rational mind.

UNACCEPTABLE PARAPHRASE (UNDERLINED WORDS ARE PLAGIARIZED)

The emotional and the rational parts of our mind operate in tight harmony for the most part as they help us make our way through our lives. Usually the two minds are balanced, with emotion feeding into and informing the operations of the rational mind, and the rational mind refining and sometimes overruling what the emotions desire. Still, the emotional and rational minds are semi-independent faculties, for as research shows, although they function separately, they are linked in the brain.

Most of the time our two minds work together, with feelings necessary for thinking and thinking necessary for feeling. Nevertheless, if strong emotions develop, it is the emotional mind that captures the upper hand, swamping the rational mind (Goleman 9).

ACCEPTABLE PARAPHRASE

According to Goleman, the emotional and rational parts of our mind work together to help us make our way through our lives. Usually, the two minds have equal input. The emotional mind provides information to the logical mind, and the logical mind processes the data and sometimes overrules emotional desires. Nevertheless, while the two minds show a biological connection in the brain, each can

```
assert some independence. Most of the time our two minds
work together, with feelings necessary for thinking and
thinking necessary for feeling. Still, if strong emotions
develop, passions overrule logical thinking (9).
```

The first attempt to paraphrase is not acceptable. The writer has simply changed a few words. What remains is plagiarized because the passage keeps most of the original's language, has the same sentence structure, and uses no quotation marks. The documentation is correct, but its accuracy does not make up for the unacceptable paraphrasing.

The second paraphrase is acceptable. It captures the essence of the original in the student's own words. Also, starting the paraphrase with the words "According to Goleman" signals readers where the paraphrase begins, just as the parenthetical page reference signals its end.

EXERCISE 31-3

Read the original material, a paragraph from "Teenagers Called Shrewd Judge of Risk" by Daniel Goleman in the *New York Times,* March 2, 1993, page C1. Then, read the unacceptable paraphrase. Point out each example of plagiarism. Finally, write your own paraphrase, starting it with words naming Goleman and ending it with this parenthetical reference: (C1).

ORIGINAL MATERIAL

In trying to help teenagers deal more successfully with the perils they face, psychologists are undertaking a search to better understand the ways adolescents think and view their world. In the process, the research is challenging many common assumptions about teenagers that have long guided parents, educators and policy makers.

UNACCEPTABLE (PLAGIARIZED) PARAPHRASE

In helping teenagers cope with the hardships they face, psychologists are striving to understand the way teenagers think and look at the world. In the process, psychologists are raising questions about the traditional beliefs held by parents, teachers, and others who help teenagers (Goleman C1).

EXERCISE 31-4

1. For a paper on how to be more productive in the workplace, paraphrase the following paragraph. Start with words mentioning the author: Sabath. End with this parenthetical reference: (35).

   Constant interruptions are not only distracting; they can put a damper on productivity. Unwelcome office interruptions can be handled in several ways. A simple yet sometimes impractical strategy is to close your door when you do not wish to be disturbed. This effectively puts a stop to any kind of interruption. If you'd rather keep your door open, or are located at an open-ended work station, consider repositioning your desk and/or work area. If your desk is now facing the entrance to your station, for example, turn it around so you won't see passers-by.

—Ann Marie Sabath, *Business Etiquette in Brief:*
The Competitive Edge for Today's Professional
(Holbrook, MA: Bob Adams, 1993)

2. In one of your sources for a research assignment, locate a paragraph that is at least 150 words in length and write a paraphrase. If you have no such assignment, choose any material suitable for a college-level paper. Your instructor may request that you submit a photocopy of the original material to accompany your paraphrase.

31e How can I summarize accurately?

A **summary** reviews the main points of a passage and gets at the gist of what an author or speaker says. A summary condenses the essentials of someone else's thought into a few statements. Summaries and paraphrases (31d) differ in one primary way: A summary is much shorter than a paraphrase and provides only the main point in the original source. Consult the guidelines for writing a summary in Box 131.

⊙ **Guidelines for writing a summary**　　　　**131**

1. Identify the main points, and condense them without losing the essence of the material.
2. Use your own words to condense the message.
3. Keep your summary short.
4. Use verbs effectively to integrate summaries into your prose (31f).
5. **Avoid plagiarism** (31a).
6. As you take notes, record all DOCUMENTATION facts about your SOURCE so that you can acknowledge your source accurately and avoid plagiarism.

Summarizing forces you to read closely and to comprehend clearly. You can learn new material by writing summaries because the process helps lock information in your memory. Summarizing is probably the most frequently used technique for taking notes and for incorporating sources into papers.

Here is a summary based on the original material by Goleman in section 31d.2. Compare it with the acceptable paraphrase in that section.

SUMMARY

```
Our emotional and rational minds work together to process
information, yet strong emotions can overrule logical
thinking (Goleman 9).
```

31e.1 Isolating the main points and condensing without losing meaning

A SUMMARY captures the entire sense of a passage in very little space, so you must read through all the content before you write. Then, isolate the main points by asking these questions: What is the subject? What is the central message on the subject? A summary excludes more than it includes, so you must make substantial deletions. A summary should reduce the original by at least half.

As you summarize, you trace a line of thought. This involves deleting less central ideas and sometimes transposing certain points into an order more suited to summary. In summarizing a longer original—say, ten pages or more—you may find it helpful first to divide the original into subsections and summarize each. Then, group your subsection summaries and use them as the basis for further condensing the material into a final summary. You will likely have to revise a summary more than once. Always make sure that a summary accurately reflects the source and its emphases.

Condensing information into a table is another option for summarizing, particularly when you are working with numerical data. (For an example, see the student research paper in Chapter 35: Table 1 summarizes many pages of a source.)

As you summarize, you may be tempted to interpret something the author says or make a judgment about the value of the author's point. Your own opinions do not belong in a summary, but do jot them down immediately so that you can recall your reactions later. Keep your own ideas visually separate from your summary by writing in the margin or in a different color ink, circling your thoughts, or otherwise making your ideas look very different on the page.

31e.2 Avoiding plagiarism when you summarize

Even though a SUMMARY is not a DIRECT QUOTATION, you must use DOCUMENTATION to credit your source. Also, you must use your own words. Compare the following passages.

SOURCE

Gardner, Howard. *The Disciplined Mind: What All Students Should Understand.* New York: Simon & Schuster, 1999. 72.

ORIGINAL

Intelligence tests typically tap linguistic and logical-mathematical intelligence—the intelligences of greatest moment in contemporary schools—perhaps sampling spatial intelligence as well. But as a species we also possess musical intelligence, bodily-kinesthetic intelligence, naturalistic intelligence, intelligence about ourselves (intrapersonal intelligence), and intelligence about other persons (interpersonal intelligence). And it is possible that human beings also exhibit a ninth, existential intelligence—the proclivity to pose (and ponder) questions about life, death, and ultimate realities. Each of these intelligences features its own distinctive form of mental representation; in fact, it is equally accurate to say that each intelligence *is* a form of mental representation.

UNACCEPTABLE SUMMARY (UNDERLINED WORDS ARE PLAGIARIZED)

<u>Intelligence tests typically tap</u> only two or three of the nine human intelligences that Gardner has identified. Furthermore, each intelligence <u>features its own distinctive form of mental representation</u> (72).

ACCEPTABLE SUMMARY

Traditional intelligence tests only evaluate two or three of the nine human intelligences that Gardner has identified. Furthermore, he believes that each intelligence has "its own distinctive form of mental representation" (72).

The unacceptable summary does not isolate the main point, and it plagiarizes by taking almost all of its language directly from the source.

The second summary is acceptable because it not only isolates the main idea but also recasts it in the student's words. One phrase ("its own distinctive form of mental representation") is borrowed, but it is set off in quotation marks. No one would charge this student with plagiarism. Also, starting the second sentence with the words "Furthermore, he believes that" signals readers where the quoted material begins, just as the parenthetical page reference signals its end.

EXERCISE 31-5

Read the original paragraph from page 42 of *Teaching Your Children Values* by Linda Eyre and Richard Eyre, published by Simon & Schuster in 1993. Then, read the unacceptable summary. Point out each example of plagiarism. Finally, write your own summary, starting it with a phrase mentioning Eyre and Eyre and ending it with this parenthetical reference: (42).

ORIGINAL MATERIAL

Be completely honest with your children. This will show them how always applicable the principle is and will demonstrate your commitment to it. Answer their questions truthfully and candidly unless it is a question that is off-limits, and then tell them simply and honestly why you won't answer it. Never let them hear you tell little "convenient lies" on the phone and never ask them to tell one for you ("My mommy isn't home"). Don't exaggerate. Don't threaten to do things you don't really intend to do.

UNACCEPTABLE PLAGIARIZED SUMMARY

It is best to be completely honest with your children in every situation that is not off-limits; do not exaggerate, threaten children, or ask them to tell little convenient lies for you. This approach will clearly demonstrate to them that the idea of honesty is always applied to every situation and relationship (Eyre and Eyre 42).

EXERCISE 31-6

1. Summarize the following paragraph by Edward O. Wilson. Start your summary by mentioning the author: Wilson. End with this parenthetical reference: (29–30).

   By repeated sampling, biologists estimate that as few as 10% of the different kinds of insects, nematode worms, and fungi have been discovered. For bacteria and other microorganisms, the number could be well below 1%. Even the largest and most intensively studied organisms are incompletely cataloged. Four species of mammals, for example, have recently been discovered in the remote Annamite Mountains along the Vietnam-Laos border. One of them, the saola or spindlehorn, is a large cowlike animal distinct enough to be classified in a genus of its own. Earth, as far as life is concerned, is still a little-known planet.

2. Write a summary of your paraphrase of the Sabath material in Exercise 31-4. Use the parenthetical reference given there.

3. Write a summary of a passage from a source you are using for a paper assigned in one of your courses, or select a passage from material suitable for a college-level paper. Your instructor may request that you submit a photocopy of the original material to accompany your summary.

31f How can I use verbs effectively to integrate source material into my prose?

The verbs listed in Box 132 help you work quotations, paraphrases, and summaries smoothly into your writing. Some of these verbs imply your position toward the source material (for example, *argue, complain, concede, deny, grant, insist,* and *reveal*); others are neutral (*comment, describe, explain, note, say,* and *write*). (The student research papers presented in Chapters 35, 36, and 37 provide many good examples of such verb use.)

⊙ **Verbs useful for integrating quotations,** **132**
paraphrases, and summaries

agree	claim	emphasize	observe	see
advise	comment	explain	offer	show
advocate	complain	find	portray	specify
analyze	concede	grant	propose	speculate
appeal	conclude	illustrate	recommend	state
argue	consider	imply	reflect	suggest
ask	contend	inquire	refute	suppose
assert	declare	insist	report	tell
assume	deny	maintain	reveal	think
believe	describe	note	say	write

31g What comes next in research writing?

This chapter covers specific advice about how to avoid PLAGIARISM in its direct forms (such as buying a paper on the Internet) and about how to avoid plagiarism using QUOTATIONS and in writing PARAPHRASES and SUMMARIES for your research papers and other source-based writing. Here's what the rest of the chapters (Chapters 32 through 38) on research writing cover:

■ **Chapter 32: Research Writing as a Process**
Information about how to organize your project, including how to create a research schedule and research log, formulate a RESEARCH QUESTION, develop a WORKING BIBLIOGRAPHY, and draft a THESIS STATEMENT for your research paper.

■ **Chapter 33: Successful Library Research**
Information about how to develop a search strategy for the library, locate useful print sources, preview sources, and compile a working bibliography, a major step in the research process.

■ **Chapter 34: Successful Online Research**
Information about how to find source material on the Internet, use online databases, and, most important, evaluate online sources. Knowing how to evaluate online—indeed, all—sources is a critical research skill.

■ **Chapter 35: MLA Documentation with Case Study**
Information about the DOCUMENTATION STYLE of the Modern Language Association (MLA), the style used most often in English courses and some of the other humanities. It provides nineteen

models for PARENTHETICAL REFERENCES within the body of your paper and sixty-two models for the WORKS CITED list at the end of your paper, along with directories to help you find the specific model you need. Also, the guidelines in Box 150 give you a detailed overview of how an MLA Works Cited is built. At the end of the chapter is the final draft of a student's completed MLA-style research paper, with a narrative of the student's research process and directed commentary, placed across from each page, to give you insight into the paper.

- **Chapter 36: APA Documentation with Case Study**
  Information about the documentation style of the American Psychological Association (APA), the style used most often in the social sciences. There are sixteen models for the parenthetical references within the body of your paper and forty-six models for the REFERENCES list at the end of your paper, along with directories to help you find the specific model you need. Also, the guidelines in Box 151 give you a detailed overview of how an APA References is built. At the end of the chapter is the final draft of a student's completed APA-style research paper, with a narrative of the student's research process.

- **Chapter 37: CM, CBE, and Columbia Online Style (COS) Documentation**
  Information and models for three other documentation styles, including *The Chicago Manual of Style* (CM), from the University of Chicago Press, a style used in history as well as the other humanities fields; Council of Biology Editors (CBE), used for biology and some other areas of science and mathematics; and the Columbia Online Style (COS), from *The Columbia Guide to Online Style* (issued by Columbia University Press), widely used for electronic sources.

- **Chapter 38: Effective Document Design**
  Information about page layout and page design for any document you write. (*Document* is a term for a piece of written material; *design* is a term for placement of tables, graphs, and other illustrations on a page, especially in relation to the printed text.) You can use this information in many ways, including for the presentation of the final draft of your research paper.

32 RESEARCH WRITING AS A PROCESS

32a What is research writing?

Research writing involves three steps: conducting research, understanding and evaluating the results of your research, and writing the research paper with accurate DOCUMENTATION. Every research project requires these steps. Moreover, research writing, as is true of the WRITING PROCESS itself, often moves forward, loops back, and jumps ahead according to what unfolds as you work.

The writing process for a research paper resembles the writing process for all academic papers. Using sources—print, electronic, and online sources—adds one more level for your attention. In planning the paper, you choose a suitable research topic; develop that topic into a research question; use a search strategy to locate and evaluate print and online sources; and take notes. In drafting and revising the paper, you present a synthesis of your findings, supported by QUOTATIONS, PARAPHRASES, and SUMMARIES of your sources.

32b What is a research question?

A **research question** is the controlling question that drives your research. Although few research paper assignments are phrased as questions, research writing calls on you to figure out an underlying question and then search to find answers to that question. By regarding research as a quest for an answer, you give your work a specific focus: You can't know whether you've found useful source material unless you know what you're looking for.

Research questions, whether stated or implied, and the strategies needed to answer them, vary widely. Your purpose might be to present and explain information: "How does penicillin destroy bacteria?" Or your purpose might be to argue one side of an issue: "Is Congress more important than the Supreme Court in setting social policy?" To find answers, you can consult various sources, using the strategies I explain in this chapter, in an attempt to understand.

Attempt is an important word in relation to research. Some research questions lead to a final, definitive answer, but some do not. The question above about penicillin leads to a reasonably definitive answer (you describe how the antibiotic penicillin destroys the cell walls of some bacteria); this means your writing has an INFORMATIVE PURPOSE. The question about social policy has no definitive answer, which means you're asked to offer an informed opinion based on facts and authoritative viewpoints gathered from your research; this means your writing has a PERSUASIVE PURPOSE.

Research is an engrossing, creative activity. By gathering information, analyzing the separate elements, and creating a SYNTHESIS of what you've learned, you come to know your subject deeply. Also, the very act of writing leads you to fresh connections and unexpected insights. All this adds up to the chance to sample the pleasures of being a self-reliant learner, an independent person with the discipline and intellectual resources to track down, absorb, synthesize, and write about your topic.

If, however, you feel somewhat overwhelmed at the prospect of research writing, you share this plight with most other students. Many researchers—inexperienced and experienced—feel intimidated at the beginning of a project. My personal approach is to break research writing into manageable chunks. Those chunks or parts are a series of steps, explained in this chapter.

32c What role do the new technologies play in research?

Not too many years ago, students and other researchers marched through each step in the same way. Today, because of computers, how you carry out the research process becomes a very individual matter. Some students use a computer only for online and CD-ROM research and for writing their papers. (In Chapter 34, "Successful Online Research," I explain how to go online and conduct research either by using the Internet or by connecting to your college library's computerized database.) These students do the rest of the steps "by hand" on index cards and sheets of paper: keeping their research log (32e), compiling their WORKING BIBLIOGRAPHY (32m), taking content notes (32n), and so forth.

Some students carry out the entire research process on computer: They set up "folders" for every phase of their project. To accumulate print sources for their working bibliography, these students download them onto a disk, or if they have a laptop computer, they download directly onto it—always carefully recording the origin of the source in the documentation style they've selected (32k). Another option is to import print sources by scanning them into their computers. Finally, they draft and revise their papers on computer, often using the "Track Changes" feature, or its equivalent, on their word processing program to keep track of their revisions.

Experiment to find whatever method works best for you. There's no right or wrong way to use the new technologies. Do what feels most comfortable to you—and always be sure to routinely save and backup your work on the computer.

32d How can I best plan my schedule for research writing?

Research writing takes time. The key to successfully completing a research project is to plan ahead and budget your time intelligently. As soon as you get an assignment for a research paper, plan your schedule, using Box 133 as a model. Because no two research paper projects are alike, adapt this schedule to your needs. You might, for example, need only one day for some steps but two weeks for others. Be flexible, but always keep your eye on the calendar.

◉ **Sample schedule for a research project**   133

Assignment received _____
Assignment due date _____

Planning   **Finish by (Date)**

1. Start my research log (32e).   _____
2. Choose a topic suitable for research (32f).   _____
3. Draft my research question (32g).   _____
4. Decide on my purpose and audience (32h).   _____
5. Take practical steps (32i):
    a. Gather equipment (32i).   _____
    b. Get to know layout of my college
        library (32i).   _____
    c. Get to know available online resources
        (Chapter 34).   _____
6. Decide what documentation style I'll use (32k). _____

                                                          ⟶

Sample schedule for a research project *(continued)*   133

Researching   **Finish by (Date)**

7. Plan my "search strategy," but modify as
   necessary (33c).   _____

8. Consult *Library of Congress Subject Headings*
   for the subject headings under my topic (33d).   _____

9. Start my list of headings and topic key words
   (33d and 34d).   _____

10. Decide the kinds of research I need to do:

    a. Print and/or electronic sources (32i–32n
       and Chapter 33).   _____

    b. Online sources (32i–32n and
       Chapter 34).   _____

    c. Field research (32j) needed? If yes,
       schedule tasks.   _____

11. Master the concept of evaluating sources
    (32l, 33k, 34f).   _____

12. Prepare to take notes from sources you find
    useful (32n).   _____

13. Do library research:

    a. Consult reference works: general (33f);
       specialized (33g).   _____

    b. Consult books (33e).   _____

    c. Consult periodicals (33i).   _____

    d. Consult electronic sources: tapes,
       CD-ROMS, etc. (33h).   _____

14. Consult online sources (Chapter 34).   _____

15. Evaluate all sources before accepting them
    (32l, 33k, 34f).   _____

Writing

16. Draft my preliminary thesis statement (32o).   _____

17. Outline, as required (32p).   _____

18. Draft my paper (32q).   _____

                                                                           →

Sample schedule for a research project *(continued)*   133

Writing   **Finish by (Date)**

19. Use correct in-text (parenthetical)
    citations (35b–35c; 36b–36c; 37a, 37c, 37e).   _____

20. Write my final thesis statement (32o).   _____

21. Revise my paper (32q).   _____

22. Compile my final bibliography: MLA Works
    Cited (35d); APA References (36f–36g); for other
    styles, see Chapter 37.   _____

Have I planned realistically for my completion date?   Yes/No
If not, revise my schedule.

32e What is a research log?

A **research log** is your diary of your research process; it is a record of your process, especially of your evolving thoughts as you move through each step. Start your research log as soon as you get your assignment. Use a separate notebook for the log to bring along as you do your research, or create a new folder using a laptop. Whichever format you rely on, I suggest that one of the first entries be your research schedule, adapted from Box 133 in 32d.

Although much of your research log will never find its way into your research paper itself, what you write in it greatly increases your efficiency. A well-kept log traces your line of reasoning as your project evolves, tells where you ended each work session, and suggests what your next steps should be. Since college students take several courses at the same time, keeping this sort of record means no wasted time retracing a research path or reconstructing a thought.

Also, a research log helps you "think on paper," especially when you use the critical thinking sequence described in Box 31 of section 5b, page 106. And as always, the physical act of writing leads you to insights not available to you by other means.

On page 507 are excerpts from Lisa Laver's research log.* Laver's research paper on multiple intelligences is at the end of Chapter 35.

---

* Notice in the log that for topic or subject searches in library material, the term used is *key word*. For any online searches, the term is *keyword*.

EXCERPTS FROM LISA LAVER'S RESEARCH LOG

`Oct. 19:` Looked for "intelligence" in `Library of Congress` `Subject Headings` (`LCSH`) located in the reference collection. Figured `LCSH` was one book. Wrong. It's quite a few big books in alpha order. Found nothing. Ready to give up. Decided to relax and let myself browse a little. Paid off. Found "intellect" (to me, same thing as "intelligence"). Went through the listing and copied down key words, especially ones marked with NT for "narrowed topic." My plan for tomorrow: Rank key words from most to least useful, and start searching the Internet.

`Oct. 21:` Looking for Internet sources. I used Yahoo.com because of my good luck with it when I needed some maps and, another time, information about a new medicine prescribed for my father. In minutes, I found tons of sites and sources. Way more than I could read and evaluate. Many of the sources listed or shown used one or two of the same words, so I used them as new keywords to narrow my search. (This doesn't always work, but I got lucky.)

32f How do I choose and narrow a research topic?

Some instructors assign a specific topic for research. Others assign a general subject area and expect you to narrow it to a topic that can be researched within the constraints of time and length imposed by the assignment. Still other instructors expect you to choose a topic on your own.

32f.1 Choosing a topic on my own

When you select any topic you want, be sure to choose one that's worthy of research writing. The topic needs to allow you to demonstrate your ability to use CRITICAL THINKING and to SYNTHESIZE ideas (see Chapter 5).

Such freedom of choice sometimes creates what can be called a "research topic block." If this happens, rest assured you can overcome it. First, force yourself to remain calm—that's the only way you can think clearly. Second, be proactive by using the suggestions in Box 134. Also, try the suggestions in Box 15 in Chapter 3, pages 50–51.

Finding ideas for research   **134**

- **Get ready.** Carry a pocket-size notebook and a pen at all times. Ideas have a way of popping into your mind when you least expect them. Jot down your thoughts on the spot, no matter where you are, so that they don't slip away.

- **Think actively.** Use STRUCTURED TECHNIQUES for gathering ideas (see 2g–2m).

- **Overcome any block that prevents you from moving ahead.** As a first step, look back at section 3b for practical ideas. Second, stop yourself from thinking about the "whole" of your research project at once. Break it into chunks, according to the small steps in your research schedule (32d).

- **Browse through textbooks.** Pick a field that interests you, and look over a textbook or two (in the bookstore, borrowed from a friend, or—at least at some colleges—on reserve in the library). See what catches your attention and makes you want to keep reading.

- **Browse the Internet.** Start with the World Wide Web because it's a user-friendly subset of the Internet, one with literally millions of sites. Brainstorm a short list of topics that interest you, and then do some subject searches or keyword searches (34c) to see where they lead.

- **Use the *Library of Congress Subject Headings,*** a multivolume reference work in print. The *LCSH* lists every single topic (and the library call number of books on each topic) with many sublists, often coded to explain their purpose. Section 33d offers help with using this reference.

- **Browse general encyclopedias.** These offer a wide-ranging survey of topics, but the articles can give you only a general, superficial sense of each subject. These reference works— available as books, on CD-ROMs, or on the Internet, as provided by each publisher—come in handy for identifying general areas and topics within those areas that interest you.

- **Browse specialized encyclopedias.** These volumes are considered "specialized" because they're devoted to only one specific area (for example, social science, history, philosophy, or the natural sciences). Their articles and chapters treat topics in some depth. Most selections mention names of major figures in the field, information that comes in handy when evaluating your sources (32l).

- **Browse through books.** Stroll through the open stacks of your library, if available, to find subjects that interest you. If your library doesn't have open stacks, browse through your library's online book list. And you can always go to a nearby public library.

32f.2 Narrowing a general topic into a workable one

Once you've found a subject that interests you (32f.1), you need to narrow it sufficiently for the time frame and other requirements of your research paper. Also, you need to be sure a narrowed topic is worthy of a college research project. Box 135 offers guidelines.

⊙ **Deciding on a workable, worthwhile**   **135**
research topic

1. **Expect to consider various topics before making your final choice.** Consult Box 134 in 32f.1 for ways to find ideas. Don't rush. Give yourself time to think. Keep your mind open to flashes of insight and to alternative ideas. At the same time, be careful not to let indecision paralyze you.

2. **Choose a topic that has a sufficient number of appropriate sources available to you.** If you can't find useful sources— ones that relate directly to your topic, and ones that are credible, not simply plentiful—drop the topic. Also, make a preliminary evaluation of the sources you've found so far (consult Box 142 in 33k, page 543, and Box 149 in 34f, pages 558–559). That way, you won't waste too much time with an inappropriate topic.

3. **Narrow the topic sufficiently.** Avoid topics that are too broad, such as "intelligence." Conversely, avoid topics that are so narrow that you can't present a suitable mix of GENERALIZATIONS and specific details. When you formulate your RESEARCH QUESTIONS (32g), you'll also be narrowing your topic.

4. **Don't choose a trivial topic.** Choose within the constraints of ACADEMIC WRITING so that you can demonstrate your ability in CRITICAL THINKING. To do this, you want to show that you can skillfully investigate ideas; ANALYZE, SUMMARIZE, and interpret them; and then—most important—SYNTHESIZE complex, perhaps conflicting, concepts (5b).

5. **Select a topic that interests you.** Your topic will be a companion for a while, sometimes most of a semester. Select a topic that arouses your interest and allows you the pleasure of satisfying your intellectual curiosity.

6. **Confer with a professor in your field of interest, if possible.** Before the meeting, read a little about your topic so that your questions and remarks show you've prepared for the conversation. Ask whether you've narrowed your topic sufficiently and productively. Also, ask for the titles of the major books and names of major authorities on your topic.

CASE STUDY

"Intelligence" was the general subject area assigned to Lisa Laver, the student whose research paper appears in Chapter 35. The paper was to be 1,800 to 2,000 words and based on about a dozen sources. It was due in six weeks.

To get started, Lisa borrowed a textbook, *Introduction to Psychology*, from a friend so that she could read the chapter on "intelligence." This helped her become familiar with general aspects of human intelligence. Then, to narrow her search, she looked in the *Library of Congress Subject Headings (LCSH)* for the term "intelligence." She found nothing there, but soon discovered that "intellect" had several subdivisions (see 33d, page 530, for an illustration of what Lisa saw in the *LCSH*). Next, she consulted a few specialized reference books for more information.

Although this report shows each of Lisa's decisions flowing smoothly, the actual process wasn't as neat and tidy. Dead ends with topic key words and frustration with book searches occurred. What looks clear cut at the end of the research process was likely a more circuitous path of backing out of dead ends and making some sharp turns in searching for answers to a research question.

A more detailed narrative, including a flowchart, of Lisa's complete research process appears in 35e.1, and the final draft of her research paper appears in 35e.2.

32g How do I formulate a research question?

Answering a **research question** is the main goal of a research process. To formulate a research question, begin by BRAINSTORMING a list of questions that comes to mind about the topic. Write your list of ideas in your research log (32e).

Some questions will naturally interest you more than others, so begin with one of those. If a question leads to a dead end, pursue another. When you find yourself accumulating answers—or in the case of un-answerable questions, accumulating viewpoints—it's likely you're look-ing at a usable research question. Once you have an explicitly stated research question, you can streamline your research by taking notes only on those sources that help you answer your research question.

Stay flexible as you work. For example, the results of your research may lead you to modify the research question slightly. Actually, such modifying is part of the "moving ahead and circling back" that charac-terizes research writing. When you've finished researching and notetak-ing based on your final research question, you have a starting place for formulating the preliminary THESIS STATEMENT for your research paper.

Suppose, for example, the topic you want to write about is "home-lessness." Here are some typical questions you might ask.

- Why can't a rich country like the United States eliminate homelessness?
- Who is homeless?
- How do people become homeless?
- Is it true that many families—not just adults—are homeless?
- Is the homeless problem getting better or worse?
- What are we doing to solve the problem of homelessness?
- What is it like to be homeless?

32h How do I determine the purpose and audience for my research paper?

Here again, your RESEARCH QUESTION (32g) comes into play. To decide whether your paper will have an INFORMATIVE PURPOSE or a PERSUASIVE PURPOSE, see what your research question asks. If the answer to it involves giving facts, information, and explanation, your purpose is to inform. For example, "How have theories of intelligence changed over time?" calls for informative writing. Conversely, if the answer involves offering an informed opinion based on contrasting views and supporting evidence, your purpose is to persuade. For example, "Why should people be aware of new theories of intelligence?" calls for persuasive writing.

You may find that your purpose shifts during your research process, as Lisa Laver's did (see 35e). Balance remaining open-minded as you work with the need to tie down your purpose before you get too far along.

AUDIENCES for research papers vary. In some situations, your paper will be read only by your instructor (1d.4). More often, your audience starts with your peers, the other students in your class. Next, it moves on to perhaps a general public audience or to specialists on your topic, with your instructor as one among many readers. Your sense of these other readers' expertise in your topic will help you make decisions about content, level of detail, and DICTION.

32i What practical steps can help me work efficiently?

To conduct your research with greatest efficiency, you need to do some footwork before you start researching. First, gather the "equipment" you need and keep it organized and ready for use at a moment's notice, referring to Box 136. Second, become familiar with your college library's layout and resources (discussed here and also in Chapter 33, "Successful Library Research"). Third, get comfortable—if you're not already so—with searching topics online (discussed in Chapter 34, "Successful Online Research").

32i.1 Gathering supplies for research

Gather the materials listed in Box 136, and for efficiency's sake, try to keep everything in one place.

⊙ **Equipment needed for research**   **136**

1. A copy of your assignment.
2. This handbook, especially Part Five, or access to the Internet so that you can read the book online. With its guidelines at hand, you can work efficiently as you evaluate sources, document your sources, and correctly handle other tasks that come up.
3. Your research log (see 32e).
4. Index cards for taking notes (unless you use a laptop). If you use different colors of index cards, you can color code the different categories of information you find. Also, if you use two sizes of cards, you can use one size for bibliography cards and the other for content note cards. Another coding strategy is to use pens of different ink colors or self-sticking dots of various colors.
5. Coins for the library's copy machines and printers.
6. Empty floppy disks for downloading material—but make sure your library allows downloading to disk.
7. A small stapler, paper clips, and rubber bands, if you use index cards and other paper.
8. A separate book bag for you to check out research project books from the library. (Librarians joke about researchers with wheelbarrows. You might need a backpack.)

32i.2 Learning how the library is organized

Learning about how your college library is organized can improve your research efficiency. Though almost all libraries in the United States and Canada are organized around the same principles for grouping information, layouts differ considerably. Your time will be well spent if you go in person to your college library for the sole purpose of figuring out what is where so that you feel comfortable and confident when you work there.

Some college libraries provide class tours for English courses; some offer individual training sessions; and most offer informative, free fliers to help students learn the library layout and the resources available to students. Box 137 provides a checklist for familiarizing yourself with your library.

Checklist for touring a library 137

1. Where is the general reference collection? (You can't check out reference books, so when you need to use them, build into your schedule extra time in the library.)
2. Where is the special reference collection? (Same rules apply as for general reference books.)
3. How does the online (or, in many cases, only computerized) book catalog work?
4. What periodical indexes does your library have? (These are lists of articles in journals and magazines, grouped by subject areas.)
5. How and where are the library's collection of journals and magazines stored? Most libraries place periodicals published in the past year in open areas, while older periodicals are on CD-ROMs, shelved in binders, or online. Become adept at using whatever system is in place at your library.
6. Are the book and journal stacks open (you can go to the shelves and browse) or closed (you must request each item by filling out a form to hand to library personnel)? If the latter, become familiar with the required procedures not only for asking for a book or journal but also for picking it up when it's ready.
7. What, if anything, is stored on microfilm or microfiche? If you think you'll use that material, take the time to learn how to use the machines. (I find that each library's machines work differently enough to stump me at first.)
8. Does the library have any special collections, such as state and federal government documents, local historical works, or the writings of persons worthy of such honor?
9. Does the library give you access to the Internet? If not, find out if this service is available in your college's computer center. When at home or in a dormitory, can you access the library's computerized systems with your computer?

32j What is field research?

Field research is primary research; it involves going into real-life situations to observe, survey, interview, or be part of some activity first-hand. A field researcher might, for example, go to a factory, a lecture, a day care center, or a mall—anywhere that people are engaged in their everyday activities. A field researcher might also conduct interviews of experts and other identified individuals. Because field research yields original data, it is a PRIMARY SOURCE.

Conducting field research takes advance planning. Be sure to allow time to gather the data you want, ANALYZE it, and then SYNTHESIZE it with other sources and with your own knowledge and experience (5e). In general, the activity of field research makes selective notetaking difficult. Therefore, go over your notes right after your research session, while your memory is fresh, and highlight major categories of information. Also, fill in any details you might not have written down. What doesn't seem useful one day might become important later.

Field research many times involves events that can't be revisited. Therefore, record as much information as possible during your research and decide afterward what information you can use. If conditions make taking notes impossible (for example, a dark performance hall), the instant you have an opportunity, find a quiet place and write down notes as fully as you can.

DOCUMENTATION is as important for field research as it is for all other research. Interviews and some performances involve another person's words, concepts, and insights. To document correctly, use the guidelines in Chapter 31 for documenting quotations, paraphrases, and summaries. If you include your own work (creating an original questionnaire, for example), say so in your paper and list it in the WORKS CITED (MLA-style) or REFERENCES (APA-style) at the end of your paper.

32j.1 Observing and surveying

To observe effectively, you must avoid injecting yourself into the situation. You should try to remain objective so that you can see things clearly. A report from someone with a bias in one direction or another makes the material useless.

If you intend to go to an event such as a concert or a play, buy your tickets immediately and be ready with alternate dates if you can't get your first choice. Similarly, if you intend to visit a museum, go as soon as possible so that you can go back again as needed.

If you want to survey a group of people on an issue, allow time to write, reflect on, and revise a questionnaire. Provide time to test the questionnaire on a few people and revise ineffective or ambiguous questions. For detailed information on the mechanics of creating a questionnaire, see Box 170 in 41a, page 733.

32j.2 Interviewing an expert

An expert can offer valuable information, a new point of view, and firsthand facts, statistics, and examples. If you want to interview an expert, probably the best place to start is with the faculty at your college. Your teachers are also scholars and researchers who have expertise in many areas. They may suggest good print and online sources, as well as other experts to contact. Indeed, your family and friends might qualify as experts, if they have been involved in any way with an issue you are researching.

Make every attempt to conduct interviews in person so that you can observe body language and facial expressions as you talk. However, if distance is a problem, you can conduct interviews over the phone or online.

To interview someone in a large corporation or an institution (an insurance company or a hospital, for example), your best approach is to contact the public relations office or customer service department. Professional organizations, such as the American Bar Association (a lawyer group), often have special staff to respond to researchers. Also, public officials are sometimes available for interviews, and many federal and state government offices have full-time representatives to provide information to the public.

Perhaps even more than with other kinds of field research, it's essential that you plan far ahead for interviews. It takes time to set up an appointment so that you can fit your research needs into other people's schedules. Part of planning is having a solid knowledge of your topic—you don't want to waste others' time or try their patience by asking information you should have gathered before the interview. Don't expect your interview to replace your doing research yourself.

Although you might not always be granted the interviews you seek, do know that many people remember their own experiences doing academic research, and they want to try to help. Box 138 provides specific suggestions for interviewing an expert.

 Interviewing an expert 138

1. Call for an appointment during office hours.
2. If you want to tape- or video-record, ask for permission when you call to set up the interview. In some cases, the person will refuse permission, for personal or legal reasons. Respect that reaction, and don't assume the person is unfriendly or unhelpful.
3. Be on time for the interview, and dress appropriately.
4. Know your equipment if you're recording. Have the equipment fully ready when you arrive, set it up, and leave it running until the end of the interview. Avoid interrupting an interview for periodic machinery checks.
5. Know why you're interviewing the person and what you want to learn. Ask questions that elicit information, not merely yes or no answers.

→

Interviewing an expert *(continued)* **138**

6. Be constructive; avoid language that conveys bias or a hostile attitude. At the same time, recognize that no one is ever totally unbiased and that an expert is entitled to a slanted point of view—or, equally important, that the person has a vested interest in what you find out.

7. Go to the appointment prepared with specific questions written out in advance. The more you know about the subject, the more specific your questions can be.

8. Pace the interview to the time you've been allotted and be prepared to leave promptly at the end of your appointment time. Be courteous and appreciative.

9. Ask permission to use quotes in your paper.

10. If an assistant set up the interview for you, thank that person as you leave.

11. Follow up, no matter how short the interview, with a brief thank-you note (e-mail isn't sufficient—send a handwritten note). That note is not just a polite gesture; it helps pave the way for the next student who might ask for an interview.

12. Immediately after the interview, take time to fill in any notes you didn't have time to finish while they are fresh in your mind. Write down all BIBLIOGRAPHY information (see the models for nonprint sources in the DOCUMENTATION STYLE you are using). Evaluate your experience in your research log to help you improve the next time you do an interview.

32k What documentation style should I use?

Ask your instructor which DOCUMENTATION STYLE you're required to use for your research paper: MLA (Chapter 35)? APA (Chapter 36)? CM, CBE, or COS (all in Chapter 37)? Another? As you compile your WORKING BIBLIOGRAPHY (32m), be sure to record all the documentation elements the required style demands. Documentation styles vary in their details, and you don't want to have to track down a source again merely to get documentation facts you didn't write down on your first pass.

32l Why do I need to evaluate my sources?

Information—whether from books, articles, the Internet, or some other resource—always requires you to carefully EVALUATE its quality (refer to the CRITICAL THINKING process in 5b). First, be sure that the material relates to your topic in more than a vague, general sense. To be useful, a SOURCE needs to help you answer your RESEARCH QUESTION (32b).

Equally important, all sources must be authoritative and reliable. The author must be an accepted authority in the field (you find this out by seeing if the author's name comes up in other material on your topic). Because anyone anywhere can put material on the Internet, you need to check all online sources for indications of accepted authority.

- To evaluate print sources, the kind you find in a library, follow the detailed directions in Box 142, which appears in Chapter 33, "Successful Library Research" (33k).

- To evaluate online sources, follow the detailed directions in Box 149, which appears in Chapter 34, "Successful Online Research" (34f).

32m What is a working bibliography?

A **working bibliography,** which emerges from your search for and evaluation of sources, is an essential part of your research process. A BIBLIOGRAPHY is a list of sources; a *working bibliography* is your preliminary list of useful sources. The list remains in flux at this relatively early stage of your search for sources.

Expect to add and drop sources as you refine your research question and locate other sources. You can record your working bibliography on 3-by-5-inch note cards or on a computer. If you use a computer, it is a good idea to routinely back up your work onto a disk. Note cards have the advantage of being easy to sift through when you're adding and discarding sources. Also, you can carry them with you to the library when you do library research. Their best use is at the end of your writing process, when you can easily sort and alphabetize cards for the final list of sources you used. Whichever method you choose—cards or computer—write only one source per card or clearly separate one entry from another in a running list.

When you come across a source that sounds usable, write a bibliography card for it immediately, while the source is in front of you. Include all the information you need to fulfill the requirements of the DOCUMENTATION STYLE that your instructor has specified. Also, record the information exactly as it would be listed in your finished paper. Spending a few extra moments at this stage can save you endless hours of work and frustration later on. Box 139 lists some of the information you should include in your working bibliography. Refer to the documentation section assigned by your professor for a more comprehensive list.

Formatting bibliography information   **139**
on each source

- For a library source, write the *call number* in the upper left corner, being careful to copy it exactly. If you conduct research at more than one library, also note the library where you found that source.

- For magazines and journals, write the exact title of the periodical and article, the date of the issue, the volume and issue numbers, and the page numbers on which the article appears.

- For an online source, write the URL (uniform resource locator) address in the upper left corner of the card, being careful to copy it exactly. Also, record any date related to the source: most recent update, date originally made available, and so forth. Most important, write down the date on which you are accessing the material and the date you are downloading the material. If you take notes directly from the screen, use the date you are taking notes. This information is required in *all* documentation styles.

- If you actually look at the source, jot two key messages to yourself on the back of the card: (a) the reason the source seems useful at the moment; and (b) the results of your evaluation of the source (5b, 33k, 34f). Here are some typical messages students have noted on their working bibliography cards:

  "One of the most credible authors about my subject."

  "Book is old, but has useful background information and definitions."

  "Article published only two months ago in scholarly journal and answers my research question perfectly!"

  "This Web page has pertinent information, but I must check whether the author is really an authority on the subject."

As a rough estimate, your working bibliography needs to be about twice as long as the list of sources you end up using. (If your assignment asks for ten to twelve sources as a minimum, you want your set of working bibliography cards to contain no fewer than twenty to twenty-five items.)

Think of compiling a working bibliography as a survey process. You want to find out what is available on a particular subject before you commit to extensive reading and notetaking. Set aside more than one span of hours to search on a given subject.

What you write on a bibliography card is very important for your future ease with your project. If eventually you use the source in your research paper, the bibliography card gives you the precise information you'll need to list the source properly in your final bibliography. Box 139 offers specific guidelines to follow.

As you track down the sources in your working bibliography, keep the following advice in mind: (1) Each time you locate a source, see if you can use it to find other sources to help you answer your research question. This serves as an excellent cross-check to help you evaluate the sources. (2) If you find a source is not useful, keep your working bibliography card anyway, and note the reason you rejected it. What seems useless now may have potential when you revise. (3) Don't be discouraged if your search goes slowly at first. As your knowledge of the topic grows, and your searching skills improve, you'll find yourself narrowing your search and becoming increasingly productive.

The working bibliography cards shown here are for two sources Lisa Laver found when she was doing the research for her paper (see 35e.1).

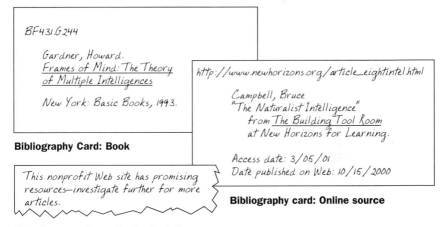

BF 431.G 244

Gardner, Howard.
<u>Frames of Mind: The Theory</u>
<u>of Multiple Intelligences</u>

New York: Basic Books, 1993.

Bibliography Card: Book

http://www.newhorizons.org/article_eightintel.html

Campbell, Bruce
"The Naturalist Intelligence"
from <u>The Building Tool Room</u>
at New Horizons for Learning.

Access date: 3/05/01
Date published on Web: 10/15/2000

Bibliography card: Online source

This nonprofit Web site has promising resources—investigate further for more articles.

Note Laver made on the back of the Campbell bibliography card

32n How do I take content notes?

If you think your preliminary search has produced enough sources in your WORKING BIBLIOGRAPHY (32m) that relate to your RESEARCH QUESTION, you're ready to take content notes. In **content notes,** record information and ideas that relate specifically to your topic. Also, write down whatever understanding you've gained from your reading. Always try to sort major information from minor information about the topic. This will help you when you organize or group ideas for DRAFTING.

On each index card, put a heading that shows a precise link to one of your bibliography cards. Include in your content notes the source's title and the number of the page or pages from which you're taking notes. Never put notes from more than one source on the same index card. If your notes on a source require more than one index card, number the cards sequentially (that is, when you need two cards, write "1 of 2" on the first card and "2 of 2" on the second card). If you take notes about more than one idea or topic from one particular source, start a new card, using the code Q for quotation, P for paraphrase, and S for summary.

To prevent PLAGIARISM, use a different font (on computer) or ink color for QUOTATIONS, PARAPHRASES, and SUMMARIES. (Every precaution you take helps you avoid the risk of plagiarism; see Chapter 31.) Also, you'll progress more quickly if, on the spot, you compose your SYNTHESIS of the material—that is, if you write down connections between the new source and other sources of which you have personal knowledge.

A content-note card written by Lisa Laver, the student whose research and writing process we are following, is shown below. The full title of the article by James Gray and Julie Viens is "The Theory of Multiple Intelligences." Laver put full information about this source in her working bibliography. On the content cards for the Gray and Viens article, Laver used a shortened form of the title. She also noted page numbers and whether the information was a quotation, paraphrase, or summary.

> Gray and Viens. "The theory of,"
> p. 22.
>
> Summary:
> Evidence that intelligence is pluralistic.

Note card summarizing a source

Some instructors require students to submit photocopies of all sources they consulted for research. Photocopying or downloading from a CD-ROM or an online database can also save you time. Having a copy of articles, book chapters, or Web pages in your research file gives you access to each item in full. Also, copies allow you to check for accuracy and prevent inadvertent misquotation or plagiarism. If you use copies, be sure to write the same bibliography information and content notes as you would if you did not have the copies. Remember to label each photo-copied or downloaded source with the author's name, the source, and other identifying information. (It's easy to think that if you have a copy, you don't need to do this or make notes). It's also a good idea to under-line (on your own copy) the section that caught your attention and write alongside it why it looks useful: The more detailed you are, the more helpful your comments will be as you narrow your working bibliography and as you draft your paper.

32o How do I draft a thesis statement for a research paper?

Drafting a thesis statement for a research paper marks the transition between the research process and the writing process. A THESIS STATE-MENT in a research paper is like the thesis statement in any essay: It sets out the central theme, which must be sustained throughout the paper (see section 2q, especially Box 12). As with any piece of writing, your research paper must fulfill the promise of its thesis statement.

At some midpoint in the research process, you might begin thinking of a preliminary thesis statement (although it's perfectly acceptable to wait until you completely finish researching). You may be able to convert your research question into a preliminary thesis. Remember, however, that a good thesis statement makes an assertion that conveys your point of view (again, see Box 12). A question is not an assertion: You want to state your thesis as a DECLARATIVE SENTENCE, not as a question. Also, expect to revise your preliminary thesis as you continue to find sources and they enlarge your knowledge of the subject.

No matter when you draft a thesis statement or how many times you revise it, your final draft should deliver the message you intend. In revis-ing your thesis statement, take charge of your material. Reread your research log (see 32e). Reread your notes (see 32n). Look for categories of information. Rearrange your note cards into logical groupings. Impose a structure on your material.

And not least, remember that you must support your thesis. Does the material you have gathered effectively make your point? If it doesn't, revise your thesis statement, conduct further research, or do both.

Lisa Laver (whose research paper appears in Chapter 35) revised her preliminary thesis statement twice before she felt that it expressed the point she wanted to make. Laver also took the key step of checking that she would be able to support it sufficiently with sources throughout her paper.

FIRST PRELIMINARY THESIS STATEMENT

There's more than one way of describing human intelligence.
[Lisa realized that this draft was too close to her research question (Can there be only one way

of describing intelligence?). She also felt it was too general in that it didn't prepare readers for the main message of her paper.]

NEXT PRELIMINARY THESIS STATEMENT

The intelligence quotient (IQ) test used today does not measure all aspects of human intelligence. [Lisa liked this thesis better but rejected it because it put too much emphasis on IQ tests when her focus was the complexity of human intelligence.]

FINAL THESIS STATEMENT

Recent studies provide convincing evidence that success increases when people use more abilities than IQ tests measure. [Lisa felt this got closer to her message; she then checked it to make sure it also satisfied the criteria for a thesis statement listed in Box 12 in section 2q.]

As you revise your thesis statement, go back to the RESEARCH QUESTION that guided your research process (see 32b). Often, your thesis statement points to the answer to that question. Here are examples of subjects narrowed to topics, focused into research questions, and then cast as thesis statements.

SUBJECT	*rain forests*
TOPIC	The importance of rain forests
RESEARCH QUESTION	What is the importance of rain forests?
INFORMATIVE THESIS STATEMENT	Rain forests provide the human race with many irreplaceable resources.
PERSUASIVE THESIS STATEMENT	Rain forests must be preserved because they offer the human race many irreplaceable resources.
SUBJECT	*nonverbal communication*
TOPIC	Personal space
RESEARCH QUESTION	How do standards for personal space differ among cultures?
INFORMATIVE THESIS STATEMENT	Everyone has expectations concerning the use of personal space, but accepted distances for that space are determined by each person's culture.
PERSUASIVE THESIS STATEMENT	To prevent intercultural misunderstandings, people must be aware of cultural differences in standards for personal space.
SUBJECT	*smoking*
TOPIC	Curing nicotine addiction
RESEARCH QUESTION	Are new approaches being used to cure nicotine addiction?

INFORMATIVE THESIS STATEMENT	Some approaches to curing nicotine addiction are themselves addictive.
PERSUASIVE THESIS STATEMENT	Because some methods of curing addiction are themselves addictive, doctors should prescribe them with caution.

32p How do I outline a research paper?

Some instructors require an OUTLINE of your research paper, either before you hand in the paper or along with the paper. In such cases, your instructor is probably expecting you to work from an outline as you write your drafts. Your research log can come in handy when you need to group and order your ideas, especially for a first draft—that is, in making an *informal outline.* An outline can serve as a guide as you plan and write your paper.

For directions on composing a *formal outline,* see section 2r (which also contains many examples). The material in 2r shows you how to head your outline with the paper's thesis statement, and it explains your choices in using either a *topic outline* (a format that requires words or phrases for each item) or a *sentence outline* (a format that requires full sentences for each item). Whatever your choice, never mix the two types. To see a sentence outline of a student's research paper, turn to section 35e.2.

32q How do I draft and revise a research paper?

The processes of DRAFTING and REVISING a research paper are much like those of drafting and revising any other piece of writing (Chapters 2 and 3), but more is demanded. You need to demonstrate that you've followed the research steps in this chapter; that you've used SOURCES correctly, employing QUOTATIONS, PARAPHRASES, and SUMMARIES without PLAGIARISM (Chapter 31); that you've moved beyond summary to SYN-THESIS of your various sources; and that you've used DOCUMENTATION correctly. To fulfill these special demands, allow ample time for drafting, thinking, redrafting, and rethinking.

Expect to write a number of drafts of your research paper. Successive drafts help you master the information you've learned and add it author-itatively to the knowledge you already had about the topic. In the first draft, organize the broad categories of your paper. Many research writers move material around within a category or from one category to another. That happens because the act of writing gives you new insights and helps you make fresh connections. A *first draft* is a rough draft. It is a prelude to revising and polishing. Box 140 suggests some ways to write your first draft.

Suggestions for drafting a research paper **140**

- Some researchers work with their notes in front of them. They use the organized piles they've made to group material into categories. They spread out each pile and work according to the subcategories of information that have emerged in the course of their research, proceeding deliberately from one pile to the next. They expect this process to take time, but they are assured of a first draft that includes much of the results of their research.

- Some researchers review all their information and then set it aside to write a *partial first draft*. This involves a quickly written first attempt at getting the material under control. This method can help you get a broad view of the material. The second step is to go back and write a *complete first draft*, with research notes at hand. When you combine the two drafts, the pieces begin to fall into place as you move material, add what's been left out, correct information, and insert in-text references.

- Some researchers write their first draft almost as if FREEWRITING (2g), writing without stopping, just getting the words down on paper. Afterward, or whenever they get a sense of how to proceed, they slow down and use their notes.

- Some researchers, when working on computer, use the "Cut" and "Paste" functions to move around the parts of their paper. (If you do this, be sure to save a copy of each draft and partial draft— even random pages—you've written so that you can refer to earlier versions later. You never know when something you've discarded can become useful again.)

- Some researchers like the physical act of working with a printout (or photocopy) of their first draft. They literally cut up the paper to move paragraphs and sentences, a kind of "unpacking" of their thinking. If a new and more readable order suggests itself, these researchers tape the paper together in its new form.

Second drafts (and subsequent versions) emerge from reading your first (or later) draft critically and then revising. If possible, distance yourself from your material by taking a break for a few days (or at least for a few hours, if you're pressed for time). Then, reread your draft, looking for ways to improve it—something that's hard to do unless you've taken time off between readings. You might ask friends or classmates to read the draft and react. Also, begin to pay attention to the document design that you want for your paper (see Chapter 38).

As you work, pay attention to any uneasy feelings you have that hint at the need to rethink or rework your material. Experienced writers know that writing is really *rewriting*. Research papers are among the most demanding composing assignments, and most writers revise several times. Consult Boxes 18 and 19 in section 3c.5 to remind yourself of general principles of revising your writing; and consult the revision checklist in Box 141 below to verify that you've remained aware of all aspects of research writing.

Once you've produced a *final draft*, you're ready to EDIT (3d), format (Chapter 38), and PROOFREAD (3e) your work. Check for correct grammar, punctuation, capitalization, and spelling. (These steps are important because no amount of careful research and good writing can make up for an incorrectly presented, sloppy, error-laden document.)

 Revision checklist for a research paper   **141**

If the answer to any question in the list is *no*, revise your draft.

1. Does your introductory paragraph lead into the body of your paper effectively (see 4b)?
2. Is your thesis statement clear, and do you fulfill its promise throughout your paper (see 2q and 32o)?
3. Do you stay on the topic?
4. Do the points you make follow logically from one another?
5. Have you answered the research question that underlies your paper?
6. Do you avoid using irrelevant or insignificant information?
7. Are there any gaps in your information?
8. Have you integrated source material without plagiarizing (see 31e.2)?
9. Have you used quotations, paraphrases, and summaries well (see Chapter 31)?
10. Are your forms for parenthetical references correct, according to the documentation style you're using (see Chapters 35–37)?
11. Does each parenthetical reference tie into a source listed in the concluding list of WORKS CITED (for MLA), or REFERENCES (for APA), or whatever bibliography form your documentation style calls for?
12. Are your citations for the concluding list of sources in your paper correct and in the right form, according to the documentation style you're using?
13. Does the concluding paragraph end your paper effectively (see 4k)?

To see one example of the research writing process in action, turn to the case study of a student's MLA-style research paper (section 35e). This MLA case study includes the final draft of an MLA-style research paper; a narrative of decisions that the student, Lisa Laver, made during her research process; and commentary (on the text page facing each page of Laver's paper) that gives you insight into specific aspects of her paper.

For an APA-style research paper, turn to the case study in section 36i. This APA case study includes the final draft of an APA-style research paper and a narrative of the decisions that the student, Carlos Velez, made during his research process. An APA-style science report is in section 41h.1.

33 SUCCESSFUL LIBRARY RESEARCH

33a What is library research?

Library research means finding sources in the library. Before the INTERNET, library research implied print sources (books, periodicals) and portable electronic sources (CD-ROMs). Sometimes print sources were stored on microfilm or microfiche instead of paper. To access these sources, a student had to go in person to the library building itself.

Since the Internet has come into widespread use, some—but not all—of what used to be physically located in a library building is now available online. In this chapter, I explain *library research* as a term that applies whether or not you access the information by going in person to the library building or by going online. In the next chapter—Chapter 34, "Successful Online Research"—I explain how to find some typically library-based sources online and how to use the Internet to access additional sources.

On your campus, the college library might now be called the Learning Resources Center or the Multimedia Center. This name change reflects the increasing overlap between traditional libraries and online resources. Always, whenever you feel unsure of how to find what you're looking for, ask a reference librarian. These professionals enjoy helping students master the art and science of research in libraries and online.

In this chapter, you will learn how to work with print SOURCES, develop a search strategy, and narrow your TOPIC in order to compile a WORKING BIBLIOGRAPHY. At that point, you will be ready to locate sources and—a critical step in the research process—EVALUATE them. You will also learn how to find sources using the library's book catalog, reference works, and indexes to periodicals.

33b What is a source?

A **source** can be a book, an article, a World Wide Web page, a CD-ROM, a videotape, a performance, or any other form of communication of information. People are also sources of information. Whatever the form you work with, any source is either a *primary* source or a *secondary* source.

A **primary source** is original work such as firsthand reports of experiments, observations, or other research; field research you carry out yourself; and documents and records, such as account books, letters, diaries, novels, poems, short stories, autobiographies, and journals. When you use a primary source, no one comes between you and your field research, firsthand reports, and an author's or compiler's own words, calculations, or records. This original or primary quality adds to a source's reliability and impact on the reader; see 5g on evaluating evidence.

A **secondary source** reports, describes, comments on, or analyzes someone else's work. This information comes to you secondhand, and it's therefore influenced by one or more people who come between you and the primary source. This does not mean secondary sources are inferior to primary sources. Indeed, scholars and other experts are excellent secondary sources. You should, however, evaluate secondary sources especially carefully. For guidelines on evaluating print sources, see 33k; for guidelines on evaluating online sources, see 34f.

33c What is a library-research search strategy?

A **search strategy** is an organized procedure that leads you from general to specific sources to answer your research question (see 32b). Planning a strategy for your search is crucial. When you search for sources according to a plan, you avoid either feeling that nothing is available or being overwhelmed by a seemingly limitless choice of sources. An effective search strategy structures your work so that you don't mistake activity for productivity. No two research processes are exactly alike. Be guided by your personal needs as you adapt the search strategies I explain. Most of all, know that no search strategy is as tidy as I describe here. Real life is more messy—and more interesting—than a flowchart or plan.

You begin by choosing one of three general search strategies or by creating one like them that meets your specific needs. You can start your search by reading articles or books by an expert in the field or by interviewing an expert; this is appropriately called the **expert method.** Or you can begin with reference books and bibliographies from current articles and use those sources to link to additional sources until you reach expert sources; this is called the **chaining method.** Or you can begin with general sources and move to increasingly specific sources; this is called the **layering method** because you build layers of information.

The layering method is especially useful for research in an unfamiliar field. Lisa Laver, the student whose research paper appears in 35e.2, started with the layering method and soon combined it with chaining. You, too, may find yourself switching or combining methods. This is perfectly acceptable. What matters is that you use a strategy and not work haphazardly. Complete your search as soon as possible after you get the assignment. Discovering early in the process what sources are available allows you time to find those that are hard to locate; to use interlibrary loan if an item is not in your library or online (Chapter 34); or to wait for someone to return books you need.

33d How can I narrow the focus of my search?

As you search for SOURCES, aim to narrow your focus continually so that your search becomes more efficient and more productive. One very helpful tool for narrowing a search is the *Library of Congress Subject Headings (LCSH)*. The *LCSH* is a multivolume catalog available, as of this handbook's publication, only in book form in the reference section of every library. The *LCSH* lists subject headings; authors and titles are not included. These subject headings are listed from most general to most narrow. Beginning your search with the *LCSH* gives you a useful hierarchy to guide your narrowing process (see 32f.2).

Subject headings are categories describing the content of books and periodical articles. Libraries arrange their collections based on *LCSH* subject headings. Another organizing tool is to find **key words,** sometimes called *descriptors* or *identifiers,* on a topic. Key words are the main words that appear in the periodical article's title; in its abstract (a brief overview), if it has one; or, in some publications, in a list before the article begins. Key words can help you search most book catalogs, periodical indexes, CD-ROMs, and Web sites.

When using key words to search for sources, chances are you will come up with a large or even overwhelming number of sources. Much of what turns up won't be relevant to your topic. For example, the topic "nuclear energy" is identified with various key words: *energy, nuclear; atomic energy; energy, atomic; nuclear power; power, nuclear;* and so on. You need to "break the code" in a sense, by figuring out which words identify the category you are seeking in each source. Expect to use a "try and see" approach. Don't get discouraged. If you're totally stumped, ask for advice from a librarian. They appreciate it when students seek help in pursuit of learning.

In your research log, keep an ongoing list of subject headings and key words that do and don't work for your topic. (For using key words for online searches, see 34d.)

Lisa Laver, the student whose research paper appears in 35e.2, looked in the *LCSH* for "intelligence," which led her to a dead end. By browsing, she found the subject heading "intellect." There she found the excerpt shown below.

Once you've developed what seems a useful list of subject headings and key words, you're ready to begin compiling your WORKING BIBLIOGRAPHY. The same procedures for this step apply to library research (this chapter) and online research (Chapter 34). Therefore, in Chapter 32, "Research Writing as a Process," section 32m, I give detailed directions on compiling a working bibliography. Please review that section.

Intellect
[BF431-BF433 (Psychology)]
UF* Human intelligence
Intelligence
Mind
BT Ability
Psychology
RT Knowledge, Theory of
Mental retardation
Thought and thinking
SA *subdivision* Intelligence levels *under classes of persons and ethnic groups*
NT Age and intelligence
Cognitive styles
Creation (Literary, artistic, etc.)
General factor (Psychology)
Heart beat and intelligence
Imagination
Logic
Memory
Mental efficiency
Motor ability and intelligence
Multiple intelligence
Perception
Reason
Self-organizing systems
Social intelligence
Stupidity
Wisdom

* *Note:* The abbreviations in the left-hand column indicate how the terms listed are related to the word you have looked up: **UF** = Used For; **BT** = Broader Topic; **RT** = Related Topic; **SA** = See Also; **NT** = Narrower Topic.

Excerpt from *Library of Congress Subject Headings*

33e How do I use a library's book catalog?

A library's online book catalog lists its holdings (its entire collection, but generally not its periodicals) in four ways: by author, by title, by subject, and by keyword (when online, *keyword* is spelled as one word). If you know an author or title, that is usually the easiest way to access a SOURCE. To use the subject headings, however, you must use the terms listed in the *Library of Congress Subject Headings* (see 33d). If you enter an *LCSH* heading only to have "nothing on this subject" appear on the computer screen, ask a reference librarian for help. Keywords can also lead you to sources. The *LCSH* headings can serve as keywords, as can the important terms in your working thesis or research question. See Box 145 in 34d, page 553, for help on refining keyword searches.

Many libraries are connected electronically to other libraries' book catalogs, giving you access to the holdings of those libraries. Some states link all their state colleges and universities into one system. Some libraries also use the Internet to connect to colleges and universities outside their state systems. Librarians can request materials from these other libraries through interlibrary loan.

An entry in the book catalog contains a great deal of useful information. Some libraries allow you to print out this information, and some even let you send the information to your e-mail account or download to a disk. Whether you choose any of these options or copy down the information yourself, it is crucial to record the call number exactly as it appears, with all numbers, letters, and decimal points. The call number tells where the book is located in the stacks (storage shelves). If you are researching in a library with *open stacks* (that is, you can go where books are shelved), the call number leads you to the area in the library where all books on the same subject can be found. Simply looking at the offerings may yield useful sources. Keep in mind that in physically browsing the stacks, you are missing sources that are checked out or at the reserve desk.

The call number is also crucial in a library or special collection with *closed stacks* (that is, you fill in a call slip, hand it in at the call desk, and wait for the book to arrive). If you fill in the wrong number or an incomplete number, your wait will be in vain. On your preliminary bibliography cards, be sure to write down all call-number information to make it easier to locate the works you want. You can see examples of an online book catalog keyword search on page 532.

At the end of every catalog entry you will find additional subjects covered in that book. In an online catalog, these additional subjects are often placed on the full record page, which can be reached from the brief record page, both shown on page 532. They can be valuable clues for further searching. If your library has a card catalog in drawers for all or part of its collection, you will find the same type of information for author, title, and subject (not for online keywords).

Screen shows
list of seach results

Search term

Screen shows
detailed
information
for first entry
in the list of
results

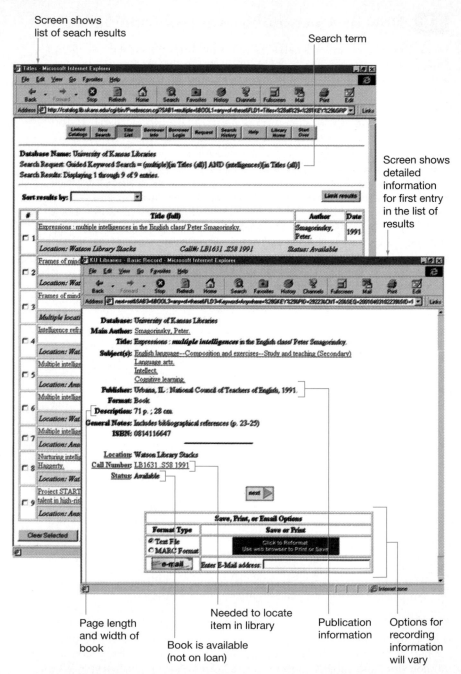

Page length
and width of
book

Needed to locate
item in library

Publication
information

Options for
recording
information
will vary

Book is available
(not on loan)

Example of online book catalog keyword search (formats will differ)

33f What are general reference works?

General reference works include encyclopedias, almanacs, yearbooks, fact books, atlases, dictionaries, biographical reference works, and bibliographies. A reference is general if it provides information on a vast number of subjects; depth on a subject isn't possible in such a compilation.

The reference book and CD-ROM reference collection in a library is the starting point for many researchers—but only the starting point. Reference works summarize, and they are, therefore, too general for an academic research study. Still, because general reference works can give you an overall picture, they are one of the best places to learn useful search words for subject headings and online catalog keyword searches. General reference works can also be helpful for finding examples and verifying facts.

Most widely used reference works are available in electronic versions, usually on CD-ROMs. Some are even online, to be accessed via the Internet. Almanacs and statistical works online are usually kept more up to date than their print or CD-ROM counterparts.

If you can't seem to find useful material, ask a reference librarian whether you're using the best source in its delivery form for your topic.

General encyclopedias

Articles in multivolume general encyclopedias, such as the *The New Encyclopaedia Britannica* or *Collier's Encyclopedia,* summarize information on a wide variety of subjects. The articles can give you helpful background information and the names of major figures and experts in the field; many articles end with a brief bibliography of major works on the subject. General encyclopedias are not the place to look for information on recent events or current research, although sometimes ongoing controversies in a field are covered.

To locate information in an encyclopedia, start with the index volume. It will give you volume and page numbers for your topic. The letters *bib* at the end of an index entry mean that the article contains a bibliography, which makes the entry worth checking for the additional sources it can lead you to. If you cannot find what you are looking for, try alternative headings or key words.

One-volume general encyclopedias, such as the *New Columbia Encyclopedia* or the *Random House Encyclopedia,* cover subjects very briefly. For college-level work, these sources are useful only for you to see whether a general subject area interests you enough for further research.

Almanacs, yearbooks, fact books

Almanacs, yearbooks, and fact books are huge compilations of facts in many subject areas. They are excellent sources for verifying information from other sources and, in some cases, for finding supporting facts and figures on the subject you're investigating.

Almanacs—such as *The World Almanac, The New York Times Almanac,* and the *Book of Facts*—present capsule accounts of a year's events and data about government, politics, economics, science and technology, sports, and many other categories. Often, the information is presented in a historical context (for example, along with who won last year's Grammy Awards in the recording industry you can see who won in the different categories since 1958, the year the awards were introduced).

Facts on File covers world events in a weekly digest and in an annual one-volume yearbook. The annual *Statistical Abstract of the United States* contains a wealth of data on the United States. *Demographic Yearbook* and the *United Nations Statistical Yearbook* carry worldwide data.

Atlases and gazetteers

Atlases contain maps of our planet's continents, seas, and skies—and whatever is known about other planets. Examples include the *Cosmopolitan World Atlas, The Times Atlas of World History,* and the *National Atlas of the United States of America.* Gazetteers provide comprehensive geographical information on topography, climates, populations, migrations, natural resources, crops, and so on. *Webster's New Geographical Dictionary* is a widely available gazetteer. Some reference works combine the two kinds of information, as does, for example, the *National Geographic Atlas of the World.*

Dictionaries

Dictionaries define words and terms. In addition to general dictionaries, specialized dictionaries exist in many academic disciplines to define words and phrases specific to a field (33g).

Biographical reference works

Biographical reference books give brief factual information about famous people—their accomplishments and pertinent events and dates in their lives. Biographical references include the *Who's Who* series, *The Dictionary of American Biography,* and *Webster's Biographical Dictionary. Current Biography: Who's News and Why* is published monthly, with six-month and annual cumulative editions.

Specialized biographical references in various fields are also available. They include *American Men and Women of Science, Contemporary Authors, Dictionary of American Negro Biography,* and *Two Thousand Notable American Women.* Because of the many different biographical sources, you may want to ask a librarian for help in locating biographical references.

Bibliographies

Bibliographies list books. *Books in Print* lists all books that are available through their publishers and certain other sources in the United States. (In other words, if a book is out of print—no longer being published—it won't be listed.) This multivolume work classifies its entries in separate volumes by author name, title, and general subject headings, but it does not describe a book's content.

The database WorldCat, available through FirstSearch, lists all the book holdings in most U.S. and some international libraries. It does not describe a book's contents, but it does list the subject headings assigned by librarians to categorize the subjects covered by the book.

The *Book Review Digest* publishes excerpts from book reviews that have appeared in major newspapers and magazines in the past year. Reputable critics' or scholars' opinions can help you evaluate a source (33k and 34f). The reviews appear in the volume that corresponds either to the year a book was published or to the one immediately following. The *Book Review Index* lists where reviews have appeared but does not carry the actual reviews. Indexes to reviews in specialized areas can also be very helpful, such as the *Index to Book Reviews in the Humanities.* Other area-specific sources, such as annual bibliographies, often list book reviews for the year as well as other publications for that field.

Consulting specialized bibliographies—ones that list many books on a particular subject—can be very helpful in your research process. Annotated or critical bibliographies describe and evaluate the works that they list and, when used with your full awareness of their potential bias, can be useful.

33g What are specialized reference works?

Specialized reference works provide more authoritative and specific information than general reference works. Specialized reference works are usually appropriate for college-level research because the information is more advanced and detailed.

Many students mistakenly overlook specialized encyclopedias in preliminary searches, moving from general references directly to books and articles. But specialized encyclopedias can be invaluable for introducing the controversies and key words in a subject area. In particular, finding authors' names in such books can help you begin to accumulate a list of credible authors. Those names become especially valuable as you search book and periodical catalogs and if you perform an Internet search.

Here are the titles of some commonly used specialized references, categorized by subject area.

BUSINESS AND ECONOMICS
A Dictionary of Economics
Encyclopedia of Advertising
Encyclopedia of Associations
Encyclopedia of Banking and Finance
Handbook of Modern Marketing

FINE ARTS
Crowell's Handbook of World Opera
International Cyclopedia of Music and Musicians
New Grove Dictionary of Music and Musicians
Oxford Companion to Art

HISTORY
Dictionary of American Biography
Encyclopedia of American History
An Encyclopedia of World History
New Cambridge Modern History

LITERATURE
Chassell's Encyclopedia of World Literature
Dictionary of Literary Biography
A Dictionary of Literary Terms
*MLA International Bibliography of Books and Articles
   on the Modern Languages and Literature*
Oxford Companion to American Literature
Oxford Companion to English Literature

PHILOSOPHY AND RELIGION
Dictionary of the Bible
Eastern Definitions: A Short Encyclopedia of Religions of the Orient
Encyclopedia of Philosophy
Encyclopedia of Religion

POLITICAL SCIENCE
Foreign Affairs Bibliography
Political Handbook and Atlas of the World
Political Science Bibliographies

SCIENCE AND TECHNOLOGY

Encyclopedia of Chemistry
Encyclopedia of Computer Science and Technology
Encyclopedia of Physics
Encyclopedia of the Biological Sciences
Larousse Encyclopedia of Animal Life
McGraw-Hill Encyclopedia of Science and Technology

SOCIAL SCIENCES

Dictionary of Anthropology
Dictionary of Education
Encyclopedia of Psychology
International Encyclopedia of the Social Sciences

FILM, TELEVISION, THEATER

International Encyclopedia of Film
International Television Almanac
Oxford Companion to the Theatre
One Hundred Greatest Films

◎ **ALERTS:** (1) Because hundreds of one-volume works are highly specific (for example, in the social sciences: *Encyclopedia of Divorce, Encyclopedia of Aging,* and *Encyclopedic Dictionary of Psychology*), I haven't listed them here. Check what one-volume specialized reference books your college library has available. (2) New specialized reference works are published throughout the year. Always keep in mind the call number for your subject area, and occasionally browse the reference collection to see if any new special reference works have arrived. ●

33h How do I use electronic databases?

Electronic databases include bibliographic files of articles, reports, and—less often—books. Each item in these databases provides information about title, author, and publisher. If a database catalogs articles from scholarly journals, the entry might also provide an abstract, or summary, of the material. Once you locate an entry that seems promising for your research, however, you must then track down the source itself. Some databases, including ERIC (Educational Resources Information Center) and NewsBank (a source of full-text newspaper articles), provide the full texts of cited articles on microfiche. With this type of a system, each citation contains an abstract as well as a catalog number (for example,

ERIC ED 139 580), which allows you to look up the microfiche that contains the entire article (ask a librarian where this is stored). ERIC is an example of a database that is also online (at <http://www.accesseric.org/>).

Keywords are essential for searching electronic databases, some of which contain as many as one hundred million references. It is important, therefore that you choose which databases will be most helpful before you begin to search. The Dialog Information System, one of the largest databases, is a compilation of more than two hundred smaller databases in the humanities, the social sciences, business, applied science and technology, medicine, economics, and current events. Restrict your search to one database at a time. A reference librarian can usually help you choose the databases best suited to your research, but first, you must be able to provide a very specific description of your research.

Electronic databases may be online and available through a library network (such as Dialog) or on CD-ROM. CD-ROM is cheaper and easier to use—an inexperienced user may follow simple on-screen instructions to search for entries. In contrast, online systems must often be used by trained librarians. Online databases require the library to pay a fee for the time used and the number of entries requested, and your library may pass the fee on to you when you use such a system. Find out whether the service is free for students and, if not, what the charge is. (Some charges are $1 or more per entry). Narrowing your search with keywords helps you avoid having to pay for a list of useless sources.

Recently, many databases previously available only online have been transferred to CD-ROM. The most popular databases on the Dialog system (such as the business, psychology, and scientific databases) are now available in this format. CD-ROM databases tend to be smaller than those online and are updated less frequently.

33i How do I use periodicals for research?

Periodicals are magazines and journals published at set intervals during the year. To use periodicals efficiently, consult indexes to periodicals first. These indexes allow you to search by subject and author. They're updated frequently and packaged in a variety of ways, often available in three formats: print index, CD-ROM index, and online index.

👁 **ALERT:** Use the correct index for your research topic. If you are using the wrong index, you may miss some of the best sources for your paper. The fact that an index is accessible on a computer does not necessarily make it the best index. If your library only has the print version of the best index for your subject, use it.●

32i.1 Using general indexes to periodicals

General indexes to periodicals list articles in journals, magazines, and newspapers. Headings and key words on the same subject vary among indexes, so think of every possible way to look up the information you seek. Large libraries have many general indexes, among them:

- *The New York Times Index* catalogs all articles printed in the *New York Times* since 1851.
- *NewsBank* covers over five hundred U.S. newspapers. It has full-text coverage from 1993 on; reproductions of articles from 1980–1992 are stored on microfiche. (It is beginning to search some newspapers' archives as well.)
- *The Readers' Guide to Periodical Literature* is the most well known index; it includes over one hundred magazines and journals for general (rather than specialized) readers. Because this index doesn't include scholarly journals, its uses are limited for college-level research. Nevertheless, it can be employed for finding topics, getting a broad overview, and for narrowing a subject. Lisa Laver used this guide in the initial stages of her student research paper, shown in 35e.2.

32i.2 Using specialized indexes to periodicals

For most college-level research, **specialized indexes** are much more appropriate when compared with general indexes. Specialized indexes help a researcher become a specialist in a particular topic. These indexes list articles published in academic and professional periodicals. Many specialized indexes carry an abstract, or summary, that was printed at the beginning of each article. Here's a sampling of specialized indexes:

BUSINESS AND ECONOMICS
Business Periodicals Index
ABI-Inform

HUMANITIES AND FINE ARTS
Art Index
Essay and General Literature Index
Humanities Index
MLA International Bibliography of Books and Articles in the Modern Languages and Literatures
Music Index

MEDICINE AND NURSING
Cumulative Index of Nursing and Allied Health Literature (CINAHL)

RELIGION AND HISTORY
Religious Index
Historical Abstracts
America: History and Life

SOCIAL SCIENCE
Education Index
Psychological Abstracts (online version is *PsycFirst*)
Social Science Index
PAIS (Public Affairs Information Service)

SCIENCE AND TECHNOLOGY
General Science Index
Applied Science and Technology Index
Biological Abstracts
Biological and Agricultural Index

On page 541, you will find three screens from a search of *PsycFirst* (the online version of the print source *Psychological Abstracts*). Lisa Laver, whose research paper appears in section 35e.2, used this source in her research on multiple intelligences.

33i.3 Locating periodicals

Indexes help you locate specific articles on your topic. Once you have that listing, though, how do you get your hands on the article itself? Most libraries include periodicals on their online catalogs, though many provide a separate list for periodicals. In either case, what you need to search for is the periodical name (for example, *American Literature* or *The Economist*), not the name of the author who wrote the article or the article title itself. If your library subscribes to that periodical, you can then use the call number to find the library's holdings. The call number, together with the citation for the particular article that you found in the index, will get you the article you are looking for.

Few libraries subscribe to all the periodicals listed in specialized indexes. Although it may not be possible to locate every article you find listed in the indexes, the interlibrary loan system (generally free of charge) or document delivery (generally at a cost to the student) allows you to request articles from other locations. Through the World Wide Web, you can access online catalogs for several other libraries as well

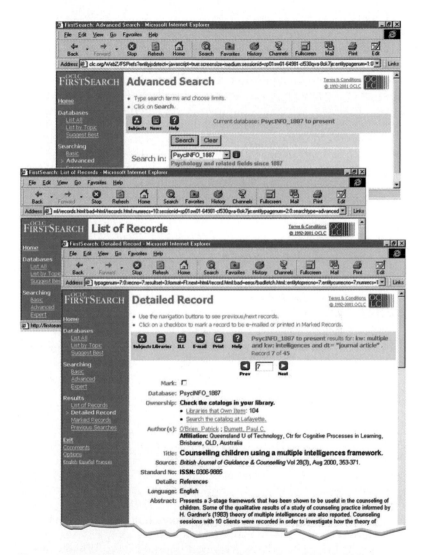

Three screens from a search of *PsycFirst* (online version of *Psychological Abstracts*) for sources on multiple intelligences

(see Chapter 34). If your library has Internet access to other library collections, take advantage of that.

33j How do I use government documents?

United States government publications are available in astounding variety. You can find information on population, weather patterns, agriculture, national parks, education, and health to name just a few topics. Government document collections are available in most reference libraries. Ask your reference librarian if your library has government publications; if it does not, ask what library nearest you houses them.

You can also order government publications that are not available through your library by consulting one of the directories listed here. Many of these publications are available at the Web site *THOMAS: Legislative Information on the Internet* (a service of the Library of Congress), available at <http://thomas.loc.gov/>. Ask a reference librarian for the best way to find the publications you need.

- The *Monthly Catalog of United States Government Publications* is an up-to-date listing of all offerings. Sources are cataloged according to subject.

- *American Statistics Index (ASI)* is published in two volumes: the index, which catalogs all statistical documents produced by government departments; and the *Abstracts,* which gives concise summaries of the documents.

- The *Congressional Information Service (CIS)* indexes all papers produced by U.S. congressional panels and committees. These documents include the texts of hearings (for example, testimony about homelessness) and reports (for example, a comparative study of temporary shelters for homeless people).

33k How should I evaluate print sources?

Sources are rarely of equal value, but how do you know which are useful and reliable and which are not? First, decide whether the information in the source relates to your topic in more than a vague, general sense. Check the table of contents, the introduction or preface, and—as you narrow your search—the index for specific subtopics. Ask how a source might help answer your research question (32g). Finally, using the criteria in Box 142, evaluate each source with a cold, critical eye.

Criteria for evaluating print sources   **142**
for research

1. **Is the source authoritative?** Generally, encyclopedias, textbooks, academic journals (*The American Scholar, Journal of Counseling and Development*), and bibliographies (see 33g) are authoritative. Books published by university presses (Northwestern University Press) and by publishers that specialize in scholarly books are also trustworthy. Material published in newspapers, general-readership magazines (*Newsweek, U.S. News and World Report*), and by large commercial publishers (Prentice Hall) may be reliable, but you should apply the other criteria in this chart with special care, cross-checking names and facts whenever possible. If the same information appears in different sources, it is likely reliable.

2. **Is the author an expert?** Biographical material in the article or book may tell you if the author is an expert on the topic. Look up the author's expertise in a reputable, up-to-date biographical dictionary in your college library (33f). Look to see if the author has a degree in this field and whether he or she is affiliated with a reliable institution. Also, if an author is often cited by professionals in the field and published in journals, he or she is probably considered an expert.

3. **Is the source current?** Check the publication date. Research is ongoing in most fields, and information is often modified or replaced by new findings. Check library catalogs (see 33e), indexes to journals (see 33i.2), and online subject directories (34d.1) to see if newer sources are available.

4. **Does the source support its information sufficiently?** Are its assertions or claims supported with sufficient evidence (5g)? If the author expresses a point of view but offers little evidence to back up that position or resorts to logical fallacies (5j), reject the source. Use wise judgment, and don't take chances.

5. **Is the author's tone balanced?** Use your critical thinking skills when you evaluate a source (see 5a–5b, 5g–5j). If the TONE (see 1e, 5c.2, 6i, and Chapter 21) is unbiased and the reasoning is logical, the source is probably useful.

34 SUCCESSFUL ONLINE RESEARCH

34a What is online research?

To go **online** means you're connected to the **Internet,** a network of computers at colleges, universities, research centers, libraries, museums, archives, government agencies, news services, businesses, and organizations around the world. The Internet offers you immediate access to vast amounts of information: newspapers, periodicals, and books; official government documents; research reports in every field by academic, government, and private organizations and institutions; some music; some videos, and so forth.

This chapter focuses on the sources available on one part of the Internet—the World Wide Web. Section 33h explains Internet connections, CD-ROMs, and other electronic sources available at your college library.

The **World Wide Web (WWW)** is the most convenient entry to the Internet. The Internet is a vast network of computers around the world. The World Wide Web (often called the **Web**) is organized around pages (called Web pages) that are linked together. The main page, called the *home page,* acts as a table of contents to all the linked Web pages, which are in turn collectively called a *Web site.* (*Web page* and *Web site* are often used interchangeably.) To be "available on the Web" means someone has to have created a Web site.

The openness of the Web is good news and bad. The good news is that anyone can have a "place in cyberspace"; the bad news is that anyone, no matter what his or her level of expertise, can create a Web site. Anyone can claim to be an expert, a prophet, or bias-free. Although many Web sites are reliable, many others are unreliable or incomplete, and still others are advertisements-in-disguise, hate-monger platforms, or even stolen material (i.e., plagiarized) from a print or other Internet source. The Web, at the moment I'm writing these words, has over 15 million sites; it'll have far more when you're reading this page. Online research demands a careful, critical eye.

My best advice is "online researcher beware." Special considerations apply when you assess the credibility of these sources, so be sure to evaluate online sources—whether on the Web or the wider Internet—using the criteria in Box 149, section 34f.

In spite of any disadvantages, researching online has several advantages. You can do some of your research from the comfort of your own desk. You might browse the Web to find ways to narrow your topic or consult online databases (of magazines, journals, and other periodicals, for example) as you assemble a working bibliography. If your topic is very current, you may have more luck if you augment any library research with online research. For example, suppose that you're researching mad cow disease and want to know whether any cases have been discovered in Italy. The World Wide Web and other Internet sites will produce source material more current than you can find in the library. For quick access to many online sources that deal with writing and research, go to these Web sites and use their direct links:

http://www.prenhall.com/english
http://www.prenhall.com/troyka

As a researcher, you need to depend on your college's library, other libraries, and the Internet. You can find many—but not all—of the same resources online that you can find in a library. Some works are found only in libraries. This is especially true if a source dates from before 1980, when the Internet became prominent. When you use the Web, always know that while sites may provide the most up-to-date information, many sites shut down suddenly. At other times, an Internet or computer glitch may prevent you from visiting the site again. Therefore, always record all the information you need for citing an online source when you access that site, in case it has shut down or is otherwise inaccessible by the time you look for it again (see 31a.2 about creating a master documentation guide).

34b How do I search the Web?

Before you can search the Web for sites that will help you answer your research question, you must get on the Web. You do this by means of a **browser,** a software program that gives you access to the Web and the SEARCH ENGINES located there. Netscape Navigator and Microsoft Internet Explorer are two popular browsers. Once on the Web, you can search for sites by using a search engine or by typing an address into the "locator" box. Explorer is pictured on page 546 and annotated to explain the main features of a browser. Other browsers have similar capabilities. Choose the "Help" menu to learn about how a particular browser operates.

Back: Takes you to the previous page visited

Locator box: Contains space for the URL (site address)

Favorites (or Bookmark): Lets you save a list of frequently visited sites

History (or Go button): Shows names of the sites you've visited

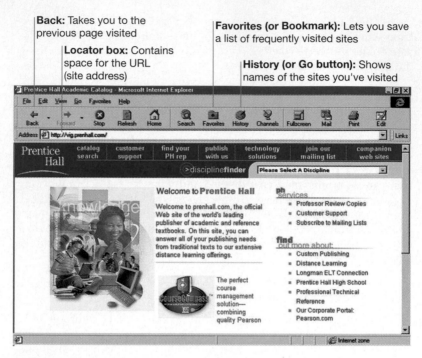

Main features of a browser

34c What is a search strategy for online research?

The principles for an online search strategy are very much like those for a library search (33c). You start with a broad subject and narrow it to arrive at a suitable topic for an academic research paper. (For what makes a "suitable topic," consult 2d and 32f.)

34c.1 Using URLs

A **URL,** for **U**niversal **R**esource **L**ocator, is a specific "address" on the Internet. Sometimes, you will have a URL that you know takes you right to the information you need. To reach a URL, type it into the locator box at the top of your screen.

34c.2 Using search engines

SEARCH ENGINES are your best entry point for online research. A search engine follows an orderly process that leads from the general to the specific. It lists Web sites related to whatever subject or keyword (34d.2) you've typed into the engine's "search strip." Box 143 lists addresses for useful search engines.

◉ **Addresses for search engines**   **143**

AltaVista http://altavista.com	Searches Web and Usenet (and its newsgroups) by keyword
Excite http://www.excite.com	Searches by keyword and subject directory
Infoseek http://guide.infoseek.com	Searches by keyword and subject directory
Lycos http://www.lycos.com	Searches by keyword and subject directory
Northern Light http://www.nlsearch.com	Categorizes the Web pages it finds into custom folders (for example, by date)
Yahoo! http://www.yahoo.com	Searches by keyword and subject directory

---

Once you finish a search using one search engine, you might want to try another. Amazingly, different search engines find somewhat—or even entirely—different lists of Web sites. This fact reflects the enormity of choices on the World Wide Web. It's up to you to pick and choose from various search engines until you find useful sources.

👁 **PUNCTUATION ALERT:** When you read or write (or type) a URL, it is suggested in MLA and APA style that you surround it with angle brackets. For example, <http://www.prenhall.com/troyka> is the URL for my publisher's Web site about my books, including this handbook. The brackets separate a URL from sentence punctuation that someone could mistake as part of the URL. However, never use angle brackets when you type a URL in the search strip at the top of your computer screen. ●

💻 **COMPUTER TIP: Meta search engines** search other engines for you. In other words, instead of using one search engine to look for sources, you can use a meta search engine to run simultaneous searches on as many as twelve search engines and subject directories. This lets you see at a glance which search engines returned the best results without having to search each one individually. Examples of meta search engines are Ask Jeeves, <http://www.ask.com>, Google, <http://www.google.com>, and Metacrawler, <http://www.metacrawler.com>. ▣

34d How do I narrow my online search for information?

Not every "hit" (an outcome or a site listed or visited in a search) will be what you are looking for. To help the search engine find the most relevant sites, therefore, you must narrow your search as much as possible. Subject directories and keyword searches are good ways to begin narrowing.

34d.1 Using a subject directory

A **subject directory** lists categories of information with links to related Web sites. In this way, directories are similar to print subject catalogs like the *Library of Congress Subject Headings* (see 33d).

One useful directory is the *Librarians' Index to the Internet (LII)*, an easy-to-use guide created by and for librarians. It groups topics both alphabetically and by category. To use the *Librarians' Index*, type its URL, <http://lii.org/>, in the search box. The first screen you see is the *lii.org* home page (shown at the top of page 549). Click on "Browse *All* Subjects" in the upper right corner to go to an alphabetical list of topics. Each topic is followed by a number in parentheses that tells you how many items are listed. When you click on a subject that interests you, you will get a list in three categories (directories, databases, and specific resources, that is, specific Web sites) and a description of each resource and its subject heading. If you click on a listing, you will go to the site, which also provides a description of its offerings, linked Web sites, and other subject resources. You can copy down and use the subject headings and linked sites for future research on that topic. In this way, subject directories let you browse subjects and start narrowing a topic.

Suppose, for example, that you are at the alphabetical list in the *Librarians' Index,* and you click to get to the subject "ballooning." The new screen lists, under "Directories," *Balloon Pages on the World Wide Web* as a link, described as "Comprehensive list of unannotated links." Clicking on this title takes you to a Web page listing titles of hundreds of Web sites about ballooning (see the second screen shot on page 549). These titles are grouped into five categories: Round the World (1 title), Round the World Attempts (19), Gordon Bennett Race (11), New on the list (27), and Published before (over 1,000). Each title is a link to its Web site. Titles of sites range from *Unicorn Balloon Company of Arizona and Colorado* to *The European Museum of Balloons and Airships* and *NOAA Profiler-Wind Profiles Data Display* to *Building a Hot Air Balloon.* If you visit a few sites, you may get ideas for an aspect of ballooning to write about. Many of these particular pages are not in English; however, such pages often include an English translation at the end.

Librarians' Index to the Internet **home page**

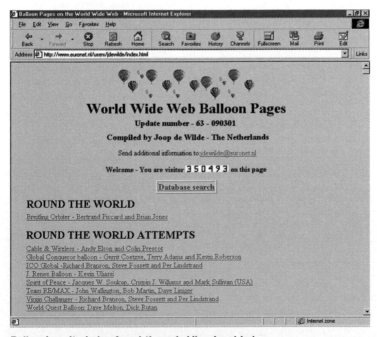

Ballooning site index found through *Librarians' Index*

Sometimes you can use a search engine as you would an online subject directory. Many search engines list categories such as Government, Health, News, Science, and so forth. Clicking on a general category will take you to lists of increasingly specific categories. Eventually, you will get a list of Web pages on the most specific subtopic you select. These search engines also allow you to click on a category and enter keywords for a search. Below is a screen shot of Yahoo! showing the categories of that search engine. Box 144 lists addresses for subject directories.

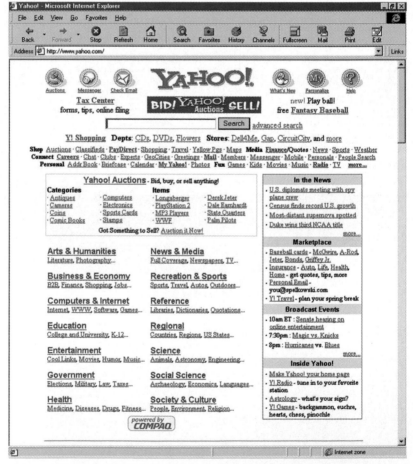

Yahoo! search page lets you find relevant sites through subject directory or through keyword search

◉ **Addresses for subject directories** 144

AskERIC Virtual Library	http://ericir.syr.edu
Libweb: Berkeley (CA) Digital Library SunSITE	http://sunsite.berkeley.edu/Libweb/
Carnegie Mellon Libraries Online Reference Tools	http://www.library.cmu.edu/ bySubject/CS+ECE/lib/reftools.html
Infomine	http://infomine.ucr.edu/
Internet Public Library	http://www.ipl.org
LibCat	www.metronet.lib.mn.us/lc/lc1.html [character preceding "html" is the numeral 1, *not* lowercase L]
Librarians' Index to the Internet	http://www.lii.org
Library of Congress	http://lcweb.loc.gov
THOR: The Virtual Reference Desk (Purdue University)	http://thorplus.lib.purdue.edu/ vlibrary/index.html
Virtual Information Center	http://www.lib.berkeley.edu
Virtual Desk Reference	http://www.refdesk.com
Virtual Reference Collection	http://www.lib.uci.edu/rraz/ genref.html
Virtual Reference Desk (University of Delaware)	http://www.lib.udel.edu/

EXERCISE 34-1

To practice using online sources, try the following activities.

1. Use your Web browser to find your college's Web site. From here, find your library's Web page. What services does the site offer? Is the page itself searchable? Is online catalog searching available?

2. Choose a subject that interests you and begin a search. Try using a subject directory to find subtopics for the subject and type a keyword to limit the search. What outcomes did you get? Did you find relevant Web pages? Why or why not? List at least eight sites that have useful material for your search and explain why they may be helpful. Keep the list for Exercise 34-2.

3. Try using a meta search engine to search for the same topic you used in question 2 above. What differences do you note in the kinds of hits and links you receive?

34d.2 Conducting a keyword search

To conduct a **keyword search,** type your topic in the search box on the opening page of the SEARCH ENGINE. The engine scans for the word(s) in Web pages, and then lists sites that contain them. Very general terms may appear on thousands of Web sites. If a search engine finds thousands of hits for your keyword, do not give up. Instead, use more specific keywords.

For example, a keyword search for *ballooning* yielded 115,000 hits, or links to Web sites, containing the one word. A search for the keywords *hot air ballooning* yielded 45,100 hits. Finally, by narrowing more and more, a search for the keywords *hot air ballooning Duluth* yielded a manageable 57 hits. The screen shot below shows the beginning of a keyword search on the search engine Google. (*Note:* The quotation marks around the keywords signal that your search is for an exact match; see explanation on page 554.)

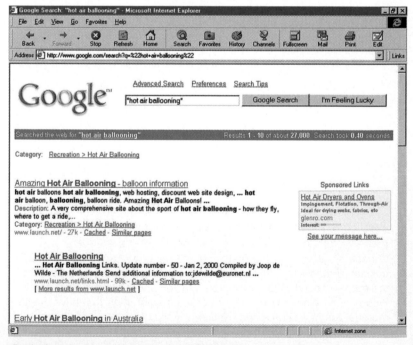

Beginning of a keyword search on the Google™ search engine

As you become more adept at using keywords, your searches will become more directed and less time-consuming. Also, the further you are in the process of drafting a thesis statement or assertion, the more specific your searches will become. The keywords in your thesis statement are likely to be good keywords for searches. In addition, most keyword search engines permit you to tailor very specific searches by means of Boolean expressions, quotation marks, and truncation.

Boolean expressions

Some search engines let you create keyword combinations that narrow and refine your search. These searches use **Boolean expressions,** the words AND, OR, NOT, and NEAR (or symbols that represent these words). Parentheses can also be used in the Boolean query box to group expressions similar to the way you would group mathematical functions. When you use Boolean expressions between keywords, you are telling the search engine to list Web sites with your keyword specifications and ignore others. When you group terms in parentheses, you direct or "force" the engine to look first at the grouped words and then at either the ungrouped or grouped words that follow.

Box 145 explains Boolean expressions in detail, using a keyword search on the subject "hot air ballooning" as an example. Without Boolean expressions, the keywords *hot air ballooning North America* would yield pages that include any of these words—and not necessarily in that order. Note the amount of weeding out that the Boolean expressions allow.

⊙ **Using Boolean expressions**   **145**

Term	Function
AND	Narrows the focus of your search because both keywords must be found. If you want to find information on "North American hot air ballooning," try the expression *hot air ballooning AND North America.*
NOT	Narrows a search by excluding texts containing the specified word or phrase. If you want to eliminate "Canadian" from your search, try *North American hot air ballooning NOT Canada.* NOT must sometimes be used with another expression, such as AND. AltaVista, for example, does not accept *North American hot air ballooning NOT Canada.* Instead, specify *North American hot air ballooning AND NOT Canada.*

→

Using Boolean expressions *(continued)*   **145**

Term   **Function**

OR   Expands a search's parameters by including more than one keyword. To expand your search to South American hot air ballooning, try the expression *hot air ballooning AND North OR South America*. Pages mentioning both "North America and hot air ballooning" and "South America and hot air ballooning" would be returned.

NEAR   Indicates that the keywords may be found close to each other or on either side of each other. If you want to localize your search on ballooning to a specific state, try *hot air ballooning NEAR Texas*. The sources returned would contain references to hot air ballooning in Texas. However, depending on which search engine you are using, NEAR will produce hits that are found in the same sentence or on the same site.

( )   If you use more than two expressions, use parentheses to group them. For example, *(hot air ballooning AND history) AND (Colorado or Kansas)* would find documents about the history of hot air ballooning in Colorado or Kansas (and both, if possible).

Box 145 is not meant to be all-inclusive. Though the expressions listed are commonly used, it is always a good idea to review the search engine's own search tips, as engines differ in how they handle expressions and formats. For example, some search engines are "case sensitive," which means that they look for keywords exactly as you type them, including capitals and lowercase letters. To be sure, check the Help box and/or "Search Tips" feature of any search engine you use.

Quotation marks for online searches

You can also use quotation marks to narrow your search. Enclosing keywords in quotations "asks" the search engine to match the exact word order on a Web page. For example, a search on AltaVista for "The World of Commercial Ballooning" nets only 39 hits, each containing the title or phrase *the world of commercial ballooning*. This is helpful when searching for a name, for example. If you search for James Joyce without using quotation marks, most engines would return pages containing words *James* and *Joyce* anywhere in the document. A search using "James Joyce" would bring you closer to finding Web sites about the Irish writer.

Truncation

A **truncation,** sometimes called *wildcarding,* allows you to look for sites by listing only the first few letters of a keyword. You can also "ask" the search engine to search for variants of a keyword by using the wild card symbol * in place of either the word ending or some of the letters in the word. For example, a truncated search for *wom*n* (or, in some cases, *wom#n*) would return hits for *woman* and *women.* This is helpful when you do not want to exclude the plural form of a noun or when a term comes in varying forms, as in the *balloon/ballooning* example.

Be careful not to use broad truncations, or you will open up your search too much. *Auto*,* for example, would return *automobile, automatic, automaton,* and so forth. In this instance, using OR might be more helpful, as in *automatic OR automation.*

Most search engines recognize the symbol * for truncation, but a few use specialized symbols such as **?, :,** or **+.** As always, check the Help screen of whichever engine you use for specific details.

If your college offers a workshop in using search engines, take it. If it does not, you might try Cornell University's *Lost in Cyberspace? A Workshop on Internet Search Engines,* <http://www.library.cornell.edu/okuref/websearch.html>. Box 146 also offers additional help in using search engines.

 Using search engines for research   146

1. Use AltaVista or another keyword engine only when you have a very specific, narrow topic with unique keywords. If you enter a general topic in AltaVista, you will be overwhelmed with thousands of returns. If this happens, switch to a subject directory such as Yahoo! and try reentering the general topic.

2. Most search engines attempt to search as much of the Web as possible. But because the World Wide Web is vast and not organized, search engines will give different results for the same search.

3. Always check the Help screen on the search engine you use. As with the rest of the Web, search engines add or change features frequently.

4. Keep trying to narrow your keywords. This cannot be said often enough.

5. Type a keyword in the "Ranking" window or box even if it duplicates the window above. If you do not do this, the search is returned in random order, and the most important source may be last.

→

Using search engines for research *(continued)*   **146**

6. If possible, limit the date range. The date on a Web site tells when it was added to the Web or last revised. That date may or may not be the same as the copyright date.

7. When you find a useful site, go to the toolbar at the top of the screen and click on "Bookmark" (or "Favorites") and then click on "Add." The Bookmark function allows you to return to a good source easily by opening Bookmarks and double-clicking on the address.

8. Use the History or Go function to track the sites you visit, in case you want to revisit one you previously thought was not helpful. You can also move a site from History to Bookmark.

34e   How can I avoid plagiarizing from online sources?

Easy access to Web sources can be a tremendous help for research. But because Web publishing is unregulated, it creates special responsibilities for the online researcher. To avoid plagiarism in all of its forms, you must become a critical reader and researcher and carefully follow the instructions in Chapter 31 of this handbook.

The special risks of plagiarism from online sources demand that you take some structured actions. Box 147 tells how you can take precautions.

◉   **Guidelines for avoiding plagiarism**   **147**
    of online sources

■ Print out immediately (or download to disk and print out later)—or create a file of—those sources you find that relate to your topic. Do this once you've narrowed your research focus, so that you will have to keep track of less information.

■ Make absolutely certain each record shows (a) the URL, (b) the name of the source, and (c) the date you accessed the source and printed it out (or the date you downloaded the source).

■ Check your required DOCUMENTATION STYLE to see exactly what details you'll need for listing the source in your IN-TEXT CITATIONS and final BIBLIOGRAPHY.

→

**Guidelines for avoiding plagiarism   147
of online sources** *(continued)*

- Write the exact reason you chose to make a copy of the source. Underline or highlight particular sections you think will be useful to you, and say why.
- Never think your instructor won't know when you're plagiarizing. Today, many Web sites are available to educators that can reveal plagiarism in a click. Most of these sites search all full and partial papers for sale on the Web or Internet, all material stored in every search engine, and the academic sites that carry scholarly books, articles, and data. The plagiarism-search site then resorts what words are plagiarized and from what sources.
- Check all the QUOTATIONS, PARAPHRASES, and SUMMARIES in your final research paper against the original material.

34f How do I evaluate online sources?

Since *anyone* can post *anything* on the Web, some sources you find may very well be PLAGIARIZED (see 31a). Also, many sources on the Web have been written by individuals posing as experts and giving false or misleading information. If you unintentionally use such a source, it nonetheless constitutes plagiarism on your part. You are always account-able for the sources you choose. To evaluate a source, use the lists in Box 148. These criteria can help you make a general survey to separate the sources worth a closer look from those not likely to be reputable.

 Judging the reliability of an online site   148

Reliable sites are from

- Educational, not-for-profit, or government organizations; Internet addresses ending in *.edu, .org, .gov,* or a country abbreviation such as *.us* or *.uk.* These organizations should list their sources. If they fail to, don't use them.

Questionable sites are from

- Commercial organizations advertising to sell a product (*.com*); Web sites that are advertisements or personal pages; junk mail. These sites may or may not list sources. If they fail to, don't use them. If they do, check that they are legitimate, not a front for the commercial enterprise.

→

Judging the reliability of an online site *(continued)* 148

Reliable sites are from

- Expert authors. They have degrees or experience in their field that you can check. See if the names appear in other reliable sources, in bibliographies on your topic, or in reference books in your college's library.

- Reliable print sources online. Online versions of the *New York Times, Time* magazine, etc., from the publisher or in a full-text index are just as reliable as the print versions.

Questionable sites are from

- Anonymous authors or authors without identifiable credentials. The reader doesn't know about them or their motives for posting to the site. Chat rooms; Usenet, discussion groups, bulletin boards, and similar networks are questionable for the same reasons.

- Excerpts and quotations from the *New York Times,* etc., that appear on a site that is not the publisher's official site may be edited in a biased or inaccurate manner. Sources may be incomplete and inaccurate.

Most sites also contain material that will help you assess their credibility, such as a bibliography or links to the author or editor. Sites that do not contain such verifying information should be discarded, however useful they may seem. It is far better to err on the side of caution than to use a plagiarized source. Box 149 gives you details on applying these general guidelines to individual online sources.

 Guidelines for evaluating each online source 149

Evaluating Authority

1. Is an author named? Are credentials listed for the author? (Look for an academic degree, an e-mail address at an academic or other institution, a credentials page, a list of publications. The last part of an e-mail address can be informative: *.edu* is an address at an educational site; *.gov* is an address at a government site; and *.com* is an address at a commercial or business site.) Be

→

Guidelines for evaluating each online source 149
(continued)

careful: Many colleges and universities now host student Web sites. These sites often end with *.edu*, as you will find in regular academic sites.

2. Is the author recognized as an authority in reputable print sources? Is the author cited in any bibliographies found in print sources?

3. Do you recognize the author as an authority from other research on your topic? Is the site cross-referenced to other credible and authoritative sites?

Evaluating Reliability

4. Do you detect from the language or layout of information either any bias or an unbalanced presentation?

5. Ask, Why does the information exist? Who gains from it? Why was it written? Why was it put on the Internet?

6. Are you asked to take action of any kind? If yes, don't use the source unless you're sure the site isn't trying to manipulate you toward its bias. For example, the World Wildlife Fund can ask for contributions and still maintain a Web site that contains reliable information. Conversely, a hate group can't be trusted as objective.

7. Is the material outdated? Is the date recent, or was the last update recent?

8. Does the author give an e-mail address for questions or comments?

Evaluating Value

9. Is the information well supported with evidence? Or do the authors express points of view without backing up their position with solid evidence?

10. Remember to read online sources using reflective reading (5c–5f) and reasoning (5a and 5b). Is the TONE unbiased (5c.2 and 21g) and the reasoning logical (5i and 5j)?

For more help with evaluating online sources, try these Web sites:

Thinking Critically About World Wide Web Resources
http://www.library.ucla.edu/libraries/college/help/critical/index.htm

Thinking Critically About Discipline-Based World Wide Web Resources
http://www.library.ucla.edu/libraries/college/help/critical/discipline.htm

Evaluating Web Resources

http://www2.widener.edu/Wolfgram-Memorial-Library/webevaluation/webeval.htm

EXERCISE 34-2

Select three of the Web sites you found for Exercise 34-1, activity 2. Evaluate these sites by applying the guidelines in Boxes 148 and 149. Write out your evaluations. Rank the sites according to their authority, reliability, and value, and tell why you support this ranking.

35 MLA DOCUMENTATION WITH CASE STUDY

35a What is MLA style?

The Modern Language Association (MLA) sponsors the **MLA style,** a DOCUMENTATION system widely used in the humanities. First, for documenting sources within the text of a research paper, MLA style calls for **parenthetical references,** explained in section 35b. Section 35c shows nineteen models that differ according to the kind of source you use.

Second, for complete bibliographic information about each source you've mentioned in your parenthetical or *in-text citations,* MLA style calls for a **Works Cited** list, placed at the end of your research paper. It includes only the sources you've actually used in your research paper, not any you've consulted but haven't used. Section 35d gives instructions for composing Works Cited pages, followed by sixty-two models based on the kind of source (book, article, Web site, etc.) you use.

For up-to-date information about MLA style for Internet sites and electronic sources—since technology seems to change daily—see MLA's Web site <http://www.mla.org>. Also, consult the fifth edition of the *MLA Handbook for Writers of Research Papers* by Joseph Gibaldi (1999) if you need more than what is covered in this chapter. The research papers in sections 35e.2 and 40e show how parenthetical citations and an MLA Works Cited work together.

35b What is an MLA in-text citation?

An MLA **in-text citation** consists of source information placed in parentheses within the body of a research paper. It signals that material has been quoted, summarized, or paraphrased from specific parts of sources.

In most in-text citations, an author's name (or, if none, a shortened title) identifies the source and the exact page numbers in that source where the reader can locate the original material. In general, introduce names of authors and titles of sources in your own sentences, and put page number information in parentheses at the end of a quotation, summary, or paraphrase.

👁 **MLA FORMAT ALERT:** Position a parenthetical citation at the end of the material it refers to, preferably at the end of a sentence, if that is not too far away from the material. At the end of a sentence, place a parenthetical reference before the sentence's end punctuation. ●

35c What are MLA guidelines for in-text citations?

The following directory corresponds to the numbered examples that follow it. The examples show how to handle various PARENTHETICAL REFERENCES or CITATIONS in the body of your paper. Remember, however, that you can usually integrate author names and titles of SOURCES into your sentences.

Directory—MLA In-text Citations

1. Paraphrased or Summarized Source—MLA
2. Source of a Short Quotation—MLA
3. Source of a Long Quotation—MLA
4. One Author—MLA
5. Two or Three Authors—MLA
6. More Than Three Authors—MLA
7. More Than One Source by an Author—MLA
8. Two or More Authors with the Same Last Name—MLA
9. Work with a Group or Corporate Author—MLA
10. Work Listed by Title—MLA
11. Multivolume Work—MLA
12. Material from a Novel, Play, or Poem—MLA
13. Work in an Anthology or Other Collection—MLA
14. Indirect Source—MLA
15. Two or More Sources in One Reference—MLA
16. An Entire Work—MLA
17. An Electronic Source with a Name or Title and Page Numbers—MLA
18. An Electronic Source That Numbers Paragraphs—MLA
19. An Electronic Source Without Page or Paragraph Numbers—MLA

1. Citing a Paraphrased or Summarized Source—MLA

According to Brent Staples, IQ tests give scientists little

insight into intelligence (293). [Author name cited in text; page

number cited in parentheses.]

In "The IQ Cult," journalist Brent Staples states that IQ tests give scientists little insight into intelligence (293). [Title of source, author name, and author credentials cited in text; page number cited in parentheses.]

IQ tests give scientists little insight into intelligence (Staples 293). [Author name and page number cited in parentheses.]

2. Citing the Source of a Short Quotation—MLA

If it is true that "thoughts, emotions, imagination and predispositions occur concurrently . . . [and] interact with other brain processes" (Caine and Caine 66), it is easy to understand why "whatever [intelligence] might be, paper and pencil tests aren't the tenth of it" (Staples 293).

👁 **MLA FORMAT ALERT:** When a quotation is no longer than four handwritten or typed lines, enclose the quoted words in quotation marks to distinguish them from your own words in the sentence. Place the parentheses after the closing quotation mark but before the sentence-ending punctuation. If a quotation ends with an exclamation point or a question mark, however, put that punctuation mark before the closing quotation mark, put the parenthetical citation next, and then put a sentence-ending period after the parenthetical citation.

Coles asks, "What binds together a Mormon banker in Utah with his brother, or other coreligionists in Illinois or Massachusetts?" (2). ●

3. Citing the Source of a Long Quotation—MLA

Gray and Viens explain how, by tapping into a student's highly developed spatial-mechanical intelligence, one teacher can bolster a student's poor writing skills:

> The teacher asked that during "journal time" Jacob create a tool dictionary to be used as a resource in the mechanical learning center. After several entries in which he drew and described tools and other materials, Jacob confidently moved on to writing about other things of import to him, such as his brothers and a recent birthday party. Rather than shy away from all things linguistic--he previously

```
had refused any task requiring a pencil--Jacob became
invested in journal writing. (23-24)
```

MLA FORMAT ALERT: When a quotation is longer than four handwritten or typed lines, do not put quotation marks around the quoted words. Instead, set the quoted words off from your own words by indenting each line of the quotation. In a typed paper, use a ten-space indent for each line of a quotation longer than four lines. If you are handwriting or using a computer, indent each line of the quotation one inch. Put one space after the last punctuation mark of the quotation, and then put in the parenthetical citation. For other examples of long quotations, see the student research papers in sections 35e and 40e. ●

4. Citing One Author—MLA

Give an author's name as it appears on the source: for a book, on the title page; for an article, directly below the title or at the end of the article. Many nonprint sources also name an author; for CDs, cassettes, tapes, or software, for example, check the printed sleeve or cover. For an online source, identify the author exactly as identified online.

```
One test asks four-year-olds to choose between one
marshmallow now or two marshmallows later (Gibbs 60).
```

5. Citing Two or Three Authors—MLA

Give the names in the same order as in the source. Spell out *and*. For three authors, use commas to separate the authors' names.

```
As children get older, they begin to express several
different kinds of intelligence (Todd and Taylor 23).
```

```
Another measure of emotional intelligence is the success of
inter- and intrapersonal relationships (Voigt, Dees, and
Prigoff 14).
```

6. Citing More Than Three Authors—MLA

With three or more authors, you can name them all or use the first author's name only, followed by *et al.*, either in a parenthetical reference or in your sentence. In citations, do not underline or italicize *et al.* No period follows *et,* but do use a period after *al.*

USAGE ALERT: The abbreviation *et al.* stands for "and others"; when an author's name followed by *et al.* is a subject, use a plural verb.

```
Carter et al. have found that emotional security varies
depending on the circumstances of the social interaction
(158). ●
```

Emotional security varies depending on the circumstances of
the social interaction (Carter et al. 158).

7. Citing More Than One Source by an Author—MLA

When you use two or more sources by an author, include the relevant
title in each citation. In parenthetical citations, use a shortened version
of the title. For example, in a paper using two of Howard Gardner's
works, *Frames of Mind: The Theory of Multiple Intelligences* and
"Reflections on Multiple Intelligences: Myths and Messages," use
Frames and "Reflections." Shorten the titles as much as possible, keeping them unambiguous to readers and starting them with the word by
which you alphabetize each work in WORKS CITED. Separate the author's
name and the title with a comma, but do not use punctuation between
the title and the page number.

Although it seems straightforward to think of multiple
intelligences as multiple approaches to learning (Gardner,
Frames 60-61), an intelligence is not a learning style
(Gardner, "Reflections" 202-203).

When you incorporate the title into your own sentences, you can
omit a subtitle, but do not shorten the title more than that.

8. Citing Two or More Authors with the Same Last Name—MLA

Use each author's first and last name in each citation, whether in your
sentences or in parenthetical citations.

According to Anne Cates, psychologists can predict how
empathetic an adult will be from his or her behavior at age
two (41), but other researchers disagree (Tyrone Cates 171).

9. Citing a Work with a Group or Corporate Author—MLA

When a corporation or other group is named as the author of a
source you want to cite, use the corporate name just as you would an
individual's name.

In a five-year study, the Boston Women's Health Collective
reported that these tests are usually unreliable (11).

A five-year study shows that these tests are usually
unreliable (Boston Women's Health Collective 11).

10. Citing a Work Listed by Title—MLA

If no author is named, use the title in citations. In your own
sentences, use the full main title and omit a subtitle, if any. For

parenthetical citations, shorten the title as much as possible (making sure that the shortened version refers unambiguously to the correct source), and always make the first word the one by which you alphabetize it. "Are You a Day or Night Person?" is the full title of the article in the following citation.

```
The "morning lark" and "night owl" connotations are typically
used to categorize the human extremes ("Are You" 11).
```

11. Citing a Multivolume Work—MLA

When you cite more than one volume of a multivolume work, include the relevant volume number in each citation. (In the Works Cited, list the multivolume work once and give the total number of volumes; see item 9 in the Works Cited examples in 35d.1.) Give the volume number first, followed by a colon and one space, followed by the page number(s).

```
By 1900, the Amazon forest dwellers had been exposed to
these viruses (Rand 3: 202).

Rand believes that forest dwellers in Borneo escaped illness
from retroviruses until the 1960s (4: 518-19).
```

12. Citing Material from a Novel, Play, or Poem—MLA

When you cite material from literary works, providing the part, chapter, act, scene, canto, stanza, or line numbers usually helps readers locate what you are referring to more than do page numbers alone. Unless your instructor tells you not to, use arabic numerals for these references, even if the literary work uses roman numerals.

For novels that use them, give part and/or chapter numbers after page numbers. Use a semicolon after the page number but a comma to separate a part from a chapter.

```
Flannery O'Connor describes one character in The Violent
Bear It Away as "divided in two--a violent and a rational
self" (139; pt. 2, ch. 6).
```

For plays that use them, give act, scene, and line numbers. Use periods between these numbers.

```
Among the most quoted of Shakespeare's lines is Hamlet's
soliloquy beginning "To be, or not to be: that is the
question" (3.1.56).
```

For poems and plays that use them, give canto, stanza, and line numbers. Use periods between these numbers.

In "To Autumn," Keats's most melancholy image occurs in the
lines "Then in a wailful choir the small gnats mourn / Among
the river swallows" (3.27-28).

⟲ **MLA ABBREVIATION ALERT:** Because the typed or typeset abbreviation
for *line* (*l.*, plural *ll.*) can be misread as the numeral 1, the *MLA
Handbook* advises beginning your first reference to lines with the word
line (or *lines*). After the first citation, omit the word and just give the
numbers. ●

13. Citing a Work in an Anthology or Other Collection—MLA

You may want to cite a work you have read in a book that contains many
works by various authors and that was compiled or edited by someone other
than the person you are citing. For example, suppose you want to cite
"Several Things" by Martha Collins, which you have read in a literature text
by Pamela Annas and Robert Rosen. Use Martha Collins's name and the
title of her work in the in-text citation and as the first block of information
for the entry in the Works Cited list (see item 11 in section 35d.1).

In "Several Things," Martha Collins enumerates what could
take place in the lines of her poem: "Plums could appear, on
a pewter plate / A dead red hare, hung by one foot. / A vase
of flowers. Three shallots" (2-4).

14. Citing an Indirect Source—MLA

When you want to quote words that you found quoted in someone
else's work, put the name of the person whose words you are quoting
into your own sentence. Indicate the work where you found the quotation either in your sentence or in a parenthetical citation beginning with
qtd. in.

⟲ **RESEARCH ALERT:** When it is possible to do so, find the PRIMARY
SOURCE for words that you want to quote rather than taking a quotation
from a SECONDARY SOURCE.

Martin Scorsese acknowledges the link between himself
and his films: "I realize that all my life, I've been an
outsider. I splatter bits of myself all over the screen"
(qtd. in Giannetti and Eyman 397).

Giannetti and Eyman quote Martin Scorsese as acknowledging
the link between himself and his films: "I realize that all
my life, I've been an outsider. I splatter bits of myself
all over the screen" (397). ●

15. Citing Two or More Sources in One Reference—MLA

If more than one source has contributed to an idea, opinion, or fact in your paper, acknowledge all of them. In a parenthetical citation, separate each block of information with a semicolon followed by one space.

```
Once researchers agreed that multiple intelligences existed,
their next step was to try to measure or define them (West
17; Arturi 477; Gibbs 68).
```

Because long parenthetical citations can disturb the flow of your paper, consider using an endnote or footnote for citing multiple sources; see section 35d.2.

16. Citing an Entire Work—MLA

References to an entire work usually fit best into your own sentences.

```
In Frames of Mind, Gardner proposes a revolutionary
expansion of our understanding of human intelligence.
```

17. Citing an Electronic Source with a Name or Title and Page Numbers—MLA

The principles that govern in-text citations of electronic sources are exactly the same as the ones that apply to books, articles, letters, interviews, or any other source you get information from on paper or in person. You put in your own sentences or in parenthetical references enough information for a reader to be able to locate full information about the source in the Works Cited list.

When an electronically accessed source identifies its author, use the author's name for in-text citations. If an electronic source does not name the author, use its title for in-text citations and for the first block of information in that source's Works Cited entry. (See item 10 in this section for an example of a work cited by its title and for advice about shortening a title for an in-text citation.)

When an electronic source has page numbers, use them exactly as you would the page numbers of a print source.

18. Citing an Electronic Source That Numbers Paragraphs—MLA

When an electronic source has numbered paragraphs (instead of page numbers), use them for in-text references as you would page numbers, with two differences: (1) Use a comma followed by one space after the name (or title), and (2) use the abbreviation *par.* for a reference to one paragraph or *pars.* for a reference to more than one paragraph, followed by the number(s) of the paragraph(s) you are citing.

Artists seem to be haunted by the fear that psychoanalysis
might destroy creativity while it reconstructs personality
(Francis, pars. 22-25).

19. Citing an Electronic Source Without Page or Paragraph Numbers—MLA

Many online sources do not number pages or paragraphs. In the Works Cited entry for such a source, include the abbreviation *n. pag.* ("no pagination"). This abbreviation serves to explain to readers why in-text references to this source do not cite page numbers. Here are two examples referring to "The Naturalist Intelligence," by Thomas Hoerr, a Web site without page numbers or paragraph numbers.

Meriwether Lewis, the legendary explorer of the United
States' Northwest Territory, certainly possessed the
naturalist intelligence (Hoerr).

Thomas Hoerr mentions Meriwether Lewis, the legendary
explorer of the United States' Northwest Territory, as
someone who possessed the naturalist intelligence.

35d How should I compile an MLA-style Works Cited list?

In MLA DOCUMENTATION, **Work Cited** pages give complete bibliographic information for each source used in a research paper. This WORKS CITED list should include only the sources from which you quote or paraphrase or summarize. Do not include sources that you have consulted but do not refer to in the paper. Box 150 gives general information about a Works Cited list, and the rest of this chapter provides models of specific kinds of Works Cited entries.

⊙ **Guidelines for an MLA-style**   **150**
     Works Cited list

■ TITLE
    Works Cited

■ PLACEMENT OF LIST
    Start a new page numbered sequentially with the rest of the
    paper, after Notes pages, if any.

                                             ⟶

MLA MLA MLA MLA MLA MLA MLA MLA MLA MLA MLA MLA

Guidelines for an MLA-style Works Cited list *(continued)* 150

■ CONTENTS AND FORMAT

Include all sources quoted from, paraphrased, or summarized in your paper. Start each entry on a new line and at the regular left margin. If the entry uses more than one line, indent all lines—beginning with the second—five spaces (or one-half inch) from the left margin. Double-space all lines.

■ SPACING AFTER PUNCTUATION

On its Web site, the MLA explains that computer type fonts have influenced many users of MLA style to leave one space rather than two spaces after punctuation at the ends of sentences. The *MLA Handbook* uses one space. Some word processing programs highlight two spaces as an error. Put one space after a comma or a colon.

■ ARRANGEMENT OF ENTRIES

Alphabetize by author's last name. If no author is named, alphabetize by the title's first significant word (not *A, An,* or *The*).

■ AUTHORS' NAMES

Use first names and middle names or middle initials, if any, as given in the source. Do not reduce to initials any name that is given in full. For one author or the first-named author in multi-author works, give the last name first. Use the word *and* with two or more authors. List multiple authors in the order given in the source. Use a comma between the first author's last and first names and after each complete author name except the last. After the last author's name, use a period: Fein, Ethel Andrea, Bert Griggs, and Delaware Rogash.

Include *Jr., Sr., II, III,* but do not include other titles and degrees before or after a name. For example, an entry for a work by Edward Meep III, M.D., and Sir Feeney Bolton would start like this: Meep, Edward, III, and Feeney Bolton.

■ CAPITALIZATION OF TITLES

Capitalize all major words in titles.

■ SPECIAL TREATMENT OF TITLES

Use quotation marks around titles of shorter works (poems, short stories, essays, articles). Underline titles of longer works (books, names of newspapers or journals containing cited articles).

→

Guidelines for an MLA-style Works Cited list *(continued)*   150

For underlining, use an unbroken line like this (unless you use software that underlines only with a broken line like this). The MLA Web site states that although computers can create italic type, in student papers underlined roman type may be more exact. Check which style your instructor prefers.

When a book title includes the title of another work that is usually underlined (as with a novel, play, or long poem), the preferred MLA style is not to underline the incorporated title: `Decoding` `Jane` `Eyre`. For a second style MLA accepts, see item 20 in section 35d.1.

If the incorporated title is usually enclosed in quotation marks (as with a short story or short poem), keep the quotation marks and underline the complete title of the book (do not underline the period): `Theme` `and` `Form` `in "I` `Shall` `Laugh` `Purely."`

Drop *A, An,* or *The* as the first word of a periodical title.

■ **PLACE OF PUBLICATION**

If several cities are listed for the place of publication, give only the first. If a U.S. city name alone would be ambiguous, also give the state's two-letter postal abbreviation (see section 30l or a standard dictionary). For an unfamiliar city outside the United States, include an abbreviated country name or an abbreviated Canadian province name.

■ **PUBLISHER**

Use shortened names as long as they are clear: *Prentice* for *Prentice Hall, Simon* for *Simon & Schuster.* For university presses, use the capital letters *U* and *P* (without periods): `Oxford` `UP;` `U` `of` `Chicago` `P`

■ **PUBLICATION MONTH ABBREVIATIONS**

Abbreviate all publication months except *May, June,* and *July.* Use the first few letters followed by a period (*Sept., Dec.*). See section 30m.

■ **PARAGRAPH AND SCREEN NUMBERS IN ELECTRONIC SOURCES**

For electronic sources that number paragraphs instead of pages, at the end of the publication information give the total number of paragraphs followed by the abbreviation *pars.:* `77` `pars.` If screens are numbered, give the total number of screens as the final information in the entry. For in-text citations, use paragraph and screen numbers for reference as you use page numbers.

→

Guidelines for an MLA-style Works Cited list *(continued)*   150

■ PAGE RANGES

Give the page range—the starting page number and the ending page number, connected by a hyphen—of any paginated electronic source and any paginated print source that is part of a longer work (for example, a chapter in a book, an article in a journal). A range indicates that the cited work is on those pages and all pages in between. If that is not the case, use the style shown next for discontinuous pages. In either case, use numerals only, without the word *page* or *pages* or the abbreviation *p.* or *pp.*

Use the full second number through 99. Above that, use only the last two digits for the second number unless it would be unclear: *113–14* is clear, but *567–602* requires full numbers.

■ DISCONTINUOUS PAGES

Use the starting page number followed by a plus sign (+): 32+.

■ WORKS CITED ENTRIES: BOOKS

Citations for books have three main parts: author, title, and publication information (place of publication, publisher, and date of publication).

    AUTHOR   BOOK TITLE   PUBLICATION INFORMATION

Didion, Joan. Salvador. New York: Simon, 1983.

■ WORKS CITED ENTRIES: PRINT ARTICLES

Citations for periodical articles contain three major parts: author, title of article, and publication information (usually periodical title, volume number, year of publication, and page range).

    AUTHOR   ARTICLE TITLE

Shuter, Robert. "A Field Study of Nonverbal

Communication in Germany, Italy, and the

             JOURNAL TITLE

United States." Communication Monographs

    PUBLICATION
    INFORMATION

44 (1977): 298-305.

→

Guidelines for an MLA-style   **150**
Works Cited list *(continued)*

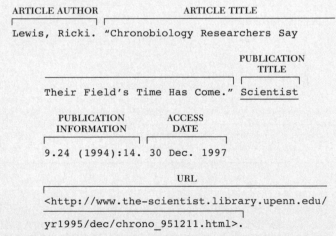

ARTICLE   JOURNAL   PUBLICATION
TITLE   TITLE   INFORMATION

"A Start." New Republic 2 May 1994: 7+.

■ **WORKS CITED ENTRIES: ONLINE SOURCES WITH URLS**

To document sources reached by entering a URL or Internet address (including World Wide Web, FTP, and Gopher sites), list as much of the following information as you can find: author, title, publication information about a print version (if there is one), publication information about the online source, the date you accessed the material, and the URL (electronic address). For these sources, the URL is required in the Works Cited entry, enclosed in angle brackets <like these>, after the access date and before the period at the end of the entry. Here is an entry for an article in a scientific news journal that appears only on the Web:

ARTICLE AUTHOR   ARTICLE TITLE

Lewis, Ricki. "Chronobiology Researchers Say

                             PUBLICATION
                             TITLE

Their Field's Time Has Come." Scientist

PUBLICATION   ACCESS
INFORMATION   DATE

9.24 (1994):14. 30 Dec. 1997

                    URL

<http://www.the-scientist.library.upenn.edu/

yr1995/dec/chrono_951211.html>.

■ **WORKS CITED ENTRIES: PORTABLE AND ONLINE SOURCES WITHOUT URLS**

Citations for electronic sources that do not have URLs contain at least six major parts: author, publication, information, title of database, publication medium, name of vendor or computer service, and electronic publication date (add access date if different). Electronic versions of sources that also appear in print start with information about the print version. Here is an entry for a journal article accessed through a computer service; it also →

Guidelines for an MLA-style **150**
Works Cited list *(continued)*

has a print version. This entry includes an online search keyword
(see items 49 and 51 in section 35d.1).

ARTICLE TITLE	TITLE OF PRINT JOURNAL	PUBLICATION INFORMATION FOR PRINT JOURNAL

"A Start." New Republic (2 May 1994): n. pag.

ELECTRONIC PUBLICATION MEDIUM	ONLINE SERVICE	ACCESS DATE

Online. America Online. 21 Apr. 1996.

KEYWORD

Keyword: new republic.

Here is an entry for an article from a CD-ROM encyclopedia:

ARTICLE AUTHOR	ARTICLE TITLE	CD-ROM TITLE

Regan, Robert. "Poe, Edgar Allan." Academic American

ELECTRONIC PUBLICATION MEDIUM	CD-ROM PUBLICATION INFORMATION

Encyclopedia. CD-ROM. Danbury, CT: Grolier

Electronic Publishing, 1993.

35d.1 Following MLA guidelines for specific sources in a Works Cited list

The directory below corresponds to the numbered examples that follow it. Not every possible documentation model is here. You may find that you have to combine features of models to document a particular source. You will also find information in the *MLA Handbook for Writers of Research Papers* (5th edition, 1999), by Joseph Gibaldi, and at <http://www.mla.org>.

Directory—MLA Style

PRINT SOURCES

34. Published and Unpublished Letters—MLA
35. Map or Chart—MLA

NONPRINT SOURCES
36. Interview—MLA
37. Lecture, Speech, or Address—MLA
38. Film, Videotape, or DVD—MLA
39. Recording—MLA
40. Live Performance—MLA
41. Work of Art, Photograph, or Musical Composition—MLA
42. Radio or Television Program—MLA
43. Microfiche Collection of Articles—MLA

PORTABLE ELECTRONIC SOURCES
44. CD-ROM Database: Abstract with a Print Version—MLA
45. CD-ROM: Article from a Periodical with a Print Version—MLA
46. CD-ROM: Selection from a Book with a Print Version—MLA
47. CD-ROM: Material with No Print Version—MLA
48. Work in More Than One Publication Medium—MLA

ONLINE SOURCES: NO URL
49. Online Service Access: Abstract with a Print Version—MLA
50. Online Service Access: Material with No Print Version—MLA
51. Online Service Access with a Keyword: Article from a Periodical with a Print Version—MLA
52. Online Service Access Showing a Path—MLA
53. Online Service Access at a Library—MLA

URL-ACCESSED ONLINE SOURCES
54. URL Access: Book—MLA
55. URL Access: Book in a Scholarly Project—MLA
56. URL Access: Government-published Books—MLA
57. URL Access: Articles in Online Periodicals—MLA
58. URL Access: Professional Home Page—MLA
59. URL Access: Personal Home Page—MLA

OTHER ONLINE SOURCES
60. Online Posting—MLA
61. Synchronous Communication—MLA
62. E-Mail Message—MLA

PRINT SOURCES
1. Book by One Author—MLA

Welty, Eudora. <u>One Writer's Beginnings</u>. Cambridge: Harvard
    UP, 1984.

2. Book by Two or Three Authors—MLA

Leghorn, Lisa, and Katherine Parker. <u>Woman's Worth</u>. Boston:
    Routledge, 1981.

Kelly, Alfred H., Winfred A. Harbison, and Herman Belz. <u>The
    American Constitution: Its Origins and Development</u>. New
    York: Norton, 1983.

3. Book by More Than Three Authors—MLA

Moore, Mark H., et al. <u>Dangerous Offenders: The Elusive
    Target of Justice</u>. Cambridge: Harvard UP, 1984.

Give only the first author's name, followed by a comma and the
phrase *et al.* ("and others"). Otherwise, you must list all authors.

4. Two or More Works by the Same Author(s)—MLA

Gardner, Howard. <u>Intelligence Reframed: Multiple Intelligences
    for the 21st Century</u>. New York: Basic, 1999.

---. <u>Multiple Intelligences: The Theory in Practice</u>. New
    York: Basic, 1993.

Give author name(s) in the first entry only. In the second and subsequent entries, use three hyphens and a period to stand for exactly the
same name(s). If the person served as editor or translator, put a comma
and the appropriate abbreviation (*ed.* or *trans.*) following the three
hyphens. Arrange the works in alphabetical (not chronological) order
according to book title, ignoring labels such as *ed.* or *trans.*

5. Book by Group or Corporate Author—MLA

The Boston Women's Health Collective. <u>Our Bodies, Ourselves</u>.
    New York: Simon, 1986.

American Psychological Association. <u>Publication Manual of the
    American Psychological Association</u>. 4th ed. Washington:
    APA, 1994.

Cite the full name of the corporate author first. When a corporate author is also the publisher, use a shortened form of the corporate name at the publisher position.

6. Book with No Author Named—MLA

The Chicago Manual of Style. 14th ed. Chicago: U of Chicago
    P, 1993.

If there is no author's name on the title page, begin the citation with the title. Alphabetize the entry according to the first significant word of the title (*Chicago,* not *The*).

7. Book with an Author and an Editor—MLA

If your paper refers to the work of the book's author, put the author's name first; if your paper refers to the work of the editor, put the editor's name first.

Brontë, Emily. Wuthering Heights. Ed. David Daiches. London:
    Penguin, 1985.

Daiches, David, ed. Wuthering Heights. By Emily Brontë.
    London: Penguin, 1985.

8. Translation—MLA

Kundera, Milan. The Unbearable Lightness of Being. Trans.
    Michael Henry Heim. New York: HarperPerennial, 1999.

9. Work in Several Volumes or Parts—MLA

Randall, John Herman, Jr. The Career of Philosophy. Vol. 1.
    New York: Columbia UP, 1962. 2 vols.

If you are citing only one volume, put the volume number before the publication information. If you wish, you can give the total number of volumes at the end of the entry. MLA recommends using arabic numerals, even if the source uses roman numerals (*Vol. 6* for Vol. VI).

10. One Selection from an Anthology or an Edited Book—MLA

Galarza, Ernest. "The Roots of Migration." Aztlan: An
    Anthology of Mexican American Literature. Ed. Luis
    Valdez and Stan Steiner. New York: Knopf, 1972. 127-32.

Give the author and title of the selection first and then the full title of the anthology. Information about the editor starts with *Ed.* (for

"Edited by"), so do not use *Eds.* when there is more than one editor.
Give the name(s) of the editor(s) in normal first name–second name
order rather than reversing first and last names. The sample papers in
section 40e provide further examples of documenting selections from
anthologies.

11. More Than One Selection from the Same Anthology or Edited Book—MLA

Gilbert, Sandra M., and Susan Gubar, eds. <u>The Norton
    Anthology of Literature by Women</u>. New York: Norton,
    1985.

Kingston, Maxine Hong. "No Name Woman." Gilbert and Gubar
    2337-47.

If you cite more than one selection from the same anthology, you can
list the anthology as a separate entry with all the publication information.
Then, list each selection from the anthology by author and title of the
selection but give only the name of the editor(s) of the anthology and the
page number(s) of the selection. Here, *ed.* stands for "editor," so it is correct to use *eds.* when more than one editor is named.

12. Signed Article in a Reference Book—MLA

Burnbam, John C. "Freud, Sigmund." <u>The Encyclopedia of
    Psychiatry, Psychology, and Psychoanalysis</u>. Ed. Benjamin
    B. Wolman. New York: Holt, 1996.

If the articles in the book are alphabetically arranged, omit volume
and page numbers. If the reference book is frequently revised, give only
the edition and year of publication.

13. Unsigned Article in a Reference Book—MLA

"Ireland." <u>Encyclopaedia Britannica</u>. 1998 ed.

If you are citing a widely used reference work, do not give full publication information. Instead, give only the edition and year of publication.

14. Second or Later Edition—MLA

Gibaldi, Joseph. <u>MLA Handbook for Writers of Research
    Papers</u>. 5th ed. New York: MLA, 1999.

If a book is not a first edition, the edition number is on the title page.
Place the abbreviated information (*2nd ed., 3rd ed.,* etc.) between the
title and the publication information. Give only the latest copyright date
for the edition you are using.

15. Anthology or Edited Book—MLA

Purdy, John L., and James Ruppert, eds. <u>Nothing But the
    Truth: An Anthology of Native American Literature</u>. Upper
    Saddle River: Prentice Hall, 2001.

Here, *ed.* stands for "editor," so use *eds.* when more than one editor is named; also see items 10 and 11.

16. Introduction, Preface, Foreword, or Afterword—MLA

Angeli, Primo. Foreword. <u>Shopping Bag Design 2: Creative
    Promotional Graphics</u>. By Judi Radice. New York: Library
    of Applied Design-PBC International, 1991. 8.

Give first the name of the writer of the part you are citing, then the name of the cited part, capitalized but not underlined or in quotation marks. After the book title, write *By* and the book author's full name, if different from the writer of the cited material. If the writer of the cited material is the same as the book author, include only the last name after *By*. Following the publication information, give inclusive page numbers for the cited part, using roman or arabic numerals as the source does.

Fox-Genovese, Elizabeth. "Mothers and Daughters: The Ties
    That Bind." Foreword. <u>Southern Mothers</u>. Ed. Nagueyalti
    Warren and Sally Wolff. Baton Rouge: Louisiana State
    UP, 1999. iv-xviii.

When the introduction, preface, foreword, or afterword has a title (as above), include it in the citation before the section name.

17. Unpublished Dissertation or Essay—MLA

Geissinger, Shirley Burry. "Openness versus Secrecy in
    Adoptive Parenthood." Diss. U of North Carolina at
    Greensboro, 1984.

State the author's name first, then the title in quotation marks (not underlined), then a descriptive label (such as *Diss.* or *Unpublished essay*), followed by the degree-granting institution (for dissertations), and, finally, the date.

18. Republished Book—MLA

Hurston, Zora Neale. <u>Their Eyes Were Watching God</u>. 1937.
    Urbana: U of Illinois P, 1978.

Republishing information can be found on the copyright page. Give the date of the original version before the publication information for the version you are citing.

19. Book in a Series—MLA

Goldman, Dorothy J. Women Writers and World War I.
    Literature and Society Ser. New York: Macmillan, 1995.

Mukherjee, Meenakshi. Jane Austen. Women Writers Ser. New
    York: St. Martin's, 1991.

20. Book with a Title Within a Title—MLA

The MLA recognizes two distinct styles for handling normally independent titles when they appear within an underlined title. In the MLA's preferred style, the embedded title should not be underlined or set within quotation marks.

Lumiansky, Robert M., and Herschel Baker, eds. Critical
    Approaches to Six Major English Works: Beowulf Through
    Paradise Lost. Philadelphia: U of Pennsylvania P, 1968.

However, the MLA now accepts a second style for handling such embedded titles. In the alternative form, the normally independent titles should be set within quotation marks, and they should be underlined.

Lumiansky, Robert M., and Herschel Baker, eds. Critical
    Approaches to Six Major English Works: "Beowulf" Through
    "Paradise Lost." Philadelphia: U of Pennsylvania P,
    1968.

Use whichever style your instructor prefers.

21. Government Publication—MLA

United States. Cong. House. Committee on Resources. Coastal
    Heritage Trail Route in New Jersey. 106th Cong., 1st
    sess. H. Rept. 16. Washington: GPO, 1999.

---. ---. Senate. Bill to Reauthorize the Congressional
    Award Act. 106th Cong., 1st sess. S 380. Washington:
    GPO, 1999.

For government publications that name no author, start with the name of the government or government body. Then, name the government agency. *GPO* is a standard abbreviation for Government Printing Office, the publisher of most U.S. government publications.

22. Published Proceedings of a Conference—MLA

Harris, Diana, and Laurie Nelson-Heern, eds. <u>Proceedings of</u>
    <u>NECC 1981: National Education Computing Conference</u>.
    17-19 June 1981. Iowa City: Weeg Computing Center,
    U of Iowa, 1981.

23. Signed Article from a Daily Newspaper—MLA

Wyatt, Edward. "A High School Without a Home." <u>New York</u>
    <u>Times</u> 3 Dec. 1999, late ed.: B11.

Omit *A* or *The* as the first word in a newspaper title. Give the day, month, and year of the issue (and the edition, if applicable). If sections are designated, give the section letter as well as the page number. If an article runs on nonconsecutive pages, give the starting page number followed by a plus sign (for example, *23+* for an article that starts on page 23 and continues on page 42).

24. Editorial, Letter to the Editor, or Review—MLA

Didion, Joan. "The Day Was Hot and Still. . . ." Rev. of
    <u>Dutch: A Memoir of Ronald Reagan</u>, by Edmund Morris. <u>New</u>
    <u>York Review of Books</u> 4 Nov. 1999: 4-6.

"Mr. Gorbachev's Role." Editorial. <u>New York Times</u> 10 Nov.
    1999: A22.

Wolfe, Cheryl. Letter. <u>Newsweek</u> 22 Nov. 1999: 22.

25. Unsigned Article from a Daily Newspaper—MLA

"A Crusade to Revitalize the City Opera." <u>New York Times</u>
    25 Jan. 2001, late ed.: B6.

"Fire Delays School Election." <u>Patriot Ledger</u> [Quincy, MA]
    14 June 1994: A1.

If the city of publication is not part of the title, put it in square brackets after the title, not underlined.

26. Signed Article from a Weekly or Biweekly Periodical—MLA

Greenfield, Karl Taro. "Giving Away the E-Store." <u>Time</u>
    22 Nov. 1999: 58-60.

27. Signed Article in a Monthly or Bimonthly Periodical—MLA

Miller, Arthur. "A Line to Walk On: The Art of a Graceful
    Exit." <u>Harper's Magazine</u> Nov. 2000: 67-71.

28. Unsigned Article from a Weekly or Monthly Periodical—MLA

"A Salute to Everyday Heroes." <u>Time</u> 10 July 1989: 461.

29. Article from a Collection of Reprinted Articles—MLA

Brumberg, Abraham. "Russia After Perestroika." <u>New York
    Review of Books</u> 27 June 1991: 53-62. Rpt. in <u>Russian
    and Soviet History</u>. Ed. Alexander Dallin. Vol. 14 of
    <u>The Gorbachev Era</u>. New York: Garland, 1992. 300-320.

30. Article from a SIRS Collection of Reprinted Articles—MLA

Curver, Phillip C. "Lighting in the 21st Century." <u>Futurist</u>
    Jan.-Feb. 1989: 29-34. <u>Energy</u>. Ed. Eleanor Goldstein.
    Vol. 4. Boca Raton: SIRS, 1990. Art. 84.

Give the citation for the original publication first, followed by the
citation for the collection.

31. Article in a Journal with Continuous Pagination—MLA

Tyson, Phyllis. "The Psychology of Women." <u>Journal of the
    American Psychoanalytic Association</u> 46 (1998): 361-64.

If the first issue of a journal with continuous pagination ends on
page 228, the second issue starts with page 229. Give only the volume
number before the year. Use arabic numerals for all numbers.

32. Article in a Journal That Pages Each Issue Separately—MLA

Hogarty, Thomas F. "Gasoline: Still Powering Cars in 2050?"
    <u>Futurist</u> 33.3 (1999): 51-55.

When each issue begins with page 1, give both the volume number
(33) and the issue number (3), separated by a period.

33. Abstract from a Collection of Abstracts—MLA

To cite an abstract, first give information for the full work: the
author's name, the title of the article, and publication information about
the full article. If a reader could not know that the cited material is an
abstract, write the word *Abstract,* not underlined, followed by a period.
Give publication information about the collection of abstracts. For abstracts identified by item numbers rather than page numbers, use the
word *item* before the item number.

Marcus, Hazel R., and Shinobu Kitayamo. "Culture and the
    Self: Implications for Cognition, Emotion, and

Motivation." Psychological Review 88 (1991): 224-53.
Psychological Abstracts 78 (1991): item 23878.

34. Published and Unpublished Letters—MLA

Sand, George. Letter to her mother. 31 May 1831. Letters
   Home: Celebrated Authors Write to Their Mothers.
   Ed. Reid Sherline. New York: Timkin, 1993. 17-20.

Brown, Theodore. Letter to the author. 7 Jan. 2000.

35. Map or Chart—MLA

The Caribbean and South America. Map. Falls Church, VA:
   AAA, 1992.

NONPRINT SOURCES

36. Interview—MLA

Friedman, Randi. Telephone interview. 30 June 1997.

For a face-to-face interview, use *Personal interview* in place of
Telephone interview. For a published interview, give the name of the
interviewed person first, identify the source as an interview, and then
give details as for any published source: author, preceded by the word
By, title, and publication details.

37. Lecture, Speech, or Address—MLA

Kennedy, John Fitzgerald. Address. Greater Houston
   Ministerial Assn. Houston. 12 Sept. 1960.

38. Film, Videotape, or DVD—MLA

Shakespeare in Love. Screenplay by Marc Norman and Tom
   Stoppard. Dir. John Madden. Prod. David Parfitt, Donna
   Gigliotti, Harvey Weinstein, Edward Zwick, and Marc
   Norman. Perf. Gwyneth Paltrow, Joseph Fiennes, and Judi
   Dench. Videocassette. Miramax/Universal, 1999.

It Happened One Night. Screenplay by Robert Riskin. Dir. and
   Prod. Frank Capra. Perf. Clark Gable and Claudette
   Colbert. 1934. Videocassette. Columbia, 1999.

Give the title first, and include the director, the distributor, and the
year. For older films subsequently released on videocassette, DVD (digital videodisc), or laser disc, provide the original release date of the

movie before the name of the distributor. Other information (writer, producer, major actors) is optional but helpful. Put first names first.

39. Recording—MLA

Smetana, Bedrich. <u>My Country</u>. Cond. Karel Anserl. Czech
    Philharmonic Orch. LP. Vanguard, 1975.

Springsteen, Bruce. "Local Hero." <u>Lucky Town</u>. Columbia, 1992.

Put first the name most relevant to what you discuss in your paper (performer, conductor, the work performed, etc.). Include the recording's title, the medium for any recording other than a CD (e.g., *LP, Audiocassette*), name of the issuer (e.g., *Vanguard*), and the year.

40. Live Performance—MLA

<u>Via Dolorosa</u>. By David Hare. Dir. Steven Daldry. Perf. David
    Hare. Lincoln Center Theater, New York. 11 Apr. 1999.

41. Work of Art, Photograph, or Musical Composition—MLA

Cassatt, Mary. <u>La Toilette</u>. Art Institute of Chicago.

Mydans, Carl. <u>General Douglas MacArthur Landing at</u>
    <u>Luzon, 1945</u>. Soho Triad Fine Art Gallery, New York.
    21 Oct.-28 Nov. 1999.

Schubert, Franz. Symphony no. 8 in B minor.

Schubert, Franz. <u>Unfinished Symphony</u>.

Do not underline or put in quotation marks music identified only by form, number, and key, but do underline any work that has a title, such as an opera or ballet or a named symphony.

42. Radio or Television Program—MLA

<u>Not for Ourselves Alone: The Story of Elizabeth Cady Stanton</u>
    <u>and Susan B. Anthony</u>. Writ. Ken Burns. Perf. Julie
    Harris, Ronnie Gilbert, and Sally Kellerman. Prod. Paul
    Barnes and Ken Burns. PBS. WNET, New York. 8 Nov. 1999.

Include at least the title of the program (underlined), the network, the local station and its city, and the date(s) of the broadcast. For a series, also supply the title of the specific episode (in quotation marks) before the title of the program (underlined) and the title of the series (neither underlined nor in quotation marks) following the program title.

43. Microfiche Collection of Articles—MLA

Wenzell, Ron. "Businesses Prepare for a More Diverse Work
    Force." <u>St. Louis Post Dispatch</u> 3 Feb. 1990.
    <u>NewsBank: Employment</u> 27 (1990): fiche 2, grid D12.

PORTABLE ELECTRONIC SOURCES

The following basic blocks of information are used to document a portable electronic source (such as a CD-ROM or a diskette) in MLA style. A period ends each block.

1. Documentation information about the print version, if any. (Many sources accessed electronically also exist in published print versions. Others exist only in electronic form.) Follow the models in directory items 1–33 above for print sources. You may not find all the details about a print version in an electronic version, but provide as much information as you can. Information about a print version usually is given at the beginning or the end of an electronic document.

2. Author (if any) and title (underlined) of the electronic source or database. If there is no print version, start your Works Cited entry with this information.

3. Electronic medium, such as *CD-ROM, Diskette,* or *Magnetic tape.*

4. Name of the producer.

5. Publication date.

44. CD-ROM Database: Abstract with a Print Version—MLA

Marcus, Hazel R., and Shinobu Kitayamo. "Culture and the
    Self: Implications for Cognition, Emotion, and
    Motivation." <u>Psychological Abstracts</u> 78 (1991): item
    23878. <u>PsycLIT</u>. CD-ROM. SilverPlatter. Sept. 1991.

All the information through *item 23878* is for the print version of this source. The volume number is 78, and the abstract's number is 23878. All the information from *PsycLIT* to the end of the entry is for the electronic version of the source. *PsycLIT* is the name of the CD-ROM database, and *SilverPlatter* is the name of the producer of the CD-ROM. The CD-ROM was issued in *September 1991.*

45. CD-ROM: Article from a Periodical with a Print Version—MLA

"The Price Is Right." <u>Time</u>. 20 Jan. 1992: 38. <u>Time Man of
    the Year</u>. CD-ROM. Compact. 1993.

Information for the print version ends with the article's page number, 38. The title of the CD-ROM is *Time Man of the Year,* its producer is the publisher Compact, and its copyright year is 1993. Both the title of the print publication and the title of the CD-ROM are underlined.

46. CD-ROM: Selection from a Book with a Print Version—MLA

"Prehistoric Humans: Earliest <u>Homo sapiens</u>." <u>The Guinness

   Book of Records 1994</u>. London: Guinness Publishing, Ltd.,

   1994. <u>The Guinness Multimedia Disk of Records</u>. CD-ROM.

   Version 2.0. Danbury, CT: Grolier Electronic Publishing,

   1994.

Version 2.0 signals that this CD-ROM is updated periodically; the producer changes version numbers rather than giving update dates.

47. CD-ROM: Material with No Print Version—MLA

"Spanish Dance." <u>Encarta 2000</u>. CD-ROM. Redmond, WA:

   Microsoft, 1999.

Encarta 2000 is a CD-ROM encyclopedia with no print version. "Spanish Dance" is the title of an article in *Encarta 2000*.

48. Work in More Than One Publication Medium—MLA

Clarke, David James. <u>Novell's CNE Study Guide</u>. Book. <u>Network

   Support Encyclopedia</u>. CD-ROM. Alameda, CA: Sybex, 1994.

This book and CD-ROM come together. Each has its own title, but the publication information—*Alameda, CA: Sybex, 1994*—applies to both.

ONLINE SOURCES: NO URL

Online sources fall into two categories: (1) those you access through an online service, such as America Online or at a library; and (2) those you access by entering a specific URL (Internet address). For source material reached through an online service, give the name of the service, and if you used a keyword (for your search), give it after the access date.

49. Online Service Access: Abstract with a Print Version—MLA

Marcus, Hazel R., and Shinobu Kitayamo. "Culture and the

   Self: Implications for Cognition, Emotion, and

   Motivation." <u>Psychological Abstracts</u> 78 (1991): item

   23878. <u>PsycINFO</u>. Dialog. 10 Oct. 1991.

This entry is for the same abstract from *Psychological Abstracts* shown in item 44, but here it is accessed from an online database (*PsycINFO*) by means of an online service (*Dialog*). This entry notes *PsycINFO*, the name of the online database, whereas item 44 notes

PsycLIT, the name of the CD-ROM database; and it notes *Dialog,* the service through which *PsycINFO* was accessed, whereas item 44 notes the CD-ROM producer, *SilverPlatter.* The last information unit —*10 Oct. 1991*—is the date that the abstract was accessed.

50. Online Service Access: Material with No Print Version—MLA

"Microsoft Licenses OSM Technology from Henter-Joyce."

WinNews Electronic Newsletter 2.6 (1 May 1995).

CompuServe. 15 May 1995.

The designation *2.6* indicates volume 2, number 6 of this electronic newsletter.

51. Online Service Access with a Keyword: Article from a Periodical with a Print Version—MLA

Kapor, Mitchell, and Jerry Berman. "A Superhighway Through

the Wasteland?" New York Times 24 Nov. 1993: Op-ed

page. New York Times Online. America Online. 5 May

1995. Keyword: nytimes.

Information applying to the print version of this article in the *New York Times* ends with *Op-ed page,* and information about the online version starts with the title of the database, *New York Times Online. America Online* is the service through which the database was accessed, and *5 May 1995* is the access date. The keyword *nytimes* was used to access *New York Times Online,* as noted after the access date.

52. Online Service Access Showing a Path—MLA

When you access a source by choosing a series of keywords, menus, or topics, end the entry with the "path" of words you used. Use semicolons between items in the path, and put a period at the end.

Futrelle, David. "A Smashing Success." Money.com 23 Dec.

1999. America Online. 26 Dec. 1999. Path: Personal

Finance; Business News; Business Publications;

Money.com.

53. Online Service Access at a Library—MLA

For a source accessed through a library's online service, first give information about the source. Then, list the name of the service, the name of the library, and the access date. Give the URL of the online service's home page, if you know it, after the access date. Enclose the URL in angle brackets and put a period after the closing bracket.

Dutton, Gail. "Greener Pigs." <u>Popular Science</u> 1999: 38-39.

    <u>ProQuest Periodical Abstracts Plus Text</u>. ProQuest

    Direct. Public Lib., Teaneck. 7 Dec. 1999 <http://

    proquest.umi.com>.

URL-ACCESSED ONLINE SOURCES

In this section, you will find models for online sources accessed when you enter a URL, or specific Internet address. These guidelines cover Web sites, FTP and Gopher sites, listservs, discussion groups, and other online sources. For such sources, provide as much of the following information as you can.

1. The author's name, if any.
2. In quotation marks, the title of a short work (poem, short story, essay, article, posted message); or underlined, the title of a book.
3. The underlined title of a scholarly project or reference database. (If the site has no title, describe it: for example, *Home page.*)
4. The name of an editor, translator, or compiler, if any, with an abbreviation such as *Ed., Trans.,* or *Comp.* before the name.
5. The date of electronic publication (including a version number, if any), or posting, or the most recent update.
6. The name of a sponsoring organization, if any.
7. The date you accessed the material.
8. The URL in angle brackets (<>), with a period after the closing bracket.

54. URL Access: Book—MLA

Chopin, Kate. <u>The Awakening</u>. 1899. 12 Dec. 1999

    <http://www.pbs.org/katechopin/library/awakening>.

55. URL Access: Book in a Scholarly Project—MLA

Herodotus. <u>The History of Herodotus</u>. Trans. George

    Rawlinson. <u>The Internet Classics Archive</u>. Ed. Daniel C.

    Stevenson. 11 Jan. 1998. Massachusetts Institute of

    Technology. 4 Dec. 1999 <http://classics.mit.edu/

    Herodotus/history.html>.

56. URL Access: Government-published Books—MLA

United States. Cong. Research Service. <u>Space Stations</u>.

    By Marcia S. Smith. 12 Dec. 1996. 4 Dec. 1999

    <http://fas.org/spp/civil/crs/93-017.htm>.

United States. Dept. of Justice. Natl. Inst. of Justice.

    Comparing the Criminal Behavior of Youth Gangs and

    At-Risk Youths. By C. Ronald Hoff. Oct. 1998. 4 Dec.

    1999 <http://www.ncjrs.org/txtfiles/172852.txt>.

For government publications that name no author, start with the name of the government or government body, and then name the government agency. For a government text, the title is followed by the writer of the publication, if available.

57. URL Access: Articles in Online Periodicals—MLA

Didion, Joan. "The Day Was Hot and Still. . . ." Rev.

    of Dutch: A Memoir of Ronald Reagan, by Edmund

    Morris. New York Review of Books 4 Nov. 1999.

    5 Dec. 1999 <http://nybooks.com/nyrev/

    www.archdisplay.cgi?19991104004R>.

Gold, David. "Ulysses: A Case Study in the Problems of

    Hypertextualization of Complex Documents." Computers,

    Writing, Rhetoric and Literature 3.1 (1997): 37 pars.

    4 Dec. 1999 <http://www.cwrl.utexas.edu/~cwrl/v3n1/

    dgold/title.htm>.

Keegan, Paul. "Culture Quake." Mother Jones Nov.-Dec. 1999.

    4 Dec. 1999 <http://www.mojones.com/mother_jones/ND99/

    quake.html>.

Lewis, Ricki. "Chronobiology Researchers Say Their Field's

    Time Has Come." Scientist 9.24 (1995): 14. 30 Dec. 1997

    <http://www.thescientist.library.upenn.edu/yr1995/dec/

    chrono-951211.html>.

Rimer, Sarah. "Retired Doctors Head Back to Work." New

    York Times on the Web 4 Dec. 1999. 4 Dec. 1999

    <http://nytimes.com/yr/mo/day/news/national/

    retired-doctors.html>.

When you cite online periodicals, give the following information:

1. The author's name, if any.
2. In quotation marks, the title of the article or editorial.
3. A description of the cited material as a *Review* (see Didion example), *Editorial,* or *Letter,* unless the title gives that information.
4. The underlined title of the periodical.

5. Volume and issue numbers, if any.
6. The date of publication.
7. The total number of pages, paragraphs, or other numbered sections, if any.
8. The date you accessed the material.
9. The URL in angle brackets (< >), with a period after the closing bracket.

58. URL Access: Professional Home Page—MLA

LEARN@PZ. Project Zero, Harvard Graduate School of
    Education. 17 Jan. 1998 <http://pzweb.harvard.edu/
    default.htm>.

LEARN@PZ is the title of the home page for Project Zero, sponsored by the Harvard Graduate School of Education.

59. URL Access: Personal Home Page—MLA

Hunter-Kilmer, Melissa. Home page. 15 Feb. 1995. 4 Dec. 1999
    <http://www.Idsonline.com/userweb/phantom/index/htm>.

For home pages, include as much of the following information as you can find:

1. If available, the name of the person who created or set up the home page. If first and last names are given, reverse the order of the first author's name.
2. The title, underlined. If there is no title, add the description *Home page*, not underlined, followed by a period.
3. For a professional home page, the name of the sponsoring organization.
4. The date you accessed the material.
5. The URL in angle brackets (< >), with a period after the closing bracket.

OTHER ONLINE SOURCES
60. Online Posting—MLA

Woodbury, Chuck. "Free RV Campgrounds." Online posting.
    4 Dec. 1999. The RV Home Page Bulletin Board. 21 Dec.
    1999 <http://www.rvhome.com/wwwboard/messages/
    4598.html>.

Be cautious about using online postings as sources. Some postings contain cutting-edge information from experts, but some contain trash.

Unfortunately, there is no way to know whether people online are who they claim to be. To cite an online message, give the author name (if any), the title of the message in quotation marks, and then *Online posting*. Give the date of the posting and the name of the bulletin board, if any. Then, give the access date and, in angle brackets, the URL.

61. Synchronous Communication—MLA

```
Bleck, Bradley. Online discussion of "Virtual First Year
     Composition: Distance Education, the Internet, and the
     World Wide Web." 8 June 1997. DaMOO. 27 Feb. 1999
     <http://DaMOO.csun.edu/CW/brad.html>.
```

Give the name of the speaker, a title for the event ("Virtual First Year Composition: Distance Education, the Internet, and the World Wide Web"), the forum (DaMOO), event or posting date, access date, and URL.

62. E-Mail Message—MLA

```
Thompson, Jim. "Bob Martin's Address." E-mail to June Cain.
     11 Nov. 1997.
```

Start with the name of the person who wrote the e-mail message. Give the title or subject line in quotation marks. Then, describe the source (*E-mail*) and identify the recipient. End with the date.

35d.2 Using content or bibliographic notes in MLA style

In MLA style, footnotes or endnotes serve two specific purposes: (1) You can use them for content (ideas and information) that does not fit into your paper but is still worth relating; and (2) you can use them for bibliographic information that would intrude if you were to include it in your text.

TEXT OF PAPER

```
Eudora Welty's literary biography, One Writer's Beginnings,
shows us how both the inner world of self and the outer
world of family and place form a writer's imagination.[1]
```

CONTENT NOTE—**MLA**

```
[1] Welty, who values her privacy, has always resisted
investigation of her life. However, at the age of seventy-
four, she chose to present her own autobiographical
reflections in a series of lectures at Harvard University.
```

TEXT OF PAPER

Barbara Randolph believes that enthusiasm is contagious (65).[1] Many psychologists have found that panic, fear, and rage spread more quickly in crowds than positive emotions do, however.

BIBLIOGRAPHIC NOTE—MLA

[1] Others who agree with Randolph include Thurman 21, 84, 155; Kelley 421-25; and Brookes 65-76.

👁 **MLA FORMAT ALERT:** Place a note number at the end of a sentence, if possible. Put it after any punctuation mark except the dash. Do not put any space before a note number, and put one space after it. In typed papers, raise the note number a little above the line of words. In word processing programs, use superscript numbers.●

35e Lisa Laver's MLA research paper

35e.1 Researching and writing the paper

Lisa Laver was given this assignment for a research paper: Write a research paper on the general subject of intelligence. The paper should be 1,800 to 2,000 words long and should be based on a variety of sources. The final paper is due in six weeks. Interim deadlines for parts of the work will be announced. To complete this assignment, you need to engage in three interrelated processes: conducting research, understanding the results of that research, and writing a paper based on the first two processes. Consult the *Simon & Schuster Handbook for Writers,* Sixth Edition, especially Chapter 32, which gives you practical, step-by-step guidance on what this assignment entails.

Lisa Laver was eager to plan her research schedule so that she could budget her time and not end up in a panic of time pressure. She knew from experience that she would likely have the most trouble in the first stages of her research process as she narrowed her topic and began to look for useful sources. She resolved to face the challenge calmly and patiently as she went along.

The general topic assigned was "intelligence." Laver realized that she had to face many steps to narrow it to a TOPIC suitable for a research paper (32f.2). Collecting possible subject headings and topic key words was her first step. She went to the library reference desk to use the

Library of Congress Subject Headings (*LCSH*) books (see 33d). She found nothing under "intelligence" but browsed a bit and found "intellect" as a main category. Its library call number, the code to lead her to all books on the subject, had a range from BF431 to BF433. She wrote down *intellect* and its call numbers in her research log (see 32e). She had taken the first step for this project.

Laver then examined the subentries at "intellect" in the *LCSH* and found the listing "human intelligence," which appealed to her as a direction to take. Then, Laver looked at the *LCSH* headings preceded by the code NT (meaning "narrowed topic"). In her research log, she listed all the NT headings as possible key words. Looking up a few of them, she soon became overwhelmed with the variety of directions she could take. She decided to try another route.

With the call numbers and topic key words in hand, Laver looked at specialized reference books (see 33g) with call numbers in the range BF431–BF433 (the call numbers she had found in the *LCSH*). In Volume 3 of *Survey of Social Science: Psychology Series*, she found an article titled "Intelligence: Definition and Theoretical Models." This proved to be Laver's first big break.

As she read the survey article, Laver's interest was captured by material on a concept of intelligence developed fairly recently by Howard Gardner of Harvard University. She wrote down Gardner's name as a possible authority (see 32l). Gardner states that human intelligence is not what people think of as IQ. He believes IQ (for "intelligence quotient") is a limited concept because it is a measure that draws on only one or two inborn human abilities. According to Gardner, the totality of human intelligence results from the interaction of eight "intelligences." Laver decided that she would pursue this topic, if she could determine that Gardner was a credible authority on the subject of intelligence. The flowchart on the facing page illustrates Laver's process of narrowing her topic.

To start checking on Gardner, Laver looked in the *Columbia Encyclopedia*, a general reference book she was familiar with from high school. Under "intelligence," Laver found Gardner and his concept of *multiple intelligences* mentioned. This gave her hope, so next she looked in the library's book catalog (see 33e) under the name "Gardner." She was delighted to find several books by him on the subject of multiple intelligences. One of them, *Frames of Mind*, became a major source on her topic. She then started writing out bibliography cards (32m and 32n).

To find out if educators had applied multiple intelligence theory, Laver checked online databases and Internet sources. The central information system of her college library uses EBSCO*host*, an online service with links to scholarly full-text databases and online journals. Through this service, she clicked on "Academic Search Elite" and "Newspaper Sources." Trial and error taught her that the "Natural Language Search" option provided better results than the "Keyword Search" option.

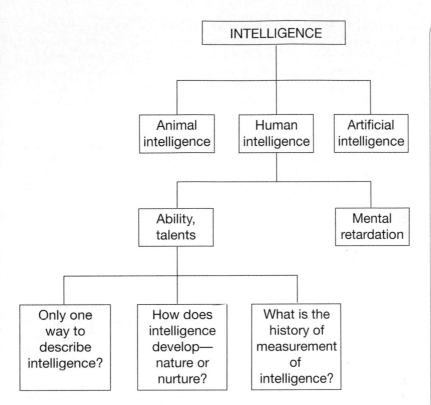

Flowchart of Lisa Laver's narrowing process

Typing in "multiple intelligences" resulted in hundreds of responses, so she added the word "Gardner." To save time, Laver also selected "full text entries only." In scrolling the results, Laver noticed that the focus of the September 1997 issue of *Educational Leadership* was multiple intelligences. She clicked on that issue, read several good articles, and printed Wendy Ecklund Lambert's article on a specific educational application of multiple intelligence theory. Typing in "multiple intelligences learning teaching" led her to Deborah Moore, whose statistics Laver could use to support Lambert's classroom activities.

Laver also used the Yahoo! search engine to locate information on Gardner's newest form of intelligence. She put in "multiple intelligences Gardner naturalist" and, at first, was overwhelmed with hundreds of matches. However, she noticed that many used the term "tool room" in the title. This led her to *The Building Tool Room* Web site and the Bruce Campbell and Thomas Hoerr sources.

As Laver read, checked the credibility of her sources, and found additional useful sources, she was at first somewhat skeptical of the concept of multiple intelligences. All her life, she had heard that intelligence was defined by IQ, which was measured by a test. In fact, she had wondered what her IQ and the IQs of her family and friends were. The more Laver thought about what she was reading, the more open she felt to the possibility of changing her viewpoint. This led Laver to form her RESEARCH QUESTION (see 32b): "Can there be only one way of describing intelligence?"

As she researched further, Laver saw references to the work of Peter Salovey and John Mayer. These names led Laver to material on "emotional intelligence," a concept that encompassed in great detail two of Gardner's eight intelligences: interpersonal and intrapersonal. Laver remembered seeing her parents reading a book by Daniel Goleman, titled *Emotional Intelligence*. Browsing through it, she saw that it drew heavily on Salovey and Mayer's work as well as on Gardner's. Laver decided to include Salovey and Mayer's work in her paper.

After taking notes, Laver was ready to DRAFT her research paper. Thinking about her PURPOSE, Laver concluded that she should inform her readers about the concept of multiple intelligences. (For a discussion of the informative purpose, see section 1c.2.) Soon after she started her second draft, however, Laver realized that her paper lacked a focus—a reason for her wanting to explain what she had learned. She decided to include her rationale for why the topic of multiple intelligences was worth writing about: Laver felt that the concept held benefits especially for students and also for the general population.

As Laver wrote, she used her note cards carefully to make sure she always knew when she was quoting a source and when she was summarizing. She made sure to put in the correct IN-TEXT CITATION (see section 35c) for each source. She also kept a WORKING BIBLIOGRAPHY (see 32m) so that she would be ready to list each one of the sources in her WORKS CITED list (see 35d.1) at the end of her paper. By the time Laver came to the final draft of her research paper, she decided to drop a few sources because they repeated what others whom she considered better authorities had said.

Laver struggled with her concluding paragraph. She wanted to assert her conviction that the ideas of Gardner, Salovey and Mayer, and Goleman on human intelligence held great promise. At first, she lacked the confidence to state her position outright; after a while, the strength of her convictions overrode her hesitancy. Here is an early draft of Laver's concluding paragraph, which you can compare to the one in her final draft that appears in section 35e.2.

Today, there is no longer a single definition of intelligence. Scientists have found new ways of describing human intelligence and seeing it in operation. Educators, in turn, can use those findings to give students more avenues to school success and, as a result, to greater self-esteem.

35e.2 Analyzing the research paper

Lisa Laver followed MLA style for format decisions on this paper.

Title page

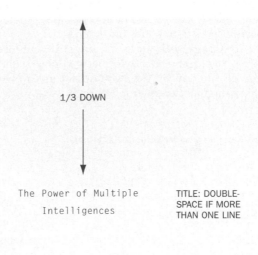

1/3 DOWN

The Power of Multiple
Intelligences

TITLE: DOUBLE-
SPACE IF MORE
THAN ONE LINE

by

Lisa Laver

BY ON SEPARATE LINE;
DOUBLE-SPACE TO NAME

COURSE, SECTION   English 101, Section C5

INSTRUCTOR   Professor Marzian

DATE SUBMITTED   23 November 2000

1 "

Title page and first page of essay with a title page. If your instructor requires a title page, you can use the format and types of information shown above for Lisa Laver's title page. Then, on page 1 of your

597

paper, put your last name followed by a space followed by the numeral 1 in the upper right corner, 1/2 inch below the top edge of the page. Then, type the paper's title, centering it 1/2 inch below the name-number heading. (See page 602.) Double-space after the title, and then start your paper, indenting the first line of each paragraph five character spaces. If you are using a computer rather than a typewriter, format for double line spacing and 1/2-inch tabs for indents.

    First page without a title page. If your instructor does not require a title page, follow MLA format guidelines, shown below, for the first page of your paper. When you do not use a title page, place identifying information in the upper left corner.

First Page for a paper without a title page

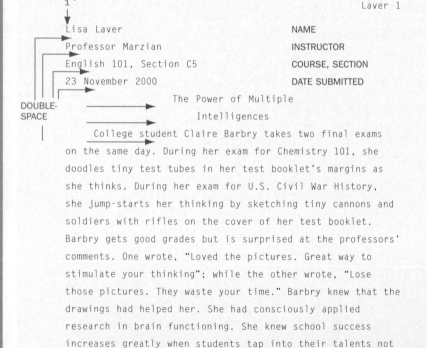

Laver 1

Lisa Laver   NAME

Professor Marzian   INSTRUCTOR

English 101, Section C5   COURSE, SECTION

23 November 2000   DATE SUBMITTED

DOUBLE-
SPACE

                  The Power of Multiple

                       Intelligences

      College student Claire Barbry takes two final exams on the same day. During her exam for Chemistry 101, she doodles tiny test tubes in her test booklet's margins as she thinks. During her exam for U.S. Civil War History, she jump-starts her thinking by sketching tiny cannons and soldiers with rifles on the cover of her test booklet. Barbry gets good grades but is surprised at the professors' comments. One wrote, "Loved the pictures. Great way to stimulate your thinking"; while the other wrote, "Lose those pictures. They waste your time." Barbry knew that the drawings had helped her. She had consciously applied research in brain functioning. She knew school success increases greatly when students tap into their talents not

Name-and-page-number heading. Except for a separate title page, give each page of a paper you prepare according to MLA format guidelines a heading in the upper right corner 1/2 inch below the top edge of the paper. Use your last name, followed by a space, followed by the page number. Number pages that come before your essay begins, such as outline pages, with lowercase roman numerals (see Lisa Laver's outline on pages 600–601). Use arabic numeral 1 on the page on which your essay begins, and then number each page consecutively through to the last page of Works Cited. Many writers take advantage of the word processing function that inserts page numbers and last name as a header, updating automatically. This feature is especially convenient when your revising causes pages to fall differently than they originally did.

Outline. Laver's instructor required a formal outline in the final draft of each student's research paper. To format her outline, Laver referred to sections 2r and 32p in this handbook. In the name–page number line in the upper right corner, she used lowercase roman numerals for the page numbers, a conventional way of showing that the outline comes before the first page of the essay itself. Laver left a 1/2-inch space below the name-number heading and then centered the word *Outline*. She double-spaced and then typed the words *Thesis statement* at the left margin, underlining them. The thesis statement in the outline matches the last sentence of the first paragraph of her paper (see page 602).

Laver developed a FORMAL OUTLINE, and she chose a sentence outline, not a topic outline (see 2r). To reflect the organization of her paper, she divided the material in the outline into three major parts, numbered I, II, and III. Within each part, she marked the main items A, B, C. When a main item went into more detail, she used 1, 2, 3, and so on, for the new level of information.

Even if your instructor does not require one, you might find that developing an outline to go with a later draft of your paper is helpful. Examining the paper's "skeleton" in such a way allows you to focus on the overall shape and organization of the paper and may reveal gaps in your paper's development that you can fill in.

1"
½"
Laver i

DOUBLE-SPACE ⟶ Outline

Thesis statement: Recent studies provide convincing evidence that success increases when people use more abilities than IQ tests measure.

I. Brain research has inspired more complex theories of intelligence.

  A. Concepts of learning and of teaching are multifaceted.

  B. The brain consists of two hemispheres, one of which is dominant.

  C. The brain performs creative and logical functions at the same time.

II. The theory of multiple intelligences (MI) is the work of Howard Gardner.

  A. Gardner has identified eight separate intelligences: musical, bodily-kinesthetic, logical-mathematical, linguistic, spatial, interpersonal, intrapersonal, and naturalistic.

  B. Gardner developed criteria for evaluating an ability as an "intelligence."

    1. It must have an identifiable core set of information-processing operations.

    2. It must have a distinctive developmental history, with a set of "end state" performances.

    3. It must have evolutionary plausibility.

    4. It must be supported by experimental and psychological tasks.

⟶

C. MI theory has affected educational practices.

    1. Teachers use Gardner's ideas and methods to help students learn traditional classroom tasks.

    2. One school reports using a variety of intelligences to study American history.

III. Other researchers have developed the concept of emotional intelligence.

    A. Emotional intelligence builds on two of Gardner's eight intelligences.

        1. Interpersonal intelligence is one.

        2. Intrapersonal intelligence is the other.

    B. Salovey and Mayer did pioneering work in the area.

    C. Daniel Goleman wrote a best-selling book on the subject.

The Power of Multiple
Intelligences

INTRODUCTION: Gets reader's attention with anecdote about a student

College student Claire Barbry takes two final exams on the same day. During her exam for Chemistry 101, she doodles tiny test tubes in her test booklet's margins as she thinks. During her exam for U.S. Civil War History, she jump-starts her thinking by sketching tiny cannons and soldiers with rifles on the cover of her test booklet.

Use ½" top margins, 1" bottom and side margins; double-space throughout

Barbry gets good grades but is surprised at the professors' comments. One wrote, "Loved the pictures. Great way to stimulate your thinking"; while the other wrote, "Lose those pictures. They waste your time." Barbry knew that the drawings had helped her. She had consciously applied research in brain functioning. She knew school success increases greatly when students tap into their talents not usually associated with academic work. She was convinced that narrow definitions of intelligence, such as those used on traditional IQ tests, can hamper a student. Recent studies provide convincing evidence that success increases when people use more abilities than IQ tests measure.

THESIS STATEMENT: Focus of paper

PARAGRAPH 2: First body paragraph begins with background information about assessing human intelligence

A review of a 1986 survey of scholarly definitions of intelligence concludes that the reader "is left with the clear impression that intelligence is such a multifaceted concept that no single quality can define it and no single task or series of tasks can capture it completely" (Urbina 1330). To everyone's benefit, the last twenty-five years of brain research have inspired broader theories of human intelligence. Caine and Caine, summarizing recent studies into the nature of intelligence, urge that educators enlarge their concepts of learning, and of teaching, to move beyond the simplistic IQ scores. These scholars note that not all new theories of diversity in intelligences are equally valid (67).

In MLA style, parentheses with page number only when author named in text

A

B

C

D, E

F

→

COMMENTARY

A. **Title.** Laver uses her title to prepare her readers for the paper's major theme (multiple intelligences) and central focus (that success increases when people use more abilities than IQ tests measure). ◎ **PROCESS NOTE:** Laver drafted a few titles as she was revising. She started with "Everyone Is Smart in Some Way," but that oversimplified the point. She later tried and rejected "Evolving Theories of Human Intelligence" because she was not writing a historical survey of human intelligence theories but rather a discussion of such theories of more recent interest. ●

B. **Introductory device.** Laver tells this anecdote, which is based on the experience of one of her friends, because she feels it illustrates her point dramatically.

C. **Thesis statement.** The last sentence of Laver's introductory paragraph is her THESIS STATEMENT. In writing it, she wants to prepare her readers, in more detail than her title does, for the message she plans to deliver. ◎ **PROCESS NOTE:** Laver tried out a few thesis statements as she moved from early to later drafts, each time trying to get closer to her central message. For evolving versions of this thesis statement, see section 32. ●

D. ◎ **PROCESS NOTE:** In an earlier draft of this paper, Laver wrote four paragraphs about the history of definitions and measurements of human intelligence. This information helped her get a better understanding of her topic. However, as she read over her draft, she realized that her coverage of the history of IQ tests was not necessary to support her thesis. Also, her draft was well over the 2,000-word limit, so she decided to delete the history paragraphs. ●

E. **Summary.** In her final draft, Laver condenses her definition and historical information into two sentences, which she places at the beginning of her second paragraph.

F. **Major source.** Laver considers the Urbina material a major source. She had found the essay in the specialized reference book located within the call number range for "intellect," found in the *Library of Congress Subject Headings* (*LCSH*). The essay, listed in the WORKS CITED at the end of Laver's paper, introduced Laver to the concept of *multiple intelligences,* the topic of her paper, and to the name Howard Gardner, the main authority on that topic.

In MLA style, header has student's last name and page number

PARAGRAPH 3: Second body paragraph provides background information about brain's hemispheres

A theory once considered "the answer" held that each person's brain consists of two hemispheres, one of which is dominant. The right side controls creative, artistic talents; the left side controls logical, language-based talents (Caine and Caine 67). This theory has some merit, but it is now considered too narrow. Other theories that are more widely accepted today are based on careful research that shows the human brain performs creative and logical functions simultaneously:

Indent block paragraph 1″ (or 10 character spaces) for a quotation longer than 4 lines

> Thought, emotions, imagination, and
> predisposition occur concurrently. They interact
> with other brain processes such as health
> maintenance and the expansion of general social
> and cultural knowledge. (Caine and Caine 66)

PARAGRAPH 4: Third body paragraph introduces Howard Gardner and his theory of multiple intelligences

The researcher who had the strongest impact on theories of human intelligence is Howard Gardner. In 1979, he was a junior member of a research team at the Harvard Graduate School of Education that investigated human potential and cognition. That experience, along with his years of additional research as a developmental psychologist, led Gardner to theorize that humans possess many different intelligences. In his book Frames of Mind, Gardner strives to disprove the idea that human intelligence consists of only the two abilities tested by standard IQ instruments: logical-mathematical and linguistic. He offers his alternative: the theory of multiple intelligences (MI). This theory questions the idea that many people learn "explicitly (from psychology or educational texts) or implicitly (by living in a culture with a strong but possibly circumscribed view of intelligence)" (5). In 1983, Gardner delineated seven intelligences: musical, bodily-kinesthetic, logical-mathematical, linguistic, visual-spatial, interpersonal, and intrapersonal (Frames 73-76). In 1996, he added an eighth intelligence to his

G

H

I

J

→

COMMENTARY

G. 👁 **PROCESS NOTE:** Laver considered whether to include the information that the "answer" had once rested almost entirely on the theory of right brain/left brain dominance. (Today, it is only one part of some intelligence theories, and it is ignored in others.) On the one hand, she worried that it might be off the topic; on the other hand, she felt that her paper needed to reflect a little of the scholarly debates that go on concerning the descriptions of human intelligence, so she decided to include it. ●

H. **Marking the repeated use of a source.** Laver indicates that she is continuing to use information from Caine and Caine by putting the page number from this source in parentheses. However, if she were to introduce information from a different source, and then want to use Caine and Caine again, she would have to include their names with the page number.

I. **Major source.** Howard Gardner is the psychologist who originated the theory of multiple intelligences. Laver decided that the central section of her paper should focus on Gardner and his work. She found his discussions of his theories in his book *Frames of Mind* and in the work of other people who refer to Gardner as the top authority in this research field.

J. **Quotation from a source.** Laver uses quotations to give her paper impact and variety. She believed that the prestige of a quotation from Gardner's landmark book, *Frames of Mind,* would bring greater authority to an idea readers might find controversial.

Key word from title in parentheses to show which of two Gardner sources is used here

list: naturalistic (Campbell). More recently, Gardner has suggested the possibility of a ninth intelligence: existential, "the proclivity to pose (and ponder) questions about life, death, and ultimate realities" (<u>Disciplined</u> 72). Table 1 lists the characteristics of eight intelligences and behaviors typical of each intelligence.

Table number and title in MLA style

Table 1

Gardner's Eight Intelligences

Type of Intelligence	Definition	Behavior
Musical	Refers to musical ability, perhaps from a biological advantage. Requires the use of symbols that are read, heard internally, and interpreted to create harmonic melody.	Person enjoys listening to music; expresses eagerness to learn from music and musicians; responds to music by conducting, performing, and/or dancing.
Bodily-kinesthetic	Refers to physical skill, including the ability to play sports, expressing emotions in dance, or otherwise displaying masterful use of the body.	Person enjoys touching and exploring objects; learns by direct involvement and participation; displays skill in acting, athletics, and dance.
Logical-mathematical	Necessitates both problem solving and synthesizing a solution in one's mind before actually articulating it.	Person enjoys logical problem solving and complex operations such as calculus, physics, computer programming; likes to study the concepts of quantity and time.
Linguistic	Encompasses the ability to master language by comprehending words and the desire to use them effectively and in a variety of ways to form well-styled and grammatically correct sentences.	Person enjoys and responds to the rhythm and variety of language; listens and reads well with the ability to comprehend, summarize, and interpret ideas.

K

L

M

N

O

→

COMMENTARY

K. **Online source.** Campbell is a source that Laver found on the Internet. Because Campbell's article does not have page numbers, Laver cannot give a page reference for her information. In the Works Cited entry at the end of her paper, Laver includes complete information, according to new MLA guidelines for documenting Internet sources, including the URL (enclosed in angle brackets).

L. ⊚ **PROCESS NOTE:** Laver almost made a serious error as a researcher as she was searching for information about Howard Gardner's theory of multiple intelligences. Early in her online research process, she found a Web site featuring a photograph of Gardner along with information about a videotape on his theories. At first, Laver was thrilled to have found something online about Gardner. But when she applied the information in Box 142 (see 33k, p. 543) and Box 150 (see 34f, pp. 558–559) for evaluating sources, she discovered that (1) the information was two years old and included only seven of the eight intelligences Gardner had identified; (2) the material was presented by a commercial enterprise that wanted to sell the videotape; and (3) the many misspellings showed that the material had not been issued by a professionally responsible group. She put the material aside and looked for more credible sources. ●

M. **Updating information.** Laver hadn't considered that Gardner might add additional intelligences to his 1993 list. However, by thoroughly researching her topic, Laver learned that to his original list of seven intelligences, Gardner had added an eighth intelligence, in 1996. In addition, she learned that he is now considering the possibility of a ninth intelligence. Including this information shows that she was persistent and careful in her research.

N. **Table.** Table 1 is a condensation of information that Laver at first took eight paragraphs to write. She found them boring to write and dull to read. As a result, she decided to present these detailed definitions in a table because she felt the material would be more concise and useful in this form.

O. **Parallelism.** In early drafts, Laver wrote out the information as it came to mind. For her final draft, however, Laver knew she needed to use parallel structures for the items in each column. In the *Definition* column, she started each definition with a verb in the present tense. In the *Behavior* column, she started each explanation with the words "Person enjoys."

Laver 4

Table 1 Gardner's Eight Intelligences, <u>continued</u>   P

Type of Intelligence	Definition	Behavior
Visual-spatial	Refers to the capacity to visualize objects without experiencing their actual existence and to recognize people, places, and fine detail.	Person enjoys navigating self and objects through space; produces mental imagery; thinks in pictures and visualizes detail; perceives space from multiple perspectives.
Interpersonal	Involves the ability to interact well with others, seek out or follow leadership, encourage human interaction, and enhance each individual's place in society.	Person enjoys interacting with others to form social relationships; communicates well verbally and non-verbally; recognizes and appreciates diverse perceptions on social and other issues.
Intrapersonal	Involves knowledge of the inner self, including the ability to use feelings and emotions as a rationale for one's behavior.	Person enjoys opportunities to explore the inner self; tends not to conform to popular opinion or peer pressure; works independently to discover meaning in experiences and thoughts.
Naturalistic	Refers to the ability to observe, understand, and organize patterns in nature; involves interest in collecting and sorting natural objects.	Person enjoys doing experiments in nature, learning names of natural objects, classifying and labeling articles from nature, and recognizing small changes in nature.

Q

Table source note in MLA style

Source: Based on Howard Gardner, <u>Frames of Mind: The Theory of Multiple Intelligences</u> (New York: Basic, 1993) and Thomas Hoerr, "The Naturalist Intelligence," <http://www.newhorizons.org/trm_hoerrmi.html>.

→

COMMENTARY

P. **Format of table.** Laver had to make some decisions about formatting this table. Advice in the *MLA Handbook for Writers of Research Papers* (5th edition) states that tables should be double-spaced. She tried that out, but the table took up six pages, overwhelming the rest of her paper. She decided to single-space the table.

Laver followed MLA guidelines by positioning the table title at the left margin and putting a broken line above and below the column headings.

She decided to repeat the table number and title, followed by the word *continued,* underlined, as well as the column headings on the second page of the table. (The *MLA Handbook* does not include guidelines for tables longer than one page, leaving format decisions for such tables up to the writer.)

Q. **More on the table format.** Following MLA style, Laver uses a broken line at the end of the information in the table.

For the source note, she includes information about Gardner's *Frames of Mind,* a print book, and Thomas Hoerr's "The Naturalist Intelligence," a source from the Internet. She gives the URL in angle brackets, as in the Works Cited entry. The entire note is double-spaced.

Laver 5

PARAGRAPH 5:
Fourth body
paragraph gives
criteria Gardner
uses to
categorize an
intelligence

Gardner does not simply make up new intelligences. He uses criteria by which to judge whether an ability deserves to be categorized as an "intelligence." Each must confer

> a set of skills of problem solving--enabling
> the individual to resolve genuine problems or
> difficulties [author's emphasis] that he or
> she encounters and laying the groundwork for the
> acquisition of new knowledge. (Frames 60-61)

R

In MLA style,
parenthetical
information
after the
period in a
block-indented
quotation

These criteria include a specific, identifiable location in the brain; identifiable stages of development; acquisition of specific new skills as development progresses; a "core set of operations," or specific ways of processing specific kinds of information; an evolutionary reason for existing; and being measurable or testable (Hoerr).

PARAGRAPH 6:
Fifth body
paragraph
provides
transition from
research to
application in
classroom

Although MI theory grew from research in psychology, educators--and their students--have begun to adopt the concept enthusiastically. Teachers using Gardner's ideas and methods today demonstrate that when unsuccessful students are taught how to tap their other intelligences to help them learn traditional classroom tasks, the students improve dramatically. Specific illustrations are often found in reports from teachers. One example comes from an American history high school class. Dealing with the Expansion Era that ran from the late eighteenth century to the middle of the nineteenth century, students chose a topic from a list prepared by the teacher, researched the topic, and then responded by using MI theory. Students used formats that allowed them to draw on their strongest intelligence among Gardner's eight. The projects created by the students included writing and performing a skit about the Lewis and Clark Expedition (linguistic and interpersonal intelligences); painting watercolors of birds and other wildlife for a project on John J. Audubon (visual-spatial

S

T

U

→

COMMENTARY

R. **Author's emphasis.** Laver knows that when underlining (or italic type) appears in a quotation, it may not be clear who is doing the emphasizing. It is prudent to insert [author's emphasis] or [emphasis added], always between square brackets, the standard way to insert information into quotations.

S. **Topic sentences.** Laver composed topic sentences to begin most of her paragraphs. She felt that they provided a useful guide to her line of reasoning and presentation of information.

T. **Specific examples.** Laver knows that well-chosen, specific examples can be clarifying and confirming illustrations of a point. Of the many examples she finds during her research, she chooses one she finds memorable and convincing.

U. 👁 **PROCESS NOTE:** In earlier drafts, Laver used full sentences for the information shown in parentheses here. This section of the paper seemed too long and wordy, so she condensed the material. Here is an excerpt from an earlier draft:

> One class project was to write and perform a skit about the Lewis and Clark Expedition. This drew on linguistic and interpersonal intelligences. Another was to paint watercolors of birds and other wildlife for a project on John J. Audubon. This drew on visual-spatial intelligence. ●

Laver 6

intelligence); creating a working telegraph (logical-
mathematical and bodily-kinesthetic intelligences); giving
a eulogy of Davy Crockett (interpersonal intelligence); and
taking on the role of a historical figure and speaking to
the class "in character" (intrapersonal, linguistic, and
interpersonal intelligences). Because of the teacher's
awareness of MI theory, the students felt "that they will
be valued for their unique qualities, that they can succeed
in their own way, and that they can have a successful

Internet sources do not require a page number. Use paragraph number, if given.

future" (Lambert). Similarly, Deborah Moore, director
of operations for the Council of Educational Facility
Planners International, endorses Gardner's ideas because
"implementing the theory of multiple intelligences will
provide eight potential pathways to learning."

PARAGRAPH 7: Sixth body paragraph makes a transition to the general public's interest in MI

Today, the general public seems increasingly intrigued
by the theory of multiple intelligences. In the last
decade, strong popular interest in two of Gardner's
intelligences has emerged. Starting with their 1990
journal article "Emotional Intelligence," Peter Salovey
and John Mayer led scientists to a substantial expansion
of Gardner's concepts of interpersonal and intrapersonal
intelligences. Salovey and Mayer avoid overusing technical
language, thus making their ideas more accessible. For
example, here is their straightforward definition of
emotional intelligence: "the ability to monitor one's own
feelings and emotions, to discriminate among them, and to

Specific example of claim at start of paragraph

use this information to guide one's thinking and actions"
[author's emphasis] (189). In 1995, a general audience "pop
psychology" book, Emotional Intelligence by Daniel Goleman,
became an immediate bestseller and remained popular for a
long time. Goleman, a journalist and writer, fleshes out
Gardner's concepts of interpersonal and intrapersonal
intelligences. He also emphasizes the close interaction
between them and the other intelligences that Gardner has
identified:

V

→

COMMENTARY

V. 👁 **PROCESS NOTE:** Serendipity (which means "luck, happenstance") led Laver to discover the work of Salovey and Mayer and of Goleman. A while before she wrote her paper, she had seen the title *Emotional Intelligence* on a book that her parents were reading. It had been recommended to them by friends who liked to read best-sellers. As Laver was learning about Gardner's concepts of different types of intelligence, the Goleman book popped into her mind, and so she checked it out of the library. It turned out to be an excellent source, and its bibliography led her to the very useful scholarly article by Salovey and Mayer. ●

Laver 7

Do not use quotation marks in block-indented excerpt unless words are in quotation marks in source

These two minds, the emotional and the rational,
operate in tight harmony for the most part,
intertwining their very different ways of knowing
to guide us through the world. Ordinarily there
is a balance between emotional and rational
minds, with emotion feeding into and informing
the operations of the rational mind, and the
rational mind refining and sometimes vetoing the
inputs of the emotions. (9)

W

PARAGRAPH 8: Seventh body paragraph gives Gardner's opinion of information in previous paragraph

Goleman, drawing mainly from the work of Salovey and
Mayer and a few others, asked Gardner his reaction to the
new public interest in emotional intelligence. Gardner
applauded the interest as a balance to trends in his
work. Gardner felt that he had tended to focus more on
cognition; yet, he told Goleman,

An ellipsis indicates words Laver omitted from the middle of one sentence to the end of another, from the source she is quoting

"When I first wrote about the personal
intelligences, I was [author's emphasis] talking
about emotion. . . . But as it has developed in
practice, the theory of multiple intelligences
has evolved to focus more on metacognition"--that
is, awareness of one's mental processes--"rather
than on the full range of emotional abilities."
(qtd. in Goleman 41)

X

CONCLUSION: Laver looks to the future with optimism

Scientists will surely continue to make new
discoveries about human intelligence. As knowledge of MI
theory spreads to educators and the public, many will
accept that human intelligence involves more than the
logical-mathematical and linguistic talents measured by
traditional IQ tests. In turn, student educational
success, as well as self-esteem, will increase
dramatically. In fact, more students and teachers might
begin to find school enjoyable and even exciting.

Y

COMMENTARY

W. **Displayed quotation.** Because the quotation by Goleman is more than four lines long, MLA style calls for it to be "displayed." This means that the quotation must have all lines in a "block" indented from the left margin. Each line should be indented 1 inch (or two tabs or ten full spaces) from the left margin.

X. **Use of ellipsis with square brackets.** Laver uses brackets here to indicate that she chose to omit words from the middle of one sentence to the end of another sentence.

Y. **Concluding paragraph.** Laver decides to end her paper with her opinion and an optimistic prediction for the future.

Laver 8

Works Cited

In MLA style, list of sources, called Works Cited, begins on a new page. Double-space throughout.

Caine, Renate Nummela, and Geoffrey Caine. "Understanding
    a Brain-based Approach to Learning and Teaching."
    Educational Leadership 48 (1990): 66-70.

List sources in alphabetical order

Campbell, Bruce. "The Naturalist Intelligence." The
    Building Tool Room. Home page. New Horizons for
    Learning. 15 Oct. 2000 <http://www.newhorizons.org/
    article_eightintel.html>.

Gardner, Howard. The Disciplined Mind: What All Students
    Should Understand. New York: Simon, 1999.

--- followed by period indicates same author as preceding entry

---. Frames of Mind: The Theory of Multiple Intelligences.
    New York: Basic, 1993.

Goleman, Daniel. Emotional Intelligence. New York: Bantam,
    1995.

Hoerr, Thomas. "The Naturalist Intelligence." The Building
    Tool Room. Home page. New Horizons for Learning.

Divide URL only after a slash

    15 Oct. 2000 <http://www.newhorizons.org/
    trm_hoerrmi.html>.

Computer Tip: Use copy-paste system for long, complicated URLs

Lambert, Wendy Ecklund. "From Crockett to Tubman:
    Investigating Historical Perspectives." Educational
    Leadership 55 (Sept. 1997): n. pag. Academic Search
    Elite. EBSCO Publishing. Kishwaukee Coll. Lib. 11 Oct.
    2000 <http://search.epnet.com>.

Moore, Deborah P. "Facilities and Learning Styles." School
    Planning and Management (Apr. 1999): 22. Academic
    Search Elite. EBSCO Publishing. Kishwaukee Coll. Lib.
    20 Oct. 2000 <http://search.epnet.com>.

Salovey, Peter, and John D. Mayer. "Emotional
    Intelligence." Imagination, Cognition and Personality
    9 (1989-90): 185-211.

Urbina, Susana P. "Intelligence: Definition and
    Theoretical Models." Survey of Social Science:

Ed. placed here stands for "Edited by"

    Psychology Series. Ed. Frank Magill. Vol. 3.
    Pasadena: Salem, 1994. 1328-33.

Z
AA
BB
CC
DD
EE
FF

COMMENTARY

Z. **General format.** Laver provides an alphabetically arranged list of all the sources referred to in the paper. It is headed *Works Cited* and follows MLA documentation style (see 35d). Entries are alphabetized by each author's last name; if no author's name is given, the work's title is the first information unit and is alphabetized by its first word (excluding *A, An,* or *The*). Any entry more than one line long has a five-space (or 1/2-inch) indent for each line after the first. Double-spacing is used within and between entries.

AA. **Journal article by two authors.** The name of the first author is inverted (last name, first name, middle name, if any), but the name of the second is not. Article title is in quotation marks, and journal title is underlined. Volume, year (in parentheses), and page numbers are given. (See also the Salovey and Mayer entry.)

BB. **Article published on a professional site on the Internet.** Author's name is inverted. Article title is in quotation marks. Title of the professional site is underlined, and the site is identified as a home page. The professional organization that maintains the site is listed. The access date is followed by the URL enclosed in angle brackets. (See the same format in the Hoerr entry.)

CC. **Book by one author.** Author's name is inverted. Title is underlined. Publisher is identified in as brief a form as possible.

DD. **Second work by an author.** Three hyphens followed by a period indicate that the author is the same as in the preceding entry. Multiple works by the same author are listed in alphabetical order by title.

EE. **Full-text article from an online service.** Author's name is inverted. Article title is in quotation marks. Title of the original source is underlined, followed by the volume number, if given. The date of the original publication and original page numbers follow. Next appears the database title, underlined, when known; the name of the computer service; the name of the library (and its city, if desired), when, as with Lisa Laver, a library has provided the service; and the date the researcher visited the site. The last item, if known, is the URL of the service's home (or log-in) page in angle brackets.

When no URL is available, write *Keyword:* (for a keyword search) after the access date, followed by the term, or write *Path:*, followed by the words you entered in series (separated by semicolons).

FF. **Signed article in a multivolume reference work.** Author is followed by title of article in quotation marks. Title of book is underlined. Abbreviation *Ed.* (for "Edited by") is followed by editor's name in regular order. Volume numbers use arabic numerals, even if the original volumes are numbered with roman numerals. Publication information is followed by inclusive page numbers for the article.

36 APA DOCUMENTATION WITH CASE STUDY

36a What is APA style?

The American Psychological Association (APA) endorses a name-year PARENTHETICAL REFERENCE documentation system that is used in its journals and has come to be used by students in the social sciences and some other disciplines. APA IN-TEXT CITATIONS alert readers to material you have used from outside sources. These citations function with an alphabetical REFERENCES list at the end of your paper that contains information which enables readers to retrieve the sources you have quoted from, paraphrased, or summarized.

36b What are APA in-text citations?

APA style requires IN-TEXT CITATIONS that identify a SOURCE by a name (usually an author's name) and a year (for print sources, usually the copyright year). You can often incorporate the relevant name, and sometimes the year, into your sentence. Otherwise, this information is placed in parentheses, which are located close by the material being credited so that a reader connects the reference to it correctly. The *Publication Manual of the American Psychological Association* (5th edition, 2001) recommends that if you refer to a work more than once in a paragraph, you give the author's name and the date at the first mention and then give only the name after that. (*Exception:* If you are citing two or more works by the same author or if two or more of your sources have the same name, each citation must include the date so that a reader knows which work is being cited.)

APA style requires page numbers for direct quotations and recommends them for paraphrases. Some instructors expect page references for any use of a source, so find out your instructor's preference.

Put page numbers in parentheses, using the abbreviation *p.* before a single page number and *pp.* when the material you are citing falls on more than one page. For a direct quotation from an electronic source that numbers paragraphs, give a paragraph number (or numbers). Handle paragraph numbers as you do page numbers, but use *para.* or ¶ (the symbol for paragraph) rather than *p.* or *pp.*

36c What are APA guidelines for in-text citations?

The directory below corresponds to the numbered examples that follow it. The examples show how to cite various kinds of sources in the body of your paper. Remember, though, that you often can introduce source names, including titles when necessary, and sometimes even years, in your own sentences rather than in parenthetical citations.

Directory—APA In-text Citations

1. Paraphrased or Summarized Source—APA
2. Source of a Short Quotation—APA
3. Source of a Long Quotation (and Format of Quotation)—APA
4. One Author—APA
5. Two Authors—APA
6. Three, Four, or Five Authors—APA
7. Six or More Authors—APA
8. Author(s) with Two or More Works in the Same Year—APA
9. Two or More Authors with the Same Last Name—APA
10. Work with a Group or Corporate Author—APA
11. Work Listed by Title—APA
12. Reference to More Than One Source—APA
13. Personal Communication, Including E-Mail and Other Nonretrievable Sources—APA
14. Reference to an Entire Online Source—APA
15. Other References to Retrievable Online Sources—APA
16. Source Lines for Graphics and Table Data—APA

1. Paraphrased or Summarized Source—APA

People from the Mediterranean prefer an elbow-to-shoulder distance from each other (Morris, 1977, p. 131). [Author name, date, and page cited in parentheses.]

Desmond Morris (1977, p. 131) notes that people from the Mediterranean prefer an elbow-to-shoulder distance from each other. [Author name cited in text; date and page cited in parentheses.]

619

2. Source of a Short Quotation—APA

A recent report of reductions in SAD-related "depression in 87 percent of patients" (Binkley, 1990, p. 203) reverses the findings of earlier studies. [Author name, date, and page reference in parentheses immediately following the quotation.]

Binkley reports reductions in SAD-related "depression in 87 percent of patients" (1990, p. 203). [Author name incorporated into the words introducing the quotation; date and page number in parentheses immediately following the quotation.]

3. Source of a Long Quotation (and Format of Quotation)—APA

Incorporate a direct quotation of fewer than forty words into your own sentence and enclose it in quotation marks. Place the parenthetical citation after the closing quotation mark and, if the quotation falls at the end of the sentence, before the sentence-ending punctuation. When you use a quotation longer than forty words, set it off from your own words by starting it on a new line and indenting each line of the quotation five spaces from the left margin. Do not enclose a displayed quotation in quotation marks. Place the parenthetical citation one space after the end punctuation of the last sentence.

DISPLAYED QUOTATION (FORTY OR MORE WORDS)

Jet lag, with its characteristic fatigue and irregular sleep patterns, is a common problem among those who travel great distances by jet airplane to different time zones:

> Jet lag syndrome is the inability of the internal body rhythm to rapidly resynchronize after sudden shifts in the timing. For a variety of reasons, the system attempts to maintain stability and resist temporal change. Consequently, complete adjustment can often be delayed for several days—sometimes for a week— after arrival at one's destination. (Bonner, 1991, p. 72)

Interestingly, this research shows that the number of flying hours is not the cause of jet lag.

The following examples show how to handle PARENTHETICAL REFER-ENCES for various sources. Remember, though, that you often can introduce source names, including titles when necessary, and sometimes even the year of publication, in your own sentences.

4. One Author—APA

```
One of his questions is, "What binds together a Mormon
banker in Utah with his brother, or other coreligionists in
Illinois or Massachusetts?" (Coles, 1993, p. 2).
```

In a parenthetical reference in APA style, a comma and a space separate a name from a year and a year from a page reference. (Examples 1 through 3 also show citations of works by one author.)

5. Two Authors—APA

If a work has two authors, give both names in each citation.

```
One report describes 2,123 occurrences (Krait & Cooper, 1994).

The results Krait and Cooper (1994) report would not
support the conclusions Davis and Sherman (1992) draw in
their review of the literature.
```

When citing two (or more) authors, use an ampersand (&) between the (final) two names in parenthetical references, but write out the word *and* for any reference in your own sentence.

6. Three, Four, or Five Authors—APA

For three, four, or five authors, use all the authors' last names in the first reference. In all subsequent references, use only the first author's last name followed by *et al.* (meaning "and others").

FIRST REFERENCE

```
In one anthology, 35% of the selections had not been
anthologized before (Elliott, Kerber, Litz, & Martin, 1992).
```

SUBSEQUENT REFERENCE

```
Elliott et al. (1992) include 17 authors whose work has
never been anthologized.
```

7. Six or More Authors—APA

For six or more authors, name the first author followed by *et al.* in all in-text references, including the first. (See page 631, model 3, for the correct References format.)

8. Author(s) with Two or More Works in the Same Year—APA

If you use more than one source written in the same year by the same author(s), alphabetize the works by their titles for the References list,

621

and assign letters in alphabetical order to the years—(1996a), (1996b), (1996c). Use the year-letter combination in parenthetical references. Note that a citation of two or more of such works lists the years in alphabetical order.

Most recently, Jones (1996c) draws new conclusions from the results of 17 sets of experiments (Jones, 1996a, 1996b).

9. Two or More Authors with the Same Last Name—APA

Include first initials for every in-text citation of authors who share a last name. Use the initials appearing in the References list. (In the second example, a parenthetical citation, the name order is alphabetical, as explained in item 12.)

R. A. Smith (1997) and C. Smith (1989) both confirm these results.

These results have been confirmed independently (C. Smith, 1989; R. A. Smith, 1997).

10. Work with Group or Corporate Author—APA

If you use a source in which the "author" is a corporation, agency, or group, an in-text reference gives that name as author. Use the full name in each citation, unless an abbreviated version of the name is likely to be familiar to your audience. In that case, use the full name and give its abbreviation at the first citation; then, use the abbreviation for subsequent citations.

This exploration will continue into the 21st century (National Aeronautics and Space Administration [NASA], 1996).

In subsequent citations, use the abbreviated form, *NASA*, alone.

11. Work Listed by Title—APA

If no author is named, use a shortened form of the title in citations. Ignoring *A, An,* or *The,* make the first word the one by which you alphabetize the title in your References. The following citation is to an article fully titled "Are You a Day or Night Person?"

The "morning lark" and "night owl" connotations are typically used to categorize the human extremes ("Are You," 1989).

12. Reference to More Than One Source—APA

If more than one source has contributed to an idea or opinion in your paper, cite the sources alphabetically by author in one set of parentheses; separate each block of information with a semicolon.

```
Conceptions of personal space vary among cultures (Morris,
1977; Worchel & Cooper, 1983).
```

13. Personal Communication, Including E-Mail and Other Nonretrievable Sources—APA

Telephone calls, personal letters, interviews, and e-mail messages are "personal communications" that your readers cannot access or retrieve. Acknowledge personal communications in parenthetical references, but not in your References list. This guideline applies as well to most discussion list postings, which are seldom fully archived.

```
Recalling his first summer at camp, one person said, "The
proximity of 12 other kids made me—an only child with
older, quiet parents—frantic for the entire eight weeks" (A.
Weiss, personal communication, January 12, 1996).
```

14. Reference to an Entire Online Source—APA

For a brief reference to an entire online source, just give the URL (Internet address) in parentheses. Do not include the source in your References list.

```
Another engaging graphic can be found on the Project Zero
home page (http://pzweb.harvard.edu/default.htm).
```

15. Other References to Retrievable Online Sources—APA

When you quote, paraphrase, or summarize an online source that is available to others, include the work in your References list and cite the author (if any) or title and the date as you would for a print source.

16. Source Lines for Graphics and Table Data—APA

If you use a graphic from another source or create a table using data from another source, give a note in the text at the bottom of the table or graphic, crediting the original author and the copyright holder. Here are examples of two source lines, one for a graphic from an article, the other for a graphic from a book.

GRAPHIC FROM AN ARTICLE—APA

Note. From [or The data in columns 1 and 2 are from] "Bridge over troubled waters? Connecting research and pedagogy in composition and business/technical communication," by J. Allen, 1992, *Technical Communication Quarterly*, *1*(4), p. 9. Copyright 1992 by the Association of Teachers of Technical Writing. Adapted with permission of the author.

GRAPHIC FROM A BOOK—APA

Note. From *How to lower your fat thermostat: The no-diet reprogramming plan for lifelong weight control* (p. 74), by D. Remington, A. G. Fisher, and E. Parent, 1983, Provo: Vitality House International. Copyright 1983 by Vitality House International. Reprinted with permission.

36d What are APA guidelines for writing an abstract?

You may be asked to include an abstract at the start of a paper you prepare in APA style. As the APA *Publication Manual* explains, "an abstract is a brief, comprehensive summary" (p. 12) of a longer piece of writing. Make a summary accurate, objective, and exact. (The APA manual estimates that an abstract should be limited in length to about 120 words or less.) You may be familiar with effective abstracts, for many disciplines have online abstracts of longer sources. Here is an abstract prepared for a paper on biological clocks.

> Circadian rhythms, which greatly affect human lives, often suffer disruptions in technological societies, resulting in such disorders as jet lag syndrome and seasonal affective disorder (SAD). With growing scientific awareness of both natural circadian cycles and the effects of disturbances of these cycles, individuals are learning how to control some negative effects.

See 36h for guidelines on formatting the Abstract page.

36e What are APA guidelines for content notes?

Content notes can be used in APA-style papers for additional relevant information that cannot be worked effectively into a text discussion. Use consecutive arabic numerals for note numbers, both within your paper and on a separate page following the last text page of your paper. See 36h for instructions on formatting the Footnotes page.

36f What are APA general guidelines for a References list?

The References list provides bibliographic information for readers who may want to access the sources you cite in your paper.

Include in a References list all the sources you quote from (31c), paraphrase (31d), or summarize (31e) in your paper so that any other person could find these same sources with reasonable effort. Do not include any source not generally available to others; see item 13 in 36c (p. 623) or, for another example, item 34 (p. 636) about personal interviews.

The general format guidelines are presented in Box 151 for quick access. A lengthy list of specific source reference models is provided in section 36g.

◉ Guidelines for an APA-style References list   151

■ TITLE
References

■ PLACEMENT OF LIST
Start a new page numbered sequentially with the rest of the paper, before Notes pages, if any.

■ CONTENTS AND FORMAT
Include all quoted, paraphrased, or summarized sources in your paper that are not personal communications, unless your instructor tells you to include all the references you have consulted, not just those you have to credit. Start each entry on a new line, and double-space all lines. On its Web page, (http://www.apastyle.org/elecref.html),* and in the 2001 edition of the *Publication Manual* (section 5.18), the APA states its recommendation that student papers follow journal formatting by using a *hanging indent* style.

* The word *online* is hyphenated in APA style, but not in MLA style or the style of this handbook. Note, too, that in APA style, URLs are separated from text with parentheses rather than angle brackets.

→

Guidelines for an APA-style References list   151
(continued)

The first line of each entry begins flush left at the margin and all other lines are indented. The hanging indent makes source names and dates prominent. Type the first line of each entry full width, and indent subsequent lines five to seven spaces (or one tab).If the tabbed hanging indent is difficult to achieve on your word processor, use the same paragraph indent already set for the paper.

> Shuter, R. (1977). A field study of nonverbal
>   communication in Germany, Italy, and the United
>   States. *Communication Monographs*, *44*, 298–305.

■ **SPACING AFTER PUNCTUATION**
The 2001 APA manual calls for one space after punctuation marks, including displayed quotations (see 36c, item 3).

■ **ARRANGEMENT OF ENTRIES**
Alphabetize by the author's last name. If no author is named, alphabetize by the first significant word (not *A, An,* or *The*) in the title of the work.

■ **AUTHORS' NAMES**
Use last names, first initials, and middle initials, if any. Reverse the order for all authors' names, and use an ampersand (&) between the second-to-last and last authors: Mills, J. F., & Holahan, R. H.
     Give names in the order in which they appear on the work (on the title page of a book; usually under the title of an article or other printed work). Use a comma between the first author's last name and first initial and after each complete name except the last, after the last author's name.

■ **DATES**
Date information follows the after name information, enclose it in parentheses. Place a period followed by one space after the closing parenthesis.
     For books, articles in journals that have volume numbers, and many other print and nonprint sources, the year of publication or production is the date to use. For articles from most magazines and newspapers, use the year followed by a comma and then the exact date that appears on the issue. Individual entries in 36g show how much information to give for various sources.

■ **CAPITALIZATION OF TITLES**
For books, articles, and chapters, capitalize the first word, the first word after a colon between a title and subtitle, and any proper nouns. For names of journals and proceedings of meetings, capitalize

→

Guidelines for an APA-style References list   151
(continued)

the first word, all nouns and adjectives, and any other words five or more letters long.

- **SPECIAL TREATMENT OF TITLES**
Use no special treatment for titles of shorter works (poems, short stories, essays, articles). Italicize titles of longer works (books, names of newspapers or journals). Underlining can be used in place of italic type if italic type face is unavailable. Draw an unbroken line that includes punctuation.
  Do not drop *A, An,* or *The* from the titles of periodicals (such as newspapers, magazines, and journals).

- **PUBLISHERS**
Use a shortened version of the publisher's name except for an association, corporation, or university press. Drop *Co., Inc., Publishers,* and the like, but retain *Books* or *Press*.

- **PLACE OF PUBLICATION**
For U.S. publishers, give the city and add the state (use the two-letter postal abbreviations listed in most dictionaries and in Box 123 in 30L) for all U.S. cities except Baltimore, Boston, Chicago, Los Angeles, New York, Philadelphia, and San Francisco. For other countries, give city and country spelled out. However, if the state or country is part of the publisher's name, omit it after the name of the city.

- **PUBLICATION MONTH ABBREVIATIONS**
Do not abbreviate publication months.

- **PAGE NUMBERS**
Use all digits, omitting none. *Only* for references to parts of books or material in newspapers, use *p.* and *pp.* before page numbers. List all discontinuous pages, with numbers separated by commas: `pp. 32, 44–45, 47–49, 53.`

- **REFERENCES ENTRIES: BOOKS**
Citations for books have four main parts: author, date, title, and publication information (place of publication and publisher).

AUTHOR   DATE   TITLE
`Didion, J. (1977). A book of common prayer.`

PUBLICATION INFORMATION
`New York: Simon & Schuster.`

→

Guidelines for an APA-style References list 151
(continued)

■ REFERENCES ENTRIES: ARTICLES
Citations for periodical articles contain four major parts: author, date, title of article, and publication information (usually, the periodical title, volume number, and page numbers).

AUTHOR   DATE   ARTICLE TITLE
Shuter, R. (1977). A field study of nonverbal

communication in Germany, Italy, and the United

PERIODICAL TITLE   VOLUME NUMBER   PAGE NUMBERS
States. *Communication Monographs*, *44*, 298–305.

■ REFERENCES ENTRIES: ELECTRONIC AND ONLINE SOURCES
Styles for documenting electronic and online sources have been changing and will continue to evolve. The 2001 APA *Publication Manual* (pp 268-281) and the APA Web page (http://www.apastyle.org/elecref.html) are the best sources for up-tp-date advice on these formats. Here are two example entries. the first is for an abstract on CD-ROM, a searchable "aggregated database" (i.e., a compilation of resources grouped for directed or simplified access). You are not required to document how you accessed the database —via portable CD-ROM, on a library server, or via a supplier Web site—but a "retrieval statement" that accurately names the source (in this case, the database) and lists the date of retrieval is required. (If you include an item or accession number, place it in parentheses.)

AUTHORS   DATE   ARTICLE TITLE
Marcus, H. F., & Kitayamo, S. (1991).Culture and

the self: Implications for cognition, emotion, and

JOURNAL TITLE AND PUBLICATION INFORMATION   RETRIEVAL INFORMATION
motivation. *Psychological Abstracts, 78.* Retrieved

October 2, 2001, from PsycLIT database Item 23873).

Guidelines for an APA-style References list   151
(continued)

The second example is for an article in a newspaper on the World Wide Web. The retrieval statement gives the access date and the URL, which "names" the source, an Internet-only publication.

```
              DATE OF PUBLICATION
   AUTHOR          ON THE WEB              TITLE OF ARTICLE
┌──────────┐┌─────────────────────────┐┌───────────────────┐
Lewis, R. (1995, December 24). Chronobiology
```

```
──────────────────────────────────────────────────────────
 researchers say their field's time has come.
```

```
    TITLE AND VOLUME      PAGE
   OF ONLINE NEWSPAPER    NUMBER        RETRIEVAL INFORMATION
┌──────────────────┐  ┌───────┐  ┌───────────────────────────
 The Scientist, 9, p. 14. Retrieved December 30, 1997,
```

```
──────────────────────────────────────────────────────────
 from http://www.the-scientist.library.upenn.
```

```
──────────────────────────────────────────
 edu/yr1995/dec/chrono_951211.html
```

Notice that the only punctuation in the URL is part of the address. Do not add a period after a URL.

36g What are APA guidelines for specific sources in a References list?

The directory below corresponds to the numbered examples that follow it. Not all documentation models are shown here. You may find that you have to combine features of models to document a particular source. More information is available in the *Publication Manual of the American Psychological Association* (5th edition, 2001) and at the APA Web site (http://www.apa.org).

Directory—APA Style

PRINT SOURCES

1. Book by One Author—APA
2. Book by Two Authors—APA
3. Book by Three or More Authors—APA
4. Two or More Books by the Same Author(s)—APA

40. Radio or Television Broadcast—APA
41. Information Services: ERIC and NewsBank—APA

ELECTRONIC AND ONLINE SOURCES
42. Article from an Encyclopedia on CD-ROM—APA
43. Computer Software—APA
44. Books Retrieved from Databases on the Web—APA
45. Article from a Periodical on the Web—APA
46. Personal or Professional Site on the Web—APA

PRINT SOURCES
1. Book by One Author—APA

Welty, E. (1984). *One writer's beginnings*. Cambridge, MA:
    Harvard University Press.

Use only the hanging indent style: the first line of an entry is flush to the left margin and all other lines are indented five to seven spaces. Here the indentation is five full spaces.

2. Book by Two Authors—APA

Leghorn, L., & Parker, K. (1981). *Woman's worth*.
    Boston: Routledge & Kegan Paul.

3. Book by Three or More Authors—APA

Moore, M. H., Estrich, S., McGillis, D., & Spelman, W.
    (1984). *Dangerous offenders: The elusive target of
    justice*. Cambridge, MA: Harvard University Press.

In the References, always list the names of the first six authors; substitute *et al.* for the seventh or more author names.

4. Two or More Books by the Same Author(s)—APA

Gardner, H. (1993). *Multiple intelligences: The theory in
    practice*. New York: Basic Books.
Gardner, H. (1999). *Intelligence reframed: Multiple intelligences
    for the 21st century*. New York: Basic Books.

References by the same author are arranged chronologically, with the earlier date of publication listed first.

5. Book by Group or Corporate Author—APA

Boston Women's Health Collective. (1986). *Our bodies,
    ourselves*. New York: Simon & Schuster.

American Psychological Association. (2001). *Publication
    manual of the American Psychological Association* (5th
    ed.). Washington, DC: Author.

Cite the full name of the corporate author first. If the author is also the publisher, use the word *Author* as the name of the publisher.

6. Book with No Author Named—APA

The Chicago manual of style (14th ed.). (1993). Chicago:
    University of Chicago Press.

7. Book with an Author and an Editor—APA

Brontë, E. (1985). *Wuthering Heights* (D. Daiches, Ed.).
    London: Penguin Books.

8. Translation—APA

Kundera, M. (1999). *The unbearable lightness of being*
    (M. H. Heim, Trans.). New York: HarperPerennial.

9. Work in Several Volumes or Parts—APA

Randall, J. H., Jr. (1962). *The career of philosophy* (Vols.
    1–2). New York: Columbia University Press.

10. One Selection from an Anthology or an Edited Book—APA

Galarza, E. (1972). The roots of migration. In L. Valdez
    & S. Steiner (Eds.), *Aztlan: An anthology of Mexican
    American literature* (pp. 127–132). New York: Knopf.

Give the author of the selection first. The word *In* introduces the larger work from which the selection is taken.

11. Selection from a Work Already Listed in References—APA

Gilbert, S., & Gubar, S. (Eds.). (1985). *The Norton
    anthology of literature by women*. New York: Norton.
Kingston, M. H. (1985). No name woman. In S. Gilbert & S.
    Gubar (Eds.), *The Norton anthology of literature by
    women* (pp. 2337–2347). New York: Norton.

Provide full information for the already-cited anthology (first example), in addition to the information about the individual selection.

12. Signed Article in a Reference Book—APA

Burnbam, J. C. (1996). Freud, Sigmund. In B. B. Wolman
(Ed.), *The encyclopedia of psychiatry, psychology, and
psychoanalysis* (p. 220). New York: Holt.

Use *In* to introduce the larger work from which the selection is taken.

13. Unsigned Article in a Reference Book—APA

Russia. (1994). In *The new encyclopaedia Britannica*. (Vol.
10, pp. 253–255). Chicago: Encyclopaedia Britannica.

14. Edition—APA

Janson, A. F. (1997). *History of Art* (5th ed., Rev.). New York: Abrams.

When a book is not the first edition, the edition number appears on
the title page. In your entry, place this information after the title and in
parentheses. Use the year of the edition you are citing.

15. Anthology or Edited Book—APA

Valdez, L., & Steiner, S. (Eds.). (1972). *Aztlan: An anthology
of Mexican American literature*. New York: Knopf.

16. Introduction, Preface, Foreword, or Afterword—APA

Fox-Genovese, E. (1999). Foreword. In N. Warren & S. Wolff (Eds.),
Southern mothers. Baton Rouge: Louisiana State
University Press.

If you are citing an introduction, preface, foreword, or afterword,
give its author's name first. After the year, give the name of the part cited.
If the writer of the material you are citing is not the author of the book,
use the word *In* and the author's name before the title of the book.

17. Unpublished Dissertation or Essay—APA

Geissinger, S. B. (1984). *Openness versus secrecy in
adoptive parenthood*. Unpublished dissertation,
University of North Carolina at Greensboro.

18. Reprint of an Older Book—APA

Hurston, Z. N. (1978). *Their eyes were watching God*. Urbana:
University of Illinois Press. (Original work published 1937)

Republishing information appears on the copyright page.

19. Book in a Series—APA

Goldman, D. J. (1995). *Women writers and World War I*. New
     York: Macmillan.

Give the title of the book, but not of the whole series.

20. Book with a Title Within a Title—APA

Lumiansky, R. M., & Baker, H. (Eds.). (1968). *Critical approaches*
     to six major English works: Beowulf *through* Paradise Lost.
     Philadelphia: University of Pennsylvania Press.

Do not italicize an incorporated title, even though it would be set in
italic typeface as a title by itself.

21. Government Publication—APA

U.S. Congress. House Subcommittee on Health and Environment
     of the Committee on Commerce. (1999). *The nursing home*
     resident protection amendments of 1999. Washington,
     DC: U.S. Government Printing Office.

U.S. Congressional Subcommittee on Technology of the
     Committee on Science. (1998). *Y2K: What every consumer*
     should know to prepare for the year 2000 program.
     Washington, DC: U.S. Government Printing Office.

U.S. Senate Special Committee on Aging. (1998). *The risk of*
     malnutrition in nursing homes. Washington, DC: U.S.
     Government Printing Office.

United States Senate Special Committee on the Year 2K
     Technical Problem. (1999). *Y2K and H_2O: Safeguarding*
     our most vital resources. Washington, DC: U.S.
     Government Printing Office.

Use the complete name of a government agency as author when no
specific person is named.

22. Published Proceedings of a Conference—APA

Harris, D., & Nelson-Heern, L. (Eds.). (1981). *Proceedings*
     of NECC 1981: National Education Computing Conference.
     Iowa City: Weeg Computing Center, University of Iowa.

23. Article from a Daily Newspaper—APA

Wyatt, E. (1999, December 3). A high school without a home.
The New York Times, pp. B1, B7.

24. Editorial, Letter to the Editor, or Review—APA

Didion, J. (1999, November 4). The day was hot and still
. . . [Review of the book *Dutch: A memoir of Ronald
Reagan*]. The New York Review of Books, 4–6.
Mr. Gorbachev's role [Editorial]. (1999, November 10). *The
New York Times*, p. A22.
Wolfe, C. (1999, November 22). [Letter to the editor].
Newsweek, 22.

25. Unsigned Article from a Daily Newspaper—APA

Female cadets gaining sway at the Coast Guard. (1999,
November 15). *The New York Times*, p. B6.
A hostess, a candidate, and a first lady fully booked.
(1999, December 5). *The New York Times*, p. 29.

26. Article from a Weekly or Biweekly Periodical—APA

Greenfield, K. T. (1999, November 22). Giving away the
e-store. *Time*, 58–60.

Use the abbreviation *p.* (or *pp.* for more than one page) for newspapers.
Do not use this abbreviation for magazines or journals. Give year, month,
and day-date for a periodical published every week or every two weeks.

27. Article from a Monthly or Bimonthly Periodical—APA

Bonner, J. T. (1999, March). The evolution of evolution.
Natural History, 108(3), 20–21.

Give the year and month(s) for a periodical published every month
or every other month.

28. Unsigned Article from a Weekly or Monthly Periodical—APA

A salute to everyday heroes. (1989, July 10). *Time*, 46–51,
54–56, 58–60, 63–64, 66.

29. Article from a SIRS Collection of Reprinted Articles—APA

Curver, P. C. (1989, January–February). Lighting in the 21st
century. *Futurist*, 29–34. Retrieved April 19,2001
from SIRS database.

30. Article in a Journal with Continuous Pagination—APA

Tyson, P. (1998). The psychology of women. *Journal of the
American Psychoanalytic Association, 46*, 361–364.

Give only the volume number after the journal title and italicize the
volume number.

31. Article in a Journal That Pages Each Issue Separately—APA

Zeleza, P. T. (1997). Visions of freedom and democracy in
postcolonial African literature. *Women's Studies
Quarterly, 25*(3–4), 10–31.

Give the volume number, italicized with the journal title. Give the
issue number in parentheses; do not italicize it.

32. Published and Unpublished Letters—APA

Sand, G. (1993). Letter to her mother. In Reid Sherline
(Ed.), *Letters home: Celebrated authors write to their
mothers* (pp. 17–20). New York: Timkin.

In the APA system, unpublished letters are considered personal communication inaccessible to general readers, so they do not appear in the
References list. Personal communications do not provide recoverable data
and so are cited only in the body of the paper, as shown in item 34 below.

33. Map or Chart—APA

The Caribbean and South America [Map]. (1992). Falls Church,
VA: American Automobile Association.

NONPRINT SOURCES

34. Interview—APA

In APA style, a personal interview is considered personal correspondence and is not included in the References list. Cite the interview in the text with a parenthetical notation that it is a personal
communication.

Randi Friedman (personal communication, June 30, 1993)
endorses this view.

35. Lecture, Speech, or Address—APA

Kennedy, J. F. (1960, September 12). Address. Speech presented to the Greater Houston Ministerial Association, Houston.

36. Motion picture—APA

Capra, F. (Director & Producer). (1934). *It happened one night* [Motion Picture]. United States: Columbia Pictures.

Capra, F. (Director & Producer). (1999). *It happened one night* [Videocassette].

Madden, J. (Director), Parfitt, D., Gigliotta, D., Weinstein, H., Zwick, E., & Norman, M. (Producers). (1999). *Shakespeare in love* [DVD].

37. Music recording—APA

Smetana, B. (1975). *My country* [With K. Anserl conducting the Czech Philharmonic Orchestra]. [Record]. London: Vanguard Records.

Springsteen, B. (Performer). (1992). Local hero. *On lucky town* [CD]. New York: Columbia Records.

38. Live Performance—APA

Hare, D. (Author), Daldry, S. (Director), & Hare, D. (Performer). (1999, April 11). *Via dolorosa* [Live performance]. New York: Lincoln Center Theater.

39. Work of Art, Photograph, or Musical Composition—APA

Cassatt, M. *La toilette* [Artwork]. Chicago: Art Institute of Chicago.

Handel, G. F. *Water music* [Musical composition].

Mydans, C. (1999, October 21–November 28). *General Douglas MacArthur landing at Luzon*. 1945 [Photograph]. New York: Soho Triad Fine Art Gallery.

40. Radio or Television Broadcast—APA

Burns, K. (1999, November 7–8). In Barnes, P., & Burns, K. (Producers), *Not for ourselves alone: The story of Elizabeth Cady Stanton and Susan B. Anthony*.

[Television broadcast] New York and Washington, D.C.:

    Public Broadcasting Service.

If you are citing a television series produced by and seen on one station, cite its call letters.

41. Information Services: ERIC and NewsBank—APA

Chiang, L. H. (1993). *Beyond the language: Native Americans'*

    nonverbal communication. (ERIC Document Reproduction

    Service No. ED368540).

Wenzell, R. (1990). *Businesses prepare for a more diverse work*

    force. (NewsBank Document Reproduction Service No. EMP 27:DIZ).

ELECTRONIC AND ONLINE SOURCES

Information from online sources that your readers cannot readily retrieve for themselves—many e-mail messages and discussion list communications, for example—should be treated as personal communication (see model 34, p.636). If you have a scholarly reason to cite a message from a newsgroup, forum, or electronic mailing list that is archived, then document an author name; the exact date of the posting; the subject line or "thread" (do not italicize it) followed by an identifier in square brackets—[Msg 23]; and a "Message posted to" statement that lists the URL of the message or of the archive.

The APA system for documenting electronic and online sources in a References list has been evolving. See the *Publication Manual* (5th edition, 2001). The APA Web site (http://www.apa.org/elecref.html). In general, APA recommends giving author, title, and publication information as for a print source. This information is followed by a "retrieval statement" that leads the reader as directly as possible to your source.

42. Article from an Encyclopedia on CD-ROM—APA

Spanish dance. (2000). *Encarta 2000.* Retrieved December 10,

    2001 from Encarta database.

The retrieval statement gives the retrieval date in full and the name of the database. The entry ends with a period.

43. Computer Software—APA

Transparent Language Presentation Program (Version 2.0 for

    Windows) [Computer software]. (1994). Hollis, NH:

    Transparent Language.

Provide an author name, if available. Standard software and program languages do not need to be listed in References. Provide the name and, in parentheses, the version number in the text.

44. Books Retrieved from Databases on the Web—APA

Adams, H. (1918). *The education of Henry Adams*. New York:

    Houghton Mifflin. Retrieved December 4, 1999, from

    Project Bartleby database: http://www.columbia.edu/acis/

    bartleby/159/index/html

The first information is for the printed version of *The Education of Henry Adams*. The retrieval statement gives the access date, the name of the database, and the URL of the specific work.

Chopin, K. (1899). *The awakening*. Retrieved December 12, 1999,

    from PBS database: http://www.pbs.org/katechopin/library/awakening

45. Article from a Periodical on the Web—APA

Parrott, Andy C. (1999). Does cigarette smoking cause stress?

    American Psychologist, 54, 817–820. Retrieved December 7,

    1999, from: http://www.apa.org/journals/amp/amp5410817.html

46. Personal or Professional Site on the Web—APA

When citing an entire Web site rather than a particular part of that site, you need only provide the Web address in a parenthetical citation, as in the following example.

Thomas is the name of an excellent source for government documents on the Web (http://thomas.loc.gov).

36h What are APA format guidelines for research papers?

Ask whether your instructor has instructions for preparing a final draft. If not, you can use the APA guidelines here.

General instructions—APA

Use 8 1/2 × 11 inch white bond paper. Double-space throughout, whether the paper is typed or prepared on a computer (the APA *Publication Manual* recommends double-spacing for a final manuscript of a student research paper but suggests that heading, titles, captions, and quotations longer than forty words may be easier to read if they are single-spaced). Set at least a 1-inch margin on the left (1 1/2 inches if you submit your paper in a binder) and leave no less than 1 inch on the right and at the bottom.

Drop down 1/2 inch from the top edge of the paper to the title-and-page-number line, described below. Then, drop down another 1/2 inch (or

1 inch from the top edge of the paper) to the next line on the page, whether that is a heading (such as "Abstract" or "Notes") or a line of your paper.

If you are typing, use indents of five to seven character spaces wherever indentation of first lines is called for (see below). If you are preparing your paper on a computer, use indents of 1/2 inch. Indent the first line of all paragraphs five to seven characters (1/2 inch), except in an abstract, the first line of which is not indented. Do not justify the right margin. Indent footnotes five to seven characters.

Order of parts—APA

Use this order for the parts of your paper: title page; abstract (if required); body of the paper; References; Appendixes, if any; Footnotes, if any; attachments, if any (such as questionnaires, data sheets, or other material your instructor asks you to include). Number all pages consecutively.

Title-and-page-number line for all pages—APA

Use a title-and-page-number line on all pages of your paper. Drop down 1/2 inch from the top edge of the paper. Type the title (use a shortened version if necessary), leave a five-character space, and then type the page number. End the title-and-page-number line 1 inch from the right edge of the paper. Ask whether your instructor wants you to include your last name in this title-and-page-number line.

Title page—APA

Use a separate title page. On it, begin with the title-and-page-number line described above, using the numeral 1 for this first page. Then, center the complete title vertically and horizontally on the page. Use two or more double-spaced lines if the title is long. Do not underline the title or enclose it in quotation marks. On the next line, center your name, and below that center the course title and section, your professor's name, and the date.

☞ **CAPITALIZATION ALERT:** (1) Use the guidelines here for capitalizing the title of your own paper and for capitalizing titles you mention in the body of your paper. (*Note:* See Box 151, page 627, "Special Treatment of Titles," on capitalization of titles in a References list, since different rules apply). (2) Use a capital letter for the first word of your title and for the first word of a subtitle, if any. Start every NOUN, PRONOUN, VERB, ADVERB, and ADJECTIVE with a capital letter. Capitalize each main word in a hyphenated COMPOUND WORD (two or more words used together to express one idea): *Father-in-Law, Self-Consciousness.* Capitalize the word after a colon or a dash. (3) Do not capitalize articles (*a, an, the*) unless one of the preceding capitalization rules applies to it. Do not capitalize PREPOSITIONS and CONJUNCTIONS unless they are five or more letters long. Do not capitalize the word *to* used in an INFINITIVE. ●

Abstract—APA

See 36d for advice about what to include in an abstract of your paper. Type the abstract on a separate page, using the numeral 2 in the title-and-page-number line. Drop down 1 inch from the top of the paper and center the word *Abstract*. Double-space below this title, and then start your abstract, double-spacing it. Do not indent the first line.

Set-off quotations—APA

Set off (display in block form) quotations of forty words or more from your own words. Double-space to start a new line for the quoted words, indenting each line of the (double-spaced) quotation five spaces from the left margin. Do not enclose the quoted words in quotation marks.

If you are quoting part of a paragraph or one complete paragraph, do not indent the first line more than five spaces. But if you quote two or more paragraphs, indent the first line of the second and subsequent paragraphs ten spaces.

When the quotation is finished, leave one space after the sentence-ending punctuation, and then give the parenthetical citation. Begin a new line to resume your own words.

References list—APA

Start a new page for your References list immediately after the end of the body of your paper. Use a title-and-page-number line. Drop down 1 inch from the top of the paper and center the word *References*. Do not underline it or put it in quotation marks. Double-space below it. Start the first line of each entry at the left margin, and indent any subsequent lines five to seven characters (or 1/2 inch) from the left margin. If the hanging indent is difficult to produce, use your paper's paragraph indent. Double-space within each entry and between entries.

Notes—APA

Whenever you use a content note in your paper (36e), try to arrange your sentence so that the note number falls at the end. The ideal place for a note number is after the sentence-ending punctuation. Use a numeral raised slightly above the line of words and immediately after the final punctuation mark.

Put your notes on a separate page after the last page of your References list. Use a title-and-page-number line. Then, drop down 1 inch from the top of the paper and center the word *Footnotes*. Do not underline it or put it in quotation marks.

On the next line, indent five characters (or 1/2 inch) and begin the note. Raise the note number slightly, and then start the words of your note leaving no space. If the note is more than one typed line, do not indent any line after the first. Double-space throughout.

36i Carlos Velez's APA-style research paper

36i.1 Researching and writing the paper

The final two sections of this chapter present a student research paper written in the DOCUMENTATION STYLE of the American Psychological Association (APA). Section 36i.1 discusses the researching, planning, drafting, and revising processes of the student, Carlos Velez. Section 36i.2 shows the final draft of the paper, including its abstract.

After Carlos Velez read his assignment, he started planning by listing various unconscious processes in humans so that he could pick one most interesting to him. Referring to his class notes and the textbook from his psychology course, he found these topics: "sleep," "dreams," "insomnia," "biological clocks," "daydreams," "hypnosis," and "meditation." He

---

Carlos Velez was given this assignment for a research paper in a course called Introduction to Psychology: Write a research paper of 1,800 to 2,000 words about an unconscious process in humans. For guidance, refer to the *Simon & Schuster Handbook for Writers,* Sixth Edition, Chapters 31 through 34. Use the documentation style of the American Psychological Association (APA) explained in Chapter 36. Your topic and working bibliography are due in two weeks. An early draft of your paper is due two weeks later (try to get it close to what you hope will be your last draft, so that comments from me and your peers can concretely help you write an excellent final draft). Your final draft is due one week after the early draft with comments is returned to you.

---

favored the topic "biological clocks" because of his experiences with jet lag whenever he traveled between his home in California (in the Pacific Time Zone) and his grandparents' home in Puerto Rico (in the Atlantic Time Zone, where it is four hours later).

Velez then checked to see whether he could find enough sources useful for research on "biological clocks." From his home computer, he went to his college's Web site and found the college library home page. He was pleased to find that the online book catalog listed several appropriate books that had not been checked out. The online databases provided the entire text of hundreds of journal, magazine, and newspaper articles. Using the Yahoo! search engine, he found even more sources. During his search, he tried a variety of terms, like "biological clocks" and "jet lag," which he thought of himself; and "circadian rhythms" and "chronobiology," which he found in articles. Skimming through the online articles, he printed ones he thought he could use. Then, he went to his college library to check out several books and to review CD-ROM and printed indexes for print periodicals available in his library.

So that he could compile a WORKING BIBLIOGRAPHY (see 32m), Velez began to read and take notes (32n). The working bibliography that he submitted consisted of twenty-six SOURCES, though he had reviewed and rejected about twelve others (he knew that this represented real progress for him). Velez did not intend to use all twenty-six sources in his paper, but he wanted them available as he wrote his early drafts. Not surprisingly, his instructor urged him to reduce the list once DRAFTING began; otherwise, Velez would risk writing too little about too much. He redoubled his efforts to read even more critically to evaluate his sources (see 5c.3, 5d, and 32l) and weed out material. He got his list down to nineteen sources, took detailed notes on each, and began to group his material into emerging subtopics.

Velez had entire books about biological clocks, so he realized that he would need to narrow the TOPIC (see 32f.2) sufficiently to shape a THESIS STATEMENT (32o). The narrowing process worried him because he had been told in other college courses that his topics for research papers were too broad. He was determined this time to avoid that same problem.

To start drafting his paper, Velez spread his note cards around him for easy reference, but he felt somewhat overwhelmed by the amount of information at hand, and he wrote only a few sentences. To break through, he decided to type a DISCOVERY DRAFT (see 3a) to see what he had absorbed from his reading and notetaking. That very rough draft became his vehicle for many things, including creating an effective thesis statement, inserting source information according to APA documentation style, and checking the logical arrangement of his material.

Revising for Velez started with his thesis statement, a process that helped him further narrow his focus. He started with "Biological clocks are fascinating," which expressed his feelings but said nothing of substance. His next version served him well, as he revised his discovery draft into a true first draft: "Biological clocks, our unconscious timekeepers, affect our lives in many ways, including compatibility in marriage, family life, jet travel, work schedules, illnesses, medical treatments, and the space program." That version proved to Velez that he was covering too much for an 1,800- to 2,000-word research paper, and he wanted to drop some material. He decided first to inform his readers about the phenomenon of biological clocks and then to discuss the effects of those clocks on people's alertness in the morning and later in the day, on travelers on jet airplanes, and on workers' performance. For his final draft, Velez used this more focused thesis statement: "Biological clocks, also known as circadian cycles, are a significant feature of human design that greatly affects people personally and professionally."

Velez used a word processing program that has a template for an APA-style document. Although this provided the overall format, he had to attend very closely to the details of correct PARENTHETICAL REFER-

ENCES (see 36b and 36c) within his paper and a correct References list (see 36f and 36g) at the end. Because he had used MLA DOCUMENTATION STYLE in other courses, he made sure not to confuse the two styles. For example, he saw that APA-style parenthetical citations require a page reference for a quotation but not for a paraphrase or summary (whereas MLA style requires a page reference for all three). For format and style details of the References list at the end of his paper, he found Box 151 in section 36f especially helpful.

As Velez checked the logical arrangement of his material, he realized that because he had dropped some aspects of biological clocks when he finally narrowed his topic sufficiently, he needed a little more depth about the aspects that he was retaining. A few hours at the computer led him to what he needed, including examples about baseball players and emergency room physicians. Velez learned from his research experiences the difference between researching a topic too broadly (and therefore gathering too many sources for the assignment) and researching a few aspects of a topic in depth by focusing on selected sources. His final draft, which appears in 36i.2, draws on sixteen sources, a number that is down considerably from the twenty-six with which he started.

Part of Velez's title page and abstract page are shown here. For guidelines on writing an abstract, see sections 36d and 36h.

36i.2 Analyzing the research paper

In APA style, always position the title-and-page-number line 1/2" from top edge of paper.

Biological Clocks   1

↕ 1/2"
←1"→

In APA style, center the following information in the middle of the page: title, your name, course title and section, the professor's name, and the date; use double-spacing

Biological Clocks:

The Body's Internal Timepieces

Carlos Velez

Introduction to Psychology 115, Section P1

Professor Robert Schmitt

November 15, 2000

APA-style Title Page

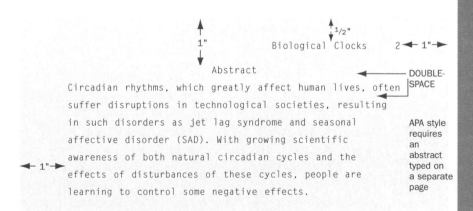

Abstract

Circadian rhythms, which greatly affect human lives, often suffer disruptions in technological societies, resulting in such disorders as jet lag syndrome and seasonal affective disorder (SAD). With growing scientific awareness of both natural circadian cycles and the effects of disturbances of these cycles, people are learning to control some negative effects.

DOUBLE-SPACE

APA style requires an abstract typed on a separate page

APA-style Abstract Page

APA STYLE:
1″ margins;
double-space
throughout

Biological Clocks:

TITLE

The Body's Internal Timepieces

INTRODUCTION:
Gets reader's
attention

Life in modern, technological societies is built around timepieces. People set clocks on radios, microwave ovens, VCRs, and much more. Students respond to bells that start and end the school day in kindergarten through twelfth grades. While carefully managing the minutes and hours each day, individuals are often forced by styles of family and work life to violate another kind of time: their

THESIS
STATEMENT:
Gives
paper's
focus

body's time. Biological clocks, also known as circadian cycles, are a significant feature of human design that greatly affects people personally and professionally.

FIRST HEADING

The Body's Natural Cycles

PARAGRAPH 2:
First body
paragraph
gives
background
information

The term *circadian*, which is Latin for "about a day," describes the rhythms of people's internal biological clocks. Circadian cycles are in tune with external time cycles such as the 24-hour period of the earth's daily rotation as signaled by the rising and setting of the sun. In fact, according to William Schwartz, professor of neurobiology and a researcher in the field of chronobiology

In APA style,
single quotation
marks inside
double
quotation
marks indicate
statement by
Schwartz is in
article by Lewis

(the study of circadian rhythm), "'All such biological clocks are adaptations to life on a rotating world'" (Lewis, 1995, p. 14). Usually, humans set their biological clocks by seeing these cycles of daylight and darkness. Studies conducted in caves or similar environments that allow researchers to control light and darkness have shown that most people not exposed to natural cycles of day and

In APA style,
summary
of two sources
is separated by
semicolon

night create cycles slightly over 24 hours (Czeisler et al., 1999; Recer, 1999). Human perception of the external day-night cycle affects the production and release of a brain hormone, melatonin, which is important in initiating and

In APA style,
no page
numbers for
paraphrases
and summaries

regulating the sleep-wake cycle, as Alfred Lewy and other scientists at the National Institutes of Health in Bethesda, Maryland, have found (Kiester & Thompson, 1997).

→

Biological Clocks   4

Each individual's lifestyle reflects that person's own circadian cycle. Scientists group people as "larks" or "owls" based on whether individuals are more efficient in the morning or at night. The idea behind the labels is that in nature larks wake early, drink dew from plants, and begin their morning song; owls, on the other hand, rest during the day and are active during the evening and night hours (Coren, 1996).

PARAGRAPH 3: Defines larks and owls

Disruptions of Natural Cycles

SECOND HEADING

"Owls," who must stay up late at night, and "larks," who must awaken early in the morning, experience mild versions of "jet lag," the disturbances that time-zone travelers often suffer from. Jet lag, which is characterized by fatigue and irregular sleep patterns, results from disruption of circadian rhythms in most people who fly in jets to different time zones:

PARAGRAPH 4: Applies terms to jet lag

> Jet lag syndrome is the inability of the internal body rhythm to rapidly resynchronize after sudden shifts in the timing. For a variety of reasons, the system attempts to maintain stability and resist temporal change. Consequently, complete adjustment can often be delayed for several days—sometimes for a week—after arrival at one's destination. (Bonner, 1991, p. 72)

In APA style, block-indented paragraph for quotations over 40 words

According to a study conducted by Josephine Arendt and Debra Skene (1997), the degree of jet lag is affected by how many time zones a traveler passes through and how quickly a traveler moves through those multiple time zones. Also, eastbound travelers generally find it harder than westbound travelers to adjust because the circadian clock tends to lag in people.

Proof of this theory can be found in the national pastime, baseball. Three researchers analyzed win-loss records to discover whether jet lag affected baseball

PARAGRAPH 5: Additional specific support for previous paragraph

In APA style, header has shortened title and page number

players' performance (Recht, Lew, & Schwartz, 1995). The study focused on the records of teams in the eastern and western United States over a period of three years. If a visiting team did not have to travel through any time zones, it lost 54% of the time. If the visiting team had traveled from east to west, it lost 56.2% of the time. But if they had traveled from west to east, the visitors lost only 37.1% of the time.

Statistics illustrate example

PARAGRAPH 6: New example describes problem as it affects another group: shift workers

Another group that suffers greatly from biological-clock disruptions consists of people whose livelihoods depend on erratic schedules. This situation affects 20% of U.S. workers whose work schedules differ from the usual morning starting time and afternoon or early evening ending time (Monk, 2000). Sue Binkley (1990) reports that Charles Czeisler, director of the Center for Circadian and Sleep Disorders at Brigham and Women's Hospital in Boston, found that 27% of the U.S. workforce does shift work. Shift work can mean, for example, working from 7:00 a.m. to 3:00 p.m. for six weeks, from 3:00 p.m. to 11:00 p.m. for six weeks, and from 11:00 p.m. to 7 a.m. for six weeks. These erratic schedules may have lasting effects on workers' health. "Shift workers suffer more cardiovascular disease and gastrointestinal disorders than does the general population" (Arendt & Skene, 1997, p. 604). In a 1989 report to the American Association for the Advancement of Science, Czeisler states that "'police officers, [medical] interns, and many others who work nights perform poorly and are involved in more on-the-job accidents than their daytime counterparts'" (Binkley, 1990, p. 26).

Specific details to illustrate example

In APA style, quotations require page number with *p*. (or *pp.* for more than one page)

PARAGRAPH 7: Additional specific support for problems caused by shift work

Other researchers confirm that safety is at risk during late-shift hours. In a study of 28 medical interns observed during late-night shifts over a one-year period, 25% admitted to falling asleep while talking on the phone, and 34% had had at least one accident or near-accident during that period (Weiss, 1989). Investigations into the

Challenger space shuttle explosion and the nuclear-reactor disasters at Three Mile Island and Chernobyl reveal critical errors made by people undergoing the combined stresses of lack of sleep and unusual work schedules (Toufexis, 1989).

Emergency room physicians experience these two stresses all the time. Their professional group, the American College of Emergency Physicians (ACEP), after investigating circadian rhythms and shift work, drafted a formal policy statement, approved by ACEP's board of directors in 1994. The policy calls for "shifts . . . consistent with circadian principles" (Thomas, 1996) to prevent burnout and keep emergency physicians from changing their medical specialty. Also, such a policy would provide the best care for patients.

If jet lag and circadian disruptions caused by shift work are obvious ways to upset a biological clock, a less obvious disruption is increasingly recognized as a medical problem: the disorder known as seasonal affective disorder (SAD). Table 1 lists some of the major symptoms of SAD.

Table 1

Common Symptoms of Seasonal Affective Disorder

Sadness	Later waking
Anxiety	Increased sleep time
Decreased physical activity	Interrupted, unrefreshing sleep
Irritability	Daytime drowsiness
Increased appetite	Decreased sexual drive
Craving for carbohydrates	Menstrual problems
Weight gain	Work problems
Earlier onset of sleep	Interpersonal problems

Note. From *The Clockwork Sparrow* (p. 204), by S. Binkley, 1990, Englewood Cliffs, NJ: Prentice Hall. Copyright 1990 by Prentice Hall.

→

PARAGRAPH 8: One group's response to information on biological clocks

APA style uses ellipsis, without brackets, to indicate words have been omitted within a direct quotation

PARAGRAPH 9: Relates problem to a medical condition

Table title

Table lists items efficiently, making them easy to read

In APA style, note below table provides source

THIRD
HEADING

Ways to Help People Affected by Cycle Disruptions

PARAGRAPH
10: Solutions
to problem
of SAD

SAD appears to be related to the short daylight (photoperiod) of winter in the temperate zones of the northern and southern hemispheres. Michael Terman, a clinical psychologist at Columbia Presbyterian Medical Center's New York State Psychiatric Institute, has studied SAD patients for many years. He has observed their

In APA style,
author's name
and year in
parentheses
when not
included
in text

inability to function at home or at work from fall to spring (Caldwell, 1999). The phenomenon of SAD not only illustrates the important role of circadian rhythms but also dramatically proves that an understanding of circadian principles can help scientists improve the lives of people who experience disruptions of their biological clocks.

Specific
method for
reducing SAD

Binkley (1990) claims that exposure to bright light for periods of up to two hours a day during the short-photoperiod days of winter reduces SAD-related "depression in 87 percent of patients . . . within a few days; relapses followed" (pp. 203-204) when light treatment ended.

PARAGRAPH
11: Applies
solution in
previous
paragraph

Lengthening a person's exposure to bright light can also help combat the effects of jet lag and shift work. Specific suggestions for using light to help reset a jet traveler's biological clock include a walk in natural light, if possible, or in hotel rooms the use of "light boxes that beam a soft white glow onto guests' faces while they work" (Bounds, 2000, p. W16).

PARAGRAPH
12: Specific
system to
reduce time-
shift problems

Establishing work schedules more sensitive to biological clocks can increase a sense of well-being and reduce certain safety hazards. A group of police officers in Philadelphia were studied while on modified shift schedules (Locitzer, 1989; Toufexis, 1989). The officers were changed between day shifts and night shifts less frequently than they had been on former shift schedules. Also, they rotated forward rather than backward in time, and they worked four rather than six consecutive days. The officers reported 40% fewer patrol car accidents and

→

decreased use of drugs or alcohol to get to sleep. Overall,
the police officers preferred the modified shift schedules.
Charles Czeisler, who conducted the study, summarizes the
importance of these results: "'When schedules are
introduced that take into account the properties of the
human circadian system, subjective estimates of work
schedule satisfaction and health improve, personnel
turnover decreases, and work productivity increases'"
(Locitzer, 1989, p. 66).

Conclusion   FOURTH
                                                      HEADING
    Scientists like Charles Czeisler are guiding
individuals about how to live harmoniously with their
biological clocks. The growing awareness of the negative
effects of shift work and travel across time zones has led
to significant advances in reducing problems caused by
disruptions of people's natural cycles. The use of light to
manipulate the body's sense of time has also helped. As
more of us realize how circadian rhythms can affect our
lifestyles, we might learn to control our biological clocks
instead of our biological clocks controlling us.

→

Begin
References
on a new
page

References

Double-space
throughout

Arendt, J. & Skene, D. (1997, December). Efficacy of melatonin
treatment in jet lag, shift work, and blindness. *Journal of
Biological Rhythms, 12,* 604–17. Retrieved October 29, 2000,
from EBSCO database (Health Source Plus).

Binkley, S. (1990). *The clockwork sparrow.* Englewood
Cliffs, NJ: Prentice Hall.

See pages
625–629 for
advice about
formatting an
APA-style
References
list in the
required or
"hanging
indent" style

Bonner, P. (1991, July). Travel rhythms. *Sky Magazine, 72–
73,* 76–77.

Bounds, W. (2000, April 7). A cure for jet lag? *The Wall
Street Journal, Weekend Journal,* pp. W1, W16.

Caldwell, M. (1999, July). Mind over time. *Discover, 20,*
52–59. Retrieved October 15, 2000, from EBSCO database
(Academic Search Elite).

Coren, S. (1996). *Sleep thieves: An eye-opening
exploration into the science and mysteries of sleep.*
New York: Free Press.

Czeisler, C., et al. (1999, June 25). Stability, precision,
and near-24-hour period of the human circadian
pacemaker. *Science,* 2177–2181.

In APA style,
italicize the
volume
number of a
journal or
magazine

Kiester, E., & Thompson, R. (1997, April). 'Traveling
light' has new meaning for jet laggards. *Smithsonian,
28,* 110+. Retrieved October 29, 2000, from EBSCO
database (Academic Search Elite).

Lewis, R. (1995, December 24). Chronobiology researchers
say their field's time has come. *The Scientist, 9,*
p. 14. Retrieved October 20, 2000, from:
http://www.the-scientist.com/yr1995/dec/chrono 951211.html

Locitzer, K. (1989, July–August). Are you out of sync

In APA style,
italicize the
comma
or other
punctuation

with each other? *Psychology Today,* 66.

Monk, T. (2000, April). What can the chronobiologist do to
help the shift worker? *Journal of Biological Rhythms,
15,* 86–94. Retrieved October 17, 2000, from EBSCO
database (Health Source Plus).

→

Biological Clocks   10

Recer, P. (1999, June 25). Study gives a new reason

for insomnia among elderly. *Philadelphia Inquirer*,

n.p. Retrieved October 31, 2000, from SIRS Knowledge

Source database.

Recht, L., Lew, R., & Schwartz, W. (1995, October 19).

Baseball teams beaten by jet lag [Letter]. *Nature*,

377, 583.

Thomas, H. A. (1996). Circadian rhythms and shift work.

ACEP Online. Retrieved October 15, 2000, from:

http://www.acep.org/library/

Toufexis, A. (1989, June 5). The times of your life. *Time*,

66–67.

Weiss, R. (1989, January 21). Safety gets short shrift on

long night shift. *Science News*, 37.

In APA style, online databases and Internet sources must include date you retrieved the source

Source is a letter appearing in publication *Nature*

37 CM, CBE, AND COLUMBIA ONLINE STYLE (COS) DOCUMENTATION

In addition to MLA and APA style, you might need to become familiar with other documentation styles used in the humanities and other disciplines. This chapter outlines three more systems of documentation, including those chosen by the University of Chicago Press (CM) and the Council of Biology Editors (CBE). Additionally, many disciplines are starting to use Columbia Online Style to document electronic sources.

CM-STYLE DOCUMENTATION

The University of Chicago Press endorses two styles of documentation. One is a name-date style similar to the MLA and APA systems of IN-TEXT CITATION; it directs readers to a BIBLIOGRAPHY, the only place where complete information on a source is listed. The other style described in this chapter in Box 152, is a note system often used in English and history as well as in other humanities disciplines.

37a What should I know about CM documentation with bibliographic notes?

The CM (for Chicago Manual) note system gives complete bibliographic information within a footnote or endnote the first time a source is cited. If the source is cited again, the note gives less information. A separate BIBLIOGRAPHY is unnecessary because each first-citation **bibliographic note** contains all the information a reader needs to identify the source. (As *The Chicago Manual of Style* points out, a separate bibliography is a convenience for readers of long works that cite many sources.)

In CM style, the notes are either at the end of a paper (*endnotes*) or at the foot of the page on which a citation falls (*footnotes*).

TEXT

```
Welty also makes this point.³
```

NOTE

```
   3. Eudora Welty, One Writer's Beginnings (Cambridge:
Harvard University Press, 1984), 17.
```

Endnotes may be easier for you to format than footnotes, especially if you are handwriting or typing your paper. Most word processing programs facilitate either system.

 **Guidelines for compiling CM-style   152
bibliographic notes**

■ TITLE

For endnotes, Notes, on a new page numbered sequentially with the rest of the paper, after the last text page of the paper. (Footnotes appear at the bottom of the page where the relevant citation occurs.)

■ CONTENTS AND FORMAT

Include a note every time you use a source. Place endnotes after the text of your paper, on a separate page titled Notes. Center the word *Notes*, neither underlined nor in quotation marks, about an inch from the top of the page, and double-space after it. Single-space the notes themselves. Indent each note's first line three characters (or one tab space in your word processing program), but do not indent the note's subsequent lines.

In the body of your paper, use raised (superscript) arabic numerals for the note numbers. Position note numbers after any punctuation marks except the dash, preferably at the end of a sentence. On the Notes page, make note numbers the same type size as the notes, and position them on, not above, the line, followed by a period. (Not all word processing programs allow you to observe these guidelines. Adapt these guidelines if necessary, using a consistent style throughout your paper.)

■ SPACING AFTER PUNCTUATION

No specific requirements.

■ ARRANGEMENT

Use sequential numerical order throughout the paper. Even if you use footnotes, do not start with 1 on each page.   →

Guidelines for compiling CM-style bibliographic notes *(continued)*   152

- **AUTHORS' NAMES**

  Give the name in standard (first name first) order, with names and initials as given in the original source. Use the word *and* before the last author's name.

- **CAPITALIZATION OF TITLES**

  Capitalize the first word and all major words.

- **SPECIAL TREATMENT OF TITLES**

  The *Chicago Manual* does not replace italics with underlining. In this handbook, however, I recommend that students underline the titles of long works, and use quotation marks around the titles of shorter works.

  Omit *A, An,* and *The* from the titles of newspapers and periodicals. For an unfamiliar newspaper title, list the city (and state, in parentheses, if the city is not well known): Newark (N.J.) Star-Ledger, for example. Note that CM style uses state name abbreviations that are different from the two-letter postal abbreviations (see page 472).

- **PUBLICATION INFORMATION**

  Enclose in parentheses. Use a colon and one space after the city of publication. Give complete publishers' names or abbreviate them according to standard abbreviations in *Books in Print*. Omit *Co., Inc.,* and the like. You can use *Univ.* for *University;* spell out *Press*. Do not abbreviate publication months.

- **PAGE NUMBERS**

  In inclusive page numbers, give the full second number for 2 through 99. For 100 and beyond, give the full second number only if a shortened version is ambiguous: *243–47, 202–6, 300–304.*

  List all discontinuous page numbers; see the model at "First Citation: Book," opposite.

  Use a comma to separate parenthetical publication information from the page numbers that follow it. Use the abbreviations *p.* and *pp.* with page numbers only for material from newspapers or from journals that do not use volume numbers and to avoid ambiguity.

- **CONTENT NOTES**

  Try to avoid using content notes. If you must use them, make footnotes, and use symbols rather than numbers: an asterisk (*) for the first note on a page and a dagger (†) for a second note on that page.

→

**Guidelines for compiling CM-style   152
bibliographic notes** *(continued)*

■ FIRST CITATION: BOOK

Citations for books include the author, title, publication information,
and page numbers when applicable.

> 1. Eudora Welty, <u>One Writer's Beginnings</u> (Cambridge:
> Harvard University Press, 1984), 25-26, 30, 43-51, 208.

■ FIRST CITATION: ARTICLE

Citations for articles include the author, article title, journal title,
volume number, year, and page numbers.

> 35. D. D. Cochran, W. Daniel Hale, and Christine P.
> Hissam, "Personal Space Requirements in Indoor versus
> Outdoor Locations," <u>Journal of Psychology</u> 117 (1984):
> 132-33.

■ SECOND CITATIONS

After giving full bibliographic information in the first note citing a
source, subsequent citations can be brief. In short papers, author
name(s) and a page reference are usually sufficient. If you have
used more than one work by the author(s), give a shortened title
as well.

37b What are CM-style guidelines for specific sources in bibliographic notes?

The directory below corresponds to the sample BIBLIOGRAPHIC NOTE
forms that follow it. Not every possible documentation model is here.
The Chicago Manual of Style, 14th edition, gives note and reference-list
forms for every imaginable source. If you cannot find the information
you need in this section, consult the *Chicago Manual.*

Directory—CM Style

1. Book by One Author—CM
2. Book by Two or Three Authors—CM
3. Book by More Than Three Authors—CM
4. Multiple Citations of a Single Source—CM
5. Book by a Group or Corporate Author—CM
6. Book with No Author Named—CM

1. Book by One Author—CM

1. Eudora Welty, <u>One Writer's Beginnings</u> (Cambridge: Harvard University Press, 1984).

CM style can combine notes with a BIBLIOGRAPHY (31b). Here is the Bibliography (usually an alphabetical list by authors' last names) entry for note 1:

Welty, Eudora. <u>One Writer's Beginnings</u>. Cambridge: Harvard
    University Press, 1984.

The format is the reverse of the bibliographic note, in which first lines indent. Also notice where periods replace commas.

2. Book by Two or Three Authors—CM

2. Lisa Leghorn and Katherine Parker, <u>Woman's Worth</u>
(Boston: Routledge & Kegan Paul, 1981).

3. Alfred H. Kelly, Winfred A. Harbison, and Herman Belz,
<u>The American Constitution: Its Origins and Development</u> (New
York: W. W. Norton, 1983).

If you are using a Bibliography as well as notes, invert only the first name listed.

Kelly, Alfred H., Winfred A. Harbison, and Herman Belz. <u>The</u>
    <u>American Constitution: Its Origins and Development</u>. New
    York: W. W. Norton, 1983.

3. Book by More Than Three Authors—CM

4. Mark H. Moore et al., <u>Dangerous Offenders: The</u>
<u>Elusive Target of Justice</u> (Cambridge: Harvard University
Press, 1984).

Give the name of the author listed first on the title page, and then put either *et al.* or *and others,* using no punctuation after the author's name.

4. Multiple Citations of a Single Source—CM

For subsequent references to a work you have already cited, give the last name of the author, followed by a comma and the page number. Note 5 shows the form for a subsequent reference to the work fully described in note 1.

5. Welty, 25.

If you cite more than one work by the same author, give the title between the name and the page number. If the title is long, you may shorten it.

6. Welty, <u>One Writer's Beginnings</u>, 25.

If you cite two or more authors with the same last name, include first names or initials in each note.

```
7. Eudora Welty, 25.
```

If you cite the same source as the source immediately preceding, you may use *Ibid.*, followed by a comma and the page number, rather than repeating the author's name.

```
8. Ibid., 25.
```

5. Book by a Group or Corporate Author—CM

```
9. Boston Women's Health Collective, Our Bodies,
Ourselves (New York: Simon & Schuster, 1986).

10. American Psychological Association, Publication
Manual of the American Psychological Association, 4th ed.
(Washington, D.C.: American Psychological Association, 1994).
```

If a work issued by an organization has no author listed on the title page, cite the name of the organization as the author of the work. The organization may also be the publisher of the work.

6. Book with No Author Named—CM

```
11. The Chicago Manual of Style, 14th ed. (Chicago:
University of Chicago Press, 1993).
```

Begin the citation with the name of the book.

7. Book with an Author and an Editor—CM

```
12. Emily Brontë, Wuthering Heights, ed. David Daiches
(London: Penguin Books, 1985).
```

In this position, the abbreviation *ed.* stands for "edited by," not "editor." Therefore, *ed.* is correct whether a work has one or more than one editor. (Also see items 10 and 15.)

8. Translation—CM

```
13. Milan Kundera, The Unbearable Lightness of Being,
trans. Michael Henry Heim (New York: HarperPerennial
Library, 1999).
```

The abbreviation *trans.* stands for "translated by," not "translator."

9. Work in Several Volumes or Parts—CM

The two notes numbered 14 show ways to give bibliographic information for a specific place in one volume of a multivolume work. Use whichever you prefer, staying consistent throughout a paper. If you are writing about the volume as a whole (as opposed to citing specific pages), end the note with the publication information.

14. Ernest Jones, The Last Phase, vol. 3 of The Life and Work of Sigmund Freud (New York: Basic Books, 1957), 97.

14. Ernest Jones, The Life and Works of Sigmund Freud, vol. 3, The Last Phase (New York: Basic Books, 1957), 97.

If you are citing an entire work in two or more volumes, use the form shown in note 15.

15. John Herman Randall, Jr., The Career of Philosophy, 2 vols. (New York: Columbia University Press, 1962).

10. One Selection from an Anthology or an Edited Book—CM

16. Ernest Galarza, "The Roots of Migration," in Aztlan: An Anthology of Mexican American Literature, ed. Luis Valdez and Stan Steiner (New York: Alfred A. Knopf, 1972), 127-32.

Give page numbers for the cited selection.

11. Two Selections from an Anthology or an Edited Book—CM

If you cite selections from an anthology or edited book, give complete bibliographical information in each citation.

12. Signed Article in a Reference Book—CM

17. John C. Burnbam, "Freud, Sigmund," in The Encyclopedia of Psychiatry, Psychology, and Psychoanalysis, ed. Benjamin B. Wolman (New York: Henry Holt and Company, 1996), 220.

13. Unsigned Article in a Reference Book—CM

18. Encyclopaedia Britannica, 15th ed., s.v. "Ireland."

The abbreviation *s.v.* stands for *sub verbo*, meaning "under the word." Capitalize the heading of the entry only if it is a proper noun. Omit publication information except for the edition number.

14. Edition—CM

19. Anthony F. Janson, History of Art, 5th ed. (New York: Harry N. Abrams, 1997).

Here the abbreviation *ed.* stands for "edition," not "edited by" (see item 7). Give the copyright date for the edition you are citing.

15. Anthology or Edited Book—CM

20. Luis Valdez and Stan Steiner, eds., Aztlan: An Anthology of Mexican American Literature (New York: Alfred A. Knopf, 1972).

16. Introduction, Preface, Foreword, or Afterword—CM

```
21. Elizabeth Fox-Genovese, foreword to Southern Mothers,
by Nagueyalti Warren and Sally Wolff, eds. (Baton Rouge:
Louisiana State University Press, 1999).
```

If the author of the book is different from the author of the cited part, give the name of the book's author after the title of the book.

17. Unpublished Dissertation or Essay—CM

```
22. Shirley Burry Geissinger, "Openness versus Secrecy in
Adoptive Parenthood" (Ph.D. diss., University of North
Carolina at Greensboro, 1984), 45-56.
```

List the author's name first, then the title in quotation marks (not underlined), a descriptive label (such as *Ph.D. diss.* or *master's thesis*), the degree-granting institution, the date, and finally the page numbers you are citing.

```
23. Kimberli M. Stafford, "Trapped in Death and
Enchantment: The Liminal Space of Women in Three Classical
Ballets" (paper presented at the annual meeting of the
American Comparative Literature Association Graduate Student
Conference, Riverside, Calif., April 1993).
```

To cite a paper read at a meeting, give the name of the meeting in parentheses, along with the location and the date.

18. Reprint of an Older Book—CM

```
24. Zora Neale Hurston, Their Eyes Were Watching God
(1937; reprint, Urbana: University of Illinois Press, 1978).
```

Republishing information is located on the copyright page. List the original date of publication first, followed by the publication information for the reprint.

19. Book in a Series—CM

```
25. Dorothy J. Goldman, Women Writers and World War I,
Literature and Society Series (New York: Macmillan
Publishing Company, 1995).
```

If the series numbers its volumes and the volume number is not part of the title, you would include the volume number after the series title. Separate the volume number from the series title with a comma.

20. Book with a Title Within a Title—CM

```
26. Aljean Harmetz, The Making of "The Wizard of Oz" (New
York: Hyperion, 1998).
```

If the name of a work that is usually underlined appears in a title, add quotation marks around it. If the name of a work that is usually in quotation marks appears in a title, keep it in quotation marks and underline it.

21. Government Publication—CM

27. House, <u>Coastal Heritage Trail Route in New Jersey</u>, 106th Cong., 1st sess., 1999, H. Rept. 16.

If a government department, bureau, agency, or committee produces a document, cite that group as the author. In a bibliography, the author is often identified as *U.S. Congress*, followed by either "House" or "Senate" and the committee or subcommittee, if any, before the title of the document.

22. Published Proceedings of a Conference—CM

28. Arnold Eskin, "Some Properties of the System Controlling the Circadian Activity Rhythm of Sparrows," in <u>Biochronometry</u>, ed. Michael Menaker (Washington, D.C.: National Academy of Sciences, 1971), 55-80.

Treat published conference proceedings as you would a chapter in a book.

23. Article from a Daily Newspaper—CM

29. Edward Wyatt, "A High School Without a Home," <u>New York Times</u>, 3 December 1999, sec. B, p. 1.

If a large paper prints more than one edition a day, identify the specific edition (such as *Southeastern edition* or *final edition*); make this the last information in the entry, preceded by a comma. For a paper that specifies sections, use *sec.* before the page number. If a paper gives column numbers, use *col.* after the page number. Separate all items with commas.

24. Editorial, Letter to the Editor, or Review—CM

30. "Mr. Gorbachev's Role," editorial, <u>New York Times</u>, 10 November 1999, sec. A, p. 22.

31. Cheryl Wolfe, letter, <u>Newsweek</u>, 22 November 1999, 22.

32. Joan Didion, "The Day Was Hot and Still . . . ," review of <u>Dutch: A Memoir of Ronald Reagan</u>, by Edmund Morris, <u>New York Review of Books</u>, 4 November 1999, 4-6.

Before page numbers, use a comma for popular magazines and a colon for journals.

25. Unsigned Article from a Daily Newspaper—CM

33. "Female Cadets Gaining Sway at the Coast Guard," New York Times, 15 November 1999, sec. B, p. 6.

26. Article from a Weekly or Biweekly Magazine or Newspaper—CM

34. Karl Taro Greenfield, "Giving Away the E-Store," Time, 22 November 1999, 58-60.

For general-readership weekly or biweekly magazines or newspapers, give the day-date, month, and year of publication. Separate page numbers from the year with a comma.

27. Article from a Monthly or Bimonthly Periodical—CM

35. John Tyler Bonner, "The Evolution of Evolution," Natural History, April 1999, 20-21.

For general-readership monthly or bimonthly magazines, give the month and year of publication. Separate page numbers from the year with a comma.

28. Unsigned Article from a Weekly or Monthly Periodical—CM

36. "A Salute to Everyday Heroes," Time, 10 July 1989, 46-51, 54-56, 58-60, 63-64, 66.

If the article is printed on discontinuous pages, give all pages in the note.

29. Article from a Collection of Reprinted Articles—CM

37. Phillip C. Curver, "Lighting in the 21st Century," Energy, Social Issues Resources Series, vol. 4 (Boca Raton, Fla.: Social Issues Resources, 1990).

Cite only the publication actually consulted, not the original source. If you use a bibliography, cite in it both the reprinted publication you consulted and the publication where the article first appeared.

30. Article in a Journal with Continuous Pagination—CM

38. Phyllis Tyson, "The Psychology of Women," Journal of the American Psychoanalytic Association 46 (1997): 361-64.

31. Article in a Journal That Pages Each Issue Separately—CM

39. Thomas F. Hogarty, "Gasoline: Still Powering Cars in 2050?" The Futurist 33, no. 3 (1999): 51-55.

The issue number of a journal is required only if each issue of the journal starts with page 1. In this example, the volume number is 33 and the issue number, abbreviated as no., is 3.

32. Personal Interview—CM

40. Randi Friedman, interview by author, Ames, Iowa, 30 June 1992.

For an unpublished interview, give the name of the interviewee and the interviewer, the location of the interview, and the date of the interview.

33. Published and Unpublished Letters—CM

41. George Sand to her mother, 31 May 1831, Letters Home: Celebrated Authors Write to Their Mothers, ed. Reid Sherline (New York: Timkin Publishers, 1993), 17-20.

42. Theodore Brown, letter to author, 7 December 1999.

For an unpublished letter, give the name of the author, the name of the recipient, and the date the letter was written.

34. Film, Videotape, or DVD—CM

43. Marc Norman and Tom Stoppard, Shakespeare in Love (New York: Miramax Films/Universal Pictures, 1999), videocassette.

44. Robert Riskin, It Happened One Night (Hollywood: Columbia Pictures, 1999), videocassette.

45. Robert Riskin, It Happened One Night (Hollywood: Columbia Pictures, 1934), filmstrip.

In note 43, the first information is the authors of the screenplay. If the point of the note was about the director or producers, then the title would be in the first position and the abbreviations *dir.* and/or *prod.* ("directed by," "produced by") would follow the comma after the title along with the relevant names.

35. Recording—CM

46. Bedrich Smetana, My Country, Czech Philharmonic, Karel Anserl, Vanguard SV-9/10.

Bedrich Smetana is the composer and Karel Anserl is the conductor.

47. Bruce Springsteen, "Local Hero," on Lucky Town, Columbia CK 53001.

36. Computer Software—CM

48. Microsoft Word Ver. 8.0, Microsoft, Seattle, Wash.

Place the version or release number, abbreviated *Ver.* or *Rel.*, directly after the name of the software. Then, list the company that owns the rights to the software, followed by that company's location.

37. ERIC Information Service—CM

49. Hunter M. Breland, Assessing Writing Skills (New York: College Entrance Examination Board, 1987), ERIC, ED 286920.

ERIC stands for Educational Resources Information Center.

38. Electronic Documents—CM

The Chicago Manual of Style (14th edition, 1993) describes electronic sources as an "exceedingly complex, fluid, and rapidly expanding field of source material" (634). The *Chicago Manual* shows samples of acceptable documentation of electronic sources. Note 50, below, shows CM style for documenting a newsgroup posting. CM style for electronic sources is based on the International Standards Organization (ISO) documentation system. If you are using CM style and do not find enough information in this book to help you document your electronic sources, consult the ISO guidelines at <www.nlc-bnc.ca/iso/tc46sc9>.

50. Dan S. Wallach, "FAQ: Typing Injuries (2/5): General Info.," in typing-injury-faq/general.z [electronic bulletin board], 1993- [cited 14 November 1993]; available from mail-server@rtfm.mit.edu; INTERNET.

39. Secondary Source—CM

51. Mary Wollstonecraft, A Vindication of the Rights of Woman (1792), 90, quoted in Caroline Shrodes, Harry Finestone, and Michael Shugrue, The Conscious Reader, 4th ed. (New York: Macmillan Publishing Company, 1988), 282.

When you quote one person's words, having found them in another person's work, give information as fully as you can about both sources. Note 51 shows the form you use when the point of your citation is Mary Wollstonecraft's words. If your point is what Shrodes, Finestone, and Shugrue have to say about Wollstonecraft's words, handle the information as in note 52.

52. Caroline Shrodes, Harry Finestone, and Michael Shugrue, The Conscious Reader, 4th ed. (New York: Macmillan Publishing Company, 1988), 282, quoting Mary Wollstonecraft, A Vindication of the Rights of Woman (1792), 90.

USING AND CITING GRAPHICS—CM

Place the credit line for a table or illustration from another source next to the reproduced material. (If you intend to publish your paper, you must receive permission to reprint copyrighted material from a source.) Spell out the terms *map, plate,* and *table,* but abbreviate *figure* as *fig.*

Reprinted, by permission, from Dennis Remington, A. Garth Fisher, and Edward Parent, <u>How to Lower Your Fat Thermostat: The No-Diet Reprogramming Plan for Lifelong Weight Control</u> (Provo, Utah: Vitality House International, 1983), 74, fig. A2-1.

CBE-STYLE DOCUMENTATION

In its 1994 style manual, *Scientific Style and Format,* the Council of Biology Editors (CBE) endorses two documentation systems widely used in mathematics and the physical and life sciences.

37c What should I know about CBE documentation?

The first system endorsed by CBE uses name-year PARENTHETICAL REFERENCES in the text of a paper, together with an alphabetically arranged Cited References (or References) list that gives full bibliographic information for each source. (This kind of IN-TEXT CITATION system is tied to a required BIBLIOGRAPHY you have already seen in both MLA and APA styles.) The second system uses numbers to mark citations in the text of a paper that correlate with a numerically arranged Cited References list. This chapter focuses on this numbered reference system, sometimes referred to as a *citation-sequence system.* Here is the way it works:

1. The first time you cite each source in your paper, assign it a number in sequence, starting with 1.
2. Mark each subsequent reference to that source with the assigned number.
3. For your Cited References list, number each entry in the order of its appearance in your paper, starting with 1. Do not list sources alphabetically.

CBE recommends using superscript numbers for source citations in your paper, although numbers in parentheses are also acceptable.

IN-TEXT CITATIONS

Sybesma[1] insists that this behavior occurs periodically, but Crowder[2] claims never to have observed it.

CITED REFERENCES LIST

1. Sybesma C. An introduction to biophysics. New York: Academic Press; 1977. 648 p.
2. Crowder W. Seashore life between the tides. New York: Dodd, Mead; 1931. New York: Dover Reprint; 1975. 372 p.

Thereafter, each citation of Sybesma's *Introduction to Biophysics* would be followed by a superscript 1, each citation of Crowder's *Seashore Life* by a superscript 2.

When you are citing more than one reference—for example, a new source and the previous three sources as well as a source from your first page—list each source number, followed by a comma but no space: `2,5-7,8`. Use a hyphen to show the range of numbers in a continuous sequence. All the numbers are raised above the line of type.

⊙ Guidelines for compiling a CBE-style Cited References list   153

■ **TITLE**

  `Cited References` or `References`

■ **PLACEMENT OF LIST**

  Start a new page numbered sequentially with the rest of the paper.

■ **CONTENT AND FORMAT**

  Include all sources quoted from, paraphrased, or summarized in your paper. Center the title about one inch from the top of the page. Start each entry on a new line. Put the number followed by a space at the regular left margin. If an entry takes more than one line, you can use a "hanging indent" for the second and all other lines, as in the models at the end of this box. The CBE does not specify an indent; unless your instructor specifies an indent, you can use five characters (typewritten papers) or about one-half inch (papers prepared on a computer). Double-space each entry and between entries.

■ **SPACING AFTER PUNCTUATION**

  Follow the spacing shown in the models in section 37d.

■ **ARRANGEMENT OF ENTRIES**

  Sequence the entries in the order that you cite the sources in your paper.

■ **AUTHORS' NAMES**

  Invert all author names, giving the last name first. You can give first names or use only initials of first and middle names. If you use initials, do not use a period or a space between first and middle initials. Use a comma to separate the names of multiple authors identified by initials; if you use full first names, use a semicolon. Do not use *and* or *&*. Place a period after the last author's name.

→

CBE CBE CBE CBE CBE CBE CBE CBE CBE CBE CBE CBE CBE CBE CBE

Guidelines for compiling a CBE-style   153
Cited References list *(continued)*

■ CAPITALIZATION OF TITLES

Capitalize a title's first word and any proper nouns. Do not capital-ize the first word of a subtitle, unless it is a proper noun.

Capitalize the titles of academic journals. If the title of a periodical is one word, give it in full; otherwise, abbreviate the title according to recommendations established by the *American National Standard for Abbreviations of Titles of Periodicals.* (An online version of this work is available at <http://www.for.gov.bc.ca/hfd/pubs/docs/mr/mr041/SG-f0045.htm>.)

Capitalize a newspaper title's major words, giving the full title, including a beginning *A, An,* or *The.*

■ SPECIAL TREATMENT OF TITLES

Do not underline titles or enclose them in quotation marks.

■ PLACE OF PUBLICATION

Use a colon after the city of publication. Add a state postal abbreviation (see Box 123 in section 30l, pages 472–473) or a country name to a city that might be ambiguous—for example, Springfield (VA) or Nijmegen (Netherlands).

■ PUBLISHER

Give the full name of the publisher, including *Co., Inc., Press, Ltd.,* and so on. Use a semicolon after the publisher's name.

■ PUBLICATION MONTH ABBREVIATIONS

Abbreviate all month names longer than three letters to their first three letters, but omit the period.

■ INCLUSIVE PAGE NUMBERS

Shorten the second number as much as possible, but do not make the number ambiguous. For example, use 233–4 for 233 to 234; 233–44 for 233 to 244; but 233–304, not 233–04. Use the abbreviation *p* without a period or underlining for "page" or "pages." Follow the guidelines in the models.

■ DISCONTINUOUS PAGE NUMBERS

Give the full numbers of all discontinuous pages, preceding the first number with the *p* abbreviation and separating successive numbers or ranges with a comma.

→

> **Guidelines for compiling a CBE-style**   **153**
> **Cited References list** *(continued)*
>
> ■ TOTAL PAGE NUMBERS
> When citing an entire book, give as the last information unit the
> total number of pages, followed by the abbreviation *p* and a period.
>
> ■ CITED REFERENCES ENTRIES: BOOKS
> Citations for books usually list author(s), title, publication informa-
> tion, and pages (either total pages when citing an entire work or
> inclusive pages when citing part of a book). Each unit of informa-
> tion ends with a period.
>
> ```
> 1. Stacy RW, Williams DT, Worden RE, McMorris RO.
>    Essentials of biological and medical sciences. New
>    York: McGraw-Hill Book Company, Inc.; 1955. 727 p.
> ```
>
> ■ CITED REFERENCES ENTRIES: ARTICLES
> Citations for articles usually list author(s), article title, and journal
> name and publication information, each section followed by a
> period. *Sci Am* is the abbreviated form of *Scientific American*. The
> volume number is 269, and the issue number, in parentheses, is 3.
>
> ```
> 1. Weissman IL, Cooper MD. How the immune system
>    develops. Sci Am 1993;269(3):65-71.
> ```

37d What are CBE guidelines for specific sources in a list of references?

The directory below corresponds to the sample references that follow it. Not every possible documentation model is here. For guidance in
citing other sources, consult CBE's *Scientific Style and Format* (6th edition, 1994) or a journal in the discipline in which you are writing.

Directory—CBE Style

7. Reprint of an Older Book—CBE
8. All Volumes of a Multivolume Work—CBE
9. Unpublished Dissertation or Thesis—CBE
10. Published Article from Conference Proceedings—CBE
11. Signed Newspaper Article—CBE
12. Unsigned Newspaper Article—CBE
13. Article in a Journal with Continuous Pagination—CBE
14. Article in a Journal That Pages Each Issue Separately—CBE
15. Journal Article on Discontinuous Pages—CBE
16. Article with Author Affiliation—CBE
17. Entire Issue of a Journal—CBE
18. Article with No Identifiable Author—CBE
19. Map—CBE
20. Unpublished Letter—CBE
21. Filmstrip—CBE
22. Videorecording—CBE
23. Slide Set—CBE
24. Electronic Sources—CBE

1. Book by One Author—CBE

1. Hawking SW. Black holes and baby universes and other essays. New York: Bantam Books; 1993. 320 p.

Use one space but no punctuation between an author's last name and the initial of the first name. Do not put punctuation or a space between first and middle initials. Do, however, keep the hyphen in a hyphenated first and middle name. See model 2, in which *Gille J-C* represents Jean-Claude Gille.

2. Book by More Than One Author—CBE

1. Wegzyn S, Gille J-C, Vidal P. Developmental systems: at the crossroads of system theory, computer science, and genetic engineering. New York: Springer-Verlag; 1990. 595 p.

3. Book by Group or Corporate Author—CBE

1. Chemical Rubber Company. Handbook of laboratory safety. 3rd ed. Boca Raton (FL): CRC; 1990. 1352 p.

4. Anthology or Edited Book—CBE

1. Heerman B, Hummel S, editors. Ancient DNA: recovery
   and analysis of genetic material from paleontological,
   archeological, museum, medical, and forensic specimens.
   New York: Springer-Verlag; 1994. 1020 p.

5. One Selection or Chapter from an Anthology or Edited Book—CBE

1. Basov NG, Feoktistov LP, Senatsky YV. Laser driver for
   inertial confinement fusion. In: Bureckner KA, editor.
   Research trends in physics: inertial confinement fusion.
   New York: American Institute of Physics; 1992. p 24-37.

6. Translation—CBE

1. Magris C. A different sea. Spurr MS, translator.
   London: Harvill; 1993. 194 p. Translation of: Un mare
   differente.

7. Reprint of an Older Book—CBE

1. Carson R. The sea around us. New York: Oxford
   University; 1951. New York: Limited Editions Club
   Reprint; 1980. 220 p.

8. All Volumes of a Multivolume Work—CBE

1. Crane FL, Moore DJ, Low HE, editors. Oxidoreduction at
   the plasma membrane: relation to growth and transport.
   Boca Raton (FL): Chemical Rubber Company; 1991. 2 vol.

9. Unpublished Dissertation or Thesis—CBE

1. Baykul MC. Using ballistic electron emission microscopy
   to investigate the metal-vacuum interface [dissertation].
   Orem (UT): Polytechnic University; 1993. 111 p.

10. Published Article from Conference Proceedings—CBE

1. Tsang CP, Bellgard MI. Sequence generation using a
   network of Boltzmann machines. In: Tsang CP, editor.
   Proceedings of the 4th Australian Joint Conference on
   Artificial Intelligence; 1990 Nov 8-11; Perth, Australia.
   Singapore: World Scientific; 1990. p 224-33.

11. Signed Newspaper Article—CBE

1. Hoke F. Gene therapy: clinical gains yield a wealth of research opportunities. The Scientist 1993 Oct 4;Sect A:1, 5, 7.

Sect stands for Section.

12. Unsigned Newspaper Article—CBE

1. [Anonymous]. Irish urge postgame caution. USA Today 1993 Nov 12;Sect C:2.

13. Article in a Journal with Continuous Pagination—CBE

1. Scott ML, Fredrickson RJ, Moorhead BB. Characteristics of old-growth forests associated with northern spotted owls in Olympic National Park. J Wildlf Mgt 1993;57:315-21.

Give only the volume number, not an issue number, before the page numbers.

14. Article in a Journal That Pages Each Issue Separately—CBE

1. Weissman IL, Cooper MD. How the immune system develops. Sci Am 1993;269(3):65-71.

Give both the volume number and the issue number (here, 269 is the volume number and 3 is the issue number).

15. Journal Article on Discontinuous Pages—CBE

1. Richards FM. The protein folding problem. Sci Am 1991;246(1):54-7, 60-6.

16. Article with Author Affiliation—CBE

1. DeMoll E, Auffenberg T (Dept. of Microbiology, Univ. of Kentucky). Purine metabolism in Methanococcus vannielii. J Bacteriol 1993;175:5754-61.

17. Entire Issue of a Journal—CBE

1. Whales in a modern world: a symposium held in London, November 1988. Mamm Rev 1990 Jan;20(9).

November 1988, the date of the symposium, is part of the title of this issue.

18. Article with No Identifiable Author—CBE

1. [Anonymous]. Cruelty to animals linked to murders of
   humans. AWI Q 1993 Aug;42(3):16.

19. Map—CBE

1. Russia and Post-Soviet Republics [political map]. Moscow:
   Mapping Production Association; 1992. Conical equidistant
   projection; 40 × 48 in.; color, scale 1:8,000,000.

20. Unpublished Letter—CBE

1. Darwin C. [Letter to Mr. Clerke, 1861]. Located at:
   University of Iowa Library, Iowa City, IA.

21. Filmstrip—CBE

1. Volcano: the eruption and healing of Mount St. Helens
   [filmstrip]. Westminster (MD): Random House; 1988.
   114 frames: color; 35 mm. Accompanied by: cassette tape;
   22 min.

After the title and description of the filmstrip, give the author, producer, and year; then give other descriptive information.

22. Videorecording—CBE

1. The discovery of the pulsar: the ultimate ignorance
   [videocassette]. London: BBC; 1983. 1 cassette: 48 min,
   sound, color.

23. Slide Set—CBE

1. Human parasitology [slides]. Chicago (IL): American
   Society of Clinical Pathologists; 1990. Color.
   Accompanied by: 1 guide.

24. Electronic Sources—CBE

In general, the CBE style book advises that you cite electronic sources by starting with a statement of the type of document, and following this, provide the information you would give for a print version. Next, supply specific information that would help a reader to locate the electronic source. End with a date: your access date for online sources or the date of the update you used for CD-ROM databases that are updated periodically.

COS DOCUMENTATION

For electronic publications, *The Columbia Guide to Online Style* (COS or CO style) by Janice R. Walker and Todd Taylor (Columbia UP, 1998) provides an alternative to other documentation styles.

37e What should I know about COS documentation?

COS uses many of the same citation elements that are present in predominantly print documentation styles such as MLA and APA. However, COS includes new format elements unique to electronic publications. COS for the humanities is similar to MLA style, while COS for the sciences shares elements of APA style. Be sure to find out from your instructor which style to use.

37e.1 Citing sources in the body of a paper in COS

In print publications, in-text or PARENTHETICAL REFERENCES include elements such as the author's last name and the page number of the reference. Many electronic sources lack such elements, and COS allows for these differences. If an author name is unknown, refer to the material by its title. Since most electronic sources are not numbered, page references may be irrelevant. Commonly, COS parenthetical citations use only the author's name for humanities style and the author's name and date of publication for scientific style.

👁 **COS CITATION ALERT:** If page numbers, sections, or other navigational aids are available, separate them with a comma and include them in the parenthetical citation as well. ●

HUMANITIES STYLE

According to the survey, over 80% of the students waited until the night before an exam to begin studying (Jani).

👁 **COS CITATION ALERT:** When the author's name is included in the sentence, the IN-TEXT CITATION is unnecessary. If there is more than one work by the author, use the work's title. ●

SCIENTIFIC STYLE

The research proved conclusively that individuals deprived of sleep were as dangerous as those driving under the influence of drugs or alcohol (Rezik, 2000).

👁 **COS CITATION ALERT:** If the publication date is unavailable, use the date of access (in day-month-year format). ●

37e.2 Creating COS bibliographic citations

Box 154 gives guidelines for a COS Works Cited list. The labeled screen below identifies elements mentioned in Chart 154.

URL   Source title   Publication date

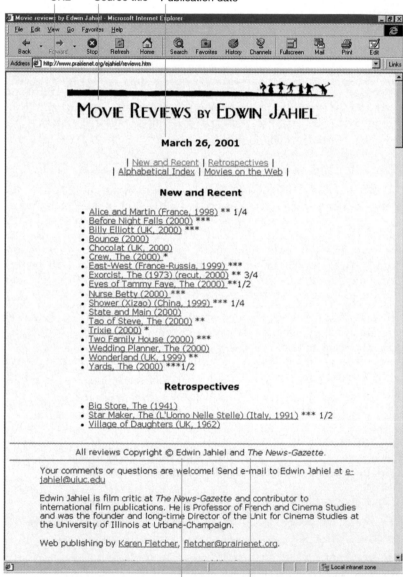

Author name   Title of print source

Web page with links to author's movie reviews

Guidelines for a COS Works Cited list 154

- **TITLE**

  Works Cited should be centered, 1 inch below the top of your bibliography page, in upper- and lowercase letters. The title should not be enclosed in quotation marks or be boldfaced, italicized, or underlined.

- **PLACEMENT OF LIST**

  If you are producing a print document, begin the Works Cited on a new page, numbered sequentially with the rest of the paper. If your document is a HYPERTEXT publication, you may use a separate file and a link to this page in the table of contents.

- **CONTENT AND FORMAT**

  See MLA guidelines in Box 150, pages 569–574.

- **ARRANGEMENT OF ENTRIES**

  See MLA guidelines in Box 150.

- **AUTHORS' NAMES**

  Finding the author of a source may not be simple. Often, online writers use an alias. List your source by these alternate names when they are the only ones you find. If an author name cannot be identified, cite the source by its title.

  In humanities style, give the author's full last name and first and middle names (if available); in scientific style, give the author's full last name and first and middle initials (if applicable). List any additional authors by first name (humanities) or first initial (scientific), followed by the full last name.

- **CAPITALIZATION AND SPECIAL TREATMENT OF TITLES**

  Use italics rather than underlining for the titles of complete works. Since hypertext links are underlined online, an underlined title may confuse your readers.

  In humanities style, enclose titles of articles and excerpts from longer works in quotation marks, and capitalize all major words. In scientific style, do not distinguish titles of articles and excerpts of longer works in any way, and capitalize only the first word of the title and proper nouns. (If a title is unavailable, use the file name.)

- **PLACE OF PUBLICATION, PUBLISHER, AND ELECTRONIC ADDRESS**

  When citing electronic sources available in fixed formats, such as software and certain electronic publications, a publisher and city are usually listed and should be cited.

  →

Guidelines for a COS Works Cited list *(continued)* 154

In online publishing, the city of publication and publisher often are not relevant to Web sites and other open-format electronic sources. In those cases, provide the URL (uniform resource locator), which is a source's entire electronic address. For long addresses that exceed a line, follow MLA style: Break only after slashes and do not hyphenate.

■ VERSION OR FILE NUMBER

When applicable, provide the specific file number or version of a program for your reference.

■ DOCUMENT PUBLICATION OR LAST REVISION DATE

Include a page's publication date or the date of its last revision, unless it is identical to the access date. For humanities style, abbreviate all month names longer than three letters to their first three letters, followed by a period. For scientific style, do not abbreviate names of months.

■ DATE OF ACCESS

With the constant updates of online material, readers may have a difficult time finding the same content in a source you cite. Always provide the date of access for an online source because it specifies the version of the page you have cited. For humanities and scientific styles, abbreviate month names to three letters, followed by a period.

■ NAVIGATION POINTS

On the World Wide Web, a given site usually occupies one page, regardless of its length. When available, list any helpful navigational aids, such as page references, paragraph numbers, or sections or parts, in your citation. Keep in mind that often these aids are not available.

■ BIBLIOGRAPHIC CITATION: HUMANITIES

Follow this form as closely as possible in your citations:

```
Author's Last Name, First Name. "Title of Document."
    Title of Complete Work [if applicable]. Version
    or File Number [if applicable]. Document date or
    date of last revision [if known and if different
    from access date]. Protocol and address, access
    path or directories (date of access).
```

→

> ## Guidelines for a COS Works Cited list *(continued)*   154
>
> ■ BIBLIOGRAPHIC CITATION: SCIENCES
> Follow this form as closely as possible in your citations:
>
> ```
> Author's Last Name, Initial(s). (Date of document
>     [if known and if different from date accessed]).
>     Title of document. Title of complete work
>     [if applicable]. Version or File number [if
>     applicable]. (Edition or revision [if
>     applicable]). Protocol and address, access
>     path or directories (date of access or visit;
>     or date of message).
> ```

37f What are COS guidelines for specific sources in a Works Cited list?

The directory below corresponds to the sample bibliographic forms that follow. COS distinguishes between humanities style and scientific style in creating a bibliography, so you will find all the models given twice, once in each style, to help you be consistent and correct when formatting your references.

Directory—COS Guidelines

1. Site on the World Wide Web—COS (see p. 676 for a labeled Web site)
2. Modified or Revised Site—COS
3. Maintained or Compiled Site—COS
4. Article from a Periodical—COS
5. Article in an Online Journal—COS
6. Work by a Group or Organization—COS
7. Corporate Home Pages and Information—COS
8. Government Information and Sites—COS
9. Book Accessed Online—COS
10. Graphic, Video, or Audio File on the Page—COS
11. Personal Electronic Mail (E-Mail)—COS
12. Posting to a Discussion List—COS

Humanities style

1. Site on the World Wide Web—COS

Blackmon, Samantha. *Cows in the Classroom?: MOOs and MUDs and MUSHes . . . Oh My!!!* 24 Aug. 2000. http://www.sla.purdue.edu/people/engl/blackmon/moo/index.html (11 Mar. 2001).

2. Modified or Revised Site—COS

Grant, William E., and Ken Dvorak. *The American 1890s: A Chronology.* Mod. Spring 2000. http://www.bgsu.edu/departments/acs/1890s/america.html (22 Nov. 2000).

If the site is revised, use the abbreviation *Rev.* in place of *Mod.*

3. Maintained or Compiled Site—COS

E-Zine-List. Maint. John Labovitz. 8 Mar. 2000. http://www.meer.net/~johnl/e-zine-list (15 Sep. 2000).

If the site is compiled, use the abbreviation *Comp.* in place of *Maint.*

4. Article from a Periodical—COS

Kaplan, Carl S. "Suit Considers Computer Files." *The New York Times* (28 Sep. 2000). http://www.nytimes.com/2000/09/28/technology/29CYBERLAW.html (13 Oct. 2000).

5. Article in an Online Journal—COS

Winickoff, Jonathan P., et al. "Verve and Jolt: Deadly New Internet Drugs." *Pediatrics* 106.4 (Oct. 2000). http://www.pediatrics.org/cgi/content/abstract/106/4/829 (10 May 2000).

6. Work by a Group or Organization—COS

GROUP

Environmental Protection Agency. "Browner Lauds Hill Action to Protect Everglades, Beaches. Urges House of Representatives to Finalize Everglades Plan." 28 Sep. 2000. http://www.epa.gov/epahome/headline_0928.htm (29 Nov. 2000).

ORGANIZATION

SIL International. "Ethnomusicology: 'Studying Music from the Outside In and from the Inside Out.'" 7 May 1999. http://www.sil.org/anthro/ethnomusicology.htm (20 Feb. 2000).

7. Corporate Home Pages and Information—COS

Pearson PLC. "Pearson Home Page." 1999. http://www.pearson.com (12 Apr. 2001).

8. Government Information and Sites—COS

Central Intelligence Agency. "Speeches and Testimony." 6 Oct. 2000. http://www.cia.gov/cia/public_affairs/speeches/speeches.html (18 Dec. 2000).

9. Book Accessed Online—COS

BOOK PUBLISHED FIRST IN PRINT VERSION

Brontë, Charlotte. *Jane Eyre*. London: Service & Paton, 1887. 1999. *University of Maryland Reading Room*. http://www.inform.umd.edu/EdRes/Reading Room/Fiction/Cbronte/JaneEyre/ (15 Sep. 2000).

BOOK PUBLISHED ONLINE

Shires, Bob. *CPR (Cardiopulmonary Resuscitation) Guide*. 17 Jan. 2000. http://www.memoware.com/Category=Medicine_ ResultSet=1.htm (17 Apr. 2000).

10. Graphic, Video, or Audio File on the Page—COS

owl.gif. 2000. "Original free clipart." *Clipart.com*. http://www.free-clip-art.net/index4.shtml (27 Oct. 2000).

11. Personal Electronic Mail (E-Mail)—COS

Torres, Elizabeth. "Re: Puerto Rican Baseball History."
    Personal e-mail (11 Sep. 2000).

12. Posting to a Discussion List—COS

Sheldon, Amy. "Re: Request for Help on Sexism Inscription."
    2 Jan. 2000. *FLING List for Feminists in Linguistics*.
    http://listserv.linguistlist.org (14 Nov. 2000).

13. Posting to a Newsgroup or Forum—COS

Markowitz, Al. "The Changing Face of Work: A Look at the
    Way We Work." 28 Sep. 2000. http://yourturn.npr.org/
    cgi-bin/WebX?50@121.HjNGardZdaj^0@.ee7a9aa
    (8 Jan. 2001).

14. Archived Posting—COS

Radev, Dragomir R. "Natural Language Processing FAQ."
    16 Sep. 1999. *Institute of Information and Computing
    Sciences*. http://www.cs.ruu.nl/wais/html/na-dir/
    natural-lang-processing-faq.html (27 Jan. 1999).

15. Online Reference Sources—COS

Reference sources such as online encyclopedias, dictionaries, thesauruses, style manuals, bibliographies, or other forms of factual material can be cited using this model.

Nordenberg, Tamar. 2000. "Make No Mistake! Medical Errors
    Can Be Deadly Serious." *Britannica.com*. Ebsco
    Publishing. http://britannica.com/bcom/original/article/
    0,5744,12430,00.html (12 Dec. 2000).

16. Computer Information Services and Online Databases—COS

Raintree Nutrition, Inc. "Pata de Vaca." Jun. 2000. *Raintree
    Tropical Plant Database*. http://www.rain-tree.com/
    patadevaca.htm (9 Sep. 2000).

17. Gopher Site—COS

"Elections." May 1996. gopher://israel-info.gov.il/
    00/facts/state/st4 (27 Dec. 2000).

18. FTP Site—COS

Project Gutenberg. 2000, Mar. 26. *Ibiblio.org.*
ftp://metalab.unc.edu/pub/docs/books/gutenberg/
(12 Aug. 2000).

19. Telnet Site—COS

Schweller, Kenneth G. "How to Design a Bot." *Collegetown
MOO.* 28 May 1999. telnet://galaxy.bvu.edu:7777
(16 Nov. 2000).

20. Synchronous Communication—COS

Dominguez, Jose. "Interchange." *Daedalus Online.* http://
daedalus.pearsoned.com (11 Mar. 2001).

21. Software—COS

Wresch, William. *Writer's Helper* Vers. 4.0. Upper Saddle
River: Prentice Hall, 1998.

Scientific style
1. Site on the World Wide Web—COS

Blackmon, S. (2000, August 24). Cows in the classroom?:
MOOs and MUDs and MUSHes . . . oh my!!! http://
www.sla.purdue.edu/people/engl/blackmon/moo/
index.html (11 Mar. 2001).

2. Modified or Revised Site—COS

Grant, W.E., and K. Dvorak. (2000). The American
1890s: a chronology. (Mod. Spring 2000). http://
www.bgsu.edu/departments/acs/1890s/america.html
(22 Nov. 2000).

If the site is revised, use the abbreviation *Rev.* in place of *Mod.*

3. Maintained or Compiled Site—COS

E-zine-list. (2000, March 8). (John Labovitz. Maint.).
http://www.meer.net/~johnl/e-zine-list (15 Sep. 2000).

If the site is compiled, use the abbreviation *Comp.* in place of *Maint.*

4. Article from a Periodical—COS

Kaplan, C. S. (2000, September 28). Suit considers computer
files. *The New York Times*. http://www.nytimes.com/2000/
09/28/technology/29CYBERLAW.html (13 Oct. 2000).

5. Article in an Online Journal—COS

Winickoff, J. P., et al. (2000, October). Verve and jolt:
deadly new Internet drugs. *Pediatrics, 106*(4).
http://www.pediatrics.org/cgi/content/abstract/106/4/829
(10 May 2000).

6. Work by a Group or Organization—COS

GROUP

Environmental Protection Agency. (2000, September 28).
Browner lauds hill action to protect Everglades,
beaches. Urges House of Representatives to finalize
Everglades plan. http://www.epa.gov/epahome/
headline_0928.htm (29 Nov. 2000).

ORGANIZATION

SIL International. (1999, May 7). Ethnomusicology:
studying music from the outside in and from the inside
out. http://www.sil.org/anthro/ethnomusicology.htm
(20 Feb. 2000).

7. Corporate Home Pages and Information—COS

Pearson PLC. (1999). Pearson home page. http://
www.pearson.com (12 Apr. 2001).

8. Government Information and Sites—COS

Central Intelligence Agency. (2000, October 6). Speeches and
testimony. http://www.cia.gov/cia/public_affairs/
speeches/speeches.html (18 Dec. 2000).

9. Book Accessed Online—COS

BOOK PUBLISHED FIRST IN PRINT VERSION

Brontë, C. (1887). *Jane Eyre*. London: Service & Paton.
(1999). *University of Maryland Reading Room.*

```
http://www.inform.umd.edu/EdRes/ReadingRoom/Fiction/
Cbronte/JaneEyre/ (15 Sep. 2000).
```

BOOK PUBLISHED ONLINE

Shires, B. (2000, January 17). *CPR (cardiopulmonary resuscitation) guide.* http://www.memoware.com/ Category= Medicine_ResultSet=1.htm (17 Apr. 2000).

10. Graphic, Video, or Audio File on the Page—COS

owl.gif [graphic file] (2000). Original free clipart. *Clipart.com.* http://www.free-clip-art.net/index4.shtml (27 Oct. 2000).

11. Personal Electronic Mail (E-Mail)—COS

Torres, E. Re: Puerto Rican baseball history. [personal e-mail]. (11 Sep. 2000).

12. Posting to a Discussion List—COS

Sheldon, A. (2000, January 2). Re: request for help on sexism inscription. *FLING List for Feminists in Linguistics.* http://listserv.linguistlist.org (14 Nov. 2000).

13. Posting to a Newsgroup or Forum—COS

Markowitz, A. (2000, September 28). The changing face of work: a look at the way we work. http://yourturn.npr.org/ cgi-bin/WebX?50@121.HjNGardZdaj^0@.ee7a9aa/ (8 Jan. 2001).

14. Archived Posting—COS

Radev, D. R. (1999, September 16). Natural language processing FAQ. *Institute of Information and Computing Sciences.* http://www.cs.ruu.nl/wais/html/na-dir/ natural-lang-processing-faq.html (27 Jan. 1999).

15. Online Reference Sources—COS

Reference sources such as online encyclopedias, dictionaries, thesauruses, style manuals, bibliographies, or other forms of factual material can be cited using the model at the top of the next page.

Nordenberg, T. (2000). Make no mistake! medical errors can be deadly serious. *Britannica.com*. Ebsco Publishing. http://britannica.com/bcom/original/article/0,5744,12430,00.html (12 Dec. 2000).

16. Computer Information Services and Online Databases—COS

Raintree Nutrition Inc. (2000, June). Pata de Vaca. *Raintree Tropical Plant Database*. http://www.rain-tree.com/patadevaca.htm (9 Sep. 2000).

17. Gopher Site—COS

Elections. (1996, May). gopher://israel-info.gov.il/00/facts/state/st4 (27 Dec. 2000).

18. FTP Site—COS

Project Gutenberg. (2000, March 26). *Ibiblio.org*. ftp://metalab.unc.edu/pub/docs/books/gutenberg/ (12 Aug. 2000).

19. Telnet Site—COS

Schweller, K. G. (1999, May 28). How to design a bot. *Collegetown MOO*. telnet://galaxy.bvu.edu:7777 (16 Nov. 2000).

20. Synchronous Communication—COS

Dominguez, J. Interchange. *Daedalus Online*. http://daedalus.pearsoned.com (11 Mar. 2001).

21. Software—COS

Wresch, W. (1998). *Writer's Helper* Vers. 4.0. Upper Saddle River: Prentice Hall.

38 EFFECTIVE DOCUMENT DESIGN

PRINT

38a How are print documents designed?

Designing a print document involves the layout you use for each page of the document. The process of **document design** includes everything from setting margins and headings to determining placement of a graphic or the use of color.

Document design is important for several reasons, not least because first impressions count. As soon as readers see your document, they form an opinion about you and your information. A well-designed document shows that you respect an assignment and have spent time formatting it so that it's attractive and readable. Making a good first impression influences readers to respond positively to your message.

You don't have to be an experienced designer to produce well-designed documents. Many software programs have easy-to-use formatting features, so writing on a computer provides multiple options for layout.

Some document design is standardized. As explained in Chapters 35, 36, and 37, discipline-related styles such as MLA, APA, and CM provide guidelines for formatting research papers. Letters, memos, and e-mail messages are also written in customary patterns (see 42a–42e). Most word processing programs have templates, or "wizards," for many standard formats.* Also, your instructor may ask you to follow a particular format.

38a.1 Using basic principles of design

The basic principles of design—of anything, from a chair to a car to a painting or a written document—are *unity, variety, balance,* and *emphasis:* UVBE.

---

* WordPerfect™ has a template for APA format.

Box 155 describes the principles of design you can use to get your message across with your document. Also, for tips on design principles from professional document designers, visit the following Web site: <http://www. peachpit.com/features/ndmonth/nddesign.html>.

 Principles of document design: UVBE   **155**

- **Unity** results from repetition and consistency. Ask: Do all elements in my document work together visually?
- **Variety** comes from a logical, appropriate break from unity that adds interest. Ask: Have I introduced design element, where appropriate, that break up monotony (e.g., inserting headings in academic papers that add to clarity or on-the-topic illustrations that add to content?
- **Balance** refers to a sense of harmony or equilibrium. Ask: Are the parts of my document in proportion to each other?
- **Emphasis** directs the eye to what is most important. Ask: Does my document design draw attention to what is most important?

38a.2 Designing with a computer

Computers now make it fairly easy for writers to vary the presentation of their writing. With new programs, writers can produce documents that would have required professional designers only a few years ago. In fact, few college instructors accept handwritten essays and research papers today. If you do not own a computer, you can use one at your college's computer lab. Find out whether the procedure is to sign up in advance or based on "first come, first served." Then, schedule enough time to get there, wait your turn, finish your work, and go there again if needed.

Box 156 lists types of software that you can use for document design.

 Computer programs used in designing   **156**
documents

Word Processing Software

Many word processing programs, such as Microsoft Word and Corel WordPerfect, have features that allow you to vary the format of

→

> **Computer programs used in designing**   **156**
> **documents** *(continued)*
>
> your document and create charts, graphs, and tables. Generally, you
> can use a word processing program to format most basic documents
> in ACADEMIC WRITING, BUSINESS WRITING, or some writing for the
> public.
>
> **Page Layout Software**
>
> Page layout software—for example, Adobe PageMaker or Microsoft
> Publisher—makes precise control of the elements of your
> document, such as text and graphic placement, possible. Though
> these programs take time to learn, they produce effective advanced
> documents, such as newsletters, brochures, and other designs you
> might use in writing for the public (Chapter 42).
>
> **Graphic Design Software**
>
> Graphic design software—for example, Macromedia Freehand or
> Adobe Photoshop—allows you to create and edit graphics, pictures,
> and other forms of art. You can then save these files in formats that
> are compatible with word processing and page layout software to
> insert into your written document.

38b What is page layout?

Layout is the arrangement of text and visuals on a page; it is a kind
of spatial composition. You use layout to reinforce the organizational
plan of your writing. For example, when you begin a new paragraph of
an essay, you begin a new line and indent from the left margin. When
using block style for a business letter, you add a double space between
paragraphs. In each case, your layout decision indicates that you are moving to a new idea. A good Web site for help with layout is *About.com*'s
template index section at <http://graphicdesign.miningco.com/arts/
graphicdesign/msubpmt.htm>. Here, you can download templates for
brochures, booklets, newsletters, and other types of documents.

38b.1 Positioning text and visuals

If you are using text and visuals in a document, arrange them so that
they balance and complement each other. Unless the style you're using
dictates otherwise, do not put all text or all visuals on one page.
Experiment with ideas for layout by creating mock-up pages on a com-

puter or by sketching some possibilities. Group together related items. If you're writing a survey questionnaire, for example, you might number each category, and use a lettered or bulleted list of questions. You might also indent the lettered lists. Such visual grouping of like items makes the information more immediately understandable to your reader.

See Box 157 for tips on page layout and positioning text and visuals.

 Page layout: Positioning text and visuals   157

- Consider the size of visuals in placing them to avoid a top-heavy or bottom-heavy page.

- Avoid splitting a chart or table between one page and the next. If possible, the entire chart or table should fit on a single page.

- Try working with layout by dividing a sheet of paper into sections. Divide it in half (either horizontally or vertically), then divide it into fourths or eighths (depending on the amount of text and size of your visuals).

- Use the "Table" feature of your computer to position text and visuals exactly where you want them. Turn the grid lines off when you are done, and the printed copy will show only the text and visuals.

- Use the "Print Preview" feature to show you what the printed version will look like.

- Print out hard copies of various layouts and look at them from different distances. Ask others to look at your layouts and tell you what they like best and least about them.

- If it is too difficult to put graphics exactly where you want them, consider grouping all the visuals in an appendix, as MLA style recommends. (This is an exception to the rule that tells you to avoid placing either all visuals or all text on one page.)

38b.2 Using white space

White space is the part of your document that is blank, and it is as important as all other elements of design. White space allows readers to navigate your document more easily and to deal with information in chunks rather than in one big block. White space also indicates breaks between ideas and focuses attention on the actual elements of your document.

For ACADEMIC WRITING, double spacing is almost always required. It gives instructors and peers space to write comments in response to your writing. In contrast, BUSINESS WRITING usually calls for single-spaced lines, with an added line of white space between paragraphs.

38b.3 Justifying and indenting

When you make your text lines either even in length or even in relation to the margins, you are **justifying** them. There are four kinds of justification, or ways to line up text lines on margins: left, right, centered, and full, as shown here.

Left justified text (text aligns on the left)

Right justified text (text aligns on the right)

Center justified text (text aligns in the center)

Full justified text (both left and right justified to full length, or measure, of the line of type)

Most documents are left justified, including ACADEMIC WRITING and BUSINESS WRITING, with unjustified, or *ragged*, right ends. This helps avoid end-of-line hyphens for broken words (see 22h). Such hyphens are correct, but distracting, to the reader. (Most textbooks are full justified, and you will see many hyphens, therefore.)

Use center, right, and full justification in designing announcements, advertising, and similar public writing to attract attention (see Chapter 42).

When you move text toward the right margin, you are **indenting.** College essays and research papers usually call for indentation of the first line in paragraphs. The standard indentation is five spaces. (See the indenting formats of student research papers in MLA and APA styles in sections 35e and 36g.) For BUSINESS WRITING, paragraphs are often in block style, which calls for no indent of first lines and single spacing, with double spacing only between paragraphs (or between the parts of the letter and its text; 42a). Do not mix these two styles by indenting the first line and double-spacing between paragraphs.

Box 158 lists some helpful tips on using justification and indentation.

⊙ **Tips on justifying and indenting**   **158**

- Use the "Increase Indent" and "Decrease Indent" functions on your computer to control the indentation of text, instead of using the tab keys. This ensures that the indents stay constant in relation to the rest of the document, even if you change the type size or font (38c.2) of the text.
- Except in ACADEMIC WRITING, use indents to indicate subsections of a document. For example, in a brochure, you could left justify headings and then indent the subsequent text.
- Indent bulleted and numbered lists (38c.3) to make them stand out.

38b.4 Setting margins and borders

Margins are the boundaries of a page, the white space or blank areas at the top, bottom, and sides. College essays call for 1 inch of space on all sides. Research papers usually require the same or more, according to the discipline-related style you are assigned (Chapters 35–37). Margins in BUSINESS WRITING are also usually 1 inch on all sides.

Borders set off information, such as a table or chart. A sales brochure, for example, might "box"—enclose in four borders, or **rules,** making a box—testimonials from satisfied customers, or a newsletter might set off upcoming events in a special box. A single rule (a simple straight line—horizontal or vertical) can emphasize breaks between major sections of a long report.

See Box 159 for more information on using margins and borders.

⊙ **Tips for using margins and borders**   **159**

- You can fit more information on a page by decreasing the margins. However, doing this also decreases the amount of white space and can make a page appear cluttered, dense, and difficult to read.
- The more you increase the margins, the less information you can fit on a page. For ACADEMIC WRITING, margins greater than 1 inch make your document look "padded."
- Depending on the type of document you are creating, you may use simple lines for borders or repeat small graphic elements (such as asterisks). Getting too fancy, though, can be distracting.
- If you use color for borders in nonacademic writing, stick to darker colors (blue or black or red) and avoid heavy (thick) rules that distract from the content.

38c How do I format text?

To format a text, you decide which typeface you will use, how you will present headings, and how you will highlight important material.

38c.1 Writing headings

Think of **headings** as headlines in your document. Headings clarify your organization; they tell your readers what to expect in each section. Longer documents, including this handbook, also use headings to break content into chunks that are easier to digest and understand. Keep headings brief and informative so that your readers can use them as cues. Also, use PARALLEL structure and consistent capitalization. Box 160 presents common types of headings, with examples showing parallel structure, and Box 161 offers additional help on writing and formatting headings.

 Common types of headings   160

- **Noun phrases can cover a variety of topics.**
  Executive Branch of Government
  Legislative Branch of Government
  Judicial Branch of Government
- **Questions can evoke reader interest.**
  When and How Does the President Use the Veto Power?
  How Does the Legislative Branch Make Laws?
  How Does the Supreme Court Decide Whether to Consider a Case?
- **-*ing* phrases can explain instructions or solve problems.**
  Submitting the Congressional Budget
  Updating the Congressional Budget
  Approving the Congressional Budget
- **Imperative sentences can give advice or directions.**
  Identify a Problem
  Poll Constituents
  Draft the Bill

Guidelines for writing and formatting   161
headings

- **Put headings in larger type than the body of your text.** You may use the same font or a contrasting typeface, if it coordinates visually and is easy to read. (See 38c.2 for more information on choosing type font and size.)
- **Use parallel structure in writing headings.** In longer documents, you can vary the form of the heading at different levels. For example, you might make all first-level heads questions and all second-level heads noun phrases. Any combination is acceptable, as long as you are consistent throughout your document.

→

> ## Guidelines for writing and formatting headings *(continued)*   161
>
> ■ **Remember to change the format for headings of different levels.** This can be done in various ways: You can center heads or left-justify them; you can vary the typeface by using boldface (heavy type), italics, or underlining; or you can use capitalization. (See 38c.2 and 38c.3.) The one rule is to be consistent in whatever style you choose in each document.
>
> - Level one heading (most important)   FIRST-LEVEL HEAD
> - Level two heading   Second-Level Head
> - Level three heading   *Third-level head*

38c.2 Choosing type fonts and sizes

Fonts are different typefaces. Most computer programs come with a variety of fonts, and you can download more from the Internet.

Fonts are divided into two major categories: serif and sans serif. *Serif* fonts have little "feet" or finishing lines at the top and bottom of each letter, and *sans serif* fonts do not (*sans* means "without"). Fonts come in different sizes (heights) that are measured in "points" (units smaller than .02 inch). Most word processing programs have font sizes ranging from 6 points to 72 points (close to an inch).

SERIF FONTS	SANS SERIF FONTS
Times New Roman 10 pt	Arial 10 pt
New Century Schoolbook 12 pt	Franklin Gothic Book 12 pt
Bookman Old Style 14 pt	Comic Sans MS 14 PT

In most ACADEMIC WRITING, it is considered standard to select fonts that range from 10 to 12 points for body text and from 14 to 18 points for headings. Be sure to consult with your instructor or with a style manual for your discipline before you format your paper. Since different font faces and sizes take up different amounts of room on a line and on a page, some instructors specify a specific typeface and size to ensure that students produce a certain amount of text per page. See Box 162 for guidelines to follow in using fonts.

⊙ **Guidelines for using type fonts** **162**

- **Choose readable fonts.** Serif fonts are more comfortable to read for long periods of time and are, therefore, used more often for body text. For body text in college work, a serif font such as Times New Roman is appropriate. Sans serif fonts are easier to read from a distance and are good choices for headings.
- **Pick different font sizes for headings.** This helps distinguish the headings from body text as well as different levels of headings; see Box 161.
- **Avoid fancy typefaces for essays and research papers.** Many instructors consider them too distracting for college work.
- **Notice the difference between how a font appears on a screen and on a printed document.** If you are designing a document to appear on the computer, choose fonts that are screen-friendly. If you are making a print document, choose a more print-friendly font.

38c.3 Highlighting

Highlighting draws attention to key words or elements of a document. You can highlight in various ways, but the one guideline that applies in all cases is this: *Use moderation.* For example, putting headings in bold is a good way to set them off, but nothing will be emphasized if too many words are in bold. This section looks at three types of highlighting—boldface, italics, and underlining; bulleted and numbered lists; and color.

Italics and underlining—they mean the same thing—have special uses in writing (for example, to indicate titles of certain works; see 30f), but they're also used for emphasis and for headings. **Boldface** is reserved for heavy emphasis.

When you discuss a series of items or steps in a complicated process or want to summarize key points or guidelines, you can sometimes use either a bulleted list (items identified by small dots or squares) or a numbered list. A list with highlighted or pinpointed items provides your reader with a way to think of the whole idea you are going to or have just communicated. In ACADEMIC WRITING, use such lists sparingly, if at all. Complete sentences and explanations are better.

Adding color to a document can change it dramatically. A flyer announcing a campus event, for example, can be as attention-getting as a magazine advertisement, especially if it incorporates this kind of visual content. Take time, however, to think about your reasons for adding color. How does color suit the genre of your document? How will it help you accomplish your purpose? What expectations does your audience have about the use of color?

Academic writing and most BUSINESS WRITING rarely call for color. Mass-mail sales letters and letters soliciting donations are exceptions because color and varying fonts (38c.2) can add appeal to their message. Use color for variety and emphasis, but never overuse it.

38d How should I incorporate visuals?

Visuals, also called *graphics,* can enhance document design, when used appropriately. A visual can condense, compare, and display information more effectively than words, but only if its content is suitable. A graph showing how sales increased over a period of time, for example, makes the point more quickly and clearly than an explanation. A photo or drawing can illustrate or reinforce a point you want to make.

Most word processing programs offer standard designs for visuals. When produced on a color printer, charts, diagrams, and other graphics can look quite dramatic. However, resist any temptation to use numerous visuals; use them only to enhance your writing, not replace it.

Two excellent Web sites on visuals can be accessed using these URLs:

http://www.colostate.edu/Depts/WritingCenter/references/graphics.htm

http://www.io.com/~hcexres/tcm1603/acchtml/graphics.html

38d.1 Using charts and graphs

Business and scientific reports rely heavily on charts and graphs. They are compact ways to present large amounts of information.

Bar graphs compare values, such as the number of different majors at a college, as shown in the graph below.

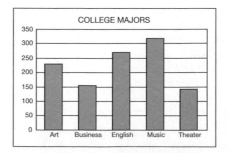

Line graphs indicate changes over time. For example, advertising revenue is shown over an eight-month period in the graph below.

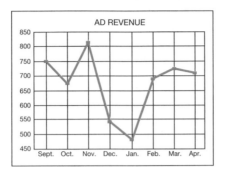

Pie charts show the relationship of each part to a whole, such as a typical budget for a college student, as shown in the chart below.

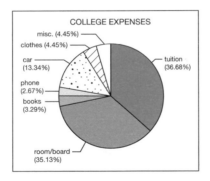

38d.2 Using other types of visuals

Time lines display events over time, such as the progress of historical events or a manufacturing process.

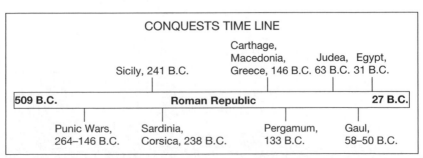

Diagrams show the parts of a whole, as in the diagram of the human brain below.

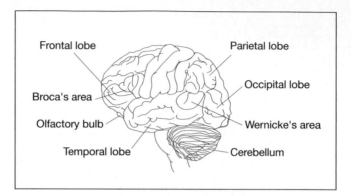

Tables present data in list form, as in the MLA-style research paper printed in Chapter 35 (pages 606–609) and the APA-style research paper printed in Chapter 36 (page 649), or as shown below.

Table 1 Total Number of Computer Lab Users by Semester		
Semester	**Number of Users**	**Percentage (%) of Student Population**
Fall 2001	2321	25.8
Spring 2002	3425	38.1
Summer 2002	592	6.6

Clip art refers to pictures, sketches, and other graphics available on some word processing programs. It can also be downloaded from the Internet. Though it is inappropriate in ACADEMIC WRITING and BUSINESS WRITING, clip art can add interest to flyers, posters, newsletters, and brochures designed for certain audiences. A Web site that is an excellent source of clip art, graphics, and fonts that can be downloaded and used free can be found at <http://dir.yahoo.com/Computers_and_Internet/ Graphics/>. Here are some samples of clip art.

Photographs can be scanned from books and articles into a computer and included in a document. Be sure to give credit to the source. You may even need to secure written permission from the source to use the photo.

Guidelines and additional help in using visuals in your documents is provided in Box 163.

⊙ Guidelines for using visuals   163

- **Design all visuals to be simple and uncluttered.** They should be clearly labeled, as needed, and easy to read.
- **Never use unnecessary visuals.** Putting cute clip art in your essay will not make your reader think it is a better essay. Including a chart that summarizes your findings might.
- **Number figures and tables, if more than one.** If possible, choose only one term: *Table 1, Table 2;* or *Figure 1, Figure 2,* and so forth).
- **Never overwhelm your text with visual elements.** If the visuals you want to use will be much larger than the text, consider putting them on separate pages or in an appendix.
- **Credit your source if a visual isn't your own.** Also, if the source indicates that it is copyrighted, you need written permission to use any part of it in your work. (Look for a source note or in the credits list for the source you are using. For a Web page, look at the top and/or bottom of the document.)

WORLD WIDE WEB

38e What should I know about writing for the Web?

The WORLD WIDE WEB (WWW), known popularly as **the Web,** is the most convenient entry to the Internet. Locations on the Web are called *Web sites,* which consist of one or a series of *Web pages.* Web pages can inform and entertain through text, images, color, and often sound and video. If you want to create your own Web page or a class assignment or group project requires one, this section will help you get started.

Print documents communicate in a *linear* fashion: You begin at page 1 and proceed to the last page, moving in a straight line. A Web document, on the other hand, is *nonlinear:* Web pages, often called **hypertext,** are

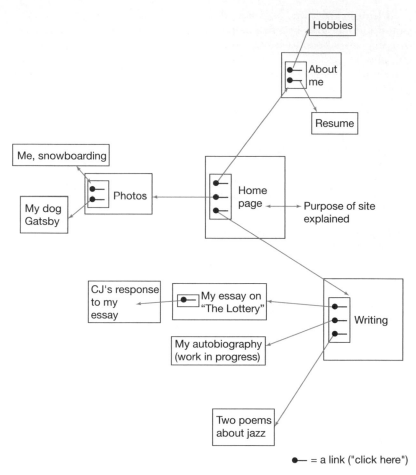

● — = a link ("click here")

A map for planning a Web site

formatted in language that allows readers to jump from one page to page (or to other linked material, such as sound) in whatever order they select. Web documents thus allow great flexibility. This flexibility means that in designing a Web page, you consider not only how each page looks but also how each page relates to the other pages on your site.

Most guidelines and principles that contribute to good design in printed documents apply equally to Web design. Basic design questions apply: Why are you creating a Web page? Who will view your Web page? What features characterize Web pages? As you plan, keep in mind the basic design principles of unity, variety, balance, and emphasis (38a.1). Also, early in your planning process, look at some Web sites that could be similar to yours. For example, if you are creating a **home page**—the opening page of a site that provides links to its other pages or parts—look at other personal home pages and note their common features. If you are putting a piece of your writing on the Web, find examples of essays posted on or written for the Web. Think about whether your Web document will be one page or several pages. If you find yourself creating a very long page, divide the content over a couple pages and connect them. This arrangement is much more readable.

Multiple-page Web sites should have a home page; it usually explains the purpose of the site and functions as a table of contents by organizing information into categories and providing links to other pages. Try sketching a map of your document; begin with a home page and then show how other pages link to it (see the example on page 700).

38f How do I plan a Web page?

Web design is similar to print design, but users will be looking at your document on a computer screen instead of separate sheets of paper. This means that your design should load quickly on viewers' screens, be easy to read and navigate, and provide just enough information—not too much and not too little.

Posting a Web page is a form of publishing. If you copyright your site, include a copyright notice by typing the word *copyright*, the copyright symbol, ©, the year of publication, and your name. If you want feedback, include your e-mail address. If you use material from sources, credit those sources and, if necessary, secure permission to use the work. PLAGIARISM is plagiarism (Chapter 31), whether the medium is print or electronic.

Box 164 provides questions to ask yourself about the special aspects of planning for Web site layout.

⊙ **Questions for Web site layout**   **164**

Navigation

How will your readers move through the content on the page? How will you arrange information so that it is clear and easy to read? How will you divide up the screen space that your page takes up? How will your readers navigate between different pages on your site? Will you provide them with links back to the home page and to the other content?

→

> ## Questions for Web site layout *(continued)*   **164**
>
> ### Grouping Content
>
> How will you arrange content on your page? How will you group related elements? How can you use headings and subheadings to help group content? Are blocks of text short? Should you arrange some elements in lists?
>
> ### Emphasizing Content
>
> How can you make the title of your page stand out? How will you draw attention to the most important material? Can you use color, sound, or animation to enhance, not detract from, the text?
>
> ### Placement of Images
>
> Where will you put images on your page? How will you arrange images so that they don't distract from the other content on the page?
>
> ### Choosing Backgrounds
>
> What background will support your content most effectively? Can your text be read easily against the background? Would a single color or a pattern be better?
>
> ### Establishing Links
>
> Are your links obvious to a reader, or are they buried in text? Will your site provide links to the other pages in your site? Do you know other reputable sites to link to that might interest your readers?

38g   How do I create a Web site?

Web sites, whether they are large commercial sites or personal home pages, are written in a computer program language. The original language format is called **HTML,** for **H**ypertext **M**arkup **L**anguage.

To write a Web page, you can use an HTML editor, a program that generates "tags," or codes, for you. HTML (or newer versions of this language) editor programs and what are called *WYSIWYG editors* (What You See Is What You Get, pronounced "whizzy-wig," editors) help you create your Web site by encoding as you type. The advantage of the WYSIWYG is that it lets you "see" the page rather than just words and codes as you type. You create your page by typing in text and inserting images and other content as you would with a word processor, and then the WYSIWYG editor generates the needed codes for you.

The most common WYSIWYG editors are Netscape Composer, which is often distributed free with versions of Netscape; Microsoft FrontPage, which comes with many versions of Microsoft Internet Explorer; and Macromedia Dreamweaver. Your school's computer lab may have these programs or others. You can also purchase an HTML editor or download one from the Internet.

Box 165 lists Web sites that offer basic information and tutorials in using HTML and WYSIWYG editors.

 Tutorials for HTML and WYSIWYG editors   165

- **HTML basics**

  http://www.jmarshall.com/easy/html

  http://www.w3.org/MarkUp/Wilbur/features.html

  http://www.ncsa.uiuc.edu/General/Internet/WWW/HTMLPrimer.html

- **Netscape Composer**

  http://www.furman.edu/~pecoy/mfl195/composer/

- **Microsoft FrontPage**

  http://msdn.microsoft.com/workshop/languages/fp/2000/tutorial2000/004fp.asp

- **Macromedia Dreamweaver**

  http://www.walkway.buffalo.edu/Workshops/Selection/Dreamweaver/dreamweaver.htm

---

38g.1 Using images

Web pages can feature many different kinds of graphics. For example, small icons such as colored balls can be used to mark off a list of items (the way bullets are used in print documents; see 38c.3). Use a scanner to scan photographs or sketches and put them online, or use a graphic design program to create your own graphics. Some WYSIWYG editors come with clip art and images. You can also download images and graphics from the Internet. The following sites offer graphics that can be downloaded free for personal use.

http://www.iconbazaar.com

http://www.clipart.com

http://www.freegraphics.com/

http://dir.yahoo.com/Computers_and_Internet/Graphics/Clip_Art/Web_Directories/

As in print documents, images on Web pages are effective only if they are used as part of communication. Simply dropping in an image here or there is more distracting than helpful. Try to find a set of graphics that provides a consistent look. Also, consider whether or not the images you are using are appropriate for your audience.

38g.2 Using tables and frames

HTML offers many options for accurately placing text and images. As with print documents, you can use the table feature to arrange text and images (see Box 157 in section 38b.1) or you may choose to create "frames" on your Web site. A frame at the far left of a page, for example, may be devoted to a single set of links or options, while new content is loaded in a larger frame on the right of the page. The following Web sites can tell you more about tables and frames:

http://hotwired.lycos.com/webmonkey/authoring/tables/index.html

http://hotwired.lycos.com/webmonkey/authoring/frames/index.html

http://html.digitalsea.net/step6.html

http://html.digitalsea.net/step7.html

38h How do I display my Web page?

Having created a Web page, you are ready to display it on the World Wide Web. To do this, you need two things: space on a Web server and files for the graphics or other nontext elements that you put on your Web page.

38h.1 Finding space on the Web

You can create HTML files (using a WYSIWYG or not) either online or offline, but you will need to upload them to a Web server for the files to be visible on the Web. In other words, you need a *host*. Your school may offer Web space to its students; check with your computing service office. If your school does not offer space, many services on the Internet offer free Web space as well as help in building Web pages. Try *Yahoo-Geocities* at <http://www.yahoo.com> or *Xoom* at <http://www.xoom.com>.

If you have a commercial Internet Service Provider (ISP) such as America Online, you may be able to use it to post your Web page.

You will also need some kind of File Transfer Protocol (FTP) program to upload the HTML files to your Web server. The host of your space should be able to advise you on the best way to upload files and which FTP program to use.

38h.2 Using nontext files

If you have used graphics, pictures, icons, or sound on your Web page, you will also need to upload those files to the Web server, where your page is now located. Otherwise, they cannot be accessed by Web browsers.

Be careful to save the files with the correct extensions. Picture files normally have *.jpg* or *.gif* extensions, and sound files normally have *.wave, .au,* or *.midi* extensions. If your files do not have the correct extensions, the Web browser will not be able to process them.

38i How should I edit my Web site?

Edit and proofread your Web site as carefully as you would a print document. Some WYSIWYG editors allow you to preview a Web page in a Web browser, but most likely you will have to upload your site to the Web server where it will be hosted. The key difference between editing a Web page and a print document is that you also need to check that all the parts of your page are working properly. Use the checklist in Box 166.

 Editing checklist for a Web site   **166**

- **Are any images broken?** Broken images will show up as small gray icons instead of the pictures you want. Broken images are usually caused by mistyping the file name or failing to upload the image to the server along with the Web page.

- **Do all the links work?** For each link to a page on your own site, be sure a file with that exact name exists on the server. For example, if you linked to a page called *essay.html* from your home page, there should be a file called *essay.html* on the server. Mistyped or mislabeled files can also cause broken links.

- **Does your site work on different browsers and computers?** Your site needs to look the same on different browsers and different computers. If it doesn't, you may want to revise your HTML. Using default settings for font, text size, and color will ensure that your page is compatible with most browsers.

- **Is the Web site highly readable?** As with print documents, the most important part of designing your Web page is making it easy to read. Ask friends and other students to give you feedback about your page.

Recheck your Web site periodically. The Internet is always changing, and links can break or change. You may also want to add new information. One of the best things about a Web page is that you can change it as often as you like, and visitors only have to reload it to see the changes. Put a date at the bottom of your page to let visitors know when you last updated the site.

There is a wealth of information about document design on the Internet. One useful site to go to when you want to get started is *About.com*'s Design page at <http://graphicdesign.miningco.com/arts/graphicdesign/>. It has links to resources for all kinds of print and Web design, including tutorials and how-tos.

Visit the Troyka Web site for information on:

- Comparing disciplines
- Writing for business
- Delivering oral presentations

You'll find access to *Giving the Perfect Presentation Using PowerPoint* by Pat Kidwell, Susan Dumond, and Martha Dumond at <bloom.ivy.tec.in.us/ivytech/aot/ studentwork/powerpt/susanpat/index.htm>. This site, which appears on the Ivy Tech State College Web site, incorporates both design issues and oral presentation skills.

PART SIX

WRITING ACROSS THE CURRICULUM

www.prenhall.com/troyka

39 COMPARING THE DISCIPLINES

39a How do the disciplines compare?

The humanities, the social sciences, and the natural sciences each have their own perspectives on the world. Each of the disciplines also has its own philosophies about academic thought and research. To understand some of the differences among the disciplines, consider these three quite different paragraphs about a mountain.

HUMANITIES

The mountain stands above all that surrounds it. Giant timbers—part of a collage of evergreen and deciduous trees—conceal the expansive mountain's slope, where cattle once grazed. At the base of the mountain, a cool stream flows over rocks of all sizes, colors, and shapes. Next to the outer bank of the stream stands a shingled farmhouse, desolate, yet suggesting its active past. Unfortunately, the peaceful scene is interrupted by billboards and chairlifts, landmarks of a modern, fast-paced life.

SOCIAL SCIENCES

Among the favorite pastimes of American city dwellers is the "return to nature." Many outdoor enthusiasts hope to enjoy a scenic trip to the mountains, only to be disappointed. They know they have arrived at the mountain that they have traveled hundreds of miles to see because huge billboards are directing them to its base. As they look up the mountain, dozens of people are riding over the treetops in a chairlift, littering the slope with paper cups and food wrappers. At the base of the mountain stands the inevitable refreshment stand, found at virtually all American tourist attractions. Land developers consider such commercialization a way to preserve and utilize natural resources, but environmentalists are appalled.

NATURAL SCIENCES

The mountain rises approximately 5,600 feet above sea level. The underlying rock is igneous, of volcanic origin, composed primarily of granites and feldspars. Three distinct biological communities are present on the mountain. The community at the top of the mountain is alpine, dominated by very short grasses and forbs. At middle altitudes, the community is a typical northern boreal coniferous forest community, and at the base and lower altitudes, deciduous forest is the dominant community. This community has, however, been highly affected by agricultural development along the river at its base and by recreational development.

These examples illustrate that each discipline has its perspective and emphasis. The paragraph written for the humanities describes the mountain from the individual perspective of the writer—a perspective both personal and yet representative of a general human response. The paragraph written for the social sciences focuses on the behavior of people as a group. The paragraph written for the natural sciences reports observations of natural phenomena.

As you study and write in each of the academic disciplines, you can experience alternate ways of thinking. As you come to know the habits of mind that characterize each discipline, you can develop specialized vocabularies to participate in the conversations of each discipline. As the range of your perspectives grows, you gain lifelong access to the major benefit of a college education. No matter what differences exist among the academic disciplines, all subject areas interconnect and overlap. Box 167 lists similarities and differences.

 ## Similarities and differences in writing   167
across the disciplines

Similarities

1. Consider your PURPOSE,* AUDIENCE, and TONE (see Chapter 1).
2. Use the WRITING PROCESS to PLAN, SHAPE, DRAFT, REVISE, EDIT, and PROOFREAD (see Chapters 2–3).
3. Develop a thesis (see Chapters 2–3).
4. Arrange and organize your ideas (see Chapter 2).
5. Use supporting evidence (see Chapters 2–4).
6. Develop paragraphs thoroughly (see Chapter 4).
7. Critically read, think, synthesize, and write (see Chapter 5).
8. Avoid confusing SUMMARY with SYNTHESIS (see Chapter 5).
9. Reason well; use good logic (see Chapter 5).
10. Write effective sentences (see Chapters 16–19).
11. Argue well (see Chapter 6).
12. Choose words well (see Chapters 19–21).
13. Use correct grammar (see Chapters 7–15).   →

---

* You can find the definition of a word printed in small capital letters (such as PURPOSE) in the Terms Glossary toward the end of this handbook.

Similarities and differences in writing   **167**
across the disciplines *(continued)*

14. Spell correctly (see Chapter 22).
15. Use correct punctuation and mechanics (see Chapters 23–30).

Differences

1. Conduct primary research and use sources for secondary research in each discipline (see 39b).
2. Select a style of documentation appropriate to each discipline (see 39c and Chapters 35–37).

For example, in a humanities class, you might read *Lives of a Cell,* a collection of essays about science and nature written by noted physician and author Lewis Thomas. As you consider the art of the writer, you will also be thinking deeply about biology and other sciences.

39b What are primary research and secondary research in the disciplines?

PRIMARY SOURCES offer you firsthand exposure to information, providing the exciting experience of discovering material on your own. But research methods differ among the disciplines when primary sources are used. In the humanities, existing documents are primary sources; the task of the researcher is to analyze and interpret these primary sources. Typical primary source material for humanities research could be a poem by Dylan Thomas, the floor plans of Egyptian pyramids, or early drafts of music manuscripts. In the social and natural sciences, primary research entails the design and undertaking of experiments involving direct observation. The task of the researcher in the social and natural sciences is to conduct experiments or to read the firsthand reports of experiments and studies by the people who conducted them.

SECONDARY SOURCES—articles and books that draw on primary sources—are important but are not firsthand reports. In the humanities, secondary sources offer analysis and interpretation; the author of a secondary source steps between you and the primary source. In the social and natural sciences, secondary sources summarize and then synthesize findings and draw parallels that offer new insights.

For a longer discussion and examples of primary and secondary sources, see Section 5g.2.

39c How do I use documentation in the disciplines?

Writers use DOCUMENTATION to give credit to the sources they have used. A writer who does not credit a source is guilty of PLAGIARISM— a serious academic offense (see 31a). Styles of documentation differ among the disciplines.

In the humanities, most fields use the DOCUMENTATION STYLE of the Modern Language Association (MLA), as explained and illustrated in Chapter 35. The student research paper in Chapter 35 and the student literary analyses in Chapter 40 use MLA documentation style. CM (Chicago Manual) style is sometimes used in the humanities; it is described in Chapter 37. In the social sciences, most fields use the documentation style of the American Psychological Association (APA), as explained and illustrated in Chapter 36. The student research paper in Chapter 36 uses APA documentation style. Research writing in the social sciences is also discussed in the first half of Chapter 41. In the natural sciences, documentation styles vary widely; consult Chapters 36 and 41 for more information. In online research, COS (Columbia Online Style) may be used to cite online publications.

www.prenhall.com/troyka

40 WRITING ABOUT LITERATURE

Literature, which includes **fiction** (novels and stories), **drama** (plays and scripts), and **poetry** (poems and lyrics), has developed from age-old human impulses to discover and communicate meaning by telling stories, reenacting events, and singing or chanting.

40a How can I understand methods of inquiry into literature?

All questions about literature require that you read a literary work closely (see 5d.2)—all **methods of inquiry** into literature begin with CRITICAL READING of the text. Often, you will be asked to answer questions that deal with the material on a literal level (see 5c.1). You might be asked to explain the meaning of a passage or to describe the historical events that took place when the work was being written.

Other questions call for inferential reasoning (see 5c.2) and evaluative thinking (see 5c.3). You might be asked to discuss the effect of sound or rhythm or rhyme in a poem or to compare and contrast characters in two plays by a particular playwright. As you write, keep in mind the principles of CRITICAL THINKING, especially the important differences between SUMMARY and SYNTHESIS (see 5b and 5e). Unlike inquiry called for by many other disciplines, literary inquiry sometimes includes asking you to describe your response or reaction to a work of literature after a close, careful reading.

In each case, your answers must reflect knowledge of the work and must be thorough, well-reasoned, and well-supported with evidence.

40b What are purposes and practices specific to writing about literature?

40b.1 Using first and third person appropriately

Many instructors require students to use the FIRST PERSON (*I, we, our*) only when writing about their personal point of view in evaluations; they want students to use the THIRD PERSON (*he, she, it, they*) for all other content. These rules are becoming less rigid, so be sure to ask about your instructor's requirements.

40b.2 Using verbs in the present tense and the past tense correctly when writing about literature

Have you ever wondered what VERB TENSE to use when writing about literature? Use the PRESENT TENSE when you describe or discuss a literary work or any of its elements: *George Henderson* [a character] *takes control of the action and **tells** the other characters when they may speak.* The present tense is also correct for discussing what the author has done in a specific work: *Because Susan Glaspell* [the author] *excludes Minnie and John Wright from the stage as speaking characters, she forces her audience to learn about them through the words of others.*

Use a PAST-TENSE VERB to discuss historical events or biographical information: *Susan Glaspell **was** a social activist who **was** strongly **influenced** by the chaotic events of the early twentieth century.*

40b.3 Using your own ideas and using secondary sources

Some assignments call only for your own ideas about the subject of your essay. Other assignments ask you to support your ideas with SECONDARY SOURCES. Secondary sources include books and articles in which an expert discusses material related to your topic. You can locate secondary sources by using the research process discussed in Chapter 32.

So that no reader mistakes someone else's ideas as your own, always document your sources (see 31b and Chapters 35–37). Otherwise, you are guilty of PLAGIARISM (31a). Also, work material from secondary sources gracefully into your writing, using VERBS effectively to integrate (31f) QUOTATIONS (31c), PARAPHRASES (31d), and SUMMARIES (31e).

40c How can I use documentation style in writing about literature?

You are required to credit your sources by using DOCUMENTATION. Many literature instructors specify that their students must use the

DOCUMENTATION STYLE of the Modern Language Association (MLA), an organization of scholars and teachers of language and literature. MLA documentation style is described in Chapter 35. Two other documentation styles sometimes required in the humanities are that of the American Psychological Association (APA), presented in Chapter 36, and that of the University of Chicago Press, known as CM STYLE, presented in Chapter 37.

40d How do I write different types of papers about literature?

Before you write about a literary work, read the work closely. Your readers can tell easily when you leave out details that are central to your message. To read closely, use your understanding of the READING PROCESS (see 5c) and engage in CRITICAL READING (see 5d).

40d.1 Writing reaction papers

A **reaction paper** is an essay in which you respond to a work of literature. For example, you might answer a central question that the work made you think about, criticize a point of view in the work, or present a problem that you see in the work. Instead, you might write about why you did or did not enjoy reading the work, what it made you think about, or how it does or does not relate to your personal experience or to your view of life. You can focus on the entire work or on part of it. Use quotations from the work as evidence for your reactions.

40d.2 Writing book reports

A **book report** first informs readers about the content of a book, using SUMMARY (see 5e). This summary is followed by your discussion of the purpose and significance of the book, its structure and style, and who might be most interested in the work. When you discuss the significance of the book, try to relate it to your field of study. For example, if the book is a classic in children's literature, your focus for a literature class would differ somewhat from your focus for a course in psychology or education.

40d.3 Writing interpretations

An **interpretation** discusses one of two things: what you think the author means by the work or what the work means personally to you. As you write an interpretation paper, keep in mind the questions in Box 168.

Questions for an interpretation paper   **168**

1. What is the theme of the work?
2. How are particular parts of the work related to the theme?
3. If patterns exist in various elements of the work, what do they mean?
4. What message does the author convey through the use of major aspects of the work, listed in Box 169?
5. Why does the work end as it does?

40d.4 Writing analyses

ANALYSIS is the examination of the relationship of a whole to its parts. In a *literary analysis,* you are expected to discuss your ideas and insights about a work of fiction, poetry, or drama. Your ideas and insights come from the thinking you do, the patterns you see, and the connections you make when you look at various aspects of the work; see a summary of points to analyze in Box 169. To get to know the work well and to gather ideas for your analysis, read the work thoroughly, again and again, looking for patterns. Write notes as you go along so that you have a record of two important resources for your writing: the patterns you find in the material and your thinking about the patterns and their meaning to the whole work.

 Major aspects of literary works to analyze   **169**

PLOT	The events and their sequence
THEME	Central idea or message
STRUCTURE	Organization and relationship of parts to each other and to the whole
CHARACTERIZATION	Traits, thoughts, and actions of the people in the plot
SETTING	Time and place of the action
POINT OF VIEW	Perspective or position from which the material is presented—sometimes by a narrator or a main character

→

Major aspects of literary works to analyze 169	
(continued)	
STYLE	How words and sentence structures present the material
IMAGERY	Pictures created by the words (similes, metaphors, figurative language; see Box 92 in section 21d)
TONE	Attitude of the author toward the subject of the work—and sometimes toward the reader— expressed through choice of words and imagery
FIGURE OF SPEECH	Nonliteral use of words, as in metaphor and simile, for enhanced vividness or effect
SYMBOLISM	Meaning beneath the surface of the words and images
RHYTHM	Beat, meter
RHYME	Repetition of similar sounds for their auditory effect

40e How should I write about literature?

This section includes three student essays of literary analysis. Two do not use SECONDARY SOURCES (40e.1 and 40e.2) and one does use them (40e.3). All three essays use MLA DOCUMENTATION STYLE (see Chapter 35).

40e.1 Student essay interpreting a plot element in a short story

The following essay interprets a plot element in Edgar Allan Poe's story "The Tell-Tale Heart."

Born in 1809, Edgar Allan Poe was an important American journalist, poet, and fiction writer. In his short, dramatic life, Poe gambled, drank, lived in terrible poverty, saw his young wife die of tuberculosis, and died himself under mysterious circumstances at age forty. He also created the detective novel and wrote brilliant, often bizarre short stories that still stimulate readers' imaginations.

When Valerie Cuneo read Poe's "Tell-Tale Heart," first published in 1843, she was fascinated by one of the plot elements: the sound of a beating heart that compels the narrator of the story to commit a murder and then to confess it to the police. In the following paper, Cuneo discusses her interpretation of the source of the heartbeat.

Cuneo 1

Valerie Cuneo

Professor Aaron

English 10B

2 February 2001

The Sound of a Murderous Heart

In Edgar Allan Poe's short story "The Tell-Tale Heart," several interpretations are possible as to the source of the beating heart that causes the narrator-murderer to reveal himself to the police. The noise could simply be a product of the narrator's obviously deranged mind. Or perhaps the murder victim's spirit lingers, heart beating, to exact revenge upon the narrator. Although either of these interpretations is possible, most of the evidence in the story suggests that the inescapable beating heart that haunts the narrator is his own.

The interpretation that the heartbeat stems from some kind of auditory hallucination is flawed. The narrator is clearly insane--his killing a kind old man because of an "Evil Eye" demonstrates this--and his psychotic behavior is more than sufficient cause for readers to question his truthfulness. Even so, nowhere else in the story does the narrator imagine things that do not exist. Nor is it likely that he would intentionally attempt to mislead us since the narrative is a confessional monologue through which he tries to explain and justify his actions. He himself describes his "disease" as a heightening of his senses, not of his imagination. Moreover, his highly detailed account of the events surrounding the murder seems to support this

→

claim. Near the end of the story, he refutes the notion
that he is inventing the sound in his mind when he says,
"I found that the noise was not within my ears" (792).
Although the narrator's reliability is questionable,
there seems to be no reason to doubt this particular
observation.

Interpreting the heartbeat as the victim's ghostly
retaliation against the narrator also presents
difficulties. Perhaps most important, when the narrator
first hears the heart, the old man is still alive. The
structure of the story also argues against the
retaliation interpretation. Poe uses the first-person
point of view to give readers immediate access to the
narrator's strange thought processes, a choice that
suggests the story is a form of psychological study. If
"The Tell-Tale Heart" were truly a ghost story, it would
probably be told in the third person, and it would more
fully develop the character of the old man and explore
his relationship with the narrator. If the heartbeat that
torments the narrator is his own, however, these
inconsistencies are avoided.

The strongest evidence that the tell-tale heart is
really the narrator's is the timing of the heartbeat.
Although it is the driving force behind the entire story,
the narrator hears the beating heart only twice. In both
of these instances, he is under immense physical and
psychological stress--times when his own heart would be
pounding. The narrator first hears the heartbeat with the
shock of realizing that he has accidentally awakened his
intended victim:

> Meantime the hellish tattoo of the heart
> increased. It grew quicker and quicker, and
> louder every instant. The old man's terror must
> have been extreme! It grew louder, I say,
> louder every moment!--do you mark me well? I

→

have told you that I am nervous: so I am. And
now at the dead hour of the night, amid the
dreadful silence of that old house, so strange
a noise as this excited me to uncontrollable
terror. (791)

As the narrator's anxiety increases, so does the
volume and frequency of the sound, an event easily
explained if the heartbeat is his own. Also, the sound of
the heart persists even after the old man is dead, fading
slowly into the background, as the murderer's own
heartbeat would after his short, violent struggle with
the old man. This reasoning can also explain why the
narrator did not hear the heart on any of the seven
previous nights when he looked into the old man's
bedchamber. Because the old man slept and the "Evil Eye"
was closed, no action was necessary (according to the
narrator-murderer's twisted logic), and, therefore, he
did not experience the rush of adrenaline that set his
heart pounding on the fatal eighth visit.

The heart also follows a predictable pattern at the
end of the story when the police officers come to
investigate a neighbor's report of the dying old man's
scream. In this encounter, the narrator's initial calm
slowly gives way to irritation and fear. As he becomes
increasingly agitated, he begins to hear the heart again.
The narrator clearly identifies it as the same sound he
heard previously, as shown by the almost word-for-word
repetition of the language he uses to describe it,
calling it "a low, dull, quick sound--much such a sound
as a watch makes when enveloped in cotton" [Poe's
emphasis] (792). As the narrator-murderer focuses his
attention on the sound, which ultimately overrides all
else, his panic escalates until, ironically, he is
betrayed by the very senses that he boasted about at the
start of the story.

→

Cuneo 4

Work Cited

Poe, Edgar Allan. "The Tell-Tale Heart." American
Literature: A Prentice Hall Anthology. Vol. 1. Ed.
Emory Elliott, Linda K. Kerber, A. Walton Litz, and
Terence Martin. Englewood Cliffs: Prentice, 1991.
789–92.

40e.2 Student essay analyzing the characters in a drama

The following essay analyzes actions and interactions of the male and female characters in *Trifles*, a one-act play written by Susan Glaspell (1882–1948). Glaspell was a feminist and social activist who wrote many plays for the Provincetown Players, a theater company she cofounded on Cape Cod, in Massachusetts. She wrote *Trifles* in 1916, four years before women were allowed to vote in the United States. In 1917, Glaspell rewrote *Trifles* as the short story "A Jury of Her Peers." In both versions of the work, two married couples and the county attorney gather at a farmhouse where a taciturn farmer has been murdered, apparently by his wife. The five characters try to discover a motive for the murder. In doing so, they reveal much about gender roles in marriage and in the larger society.

After reading *Trifles*, Peter Wong said to his instructor, "No male today could get away with saying some of the things the men in that play say." The instructor encouraged Wong to analyze that reaction.

Wong 1

Peter Wong

Professor Minoc

Drama 250

12 December 2000

        Gender Loyalties: A Theme in Trifles

    Susan Glaspell's play Trifles is a study of
character even though the two characters most central to

→

the drama never appear on stage. By excluding Minnie and John Wright from the stage as speaking characters, Glaspell forces us to learn about them through the observations and recollections of the group visiting the farmhouse where the murders of Minnie Wright's canary and of John Wright took place. By indirectly rounding out her main characters, Glaspell invites us to view them not merely as individuals but also as representatives in a conflict between the sexes. This conflict grows throughout the play as characters' emotions and sympathies become increasingly polarized and oriented in favor of their own gender. From this perspective, each of the male characters can be seen to stand for the larger political, legal, and domestic power structures that drive Minnie Wright to kill her husband.

George Henderson's speaking the first line of the play is no accident. Although his power stems from his position as county attorney, Henderson represents the political, more than the legal, sphere. With a job similar to a district attorney's today, he is quite powerful even though he is the youngest person present. He takes control of the action, telling the other characters when to speak and when not to and directing the men in their search for evidence that will establish a motive for the murder. As the person in charge of the investigation, George Henderson orders the other characters about. Mrs. Peters acknowledges his skill at oratory when she predicts that Minnie Wright will be convicted in the wake of his "sarcastic" cross-examination (speech 63).

Glaspell reveals much of the conflict in the play through the heated (but civil) exchanges between George Henderson and Mrs. Hale. His behavior (according to the stage directions, that of a gallant young politician)

→

does not mask his belittling of Minnie Wright and of women in general:

> COUNTY ATTORNEY. I guess before we're through she may have something more serious than preserves to worry about.
>
> HALE. Well, women are used to worrying over trifles. [The two women move a little closer together.]
>
> COUNTY ATTORNEY. [With the gallantry of a young politician.] And yet, for all their worries, what would we do without the ladies? [The women do not unbend. He goes to the sink, takes a dipperful of water from the pail, and pouring it into a basin, washes his hands. Starts to wipe them on the roller-towel, turns it for a cleaner place.] Dirty towels! [Kicks his foot against the pans under the sink.] Not much of a housekeeper, would you say, ladies? (speeches 29–31)

As this excerpt shows, George Henderson seems to hold that a woman's place is in the kitchen, even when she is locked up miles away in the county jail. He shows so much emotion at the discovery of dirty towels in the kitchen that it is almost as if he has found a real piece of evidence that he can use to convict Minnie Wright, instead of an irrelevant strip of cloth. It is apparent that his own sense of self-importance and prejudicial views of women are distracting him from his real business at the farmhouse.

Sheriff Henry Peters, as his title suggests, represents the legal power structure. Like the county attorney, Henry Peters is also quick to dismiss the "trifles" that his wife and Mrs. Hale spend their time discussing while the men conduct a physical search of the premises. His response to the attorney's asking whether he is absolutely certain that the downstairs contains no relevant clues to the motive for the murder is a curt "Nothing here but kitchen things" (speech 25). Ironically, the women are able to reconstruct the entire murder, including the motive, by beginning their inquiries with these same "kitchen things." Sheriff Peters and the other men all completely miss the unfinished quilt, the bird cage, and the dead bird's body. When the sheriff overhears the women talking about the quilt, his instinctive reaction is to ridicule them, saying, "They wonder if she was going to quilt it or just knot it!" (speech 73). Of course, the fact that Minnie Wright was going to knot the quilt is probably the single most important piece of evidence that the group could uncover, since John Wright was strangled with what we deduce is a quilting knot. Although he understands the law, the sheriff seems to know very little about people, and this prevents him from ever cracking this case. His blindness is made clear when he chuckles his assent to the county attorney's observation that Mrs. Peters is literally "married to the law" (speech 145) and therefore beyond suspicion of trying to hinder the case against Minnie Wright. This assumption is completely wrong, for Mrs. Peters joins Mrs. Hale in suppressing the evidence and lying to the men.

Rounding out the male characters is Lewis Hale, a husband and farmer who represents the domestic sphere. Although Lewis Hale may not be an ideal individual, he provides a strong foil for John Wright's character. We might expect Lewis Hale, as Mrs. Hale's spouse, to be a good (or at least a tolerable) person, and, on the whole, he is. Although he, too, misses the significance of the "trifles" in the kitchen and mocks the activities of his wife and Mrs. Peters, he seems less eager than the other men to punish Minnie Wright--possibly because he knew

→

John Wright better than they did. Lewis Hale is clearly
reluctant to provide evidence against Minnie Wright when
he speaks of her behavior after he discovers the body:

> HALE. She moved from that chair to this one
> over here [Pointing to a small chair in the
> corner.] and just sat there with her hands
> held together and looking down. I got
> a feeling that I ought to make some
> conversation, so I said I had come in to
> see if John wanted to put in a telephone,
> and at that she started to laugh, and then
> she stopped and looked at me--scared. [The
> county attorney, who has had his notebook
> out, makes a note.] I dunno, maybe it
> wasn't scared. I wouldn't like to say it
> was. . . . (speech 23)

Lewis Hale is the only man who tries to bring up
the incompatibility in the Wrights' marriage, citing John
Wright's dislike for conversation and adding, "I didn't
know if what his wife wanted made much difference to
John--" (speech 9), but George Henderson cuts him off
before he can pursue this any further. Lewis Hale is a
personable and talkative man--not at all like John
Wright, whom Mrs. Hale likens to "a raw wind that gets
to the bone" (speech 103). Lewis Hale is a social being
who wants to communicate with the people around him, as
his desire for a telephone party line indicates. The
Hales' functional marriage shows that gender differences
need not be insurmountable, but it also serves to
highlight the truly devastating effect that a completely
incompatible union can have on two people's lives. Mrs.
Hale reminds us that even a marriage that "works" can be
dehumanizing:

> MRS. HALE. I might have known she needed
> help! I know how things can be--for women.

→

I tell you it's queer, Mrs. Peters. We live
close together and we live far apart. We
all go through the same things--it's all
just a different kind of the same thing.
(speech 136)

The great irony of the drama is that the women are
able to accomplish what the men cannot: They establish
the motive for the murder. They find evidence suggesting
that John Wright viciously killed his wife's canary--her
sole companion through long days of work around the
house. More important, they recognize the damaging nature
of a marriage based on the unequal status of the
participants. Mrs. Hale and Mrs. Peters decide not to
help the case against Minnie Wright, not because her
husband killed a bird, but because he isolated her, made
her life miserable for years, and cruelly destroyed her
one source of comfort. Without hope of help from the
various misogynistic, paternalistic, and uncomprehending
political, legal, and domestic power structures
surrounding her, Minnie Wright took the law into her own
hands. As the characters of George Henderson, Henry
Peters, and Lewis Hale demonstrate, she clearly could not
expect understanding from the men of her community.

Work Cited

Glaspell, Susan. Trifles. Literature: An Introduction to
Reading and Writing. 4th ed. Ed. Edgar V. Roberts
and Henry E. Jacobs. Englewood Cliffs: Prentice,
1995. 1038-48.

40e.3 Student research paper analyzing two poems

The student essay that follows here is a literary analysis that uses secondary sources.

Born in 1889 on the Caribbean island of Jamaica, Claude McKay moved to the United States in 1910 and became a highly respected poet. Paule Cheek chose to write about Claude McKay's nontraditional use of a very traditional poetic form, the sonnet. A sonnet has fourteen lines in a patterned rhyme and develops one idea. In secondary sources, Cheek found information about McKay's life that she felt gave her further insights into both the structure and the meaning of McKay's sonnets "The White City" and "In Bondage."

Cheek 1

Paule Cheek

Professor Scotia

English 112, Section 03

14 February 2001

Words in Bondage: Claude McKay's

Use of the Sonnet Form in Two Poems

    The sonnet has remained one of the central poetic forms of Western tradition for centuries. This fourteen-line form is easy to learn but difficult to master. With its fixed rhyme schemes, number of lines, and meter, the sonnet form forces writers to be doubly creative while working within it. Many poets over the years have modified or varied the sonnet form, playing upon its conventions to keep it vibrant and original. One such writer was Jamaican-born Claude McKay (1889–1948).

    The Jamaica of McKay's childhood was very different from turn-of-the-century America. Slavery had ended there in the 1830s, and McKay was able to grow up "in a society whose population was overwhelmingly black and largely free of the overt white oppression which constricted the lives of black Americans in the United States during this same period" (Cooper, Passion 5-6). This background could not have prepared McKay for what he

→

encountered when he moved to America in his twenties.
Lynchings, still common at that time, were on the rise,
and during the Red Scare of 1919, there were dozens of
racially motivated riots in major cities throughout the
country. Thousands of homes were destroyed in these
riots, and several black men were tortured and burned at
the stake (Cooper, Claude McKay 97). McKay responded to
these atrocities by raising an outraged cry of protest in
his poems. In two of his sonnets from this period, "The
White City" and "In Bondage," we can see McKay's mastery
of the form and his skillful use of irony in the call
for social change.

McKay's choice of the sonnet form as the vehicle
for his protest poetry at first seems strange. Since his
message was a radical one, we might expect that the form
of his poetry would be revolutionary. Instead, McKay
gives us sonnets--a poetic form that dates back to the
early sixteenth century and was originally intended to be
used exclusively for love poems. Critic James R. Giles
notes that this choice

> is not really surprising, since McKay's
> Jamaican education and reading had been based
> firmly upon the major British poets. From the
> point quite early in his life when he began to
> think of himself as a poet, his models were
> such major English writers as William
> Shakespeare, John Milton, William Wordsworth.
> He thus was committed from the beginning to the
> poetry which he had initially been taught to
> admire. (44)

McKay published both "The White City" and "In
Bondage" in 1922, and they are similar in many ways. Like
most sonnets, each has fourteen lines and is in iambic
pentameter. The diction is extremely elevated. For

→

example, this quatrain from "In Bondage" is almost
Elizabethan in its word choice and order:

> For life is greater than the thousand wars
> Men wage for it in their insatiate lust,
> And will remain like the eternal stars,
> When all that shines to-day is drift and dust.
> (lines 8-12)

If this level of diction is reminiscent of
Shakespeare, it is no accident. Both poems employ the
English sonnet rhyme scheme (a b a b c d c d e f e f
g g) and division into three quatrains and a closing
couplet. McKay introduces a touch of his own, however.
Although the English sonnet form calls for the "thematic
turn" to fall at the closing couplet, McKay defies
convention. He incorporates two turns into each sonnet
instead of one. This allows him to use the first "mini-
turn" to further develop the initial theme set forth in
the first eight lines while dramatically bringing the
poem to a conclusion with a forcefully ironic turn in the
closing couplet. Specifically, in "The White City," McKay
uses the additional turn to interrupt his description of
his "Passion" with a vision of "a mighty city through the
mist" (9). In "In Bondage," he uses the additional turn
to justify his desire to escape the violent existence
that society has imposed on his people.

McKay also demonstrates his poetic ability through
his choice of words within his customized sonnets.
Consider the opening of "In Bondage":

> I would be wandering in distant fields
> Where man, and bird, and beast, lives leisurely,
> And the old earth is kind, and ever yields
> Her goodly gifts to all her children free;
> Where life is fairer, lighter, less demanding,
> And boys and girls have time and space for play

→

Cheek 4

Before they come to years of understanding--

Somewhere I would be singing, far away. (ll. 1-8)

The conditional power of would in the first line,
coupled with the alliterative wandering, subtly charms us
into a relaxed, almost dreamlike state in which the poet
can lead us gently through the rest of the poem. The
commas in the second line force us to check our progress
to a "leisurely" crawl, mirroring the people and animals
that the line describes. By the time we reach the eighth
line, we are probably ready to join the poet in this
land of "somewhere . . . far away."

Then, this optimistic bubble is violently burst by
the closing couplet:

But I am bound with you in your mean graves,

O black men, simple slaves of ruthless slaves.

(ll. 13-14)

In "The White City," McKay again surprises us. This
time, he does so by turning the traditional love sonnet
upside down; instead of depicting a life made unendurable
through an overpowering love, McKay shows us a life made
bearable through a sustaining hate:

I will not toy with it nor bend an inch.

Deep in the secret chambers of my heart

I muse my life-long hate, and without flinch

I bear it nobly as I live my part.

My being would be a skeleton, a shell,

If this dark Passion that fills my every mood,

And makes my heaven in the white world's hell,

Did not forever feed me vital blood. (ll. 1-8)

If it were not for the presence of "life-long hate"
in the third line, this opening would easily pass as part
of a conventional love sonnet. The emotion comes from
"deep in the secret chambers" of the speaker's heart (2),
it allows him to transcend "the white world's hell" (7),

→

and it is a defining "Passion." Once again, however,
McKay uses the couplet to defy our expectations by making
it plain that he has used the form of the love sonnet
only for ironic effect: "The tides, the wharves, the dens
I contemplate, / Are sweet like wanton loves because I
hate" (ll. 13—14).

McKay's impressive poetic ability made him a master
of the sonnet form. His language could at times rival
even Shakespeare's, and his creativity allowed him to
adapt the sonnet to his own ends. His ironic genius is
revealed in his use of one of Western society's most
elevated poetic forms in order to critique that same
society. McKay once described himself as "a man who was
bitter because he loved, who was both right and wrong
because he hated the things that destroyed love, who
tried to give back to others a little of what he had got
from them . . ." (Barksdale and Kinnamon 491). As these two
sonnets show, McKay gave back very much indeed.

→

Cheek 6

Works Cited

Barksdale, Richard, and Kenneth Kinnamon, eds. <u>Black</u>
   <u>Writers of America: A Comprehensive Anthology</u>. New
   York: Macmillan, 1972.

Cooper, Wayne F. <u>Claude McKay: Rebel Sojourner in the</u>
   <u>Harlem Renaissance</u>. Baton Rouge: Louisiana State UP,
   1987.

---, ed. <u>The Passion of Claude McKay</u>. New York: Schocken,
   1973.

Giles, James R. <u>Claude McKay</u>. Boston: Twayne, 1976.

McKay, Claude. "In Bondage." <u>Literature: An Introduction</u>
   <u>to Reading and Writing</u>. 4th ed. Ed. Edgar V. Roberts
   and Henry E. Jacobs. Englewood Cliffs: Prentice,
   1995. 772-73.

---. "The White City." <u>Literature: An Introduction to</u>
   <u>Reading and Writing</u>. 4th ed. Ed. Edgar V. Roberts
   and Henry E. Jacobs. Englewood Cliffs: Prentice,
   1995. 967.

41 WRITING IN THE SOCIAL SCIENCES AND NATURAL SCIENCES

SOCIAL SCIENCES

41a How do I gather information in the social sciences?

The **social sciences** focus on the behavior of people as individuals and in groups. The social science field includes disciplines such as economics, education, geography, political science, psychology, and sociology. At some colleges, history is included in the social sciences; at others, it is part of the humanities.

Observation is a common method for inquiry in the social sciences. To make observations, use whatever tools or equipment you might need: writing utensils, sketching materials, tape recorders, cameras. As you observe, take complete and accurate notes. In a report of your observations, tell what tools or equipment you used, because your method might have influenced what you saw (for example, your taking photographs may make people act differently than is usual for them).

Interviewing is another common method of inquiry that social scientists use. Interviews are useful for gathering people's opinions and impressions of events. If you interview, remember that interviews are not always a completely reliable way to gather factual information, because people's memories are not precise or people's first impulse is to present themselves in the best light. If your only source of factors is interviews, try to interview as many people as possible so that you can cross-check the information.

NOTETAKING ALERTS: (1) If you use abbreviations to speed your notetaking, be sure to write down what they stand for so that you will be able to understand them later when you write up your observations. (2) Before you interview anyone, master any equipment you might need to use so that mechanical problems do not intrude on the interview process (32j). ●

Questionnaires are also a useful method of inquiry in the social sciences. To write questions for a questionnaire, use the guidelines in Box 170. When you give people a questionnaire, be sure to ask enough people so that you do not reach conclusions based on too small a sample of responses.

⊙ **Guidelines for writing questions**   **170**
for a questionnaire

1. Define what you want to find out and then write questions that will elicit the information you seek.
2. Phrase questions so that they are easy to understand.
3. Use appropriate language (21b) and avoid artificial language (21h–21m).
4. Be aware that how you phrase your questions will determine whether the answers that you get truly reflect what people are thinking. Make sure that your choice of words does not imply what you want to hear.
5. Avoid questions that invite one-word answers about complex matters that call for a range of responses.
6. First test a draft of the questionnaire on a small group of people. If any question is misinterpreted or hard to understand, revise and retest it.

41b How can I understand writing purposes and practices in the social sciences?

SUMMARY and SYNTHESIS (5e) are fundamental and important strategies for analytical writing in the social sciences.

ANALYSIS (4i.6 and 5b) helps social scientists write about problems and their solutions. For example, an economist writing about financial troubles in a major automobile company might start by breaking the situation into parts: analyzing employee salaries and benefits, the selling price of cars, and the costs of doing business. Next, the economist might show how these parts relate to the financial health of the whole company. Finally, the economist might suggest how specific changes would help solve the company's financial problems.

Social scientists often also use ANALOGY (4i.9) to make unfamiliar ideas clear. When an unfamiliar idea is compared to one that is more familiar, the unfamiliar idea becomes easier to understand. For example, sociologists may talk of the "culture shock" that some people feel when they enter a new society. The sociologists might compare this shock to the reaction of someone suddenly being moved hundreds of years into the future or the past.

Social scientists are particularly careful to **define their terms** when they write, especially when they discuss complex social issues. For example, if you are writing a paper on substance abuse in the medical profession, you must first define what you mean by the terms *substance abuse* and *medical profession.* Does *substance* mean alcohol and drugs or only drugs? What defines *abuse,* and how do you measure it? By *medical profession,* do you mean nurses and doctors or only doctors? Without defining such terms, you confuse readers or lead them to wrong conclusions.

In college courses in the social sciences, using the FIRST PERSON (*I, we, our*) is acceptable, but only to write about your reactions and experiences. Your goal is usually to be a neutral observer, so most of the time you should use the THIRD PERSON (*he, she, it, one, they*). Some writing in the social sciences overuses the PASSIVE VOICE (8o and 8p). Style manuals for the social sciences, however, recommend the ACTIVE VOICE whenever possible.

41c How can I use documentation style in the social sciences?

If you use SOURCES when writing about the social sciences, you must credit these sources by using DOCUMENTATION. The most commonly used DOCUMENTATION STYLE in the social sciences is that of the American Psychological Association (APA). APA documentation style uses PARENTHETICAL REFERENCES in the body of a paper and a REFERENCES list at the end of a paper. APA documentation style is described in detail in Chapter 36. You can also find a sample student research paper using APA documentation style in section 36i.2.

The Chicago Manual (CM) style of documentation is sometimes used in the social sciences. CM BIBLIOGRAPHIC NOTE style is described in detail in Chapter 37.

41d How can I write different types of papers in the social sciences?

Case studies and research papers are the two major types of papers written in the social sciences.

41d.1 Writing case studies in the social sciences

A **case study** is an intensive study of one group or individual. If you write a case study, describe situations as a *neutral observer.* Refrain from interpreting them unless your assignment says that you can add your interpretation after your report. Also, always differentiate between fact and opinion (5c.2). For example, you may observe nursing home patients lying in bed on their sides facing the door. Describe exactly what you see: If you interpret or read into this observation that patients are lonely and are watching the door for visitors, you could be wrong. Perhaps medicines are injected in the right hip, and patients are more comfortable lying on their left side, which just happens to put them in a position facing the door. Such work requires FIELD RESEARCH (32j).

A case study is usually presented in a relatively fixed format, but the specific parts and their order vary. Most case studies contain the following components: (1) basic identifying information about the individual or group; (2) a history of the individual or group; (3) observations of the individual's or group's behavior; and (4) conclusions and, perhaps, recommendations as a result of the observations.

41d.2 Writing research papers in the social sciences

RESEARCH PAPERS in the social sciences can be based on your FIELD RESEARCH (41d.1 on case studies; 32j and 41a on interviews and questionnaires). Also, and more often for students, social science research paper writing can require that you consult SECONDARY SOURCES (see Chapters 33 and 34, especially 33g on using specialized reference books and 33i.2 on using specialized indexes). These sources are usually articles and books that report, summarize, and otherwise discuss the findings of other people's research. You can find a sample of a student research paper using secondary sources, written for an introductory psychology course, in Chapter 36.

NATURAL SCIENCES

41e How do I gather information in the sciences?

The **natural sciences** include disciplines such as astronomy, biology, chemistry, geology, and physics. The sciences focus on natural phenomena. Scientists form and test **hypotheses,** which are, assumptions made to prove their logical soundness and consequences in the real world. They do this to explain CAUSE AND EFFECT (5h) as systematically and objectively as possible.

The **scientific method,** commonly used in the sciences to make discoveries, is a procedure for gathering information related to a specific hypothesis. The scientific method is the cornerstone of all inquiry in the sciences. Guidelines for using the scientific method are presented in Box 171 on the next page.

◉ **Guidelines for using the scientific method**   171

1. Formulate a tentative explanation—known as a *hypothesis*—for a scientific phenomenon. Be as specific as possible.
2. Read and summarize previously published information related to your hypothesis.
3. Plan and outline a method of investigation to uncover the information needed to test your hypothesis.
4. Experiment, exactly following the investigative procedures you have outlined.
5. Observe closely the results of the experiment, and write notes carefully.
6. Analyze the results. If they prove the hypothesis to be false, rework the investigation and begin again. If the results confirm the hypothesis, say so.
7. Write a report of your research. At the end, you can suggest additional hypotheses that might be investigated.

41f What are writing purposes and practices in the natural sciences?

Because scientists usually write to inform their AUDIENCES about factual information, SUMMARY and SYNTHESIS are fundamental, important techniques (5e).

Exactness is extremely important in scientific writing. Readers expect precise descriptions of procedures and findings, free of personal biases. Scientists expect to be able to *replicate*—repeat step by step—the experiment or process the researcher carried out and obtain the same outcome.

Completeness is as important as exactness in scientific writing. Without complete information, a reader can misunderstand the writer's message and reach a wrong conclusion. For example, a researcher investigating how plants grow in different types of soil needs to report all these facts: an analysis of each soil type, the amount of daylight exposure for each plant, the soil's moisture content, the type and amount of fertilizer used, and all other related facts. By including all this information, the researcher tells the reader how the conclusion in the written report was founded in the experiment or analysis. Specifically, in the soil example just described, plant growth turns out to depend on a combination of soil type, fertilizer, and watering.

Because science writing depends largely on objective observation, rather than subjective comments, scientists generally avoid using the FIRST PERSON (*I, we, our*) in their writing. Another reason to avoid the first person is that the sciences generally focus on the experiment rather than on the person doing the experimenting.

When writing for the sciences, you are often expected to follow fixed formats, which are designed to summarize a project and present its results efficiently. In your report, organize the information to achieve clarity and precision. Writers in the sciences sometimes use charts, graphs, tables, diagrams, and other illustrations to present material. In fact, illustrations in many cases can explain complex material more clearly than can words.

41g How do I use documentation style in the natural sciences?

If you use SECONDARY SOURCES when you write about the sciences, you are required to credit your sources by using DOCUMENTATION. DOCUMENTATION STYLES in the various sciences differ somewhat. Ask your instructor which style you should use.

The Council of Biology Editors (CBE) has compiled style and documentation guidelines for the life sciences, the physical sciences, and mathematics in *Scientific Style and Format: The CBE Manual for Authors, Editors, and Publishers* (6th edition, 1994). CBE documentation guidelines are described in sections 37c and 37d.

41h How do I write different types of papers in the natural sciences?

Two major types of papers in the sciences are reports and reviews.

41h.1 Writing science reports

Science reports tell about observations and experiments; such reports may also be called *laboratory reports* when they describe laboratory experiments. Formal reports feature the eight elements identified in Box 172. Less formal reports, which are sometimes assigned in introductory college courses, might not include an abstract or a review of the literature. Ask your instructor which sections to include in your report.

⊙ **Parts of a science report** 172

1. **Title.** This is a precise description of what your report is about. (Your instructor may require a *title page* that lists the title, your name, the course name and section, your instructor's name, and the date. If so, there is no recommended format in CBE style; generally, students use APA format [36i.2] or their instructor's.)

2. **Abstract.** This is a short overview of the report. Readers may review this to decide whether or not your research is of interest to them.

3. **Introduction.** This section states the purpose behind your research and presents the hypothesis. Any needed background information and a review of the literature appear here.

4. **Methods and Materials.** This section describes the equipment, material, and procedures used.

5. **Results.** This section provides the information obtained from your efforts. Charts, graphs, and photographs help present the data in a way that is easy for readers to grasp.

6. **Discussion.** This section presents your interpretation and evaluation of the results. Did your efforts support your hypothesis? If not, can you suggest why not? Use concrete evidence in discussing your results.

7. **Conclusion.** This section lists conclusions about the hypothesis and the outcomes of your efforts, with particular attention given to any theoretical implications that can be drawn from your work. Be specific in suggesting further research.

8. **Cited References.** This list presents references cited in the review of the literature, if any. Its format conforms to the requirements of the documentation style in the particular science that is your subject.

Sample student science report

The sample student report here is by Adam Furman, a student in an introductory course in biology. The report follows APA format for margins, page numbering, and title page. The text and references follow CBE-style recommendations.

Effectiveness 1

The Effectiveness of Common Antibiotics
(ABSTRACT OMITTED)
Introduction

The purpose of this experiment was to test the effectiveness of antibiotics against two common bacteria.

Antibiotics are substances that inhibit life processes of bacteria. There are two types of antibiotics. One interferes with cell wall synthesis, causing death. The other disrupts protein synthesis, thus preventing replication.

~~Escherichia coli~~ is a gram-negative bacterium. It is found in the colon of many mammals, including humans. Commonly, it contaminates beef and chicken products. ~~Staphylococcus epidermidis~~ is a gram-positive bacterium found naturally on the skin. This bacterium is often the cause of infected burns and cuts. Both bacteria were used in this experiment.

It is hypothesized that five chemical antibiotics will be effective against both bacteria. Also hypothesized is that two natural antimicrobials, Echinacea and garlic, would not work very well.

Methods and Materials

Using aseptic techniques, two petri dishes were inoculated. ~~Staphylococcus epidermidis~~ was used on one dish and ~~Escherichia coli~~ on a second dish. A sterile paper disc was saturated with Streptomycin. The disc was placed on one of the dishes. The process was repeated for the other dish. Both dishes were marked with identification and location of the paper discs. Each of the following was also saturated on paper discs and placed into its own zone on both dishes: sterile water (control), Ampicillin, Erythromycin, Chloramphenicol, Tetracycline, Gentamycin, Echinacea, and garlic.

The dishes were incubated overnight at room temperature. The zone of inhibition of growth in centimeters was measured and recorded.

→

Results

Streptomycin, a protein synthesis disrupter, worked effectively to prevent growth of the S. epidermidis and the E. coli. Tetracycline inhibited the reproduction of the S. epidermidis and the E. coli. Ampicillin, a common bactericide, worked better on the S. epidermidis than the E. coli, because the S. epidermidis is gram positive and the E. coli is gram negative. Gentamycin effectively prevented the growth of E. coli. Erythromycin and Chloramphenicol behaved similarly to the Ampicillin.

The antibiotics behaved as expected in regard to effectiveness against gram-positive and gram-negative bacteria. As hypothesized, the Echinacea inhibited growth only slightly, indicating that it probably would not function as an antibiotic. The garlic had a zone of inhibition greater than expected for a non-antibiotic. Zero centimeters of inhibition from the sterile water control demonstrates that there was no contamination of the experiment.

(DISSUSSION SECTION OMITTED)

Conclusion

The results imply that the Ampicillin would be an effective treatment against ~~S. epidermidis~~ infection and Gentamycin would prove effective in treating an infection of ~~E. coli.~~

As with any experiment, it would be wise to repeat the tests again to check for accuracy. Other antibiotics could be tested against a larger range of bacteria for broader results.

41h.2 Writing science reviews

A **science review** is a paper discussing published information on a scientific topic or issue. The purpose of the review is SUMMARY: to assemble for readers all the current knowledge about the topic or issue. Sometimes, the purpose of a science review is SYNTHESIS: to suggest a new interpretation of the old material. Reinterpretation combines the older views with new and more complete or more compelling information. In such reviews, the writer must present evidence to persuade readers that the new interpretation is valid.

If you are required to write a science review, you should (1) choose a very limited scientific issue currently being researched; (2) use information that is current—the more recently published the articles, books, and journals you consult, the better; (3) accurately PARAPHRASE and summarize material (31d and 31e); and (4) DOCUMENT your sources (Chapters 35–37). If your review runs longer than two or three pages, you might want to use headings to help your reader understand the organization and idea progression of your paper. See Chapters 32–34 for advice on finding sources.

www.prenhall.com/troyka

42 BUSINESS AND PUBLIC WRITING

Business and public writing start where writing in all other disciplines does, with thinking about your PURPOSE and your AUDIENCE. This chapter explains routine BUSINESS WRITING, that is, how to write typical business correspondence—letters, memos, resumes, job application letters, and e-mail messages. The second part of the chapter discusses types of PUBLIC WRITING, writing intended for members of your community, for the community as a whole, or for public officials. Box 173 gives you general guidelines for business and public writing.

◉ **Guidelines for business and public writing**   173

- Consider your audience's needs and expectations.
- Have a clear purpose. Understand the context for your communication.
- Put essential information first.
- Make your points clearly and directly.
- Use conventional formats.

BUSINESS WRITING

42a How do I write and format a business letter?

Business letters give information, build goodwill, or establish a foundation for discussions or transactions. Experts in business and government agree that the letters likely to get results are short, simple, direct, and human. Here is basic advice: (1) Address the person by name; (2) tell what your letter is about in the first paragraph; (3) be honest; (4) be clear and specific; (5) use correct EDITED AMERICAN ENGLISH; (6) be positive and natural; and (7) edit ruthlessly. Also keep the following points in mind when writing a business letter:

- **Format:** Select block style (in which all lines begin at the left margin) or modified block style (lines for inside address and body begin at left margin; heading, closing, and signature begin about halfway across the page).

- **Paper:** Use only 8 1/2-by-11-inch paper. The most professional colors are white or very light beige.

- **Letterhead:** When writing from a company, use its official letterhead. If you're writing on your own behalf, use or create your own letterhead. Center your full name, address, and phone number at the top of the page. Use a larger size font than you use for the content of the letter. Avoid any font that is fancy or loud when your letter carries a serious message, such as following up on a meeting, relaying information, requesting information, making a complaint, or writing to the editor of a newspaper or magazine. (If you do not prepare a personal letterhead, your heading is part of the block or modified style indicated above.)

- **Name of recipient:** Be as specific as possible. An exact name (or at least a specific category of people) tells readers you have taken the time to do some research. If you use a category, place the key word first: For example, use "Billing Department," not "Department of Billing." Try to avoid using "To Whom It May Concern," which implies you expect the person who receives the letter to do the work of figuring out the specific recipient. Such letters are often ignored. See Box 174 for ways to avoid sexist or otherwise inappropriate salutations.

- **Spacing:** Use single spacing except between paragraphs.

- **Content:** Write using CONCISE and clear language. Explain your purpose in the beginning. Check that your information is accurate and that it includes all relevant facts. Never repeat yourself, and keep your entire message as evenhanded in TONE as possible. You can express disappointment or make a complaint without using inflammatory language. A reasonable approach always gets the best results.

- **Tone:** Use a medium LEVEL OF FORMALITY in word choice and style, unless you're certain that INFORMAL LANGUAGE is appropriate.

- **Final copy:** Proofread carefully. Your neat, error-free letter reflects well on you and your company or organization. Also your reader is more likely to read it.

In a business letter, always use GENDER-NEUTRAL LANGUAGE in the salutation (the opening "To" or "Dear"). If you don't know the specific person to whom you need to address your letter, take the steps listed in Box 174; see also 21g.

⊙ Writing a gender-neutral salutation   174

1. Telephone the company to which you are sending the letter. State your reason for sending the letter and ask for the name of the person who should receive it.
2. Do not address the person by first name. For a man, use *Mr.* or another appropriate title. For a woman, use *Ms.* or another appropriate title, unless you are specifically told to use *Miss* or *Mrs.* or another title such as *Dr.*
3. If you use a title alone instead of a name, keep the title generic and gender-neutral.

NO   Dear Sir: [obviously sexist]
     Dear Sir or Madam: [*Madam* is an out-of-date term, and few women like its connotation]

YES   Dear Human Resources Officer:
     Dear IBM Sales Manager:

The sample envelope below and sample business letter on the opposite page are models of typical formats you can use.

```
Jan Dubitz
742 Lincoln Hall
Northeast College
2038 Washington Blvd.
Chicago, IL 60312
```

ENVELOPE: Fold letter in thirds horizontally and insert in an appropriate-size envelope. Place your return address in the upper left corner and the mailing address in the middle of the envelope.

```
Ms. Yolanda Harper
Abco Rental Company
1249 Logan Rd.
Chicago, IL 60312
```

Sample envelope

Jan Dubitz
742 Lincoln Hall Northeast College
2038 Washington Blvd.
Chicago, IL 60312
(210) 555-3723

September 14, 2000

▲
4 spaces
▼

Ms. Yolanda Harper
Abco Rental Company
1249 Logan Rd.
Chicago, IL 60312

SALUTATION: Use an appropriate title (*Mr., Ms., Dr., Professor*) and the person's name. If you do not know the name, use a title (*Dean of Students, Human Resources Coordinator*). Add a colon at the end of the salutation.

Dear Ms. Harper:

▲
2 spaces
▼

I rented a refrigerator from your company on August 27. After only two weeks, the freezer compartment no longer keeps food frozen. Per the rental agreement, this is my written request for a replacement refrigerator. The agreement states that you will replace the refrigerator within five business days from the receipt of my letter.

I will call you next week to arrange the exchange. Thank you for your prompt attention.

Sincerely,

CLOSING: Capitalize only the first word (*Yours truly, Sincerely yours*) and follow with a comma.

4 spaces *Jan Dubitz*

SIGNATURE: If you have a title, type it underneath your name. Sign letter in space above your name.

Jan Dubitz

Enc: Copy of rental agreement

OTHER: Use *Enc:* or *Enclosure:* if you include material *with* your letter. Use *cc:* to indicate that you have sent any courtesy copies.

Sample business letter

42b How do I write a memo?

Memos can be sent on paper or via e-mail. Readers need to quickly determine the importance of a memo by reading the headings at the top. A memo from a supervisor asking for sales figures will receive prompt attention, whereas a memo from the office manager about new forms for ordering supplies probably will not receive a careful reading until it is time to order more supplies.

The AUDIENCE for a memo is usually "local." For example, in the workplace, local audiences can be senior management, other levels of supervisors or managers, people at your level, all employees, or customers. Other audiences can be people who share interests (religious, political, or leisure-time groups) or causes (environment, education, or health care). Be as specific as possible in naming your memo's audience.

Memos are written to give new information; SUMMARIZE, clarify, or SYNTHESIZE known information; put information officially on the record; make a request or suggestion; and record recent activities and outcomes. Most word processing software provides formats for memos. For example, in versions of Microsoft Word™, you can click on "File" on the Menu bar, then "New," then "Memo." Select the style you want—"Professional" is a good choice for workplace use. A memo has the following parts:

- **Headings:**

  TO: [Your audience, named as specifically as possible]

  FROM: [Your name]

  DATE: [Month, day, and year you're writing]

  SUBJECT: [Memo's topic, concisely stated]

- **Contents:**

  Introductory paragraph: State the memo's purpose and give needed background information.

  Body paragraph(s): State the point you are making in the memo and why it's worth readers' time. Or, as the sample memo on the opposite page shows, give the data required.

  Conclusion: End with a one- or two-sentence summary or with a specific recommendation. If the memo is short, like the sample memo on the opposite page, end either with instructions or a thank-you line.

One or at most two pages is the expected length of a memo. If you need more pages, you are writing a report (see 42f).

TO: English Teaching Assistants
FROM: Professor Thomas Nevers, Director,
           First-Year Composition
DATE: December 1, 2001
SUBJECT: New Computer Programs

Several new writing programs will be installed
in the English computer labs. Training sessions
are scheduled during the week before classes begin
next semester.

      Tuesday, January 8   9:00-11:00 a.m.

      Wednesday, January 9   1:00-3:00 p.m.

      Thursday, January 10   8:30-10:30 a.m.

      Friday, January 11   1:30-3:30 p.m.

Please stop by my office by December 12 to sign up
for one of the two-hour workshops.

Sample memo

42c How do I create a resume?

A **resume** details your employment experience, education, and other accomplishments for a potential employer. Since your resume will be compared to those of numerous other applicants, take time to make a favorable impression. Format your resume so it is easy to read and include only information relevant to the position for which you are applying. A worksheet to help you think through what to say, and not say, in a resume appears on pages 750–751. Proofread the document for accuracy and ask others to review it for clarity.

Follow the guidelines below for writing a resume; also, examine the sample on the facing page. A helpful Web site for writing resumes is <http://www.umn.edu/ohr/ecep/resume/>.

- Use the Resume Worksheet on pages 750–751 to draft your resume.
- Adjust the emphasis in your resume to fit your purpose: For a job as a computer programmer, you need to emphasize different facts about yourself than if you were applying to be a retail salesperson.
- Fit all information on one page by stressing what will interest your potential employer. If you must use a second page, put the most important information on the first page.
- Use clear headings to separate blocks of information.
- Under the headings, write telegram-style. Start with verb phrases, not with the word *I;* also omit *a, an, the.* Write, for example, "Created new computer program to organize company's spreadsheets," not "*I* created *a* new computer program to organize *the* company's spreadsheets."
- Put the most recent item first in each category.
- Don't pad entries with irrelevant information or wordy writing.
- *Never* lie.
- Include references or state that you can provide them "upon request" (and have them ready to go).
- Print your resume on high-quality, white or very light beige paper.
- *Multilingual writers:* For a job in the United States, do not include personal information that may be expected in other countries. For example, do not give your age, marital status, or religion.

Margaret Lorentino
1338 Sunflower Lane
Rochelle, IL 61068
(815) 555-3756

OBJECTIVE: Seeking a full/part-time position as a medical transcriptionist to utilize my medical, computer, and office skills

EDUCATION: Certificate of Completion, Medical Transcription
Kishwaukee College, Malta, IL, December 2000
Bachelor of Science, Marketing
Northern Illinois University, DeKalb, IL, May 2000
Associate in Arts; Studied Nursing and Business
Harper Junior College, Palatine, IL, December 1987

EMPLOYMENT: Kishwaukee College, Malta, IL, January 2000–Present
Lab Assistant and Computer Skills Teacher
RTD Real Estate, Muncie, IN, August 1994–August 1995
Receptionist, Accounting Assistant
Northwestern Mutual Life, Schaumburg, IL,
May 1991–July 1992
Sales Assistant
Reliable Personnel, Park Ridge, IL, May 1990–May 1991
Temporary Employment Manager

SKILLS: Computer
- Experienced with Microsoft Office 2000 and WordPerfect
- Type 60 wpm
- Have experience with Lotus, Excel, and Access
- Teach WordPerfect and basic computer skills in first-year college English classes

Organizational
- Girl Scout leader, soccer coach, Sunday school teacher
- Trained employees in data entry and accounting principles
- Managed a temporary workforce of 20–30 employees

REFERENCES: Available upon request

Sample resume

RESUME WORKSHEET

Photocopy and fill in this resume worksheet to help you create your own resume.

(Name) _____

(Address) _____

(City, State, Zip) _____

(Home Telephone) _____

(Work Telephone) _____

(Fax Number, if one) _____

(E-mail Address) _____

Position Desired or Career Objective _____
_____
_____

[Include below only if relevant and meaningful; add more lines in a category, as necessary.]

Education (most recent education first)

1. (Degree or Certificate) _____ (Dates) _____
   (Institution) _____
   (Major or Area of Concentration) _____

2. (Degree or Certificate) _____ (Dates) _____
   (Institution) _____
   (Major or Area of Concentration) _____

Experience (most recent experience first)

1. (Job Title) _____ (Dates) _____
   (Employer) _____
   (Responsibilities and Accomplishments) _____
   _____
   _____

2. (Job Title) _____ (Dates) _____
   (Employer) _____
   (Responsibilities and Accomplishments) _____
   _____
   _____

License or Certification, if any (nursing, accounting, massage therapy, etc.)

1. (License) _____ (Dates) _____
   (Issuing Agency) _____

2. (License) _____ (Dates) _____
   (Issuing Agency) _____

Related Experience

(Description) _____ (Dates) _____
(Organization or Company) _____
(Duties/Accomplishments) _____

Honors/Awards, if any

_____

_____

_____

Publications/Presentations, if any

_____ (Dates) _____
_____ (Dates) _____

Activities/Interests (clubs, organizations, volunteer work)

_____

_____

_____

Special Abilities, Skills, Knowledge (languages, computer, travel)

_____

_____

_____

References (personal, professional)

_____

_____

_____

42d How do I compose a job application letter?

A job application letter always needs to accompany your resume. Avoid simply repeating what is already in the resume. Acquaint yourself with available descriptions of the position and its responsibilities and connect the company's expectations and your experience. Highlight how your background has prepared you for this position. Here are guidelines.

- Use one page only.
- Use the same name, content, and format guidelines as for a business letter (42a).
- Open by identifying the position you are applying for.
- Address the letter to a specific person. If you cannot get a name, use a title (e.g., "Human Resources Coordinator"). Avoid using "To Whom It May Concern" (42a).
- Think of your letter as a polite sales pitch about you. Don't be shy, but don't exaggerate what you can do for the company if you get the job.
- Explain how your background will meet the requirements of the job at this workplace in particular.
- Stress your qualifications for the position.
- If the job will be your first, give your key attributes—if they are relevant and true—such as that you are punctual, self-disciplined, a "team player," eager to learn and to work hard for the company.
- State when you're available for an interview and also how you can be reached.
- Edit and proofread carefully. Even one misspelled word can hurt your chances.

The sample letter on page 753 is by Margaret Lorentino, a mother with young children, who seeks a position that would allow her to work at home. She is responding to a newspaper ad for a medical transcription position. The format is modified block style.

1338 Sunflower Lane
Rochelle, IL 61068
December 1, 2000

Ms. Arlene Chang
Employment Coordinator
Rockford Medical Center
820 N. Main St.
Rockford, IL 61103

Dear Ms. Chang:

I had a chance to talk with you last spring about your company at the Kishwaukee College Job Fair. I am very interested in the medical transcription position that I noticed in the Rockford Register Star on November 29.

I will be completing my Medical Transcription Certificate at the end of December. I have taken courses in medical transcription, medical office procedures, and keyboarding, as well as numerous computer courses. I have a bachelor's degree in marketing from Northern Illinois University and also studied nursing for almost a year at Harper Junior College. I believe that this background would help me in this position.

The enclosed resume will give you the details of my experience and qualifications. I think that my experience and education make a great combination for this position. I am available for an interview at your convenience. My home phone number is (815) 555-3756.

Sincerely yours,

Margaret Lorentino

Margaret Lorentino

Sample job application letter

42e What are guidelines for writing e-mail?

E-mail stands for "electronic mail." Today, a great deal of business and local communication is conducted by e-mail. Though e-mail is less formal than a letter, certain conventions still apply, as follows:

- Write a subject in the Subject box to tell your reader the topic.
- Single-space within paragraphs; double-space between paragraphs.
- Do not use ALL CAPITALS. They are hard to read and generally considered the written equivalent of shouting.
- Use bulleted or numbered lists when itemizing.
- Keep your message brief and your paragraphs short. (Reading a screen is harder on the eyes than reading from a printed document, so people have a tendency to skim e-mail.)
- Be cautious what you say in an e-mail. It can be forwarded to others without your permission, although this practice is unethical. Never give personal information to strangers. Never give credit information on a nonsecure site.
- Forward an e-mail message *only* if you ask the original sender for permission.
- Check your document to make sure your message is clear, your TONE is appropriate, and spelling, grammar, and punctuation are correct.
- Use "emoticons" only if you are sure the reader appreciates them. :-) Some people do not. :-(
- Never "flame" (make personal attacks on others).
- Never "spam" (send unsolicited, or "junk," mail).

For longer documents, such as academic papers, you can compose in a word processing program and then attach the document to an e-mail message to be sent to your instructor or others. Attached documents look better because they maintain original formatting (margins, spacing, italics). One word of caution: Be sure your intended recipient will be able to download your attached file.

In the sample e-mail on the facing page, a reporter is writing to MP3 users on a listserv (Internet discussion group) for the first time.

PUBLIC WRITING

In addition to ACADEMIC WRITING and BUSINESS WRITING, you may also find occasion to do **public writing**—writing addressed either to members of your community, the community as a whole, or public officials. Writing for the public can include a letter to the editor of a newspaper or

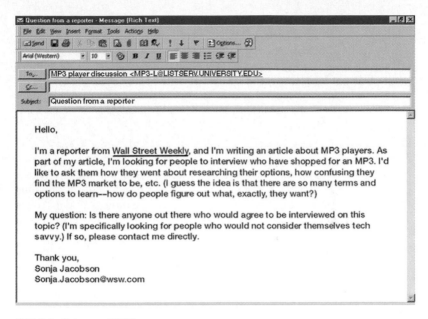

E-Mail to listserv of MP3 users

magazine or to your congressional representative. You might write a newspaper article to publicize a local theater group or a proposal to your town government for building a park at the site of a burned-down warehouse. On the Internet, you might post a book review on a bookseller's Web site or a message about an upcoming concert to a newsgroup.

In all of these examples—and you could add many more of your own—you are writing for an AUDIENCE you do not know personally and one that does not know you. You are also discussing subjects that you think affect others, not just you alone. For these reasons, public writing requires that you take special care in analyzing your audience and establishing your credibility.

In a piece of public writing, "establishing credibility" means convincing your readers that they should listen to you. You do this by knowing the answers to some key questions: Do you have something in common with them? Does your experience make you a reputable source? or, Have you done research to become a knowledgeable source? Can you cite other authorities who agree with your perspective?

For example, if you are writing a letter to the editor of your local newspaper, you will gain credibility if you begin, "As a resident of Green County for 12 years" and then go on to give your opinion. By establishing yourself first as a member of your audience's community, you convey that you have a sincere and long-standing interest in the welfare of that community. Or suppose you are writing to ask one of your state senators to support a bill for a new wildlife refuge. You might present your argument on the basis of your research into the benefits and drawbacks of setting aside the land. In this way, you make yourself credible by demonstrating that you understand the complexities of the issue.

The following sections describe three common types of public writing: reports, letters to the editor, and letters to political representatives.

42f How do I write reports for the public?

Reports for the public vary in length, format, and content. An "action brief" from a political organization might consist of a few pages detailing recent developments on an issue of concern. A "technology update" from a local association of people with a shared, specialized hobby might contain news of technological advances, along with critical reviews and, perhaps, information where to purchase each item. A report to a journal read mainly by those in a certain profession may take up an issue or methodology currently being debated.

Write your material in an evenhanded TONE so that your credibility is supported by your fairness. If you take a critical stance (see Chapter 5), be sure it's well reasoned and supported and that it lacks bias or malice toward a person (or persons) or specific ideas. None of this means your writing style needs to be limp. Choose nonbiased language (21g) that is spirited, enthusiastic, and even stirring.

To write a report, follow the guidelines in Box 175.

◉ **Writing a public report**   **175**

■ Decide how far to go in your report. Will you only inform, or will you also analyze the information you present? Or—going one step further—will you make a recommendation based on the information and your analysis?

■ State your findings in an objective tone of voice. Though you may later bring in your opinion by interpreting the data or recommending a course of action, your credibility depends on first reporting accurately.

■ A formal report usually follows the organization listed below. Depending on the purpose of your report, however, you might combine or expand any of the sections.

   • **Introduction:** Explains the purpose of the report or describes the problem studied; often outlines the organization of the entire report

→

Writing a public report *(continued)* **175**

- **Methods:** Describes how the data were gathered
- **Results:** Presents the findings of the report
- **Discussion:** States the implications of your findings
- **Conclusion:** Makes recommendations or simply summarize the findings

---

The following excerpt is the introduction to a report on teaching in a foreign country. The entire report, which follows the organization described in Box 175, appeared in a journal for teachers, called *Teaching of Psychology.*

Teaching Psychology in Estonia*

Lawrence T. White
Beloit College

Sarah Ransdell
Florida Atlantic University

Many lessons learned abroad also apply at home. In that spirit, we report the lessons we learned. . . . We describe our experiences as teachers of psychology in Estonia and discuss some of the benefits that teachers reap when they become more aware of themselves and their audiences.

From August 1997 to January 1998, we were privileged to teach in the Republic of Estonia as part of the Fulbright scholars program. As teachers of psychology in a foreign country, we gained experience and learned lessons that we want to share with other teachers of psychology. In this article, we aim to achieve two goals: (a) describe our experiences as teachers of psychology in Estonia and (b) discuss some of the benefits teachers reap when they become more aware of themselves and their audiences.

The Soviet Union occupied Estonia between 1940 and 1991. Under Soviet rule, Estonia's connections to Western psychology were formally severed—individuals were not allowed to buy Western books, libraries were not allowed to subscribe to Western periodicals. . . .

* From "Teaching Psychology in Estonia," by L.T. White and S. Ransdell, 2000, *Teaching Psychology, 27,* p. 217. Copyright © 2000 by Lawrence Erlbaum Associates, Inc. Reprinted with permission.

42g How do I write letters to my community or its representatives?

Letters to your community include letters to editors of newspapers and magazines, statements of position for a local or national newsletter, and material you self-publish (Chapter 38). Such letters allow you to participate in a discussion with a community of peers. When writing in response to a particular piece of writing in the same publication, always begin by referring precisely to what you are responding to.

In the following example, a resident of Brooklyn, New York, argues for preserving a museum building.

To the Editor:

Re "City Museum Plans to Move Downtown" (news article, Dec. 14):

A museum visit should be a kind of time travel. Certainly the artifacts are from another time, but just as important, the building itself echoes with the footfalls of generations of visitors eager to witness and digest their common history.

The very displays are a reflection of the time when they were conceived. This is why I am heartbroken that the Museum of the City of New York plans to leave its splendid old mansion opposite Central Park's Conservatory Garden.

So little of the city we once knew is still recognizable. Can't we at least preserve the museums?

The 19th-century doll houses and toys, the period rooms, the old fire engine next to restrooms with marble and enamel fixtures, thick wooden doors, brass door handles, the great sweeping staircase with its ironwork—surely there are more of us who would contribute to save this building for its museum and the ghosts of visitors past.

KATHARINE FLANDERS
MUKHERJI
Brooklyn, Dec. 14, 2000

Many letters to the editor propose solutions to a community problem. These letters aim to persuade other readers that a problem exists and that a particular solution is not only feasible but also the most advantageous of all the possible alternatives. Keep the following guidelines in mind when writing to propose a solution:

■ Briefly explain the specific problem you are attempting to solve.

■ Tell how your solution will solve all elements of the problem.

■ Briefly address possible objections or alternatives to your proposed solution.

■ State why your solution offers the most advantages of all the alternatives.

Letters to your civic and political leaders can influence their opinions and actions. You might write in reaction to a proposed law or course of action, to object to an existing law or situation, or to thank or compliment the person for action taken. State your purpose at the outset; be concise; and end by clearly stating what action you request so that a response, if given, can be on-point.

www.prenhall.com/troyka

43 WRITING UNDER PRESSURE

The demands of **writing under pressure** can sometimes seem overwhelming, but if you break the challenge into small, sequential steps and then focus on each step in turn, you can succeed. When you write under the pressure of time constraints, you are expected to write as completely and clearly as possible. If you tend to freeze under pressure, force yourself to take some slow, deep breaths or to use a relaxation technique such as counting backward from ten. When you turn to the task, remember to break the whole into parts so that the process is easier to work through.

Writing answers for essay tests is one of the most important writing tasks that you face in college. Common in all disciplines, including the natural sciences, essay tests demand that you recall information and also put assorted pieces of that information into contexts that lead to GENERALIZATIONS you can support. Essay tests give you the chance to SYNTHESIZE and apply your knowledge, helping your instructor determine what you have learned.

43a What are cue words and key words?

Most essay questions contain what is called a **cue word,** a word of direction that tells what the content of your answer is expected to emphasize. Knowing the major cue words and their meanings can increase your ability to plan efficiently and write effectively. Be guided by the list of cue words and sample essay test questions in Box 176.

⊙ **Cue words found in questions for essay tests   176**

■ *Analyze:* **to separate something into parts and then discuss the parts and their meanings**
Analyze Socrates' discussion of "good life" and "good death."

→

760

Cue words found in questions for essay tests   **176**
(continued)

- *Clarify:* **to make clear, often by giving a definition of a key term and by using examples to illustrate it**
  Clarify T. S. Eliot's idea of tradition.

- *Classify:* **to arrange into groups on the basis of shared characteristics**
  Classify the different types of antipredator adaptations.

- *Compare and contrast:* **to show similarities and differences**
  Compare and contrast the reproductive cycles of a moss and a flowering plant.

- *Criticize:* **to give your opinion concerning the good points and bad points of something**
  Criticize the architectural function of modern football stadiums.

- *Define:* **to state precisely what something is and thereby to differentiate it from similar things**
  Define the term "yellow press."

- *Describe:* **to explain features to make clear an object, procedure, or event**
  Describe the chain of events that constitutes the movement of a sensory impulse along a nerve fiber.

- *Discuss:* **to consider as many elements as possible concerning an issue or event**
  Discuss the effects of television viewing on modern attitudes toward violence.

- *Evaluate:* **to give your opinion about the importance of something**
  Evaluate Margaret Mead's contribution to anthropology.

- *Explain:* **to make clear or intelligible something that needs to be understood or interpreted**
  Explain how the amount of carbon dioxide in the blood regulates rates of heartbeat and breathing.

- *Illustrate:* **to give examples of something**
  Illustrate the use of symbolism in Richard Wright's novel *Native Son.*

→

Cue words found in questions for essay tests   176
(continued)

■ *Interpret:* **to explain the meaning of something**
Give your interpretation of Maxine Kumin's poem "Beans."

■ *Justify:* **to show or prove that something is valid or correct**
Justify the existence of labor unions in today's economy.

■ *Prove:* **to present evidence that cannot be refuted logically or with other evidence**
Prove that smoking is a major cause of lung cancer.

■ *Relate:* **to show the connections between two or more things**
Relate increases in specific crimes in the period 1932–1933 to the prevailing economic conditions.

■ *Review:* **to evaluate or summarize something critically**
Review the structural arrangements in proteins to explain the meaning of the term *polypeptide.*

■ *Show:* **to point out or demonstrate something**
Show what effects pesticides have on the production of wheat.

■ *Summarize:* **to identify the major points of something**
Summarize the major benefits of compulsory education.

■ *Support:* **to argue in favor of something**
Support the position that destruction of rain forests is endangering the planet.

Each essay question also has one or more **key words** that tell you the information, topics, and ideas you are to write about. For example, in the question "Criticize the architectural function of the modern football stadium," the cue word is *criticize,* and the key words are *architectural function* and *football stadium.* To answer the question successfully, you must first define the term *architectural function;* then describe the typical modern football stadium (mentioning major variations when important); and then discuss how well the typical modern football stadium fits your definition of architectural function.

43b How do I write effective responses to essay test questions?

An **effective response** to an essay test question is complete and logically organized. Here are two answers to the question "Classify the different types of antipredator adaptations." The first one is successful; the second is not. The sentences are numbered for your reference, and they are explained in the text.

ANSWER 1

(1) Although many antipredator adaptations have evolved in the animal kingdom, all can be classified into four major categories according to the prey's response to the predator. (2) The first category is hiding techniques. (3) These techniques include cryptic coloration and behavior in which the prey assumes characteristics of an inanimate object or part of a plant. (4) The second category is early enemy detection. (5) The prey responds to alarm signals from like prey or other kinds of prey before the enemy can get too close. (6) Evasion of the pursuing predator is the third category. (7) Prey that move erratically or in a compact group are displaying this technique. (8) The fourth category is active repulsion of the predator. (9) The prey kills, injures, or sickens the predator, establishing that it represents danger to the predator.

ANSWER 2

(1) Antipredator adaptations are the development of the capabilities to reduce the risk of attack from a predator without too much change in the life-supporting activities of the prey. (2) There are many different types of antipredator adaptations. (3) One type is camouflage, hiding from the predator by cryptic coloration or imitation of plant parts. (4) An example of this type of antipredator adaptation is the praying mantis. (5) A second type is the defense used by monarch butterflies, a chemical protection that makes some birds ill after eating the butterfly. (6) This protection may injure the bird by causing it to vomit, and it can educate the bird against eating other butterflies. (7) Detection and evasion are also antipredator adaptations.

Here is an explanation of what happens, sentence by sentence, in the two answers to the question about antipredator adaptations.

SENTENCE	ANSWER 1	ANSWER 2
1	Sets up classification system and gives number of categories based on key word	Defines key word
2	Names first category	Throwaway sentence—accomplishes nothing

SENTENCE	ANSWER 1	ANSWER 2
3	Defines first category	Names and defines first category
4	Names second category	Gives an example for first category
5	Defines second category	Gives an example for second (unnamed) category
6	Names third category	Continues to explain example
7	Defines third category	Names two categories
8	Names fourth category	
9	Defines fourth category	

Answer 1 sets about immediately answering the question by introducing a classification system, as called for by the cue word *classify.* Answer 2, by contrast, defines the key word, a waste of time on a test that will be read by an audience of specialists. Answer 1 is tightly organized, easy to follow, and to the point. Answer 2 rambles, never names the four categories, and says more around the subject than on it.

43c What strategies can I use when writing under pressure?

If you use specific **strategies** when writing under pressure, you can be more comfortable and your writing will likely be more effective. As you use the strategies listed in Box 177, remember that your purpose in answering questions is to show what you know in a clear, direct, and well-organized way. When you are studying for an essay exam, write out one-sentence summaries of major areas of information. This technique helps fix the ideas in your mind, and a summary sentence may become a thesis sentence for an essay answer.

◎ **Strategies for writing essay tests**   **177**

1. Do not start writing immediately.
2. If the test has two or more questions, read them all at the start. Determine whether you are supposed to answer all the questions. Doing this gives you a sense of how to budget your time, either by dividing it equally or by allotting more time for some questions than for others. If you have a choice, select questions about which you know the most and can write about most completely in the time limit.

→

> **Strategies for writing essay tests** *(continued)*   **177**
>
> 3. Analyze each question that you answer by underlining the *cue words* and *key words* (see 43a) to determine exactly what the question asks.
> 4. Use the writing process as much as possible within the constraints of the time limit. Try to allot time to plan and revise. For a one-hour test on one question, take about ten minutes to jot down preliminary ideas about content and organization, and save ten minutes to reread, revise, and edit your answer. If you are pressed suddenly for time—but try to avoid this—consider skipping a question that you cannot answer well or a question that counts less toward your total score. If you feel blocked, try FREEWRITING (see 2g) to get your hand and your thoughts moving.
> 5. Support any GENERALIZATIONS with specifics (see 4f about using the formula RENNS for being specific).
> 6. Beware of going off the topic. Respond to the cue words and key words in the question, and do not try to reshape the question to conform to what you might prefer to write about. Remember, your reader expects a clear line of presentation and reasoning that answers the stated question.

The more you use the strategies in the box and adapt them to your personal needs, the better you will use them to your advantage. Try to practice them, make up questions that might be on your test, and time yourself as you write the answers. Doing this offers you another benefit: If you study by anticipating possible questions and writing out the answers, you will be very well prepared if one or two of them show up on the test.

EXERCISE 43-1

Look back at an essay that you have written under time pressure. Read it over and decide whether you would change the content of your answer or the strategies you used as you were writing under pressure. List these specific strategies, and if you think they were useful, add them to Box 177.

44 ORAL PRESENTATIONS

Preparing an **oral presentation** and writing an essay involve some of the same processes. In each, you determine your PURPOSE, analyze your AUDIENCE, and work to deliver a clear, controlling idea. This chapter will help you move from written to oral delivery and show you how to use what you know about writing to prepare effective oral presentations. You will also learn about the special considerations that apply to speaking, instead of writing, your thoughts.

PREPARING AN ORAL PRESENTATION

44a How do I determine my purpose and topic?

Just as writing purposes change from one situation to the next, so do speaking purposes. You might address students living in your dorm to *inform* them about a film club you are starting on Monday nights. You might try to *persuade* the history department or registrar to transfer credits from a class you took overseas. The toast you give at a friend's wedding is meant, in part, to *entertain* the wedding guests.

In the academic setting, to inform and to persuade are the most common PURPOSES: To *inform* is to help your audience understand something; to *persuade* is to influence the attitudes and behaviors of your audience.

With a general purpose in mind, you are ready to think about your TOPIC. Sometimes your topic will be assigned, but if not, follow these guidelines: Select a topic that you care about and that your audience will care about also. Choose one that you either already know about or that you can learn about in the time you have to prepare. Be sure you can do justice to your topic within the time constraints of the presentation itself.

Now, narrow your topic to the one main point you want to make, and state the specific purpose of your speech. Write your specific purpose as an INFINITIVE PHRASE: *to inform about . . . , to convince that . . . , to show how . . . , to explain why . . .* Use specific terms and precise language.

44b How do I adapt my message to my audience?

To determine how best to approach your TOPIC, consider your AUDI-ENCE and adapt your message accordingly. Begin by asking yourself these questions: How much does my audience already know about this topic? What terms and concepts will they not know? What information must I provide as a foundation for my message? Does my audience have a particular bias toward my topic that I need to consider?

Based on your responses to these questions, you will probably find that your audience falls into one of three categories: *uninformed, informed,* or *mixed.* Box 178 offers help in adapting your message to each type of audience.

 Adapting oral presentations to the audience   178

Uninformed Audience

Limit the number of new ideas you present. Use visual aids to establish the basics, avoiding technical terms as much as possible. Define new terms and concepts. Repeat key ideas and use vivid examples.

Informed Audience

Do not waste their time with the basics, but introduce new ideas and concepts. From the beginning, reassure them that you will be covering new ground.

Mixed Audience

Start with simple concepts and move toward more complex ones. In the introduction, acknowledge the presence of the more informed members of the audience and explain that you are only reviewing the basics so that everyone can build from the same knowledge base.

Adapting your presentation to the general needs and expectations of your audience does not mean catering to their views and saying only what they might want to hear. It means rather that you need to consider their knowledge of your topic and their interest in it. You can then make your message understandable and relevant by using appropriate language and examples.

44c   How do I formulate a working thesis?

As with the THESIS STATEMENT of an essay, the **working thesis** for an oral presentation makes clear the main idea and the speaker's PURPOSE. It also reflects the speaker's AUDIENCE analysis in its content (neither too sophisticated nor too simple) and its language (the word choice is at the right level). In addition, a working thesis is a practical preparation step because it helps you stay on your topic, and it introduces and connects the key concepts of your presentation.

Box 179 demonstrates how a student speaking on infertility worked from a general purpose and topic to arrive at a specific purpose and working thesis.

⊙   **Formulating a working thesis**   **179**

GENERAL PURPOSE	To inform
TOPIC	"infertility"
SPECIFIC PURPOSE	To explain medical advancements in the treatment of infertility
WORKING THESIS	The sorrow of infertility is becoming a thing of the past for many couples thanks to medical procedures such as donor insemination, in vitro fertilization, and egg harvesting.

44d   How do I organize my presentation?

When you have compiled the information you will use in your oral presentation, develop an organizational outline. An **organizational outline** shows the three-part structure of an oral presentation—introduction, body, conclusion—and lists major points (as lettered headings) with two to three supporting points (as numbered subheadings). Use sentences for your main points to sharpen your thinking as you DRAFT. Box 180 presents a typical organizational outline.

⊙ **Organizational outline for an oral**   180
    presentation

Title

General purpose:

Topic:

Specific purpose:

Thesis statement:

Introduction

  A. _____

  B. _____

(transition)

Supporting material

  A. _____

    1. _____

    2. _____

(transition)

  B. _____

    1. _____

    2. _____

(transition)

  C. _____

    1. _____

    2. _____

(transition)

Conclusion

  A. _____

  B. _____

  C. _____

Introduction

The members of an audience waiting to hear a speaker have three questions in mind: Who are you? What are you going to talk about? Why should I listen? They are good questions, and you should respond to them in the introduction to your talk. Here are some suggestions:

- Grab your audience's attention with a question, quotation, fascinating statistic, anecdote, background information, or compliment. Whether someone introduces you or not, tell your audience what qualifies you to speak on your particular subject.
- Briefly explain the organization of your talk. This gives your audience a road map so that they know where you are starting, where you are going, and what they have to look forward to as you speak.

Supporting material

Though much of the advice given for oral presentations applies to written communication as well, audiences for oral presentations generally need some special help from the speaker. When you are reading an article and lose sight of the main point, you can turn back to the first few paragraphs and reread. But when you are listening to a speech and your mind wanders, you cannot ask the speaker to go back and repeat.

As a speaker, there are strategies you can employ to keep listeners interested and aware of what your purpose is and where you are. Below are some suggestions.

- Give signals to show where you are on the road map. Use *first, second,* and *third* appropriately. Show CAUSE AND EFFECT with words such as *subsequently, therefore,* and *furthermore.* If you are telling a story, use signpost terms such as *before, then,* and *next.*
- Define unfamiliar terms and give vivid examples to help the audience understand these new ideas and concepts.
- Comment on your own material. Tell the audience what is significant, memorable, or relevant—and why.
- Repeat key ideas. If you do so sparingly, you can emphasize the importance of the idea and help the audience remember it.
- Provide internal summaries. Every so often, take a moment to recap what you have covered as reassurance for both yourself and your audience.

Conclusion

In the conclusion of a speech, an audience looks for a sense of closure. Here are some ways to conclude your presentation.

- Signal the end with verbal ("In conclusion,") and nonverbal (facial expressions, gestures) cues.

- Offer a fresh restatement of your main message—but do not introduce new ideas.

- Use a dramatic clincher statement, cite a memorable quotation, or issue a challenge.

- When you say "Finally," make sure you mean it. In other words, do not conclude more than once.

44d.1 Researching the speech

Doing research for an oral presentation requires the same kind of planning as doing research for written documents. To keep yourself calm and focused, divide the preparation into manageable tasks, according to a realistic time line (32d). Set small goals and stick to your calendar in order to give yourself enough time to research, organize, and practice your presentation (44i). Review Chapters 31 through 34 for help on finding and evaluating sources, taking notes, planning a research strategy, and documenting sources.

44d.2 Drafting the speech

Most of the preparation involved in an oral presentation is written work. Writing helps you take four important steps in your preparation: (1) organize your thoughts; (2) distance yourself from the ideas and remain objective; (3) pay attention to words and language; and (4) polish for clarity and impact.

When drafting your speech, it may help you to review Chapters 20 through 22 on usage and the impact and correct form of words. In particular, see section 21b for a discussion of a medium LEVEL OF FORMALITY in language, which is an appropriate level for most public speaking. Careful DICTION (21e) will make your speech easy for your audience to listen to and memorable. Box 181 presents some tips on language that apply specifically to oral presentations.

◎ **Using language effectively in oral**   **181**
  presentations

- **Recognize the power of precise words.**
  "Never in the field of human conflict was so much owed by so many to so few."

  —Winston Churchill
  →

Using language effectively in oral   **181**
presentations *(continued)*

Substitute *history* for *field of human conflict,* and note the diminished effect.

- **Take care not to offend.** If there is any chance a word, phrase, or example could offend anyone in your audience, do not use it. Avoid SEXIST PRONOUNS and NOUNS (10r and 21g).
- **Use guide phrases.** Words such as *now, first, my next point,* and so on help listeners follow your organization.
- **Use the active voice.** The ACTIVE VOICE is generally preferred in writing (8o), but it is crucial in oral presentations. Listeners will have an easier time grasping your point if you state the subject at the beginning of a sentence. Consider the following two sentences:

Gun control is an issue that must be considered by all citizens. [passive]

All citizens must consider the issue of gun control. [active]

44e How do I present collaboratively?

At some point, you might be asked to present an oral report as part of a group. As with collaborative projects of any sort, special considerations apply.

- When choosing a topic, be sure that most members of the group are familiar with the subject. All members of the group should be able to contribute in some way.
- Find out whether all members of the group are required to speak for an equal amount of time. If so, agree on firm time limits for each person, so that everyone can participate in the delivery. If there is no such requirement, students who enjoy public speaking can take more responsibility for delivery, while others do more of the preparatory work or contribute in other ways.
- Lay out clearly what each member's responsibilities are in preparing the presentation. Try to define roles that complement one another; otherwise, you may end up with overlap in one area and no coverage in another.
- As with individual presentations, allow enough time for practice. Though each member can practice on his or her own part alone,

schedule practice sessions for the entire presentation as a group. This will help you (a) work on transitions, (b) make sure the order of presenters is effective, and (c) time the length of the presentation.

DELIVERING AN ORAL PRESENTATION

When you write a document to be read, you not only consider the information you present, you also think about DOCUMENT DESIGN—the "how" of presentation for written documents (Chapter 38). When preparing an oral presentation, you also must consider how—not just what—you present. In oral presentations, the "how" is called **delivery.**

44f How do I choose a presentation style?

Presentation style is the way you deliver your speech: You may memorize it, read it, or speak *extemporaneously*—that is, without a text. (An extemporaneous speech can be spur of the moment or carefully prepared, but it is delivered free of text, possibly using notes, but never reading from them, word by word.)

Memorized speeches often sound unnatural, and there is no safety net if you forget a word or sentence. Fortunately, memorization is not necessary in most academic and professional speaking situations.

Reading as a presentation style is often boring for listeners, and it can create an uncomfortable barrier between you and your audience. If you must read your speech, remember to make frequent eye contact with the audience, vary your tone of voice, and use appropriate gestures.

Presenting extemporaneously is usually your best choice. You are well prepared but have an outline or index cards to keep you focused. A **presentation outline,** which is not the same as an organizational outline (44d), lists the major points you want to make, but the language you use to develop these points is "of the moment." The outline or index cards should also include the names of any sources so that you can correctly cite their contributions to your speech. Box 182 gives specific help in preparing the two main types of presentation aids. Choose whichever feels more comfortable to you.

◎ **Preparing oral presentation aids**   **182**

For a presentation outline, follow the same style as the organizational outline (see Box 180, in 44d), with these changes:

- Type the outline in a large font for easier reading.

→

Preparing oral presentation aids *(continued)* **182**

- Clearly label or separate the introduction, supporting material, and conclusion.
- Try to use key words and phrases only, or you will end up typing a script.
- Put in cues for pauses, use of visuals, or emphasis.
- Use only one side of the page to avoid shuffling paper.
- Highlight key points you cannot afford to skip.

Presentation index cards are another option:

- Number or label the order of the index cards, in case they somehow become shuffled.
- Use one index card per major point and one per minor point. Use only one side of each card.
- Use various colors of pen on white cards or different card colors to separate topics or segments of your speech.
- Highlight key points that you cannot afford to skip—small self-stick notes are good for this.
- Note on your card when to use a visual.

44g How do I vary my voice and use nonverbal communication?

Your voice is the focus of the presentation, so be aware of it and project. If you are unsure of your volume, it is fine to ask the audience if they can hear you. Articulate—speak slowly and deliberately—but not so slowly that there is no rhythm or pace to the speech. Change the tone of your voice for emphasis and clarity. Insert planned pauses. In general, try to sound like yourself, but an intensified version. Remember that if you are using a microphone, you do not need to raise your voice.

Eye contact is the most important **nonverbal communication** tool. Try to make eye contact with your audience immediately. If you have to walk up to a podium, do not begin speaking before you are standing squarely behind the podium, looking directly at the audience. Eye contact communicates confidence.

Your body language will either add or detract from your overall message. Use appropriate facial expressions to mirror the emotions of your message. Gestures, if not overdone, contribute to your message by adding emphasis. The best gestures appear natural rather than forced or timed. If you are unsure of where to place your hands, rest them on the podium—try not to primp or fidget. Body movements should be kept to a minimum and be used in pace with the speech. Step forward or backward to indicate transitions, but do not sway side to side. Of course, dress appropriately for your audience and venue.

44h How do I incorporate visual aids into my presentation?

Good **visual aids** make ideas clear and understandable, but they should not take the place of a well-prepared speech. They add interest to an already interesting topic. They reinforce key ideas by providing illustrations or concrete images for the audience, and if done well, they can make long explanations unnecessary and add to your credibility. Here are the various types of visual aids and their uses.

- **Posters.** Posters can be very effective because they are large and can dramatize a point. To be sure they do not distract from your presentation or lose their impact, keep them covered until you are ready for them.

- **Dry-erase boards.** These are preferable to chalkboards because their colors are visually appealing. Use them to emphasize an occasional technical word or to do a rough sketch when illustrating a process. More complicated graphics should be prepared in advance as transparencies for projection or as handouts.

- **Slides.** Before your speech, be sure the slides are in the proper order and correctly placed (upright) in the machine. Try to arrive early to double-check that the slide projector is working and in focus. If the screen you will be using will not be up for your entire presentation, check that it goes up and down easily.

- **Transparencies.** Transparencies used with an overhead projector combine the advantages of posters and dry-erase boards. You can prepare a graphic in advance and then write on that sheet to emphasize a point. You can also use a blank transparency sheet on the projector to make a rough illustration from scratch.
    When using an overhead projector, dim the lights in the room without turning them completely off. This allows you to see your presentation notes and your audience to continue taking their own notes. Number and label your transparencies—self-stick notes are good for this. Before your speech, put a transparency on the screen to be sure you know how to make it appear right-side up.

- **PowerPoint.** If you are making a PowerPoint presentation, the most important thing to do is double-check the in-place computer system before you begin. If possible, bring your own laptop in case the software or a specific computer is not compatible with your disk. PowerPoint technology is very impressive, but remember, it is only an enhancement. Your information—spoken with clarity and authority—is the main attraction.

■ **Handouts.** Handouts are preferable to other visual aids when the subject is a longer text or when you want to give your audience something to take home. If you distribute handouts during the speech, wait until everyone has one before you begin speaking, and do not distribute the handout until you are ready to discuss it. Short and simple handouts work best during a presentation; save longer and more detailed ones for the end, if possible. Include documentation information for your source on the handout if it is not your own writing or graphic (see Chapters 35–37).

Visuals enhance a speech, but you should be able to give your presentation without them if the need arises. Bringing backup material can help you in a pinch. You might, for example, put key illustrations on transparencies in addition to a PowerPoint file. If something does go noticeably wrong during your presentation, relax. It happens to everyone! Take a deep breath, briefly apologize to the audience (if necessary), and keep going. Box 183 offers tips on using visuals.

◎ **Tips for using visuals in oral presentations**   **183**

■ Practice with the visuals you plan to use.
■ Try to keep your focus on the audience, not the visual aid.
■ Do not let visuals distract the audience from your speech.
■ Do not use too many visuals.
■ Proofread your written visuals just as carefully as you would a formal essay.
■ Make visuals large enough for the entire audience to see.
■ Use simple layouts or drawings—nothing cluttered or overly complicated.
■ If possible, arrive early to check the equipment.

44i **What can I do to practice for my presentation?**

Good delivery requires practice. In preparing to speak, figure in enough time for at least four complete run-throughs of your entire presentation, using visuals if you have them. When you practice, keep the following in mind:

- Practice conveying ideas rather than particular words so that your tone does not become stilted.
- Time yourself and cut or expand material accordingly.
- Practice in front of a mirror or videotape yourself. As you watch yourself, notice your gestures. Do you look natural? Do you make nervous movements that you were not aware of as you spoke?
- Practice in front of a friend. Ask for constructive feedback by posing these questions: What was my main point? Did the points flow? Did any information seem to come from out of nowhere or not fit in with the information around it? Did I sound natural? Did I look natural? How did the visuals add to my message?

If you suffer from stage fright—as almost everyone does—remember that the more prepared and rehearsed you are, the less frightened you will be. Keep in mind that your aim is to communicate, not perform. Box 184 suggests some ways to overcome physical signs of anxiety.

◉ **Overcoming anxiety in an oral presentation   184**

- **Pounding heart.** Don't worry. No one else can hear it!
- **Trembling hands.** Rest them on the podium. If there is no podium, hold your presentation outline or note cards.
- **Shaky knees.** Stand behind the desk or podium. If there is no desk, step forward to emphasize a point. Walking slowly from one place to another can also help you get rid of nervous energy.
- **Dry throat and mouth.** Keep water at the podium and take an occasional sip.
- **Quivering voice.** Speaking louder can help until this disappears on its own.
- **Flushed face.** It is not as noticeable as it feels, and it will fade as you continue speaking.

When you are in place and ready to begin, pause for a moment before speaking. Count to five. Take a deep breath. Look at the audience, then begin. Stop thinking that the audience is there to critique you. Instead, concentrate on delivering your message and you will appear sincere and confident.

PREFACE FOR ESL STUDENTS

If you ever worry about your English writing, you have much in common with me and with many U.S. college students. The good news is that errors you make demonstrate the reliable truth that you are moving normally through the unavoidable, necessary stages of second-language development. Unfortunately, there are no shortcuts. The process is like learning to play a musical instrument. Few people learn to play fluently without making lots of errors.

What can you do to progress as quickly as possible from one writing stage to another? I recommend that you start by bringing to mind what school writing is like in your first language. Specifically, recall how ideas are presented in your written native language, especially when information is explained or a topic requires a logical argument.

Most college writing in the United States is very direct in tone and straightforward in structure. In a typical essay or research paper, the reader expects to find a THESIS STATEMENT that clearly states the central message of the entire piece of writing. Usually, the thesis statement falls in the first paragraph, or in a longer piece, perhaps in the second paragraph. Then, each paragraph that follows relates in content directly to the essay's thesis statement. Also, each paragraph begins with a TOPIC SENTENCE that contains the main point of the paragraph, and the rest of the paragraph supports the point made in the topic sentence. This support consists of RENNS (8d) that provide specific details. The final paragraph brings the piece of writing to a logical conclusion.

Writing structures typical of your native language most likely differ from those in the United States. Always honor your culture's writing traditions and structures, for they reflect the richness of your heritage. At the same time, try to adapt to and practice the academic writing style characteristic of the United States. Later, some college instructors might encourage you to practice other, more subtle English writing styles that allow greater liberty in organization and expression.

Distinctive variations in school writing styles among people of different cultures and language groups have interested researchers for the past thirty years. Such research is ongoing, so scholars hesitate to generalize. Even so, interesting differences have been observed. Many Spanish-speaking students feel that U.S. school writing lacks grace because writers do not include any wide-ranging background material: in fact, U.S. writing teachers usually say such broad introductory material is wordy or not really relevant to the central message. Japanese school writing customarily begins with references to nature. In some African nations, a ceremonial, formal opening is expected to start school writing as an expression of respect for the reader. As a person, I greatly enjoy discovering the rich variations in the writing traditions of the many cultures of the world. As a college teacher, however, my responsibility is to explain the expectations in the United States.

If you were in my class, I would say "Welcome!" and then ask you to teach me about writing in your native language. Using that knowledge, I would respectfully teach you the U.S. approach to writing so that I could do my best to help you succeed in a U.S. college.

L.Q.T.

Visit the Troyka Web site for information on:

- Distinguishing between singular and plural nouns
- Understanding word order
- Using verbs

You'll find access to *The Internet TESL Journal's Self-Study Quizzes for ESL Students* at <www.aitech.ac.jp/~iteslj/quizzes/grammar.html>. This site offers quizzes on plurals, word order, verbs, and a host of other ESL topics.

PART SEVEN

WRITING WHEN ENGLISH IS A SECOND LANGUAGE

45 SINGULARS AND PLURALS

HOW TO USE CHAPTER 45 EFFECTIVELY

1. Use this chapter together with these handbook sections:
   - 7b, NOUNS
   - 8c, -*s* form of VERBS
   - 10a–10m, SUBJECT-VERB AGREEMENT
   - 11f, nouns as MODIFIERS

2. Remember that throughout this handbook, you can find the definitions of words printed in SMALL CAPITAL LETTERS in the Terms Glossary toward the back of this handbook.

3. Use **cross-references** (often given in parentheses) to find full explanations of key concepts.

This chapter can help you choose between using SINGULAR (one in NUMBER) and PLURAL (more than one). Section 45a discusses the concept of COUNT and NONCOUNT NOUNS. Section 45b discusses DETERMINERS and nouns. Section 45c discusses particularly confusing instances of the choice between singular and plural. Section 45d discusses some nouns with irregular plural forms.

45a What are count and noncount nouns?

Count nouns name items that can be counted: *a radio* or *radios*, *a street* or *streets, an idea* or *ideas, a fingernail* or *fingernails*. Count nouns can be SINGULAR or PLURAL.

Noncount nouns name things that are thought of as a whole and not split into separate, countable parts: *rice, knowledge, traffic*. There are two important rules to remember about noncount nouns: (1) They are never preceded by *a* or *an*, and (2) they are never plural. Box 185 lists eleven categories of uncountable items, giving examples in each category.

> ◉ **Uncountable items** 185
>
> | | |
> |---|---|
> | GROUPS OF SIMILAR ITEMS | clothing, equipment, furniture, jewelry, junk, luggage, mail, money, stuff, traffic, vocabulary |
> | ABSTRACTIONS | advice, equality, fun, health, ignorance, information, knowledge, news, peace, pollution, respect |
> | LIQUIDS | blood, coffee, gasoline, water |
> | GASES | air, helium, oxygen, smog, smoke, steam |
> | MATERIALS | aluminum, cloth, cotton, ice, wood |
> | FOOD | beef, bread, butter, macaroni, meat, pork |
> | PARTICLES OR GRAINS | dirt, dust, hair, rice, salt, wheat |
> | SPORTS, GAMES, ACTIVITIES | chess, homework, housework, reading, sailing, soccer |
> | LANGUAGES | Arabic, Chinese, Japanese, Spanish |
> | FIELDS OF STUDY | biology, computer science, history, literature, math |
> | EVENTS IN NATURE | electricity, heat, humidity, moonlight, rain, snow, sunshine, thunder, weather |

Some nouns can be countable or uncountable, depending on their meaning in a sentence. Most of these nouns name things that can be meant either individually or as "wholes" made up of individual parts.

COUNT You have **a hair** on your sleeve. [In this sentence, *hair* is meant as an individual, countable item.]

NONCOUNT Kioko has black **hair.** [In this sentence, all the strands of *hair* are referred to as a whole.]

COUNT **The rains** were late last year. [In this sentence, *rains* is meant as individual, countable occurrences of rain.]

NONCOUNT **The rain** is soaking the garden. [In this sentence, all the particles of *rain* are referred to as a whole.]

When you are editing your writing (see Chapter 3), be sure that you have not added a plural -*s* to any noncount nouns, for they are always singular in form.

👁 **VERB ALERT:** Be sure to use a singular verb with any noncount noun that functions as a SUBJECT in a CLAUSE. ●

To check whether a noun is count or noncount, look it up in a dictionary such as the *Dictionary of American English* (Heinle & Heinle). In this dictionary, count nouns are indicated by [C], and noncount nouns are indicated by [U] (for "uncountable"). Nouns that have both count and noncount meanings are marked [C;U].

45b How do I use determiners with singular and plural nouns?

Determiners, also called *expressions of quantity,* are used to tell how much or how many with reference to NOUNS. Other names for determiners include *limiting adjectives, noun markers,* and ARTICLES. (For information about articles—the words *a, an,* and *the*—see Chapter 46.)

Choosing the right determiner with a noun can depend on whether the noun is NONCOUNT or COUNT (see 45a). For count nouns, you must also decide whether the noun is singular or plural. Box 186 lists many determiners and the kinds of nouns that they can accompany.

◉ **Determiners to use with count
and noncount nouns**   **186**

Group 1: Determiners for Singular Count Nouns

With every **singular count noun,** always use one of the determiners listed in Group 1.

a, an, the	**a house**	**an egg**	**the car**
one, any, some,	**any house**	**each egg**	**another car**
every, each, either,			
neither, another,			
the other			
my, our, your, his,	**your house**	**its egg**	**Connie's car**
her, its, their,			
nouns with 's or s'			
this, that	**this house**	**that egg**	**this car**
one, no, the first,	**one house**	**no egg**	**the fifth car**
the second, etc.			

→

Determiners to use with count and noncount nouns *(continued)*   186

Group 2: Determiners for Plural Count Nouns

All the determiners listed in Group 2 can be used with **plural count nouns.** Plural count nouns can also be used without determiners, as discussed in section 46b.

the	the bicycles	the rooms	the idea
some, any, both, many, more, most, few, fewer, the fewest, a lot of, a number of, other, several, all, all the	some bicycles	many rooms	all ideas
my, our, your, his, her, its, their, nouns with '*s* or *s*'	our bicycles	her rooms	student's ideas
these, those	these bicycles	those rooms	these ideas
no, two, three, etc.; the first, the second, the third, etc.	no bicycles	four rooms	the first ideas

Group 3: Determiners for Noncount Nouns

All the determiners listed in Group 3 can be used with **noncount nouns** (always singular). Noncount nouns can also be used without determiners, as discussed in section 46b.

the	the rice	the rain	the pride
some, any, much, more, most, other, the other, little, less, the least, enough, all, all the, a lot of	enough rice	a lot of rain	more pride
my, our, your, his, her, its, their, nouns with '*s* or *s*'	their rice	India's rain	your pride
this, that	this rice	that rain	this pride
no, the first, the second, the third, etc.	no rice	the first rain	no pride

👁 **USAGE ALERT:** The phrases *a few* and *a little* convey the meaning "some": *I have **a few** rare books* means "I have *some* rare books." *They are worth **a little** money* means "They are worth *some* money." Without the word *a*, the words *few* and *little* convey the meaning "almost none": *I have **few** [or *very few*] books* means "I have *almost no* books." *They are worth **little** money* means "They are worth *almost no* money." ●

45c How do I use *one of*, nouns as adjectives, and *states* in names or titles?

One of *constructions*

One of constructions include *one of the* and a NOUN or *one of* followed by an ADJECTIVE-noun combination (*one of my hats, one of those ideas*). Always use a plural noun as the OBJECT when you use *one of the* with a noun or *one of* with an adjective-noun combination.

NO	*One of the **reason** to live here is the beach.*
YES	*One of the **reasons** to live here is the beach.*
NO	*One of her best **friend** has moved away.*
YES	*One of her best **friends** has moved away.*

The VERB in these constructions is always singular because it agrees with the singular *one*, not with the plural noun: ***One** of the most important inventions of the twentieth century **is** [not *are*] television.*

For advice about verb forms that go with *one of the . . . who* constructions, see section 10k.

Nouns used as adjectives

ADJECTIVES in English do not have plural forms. When you use an adjective with a PLURAL NOUN, make the noun plural but not the adjective: *the **green** [not *greens*] leaves.* Be especially careful when you use a word as a MODIFIER that can also function as a noun.

The bird's wingspan is ten inches. [*Inches* is functioning as a noun.]
The bird has a ten-inch wingspan. [*Inch* is functioning as a modifier.]

Do not add *-s* (or *-es*) to the adjective even when it is modifying a plural noun or pronoun.

| **NO** | Many **Americans** students are basketball fans. |
| **YES** | Many **American** students are basketball fans. |

Names or titles that include the word *states*

States is a plural word. However, names such as *United States* or *Organization of American States* refer to singular things—one country and one organization, even though made up of many states. When *states* is part of a name or title referring to one thing, the name is a SINGULAR NOUN and therefore requires a SINGULAR VERB.

NO The **United States have** a large entertainment industry.

NO The **United State has** a large entertainment industry.

YES The **United States has** a large entertainment industry.

45d How do I use nouns with irregular plurals?

Some English nouns have irregularly spelled plurals. In addition to those discussed in section 22c, here are others that often cause difficulties.

Plurals of foreign nouns and other irregular nouns

Whenever you are unsure whether a noun is plural, look it up in a dictionary. If no plural is given for a singular noun, add *-s* to form the plural.

Many nouns from other languages that are used unchanged in English have only one plural. If two plurals are listed in the dictionary, look carefully for differences in meaning. Some words, for example, keep the plural form from the original language for scientific usage and have another, English-form plural for nonscientific contexts: *formula, formulae, formulas; appendix, appendices, appendixes; index, indices, indexes; medium, media, mediums; cactus, cacti, cactuses; fungus, fungi, funguses.*

Words from Latin that end in *-is* in their singular form become plural by substituting *-es: parenthesis, parentheses; thesis, theses; oasis, oases.*

Other words

Medical terms for diseases involving an inflammation end in *-itis: tonsillitis, appendicitis.* They are always singular.

The word *news*, although it ends in *s*, is always singular: *The **news is** encouraging.* The words *people, police,* and *clergy* are always plural even though they do not end in *s: The **police are** prepared.*

EXERCISE 45-1

Consulting all sections of this chapter, select the correct choice from the words in parentheses and write it in the blank.

EXAMPLE At the beginning of every school year, all (student, students) <u>students</u> can expect (homework, homeworks) <u>homework</u> that teaches them about the toll-free No Bully hot line.

1. One of the main (reason, reasons) _____ for such a hot line is the change in tempers and violent capacities of (American, Americans) _____ students.

2. Because students are often bullied by a fellow classmate when outside the classroom, it is important that they receive (information, informations) _____ about how to react when confronted by such a threat.

3. Many a child in the (United State, United States) _____ is in danger not only of being teased and taunted by others but also of being the victim of a crime in which (blood, bloods) _____ is spilled, such as assault or robbery.

4. Because (many, much) _____ classrooms are unsupervised after school hours, this (time, times) _____ is especially dangerous.

5. In a moment of danger, (ignorance, ignorances) _____ can be deadly, so the No Bully hot line was set up to give students (advice, advices) _____ on how to handle bullies and other threatening situations.

EXERCISE 45-2

Consulting all sections of this chapter, select the correct choice from the words in parentheses and write it in the blank.

EXAMPLE   Because of their innate (intelligence, intelligences) <u>intelligence,</u> many (pet, pets) <u>pets</u> can often be very protective of the humans they love.

1. One of the most frightening (animal, animals) _____ is a poisonous (rattlesnake, rattlesnakes) _____, but not to a twelve-year-old retriever, Partner.

2. Longtime friends Nick and Ross, both eight years old, were chopping down a tree for a campfire when a (six-foot, six-feet) _____ rattlesnake fell from a branch.

3. Partner leaped over (dirt, dirts) _____ and (leave, leaves) _____ to get to the poisonous snake, which he attacked.

4. Verle, Nick's father and Partner's owner, was (many, much) _____ yards away when he heard the racket, and he rushed over just in time to see the rattler sink its fangs into Partner's nose.

5. Within minutes, the rattler was killed by a bystander; and Partner, who showed a lot of (courage, courages) _____ and has now recovered, has become one of the best (friend, friends) _____ Nick and Ross have ever had.

46 ARTICLES

HOW TO USE CHAPTER 46 EFFECTIVELY
1. Use this chapter together with these handbook sections:
   - 7b, NOUNS
   - 45a, SINGULARS and PLURALS with COUNT and NONCOUNT NOUNS
   - 45b, DETERMINERS with count and noncount nouns
2. Remember that throughout this handbook, you can find the definitions of words printed in SMALL CAPITAL LETTERS in the Terms Glossary toward the end of this handbook.
3. Use **cross-references** (often given in parentheses) to find full explanations of key concepts.

This chapter gives you guidelines for using **articles.** Section 46a discusses using articles with singular count nouns. Section 46b discusses using articles with plural count nouns and with noncount nouns (which are always singular). Section 46c discusses using articles with PROPER NOUNS and with GERUNDS.

46a How do I use *a, an,* or *the* with singular count nouns?

The words *a* and *an* are called **indefinite articles.** The word *the* is called the **definite article.** Articles are one type of DETERMINER. (For more on determiners, see section 7f; for other determiners, see Box 186 in section 45b, pages 782–783.) Articles signal that a NOUN will follow and that any MODIFIERS between the article and the noun refer to that noun.

a chair	**the** computer
a cold, metal chair	**the** lightning-fast computer

Every time you use a SINGULAR COUNT NOUN, a COMMON NOUN that names one countable item, the noun requires some kind of determiner;

see Group 1 in Box 186 (in 45b) for a list. To choose between *a* or *an* and *the*, you need to determine whether the noun is **specific** or **nonspecific**. A noun is considered specific when anyone who reads your writing can understand exactly and specifically to what item the noun is referring. If the noun refers to any of a number of identical items, it is nonspecific.

For nonspecific singular count nouns, use *a* (or *an*). When the singular noun is specific, use *the* or some other determiner. Box 187 can help you decide when a singular count noun is specific and therefore requires *the*.

 ## When a singular count noun is specific and requires *the*   187

- **Rule 1: A noun is specific and requires *the* when it names something unique or generally and unambiguously known.**

  The sun has risen above **the horizon.** [Because there is only one *sun* and only one *horizon*, these nouns are specific in the context of this sentence.]

- **Rule 2: A noun is specific and requires *the* when it names something used in a representative or abstract sense.**

  Benjamin Franklin favored **the turkey** as **the national bird** of the United States. [Because *turkey* and *national bird* are representative references rather than references to a particular turkey or bird, they are specific nouns in the context of this sentence.]

- **Rule 3: A noun is specific and requires *the* when it names something defined elsewhere in the same sentence or in an earlier sentence.**

  The ship *Savannah* was the first steam vessel to cross the Atlantic Ocean. [*Savannah* names a specific ship.]

  The carpet in my bedroom is new. [In *my bedroom* defines exactly which carpet is meant, so *carpet* is a specific noun in this context.]

  I have **a computer** in my office. **The computer** is often broken. [*Computer* is not specific in the first sentence, so it uses *a*. In the second sentence, *computer* has been made specific by the first sentence, so it uses *the*.]

- **Rule 4: A noun is specific and requires *the* when it names something that can be inferred from the context.**

  Monday, I had to call **the technician** to fix it. [*A technician* would be any of a number of individuals; *the technician* implies the same person has been called before, and so it is specific in this context.]

⬙ **ALERT:** Use *an* before words that begin with a vowel sound. Use *a* before words that begin with a consonant sound. Go by the sound, not the spelling. For example, words that begin with *h* or *u* can have either a vowel or a consonant sound. Make the choice based on the sound of the first word after the article, even if that word is not the noun.

an idea	**a g**ood idea
an umbrella	**a u**seless umbrella
an honor	**a h**istory book⬤

One common exception affects Rule 3 in Box 187. A noun may still require *a* (or *an*) after the first use if more information is added between the article and the noun: *I bought **a sweater** today. It was **a** (not the) red sweater.* (Your audience has been introduced to *a sweater* but not *a red sweater,* so *red sweater* is not yet specific in this context and cannot take *the.*) Other information may make the noun specific so that *the* is correct. For example, *It was **the red sweater that I saw in the store yesterday*** uses *the* because the *that* CLAUSE makes specific which red sweater is meant.

46b How do I use articles with plural nouns and with noncount nouns?

With PLURAL NOUNS and NONCOUNT NOUNS, you must decide whether to use *the* or to use no article at all. (For guidelines about using DETERMINERS other than articles with nouns, see Box 186 in section 45b, pages 782–783.) What you learned in section 46a about NONSPECIFIC and SPECIFIC NOUNS can help you make the choice between using *the* or using no article. Box 187 in section 46a explains when a singular count noun's meaning is specific and calls for *the.* Plural nouns and noncount nouns with specific meanings usually use *the* in the same circumstances. However, a plural noun or a noncount noun with a general or nonspecific meaning usually does not use *the.*

Geraldo grows **flowers** but not **vegetables** in his garden. He is thinking about planting **corn** sometime. [three nonspecific nouns]

Plural nouns

A plural noun's meaning may be specific because it is widely known.

The oceans are being damaged by pollution. [Because there is only one possible meaning for *oceans*—the oceans on the earth—it is correct to use *the.* This example is related to Rule 1 in Box 187.]

789

A plural noun's meaning may also be made specific by a word, PHRASE, or CLAUSE in the same sentence.

Geraldo sold **the daisies from last year's garden** to the florist. [Because the phrase *from last year's garden* makes *daisies* specific, *the* is correct. This example is related to Rule 3 in Box 187.]

A plural noun's meaning usually becomes specific by its use in an earlier sentence.

Geraldo planted **tulips** this year. **The tulips** will bloom in April. [*Tulips* is used in a general sense in the first sentence, without *the*. Because the first sentence makes *tulips* specific, *the tulips* is correct in the second sentence. This example is related to Rule 3 in Box 187.]

A plural noun's meaning may be made specific by the context.

Geraldo fertilized **the bulbs** when he planted them last October. [In the context of the sentences about tulips, *bulbs* is understood as a synonym for *tulips*, which makes it specific and calls for *the*. This example is related to Rule 4 in Box 187.]

Noncount nouns

Noncount nouns are always singular in form (see 45a). Like plural nouns, noncount nouns use either *the* or no article. When a noncount noun's meaning is specific, use *the* before it. If its meaning is general or nonspecific, do not use *the*.

Kalinda served us **rice**. She flavored **the rice** with curry. [*Rice* is a noncount noun. This example is related to Rule 3 in Box 187. By the second sentence, *rice* has become specific, so *the* is used.]

Kalinda served us **the rice that she had flavored with curry**. [*Rice* is a noncount noun. This example is related to Rule 3 in Box 187. *Rice* is made specific by the clause *that she had flavored with curry*, so *the* is used.]

Generalizations with plural or noncount nouns

Rule 2 in Box 187 tells you to use *the* with singular count nouns that carry general meaning. With GENERALIZATIONS using plural or noncount nouns, omit *the*.

NO **The tulips** are **the flowers** that grow from **the bulbs**.

YES **Tulips** are **flowers** that grow from **bulbs**.

NO **The dogs** require more care than **the cats** do.

YES **Dogs** require more care than **cats** do.

46c How do I use *the* with proper nouns and with gerunds?

Proper nouns

PROPER NOUNS name specific people, places, or things (see 7b). Most proper nouns do not require ARTICLES: *We visited **Lake Mead** with **Asha** and **Larry**.* As shown in Box 188, however, certain types of proper nouns do require *the*.

⊙ Proper nouns that use *the*   188

■ **Nouns with the pattern *the . . . of . . .***
  the United States **of** America   **the** Fourth **of** July
  the Republic **of** Mexico   **the** University **of** Paris

■ **Plural proper nouns**
  the United Arab Emirates
  the Johnsons
  the Rocky Mountains [*but* Mount Fuji]
  the Chicago Bulls
  the Falkland Islands [*but* Long Island]
  the Great Lakes [*but* Lake Superior]

■ **Collective proper nouns (nouns that name a group)**
  the Modern Language Association
  the Society of Friends

■ **Some (but not all) geographical features**
  the Amazon   **the** Gobi Desert   **the** Indian Ocean

■ **Three countries**
  the Congo   **the** Sudan   **the** Netherlands

Gerunds

GERUNDS are PRESENT PARTICIPLES (the *-ing* form of VERBS) used as nouns: ***Skating** is challenging.* Gerunds are usually not preceded by *the*.

NO   **The constructing** new bridges is necessary to improve traffic flow.

YES   **Constructing** new bridges is necessary to improve traffic flow.

Use *the* before a gerund when two conditions are met: (1) The gerund is used in a specific sense (see 46a), and (2) the gerund does not have a DIRECT OBJECT.

> **NO** **The designing fabric** is a fine art. [*Fabric* is a direct object of *designing,* so *the* should not be used.]

> **YES** **Designing** fabric is a fine art. [*Designing* is a gerund, so *the* is not used.]

> **YES** **The designing of** fabric is a fine art. [*The* is used because *fabric* is the OBJECT OF THE PREPOSITION *of* and *designing* is meant in a specific sense.]

EXERCISE 46-1

Consulting all sections of this chapter, select the correct article from the words in parentheses and write it in the blank.

EXAMPLE   Be forewarned: (A, An, The) <u>The</u> camera as we know it may soon be obsolete.

1. At (a, an, the) _____ dawn of (a, an, the) _____ twenty-first century comes (a, an, the) _____ invention so advanced that it may completely rid (a, an, the) _____ United States of America of every camera that has come before it.
2. (A, An, The) _____ digital camera, which allows photos to appear on (a, an, the) _____ computer monitor, takes up virtual space, not physical space.
3. As (a, an, the) _____ result, if you see (a, an, the) _____ bad photo on (a, an, the) _____ screen, you can simply erase (a, an, the) _____ poor photo to make room for (a, an, the) _____ new one.
4. With this new technology, (a, an, the) _____ aunt can even e-mail photos to her niece or nephew, or she can post photos to (a, an, the) _____ Web page.
5. Digital cameras also allow people to alter (a, an, the) _____ appearance of people or things, which, according to many critics, is (a, an, the) _____ chief disadvantage of (a, an, the) _____ digital camera.

EXERCISE 46-2

Consulting all sections of this chapter, decide which of the words in parentheses is correct and write it in the blank. If no article is needed, leave the blank empty.

EXAMPLE   For (a, an, the) _____ years, people have worked under (a, an, the) <u>the</u> assumption that (a, an, the) <u>the</u> best remedy for (a, an, the) <u>a</u> burn is butter.

1. This kind of treatment seems to be (a, an, the) _____ good idea because butter looks and feels like ointment, but butter doesn't contain (a, an, the) _____ antibacterial property like ointment does.

2. In using butter to treat (a, an, the) _____ burns, you are coating (a, an, the) _____ skin with debris that must be removed later to keep it from interfering with (a, a, the) _____ healing process.

3. In actuality, cold water without ice will not only ease (a, an, the) _____ pain but also prevent scarring and further damage.

4. In fact, (a, an, the) _____ person who keeps the finger submerged for at least several minutes and as long as half an hour will have (a, an, the) _____ least painful or scarred burn, according to doctors.

5. However, if (a, an, the) _____ burn is serious, (a, an, the) _____ first person to be consulted should be a doctor.

47 WORD ORDER

HOW TO USE CHAPTER 47 EFFECTIVELY

1. Use this chapter together with these handbook sections:
   - 7f, ADJECTIVES
   - 7g, ADVERBS
   - 7k–7q, SENTENCE TYPES and patterns
   - 7n, MODIFIERS
   - 7p, CLAUSES
   - 10g, VERBS with INVERTED WORD ORDER
2. Remember that throughout this handbook, you can find the definitions of words printed in SMALL CAPITAL LETTERS in the Terms Glossary toward the back of this handbook.
3. Use **cross-references** (often given in parentheses) to find full explanations of key concepts.

This chapter can help you with several issues of **word order** in sentences. Section 47a discusses STANDARD WORD ORDER for English sentences and important variations. Section 47b discusses the placement of adjectives. Section 47c discusses the placement of adverbs.

47a How do I understand standard and inverted word order in sentences?

In STANDARD WORD ORDER, the most common pattern for DECLARATIVE SENTENCES in English, the SUBJECT comes before the VERB. (To understand these concepts more fully, review sections 7l–7p.)

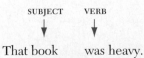

With INVERTED WORD ORDER, the MAIN VERB or an AUXILIARY VERB comes before the subject. The most common use of inverted word order in English is in forming DIRECT QUESTIONS. Questions that can be answered with a yes or no begin with a form of *be* used as a main verb, with an auxiliary verb (*be, do, have*), or with a MODAL AUXILIARY (*can, should, will*, and others; see Chapter 50).

Questions that can be answered with a yes *or* no

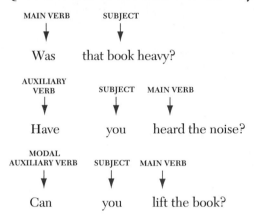

MAIN VERB	SUBJECT
↓	↓
Was	that book heavy?

AUXILIARY VERB	SUBJECT	MAIN VERB
↓	↓	↓
Have	you	heard the noise?

MODAL AUXILIARY VERB	SUBJECT	MAIN VERB
↓	↓	↓
Can	you	lift the book?

To form a yes-or-no question with a verb other than *be* as the main verb and when there is no auxiliary or modal as part of a VERB PHRASE, use the appropriate form of the auxiliary verb *do*.

AUXILIARY VERB	SUBJECT	MAIN VERB
↓	↓	↓
Do	you	want me to put the book away?

A question that begins with a question-forming word like *why, when, where,* or *how* cannot be answered with a yes or no: **Why** *did the book fall?* Some kind of information must be provided to answer such a question; the answer cannot be simply yes or no because the question is not "*Did the book fall?*" Information on *why* it fell is needed: for example, *It was too heavy for me.*

Information questions: Inverted order

Most information questions follow the same rules of inverted word order as yes-or-no questions.

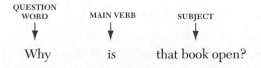

QUESTION WORD	MAIN VERB	SUBJECT
↓	↓	↓
Why	is	that book open?

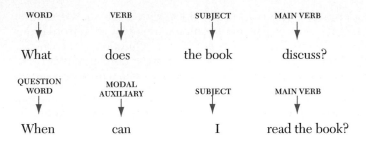

WORD	VERB	SUBJECT	MAIN VERB
What	does	the book	discuss?

QUESTION WORD	MODAL AUXILIARY	SUBJECT	MAIN VERB
When	can	I	read the book?

Information questions: Standard order

When *who* or *what* functions as the subject in a question, use standard word order.

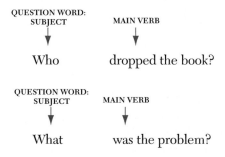

QUESTION WORD: SUBJECT	MAIN VERB
Who	dropped the book?

QUESTION WORD: SUBJECT	MAIN VERB
What	was the problem?

👁 **ALERT:** When a question has more than one auxiliary verb, put the subject after the first auxiliary verb. ●

FIRST AUXILIARY	SUBJECT	SECOND AUXILIARY	MAIN VERB
Would	you	have	replaced the book?

The same rules apply to emphatic exclamations: ***Was*** *that book heavy!* ***Did*** *she enjoy that book!*

Negatives

When you use negatives such *as never, hardly ever, seldom, rarely, not only,* or *nor* to start a CLAUSE, use inverted order. These sentence pairs show the differences, first in standard order and then in inverted order.

I have never seen a more exciting movie. [standard order]

Never have I seen a more exciting movie. [inverted order]

She is not only a talented artist **but also** an excellent musician.

Not only is she a talented artist, **but she is also** an excellent musician.

I didn't like the book, and **my husband didn't either.**

I didn't like the book, and **neither did my husband.**

👁 **USAGE ALERT:** With INDIRECT QUESTIONS, use standard word order: *She asked **how I dropped the book*** [not *She asked **how did I drop** the book*]. ●

👁 **STYLE ALERT:** Word order deliberately inverted can be effective, when used sparingly, to create emphasis in a sentence that is neither a question nor an exclamation (also see 19e). ●

47b How can I understand the placement of adjectives?

ADJECTIVES modify—describe or limit—NOUNS, PRONOUNS, and word groups that function as nouns (see 7f). In English, an adjective comes directly before the noun it describes. However, when more than one adjective describes the same noun, several sequences may be possible. Box 189 shows the most common order for positioning several adjectives.

🎯 **Word order for more than one adjective**   **189**

1. **Determiners, if any:** *a, an, the, my, your, this, that, these, those,* and so on
2. **Expressions of order, including ordinal numbers, if any:** *first, second, third, next, last, final,* and so on
3. **Expressions of quantity, including cardinal (counting) numbers, if any:** *one, two, few, each, every, some,* and so on
4. **Adjectives of judgment or opinion, if any:** *pretty, happy, ugly, sad, interesting, boring,* and so on
5. **Adjectives of size or shape, if any:** *big, small, short, round, square,* and so on
6. **Adjectives of age or condition, if any:** *new, young, broken, dirty, shiny,* and so on
7. **Adjectives of color, if any:** *red, green, blue,* and so on
8. **Adjectives that can also be used as nouns, if any:** *French, Protestant, metal, cotton,* and so on
9. **The noun**

1	2	3	4	5	6	7	8	9
a		few		tiny		red		ants
the	last	six					Thai	carvings
my			fine		old		oak	table

47c How can I understand the placement of adverbs?

ADVERBS modify—describe or limit—VERBS, ADJECTIVES, other adverbs, or entire sentences (see 7g). Adverbs may be positioned first, in the middle, or last in CLAUSES. Box 190 summarizes adverb types, what they tell about the words they modify, and where each type can be placed.

◉ Types of adverbs and where to position them   190

ADVERBS OF MANNER	■ describe *how* something is done	Nick **carefully** groomed the dog.
	■ are usually in middle or last position	Nick groomed the dog **carefully.**
ADVERBS OF TIME	■ describe *when* or *how long* about an event	**First,** he shampooed the dog.
	■ are usually in first or last position	He shampooed the dog **first.**
	■ include *just, still, already,* and similar adverbs, which are usually in middle position	He had **already** brushed the dog's coat.
ADVERBS OF FREQUENCY	■ describe *how often* an event takes place	Nick has **never** been bitten by a dog.
	■ are usually in middle position	
	■ are in first position when they modify an entire sentence (see "Sentence adverbs" on page 799)	**Occasionally,** he is scratched while shampooing a cat.
ADVERBS OF DEGREE OR EMPHASIS	■ describe *how much* or *to what extent* about other modifiers	Nick is **extremely** calm around animals. [*Extremely* modifies *calm.*]
	■ are directly before the word they modify	
	■ include *only,* which is easy to misplace (see 14a.2)	

→

Types of adverbs and where to position them *(continued)*		190
SENTENCE ADVERBS	■ modify the entire sentence rather than just one word or a few words ■ include transitional words and expressions (see 4g.1), as well as such expressions as *maybe, probably, possibly, fortunately, unfortunately,* and *incredibly* ■ are in first position	**Incredibly,** he was once asked to groom a rat.

👁 **USAGE ALERT:** Do not let an adverb separate a verb from its DIRECT OBJECT or INDIRECT OBJECT. ●

EXERCISE 47-1

Consulting all sections of this chapter, find and correct any errors in word order.

1. For two hundred years almost, the North Pacific humpback whales have returned to the tropic waters of Hawaii.
2. Why they are returning to these particular waters year after year?
3. The humpbacks do not accidentally arrive in Hawaiian waters; they are precise extremely in searching for this specific location, where they gather to complete their breeding rituals.
4. The whales first to arrive are sighted sometime in late November, after completing a 3,000-mile journey.
5. The humpbacks last to migrate to Hawaii arrive by December late or January early.

EXERCISE 47-2

Consulting all sections of this chapter, find and correct any errors in word order.

1. A beautiful few flowers began to bloom in my garden this week.
2. A neighbor asked me, "You did grow all these yourself?"
3. "Yes," I replied, "the roses are my favorite husband's, but my favorite are the tulips."
4. My neighbor, who extremely was impressed with my gardening efforts, decided to grow some flowers of her own.
5. Weeks later, as I strolled by her house, I saw her planting happily seeds from her favorite type of plant—petunias.

48 PREPOSITIONS

HOW TO USE CHAPTER 48 EFFECTIVELY

1. Use this chapter together with these handbook sections:
   - 7h, PREPOSITIONS
   - Chapter 21, using appropriate language
2. Remember that throughout this handbook, you can find the definitions of words printed in SMALL CAPITAL LETTERS in the Terms Glossary toward the end of this handbook.
3. Use **cross-references** (often given in parentheses) to find full explanations of key concepts.

Prepositions function with other words in PREPOSITIONAL PHRASES (7o). Prepositional phrases usually indicate *where* (direction or location), *how* (by what means or in what way), or *when* (at what time or how long) about the words they modify.

This chapter can help you with several uses of prepositions, which function in combination with other words in ways that are often idiomatic—that is, peculiar to the language. The meaning of an IDIOM differs from the literal meaning of each individual word. For example, the word *break* usually refers to shattering, but the sentence *Yao-Ming broke into a smile* means that a smile appeared on Yao-Ming's face. Knowing which preposition to use in a specific context takes much experience in reading, listening to, and speaking the language. A dictionary like the *Dictionary of American English* (Heinle & Heinle) can be especially helpful when you need to find the correct preposition to use in cases not covered by this chapter. Section 48a lists many common prepositions. Section 48b discusses prepositions with some expressions of time and place. Section 48c discusses combinations of verbs and prepositions called PHRASAL VERBS. Section 48d discusses common expressions using prepositions.

48a How can I recognize prepositions?

Box 191 lists many common prepositions.

◎ **Common prepositions** 191

about	before	except for	near	through
above	behind	excepting	next	throughout
according to	below	for	of	till
across	beneath	from	off	to
after	beside	in	on	toward
against	between	in addition to	onto	under
along	beyond	in back of	on top of	underneath
along with	but	in case of	out	unlike
among	by	in front of	out of	until
apart from	by means of	in place of	outside	up
around	concerning	inside	over	upon
as	despite	in spite of	past	up to
as for	down	instead of	regarding	with
at	during	into	round	within
because of	except	like	since	without

48b How do I use prepositions with expressions of time and place?

Box 192 shows how to use the prepositions *in, at,* and *on* to deliver some common kinds of information about time and place. The box, however, does not cover every preposition that indicates time or place, nor does it cover all uses of *in, at,* and *on.* Also, the box does not include expressions that operate outside the general rules. (Both these sentences are correct: *You ride **in** the car* and *You ride **on** the bus.*)

◎ **Using *in, at,* and *on* to show time and place** 192

Time

■ ***in* a year or a month** (*during* is also correct but less common)

   in 1995   **in** May

→

Using *in*, *at*, and *on* to show time and place *(continued)* 192

- *in* **a period of time**
  in a few months (seconds, days, years)

- *in* **a period of the day**
  in the morning (afternoon, evening)
  in the daytime (morning, evening) *but* at night

- *at* **a specific time or period of time**

at noon	at 2:00	at dawn	at nightfall

  at takeoff (the time a plane leaves)
  at breakfast (the time a specific meal takes place)

- *on* **a specific day**

on Friday	on my birthday

Place

- *in* **a location surrounded by something else**

in the province of Alberta	in the kitchen
in Utah	in the apartment
in downtown Bombay	in the bathtub

- *at* **a specific location**

at your house	at the bank

  at the corner of Third Avenue and Main Street

- *on* **a surface**
  on page 20
  on the second floor *but* in the attic *or* in the basement
  on Washington Street
  on the mezzanine
  on the highway

48c How do I use prepositions in phrasal verbs?

Phrasal verbs, also called *two-word verbs* and *three-word verbs,* are VERBS that combine with PREPOSITIONS to deliver their meaning. In some phrasal verbs, the verb and the preposition should not be separated by other words: **Look at** *the moon* [not **Look** *the moon* **at**]. In **separable phrasal verbs,** other words in the sentence can separate the verb and the preposition without interfering with meaning: *I* ***threw away*** *my homework* is as correct as *I* ***threw*** *my homework* ***away.***

Here is a list of some common phrasal verbs. The ones that cannot be separated are marked with an asterisk (*).

SELECTED PHRASAL VERBS

ask out	get along with*	look into
break down	get back	look out for*
bring about	get off*	look over
call back	go over*	make up
drop off	hand in	run across*
figure out	keep up with*	speak to*
fill out	leave out	speak with*
fill up	look after*	throw away
find out	look around	throw out

Position a PRONOUN OBJECT between the words of a separable phrasal verb: *I threw* ***it*** *away.* Also, you can position an object PHRASE of several words between the parts of a separable phrasal verb: *I threw* ***my research paper*** *away.* However, when the object is a CLAUSE, do not let it separate the parts of the phrasal verb: *I threw away* ***all the papers that I wrote last year.***

Many phrasal verbs are informal and are used more in speaking than in writing. For ACADEMIC WRITING, a more formal verb is usually more appropriate than a phrasal verb. In a research paper, for example, *propose* or *suggest* might be a better choice than *come up with.* For academic writing, acceptable phrasal verbs include *believe in, benefit from, concentrate on, consist of, depend on, dream of* (or *dream about*), *insist on, participate in, prepare for,* and *stare at.* None of these phrasal verbs can be separated.

EXERCISE 48-1

Consulting the preceding sections of this chapter and using the list of phrasal verbs in section 48c, write a one- or two-paragraph description of a typical day at work or school in which you use at least five phrasal verbs. After checking a dictionary, revise your writing, substituting for the phrasal verbs any more formal verbs that you think might be more appropriate for academic writing.

48d How do I use prepositions in common expressions?

In many common expressions, different PREPOSITIONS convey great differences in meaning. For example, four prepositions can be used with the verb *agree* to create five different meanings.

agree to means "to give consent": *I cannot **agree to** my buying you a new car.*

agree about means "to arrive at a satisfactory understanding": *We **agree about** your needing a car.*

agree on means "to concur": *You and the seller must **agree on** a price for the car.*

agree with means "to have the same opinion": *I **agree with** you that you need a car.*

agree with means "be suitable or healthful": *The idea of having such a major expense does not **agree with** me.*

You can find entire books filled with English expressions that include prepositions. The following list shows a few that you are likely to use often.

SELECTED EXPRESSIONS WITH PREPOSITIONS

ability in	different from	involved with [*someone*]
access to	faith in	knowledge of
accustomed to	familiar with	made of
afraid of	famous for	married to
angry with *or* at	frightened by	opposed to
authority on	happy with	patient with
aware of	in charge of	proud of
based on	independent of	reason for
capable of	in favor of	related to
certain of	influence on *or* over	suspicious of
confidence in	interested in	time for
dependent on	involved in [*something*]	tired of

49 GERUNDS, INFINITIVES, AND PARTICIPLES

HOW TO USE CHAPTER 49 EFFECTIVELY

1. Use this chapter together with these handbook sections:
   - 7e, VERBALS
   - 7l–7m, SUBJECTS and OBJECTS
   - 8b, principal parts of VERBS
   - 10b, SUBJECT-VERB AGREEMENT
   - Chapter 18, PARALLELISM

2. Remember that throughout this handbook, you can find the definitions of words printed in SMALL CAPITAL LETTERS in the Terms Glossary found toward the end of this handbook.

3. Use **cross-references** (often given in parentheses) to find full explanations of key concepts.

PARTICIPLES are verb forms (see 8b). A verb's *-ing* form is its PRESENT PARTICIPLE. The *-ed* form of a regular verb is its PAST PARTICIPLE; IRREGULAR VERBS form their past participles in various ways (for example, *bend, bent; eat, eaten; think, thought*—for a complete list, see Box 61 in section 8d, pages 186–189). Participles can function as ADJECTIVES (*a smiling face, a closed book*).

A verb's *-ing* form can also function as a NOUN (***Sneezing** spreads colds*), which is called a GERUND. Another verb form, the INFINITIVE, can also function as a noun. An infinitive is a verb's SIMPLE or base FORM, usually preceded by the word *to* (*We want everyone **to smile***). Verb forms—participles, gerunds, and infinitives—functioning as nouns or MODIFIERS are called VERBALS, as explained in section 7e.

This chapter can help you make the right choices among verbals. Section 49a discusses gerunds and infinitives used as subjects. Section 49b discusses verbs that are followed by gerunds, not infinitives. Section 49c discusses verbs that are followed by infinitives, not gerunds. Section 49d discusses meaning changes that depend on whether certain verbs are followed by a gerund or by an infinitive. Section 49e explains that meaning does not change for certain sense verbs no matter whether they are followed by a gerund or an infinitive. Section 49f discusses differences in meaning between the present participle form and the past participle form of some modifiers.

49a How can I use gerunds and infinitives as subjects?

Gerunds are used more commonly than infinitives as subjects. Sometimes, however, either is acceptable.

Choosing the right health club is important.

To choose the right health club is important.

◉ **VERB ALERT:** When a gerund or an infinitive is used alone as a subject, it is SINGULAR and requires a singular verb. When two or more gerunds or infinitives create a COMPOUND SUBJECT, they require a plural verb. (See sections 7l and 10e.) ●

49b When do I use a gerund, not an infinitive, as an object?

Some VERBS must be followed by GERUNDS used as DIRECT OBJECTS. Other verbs must be followed by INFINITIVES. Still other verbs can be followed by either a gerund or an infinitive. (A few verbs can change meaning depending on whether they are followed by a gerund or an infinitive; see section 49d.) Box 193 lists common verbs that must be followed by gerunds, not infinitives.

Yuri **considered** *calling* [not *to call*] the mayor.

He **was having trouble** *getting* [not *to get*] a work permit.

Yuri's boss **recommended** *taking* [not *to take*] an interpreter to the permit agency.

◉ **Verbs and expressions that must be followed by gerunds**   **193**

acknowledge	detest	mind
admit	discuss	object to
advise	dislike	postpone

➡

> **Verbs and expressions that must be** 193
> **followed by gerunds** *(continued)*
>
> | | | |
> |---|---|---|
> | anticipate | dream about | practice |
> | appreciate | enjoy | put off |
> | avoid | escape | quit |
> | cannot bear | evade | recall |
> | cannot help | favor | recommend |
> | cannot resist | finish | regret |
> | complain about | give up | resent |
> | consider | have trouble | resist |
> | consist of | imagine | risk |
> | contemplate | include | suggest |
> | defer from | insist on | talk about |
> | delay | keep (on) | tolerate |
> | deny | mention | understand |

Gerund after go

The word *go* is usually followed by an infinitive: *We can* **go to see** [not *go seeing*] *a movie tonight.* Sometimes, however, *go* is followed by a gerund in phrases such as *go swimming, go fishing, go shopping,* and *go driving: I will* **go shopping** [not *go to shop*] *after work.*

Gerund after be + *complement* + *preposition*

Many common expressions use a form of the verb *be* plus a COMPLEMENT plus a PREPOSITION. In such expressions, use a gerund, not an infinitive, after the preposition. Here is a list of some of the most frequently used expressions in this pattern.

SELECTED EXPRESSIONS USING BE + COMPLEMENT + PREPOSITION

be (get) accustomed to	be interested in
be angry about	be prepared for
be bored with	be responsible for
be capable of	be tired of
be committed to	be (get) used to
be excited about	be worried about

We **are excited about** *voting* [not *to vote*] in the next election.

Who **will be responsible for** *locating* [not *to locate*] our polling place?

👁 **USAGE ALERT:** Always use a gerund, not an infinitive, as the object of a preposition. Be especially careful when the word *to* is functioning as a preposition in a PHRASAL VERB (see 48c): *We are committed **to changing*** [not *to change*] *the rules.* ●

49c When do I use an infinitive, not a gerund, as an object?

Box 194 lists selected common verbs and expressions that must be followed by INFINITIVES, not GERUNDS, as OBJECTS.

She **wanted *to go*** [not *wanted going*] to the lecture.

Only three people **decided *to question*** [not *decided questioning*] the speaker.

◎ **Verbs and expressions that must be followed by infinitives**   **194**

afford	claim	hope	promise
agree	consent	intend	refuse
aim	decide	know how	seem
appear	decline	learn	struggle
arrange	demand	like	tend
ask	deserve	manage	threaten
attempt	do not care	mean	volunteer
be left	expect	offer	vote
beg	fail	plan	wait
cannot afford	give permission	prepare	want
care	hesitate	pretend	would like

Infinitives after be + complement

Gerunds are common in constructions that use forms of the verb *be*, a COMPLEMENT, and a PREPOSITION (see 49b). However, use an infinitive, not a gerund, when *be* plus a complement is not followed by a preposition.

We **are eager *to go*** [not *going*] camping.

I **am ready *to sleep*** [not *sleeping*] in a tent.

Infinitives to indicate purpose

Use an infinitive in expressions that indicate purpose: *I read a book to learn more about Mayan culture.* This sentence means "I read a book for the purpose of learning more about Mayan culture." *To learn* delivers the idea of purpose more concisely (see Chapter 16) than expressions such as *so that I can* or *in order to.*

Infinitives with the first, the last, the one

Use an infinitive after the expressions *the first, the last,* and *the one: Nina is the first to arrive* [not *arriving*] *and the last to leave* [not *leaving*] *every day. She's always the one to do the most.*

Unmarked infinitives

Infinitives used without the word *to* are called **unmarked infinitives,** or sometimes *bare infinitives.* An unmarked infinitive may be hard to recognize because it is not preceded by *to.* Some common verbs followed by unmarked infinitives are *feel, have, hear, let, listen to, look at, make* (meaning "compel"), *notice, see,* and *watch.*

Please let me **take** [not *to take*] you to lunch. [unmarked infinitive]

I want **to take** you to lunch. [marked infinitive]

I can have Kara **drive** [not *to drive*] us. [unmarked infinitive]

I will ask Kara **to drive** us. [marked infinitive]

The verb *help* can be followed by a marked or an unmarked infinitive. Either is correct: *Help me **put** [or **to put**] this box in the car.*

👁 **USAGE ALERT:** Be careful to use parallel structure (see Chapter 18) correctly when you use two or more gerunds or infinitives after verbs. If two or more VERBAL OBJECTS follow one verb, put the verbals into the same form.

NO We went **sailing** and **to scuba dive.**
YES We went **sailing** and **scuba diving.**

NO We heard the wind **blow** and the waves **crashing.**
YES We heard the wind **blow** and the waves **crash.**
YES We heard the wind **blowing** and the waves **crashing.**

Conversely, if you are using verbal objects with COMPOUND PREDICATES, be sure to use the kind of verbal that each verb requires.

NO We enjoyed **scuba diving** but do not plan **sailing** again.
[*Enjoyed* requires a gerund object, and *plan* requires an infinitive object; see Boxes 193 and 194.]
YES We enjoyed **scuba diving** but do not plan **to sail** again. ●

49d How does meaning change when certain verbs are followed by a gerund or an infinitive?

With stop

The VERB *stop* followed by a GERUND means "finish, quit." *Stop* followed by an INFINITIVE means "interrupt one activity to begin another."

We **stopped** *eating.* [We finished our meal.]

We **stopped** *to eat.* [We stopped another activity, such as driving, in order to eat.]

With remember *and* forget

The verb *remember* followed by an infinitive means "not to forget to do something": *I must **remember to talk** with Isa. Remember* followed by a gerund means "recall a memory": *I **remember talking** in my sleep last night.*

The verb *forget* followed by an infinitive means "fail to do something": *If you **forget to put** a stamp on that letter, it will be returned. Forget* followed by a gerund means "do something and not recall it": *I **forget having put** the stamps in the refrigerator.*

With try

The verb *try* followed by an infinitive means "make an effort": *I **tried to find** your jacket.* Followed by a gerund, *try* means "experiment with": *I **tried jogging** but found it too difficult.*

49e Why is the meaning unchanged whether or not a gerund or an infinitive follows sense verbs?

Sense VERBS include words such as *see, notice, hear, observe, watch, feel, listen to,* and *look at.* The meaning of these verbs is usually not affected by whether a GERUND or an INFINITIVE follows as the OBJECT. *I **saw** the water **rise** and I **saw** the water **rising*** both have the same meaning in American English.

EXERCISE 49-1

Consulting sections 49b through 49e, write the correct form of the verbal object (either a gerund or an infinitive) for each verb in parentheses.

EXAMPLE   People like (think) <u>to think</u> that they have a good memory, but everybody shows signs of forgetfulness from time to time.

1. Think about (ride) _____ the railroad to work on a rainy Monday morning.
2. The comfortable reclining seats let passengers (take) _____ a relaxing nap on the way to work.
3. Because of the rain, commuters are forced (bring) _____ an umbrella and a raincoat, along with their usual traveling items.
4. Once they reach their destination, passengers forget that they need their umbrellas and raincoats (walk) _____ the few blocks to work.
5. (Step) _____ out into the rain makes them suddenly realize that they've left their umbrellas and raincoats on the train, which has already left the station.
6. However, they need not be angry about (lose) _____ the forgotten item.
7. Many railroads have lost-and-found offices that help (reunite) _____ the rightful owners with their lost possessions.
8. After losing a possession, passengers tend (call) _____ the lost-and-found office in search of the missing article.
9. Some commuters even acknowledge (leave) _____ gifts, false teeth, wooden legs, and bicycles aboard the train.
10. Most times, people can claim their possessions either by (answer) _____ a few questions to ensure proper ownership or by (identify) _____ the lost item.

49f How do I choose between -*ing* and -*ed* forms for adjectives?

Deciding whether to use the -*ing* form (PRESENT PARTICIPLE) or the -*ed* form (PAST PARTICIPLE of a regular VERB) as an ADJECTIVE in a specific sentence can be difficult. For example, *I am **amused*** and *I am **amusing*** are both correct in English, but their meanings are very different. To make the right choice, decide whether the modified NOUN or PRONOUN is causing or experiencing what the participle describes.

Use a present participle (-*ing*) to modify a noun or pronoun that is the agent or the cause of the action.

Micah described your **interesting** plan. [The noun *plan* causes what its modifier describes—interest; so *interesting* is correct.]

I find your plan **exciting.** [The noun *plan* causes what its modifier describes—excitement; so *exciting* is correct.]

Use a past participle (-*ed* in regular verbs) to modify a noun or pronoun that experiences or receives whatever the modifier describes.

An **interested** committee wants to hear your plan. [The noun *committee* experiences what its modifier describes—interest; so *interested* is correct.]

Excited by your plan, they called a board meeting. [The pronoun *they* experiences what its modifier describes—excitement; so *excited* is correct.]

811

Here are frequently used participles that convey very different meanings, depending on whether the *-ed* or the *-ing* form is used.

amused, amusing	frightened, frightening
annoyed, annoying	insulted, insulting
appalled, appalling	offended, offending
bored, boring	overwhelmed, overwhelming
confused, confusing	pleased, pleasing
depressed, depressing	reassured, reassuring
disgusted, disgusting	satisfied, satisfying
fascinated, fascinating	shocked, shocking

EXERCISE 49-2

Consulting section 49f, choose the correct participle from each pair in parentheses.

EXAMPLE   It can be a (satisfied, satisfying) <u>satisfying</u> experience to learn about the lives of artists.

1. Artist Frida Kahlo led an (interested, interesting) _____ life.
2. When Kahlo was eighteen, (horrified, horrifying) _____ observers saw her (injured, injuring) _____ in a streetcar accident.
3. A (disappointed, disappointing) _____ Kahlo had to abandon her plan to study medicine.
4. Instead, she began to create paintings filled with (disturbed, disturbing) _____ images.
5. Some art critics consider Kahlo's paintings to be (fascinated, fascinating) _____ works of art, though many people find them (overwhelmed, overwhelming) _____.

EXERCISE 49-3

Consulting section 49f, choose the correct participle from each pair in parenthesis.

EXAMPLE   Learning about the career of a favorite actor or actress is always an (interested, interesting) <u>interesting</u> exercise.

1. Canadian Jim Carrey is an actor-comedian with a very (fascinated, fascinating) _____ history.
2. (Raised, Raising) _____ by his parents in southern Ontario, Carrey grew up in one of the most media-rich areas in North America.
3. Biographies reveal the (surprised, surprising) _____ news that this bright and talented student dropped out of school during the tenth grade.

4. After relocating to Los Angeles in the 1980s, the (disappointed, disappointing) _____ Carrey discovered the difficulties of acting after his first (canceled, canceling) _____ TV series left him briefly out of work.

5. Carrey's career skyrocketed with his (amused, amusing) _____ appearances on *In Living Color,* a TV show that led to a string of box-office hits like *Ace Ventura: Pet Detective, The Mask,* and *The Truman Show.*

EXERCISE 49-4

Consulting section 49f, choose the correct participle from each pair in parentheses.

EXAMPLE   Studying popular myths that turn out to be false can be a (fascinated, fascinating) *fascinating* experience.

1. While doing research for a paper about birds, I discovered some (interested, interesting) _____ information about ostriches.

2. I encountered an (unsettled, unsettling) _____ passage in a book, which said that ostriches do not, in fact, stick their heads into the sand for protection when they feel fear.

3. This myth about (frightened, frightening) _____ ostriches began among the ancient Arabs and has since been passed on by many reputable writers.

4. In reality, an ostrich does not have to do something as useless as bury its head in the sand when a predator approaches, because a (hunted, hunting) _____ ostrich can reach speeds of nearly 35 mph and can thus outrun most other animals.

5. A (threatened, threatening) _____ ostrich can also kick its way out of many dangerous situations with its powerful legs, and with its 8-foot-tall frame, it presents itself as a (frightened, frightening) _____ opponent.

50 MODAL AUXILIARY VERBS

HOW TO USE CHAPTER 50 EFFECTIVELY

1. Use this chapter together with these handbook sections:

   - 7d, recognizing VERBS
   - 8e, AUXILIARY VERBS
   - 8g-8i, VERB TENSE
   - 8j, PROGRESSIVE TENSES
   - 8m, SUBJUNCTIVE MOOD

2. Remember that throughout this handbook, you can find the definitions of words printed in SMALL CAPITAL LETTERS in the Terms Glossary toward the end of the handbook.

3. Use **cross-references** (often given in parentheses) to find full explanations of key concepts.

   Auxiliary verbs are known as *helping verbs* because adding an auxiliary verb to a MAIN VERB helps the main verb convey additional information (see 8e). For example, the auxiliary verb *do* is important in turning sentences into questions. *You have to sleep* becomes a question when *do* is added: *Do you have to sleep?* The most common auxiliary verbs are forms of *be, have,* and *do.* Boxes 63 and 64 in section 8e (see pages 191–192) list the forms of these three verbs.

   MODAL AUXILIARY VERBS are one type of auxiliary verb. They include *can, could, may, might, should, had better, must, will, would,* and others discussed in this chapter. Modals differ from *be, have,* and *do* used as auxiliary verbs in the specific ways discussed in Box 195.

   This chapter can help you use modals to convey shades of meaning. Section 50a discusses using modals to convey ability, necessity, advisabil-

814

◎ Modals and their differences   195 <br> from other auxiliary verbs

- Modals in the present future are always followed by the SIMPLE FORM of a main verb: *I **might** go* tomorrow.

- One-word modals have no *-s* ending in the THIRD-PERSON SINGULAR: *She **could** go with me; you **could** go with me; they **could** go with me.* (The two-word modal *have to* changes form to agree with its subject: *I **have to** leave; she **has to** leave.*) Auxiliary verbs other than modals usually change form for third-person singular: *I **do** want to go; he **does** want to go.*

- Some modals change form in the past. Others (*should, would, must,* which convey probability, and *ought to*) use *have* + a PAST PARTICIPLE. *I **can** do it* becomes *I **could** do it* in PAST-TENSE CLAUSES about ability. *I **could** do it* becomes *I **could have done** it* in clauses about possibility.

- Modals convey meaning about ability, necessity, advisability, possibility, and other conditions: For example, *I can go* means "I am able to go." Modals do not describe actual occurrences.

---

ity, possibility, and probability. Section 50b discusses using modals to convey preferences, plans or obligations, and past habits. Section 50c introduces modals in the PASSIVE VOICE.

50a How do I convey ability, necessity, advisability, possibility, and probability with modals?

Conveying ability

The MODAL *can* conveys ability now (in the present), and *could* conveys ability before (in the past). These words deliver the meaning "able to." For the future, use *will be able to*.

We **can** work late tonight. [*Can* conveys present ability.]

I **could** work late last night, too. [*Could* conveys past ability.]

I **will be able to** work late next Monday. [*Will be able* is the future tense; *will* here is not a modal.]

Adding *not* between a modal and the MAIN VERB makes the CLAUSE negative: *We **cannot** work late tonight; I **could not** work late last night; I **will not be able to** work late next Monday.*

👁 **USAGE ALERT:** You will often see negative forms of modals turned into CONTRACTIONS: *can't, couldn't, won't, wouldn't,* and others. Because contractions are considered informal usage by some instructors, you will never be wrong if you avoid them in ACADEMIC WRITING, except when you are reproducing spoken words. ●

Conveying necessity

The modals *must* and *have to* convey a need to do something. Both *must* and *have to* are followed by the simple form of the main verb. In the present tense, *have to* changes form to agree with its subject.

You **must** leave before midnight.

She **has to** leave when I leave.

In the past tense, *must* is never used to express necessity. Instead, use *had to.*

PRESENT TENSE   We **must** study today. We **have to** study today.

PAST TENSE   We **had to** [not *must*] take a test yesterday.

The negative forms of *must* and *have to* also have different meanings. *Must not* conveys that something is forbidden; *do not have to* conveys that something is not necessary.

You **must not** sit there. [Sitting there is forbidden.]

You **do not have to** sit there. [Sitting there is not necessary.]

Conveying advisability or the notion of a good idea

The modals *should* and *ought to* express the idea that doing the action of the main verb is advisable or is a good idea.

You **should** go to class tomorrow morning.

In the past tense, *should* and *ought to* convey regret or knowing something through hindsight. They mean that good advice was not taken.

You **should have** gone to class yesterday.

I **ought to have** called my sister yesterday.

The modal *had better* delivers the meaning of good advice or warning or threat. It does not change form for tense.

You **had better** see the doctor before your cough gets worse.

Need to is often used to express strong advice, too. Its past-tense form is *needed to*.

You **need to** take better care of yourself. You **needed to** listen.

Conveying possibility

The modals *may, might,* and *could* can be used to convey an idea of possibility or likelihood.

We **may** become hungry before long.

We **could** eat lunch at the diner next door.

For the past-tense form, use *may, might,* and *could,* followed by *have* and the past participle of the main verb.

I **could have studied** French in high school, but I studied Spanish instead.

Conveying probability

In addition to conveying the idea of necessity (see page 816), the modal auxiliary verb *must* can also convey probability or likelihood. It means that a well-informed guess is being made.

Marisa **must** be a talented actress. She has been chosen to play the lead role in the school play.

When *must* conveys probability, the past tense is *must have* plus the past participle of the main verb.

I did not see Boris at the party; he **must have left** early.

EXERCISE 50-1

Consulting section 50a, fill in the blanks with the past-tense modal auxiliary that expresses the meaning given in parentheses.

EXAMPLE I (advisability) <u>should have</u> gone straight to the doctor the instant I felt a cold coming on.

1. Since I (necessity, no choice) _____ work late this past Monday, I could not get to the doctor's office before it closed.
2. I (advisability) _____ fallen asleep after dinner, but I stayed awake for a while instead.
3. Even after I finally got into bed, I (ability) _____ not relax.
4. I (making a guess) _____ not _____ heard the alarm the next morning, because I overslept nearly two hours.
5. When I finally arrived at work, my boss came into my office and said, "Julie, you (necessity) _____ stayed home and rested if you are sick."

50b How do I convey preferences, plans, and past habits with modals?

Conveying preferences

The modal *would rather* expresses a preference. *Would rather,* the PRESENT TENSE, is used with the SIMPLE FORM of the MAIN VERB, and *would rather have,* the PAST TENSE, is used with the PAST PARTICIPLE of the main verb.

We **would rather see** a comedy than a mystery.

Carlos **would rather have stayed** home last night.

Conveying plan or obligation

A form of *be* followed by *supposed to* and the simple form of a main verb delivers a meaning of something planned or of an obligation.

I **was supposed to meet** them at the bus stop.

Conveying past habit

The modals *used to* and *would* express the idea that something happened repeatedly in the past.

I **used to** hate going to the dentist.

I **would** dread every single visit.

◎ **USAGE ALERT:** Both *used to* and *would* can be used to express repeated actions in the past, but *would* cannot be used for a situation that lasted for a period of time in the past.

NO   I **would** live in Arizona.

YES   I **used to** live in Arizona. ●

50c How can I recognize modals in the passive voice?

MODALS use the ACTIVE VOICE, as shown in sections 50a and 50b. In the active voice, the subject does the action expressed in the MAIN VERB (see 8n and 8o).

Modals can also use the PASSIVE VOICE (8p). In the passive voice, the doer of the main verb's action is either unexpressed or is expressed as an OBJECT in a PREPOSITIONAL PHRASE starting with the word *by.*

PASSIVE   The waterfront **can be seen** from my window.

ACTIVE   I **can see** the waterfront from my window.

PASSIVE   The tax form **must be signed** by the person who fills it out.

ACTIVE   The person who fills out the tax form **must sign** it.

EXERCISE 50-2

Consulting section 50a, fill in the blanks with the past-tense modal auxiliary that expresses meaning given in parentheses.

EXAMPLE   I (advisability) <u>should have</u> waited for a rainy afternoon to visit the Empire State Building.

1. Since I (necessity, no choice) _____ work all week, Sunday was my only free day to visit the Empire State Building.
2. I (advisability) _____ known that because it was such a clear, beautiful day, everyone else would want to visit this New York City landmark, too.
3. The lines for the elevator were terribly long, and even though I am physically fit, I (ability) _____ not possibly climb the eighty-six flights of stairs to the observation deck near the top of the building.
4. The other visitors to the Empire State Building (probability) _____ noticed how impatient I was becoming by the look on my face.
5. Then I heard the security guard say to the woman in line ahead of me, "You (advice, good idea) _____ come yesterday. Because of the light drizzle, hardly anyone was here."

EXERCISE 50-3

Consulting all sections of this chapter, select the correct choice from the words in parentheses and write it in the blank.

EXAMPLE   When I was younger, I (would, used to) <u>used to</u> love to go bicycle riding.

1. You (ought to have, ought have) _____ called yesterday as you had promised you would.
2. Judging by the size of the puddles in the street outside, it (must be rained, must have rained) _____ all night long.
3. Ingrid (must not have, might not have been) _____ as early for the interview as she claims she was.
4. After all the studying he did, Pedro (should have, should have been) _____ less frightened by the exam.
5. I have to go home early today, although I really (cannot, should not) _____ leave before the end of the day because of all the work I have to do.

EXERCISE 50-4

Consulting all sections of this chapter, select the correct choice from the words in parentheses and write it in the blank.

EXAMPLE   We (must have, must) <u>must</u> study this afternoon.

1. Unfortunately, I (should not, cannot) _____ go to the movies with you because I have to take care of my brother tonight.
2. Juan (would have, would have been) _____ nominated class valedictorian if he had not moved to another city.
3. You (ought not have, ought not to have) _____ arrived while the meeting was still in progress.
4. Louise (must be, must have been) _____ sick to miss the party last week.
5. Had you not called in advance, you (may not have, may not have been) _____ aware of the traffic on the expressway.

TERMS GLOSSARY

This glossary defines important terms used in this handbook, including the ones that are printed in small capital letters. Many of these glossary entries end with parenthetical references to the handbook section(s) or chapter(s) where the specific term is fully discussed.

absolute adjective An adjective that communicates a noncomparable quality or state, such as *unique* or *perfect*. (11e.2)

absolute phrase A phrase containing a subject and a participle that modifies an entire sentence. (7o)

- **The semester** [subject] **being** [present participle of *be*] **over,** the campus looks deserted.

abstract noun A noun that names something not knowable through the five senses: *idea, respect*. (7b)

academic writing Writing you do for college classes. (1d)

action verbs Strong verbs that increase the impact of your language and reduce wordiness. *Weak verbs*, such as *be* or *have*, increase wordiness. (16e)

active voice An attribute of verbs showing that the action or condition expressed in the verb is done by the subject, in contrast with the *passive voice*, which conveys that the action or condition of the verb is done to the subject. (8n, 8o)

adjective A word that describes or limits (modifies) a noun, a pronoun, or a word group functioning as a noun: *silly, three*. (7f, Chapter 11)

adjective clause A dependent clause, also known as a *relative clause*. An adjective clause modifies a preceding noun or pronoun and begins with a relative word (such as *who, which, that,* or *where*) that relates the clause to the noun or pronoun it modifies. Also see *clause*. (7p.2)

adverb A word that describes or limits (modifies) verbs, adjectives, other adverbs, phrases, or clauses: *loudly, very, nevertheless, there*. (4g, Chapter 11)

adverb clause A dependent clause beginning with a subordinating conjunction that establishes the relationship in meaning between the adverb clause and its independent clause. An adverb clause modifies the independent clause's verb or the entire independent clause. Also see *clause, conjunction*. (7p.2)

agreement The required match of number and person between a subject and verb or a pronoun and antecedent. A pronoun that expresses gender must match its antecedent in gender also. (Chapter 10)

analogy An explanation of the unfamiliar in terms of the familiar. Like a simile, an analogy compares things not normally associated with each other; but unlike a simile, an analogy does not use *like* or *as* in making the comparison. Analogy is also a rhetorical strategy for developing paragraphs. (4i.9, 21d, 41b)

analysis A process of critical thinking that divides a whole into its component parts in order to understand how the parts interrelate. Sometimes called *division*, analysis is also a rhetorical strategy for developing paragraphs. (4i.6, 5b, 40d.4, 41b)

antecedent The noun or pronoun to which a pronoun refers. (9m–9s, 10n–10s)

APA style See *documentation style*.

appeals to reason Tools a writer uses to convince the reader that the reasoning in an argument is sound and effective; there are three types—logical, emotional and ethical appeals. (6h)

appositive A word or group of words that renames a preceding noun or noun phrase: *my favorite month,* **October.** (7n.3)

argument A rhetorical attempt to convince others to agree with a position about a topic open to debate. (1b, Chapter 6)

articles Also called *determiners* or *noun markers,* articles are the words *a, an,* and *the. A* and *an* are indefinite articles, and *the* is a definite article; also see *determiner.* (7f, Chapter 46)

assertion A statement. In developing a thesis statement, an assertion is a sentence that makes a statement and expresses a point of view about a topic; in writing argument, an assertion is the position you want to argue. (2q, 6c)

audience The readers to whom a piece of writing is directed; the three types include *general audience, peer audience,* and *specialist audience.* (1d)

auxiliary verb Also known as a *helping verb,* an auxiliary verb is a form of *be, do, have, can, may, will,* or certain other verbs, that combines with a main verb to help it express tense, mood, and voice. Also see *modal auxiliary verb.* (8e)

biased language Language that conveys or appeals to prejudice or stereotypes. Also see *sexist language.* (3c.5, 6h, 21h, 42f)

bibliographic notes In a note system of documentation, a *footnote* or *endnote* gives the bibliographic information the first time a source is cited. (31b, 35d.2, Chapter 37)

bibliography A list of information about sources. (Chapters 35, 36, and 37)

body paragraphs Paragraphs that provide the substance of your message in a sequence that makes sense. (2n, 3b, 4a, 4c)

Boolean expressions In a search engine, symbols or words such as And, Or, Not, and Near that let you create keyword combinations that narrow and refine your search. (2l, 34d.2)

brainstorming Listing all ideas that come to mind on a topic and then grouping the ideas by patterns that emerge. (2h)

browser A program that gives you access to the World Wide Web and the search engines located there. (34b)

bureaucratic language Sometimes called *bureaucratese;* language that is overblown or overly complex. (21m)

business writing Writing designed for business, including letters, memos, resumes, job application letters, and e-mail messages. (1e, 4a, Chapter 42)

case The form of a noun or pronoun in a specific context that shows whether it is functioning as a subject, an object, or a possessive. In modern English, nouns change form in the possessive case only (*city* = form for subjective and objective cases; *city's* = possessive-case form). Also see *pronoun case.* (9a–9j)

cause and effect The relationship between outcomes (effects) and the reasons for them (causes). Cause-and-effect analysis is a rhetorical strategy for developing paragraphs. (4l.10, 5h, 5i, 5k)

chronological order Also called time order, an arrangement of information according to time sequence; an organizing strategy for sentences, paragraphs, and longer pieces of writing. (4h)

citation Information to identify a source quoted, paraphrased, summarized, or referred to in a piece of writing; *in-text citations* are in *sentences* or *parenthetical references.* Also see *documentation.* (Chapters 31, 33, and 35)

classification A rhetorical strategy for paragraph development that organizes information by grouping items according to underlying shared characteristics. (4i.7)

clause A group of words containing a subject and a predicate. A clause that delivers full meaning is called an *independent* (or *main) clause.* A clause that lacks full meaning by itself is called a *dependent* (or *subordinate) clause.* Also see *adjective clause, adverb clause, nonrestrictive element, noun clause, restrictive element.* (7p)

cliché An overused, worn-out phrase that has lost its capacity to communicate effectively: *flat as Kansas, ripe old age.* (21h, 21j)

climactic order Sometimes called *emphatic order,* climactic order is an arrangement of ideas or other kinds of information from least important to most important. (4h.5, 6e)

clustering See *mapping.*

coherence The clear progression from one idea to another using transitional expressions, pronouns, selective repetition, or parallelism to make connections between ideas. (3c.4, 4g)

823

collaborative writing Students working together to write a paper. (1d, 3f)

collective noun A noun that names a group of people or things: *family, committee.* Also see *noncount noun.* (7b, 10i, 10s)

colloquial language Casual or conversational language. Also see *slang.* (21h)

comma splice The error that occurs when only a comma connects two independent clauses; also called a *comma fault.* (Chapter 13)

common noun A noun that names a general group, place, person, or thing: *dog, house.* (7b)

comparative The form of a descriptive adjective or adverb that expresses a different degree of intensity between two: *bluer, less blue; more easily, less easily.* Also see *positive, superlative.* (11e.1)

comparison and contrast A rhetorical strategy for organizing and developing paragraphs by discussing similarities (*comparison*) and differences (*contrast*). It has two patterns: *point-by-point* or *block organization.* (4i.8)

complement An element after a verb that completes the predicate, such as a direct object after an action verb or a noun or adjective after a linking verb. Also see *object complement, predicate adjective, predicate nominative, subject complement.* (7n)

complete predicate See *predicate.*

complete subject See *subject.*

complex sentence See *sentence types.*

compound-complex sentence See *sentence types.*

compound noun See *subject.*

compound predicate See *predicate.*

compound sentence See *coordinate sentence, sentence types.*

compound subject See *subject.* (7l, 10e)

compound word Two or more words placed together to express one concept. (22j)

conciseness An attribute of writing that is direct and to the point. (Chapter 16)

conclusion See *syllogism.* (5i.2)

concrete noun A noun naming something that can be seen, touched, heard, smelled, or tasted: *smoke, sidewalk.* (7b)

conjunction A word that connects or otherwise establishes a relationship between two or more words, phrases, or clauses. Also see *coordinating conjunction, correlative conjunction, subordinating conjunction.* (7l)

conjunctive adverb An adverb, such as *therefore* or *meanwhile,* that communicates a logical connection in meaning. (7g)

connotation An idea implied by a word, involving associations and emotional overtones that go beyond the word's definition.

content note A note that records information and ideas that relate specifically to your topic. (32n)

contraction A word where an apostrophe takes the place of one or more omitted letters. (27d)

coordinate adjective Two or more adjectives of equal weight that modify a noun. (24e)

coordinate sentence Two or more independent clauses joined by either a semicolon or a comma with coordinating conjunction showing their relationship; also called a *compound sentence*. Also see *coordination*. (17b)

coordinating conjunction A conjunction that joins two or more grammatically equivalent structures: *and, or, for, nor, but, so, yet*. (7i, 13c.3, 17b, 17c)

coordination The use of grammatically equivalent forms to show a balance or sequence of ideas. (17a–17d, 17l)

correlative conjunction A pair of words that joins equivalent grammatical structures, including *both . . . and, either . . . or, neither . . . nor, not only . . . but* (or *but also*). (7i)

count noun A noun that names an item or items that can be counted: *radio, streets, idea, fingernails*. (7b, 45a, 45b, 46a, 46b)

critical reading A parallel process to critical thinking where you think about what you're reading while you're reading it. (5d, 40d)

critical response Formally, an essay summarizing a source's central point or main idea. It includes a *transitional statement* that bridges this summary and the writer's synthesized reactions in response. (5f)

critical thinking A form of thinking where you take control of your conscious thought processes. (5a, 5b, 31a.1, 32e, 32f.1, 33k)

cumulative adjectives Adjectives that build meaning from word to word: *distinctive musical style*. (24e)

cumulative sentence The most common structure for a sentence, with the subject and verb first, followed by modifiers adding details; also called a *loose sentence*. (19g)

dangling modifier A modifier that attaches its meaning illogically, either because it is closer to another noun or pronoun than to its true subject or because its true subject is not expressed in the sentence. (14d)

declarative sentence A sentence that makes a statement: *Sky diving is exciting*. Also see *exclamatory sentence, imperative sentence, interrogative sentence*. (7k)

deduction The process of reasoning from general claims to a specific instance. (5i.2)

definite article See *articles.*

definition A rhetorical strategy in which you define or give the meaning of words or ideas. Includes *extended definition.* (4i.5)

demonstrative pronoun A pronoun that points out the antecedent: *this, these; that, those.* (7c, 7f)

denotation The dictionary definition of a word. (21e.1)

dependent clause A clause that cannot stand alone as an independent grammatical unit. Also see *adjective clause, adverb clause, noun clause.* (7p.2, 12b)

description A rhetorical strategy that appeals to a reader's senses—sight, sound, smell, taste, and touch. (4i.2)

descriptive adjective An adjective that describes the condition or properties of the noun it modifies and (except for a very few such as *dead* and *unique*) has comparative and superlative forms: *flat, flatter, flattest.* (5e)

descriptive adverb An adverb that describes the condition or properties of whatever it modifies and that has comparative and superlative forms: *happily, more happily, most happily.* (7g)

determiner A word or word group, traditionally identified as an adjective, that limits a noun by telling how much or how many about it. Also called *expression of quantity, limiting adjective,* or *noun marker.* (7f, 45b, Chapter 46)

diction Word choice. (21e)

direct address Words naming a person or group being spoken to. Written words of direct address are set off by commas. (24g)

- The answer, **my friends,** lies with you. Go with them, **Gene.**

direct discourse In writing, words that repeat speech or conversation exactly and so are enclosed in quotation marks. (15e, 24g, 28e)

direct object A noun or pronoun or group of words functioning as a noun that receives the action (completes the meaning) of a transitive verb. (7m)

direct question A sentence that asks a question and ends with a question mark: *Are you going?* (23a, 23c)

direct quotation See *quotation.*

direct title A title that tells exactly what the essay will be about. (3c.3)

discovery draft A first draft developed from focused freewriting. (2g, 3a)

documentation The acknowledgment of someone else's words and ideas used in any piece of writing by giving full and accurate information about the person whose words were used and where those words were found. For example, for a print source, documentation usually includes names of all authors, title of the source, place and date of publication, and related information. (31b–31f, Chapters 35–37)

documentation style A system for providing information about the source of words, information, and ideas quoted, paraphrased, or summarized from some source other than the writer. Documentation styles discussed in this handbook are *MLA, APA, CM, CBE* and COS. (31b, Chapters 35–37)

document design A term for the placement of tables, graphs, and other illustrations, on printed and online material. (Chapter 38)

double negative A nonstandard negation using two negative modifiers rather than one. (11c)

drafting A part of the writing process in which writers compose ideas in sentences and paragraphs. *Drafts* are versions—*first* or *rough, revised,* and *final*—of one piece of writing. (3a)

Drop Test A method of checking for correct case in compound constructions. (9f, 9g, 9i)

edited American English English language use that conforms to established rules of grammar, sentence structure, punctuation, and spelling; also called *standard English.* (21c)

editing A part of the writing process in which writers check the technical correctness of grammar, spelling, punctuation, and mechanics. (3d)

elliptical construction A sentence or clause structure that deliberately omits words expressed elsewhere or that can be inferred from the context. (7p.2, 15h, 16d)

essential element See *restrictive element.*

euphemism Language that attempts to blunt certain realities by speaking of them in "nice" or "tactful" words. (21e)

evaluate A step in the critical thinking process where you judge the quality of the material you are assessing. (5b, 5c.2, 5g)

evidence Facts, data, examples, and opinions of others used to support assertions and conclusions. Also see *source.* (5g)

example A rhetorical strategy for paragraph development that presents particular instances of a larger category. *Extended example* or *illustration* presents additional details to make vivid an example. (4i.4)

exclamatory sentence A sentence beginning with *What* or *How* that expresses strong feeling: *What a ridiculous statement!* (7k)

expletive The phrase *there is (are), there was (were), it is,* or *it was* at the beginning of a clause, changing structure and postponing the subject:

■ **It is** Mars that we hope to reach. [Compare: *We hope to reach Mars*]. (9q.3, 16c)

expository writing See *informative writing.*

expression of quantity See *determiner.*

expressive purpose See *expressive writing.*

expressive writing Writing that reflects your personal thoughts and feelings. (1c.1)

faulty parallelism Grammatically incorrect writing that results from non-matching grammatical forms linked with coordinating conjunctions. (18e)

faulty predication A grammatically illogical combination of subject and predicate. (15g)

field research Primary research that involves going into real-life situations to observe, survey, interview, or be part of some activity. (32j, 41d.1)

figurative language Words that make connections and comparisons and draw on one image to explain another and enhance meaning. (21d)

finite verb A verb form that shows tense, mood, voice, person, and number while expressing an action, occurrence, or state of being.

first person See *person.*

focused freewriting A technique that may start with a set topic or may build on one sentence taken from earlier freewriting. (2g)

freewriting Writing nonstop for a period of time to generate ideas by free association of thoughts. Also see *discovery draft.* (2g)

fused sentence See *run-on sentence.*

future perfect progressive tense The form of the future perfect tense that describes an action or condition ongoing until some specific future time: *I will have been talking.* (8j)

future perfect tense The tense indicating that an action will have been completed or a condition will have ended by a specified point in the future: *I will have talked.* (8g, 8i)

future progressive tense The form of the future tense showing that a future action will continue for some time: *I will be talking.* (8j)

future tense The form of a verb, made with the simple form and either *shall* or *will,* expressing an action yet to be taken or a condition not yet experienced: *I will talk.*

gender Concerning languages, the classification of words as masculine, feminine, or neutral. In English, a few pronouns show changes in gender in third-person singular: *he, him, his; she, her, hers; it, its.* A few nouns naming roles change form to show gender difference: *prince, princess,* for example. (10r, 21b)

gender-neutral language See *sexist language.*

generalization A broad statement without details. (1c.3, 1d)

gerund A present participle functioning as a noun: ***Walking*** *is good exercise.* Also see *verbal.* (7e, 46c, Chapter 49)

gerund phrase A gerund, with its modifiers and objects, that functions as a subject or an object. (7o)

helping verb See *auxiliary verb*.

homonyms Words spelled differently that sound alike: *to, too, two*. (22f)

hyperbole See *overstatement*.

hypertext Web pages formatted in language that allows readers to jump from one page to another. (38e)

idiom A word, phrase, or other construction that has a different meaning from its usual meaning:

- He lost his head. She hit the ceiling. (Chapter 48)

idiomatic expression Words that depart from normal use; such as using *it* as the sentence subject when writing about time. (9q.3)

illogical predication See *faulty predication*.

imperative mood The mood that expresses commands and direct requests, using the simple form of the verb and often implying but not expressing the subject, you: *Go*. (8l)

imperative sentence A sentence that gives a command:

- Go to the corner to buy me a newspaper. (7k, 12b.3)

incubation The prewriting technique of giving ideas time to develop and clarify. (2m)

indefinite article See *articles, determiner*.

indefinite pronoun A pronoun, such as *all, anyone, each*, and *others*, that refers to a nonspecific person or thing. (7c, 7f, 10h)

independent clause A clause that can stand alone as an independent grammatical unit. (7p.1)

indicative mood The mood of verbs used for statements about real things or highly likely ones:

- I think Grace is arriving today. (8l, 15d)

indirect discourse Reported speech or conversation that does not use the exact structure of the original and so is not enclosed in quotation marks. (15e, 24h)

indirect object A noun or pronoun or group of words functioning as a noun that tells to whom or for whom the action expressed by a transitive verb was done. (7m)

indirect question A sentence that reports a question and ends with a period:

- I asked if you are leaving. (23a, 23c, 47a)

indirect quotation See *quotation*.

induction The reasoning process of arriving at general principles from particular facts or instances. (5i.1)

inductive reasoning A form of reasoning that moves from particular facts or instances to general principles. (5j.1)

inference What is suggested or implied but not stated. (5c.2)

infinitive A verbal made of the simple form of a verb and usually, but not always, *to* that functions as a noun, adjective, or adverb. Infinitives without the word *to* are called *unmarked* (or *bare*) *infinitives*. (7e, 8k, Chapter 49)

infinitive phrase An infinitive, with its modifiers and object, that functions as a noun, adjective, or adverb. Also see *verbal phrase*. (7e)

informal language Word choice that creates a tone appropriate for casual writing or speaking. (1e, 21h)

informative purpose See *informative writing*.

informative writing Writing that gives information and, when necessary, explains it; also known as *expository writing*. (1c.2)

intensive pronoun A pronoun that ends in *-self* and that intensifies its antecedent. Also called *reflexive pronoun:*

- Vida **himself** argued against it.

interjection An emotion-conveying word that is treated as a sentence, starting with a capital letter and ending with an exclamation point or a period: *Oh! Ouch!* (7j, 24j)

Internet A vast, international network of computers. An online server allows individuals to access information on the network and view it on their own computer. Also simply called the *Net*. An *Internet search* provides sources for writing. Also see *search engine*. (33h, 34a)

interrogative pronoun A pronoun, such as *whose* or *what*, that implies a question:

- **Who** called? (7c, 12b.1)

interrogative sentence A sentence that asks a direct question:

- Did you see that? (7k)

in-text citation Source information placed in parentheses within the body of a research paper. Also see *citation, parenthetical reference*. (35b, 36b)

intransitive verb A verb that does not take a direct object. (8f)

invention techniques Ways of gathering ideas for writing. Also see *planning, structured techniques*. (2g–2m)

inverted word order In contrast to standard order, the main verb or an auxiliary verb comes before the subject in inverted word order. Most questions and some exclamations use inverted word order. (10g, 19e, Chapter 47)

irony Words used to imply the opposite of their usual meaning. (21d)

irregular verb A verb that forms the past tense and past participle in some way other than by adding *-ed* or *-d*. (8d)

jargon A particular field's or group's specialized vocabulary that a general reader is unlikely to understand. (21k)

layout The arrangement of text and visuals on a page. (38b)

levels of formality Word choices and sentence structures reflecting various degrees of formality of language. A formal level is used for ceremonial and other occasions when stylistic flourishes are appropriate. A medium level, neither too formal nor too casual, is acceptable for most academic writing. (21b)

levels of generality Degrees of generality used to group or organize information or ideas as you write, as when moving from the most general to the least specific. Conversely, *levels of specificity* move from the most specific to the most general. (2o)

limiting adjective See *determiner.*

linking verb A main verb that links a subject with a subject complement that renames or describes the subject. Linking verbs, sometimes called *copulative verbs,* convey a state of being, relate to the senses, or indicate a condition. (8a, 8c)

logical fallacies Flaws in reasoning that lead to illogical statements. (5j)

main clause See *independent clause.*

main verb A verb that expresses action, occurrence, or state of being and that shows mood, tense, voice, number, and person. (8b)

mapping An invention technique based on thinking about a topic and its increasingly specific subdivisions; also known as *clustering* or *webbing.* (2j)

mechanics Conventions governing matters such as the use of capital letters, italics, abbreviations, and numbers. (Chapter 30)

metaphor A comparison implying similarity between two things; a metaphor does not use words such as *like* or *as,* which are used in a simile and which make a comparison explicit: *a mop of hair* (compare the simile *hair like a mop*). (21d)

misplaced modifier Describing or limiting words that are wrongly positioned in a sentence so that their message is either illogical or relates to the wrong word or words. Also see *squinting modifier.* (14a)

mixed construction A sentence that unintentionally changes from one grammatical structure to another, incompatible one, so that the meaning is garbled. (15f)

mixed metaphors Incongruously combined images. (21d)

MLA style See *documentation style, parenthetical reference.*

modal auxiliary verb A group of nine auxiliary verbs that add information such as a sense of needing, wanting, or having to do something or a sense of possibility, likelihood, obligation, permission, or ability. (8e, Chapter 50)

modifier A word or group of words functioning as an adjective or adverb to describe or limit another word or word group. Also see *misplaced modifier*. (7n.2, Chapter 11, 19e)

mood The attribute of verbs showing a speaker's or writer's attitude toward the action by the way verbs are used. English has three moods: imperative, indicative, and subjunctive. Also see *imperative mood, indicative mood, subjunctive mood*. (8l, 8m)

narrative (narration) A rhetorical strategy that tells a story; a *narration* deals with what is or what has happened. (4i.1)

noncount noun A noun that names a thing that cannot be counted: *water, time*. Also see *collective noun*. (7b, Chapters 45 and 46)

nonessential element See *nonrestrictive element*.

nonrestrictive clause See *nonrestrictive element*.

nonrestrictive element A descriptive word, phrase, or dependent clause that provides information not essential to understanding the basic message of the element it modifies and so is set off by commas. Also see *restrictive element*. (24f)

nonsexist language See *sexist language*.

nonspecific noun A noun that refers to any of a number of identical items; it takes the indefinite articles *a, an*. (46a)

nonstandard English Language usage other than *edited American English*. (21c)

noun A word that names a person, place, thing, or idea. Nouns function as subjects, objects, or complements. (7b)

noun clause A dependent clause that functions as a subject, object, or complement. (7p.2)

noun complement See *complement*.

noun determiner See *determiner*.

noun phrase A noun and its modifiers functioning as a subject, object, or complement. (7o)

number The attribute of some words indicating whether they refer to one (*singular*) or more than one (*plural*). (8a, 10b, 15b, Chapter 45)

object A noun, pronoun, or group of words functioning as a noun or pronoun that receives the action of a verb (*direct object*); tells to whom or for whom something is done (*indirect object*); or completes the meaning of a preposition (*object of a preposition*). (7m)

object complement A noun or adjective renaming or describing a direct object after verbs such as *call, consider, name, elect,* and *think:*

- I call some joggers **fanatics.** (7n.1)

objective case The case of a noun or pronoun functioning as a direct or indirect object or object of a preposition or of a verbal. A few pronouns change form to show case (*him, her, whom*). Also see *case.* (Chapter 9)

outline Technique for laying out ideas for writing. An outline can be formal or informal. (2r, 32p)

overstatement Deliberate exaggeration for emphasis; also called *hyperbole.* (21d)

paragraph A group of sentences that work together to develop a unit of thought. They are the structured elements of an essay, which is composed of an *introductory paragraph, body paragraphs,* and a *concluding paragraph.* Also see *shaping.* (2n, Chapter 4)

paragraph arrangement Ordering sentences by specific techniques to communicate a paragraph's message. (4h)

paragraph development Using specific, concrete details (RENNS) to support a generalization in a paragraph; rhetorical strategies or patterns for organizing ideas in paragraphs. (4f, 4i)

parallelism The use of equivalent grammatical forms or matching sentence structures to express equivalent ideas and develop coherence. (4g.4, Chapter 18)

paraphrase A restatement of someone else's ideas in language and sentence structure different from those of the original. (31d)

parenthetical reference Information enclosed in parentheses following quoted, paraphrased, or summarized material from a source to alert readers to the use of material from a specific source. Parenthetical references function together with a list of bibliographic information about each source used in a paper to document the writer's use of sources. Also see *citation.* (35a)

participial phrase A phrase that contains a present participle or a past participle and any modifiers and that functions as an adjective. Also see *verbal phrase.* (7o)

passive construction See *passive voice.*

passive voice The form of a verb in which the subject is acted on; if the subject is mentioned in the sentence, it usually appears as the object of the preposition *by:*

- **I was frightened by** the thunder. [Compare: the active-voice version The thunder **frightened me.**]

The passive voice emphasizes the action, in contrast to the *active voice,* which emphasizes the doer of the action. (8n–8p)

past participle The third principal part of a verb, formed in regular verbs, like the past tense, by adding *-d* or *-ed* to the simple form. In irregular verbs, it often differs from the simple form and the past tense: *break, broke, broken.* (7e, 8b, 49f)

past perfect progressive tense The past perfect tense form that describes an ongoing condition in the past that has been ended by something stated in the sentence: *I had been talking.* (8j)

past perfect tense The tense that describes a condition or action that started in the past, continued for a while, and then ended in the past: *I had talked.* (8g, 8i)

past progressive tense The tense that shows the continuing nature of a past action: *I was talking.* (8j)

past tense The tense that tells of an action completed or a condition ended. (8g)

past-tense form The second principal part of a verb, in regular verbs formed by adding *-d* or *-ed* to the simple form. In irregular verbs, the past tense may change in several ways from the simple form. (8b, 8d)

peer-response group A group of students formed to give each other feedback on writing. (1d.1)

perfect infinitive A tense used to describe an action that occurs before the action in the main verb. (8k)

perfect tenses The three tenses—the present perfect (*I have talked*), the past perfect (*I had talked*), and the future perfect (*I will have talked*)—that help show complex time relationships between two clauses. (8g, 8i)

periodic sentence A sentence that begins with modifiers and ends with the independent clause, thus postponing the main idea—and the emphasis—for the end; also called a *climactic sentence.* (19g)

person The attribute of nouns and pronouns showing who or what acts or experiences an action. *First person* is the one speaking (*I, we*); *second person* is the one being spoken to (*you, you*); and *third person* is the person or thing being spoken about (*he, she, it, they*). All nouns are third person. (8a, 10b, 40b.1)

personal pronoun A pronoun that refers to people or things, such as *I, you, them, it.* (7c, 9q.3)

personification A type of figurative language in which a human trait is assigned to a nonhuman thing. (21d)

persuasive purpose See *persuasive writing.*

persuasive writing Writing that seeks to convince the reader about a matter of opinion. It is also known as *argumentative writing.* (1c.3, Chapter 6)

phrasal verb A verb that combines with one or more prepositions to deliver its meaning: *ask out, look into.* (48c)

phrase A group of related words that does not contain a subject and predicate and thus cannot stand alone as an independent grammatical unit. A phrase functions as a noun, verb, or modifier. (7o)

plagiarism A writer's presenting another person's words or ideas without giving credit to that person. Documentation systems allow writers to give proper credit to sources in ways recognized by scholarly communities. Plagiarism is a serious offense, a form of intellectual dishonesty that can lead to course failure or expulsion. (1f, 31a)

planning An early part of the writing process in which writers gather ideas. Along with shaping, planning is sometimes called *prewriting.* (Chapter 2)

plural See *number.*

positive The form of an adjective or adverb when no comparison is being expressed: *blue, easily.* Also see *comparative, superlative.* (11e)

possessive A determiner or limiting adjective that shows possession or ownership: *my, your, their,* and so on. (7f)

possessive case The case of a noun or pronoun that shows ownership or possession. Also see *case, pronoun case.* (Chapter 9, 27a–27d)

predicate The part of a sentence that contains the verb and tells what the subject is doing or experiencing or what is being done to the subject. A *simple predicate* contains only the main verb and any auxiliary verbs. A *complete predicate* contains the verb, its modifiers, objects, and other related words. A *compound predicate* contains two or more verbs and their objects and modifiers, if any. (7l)

predicate adjective An adjective used as a subject complement:
■ That tree is **leafy.** (7n.1)

predicate nominative A noun or pronoun used as a subject complement:
■ That tree is a **maple.** (7n.1)

prediction A major activity of the *reading process,* in which the reader guesses what comes next. (5c)

prefix A syllable added before a root word that changes the word's meaning. (21i)

premises In a deductive argument expressed as a syllogism, statements presenting the conditions of the argument from which the conclusion must follow. (5i.2)

preposition A word that conveys a relationship, often of space or time, between the noun or pronoun following it and other words in the sentence. The noun or pronoun following a preposition is called its *object.* (7h, Chapter 48)

prepositional phrase A preposition and the word it modifies. Also see *phrase, preposition.* (7h, 7o)

present participle A verb's *-ing* form. Used with auxiliary verbs, present participles function as main verbs. Used without auxiliary verbs, present participles function as nouns or adjectives. (8b, 7e, 49f)

present perfect progressive tense The present perfect tense form that describes something ongoing in the past that is likely to continue into the future: *I have been talking.* (8j)

present perfect tense The tense indicating that an action or its effects, begun or perhaps completed in the past, continue into the present: *I had talked.* (8g, 8i)

present progressive tense The present-tense form of the verb that indicates something taking place at the time it is written or spoken about: *I am talking.* (8j)

present tense The tense that describes what is happening, what is true at the moment, and what is consistently true. It uses the simple form (*I talk*) and the *-s* form in the third-person singular (*he, she, it talks*). (8g, 8h)

prewriting All activities in the writing process before drafting. Also see *planning, shaping.* (2e–2m)

primary sources Firsthand work: write-ups of experiments and observations by the researchers who conducted them; taped accounts, interviews, and newspaper accounts by direct observers; autobiographies, diaries, and journals; expressive works (poems, plays, fiction, essays); also known as *primary evidence.* Also see *secondary source.* (5g.2, 32j, 33b)

process A rhetorical strategy in writing that reports a sequence of actions by which something is done or made. (4i.3)

progressive forms Verb forms made in all tenses with the present participle and forms of the verb *be* as an auxiliary. Progressive forms show that an action, occurrence, or state of being is ongoing. (8g, 8j)

pronoun A word that takes the place of a noun and functions in the same ways that nouns do. Types of pronouns are *demonstrative, indefinite, intensive, interrogative, personal, reciprocal, reflexive,* and *relative.* The word (or words) a pronoun replaces is called its *antecedent.* (7c, Chapter 9, 11m–11r)

pronoun-antecedent agreement The match in expressing number and person—and for personal pronouns, gender as well—required between a pronoun and its antecedent. (10n–10s)

pronoun case The way a pronoun changes form to reflect its use as the agent of action (*subjective case*), the thing being acted upon (*objective case*), or the thing showing ownership (*possessive case*). (9a–9k)

pronoun reference The relationship between a pronoun and its antecedent. (9l–9r)

proofreading Reading a final draft to find and correct any spelling or mechanics mistakes, typing errors, or handwriting illegibility; the final step of the writing process. (3e)

proper adjective An adjective formed from a proper noun: *Victorian, American.* (30e)

proper noun A noun that names specific people, places, or things and is always capitalized: *Dave Matthews, Buick.* (7b, 30e, 46c)

public writing Writing intended for members of your community, the community as a whole, or public officials. (42f–h).

purpose The goal or aim of a piece of writing: to express oneself, to provide information, to persuade, or to create a literary work. (1b, 1c)

quotation Repeating or reporting another person's words. *Direct quotation* repeats another's words exactly and encloses them in quotation marks. *Indirect quotation* reports another's words without quotation marks except around any words repeated exactly from the source. Both *direct* and *indirect quotation* require *documentation* of the *source* to avoid *plagiarism.* Also see *direct discourse, indirect discourse.* (Chapter 28, 31c)

reader See *audience.* (1b, 1c)

reading process Critical reading that requires the reader to read for *literal meaning,* to draw *inferences,* and to *evaluate.* (5c)

reciprocal pronoun The pronouns *each other* and *one another* referring to individual parts of a plural antecedent:

- We respect **each other.** (7c)

References In many documentation styles, including APA, the title of a list of sources cited in a research paper or other written work. (33d, 33e, 33f, 36)

reflexive pronoun A pronoun that ends in *-self* and that reflects back to its antecedent:

- They claim to support **themselves.** (7c)

regional language Language specific to a geographic area. (21i)

regular verb A verb that forms its past tense and past participle by adding *-ed* or *-d* to the simple form. Most English verbs are regular. (8b, 8d)

relative adverb An adverb that introduces an adjective clause:

- The lot **where** I usually park my car was full. (7g)

relative clause See *adjective clause.*

relative pronoun A pronoun, such as *who, which, that, whom,* or *whoever,* that introduces an adjective clause or sometimes a noun clause. (7c)

RENNS Test See *paragraph development.* (4f)

research question The controlling question that drives research. (32b)

research writing A process in three steps: conducting research, understanding and evaluating the results of the research, and writing the research paper with accurate documentation. (Chapter 31, 32a)

restrictive clause See *restrictive element.*

restrictive element A word, phrase, or dependent clause that contains information that is essential for a sentence to deliver its message. Do not set off with commas. (24f)

revision A part of the writing process in which writers evaluate their rough drafts and, based on their assessments, rewrite by adding, cutting, replacing, moving, and often totally recasting material. (3c)

rhetoric The area of discourse that focuses on arrangement of ideas and choice of words as a reflection of both the writer's purpose and the writer's sense of audience. (Chapter 1)

rhetorical strategies In writing, various techniques for presenting ideas to deliver a writer's intended message with clarity and impact. Reflecting typical patterns of human thought, rhetorical strategies include arrangements such as chronological and climactic order; stylistic techniques such as parallelism and planned repetition; and patterns for organizing and developing writing such as description and definition. (4k)

Rogerian argument An argument technique adapted from the principles of communication developed by psychologist Carl Rogers. (6d)

root A word's core that carries its meaning or origin. (22i)

run-on sentence The error of running independent clauses into each other without the required punctuation that marks them as complete units; also called a *fused sentence* or *run-together sentence.* (Chapter 13)

search engine An Internet-specific software program that can look through all files at Internet sites. (34b, 34c.2)

secondary source A source that reports, analyzes, discusses, reviews, or otherwise deals with the work of someone else, as opposed to a primary source, which is someone's original work or firsthand report. A reliable secondary source should be the work of a person with appropriate credentials, should appear in a respected publication or other medium, should be current, and should be well reasoned. (5g.2, 32j, 33b, 39b, 40b.3)

second person See *person.*

sentence See *sentence types.*

sentence fragment A portion of a sentence that is punctuated as though it were a complete sentence. (Chapter 12)

sentence types A grammatical classification of sentences by the kinds of clauses they contain. A *simple sentence* consists of one independent clause. A *complex sentence* contains one independent clause and one or more dependent clauses. A *compound-complex sentence* contains at least two independent clauses and one or more dependent clauses. A *compound* or *coordinate sentence* contains two or more independent clauses joined by a coordinating conjunction. Sentences are also classified by their grammatical function; see *declarative sentence, exclamatory sentence, imperative sentence, interrogative sentence.* (7k, 7q, 17b)

sentence variety Writing sentences of various lengths and structures; see *coordinate sentence, cumulative sentence, periodic sentence, sentence types.* (19a)

sexist language Language and tone that unfairly or unnecessarily assign roles or characteristics to people on the basis of gender. Language that avoids gender stereotyping is called *nonsexist language* or *gender-neutral language.* (10r, 21g)

shaping An early part of the writing process in which writers consider ways to organize their material. Along with planning, shaping is sometimes called *prewriting.* (2n–2r)

shift Within a sentence, an unnecessary abrupt change in *person, number, subject, voice tense, mood,* or *direct* or *indirect discourse.* (15a–15c)

simile A comparison, using *like* or *as,* of otherwise dissimilar things. (21d)

simple form The form of the verb that shows action, occurrence, or state of being taking place in the present. It is used in the singular for first and second person and in the plural for first, second, and third person. It is also the first principal part of a verb. The simple form is also known as the *dictionary form* or *base form.* (8b)

simple predicate See *predicate.*

simple sentence See *sentence types.*

simple subject See *subject.*

simple tenses The present, past, and future tenses, which divide time into present, past, and future. (8g, 8h)

singular See *number.*

slang A kind of colloquial language, it is coined words and new meanings for existing words, which quickly pass in and out of use; not appropriate for most academic writing. (21a.3)

slanted language Language that tries to manipulate the reader with distorted facts. (21h)

source A book, article, print or Internet document, other work, or person providing credible information. In *research writing,* often called *outside sources.* (1f, Chapters 31, 33, and 34)

spatial order An arrangement of information according to location in space; an organizing strategy for sentences, paragraphs, and longer pieces of writing. (4h.2)

specific noun A noun understood to be exactly and specifically referred to; uses the definite article *the*. (46a)

split infinitive One or more words coming between the two words of an infinitive. (14b)

squinting modifier A modifier that is considered misplaced because it is not clear whether it describes the word that comes before it or the word that follows it.

standard English See *edited American English.*

standard word order The most common order for words in English sentences: The subject comes before the predicate. Also see *inverted word order.* (19e, Chapter 47)

stereotype A kind of hasty generalization (a *logical fallacy*) in which a sweeping claim is made about all members of a particular ethnic, racial, religious, gender, age, or political group. (5j)

structured techniques See *invention techniques, planning, prewriting strategies..* (2e–2m)

subject The word or group of words in a sentence that acts, is acted upon, or is described by the verb. A *simple subject* includes only the noun or pronoun. A *complete subject* includes the noun or pronoun and all its modifiers. A *compound subject* includes two or more nouns or pronouns and their modifiers. (7l)

subject complement A noun or adjective that follows a linking verb, renaming or describing the subject of the sentence; also called a *predicate nominative.* (7n.1)

subjective case The case of the noun or pronoun functioning as a subject. Also see *case, pronoun case.* (Chapter 9)

subject tree A prewriting technique that shows you visually whether you have sufficient content, at varying levels of generality or specificity, to start a first draft of writing. (2p)

subject-verb agreement The required match between a subject and verb in expressing number and person. (10b–10m)

subjunctive mood A verb mood that expresses wishes, recommendations, indirect requests, speculations, and conditional statements.

■ I wish you **were** here. (8l, 8m)

subordinate clause See *dependent clause.*

subordinating conjunction A conjunction that introduces an adverb clause and expresses a relationship between the idea in it and the idea in the independent clause. (7i, 13c.4, 17f, 17g)

subordination The use of grammatical structures to reflect the relative importance of ideas. A sentence with logically subordinated information expresses the most important information in the independent clause and less important information in dependent clauses or phrases. (17e–17i)

suffix An ending added to a word that changes the word's meaning. (7f, 22d)

summary A brief version of the main message or central point of a passage or other discourse; a critical thinking activity preceding synthesis. (5e, 31e)

superlative The form of an adjective or adverb that expresses comparison among three or more things: *bluest, least blue; most easily, least easily.* (11e.1)

syllogism The structure of a deductive argument expressed in two *premises* and a *conclusion.* The first premise is a generalized assumption or statement of fact. The second premise is a different assumption or statement of fact based on evidence. The conclusion is also a specific instance that follows logically from the premises. (5i.2)

synonym A word that is very close in meaning to another word: *cold* and *icy.* (21e)

synthesis A component of critical thinking in which material that has been summarized, analyzed, and interpreted is connected to what is already known (one's prior knowledge) or to what has been learned from other authorities. (5b, 5e)

tag question An inverted verb-pronoun combination added to the end of a sentence, creating a question that asks the audience to agree with the assertion in the first part of the sentence. A tag question is set off from the rest of the sentence with a comma:

■ You know what a tag question is, **don't you?** (24g)

tag sentence See *tag question.*

tense The time at which the action of the verb occurs: the present, the past, or the future. Also see *perfect tenses, simple tenses.* (8g–8k)

tense sequence In sentences that have more than one clause, the accurate matching of verbs to reflect logical time relationships. (8k)

thesis statement A statement of an essay's central theme that makes clear the main idea, the writer's purpose, the focus of the topic, and perhaps the organizational pattern. (2q)

third person See *person.*

title The part of an essay that clarifies the overall point of the piece of writing. It can be *direct* or *indirect.* (3c.3)

tone The writer's attitude toward his or her material and reader, especially as reflected by word choice. (1e, 5c.2, 6i)

841

topic The subject of discourse. (2c, 2d)

topic sentence The sentence that expresses the main idea of a paragraph. A topic sentence may be implied, not stated. (4e)

Toulmin model A model that defines the essential parts of an argument as the *claim* (or *main point*), the *support* (or *evidence*), and the *warrants* (or *assumptions behind the main point*). (6f)

transition The connection of one idea to another in discourse. Useful strategies within a paragraph for creating transitions include transitional expressions, parallelism, and planned repetition of key words and phrases. In a long piece of writing, a *transitional paragraph* is the bridge between discussion of two separate topics. Also see *critical response*. (4g.1, 4j)

transitional expressions Words and phrases that signal connections among ideas and create coherence. (4g.1)

transitive verb A verb that must be followed by a direct object. (8f)

truncation A technique that allows the researcher to look for Internet sites by listing only the first few letters of a keyword. Also called *wildcarding*. (34d.2)

understatement Figurative language in which the writer uses deliberate restraint for emphasis. (21d)

unity The clear and logical relationship between the main idea of a paragraph and the evidence supporting the main idea. (3c.4, 4d, 4e)

unstated assumptions Premises that are implied but not stated. (5i.2)

URL The *uniform resource locator,* the address of a specific Web page. (34c.1)

usage A customary way of using language. (Chapter 20)

valid Correctly and rationally derived; applied to a deductive argument whose conclusion follows logically from the premises. Validity applies to the structure of an argument, not its truth. (5i.2)

verb Any word that shows action or occurrence or describes a state of being. Verbs change form to convey time (*tense*), attitude (*mood*), and role of the subject (*voice,* either *active* or *passive*). Verbs occur in the predicate of a clause and can be in verb phrases, which may consist of a main verb, auxiliary verbs, and modifiers. Verbs can be described as *transitive* or *intransitive,* depending on whether they take a direct object. Also see *voice.* (Chapters 8 and 44)

verbal A verb part functioning as a noun, adjective, or adverb. Verbals include *infinitives, present participles* (functioning as adjectives), *gerunds* (present participles functioning as nouns), and *past participles.* (7e, Chapter 49)

verbal phrase A group of words that contains a verbal (an infinitive, participle, or gerund) and its modifiers. (7o)

verb phrase A main verb, any auxiliary verbs, and any modifiers. (7o)

verb tense See *verb tense.*

voice An attribute of verbs showing whether the subject acts (*active voice*) or is acted on (*passive voice*). Verbs are sometimes referred to as *strong* or *action verbs* or *weak verbs.* (8n–8p)

warrant One of three key terms in the *Toulmin model* for argument; refers to implied or inferred assumptions. They are based on *authority, substance,* and *motivation.* (6f)

Web See *World Wide Web.*

webbing See *mapping.*

Web page On the Internet, a file of information. Such a file is not related in length to a printed page, as it may be a paragraph or many screens long. (39a)

wordiness An attribute of writing that is full of empty words and phrases that do not contribute to meaning. The opposite of *conciseness.* (43b)

World Wide Web A user-friendly computer network used to access information in the form of text, graphics, and sound on the Internet. Also simply called the *Web.* (39a)

working bibliography A preliminary list of useful sources in research writing. (32m)

Works Cited In MLA documentation style, the title of a list of all sources cited in a research paper or other written work. (33b)

writer's block The desire to start writing, but not doing so. (3b)

writing process Stages of writing in which a writer gathers and shapes ideas, organizes material, expresses those ideas in a rough draft, evaluates the draft and revises it, edits the writing for technical errors, and proofreads it for typographical accuracy and legibility. The stages often overlap; see *planning, shaping, drafting, revision, editing, proofreading.* (Chapters 1, 2, and 3)

writing situation The beginning of the writing process for each writing assignment as defined by four elements: topic, purpose, audience, special requirement (TPAS). (2c)

INDEX

845

853

Index

Social sciences (continued)
  writing purposes and practices,
    207, 708, 733–734
Software
  APA-style documentation for, 638
  capitalization of titles, 466
  CM-style documentation for, 665
  COS/humanities-style
    documentation for, 683
  COS/scientific-style
    documentation for, 686
  for document design, 688–689
  no quotation marks or italics with,
    468
some
  comparative and superlative forms,
    252
  subject-verb agreement, 234, 235
sometime, sometimes, some time,
  355
Song titles, quotation marks for,
  442–443
sort, kind, 351
sort of, kind of, 351
Sources. See also Bibliographies;
    Documentation; Library
    resources
  defined, 480, 527–528, 839
  evaluation of, 124–126, 516–517,
    542–543, 557–560
  field research and, 513–516
  government agencies as, 542
  obligations toward, 16–17
  primary and secondary, 124–126,
    528, 710
  for writing, 16–17
Spatial order, 90, 388, 840
Specialist audience, 8, 13
Specialized dictionaries, 363
Specialized indexes to periodicals,
  539–542
Specialized language, 371–372
Special pleading, as logical fallacy,
  136
Specific details, developing
  paragraphs with, 82–83
Specific nouns, 787–789, 840
Specific-to-general arrangement, 91
Specific words, 365–366
Spell-check program, 19

Spelling, 374–388. See also
    Hyphen(s)
  of compounds, 386–387
  in dictionary entries, 363
  errors in
    proofreading for, 375
    in quoted sources [sic], 453
  homonyms, 378–383
  and hyphenation, 384–388
  ie/ei rules, 377
  mnemonic aids, 378
  of plurals, 375–376
  and pronunciation, 378
  with suffixes, 376–377
Split infinitives, 284–285, 840
Squinting modifiers, 283, 840
Standard English, 360
Standard word order, 337, 794–799, 840
State names
  abbreviation of, 472–473
  after city names, commas with, 473
states, 784–785
stationary, stationery, 355, 382
Statistics, numbers, 477
Stereotyping, 840
  by gender, 366–368, 367
  as logical fallacy, 133
Strong commands, 203, 335, 394
Structure
  literary analysis of, 715
  for written argument, 142–143
Structured techniques, 27–34, 840
Style, literary analysis of, 716
Style-check programs, 19
Subject(s), 167–168, 840. See also
    Subjective case
  awkward separation from verbs,
    287–288
  in clauses, 175
  emphasizing, 337
  implied, 203, 257, 259
  of infinitives, 218
  noun clauses as, 177–178
  plural, 228–229, 231–232
  required for completeness,
    257, 259
  separation from verbs, 419
  shifts in, 291
  simple, 167
  after verb, 794–799

878

List of Boxes by Content

List of Boxes by Content (*continued*)

List of Boxes by Content (*continued*)

List of Boxes by Content (*continued*)

Summary of Changes to the *MLA Handbook for Writers of Research Papers*, Sixth Edition (2003)

The *MLA Handbook for Writers of Research Papers* was recently published in a new sixth edition. Some forms of documentation and citation have been changed. This insert is intended to detail these changes and provide you with the most up-to-date information about MLA style. Be sure to speak with your instructor if you need additional clarification.

PREPARING THE LIST OF WORKS CITED

Full-Text Databases

Most college and university libraries subscribe to full-text periodical and book databases such as the *New York Times Online* and *American National Biography* and to general databases such as JSTOR, InfoTrac, and Lexis-Nexis that provide a wide range of bibliographic and full-text sources. When you cite works from databases, observe the following changes in MLA style.

1. *URL-Specific Document:* When you cite an online source that can be accessed by a short and logical URL, include the full URL in your citation of the source. An article from the *New York Times,* for example, can be easily accessed by the reader using the URL specified in your Works Cited list.

   ```
   Petersen, Melody. "A Respected Face, but Is It News

       or an Ad?" New York Times on the Web 7 May

       2003. 8 May 2003 <http://www.nytimes.com/2003/

       05/07/business/media/07DRUG.html>.
   ```

2. *URL of Search Page:* If the URL of your document is long and convoluted, it will be quite difficult for your reader to access the source. Consider this example of a URL from a journal accessed through JSTOR.

   ```
   http://links.jstor.org/sici?sici=00290564%28197512%

   2930%3A3%3C305%3AATSOPJA%3E2.0CO%3B2-5
   ```

When this problem arises, MLA suggests that it is more convenient to supply the URL of the database's search page, as shown here.

```
Hart, Francis R. "The Spaces of Privacy: Jane Austen."

    Nineteenth-Century Fiction 30.3 (1975): 305-33.

    JSTOR. 5 Feb. 2003 <http://www.jstor.org/search>.
```

3. *No URL:* If your source does not have an accessible URL or the URL is unique to the library, cite the URL for the home page of the subscription service that you used to find your source.

```
Youakim, Sami. "Work-Related Asthma." American

    Family Physician 64 (2001): 1839-53. Health

    Reference Center. InfoTrac. Bergen County

    Cooperative Lib. System, NJ. 14 Mar. 2003

    <http://www.galegroup.com/>.
```

Internet Sources

The new edition of the *MLA Handbook* does not change the style for Internet citations, but it does expand the information to be included. The following citation exhibits the necessary components of an Internet citation.

```
           ❶                        ❷
Hart, Francis R. "The Spaces of Privacy: Jane Austen."
    Nineteenth-Century Fiction 30.3 (1975): 305-33. ❸
    JSTOR. 5 Feb. 2003 <http://www.jstor.org/search>.
       ❹        ❺                      ❻
```

❶ Name of author, editor, translator, or compiler of the source.

❷ Title of the article or other short work, enclosed in quotation marks. For a posting to a discussion list or forum, use the subject line as the title.

❸ Publication information for the print version of the source.

❹ Title of the Internet site (scholarly project, database, online periodical, or Web site, underlined).

❺ Date of access.

❻ URL of the source or URL of the site's search page if the URL is exceptionally long.

Remember to include the following details in your citation if such information is given or available for your source.

- Include the name of the editor, translator, or compiler of the source in addition to the author's name.

- Note the name of the editor of the Web site.

- Include the date of electronic publication, latest update, or posting.

- Give the name and location of the library if your site was accessed through a library subscription service.

- Name the list or forum, if your source is a posting to a discussion list or forum.

- Include the name of the site's sponsoring institution or organization.

Other Important Points Concerning the List of Works Cited

1. *Work from a Library Subscription Service:* When you cite material from a library service, be sure to cite the name of the database used, the name of the service, the name and location of the library, the date of access, and the URL of the subscription service home page if it is available.

   Dutton, Gail. "Greener Pigs." Popular Science

       255.5 (1999): 38-39. ProQuest Direct.

       Public Lib., Teaneck, NJ. 7 Dec. 2002

       <http://proquest.umi.com>.

2. *Work from a Personal Subscription Service:* To cite a source that you found via a personal subscription service that allows you to retrieve information through a keyword search, end the citation with *Keyword,* followed by a colon and the date of access. If you used a series of topic labels rather than a keyword end the citation with *Path,* followed by a colon, and the sequence of topics that you used to locate your source. Use semicolons to separate the topics.

   Futurelle, David. "A Smashing Success." Money.com

       23 Dec. 1999. America Online. 4 Oct. 2002.

       Path: Personal Finance; Business News;

       Business Publications; Money.com.

THE MECHANICS OF WRITING: ELLIPSES

The most significant difference between the fifth and sixth editions of the *MLA Handbook* is in the style of ellipses. The fifth edition required that ellipses (three spaced periods used to indicate an omission from quoted material) be enclosed in square brackets. Now the style is to omit the brackets. You should, however, check which ellipsis style your instructor prefers.

Preferred Ellipsis Style of the 6th Edition:

```
In her article "Living in Two Cultures," Jeanne
Wakatsuki Houston notes: "My husband and I often joke
that the reason we have stayed married for so long is
that we . . . mystify each other with responses and
attitudes that are plainly due to our different
backgrounds" (191).
```

Preferred Ellipsis Style of the 5th Edition:

```
In her article "Living in Two Cultures," Jeanne
Wakatsuki Houston notes: "My husband and I often joke
that the reason we have stayed married for so long is
that we [. . .] mystify each other with responses and
attitudes that are plainly due to our different
backgrounds" (191).
```

Exception: Do enclose ellipses in square brackets if the original passage you are quoting contains its own ellipsis points. The brackets will distinguish your ellipses from those in the source.

Original Source:

```
In "Living in Two Cultures," Jeanne Wakatsuki
Houston discusses her early questions about marital
roles. She notes:

        When we first married I wondered if I should lay
        out his socks and underwear every morning like
        my mother used to do for my father. But my
        brothers' warning would float up from the past:
```

don't be subservient to Caucasian men or they
will take advantage. So I compromised and laid
them out sporadically, whenever I thought to do
it . . . which grew less and less often as the
years passed. (224)

Quoted Source:

In "Living in Two Cultures," Jeanne Wakatsuki
Houston discusses her early questions about marital
roles. She notes:

When we first married I wondered if I should
lay out his socks [. . .]. But my brothers'
warning would float up from the past: don't be
subservient to Caucasian men or they will take
advantage. So I compromised and laid them
out sporadically, whenever I thought to do
it . . . which grew less and less often as the
years passed. (224)

The following paper by first-year student Chassey Wilkins-Hicks
demonstrates the changes to MLA guidelines. The format shown in
this paper is reflective of MLA style but has been slightly modified to
accommodate the space limitations of the trim in this book. Note
that MLA-style student papers should be double-spaced throughout.
As always, see your instructor if you have any questions regarding the
arrangement of this paper.

↑
1"
↓

↕ ½"
Hicks 1 ← 1" →

Chassey Wilkins-Hicks

Professor Ezzell

English 112

17 April 2003

Peace by Prescription

← 5 → "Sit down at the dinner table!" "Stop
spaces
fidgeting and finish your homework!" "Didn't

you hear a single word I said?" Do these

demands sound familiar? Perhaps you remember

hearing those same words as a child, or

maybe you have even spoken them to your own

son or daughter. They are not uncommon

phrases in the home of a lively, vivacious

child doing nothing more than enjoying life

and burning the energy many adults wish they

← 1" →   ← 1" →

could bottle. Yet many adults are beginning

to view any type of bubbly, rambunctious

behavior as unacceptable. More parents are

being swayed toward the idea that if you

have to speak to your children in such a

manner, there must be something wrong with

them. Enter attention deficit hyperactivity

disorder (ADHD). In the past two decades the

diagnosis of ADHD has been on a steady rise.

Independent academic studies as well as

numerous years of research by organizations

such as the National Institute on Drug Abuse

(NIDA) place the proportion of the general

public affected at approximately 3 to 5

percent (United States). The American

↑
1"
↓

Hicks 2

Academy of Pediatrics reports that 4 to 12
percent of the nation's school-age children
are affected (1).

A considerable number of the diagnosed
children are prescribed some form of
psychostimulant, such as methylphenidate, to
treat their symptoms. One brand is so
commonly used, it has practically become a
household name--Ritalin. These drugs,
however, do not pave the path to recovery.
Instead, they chemically alter some of the
behavior symptoms associated with ADHD. As I
intend to prove, behavior therapy is a much
safer alternative than psychostimulants in
treating children diagnosed with ADHD. The
process can also prove to be a learning and
rewarding experience for children, as well
as their parents.

A comprehension of exactly how the
diagnosis of ADHD is determined is needed to
understand the treatments offered. Even with
the countless hours of research dedicated to
the study of ADHD, the cause remains a
mystery. Zwi, Ramchandani, and Joughin
attribute the symptoms to a collection of
neurobiological problems in the function and
makeup of the brain rather than just one
disorder (975). Unfortunately, none of my
research reveals a conclusive opinion that
the brains of those classified with ADHD

function differently than the brains of
those who are considered normal. And,
because there is no proven medical
examination or test that can confirm ADHD,
the chance of misdiagnosis remains high.

Jaydene Morrison, a nationally certified
school psychologist and teacher, does a
fantastic job of outlining the standard
practice of diagnosing ADHD in her book
Coping with ADD/ADHD. It requires several
steps and a wide range of IQ and aptitude
tests. A doctor may first want to rule out any
medical disorder or learning disability (9).
The frustration experienced or what
may appear as lack of attention due to a
hearing impairment can be a misconception
of an unruly student. Teachers are often
requested to assist by completing lengthy
questionnaires on the child's behavior as
well as study habits and moods. The next step
is determining whether the child falls within
the academic level of his or her peers.
Reading, writing, spelling, and mathematic
capabilities are analyzed for correctness as
well as speed. IQ testing such as problem and
puzzle solving is utilized in a verbal and
hands-on setting. These different aspects of
testing demonstrate the process by which the
mind computes the problem and transfers the
information to paper (11).

Hicks 4

Symptoms of ADHD include a wide variety
of behavior and learning traits. Some of
these include being inattentive, easily
distracted, unable to organize, forgetful,
overtalkative, fidgety, and impatient. Many
argue that this list also describes most
typical, healthy children at some point in
time. In an October 2000 issue of US News
and World Report, Nancy Shute quotes Dickie
Scruggs as saying, "[T]he diagnosis of ADHD
would fit every child in America."

Ritalin, a central nervous system
stimulant, is used to treat ADHD based on
the speculation that it increases the
release of dopamine in the brain. This
assumption is founded on laboratory research
performed on healthy adults. The InfoFacts
sheet on methylphenidate (Ritalin) explains
that by use of a type of brain scan called
positron emission tomography (PET),
researchers confirmed an increase in dopamine
levels in what were considered normal,
healthy subjects administered with

←—10—→ therapeutic doses of
  spaces
          methylphenidate. . . . The
          researchers speculate that
          methylphenidate amplifies the
          release of dopamine, a
          neurotransmitter, thereby
          improving attention and focus in

Hicks 5

individuals who have dopamine
signals that are weak, such as
individuals with ADHD. (United
States)

Like many others who disagree with the
use of psychostimulants as a primary
treatment for ADHD, I am not out to disprove
the effects of these drugs. In fact, as
described in the research above, Ritalin and
similar drugs can improve attentiveness and
concentration in almost anyone. In a
personal interview, Thomas Mates, PhD, a
respected child psychologist here in
Wilmington, North Carolina, told me that
many college students have admitted taking
these types of pharmaceuticals to improve
their study habits. Improving only the
ability to focus, however, does not teach a
child good learning habits. The chemicals
merely subdue the individual and the
undesirable behavior. David Stein, PhD,
author of Ritalin Is Not the Answer and an
advocate for behavior therapy, asserts, "The
drugs do control the behaviors, but then
they serve to mask the problem behaviors and
thus block the way for effective change"
(35). What parent would envision spending
quality time with an eight-year-old child
that was under the influence of cocaine?
Amazingly enough, though, parents of

millions of children have been convinced
that giving Ritalin to their child is
acceptable. The comparison with cocaine is
not so outrageous when you consider that the
NIDA has placed a Schedule II narcotics
control label on methylphenidate.

As with any drug, the risks of
adverse reactions are always present. A
long list of side effects accompanies these
stimulant medications, including "decreased
appetite/weight loss, . . . transient tics,
stuttering, increased blood pressure or heart
rate, and growth delay" (American Academy of
Pediatrics 12). I can speak only for myself,
but I hope I represent all cautious parents
when I say that I would take dealing with my
child's behavior problem over inducing these
side effects in her.

I question, is the tranquility these
drugs create for the children or for the
parents? The choices between two minutes
of the parents' day to administer the dose of
a tiny pill versus the countless hours of
one-on-one attention needed to find the root
of the problem could appear too easy. The
answer is obvious for those who are willing
to take the time. I don't deny that there
may be children with extreme cases of
inattentiveness and/or hyperactivity that may
require a medical approach. This, however,

should be the last option and used after all
other means, methods, and programs have been
exhausted. Mind-altering drugs are not a safe
alternative in treating children for what is
more often than not a behavior problem.

Behavior therapy does work. Stein notes
that the treatment of Helen Keller by Annie
Sullivan is the "first documented behavior
modification case" (13). Helen Keller's
motivation and drive were eliminated by a
family who pampered her and overcompensated
for what they thought were her inabilities
to function for herself. Ms. Sullivan
removed Helen from these detrimental
surroundings and required her to perform
activities necessary to everyday existence.
In doing so, Helen was able to gain and
retain the knowledge to lead a self-
fulfilling life.

I recently took my nine-year-old
daughter to a psychologist. I was relieved
to hear that she does not exhibit the
characteristics or enough of the symptoms
to be diagnosed with ADHD. Why then was I
prompted to have her tested? More than
likely it was for the same reasons most
parents are succumbing to this decision. She
was almost unmanageable at times and seemed
easily distracted or frustrated when it came
to schoolwork or long projects. Thinking

back, I was looking for the easy way out.
The term "spoiled" now looms in my mind.
After reviewing the results of her tests
and discussing the doctor's analysis, we
concluded she needs more direction in
controlling her behavior, study habits, and
thinking patterns. The doctor also explained
that I may be too lenient with her at times,
allowing her to feel entitled to get what
she wants. In looking for a way out, I,
probably like many other parents, was
searching for a cause rather than looking at
my parenting skills. We are looking,
however, in the wrong direction if looking
for a medical answer. Stein writes,
"I deeply believe that nothing medical
causes children to not pay attention and to
misbehave. They simply do not pay attention
and they do misbehave" (22). Behavior
therapy, therefore, can be a learning and
growing experience for the child and for the
parent, as well.

    There are many behavior therapy
treatment programs geared toward and
created specifically for children suffering
from ADHD. The programs may differ in
structure, but are based on modifying the
child's current behavior by applying the
techniques frequently and consistently.
Some programs set goals and rewards for

Hicks 9

good behavior and have consequences for inappropriate behavior. These rewards and consequences vary depending on the present and long-term goals set by the parent and child. The program is individualized to the child by allowing him or her to participate. Recognizing behavior, both good and bad, is an important step in allowing the child to assist in setting goals and choosing punishments.

Another program, the Caregivers' Skill Program, works "by first getting [children's] behavior under control, so we can get their full attention, so we can inspire their motivation" (Stein 41). Lack of interest, and thus motivation, can cause anyone to be inattentive, fidgety, forgetful, and easily distracted. No, it is not a coincidence that you have heard these descriptions before. This only reinforces the fact that these are not symptoms of ADHD alone. As stated above, the first goal is to get a handle on the current behavior. This is achieved in a manner similar to other programs by identifying the problem behavior and using reinforcements such as spending more time with the child and praising the child. Material reinforcements such as special privileges and objects are also an option, but their effects are

Hicks 10

short-lived and can cause another form of
entitlement expectancy. Immediate
reinforcement of positive behavior leads to
a much more pleasant atmosphere than
discipline for bad behavior. Ponder this:
If your employer only pointed out the
shortcomings of your work performance
without praising your accomplishments,
would you not have a bad attitude?

Stop and smell the roses. The roses in
this story are the children. We would not
unnecessarily poison our roses just as we
should not poison our children. Drugs such
as methylphenidate and amphetamines used
needlessly are poison to a child's mind and
body. Encouragement, interaction, and
positive reinforcement are the keys to a
healthy, motivated child. Who knows? Many
parents may find their children need them
more than anything a prescription could
ever offer.

↑
1"
↓

↑½"
↓
Hicks 11

Works Cited

← 1" → American Academy of Pediatrics.   ← 1" →

←5→ <u>Understanding ADHD</u>. Elk Grove
spaces
        Village: American Academy of

        Pediatrics, 2001.

Mates, Thomas. Personal interview. 27 Mar.

        2003.

Morrison, Jaydene. <u>Coping with ADD/ADHD</u>.

        New York: Rosen, 1996.

Shute, Nancy. "Pushing Pills on Kids?" <u>US</u>

        <u>News and World Report</u> 2 Oct. 2000:

        60. <u>Academic Search Elite</u>. EBSCO.

        Cape Fear Community Coll. Lib.,

        Wilmington, NC. 24 Mar. 2003

        <http://www.epnet.com>.

Stein, David B. <u>Ritalin Is Not the Answer</u>.

        San Francisco: Jossey-Bass, 1999.

United States. National Institute on

        Drug Abuse. <u>NIDA InfoFacts:</u>

        <u>Methylphenidate (Ritalin)</u>. 17 Mar.

        2003 <http://www.nida.nih.gov/

        infofax/ritalin.html>.

Zwi, Morris, Paul Ramchandani, and Carol

        Joughin. "Evidence and Belief in

        ADHD." <u>British Medical Journal</u>

        321.7267 (2000): 975-76. <u>Academic</u>

        <u>Search Elite</u>. EBSCO. Cape Fear

        Community Coll. Lib., Wilmington, NC.

        20 Mar. 2003 <http://www.epnet.com>.

HOW TO FIND INFORMATION
IN THIS HANDBOOK

You can use your **Simon & Schuster Handbook for Writers** as a reference book, just as you use a dictionary or an encyclopedia. At each step, use one or more suggestions to find the information you want.

STEP 1: Use lists to decide where to go.

- Scan the Overview of Contents (on inside front cover).

- Scan the longer Table of Contents.

- Scan the Index at the back of the book for a detailed alphabetical list of all major and minor topics.

- Scan the List of Boxes, starting on page 887, that highlight and summarize all major subjects.

STEP 2: Locate the number that leads to the information you seek.

- Find a chapter number.

- Find a number–letter combination for a section in a chapter and the question it asks.

- Find a box number.

- Find a page number.

STEP 3: Check elements on each page, illustrated on the inside back cover, to confirm where you are in the book.

- Look at the top of each page for the color bar that identifies the part.

- Look for the shortened title at the top of each page (left page for chapter title and right page for section title).

- Look for a section's number-letter combination in white inside a blue rectangle.

- Look for a box title and number.

- Look for a page number at the bottom of the page.

STEP 4: Locate and read the information you need. Use special features, illustrated on the opposite page, to help you.

- Use cross-references to related key concepts.

- Find the definition for any word printed in small capital letters in the Terms Glossary starting on page 821.

- Use 👁 ALERTS● , ⊕ ESL NOTES ✦ , and 🖥 COMPUTER TIPS◻ for pointers about related matters of usage, grammar, punctuation, and writing.

COLOR GUIDE TO THIS HANDBOOK

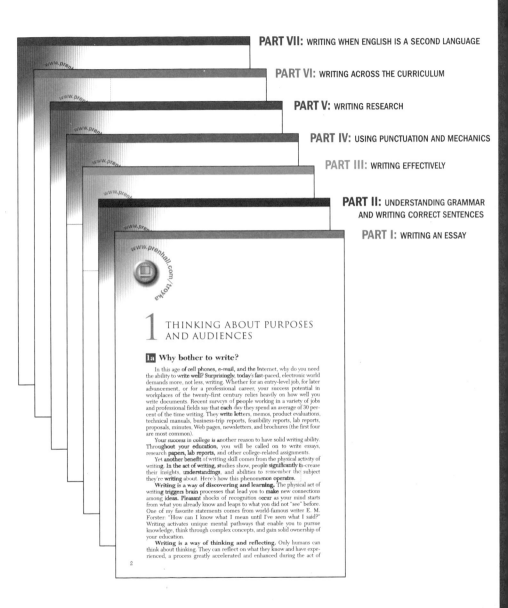

PART VII: WRITING WHEN ENGLISH IS A SECOND LANGUAGE

PART VI: WRITING ACROSS THE CURRICULUM

PART V: WRITING RESEARCH

PART IV: USING PUNCTUATION AND MECHANICS

PART III: WRITING EFFECTIVELY

PART II: UNDERSTANDING GRAMMAR AND WRITING CORRECT SENTENCES

PART I: WRITING AN ESSAY

1 THINKING ABOUT PURPOSES AND AUDIENCES

1a Why bother to write?

In this age of cell phones, e-mail, and the Internet, why do you need the ability to write well? Surprisingly, today's fast-paced, electronic world demands more, not less, writing. Whether for an entry-level job, for later advancement, or for a professional career, your success potential in workplaces of the twenty-first century relies heavily on how well you write documents. Recent surveys of people working in a variety of jobs and professional fields say that each day they spend an average of 30 percent of the time writing. They write letters, memos, product evaluations, technical manuals, business-trip reports, feasibility reports, lab reports, proposals, minutes, Web pages, newsletters, and brochures (the first four are most common).

Your success in college is another reason to have solid writing ability. Throughout your education, you will be called on to write essays, research papers, lab reports, and other college-related assignments.

Yet another benefit of writing skill comes from the physical activity of writing. In the act of writing, studies show, people significantly in-crease their insights, understandings, and abilities to remember the subject they're writing about. Here's how this phenomenon operates.

Writing is a way of discovering and learning. The physical act of writing triggers brain processes that lead you to make new connections among ideas. Pleasant shocks of recognition occur as your mind starts from what you already know and leaps to what you did not "see" before. One of my favorite statements comes from world-famous writer E. M. Forster: "How can I know what I mean until I've seen what I said?" Writing activates unique mental pathways that enable you to pursue knowledge, think through complex concepts, and gain solid ownership of your education.

Writing is a way of thinking and reflecting. Only humans can think about thinking. They can reflect on what they know and have experienced, a process greatly accelerated and enhanced during the act of

2

ICONS FOR BOXES

 checklist

 summary

 pattern

RESPONSE SYMBOLS AND PROOFREADING MARKS

Instructors often use correction symbols to show students where they need to revise and edit their writing. Listed below are standard symbols and the chapter and/or section numbers in this handbook you can go for help with corrections. A list of proofreading symbols follows so you can mark your own drafts for improvement.

Correction Symbols

ab	abbreviation error, **23b, 30i–30n**
ad	adjective or adverb error, **11**
agr	agreement error, **10**
ca	case error, **9**
cap	needs capital letter, **30a–30e**
cl	avoid cliché, **21j**
coh	needs coherence, **4g**
coord	faulty coordination, **17a–17d**
cs	comma splice, **13a–13c.4**
dev	needs development, **4a, 4g, 4i**
dm	dangling modifier, **14d, 14e**
e	needs exact language, **21e**
emph	needs emphasis, **19**
frag	sentence fragment, **12**
hyph	hyphenation error, **22g, 22k**
inc	incomplete sentence, **15h–15j**
ital	italics (underlining) error, **30f–30i**
k	awkward construction, **14, 15**
lc	needs lowercase letter, **30a–30e**
mixed	mixed construction, **15f, 15g**
mm	misplaced modifier, **14a–14c**
num	number use error, **30l–30m**
¶	start new paragraph, **4**
no ¶	do not start new paragraph, **4**
//	parallelism, **18**
pl	plural error, **22c–22f**

pro ref	pronoun reference error, **9**
pro agr	pronoun agreement error, **10**
pe	punctuation error, **23–29**
ref v	reference vague, **9**
rep	repetitious (redundant), **16d**
ro	run-on sentence, **14**
shift	shift, **15a–15e**
sl	avoid slang, **21h**
sp	spelling error, **22**
subord	faulty subordination, **17e–17i**
sxt	sexist language use, **10r, 21g**
t, tense	verb tense error, **8g–8k**
trans	needs transition, **4g.1, 4j**
u	needs unity, **4d, 4e**
us	usage error, **20**
v	verb form error, **8b–8f**
v agr	verb agreement error, **10a–10m**
var	needs sentence variety, **19**
vo	voice change, **8n–8p**
w	wordy, **16d**
wc	word choice error, **21e**
ww	wrong word, **21**
,/	comma error, **24**
;/	semicolon error, **25**
:/	colon error, **26**
ᵛ	apostrophe error, **27**
"/"	quotation marks error, **28**
?	meaning unclear

Proofreading Marks with Examples

ℒ delete	rom use roman type	caret A∧signals an addition
¶ new paragraph	ital use italic type	add#space
∽ transpose letters	cap use capital letters	clo se up space
⌐ transpose words	lc use lowercase letters	They live in WI. SP
∧ insert	take the this out	That sounds silly rom
# add space	This is the end.¶This is a new beginning.	Washington Post ital
○ close up space	transpose letters	anne tyler cap
SP spell out	words transpose	Drive North and then East. lc